Anonymous

Pulpit Themes and Preacher's Assistant

Anonymous

Pulpit Themes and Preacher's Assistant

ISBN/EAN: 9783337169862

Printed in Europe, USA, Canada, Australia, Japan

Cover: Foto ©Lupo / pixelio.de

More available books at **www.hansebooks.com**

AND

PREACHER'S ASSISTANT.

OUTLINES OF SERMONS,

BY

THE AUTHOR OF "HELPS FOR THE PULPIT."

PHILADELPHIA:
SMITH, ENGLISH & CO.,
No. 23 NORTH SIXTH STREET.
NEW YORK: PHINNEY, BLAKEMAN & MASON.
BOSTON: GOULD & LINCOLN.
1860.

PULPIT THEMES;

OR

OUTLINES OF SERMONS.

"I AM SET FOR THE DEFENCE OF THE GOSPEL."—PAUL.

PREFACE.

CHRISTIANITY is the greatest blessing ever bestowed upon this world. It brings glad tidings of good things to lost and fallen men: it turns the curse of the law into a rich, consoling, ennobling, and everlasting blessing. It has the promise of the life that now is, and of that which is to come. But Christianity is assailed by enemies on every hand. Most determined and virulent is their opposition to the holy verities of the gospel. Hence it becomes ministers of the gospel *to be up to the times* in which they live; and to be able, from their literary attainments, and accumulation of philosophical and biblical knowledge, to say, "I am set for the defence of the gospel."

Infidel philosophers have placed in hostile attitude against Christianity, geology from beneath, and from the altitudes of the upper firmament, astronomy. Then from the mysteries of the human spirit, attempts have been made to discover some wondrous spell, by which to disenchant the world of its confidence in the gospel of Christ. From lecture-rooms of anatomy, the lessons of materialism have been inculcated, for the purpose of ridiculing religion, and expelling it from the earth. Others attempt to associate the doctrines of phrenology with their denial of the Christian revelation, as if there were any earthly connection between the form of the human skull and the truth or falsehood of our religion. Christianity has been made a sort of play-ground for all manner of inroads of human speculation.

Nevertheless, while this opposition shows the necessity of adequate ministerial qualification, Christianity carries with it an evidence which is unassailable, and which places it beyond the reach of external violence. It is not the hammer of the mineralogist that can break this evidence. It is not the telescope of the astronomer that can enable us to descry in it any character of falsehood. It is not by the knife of the anatomist that we can find our way to the alleged rottenness which lies at its core. It is not by a dissecting of metaphysics that the mental philosopher can probe his way to the secret of its insufficiency, and make exposure to the world of the yet unknown flaw, which vitiates the proof of the Christian faith. All these sciences have, at one period or another, cast their missiles at the stately fabric of our Christian philosophy and erudition, but they have dropped harmless and impotent at its base.

Still the minds of the simple and unwary are in danger of being seduced, and therefore ministers of the gospel are to nerve themselves for the fight with the girdle of truth, and the sword of the Spirit. They are to become familiar with infidel objections to Christianity, and to be able to meet them.

Some of the following outlines are designed to supply arguments by which to withstand infidel opposition, to establish the minds of the wavering, and to comfort those who are weak and tremble for Zion. Such as they are, the Author leaves them to the judgment of the reader; and hopes that they may at least become suggestive of better thoughts, brighter ideas, and more powerful arguments, by which to secure the above objects. In that case, the author will have his reward.

W. N.

PULPIT THEMES.

I.—THE FAITHFUL AND ACCEPTABLE SAYING.

"This is a faithful saying, and worthy of all acceptation, that Jesus Christ came into the world to save sinners; of whom I am chief."—1 TIM. i. 15.

If a man has received special benefit from a medical prescription, he will very cordially recommend it to others.——The Apostle Paul had received great benefit from Jesus Christ, the great Physician of souls, for which he was willing to magnify him by life and by death. The grace of God had cured him of Pharisaism, of guilt and condemnation, of wretchedness and ruin, and had given him moral and spiritual health—Divine enjoyment—dignity of office—Christian usefulness, and heavenly hope. He had cause therefore to praise his Physician, and to recommend him to others.

The text has the character of a parenthesis; and seems to have been introduced into the narrative, because the mind of the Apostle was full of the subject. He, the chief of sinners, had obtained mercy, through "Christ Jesus, who had come into the world to save sinners." This doctrine to him was interesting and glorious, for he had felt its benefit; he regarded it as a sovereign remedy for the woes of humanity. It was "worthy of all acceptation." Consider,

I. THE GLORIOUS DOCTRINE: "*That Christ Jesus came into the world to save sinners.*"

The word "saying" means in this place, *doctrine, position,* or *declaration.*

This Doctrine divides itself thus: The Person delegated—the place into which he came—the design of his delegation—the extent of his saving power.

1. *The Person delegated to save sinners.* "Christ Jesus." A person of unparalleled dignity and glory, as declared by the pro-

phets, evangelists, and apostles. They speak of him as *Christ Jesus*,* as the anointed of God, and as the Saviour of the world. ——To save sinners — to save them for ever, it was necessary that the person delegated should be superior to men, the sinners, and to angels, the created — a Being super-human and super-angelic. Such was Christ Jesus, the Son of God—equal with him. Hence in accordance with his matchless dignity and glory, Moses speaks of him in these emphatical terms: "The Lord thy God," etc. Deut. viii. 15.——David in the most glowing terms, declares his royal and priestly character, Ps. cx. 1 — 4.—— The life-giving strains of Isaiah's harp announce his glory, as if the prophet had actually taken his stand by the Babe of Bethlehem, and eyed him in every step of his onward course, till, as the "Man of sorrows," he "poured out his soul unto death." O what strains are these! — "Unto us a child is born," etc. Isa. ix. 6, 7.——This is he of whom Jehovah speaks by the prophet Jeremiah: "Behold, the days come," etc. Jer. xxiii. 5, 6.—— This is that Messiah, of whom Gabriel speaks to Daniel the prophet, Dan. ix. 24.——This is that *Messenger*, or *Angel of the Covenant*, of whom Malachi, the last of the prophets, speaks. Mal. iii. 1.——And then if we come down to the writings of the Evangelists and Apostles, as they narrate his marvellous acts and teaching, and describe his gracious character, we behold "his glory as the only begotten of the Father, full of grace and truth." The language of the Apostle Paul speaks volumes; "Without controversy," etc. 1 Tim. iii. 16.—— This then is that glorious *Messiah*, that *Anointed One*, whom God the Father has consecrated, or set apart, as the great Prophet, Priest, and King of the church, that he may, by the efficient discharge of these offices, save sinners, even the chief.

2. *The Place into which he came:* "the world." This implies his pre-existence, and then his humility and condescension in coming into such a vile world as this. This is stated, John i. 1, 2; Phil. ii. 6 — 9. He came from heaven, that vast, pure, magnificent, and felicitous abode, to this fallen, sin-trodden, and sin-cursed world — from those realms of light to this region of darkness and shadow of death — from the greetings and adoration of the cherubim and seraphim to the lamentation, mourning and woe of wretched sinners — from association with pure ethereal spirits to mingle with publicans and sinners — from the throne of the King, to the manger, the cross, and the grave—from the Father in whose bosom he dwelt, to do battle with the Prince of this world —with the Prince of darkness. O what a transition! From heaven to earth! That pure Being! The Holy Son of God! to tabernacle here! Yet did the King eternal, immortal, and invisible, surrounded as he is with the splendour of a wide and everlasting monarchy, bend his steps to our humble habitation; yes, the foot-

---

* CHRIST. A Greek word answering to the Hebrew Messiah, signifying the *anointed*, or the consecrated one, or the Messiah, three terms of similar import. John i. 41.—— JESUS, means the Son of God, the Saviour of the world. This name is compounded of *Yah*, or *Jah*, a name of God, and *Houshaia*, the Saviour, and may therefore be read *Jehovah the Saviour.*— *Nicholson's Bible Companion.*

steps of God manifest in the flesh have been on this earth which sin has made like unto hell. Yes, defiled, loathsome, and miserable as this world was—and small though this planet be amid the orbs and the systems of immensity, yet hither hath the King of glory bent his mysterious way, and entered the tabernacle of vile men, and in the disguise of a servant did he sojourn for years under the roof which canopies our obscure and solitary world.* It was here that he clothed himself with the vile rags of humanity, and performed every part of his prophetical and priestly office, in a state of deep abasement, in order to obtain eternal redemption for us, and to lay the foundation of earth's future happiness, and his own inconceivable and everlasting mediatorial glory. Eph. iv. 9, 10.

3. *The Design of Christ Jesus in coming into the world.* "To save sinners."

His name, as before stated, indicates his gracious design. Matt. i. 20, 21.——Consider,

(1) *The persons he came to save.* "Sinners." It is evidently implied that those whom Christ came to save *needed salvation.* Hence Christ said, "For the Son of man is come to seek and to save that which was lost."

The Sinner is lost as to the *service of God and fellowship with him.* "Your sins and iniquities have separated between you and your God." Isa. lix. 2; Eph. iv. 18. The sinner has no love for God—no relish for his service—no desire for fellowship with him.

The sinner is lost as to *his body and the powers of his mind.* The body, by reason of sin, is decaying, and must die, Rom. v. 12; but while he lives, he yields every member of his body as an instrument of unrighteousness. Rom. vi. 13.——The powers of his mind too are prostrated to the service of sin. God has an absolute propriety in all his powers, but he will not have God to reign over him. The understanding, the will, the affections, the desires, are all captivated by sin, and drawn away from God. The sinner then is lost.

---

* Yes, this world is but a twinkling atom in the peopled infinity of worlds around it. But look to the moral grandeur of the transaction, and not to the material extent of the field upon which it was executed — and from the retirement of our dwelling-place, there may issue forth such a display of the God-head, as will circulate the glories of his name amongst all his worshippers. Here sin entered. Here was the kind and unwearied beneficence of a Father repaid by the ingratitude of a whole family. Here the law of God was dishonoured, and that too in the face of its proclaimed and unalterable sanctions. Here the mighty contest of the attributes was ended—and when justice put forth its demands, and truth called for the fulfilment of its warnings, and the immutability of God would not recede by a single iota from any one of its positions, and all the severities he ever uttered against the children of iniquity, seemed to gather into one cloud of impending vengeance on the tenement that held us—did the visit of the only-begotten Son chase away all these obstacles to the triumph of mercy — and humble as the tenement may be, deeply shaded in the obscurity of insignificance as it is, among the statelier mansions on every side of it — yet will the recall of its exiled family never be forgotten, and the illustration that has been given in this orb of the mingled grace and majesty of God, will never lose its place among the themes and acclamations of eternity. — *Dr. Chalmers.*

Lost as *a transgressor of God's holy law*, and condemned to suffer the fearful penalty denounced against the sinner. Jehovah will not allow his holy and righteous law to be broken with impunity.——Therefore he has declared, "The soul that sinneth shall die." See also Rom. iii. 19, 20; Gal. iii. 10.

The sinner then has lost the Divine favour—is under the curse, and therefore must be wretched.——It is impossible for a creature to be happy, who is conscious of his own depravity, and his liability to suffer all the consequences of sin. In the absence of God, and of innocence, there is in the soul of man an aching void, that cannot be filled from the haunts of pleasure and dissipation. "There is no peace, saith my God, to the wicked."

The sinner is *absolutely* lost—his ruin is complete—he cannot save himself—nor can he be saved by any other being, human or angelic. Neither he, nor any one for him, can honour the broken law and satisfy the claims of Divine justice. His impurity is deep and abominable in the sight of God; but he cannot cleanse himself; he cannot restore the beauteous image of God, which sin has defaced, nor make himself a new creature.

(2) *How the coming of Christ was conducive to the salvation of sinners.*

Prompted by infinite love the Saviour came from the most excellent glory to save sinners, when he was under no necessity of coming; he came to save, not to destroy; to reveal mercy, not to denounce judgment; to save sinners—the poor, the lost, the wandering—not to condemn them; he came to restore them to the favour of God, to raise them up from their degradation, and exalt them to heaven's eternal felicities. He effected this

By placing himself in the sinner's state and circumstances. His incarnation allied him to humanity. The Son of God became the "Babe of Bethlehem." He was poor, despised, persecuted, and misrepresented. By assuming human nature, he was able to sympathize, and capable of suffering and death. John i. 14; Heb. ii. 14—18.

He honoured the law by his perfect obedience to all its precepts. See Heb. vii. 26—28.

He came as a Prophet, as the *Light of the world*, to remove the sinner's ignorance by revealing to him his lost estate—the way of salvation—the path of obedience—and the hope of eternal life—accompanying all with the gift of his Holy Spirit to make wise unto salvation. Luke i. 76—79.

He came as a priest to make atonement for sinners. He ascended the cross, and there endured the penalty due to lost men. He endured the curse himself for guilty man. See Isa. liii. et cum multis.

He came as a King to expel every foe from the heart, to subdue every lust, and to reign there as supreme—and to conquer all the foes of his saved people.

4. *The extent of his Saving Power.* "Of whom I am chief," or the first, denoting that he occupied the first rank among sinners. Even his strict regard to the moral law was prompted by great pride of heart. See Phil. iii. 4—8. But that which particularly aggravated his guilt was the part which he had taken in putting the saints to death. 1 Tim. i. 13; Acts viii. 3; xxvi. 9—11; 1 Cor. xv. 9.——A true penitent will always retain an abasing sense of his past guilt; and such a conviction is not inconsistent with evidence of piety, and high Christian attainments.

But the conversion and salvation of Saul of Tarsus proves that Christ Jesus came to save the vilest of the vile. His grace is infinite, sovereign, and free. "Able to save to the uttermost." Heb. vii. 25. "Mighty to save." Isa. lxiii. 1. Hence he saved such characters as the Corinthians, 1 Cor. vi. 9, 10.——No sins are of too deep a dye for the atoning blood of Christ to wash away; no habits of vice are too strong for his victorious grace to subdue; no former crimes shall prevent the exercise of the Divine clemency through Christ Jesus. He will make his grace to superabound where sin has most abounded. Rom. v. 20. He that could extend his mercy to the furious, cruel, and bloody persecutor, Saul, and make him a vessel of honour, and a successful Apostle, what cannot his grace do? He that could save a Magdalene, etc., what cannot his grace do? Verily it is boundless. "Though your sins be as scarlet," etc. Isa. i. 18.

II. THE CHARACTER OF THIS SAYING: "Faithful" and "worthy of all acceptation."

1. *It is a true Saying.* "Faithful," or true, credible, that which may safely be depended on. The Apostle uses the phrase several times; 1 Tim. iii. 1; iv. 9; Titus iii. 8. This phrase appears to have been used by the Apostle when he delivered a truth of vast importance. The truth of this Doctrine is proved

(1) *By prophecy.* Prophecy foretold that Christ Jesus should come into the world, and subsequent history proves that he did. The *time of his coming was exactly foretold.* It was when the Sceptre had departed, etc. Gen. xlix. 10, or when the Jews had no kings of their own nation, but were governed by strangers. This was foretold by Jacob on his dying bed 1700 years before the event. Daniel too predicted the time of Christ's coming, Dan. ix. 24, etc. The "seventy weeks" meaning weeks of years, or 490 years. At the expiration of that time Christ Jesus came, according to Sir Isaac Newton, and other learned chronologers.——The exact *place of his birth* was foretold by the prophet Micah, v. 2, *Bethlehem.* There he was born, and by means of a very special providence, the promulgation of an edict by Augustus Cæsar, requiring all persons to repair to the places of their nativity in order to be enrolled or registered there.—— The birth of Christ was miraculous, and accorded with the spirit of prophecy, Isa vii. 14; Matt. i. 18, etc. So did the character of Christ, the treatment he received from men, and the nature of his sufferings, death, resur-

rection, and ascension. See Ps. xxii; Ps. lxix; Isa. liii; Ps. lxviii. 18.

(2) The *miracles* which Christ performed, and the *miraculous power* with which he endowed his disciples, prove the gospel to be true. See 2 Pet. i. 16, 17.

The apostles were not deceivers—they had nothing to gain—on the other hand, for the truth's sake they were exposed to contempt, to imprisonment, to torture, and to death. If the gospel had been false, if they had not been eye-witnesses of Christ's majesty and glory, would they have endured all this?

(3) Proved by the holy, benevolent, and disinterested life of Christ. He did no sin — went about doing good — sought not the praise of men, but the approbation of God. Deceivers are never good and disinterested.

(4) *The truth of the gospel is proved by its efficacy.* It is not a mere pretence. It really answers the design announced — to save the sinner. It is an efficient specific for the woes of humanity. Millions of patients have taken the medicine, and their spiritual diseases have in consequence been healed.———

(5) The Gospel is true because all history shows that Providence has determined to secure its ultimate influence and glory.———The hand of persecution has not been able to arrest and stay its progress.———Neither the waters nor the fires of persecution have drowned or consumed it. Providence has guarded it and secured its triumphs. What inventions of cruelty, what machinations of evil have been called into requisition to destroy the gospel, but it still lives, and gives evidence of still more splendid conquests!

2. *It is worthy of all Acceptation.* It is so full of joyful and heavenly intelligence — so replete with salvation here and eternal life hereafter, that it is worthy of being received with the most fervid gratitude, with all possible readiness of mind, and with a joyful exulting heart. It is worthy of all acceptation

(1) *Because it is true.* It would not matter however rich the blessings of the gospel were stated to be, if they were not true. But as the salvation is great, — the riches of Christ unsearchable, and the weight of glory inconceivably vast and eternal, this is their further and greatest recommendation, they are strictly true. "A faithful saying." Not a "cunningly devised fable."

(2) This saying or doctrine being of *the highest interest to us* makes it worthy of all acceptation. We are the "*sinners*" needing salvation — we cannot save ourselves — if not saved by Christ we must perish. Is not wealth acceptable to the poor man — a physician to the diseased or dying, liberty to the captive, pardon to the condemned? etc. The state of a sinner is more abject and perilous. This "saying" is the only ground of a sinner's hope.

(3) It is worthy of all acceptation from *the nature of salvation itself.* It gives complete pardon—full justification—peace—joy—likeness to God—fellowship with him—hope of heaven—victory over death and the grave—an abundant entrance into heaven

itself. Is not this worthy of a cheerful, prompt, and joyful acceptance?——Men would readily accept of gold and silver, of a coronet or a crown, a splendid mansion, and a vast domain, if freely tendered them, but what trifles are these compared with an interest in God here, and heaven and glory for ever!

It is a doctrine which in its causes and consequences will occupy the attention of eternity itself, and become the theme, the song of heaven for ever, Rev. v. 9—14.

Lastly. The way of accepting it is *by faith*. First to feel the need of it—to comprehend its simple yet glorious import—then to rely on the glorious statement that "Christ Jesus came into the world to save sinners." This is believing, this is faith. So the jailor acted. Acts xvi.

II.—CHRIST THE FRIEND OF SINNERS.

"A Friend of publicans and sinners."—LUKE vii. 34.

That which may be deemed reproachful by some men, may be esteemed honourable by others.——In spiritual things this is true. Sinners account that dishonourable which God regards and pronounces to be honourable. The Pharisees in the context thought it disreputable for Christ to associate with publicans and sinners. But they mistook his character, and the design of his mission. With him the soul of a publican was as valuable as the soul of a prince. The one needs salvation as much as the other.——To be the Friend of publicans and sinners was a glorious trait in the Redeemer's character and not a reproach. It will be the joy of the church on earth to the end of time, and the admiration of heaven for ever, that Jesus Christ is the Friend of publicans and sinners—the Friend of the vilest of the vile.

The gracious statement in the text may be proved and illustrated by the following observations:—

I. *How different was the procedure of Christ from that of men!*

They love to associate with men of equal or of superior birth and station. To the poor man, to the vile and outcast, they often say by their conduct, " Stand by thyself, I am holier than thou." ——But Christ associated with publicans and sinners, v. 29.

·A publican was one appointed by the Romans to collect taxes, the Jewish tribute, etc. They were generally great extortioners, and detested by the Jews, Matt. v. 46. They were sinners, and Christ longed to save them. He delighted to bless those who did not merit his blessing. The poor, the lame, the blind, the sick, and all the wretched sons of woe, were the objects of his anxious solicitude. "I came not to call the righteous, but sinners to repentance."

II. *The wretched circumstances of publicans and sinners required an Almighty Friend.* "Sin is the transgression of the law," and that is followed by "*the curse.*" Gal. iii. 10. Sin defiles and ruins the soul. The sinner, then, needs a Friend. —— Does a sick man need a physician — an insolvent man a friend — a man liable to perish a deliverer? Much more does the sinner need a Saviour; else there can be no meaning in the terrible denunciations of the law, and the sweet promises of the gospel. Rom. iii. 9—26.

III. *To be the Friend of Publicans and sinners accorded with the design of Christ's mission.*

For this he was ordained, for this he was qualified, and sealed. He came to "save sinners," "the ungodly," "the unrighteous." 1 Tim. i. 15. He said at Nazareth, "The Spirit of the Lord," etc. Luke iv. 18.

IV. *Christ has proved himself the Friend of publicans and sinners*

1. *By assuming their nature.* John i. 14.

2. *By becoming their Surety*—dying in their stead, and rising for their justification. For them he endured the penalty due to transgression.——A poor publican—the chief of sinners, may look to the Lamb slain on the cross, and say, "He loved me, and gave himself for me."

3. *By the operations of his grace upon their hearts.* He enlightens and quickens them to see their fall and ruin — he draws them to himself. They believe on his name; they fall and rest upon his sacrifice. He sprinkles his precious blood upon their consciences. He absolves them from all their sins. They are free.——He gives them his sanctifying and comforting Spirit. 1 John i. 7, 9.

4. *By what he is doing for them in heaven*—pleading their cause —and sympathizing with them in their sorrows.

5. *By his gracious purpose to guard and guide them through all the dangers of their earthly state.* "Lo! I am with you alway, even to the end of the world." "Thou shalt guide me with thy counsel, and afterwards receive me to glory."

V. *The Character of Christ as the Friend of publicans and sinners*

1. *He is Divine.* An earthly friend is valuable. But Christ is a Divine Friend with infinite resources to save and bless publicans and sinners. He who befriends us — he who saves, is God. John i. 1—3; Heb. i. 1, etc.

2. *He is an Almighty Friend.* Almighty to subdue the sinful heart and all its hateful lusts — to conquer all spiritual foes — to calm all mental fears — and to fill with peace and joy through believing.

3. *He is a constant and unvarying Friend* — in adversity as well as prosperity; in sickness and in health, etc. "A true friend loveth at all times." This is true of Christ. "I will never leave thee," etc. —— His friendship is effectual; it is prompt, and not

merely professional. He promises much, and he is ever ready to do abundantly above all we can ask or think.

4. *He is an everlasting friend.* His friendship here is consummated by eternal life in heaven, in his immediate presence.

APPLICATION.

1. How encouraging this statement to the penitent sinner,—to one desponding on account of the malignity of his case!——If the salvation of a sinner depended upon man, he would be rejected on account of his vileness.

2. The conduct of Christ is worthy of imitation. He was not ashamed of the poor sinner. Be like him. Angels thought themselves highly honoured when they conveyed the soul of a beggar to Abraham's bosom. Seek to bless the poor, the wretched, the vile. "Go into the highways," etc.

3. Blessed are they who have Christ for their Friend. Is he your Friend?

III.—THE GLORIOUS MANIFESTATION OF CHRIST AND HIS PEOPLE.

"WHEN Christ, who is our life, shall appear, then shall ye also appear with him in glory."—COL. iii. 4.

GLORIOUS are the privileges and distinctions of God's people in this world; but greater honours await them in the next. For the enjoyment of future glory, they are not at present constituted, and the world could not bear its manifestation.——Divine grace has been infused into their souls in this life, and has had its transforming and elevating influence. But grace is but the bud of glory hereafter to be expanded. In the great day of eternity, God will finish his work, and perfect all that which concerns his people. Then the bud of grace will open into an immortal flower, and exhibit its unfading beauties, and yield its undying fragrance, amid all the solemnities of the Last Day. "When Christ, who is our Life," etc.

I. THE CHARACTER OF CHRIST. "Our Life."

This character is frequently given to him. "In him was life, and the life was the light of men." John i. 4. He is spoken of as the giver of life, John x. 28.

This character is represented figuratively. Christ is the Head. Believers are the members of his body, Eph. iv. 15, 16; Col. i. 18. He is called the "Vine," and believers are the "branches," John xv.

This representation implies,

1. That Christ is the *Author of spiritual life*. The life of a sinner is carnal, worldly, wicked.——But Christ by his word and Spirit, regenerates the soul. It is dead to all spiritual or holy life. He quickens it, and raises it to a new state of holy existence. "Therefore if any man be in Christ Jesus, he is a new creature." He has "passed from death unto life." He gives power, energy, to the means of grace—to human instrumentality, for the quickening of dead souls.——Now they are changed. Different from what they were before.

2. Christ is the Author of their *justified life*. This is stated, Acts xiii. 38, 39. Freedom from condemnation. Rom. viii. 1. Peace. Rom. v. 1.

3. He is the Author of their *sanctification*. The Life of their holiness. He is "made unto them sanctification." At v. 3, they are said to be "dead." Dead to the world, to sin, to earthly pleasures. Just as Christ became virtually dead in the tomb, so they in virtue of their connection with him, have become dead to sin, etc. See Rom. vi.

4. He is the Author of a life of *spiritual privilege and joy* to all his people. Adoption — communion with God — manifestations of his love and power to their hearts — the Life of all their graces, faith, hope, patience, joy in the Holy Ghost.

5. He is their *sustaining Life*. Maintains his life in their souls, in opposition to worldly, depraved, and Satanic influence. Phil. i. 6.

6. He is their *Resurrection* Life. See John xi. 25; Rom. viii. 11. How different then will the body be — "fashioned like unto his glorious body."

7. He is the Author of *Eternal Life*. Rom. vi. 23.

II. THE SECOND APPEARANCE OF CHRIST. "Shall appear."

The appearance of Christ to judge the world and glorify his people may be argued on several grounds—from reason—from the justice of God—from the unequal distribution of things—from the responsibility of man. But the voice of scripture alone is sufficient. "Thus saith the Lord."

He shall appear. So said Enoch, the seventh from Adam. Jude 14, 15.

He shall appear. Holy Job anticipated it. Job xix. 25, 26, 29.

He shall appear. "Our God shall come," says the Psalmist. Ps. l. 3, 4, 6.

He shall appear. It was announced by Christ and his apostles. Matt. xxv. 31, etc. Acts xvii. 31. 2 Cor. v. 10, etc. etc.

His appearance will be glorious. Glorious in his person. How different from his first appearance! Glorious in his attendants, angels.—Glorious in his office and authority.

III. THAT ALL TRUE BELIEVERS SHALL APPEAR WITH CHRIST IN GLORY. "Then shall ye also appear with him in glory."

1. Christ will account it an honour, when he appears in glory to have all his redeemed with him. It will be the day for the "manifestation of the sons of God." "They shall come from the east," etc. "A great company which no man can number." This glorified multitude will illustrate the power of his grace— the efficacy of his blood — and the greatness and glory of his salvation. "He shall come to be glorified in his saints, and to be admired in all them that believe."

2. They shall appear in his glorious likeness. Like him in body and soul. 1 John iii. 2.

3. They will appear with him in glory, as the participants in his honour, joy, and felicity. Whatever gladdens him will gladden them. Then will he realize "the joy set before him."

4. They will appear with him in glory as the honoured instruments whom he has employed to carry on the interests of his kingdom. Like some great conqueror returning from the field of battle, and recognizing the military prowess of all the soldiers whom he has commanded, and whom he commends to the attention of his sovereign—so Christ will own the labours of his people—the least service—the cup of cold water—the feeble offering, shall not lose its reward. "God is not unrighteous to forget," etc.

5. They will appear with him in glory, publicly, before angels, demons, and mankind, to receive his approval and the rewards of his grace — to "inherit the kingdom prepared," etc. — to "enter into the joy of their Lord."

6. They shall appear with him in glory, while sinners — the great, the noble, the illustrious, the proud oppressor, shall be "clothed with shame and everlasting contempt."

APPLICATION.

1. The key to heavenly glory. "Christ our life."
2. The glorious result of serving Christ. "Glory."
3. A proper estimate of the world. It is mean and worthless when compared with future glory.

IV.—PRAYER OF THE DISEASED SOUL TO THE DIVINE PHYSICIAN.

"LORD, be merciful unto me, heal my soul, for I have sinned against thee."—Ps. xli. 4.

WHAT dreadful havoc has sin produced upon the body and soul of man. At his creation he came forth from the hands of his Creator pure and happy, and when Jehovah gazed on him, and saw his image reflected by him, he pronounced him to be very good.——But, alas! what a change! "The pure gold has become dim." Sin has marred and defiled the beauty of man. It has diseased both body and soul, and he is now a compound of pain and sorrow, of condemnation and ruin.

This Psalm appears to have been written by David when afflicted in body, and persecuted by his enemies: v. 6—10. A time of sickness is favourable to the duty of self-examination; for then the mind is solemnized by thoughts of death and eternity. David examined himself, and found himself imperfect and sinful. He regarded sin as a hateful disease, and earnestly prayed to be delivered from it. Doubtless he was anxious about his body; but the welfare of his immortal soul claimed his supreme attention. Whereas the majority of mankind care but for the body. Consider,

I. SIN AS A DISEASE. Moral evil is in this petition described as a disease.

As there is some analogy between the body and the soul, so there is between the diseases of the one and the other.

This disease is a spiritual one, affecting the nature, beauty, health, vigour, and happiness of the soul. Thus David says, "Bless the Lord, O my soul, who healeth all thy diseases."

1. Bodily disease consists in *disorder*, or some derangement in the system. Perspiration may be obstructed, the circulation of the blood impeded or rapidly increased by febrile affection, muscular action relaxed, and the strength of the animal frame prostrated. The disease of the soul is something akin to this. The soul is altogether diseased. All its powers are perverted. "From the crown," etc. Isa. i. 6.

The *understanding* is diseased. What is the disease of the understanding, but ignorance and folly? Originally it was a lamp of moral and intellectual brightness. But how is it now? 1 Cor. ii. 14.

The *memory* is diseased. Proved by the quickness with which it remembers sinful things, and the quickness with which it forgets holy things. It is like the husbandman's sieve, which retains the chaff, and allows the good grain to escape. It was once a cabinet of jewels, it is now a receptacle of dross.

The will is *diseased*. Proved by its opposition to the will of God. The will of God is infinitely good, that which opposes it must be infinitely evil.

The *affections* are diseased. Look at its love. It loves the creature in preference to the Creator — the husks of the swine instead of the heavenly manna.—— Look at its desires. A man diseased in body, often desires what would injure him, and which the wise physician peremptorily forbids. So it is with the diseased soul; it desires those objects which accelerate its ruin. As to the affection of grief, the diseased soul weeps over the loss of that which can do it no good—which can ruin it—and it discovers no grief for the loss of invaluable blessings designed to enrich the soul for ever. As it respects its joys, they arise from the pursuit of vanity —shadows. Joy in the creature—in the possession of perishing trifles, etc.——Is not the soul diseased?

The *conscience* is diseased. If sin had left any part uninjured, it would seem to be the conscience. Not so; *the very conscience is defiled;* and nothing has been too vile to be perpetrated under its permission, and in obedience to its dictates. Sin sometimes makes the conscience speak erroneously, and at other times it strikes it dumb.——

2. This Disease *has been derived from Adam*, who lost his first estate, and is now *inherent in the human constitution*. Man comes into the world with the seeds of evil in his very nature. " He goes astray from his birth, speaking lies." *

3. It is a disease characterized by *offensiveness*, and *unfitness for society*.——So David viewed the disease of sin. Ps. xxxviii. 5—8. This offensiveness is found in their language, in their disposition, tempers, practices. They yield the members of their bodies, and the powers of their minds as instruments of uncleanness. Rom. vi.——How offensive a diseased sinner to a real godly man—to an angel—to a pure spirit—to God.†——

4. *This disease is infectious.* Satan, who was first diseased, communicated the infection to the angels who fell from heaven, and soon after the fair structure of earth was finished, he inoculated

---

* 'Who can bring a clean thing out of an unclean?' It is a law pervading all nature that "like begets like." A viper brings forth a poisonous brood. Swine produce something that loves the mire. The skin of an Ethiopian will be black. What but depraved offspring can descend from sinful parents? Therefore, says Job, 'What is man, that he should be clean, or he that is born of a woman, that he should be righteous!' The scripture assures us that 'all have sinned and come short of the glory of God.' It teaches us, that 'the heart is deceitful above all things and desperately wicked.' It assures us that it is not the life which defiles the heart; but the heart the life: 'For from within, out of the heart of men, proceed evil thoughts, adulteries, fornications, murders, thefts, covetousness, wickedness, deceit, lasciviousness, an evil eye, blasphemy, pride, foolishness: all these evil things come from within, and defile the man.' It requires no less than a change of nature, to show that our nature is depraved; and it requires this change in every man, to show that this depravity is universal.—*Jay.*

† And sin *is* uncleanness. Its very nature is contamination. The moment it touched a number of angels in heaven, it turned them into devils, and expelled them from their first estate. It is so contagious, that it infects every thing in contact with it, so that, as the house of the leper was to be taken down because of the inhabitant, 'the heavens shall pass away with a great noise, and the elements shall melt with fervent heat, the earth, also, and all the works that are therein shall be burned up'—not because they are guilty— but because they have been the witnesses, the instruments, the abodes of sin.

Sin is a pollution the most deep and diffusive; it stops not at the surface, but penetrates the inner man of the heart; it spreads through every power, from the highest intellectual faculty, down to the lowest animal appetite. It is a pollution the most horrible and dangerous, as it disfigures us before God; and renders us odious in his sight. And nothing else does this. Poverty does not; meanness does not; disease does not—Lazarus full of sores, begging at the rich man's gate, and Job covered with boils among the ashes, were dear to God, and lay in his bosom. But sin is the *abominable thing* which his *soul hates*. Men often roll it, as a sweet morsel, under their tongue; but it is more poisonous than the gall of asps. They think lightly of it; but can *that* be a trifling thing which causes God to hate the very work of his own hands—(my soul loathed them!)—and induce the very 'Father of mercies' to say at last, ' Depart, ye cursed, into everlasting fire, prepared for the devil and his angels!' —*Jay.*

the spotless nature of man with the foul contagion. Great is the influence of evil example.——

5. *It is universal.* It has spread itself over the whole world. "All have sinned," etc. Rom. iii. 23.

6. *It is painful.* Nearly all diseases of the body are painful. So it is with the soul — when evil is done, and conscience awakes — when death and judgment are near.

Lastly, Its *influence is destructive* and leads to death. Even as disease wastes and destroys the body. So with sin. Sin destroys the strength of the soul; it mars the beauty of the soul, changing all its glory into deformity; it destroys the spiritual appetite, causes it to loathe the pure delights of heaven. It destroys the enjoyments of the soul!

And then sin, when it is finished, bringeth forth *death!* Sin is the mortal poison of the soul which introduces into the body the principles of its destruction, and into the soul those evil propensities which will issue in eternal perdition. This is its natural tendency, and nothing can counteract it but the grace of God.—— Consider,

II. THE PRAYER OF DAVID. "Lord, be merciful," etc.

1. *It was the prayer of a man who felt his disease.* "Heal my soul," implying that he felt that his soul was diseased.—— The whole system of the gospel is founded in the fact of our guilt and depravity, and till a man is convinced of this, he will never apply for Divine mercy. Pardon offered to the innocent will be deemed an insult. Alms presented to the affluent will be rejected with disdain. O what a mercy to feel the need of mercy!

2. It was the prayer of a man who *despaired of saving himself,* and who sought help from God. "Lord, be merciful unto me. I cannot save myself from this dreadful disease. It is too firmly fixed in my soul for me to remove. Ceremonial law observances will not remove it. I cannot destroy it by munificent gifts. In ordinary things 'where the word of a king is, there is power;' but I have no power over this disease." Such was the experience of Paul, Phil. iii. and that of every true Christian: "By the deeds of the law," etc.

3. It was the *prayer of penitence, and confession of sin to God.* "I have sinned against thee." He regarded sin as not only injurious to himself, but as offensive to God, and meriting his displeasure and wrath. See Ps. li. He was contrite—he was humbled — he mourned the effects of sin. "If we confess our sins," etc. 1 John i. 8, 9.

4. It was a prayer for the *application of the healing art of the Almighty Physician of souls.* "Lord, be merciful unto me: heal my soul."

The disease of sin is not incurable. It is so indeed to us, but not to the Lord, Matt. xvii. 14 — 17. Like the leprosy of old, it yields to no human application.

(1) It was a recognition of Divine Mercy flowing through the mediation of Christ. It is only by and through him "that God can be just, and yet the justifier of him that believeth in Jesus." He is called "the mercy promised to the Fathers." And the nature of this mercy is beautifully stated, Tit. iii. 4—7.——Christ has honoured the law—he has removed the curse—"broken down the middle wall of partition," Eph. ii. 14, 15, and therefore God can be merciful. "Behold the Lamb of God," etc., for there is mercy, and pardon, and justification, and all the sin-sick soul can need. Christ is the Physician—his blood the cure.

(2) It was a recognition of Divine power. "Heal my soul." Rectify all its disorders—subjugate every symptom of my disease —cleanse me from all impurity—give me a disposition to hate sin — and strength to resist its influence. "Create within me," etc. Give me thy Spirit to work thy will in me, and to bear witness, etc. Then shall I be healed.

(3) It is the *prayer of faith*. Prayer is nothing without faith, and faith is always connected with successful prayer. David was a believer—a believer in that Saviour whom he predicted. "Believe in the Lord Jesus Christ, and thou shalt be saved."

APPLICATION.

1. Be thankful that sin can be healed.
2. Avoid all unscriptural means of healing.
3. The time for being healed will soon come to an end. "The harvest will soon be past."

V.— SWEETNESS OF DIVINE MEDITATION.

"My meditation of him shall be sweet."— Ps. civ. 34.

AMONG all the subjects of contemplation presented to the mind, there is none that can in any degree be compared with God, the only Fountain of true and enduring happiness. His "favour is life," and his "loving-kindness is better than life."

The Psalm was written by David; and in it he celebrates the omnipotence and unbounded benevolence of God in the fabric of the world, and the operations of Divine Providence. The Psalmist shows that we need not to enter into heaven to seek God; for all the works of nature, and their complete order, are most lively mirrors which reflect his majesty. What a broad field for meditation does this Psalm afford! The Psalmist contemplates God. Consider

I. THE OBJECT OF CHRISTIAN MEDITATION.

A good man loves to think that there is such a great and glorious Being as God, and he delights to meditate on his nature, attributes, word, and works. With great pleasure he dwells on all the arrangements of his love, and the gracious relationship to himself, to which he has condescended to admit the chief of sinners. The Christian meditates upon God as the self-existent God, the Creator, and Governor of the universe. And it is sweet and comfortable to his mind, to think that the world and all its affairs are superintended and managed by infinite wisdom and love, and not left to blind contingency or chance. While the belief of the existence and government of God is the source of comfort, Atheism throws a dark and most melancholy aspect over human existence. If there is no God, there is no soul, no future state of existence, no responsibility. Atheism may harmonize with the feelings and wishes of a depraved heart, — and that is the real source of all infidelity — but it does not harmonize with the dictates of reason, and of an enlightened and sanctified judgment. Indeed, what is human existence — what is this world — what are all human possessions — what is life, if there is no God? A perfect blank; nothing, worse than nothing — answering no purpose — leading to no result.

But there is a God. Our reason would have it so — conscience enunciates it — all the works of creation proclaim it. All manifest design, contrivance, and the exercise of infinite intelligence, and Almighty power and love.——And man is immortal; he aspires after eternity. This is a constituent part of his nature. A desire to live for ever is inwoven in his soul.*

More particularly, As the Christian is fully persuaded as to the existence of God, he meditates

---

* "Modern atheists and infidels are the advocates of Nature-worship. Here we have a Carlyle shouting out his wild wolf-like '*Eureka*' about earth, 'She is my mother and divine.' There Emerson sings his hymns to 'Nature,' and as he steps over puddles and barren moors, under dull and dripping skies, almost fears to say how glad he is. Yonder, poets and poetasters, are emulously contending which of them shall most extravagantly praise the stars, and the smoke of ten thousand censers in steaming up the unconscious midnight. And even a lady steps forth, and proposes in very bad verse that we shall henceforth worship the sun. And in remoter distance stand the authors of the 'Vestiges,' and the 'Constitution of Man,' surrounded by their many-eyed votaries, declaring that man has crawled up to his present position from the low level of the brute, and that forsooth a fungus can develop into a Foster, a worm into a Wadsworth, an ape into a Newton!"

A writer in the *Eclectic Review* for May, 1854, thus writes, and also the following beautiful remarks deserve attention: "The creation, large and magnificent as it is, is not equal in grandeur or worth to one immortal mind. Majestic the universe is, but can it think, or feel, or reason, or imagine, or hope, or love?" talk to me of the sun! One might say, standing up in all the conscious dignity of his own nature: 'The sun is not alive: he is but a dead luminary after all; I am alive; I never was dead; I never can die. I may therefore put my foot on that proud orb and say, I am greater than thou. The sun cannot, with all his rays, write on flower, or grass, or the broad page of ocean, the name of God. A child of seven can, and is therefore greater than the sun. The sun cannot from his vast surface utter an articulate sound. He is a magnificent mute; but out of the mouths of babes and sucklings God perfects praise. The sun shall perish; but I have that within me that shall never die. He might, indeed, or the universe of which he is a part, arise and "crush me; but I should *know* he was crushing me. I should be conscious of the defeat; he should not be conscious of the victory." The whole material universe, in short, is only the nursery to my immortal mind; and whether is greater, the nursery, or the child? I am a spirit, and *it* is only a great and glorious clod.'

1. Upon the perfections of God.

He is eternal. Ps. xc. 1, 2. With what awe and pleasure should we meditate on a Being whose duration had no beginning, nor shall have an end! Isa. lviii. 15; 1 Tim. i. 17. He "only hath immortality," that is, originally, essentially, and independently. See also Deut. xxxiii. 27; Isa. xli. 4; and Rev. i. 8. The God whom the Christian has chosen for his portion, must be a satisfying portion. He loves them with an everlasting love.

He is immutable. If God is eternal, he is unchangeable. James i. 17. He says concerning himself, "I am the Lord, I change not." — See Hebrews i. 10. How sweet is this thought! — every thing around me changes — my affairs, my family, my health, etc., are all mutable. I turn to my God, and find there an abiding refuge.

He is omnipresent. He is an infinite Being, and space with him is nothing. 1 Kings viii. 27; Ps. cxxxix. 7 — 10; Jer. xxiii. 23, 24. Precious thought! Wherever I am, the God of salvation is there. On land, on sea, in all perils, in persecution, in prison, in famine and distress, in sickness, in death, my God is there.

He is omniscient. Infinite in knowledge. 1 Sam. ii. 2. "His understanding is infinite." Ps. cxlvii. 5; Heb. iv. 13. To the believer the omniscience of God is a precious attribute. God knows all about him at any time, and overshadows him with the wings of Divine love. "I am poor and needy, yet the Lord thinketh on me." "Lord, all my desire is before thee," etc. Ps. xxxviii. 9.

He is omnipotent. This perfection is magnificently proclaimed by the sacred penmen. Ps. clviii. 5; Job. ix. 4 and 19; xxxvii. 23; Gen. xvii. 1. How safe, then, must the Christian be, when exposed to dangers, enemies! God can and will deliver and preserve him.

And *every other attribute* affords the greatest scope for sweet and rapturous meditation. His unspotted purity — his impartial justice and righteousness — his goodness and mercy — his truth and faithfulness. These attributes of God are manifested

2. In the *works of creation,* upon which the Christian delights to meditate.* Every object that he beholds leads him up to its Almighty Creator, and declares his glory. "The invisible things of God, even his eternal power and Godhead," are revealed to the pious meditant, "by the things which do appear." He reflects upon his body, and sees the most exquisite skill, etc. He extends his thoughts to the orb which he inhabits, — its continents and oceans; its varying climes and changing seasons; its numerous productions, and its myriads of inhabitants; the regularity of the laws by which it is governed, and the harmony of every operation

---

* Nature seen by meditation, through the medium of revelation, assumes a new appearance. It is then no longer an effect without a known cause, nor a means without any visible tendency to an end; but it is recognized as the work of an intelligent Being, displaying, upon a grand and extensive scale, his infinite wisdom, power, and beneficence. — *Richard Watson.*

of that energy by which it is supported. Thus he discovers the works of the Lord, and the operations of his hands, and exclaims, "O Lord, how manifold are thy works! in wisdom hast thou made them all," etc. Ps. civ. 24. Lifting up his eyes to the celestial expanse above him, the wonders which this interior part of the temple of the universe discloses, confirm these sentiments, and enlarge these conceptions: — "The heavens declare," etc. Ps. xix. 1; viii. 3, 4. The Christian meditates

3. On the *operations of Divine Providence.* That Providence governs a boundless universe, and yet cares for the meanest saint. "Casting all your care upon him, for he careth for you." Carnal men witness the operations, and feel the influence of the Divine government; but they see not its secret springs, and are unable to trace its effects. Empires rise and fall; wars and tumults shake the nations of the earth; princes and noblemen, by counsel in the cabinet, or by military prowess in the field, appear to "ride on the whirlwind and direct the storm." These are the only causes which the majority of men recognize.——But the Christian who reflects upon God, enters into the counsels of Heaven, and, in some measure, learns the motives of the Divine Governor. "The secret of the Lord is with them that fear him." "Shall I hide from Abraham the thing that I do?" Where others mark the operation of second causes only, he contemplates the universal influence of the first. Where they see an agent only, he sees a Principal directing it. Where they see confusion, he sees order,—a regular and continued plan executed by Deity in every age. Many things indeed to him are mysterious, because his powers are limited, yet he confides in the wisdom of God.

The Christian delights to meditate on the special providence which has characterized his life. He finds, on reflection, that God has "crowned his life with loving-kindness," etc.——that he has saved his soul from the snare of the Evil One, and brought him into a spiritual alliance with himself. Again, the Christian meditates

4. On *Redemption by Christ Jesus.* This is a wondrous and all-absorbing theme. It has interested the church in every age; for "the gospel was preached unto them as well as unto us; and though the medium was too dim for the object to be seen very distinctly through it, yet enough was discovered to interest the soul. David says, "In thy law do I meditate day and night;" not in the moral law only, but in the Levitical, that by an attentive perusal of the shadow, his conception of the substance might become more correct and extensive. On this subject all the prophets loved to dwell. "Of which salvation," etc. See 1 Pet. i. 10, 11.——But the shadows have passed away, and the true substance is manifested. Jesus has appeared—died, risen, ascended, intercedes, and reigns. Every Christian delights to dwell on this mighty redemption. He regards himself as a transgressor, deserving infinite wrath; but sees Jesus interposing as

the willing victim to endure that wrath in his stead. He sees him smitten of God and afflicted for him. It pleased the Father to bruise him, and put him to grief; and he, by the power of love unparalleled, love stronger than death, became "obedient unto death," etc. He sees suspended from that cross all that his soul needs in time and in eternity,—a free, full, rich, soul-exalting, and everlasting salvation. "He loved me, and gave himself for me."

5. Upon vanquished death, a glorious resurrection, and a purchased heaven of immortal life and bliss. The sacrifice of Christ secures the conquest of death. "He hath abolished death." 1 Cor. xv. 55, etc.——His resurrection is the pledge that his people shall be raised, and leave behind them all sin, sorrow, and death. ——Christ has entered heaven as the Forerunner of his people——they shall soon follow, and reign with him in that bright and happy world. It is sweet for the saint to meditate on his Father's house above—"eternal in the heavens." Oppressed with sin, and many woes, he contemplates "THE REST." Groaning in a tabernacle full of infirmity and imperfection, he rejoices in the reversion of "a house not made with hands," a state of perfection and love, a permanency of felicitous condition.

II. WHAT IS NECESSARY TO RENDER MEDITATION ON GOD SWEET.

1. *A proper estimate of the Duty.* It must be regarded as important, and as fraught with great advantages, or it will not be sweet.

2. That it be *congenial to the mind.* This is the effect of regeneration, by which man's enmity to God is removed. Now there is true affinity. To meditate on God is agreeable and pleasant. "The carnal mind is enmity against God." But the believer is brought into a covenant relation with God. He can say, the God who created the heavens and the earth—the Governor of the universe—is my Father and my God.

3. The diligent use of means to acquire a knowledge of God—observation and survey of his works in creation, providence and grace—reading the Scriptures, and prayer for Divine enlightenment.

III. THE HAPPY EFFECTS OF CHRISTIAN MEDITATION. "It is sweet."

1. It increases our knowledge of God, and of ourselves.

2. It is consolatory and supporting. In affliction—in all trouble—in national calamities. "In the multitude of thy thoughts within me, thy comforts delight my soul." Ps. xciv. 19. The thoughts of God's infinite wisdom reconcile the mind to the conduct of Divine Providence. The thoughts of Divine omnipotency establish and strengthen. The thoughts of his eternal love and mercy produce triumphant hope and joy.

3. It is therefore a source of refined and exalted pleasure. It

leads to communion with God. Purity and intercourse with him must yield happiness.

4. It never satiates. The mind may exhaust some subjects, but never this. The novelty and interest of other subjects are but short-lived. This is everlasting.

5. It prepares for heaven. It is a heavenly duty. It is a practice that links the soul to heaven. It makes it familiar with the heavenly inheritance, and this sublimates the mind, and makes it aspire after heaven. It assimilates the soul to heaven. In connection with Divine communion or prayer, it brings down a rich stream of heavenly mercy, which renders the soul a "fit habitation of God through the Spirit." Those who live in the habit of an exercise so morally productive as this must be rapidly preparing for the kingdom of glory. They grow familiar with those objects which will be the foremost to engage the mind in a state of future felicity, and they are forming their characters to the models of those who are already in possession of it.

VI. — THE APOSTOLIC BENEDICTION.

"GRACE be with all them that love our Lord Jesus Christ in sincerity."—EPH. vi. 24.

ONE good evidence that we are the Lord's people is love for our fellow-Christians. Where this love reigns there will be fervent prayer and corresponding exertions to promote their welfare. For this is Christ's "commandment, that we should believe on the name of his Son Jesus Christ, and love one another." 1 John iii. 23.——How excellent was the spirit breathed by the Apostle! and how worthy it is of being imitated! It was a spirit of fervent, impartial, and untiring love. This he cherished towards the Christians at Ephesus. Hence the counsels which he gave them, and the prayers he offered to God on their behalf, evince the deep solicitude of his love.

I. THE SUBJECTS OF THE APOSTOLIC BENEDICTION; "all them that love our Lord Jesus Christ in sincerity."

1. *The Object of their love.* "Our Lord Jesus Christ." The phrase denotes the excellency and suitableness of the Object of a Christian's love. It is the dictates of an enlightened mind to love that which is excellent, and to "abhor that which is evil." In Christ all good meets; it exists in absolute perfection, and can have no addition. And here we speak not so much of his glories as seen in his Godhead, — they are too dazzling for us to approach near them — but of their manifestation as tempered by passing through the veil of his pure humanity.

Look at Jesus Christ in his various offices which he sustained, and he is equally lovely and attractive in them all.

Look at the virtues which adorned his character — how godlike they appear! How superior was his wisdom—how great his knowledge! How tender was his compassion, and disinterested his benevolence, the many eventful scenes in his life declare. Think too of his humility, and condescension. All moral virtues were in him. He was "holy, harmless, undefiled." He was "altogether lovely." And all the stronger virtues of religion; such as meekness, patience, resignation, devotion, lived in him.

Here, then, is a reason for love as strong and unbounded as the supreme excellence of the character to which it is attached.

Christ is loved by his people on account of his *redeeming love.* "We love him," etc. 1 John iv. 19. The love of the Redeemer is stated, Rom. v. 7, 8; 1 John iv. 10. The Apostles state man's unworthiness in contrast with a generous, suffering love. Though man was a monster of vice, yet we see Jesus suffering death for him. Shrouding his glory in humanity, willingly scoffed and persecuted, the day witnessed his labours, and cold mountains and the midnight air witnessed his prayers for sinners. He was mocked, that they might be honoured; condemned, that they might be justified; and died a cruel and shameful death that they might live, yea, live for ever.*

2. *The Character of their love.* They "love the Lord Jesus Christ in sincerity." It is love "without dissimulation." It naturally flows from having an interest in Christ, and union with him. All who have been enlightened by his Spirit, and pardoned through his blood, will be sure to love him in sincerity.

Many profess to love Christ, but do not love him in sincerity. "But if any man love God, the same is known of him." The term "sincerity" is used, 1 Cor. v. 8; 2 Cor. i. 12; ii. 17; viii. 8.†

---

* The immense benefits derived from Christ must ever induce love to him. "It is impossible to think of him without having some relation, in which our highest interest is connected, presented to our thoughts. His names attest this. 'Jesus,' 'Redeemer.' 'Christ.' The offices to which he was anointed attest it. Is he a Prophet? He still teaches us by his word and Spirit. Is he a Priest? 'He ever liveth,' etc. Is he a King? He rules angels that they may minister to us; the world, for the preservation and extension of the religion which is our light and life; he rules our affairs in mercy. Every object and state reminds us of his love.

"Do we think of life? We owe it to his intercession. Of spiritual mercies? They are the fruits of his redemption; for we deserve nothing. Of the ordinances? They are the visitations of his grace.

"Do we regard the future as well as the present? We expect his kingdom. Do we anticipate death? We have the victory by him. Judgment? We have justification through his blood. What then can we plead besides? Do we think of heaven? We view him as the grand source of light, love, and joy. Should constant benefits excite love? Then *our love ought to be supreme.* And are they never to cease? Then *ought our love to be eternal.*"—*Richard Watson.*

† Sincerity is an essential attribute of personal religion; it is produced by faith in Christ, supported by Divine love and filial fear, and distinguished by an amiable self-diffidence, and a firm reliance on the free grace of God; all other virtues derive not only their lustre, but their existence from sincerity. The consciousness of godly sincerity is the grand support of true courage, and is productive of more solid and lasting happiness in a time of trouble, than any thing else in the world. Insincere professors are as clouds without water, trees without fruit, or lamps without oil; but those who love God with undivided hearts have a constant succession of pleasure from the Divine approbation, and the testimony of their own conscience.

The sincerity of this love is proved by the effects it produces. "A tree is known by its fruit," etc.

(1) It evidences itself *by love to God's word.* "O how I love thy law," etc.

(2) *By hatred to sin.* They who "name the name of the Lord Jesus Christ will depart from all iniquity."

(3) *By cheerful and prompt obedience* to his precepts. "If ye love me, keep my commandments."

(4) *By brotherly love.* He loves those who love Christ. 1 John iv. 20, 21.

(5) *By zeal for God's house.* Loves to be there — loves its worship — prays for it, and seeks its prosperity. "How amiable are thy tabernacles," etc.

The labours of a sincere Christian will be of a disinterested character. Not done for gain, or for human applause. They will sometimes be connected with opposition—self-sacrifice—self-denial—persecution. These test the sincerity of a man's love.

II. THE NATURE OF THE BENEDICTION. "Grace be with you," etc. This was the earnest desire and prayer of the Apostle, an indication of the extensive benevolence of his soul, which was always panting after the happiness of man. See Rom. x. 1.

1. His prayer embraced the communication of *Divine Grace.* That is, the free and unmerited favour of God. It embraces all arrangements of Divine Love on man's behalf. It includes all the guidance and superintendance of Providence. It includes all the work of Christ—his life—his death—his intercession, etc. It includes all the rich and varied blessings which he can and will bestow on his church. See 2 Tim. i. 9; 2 Cor. viii. 9.

2. All Christians *need the grace of God.* Because they are weak and helpless, and can never conquer their foes, perform their duties, and realize spiritual enjoyment, without it. It is this that strengthens, quickens, animates, and constrains.

(1) Grace be with them in all the trials peculiar to the age in which they lived. It was a time of persecution, etc.

(2) Grace be with them to support them in the time of personal and relative affliction.

(3) Grace be with them in the time of temptation, and in the hour of spiritual darkness. "When the enemy comes in like a flood," etc. 1 Pet. i. 6, 7. May God "bruise" Satan under your feet.

(4) Grace be with them in the discharge of Christian duties.

(5) Grace be with them to sanctify, refine, and make them meet for the inheritance of the saints in light.

(6) Grace be with them in their dying hour.

Lastly, his prayer embraces *heaven* itself. Grace be with them till it has effectually done its work, and raised them to endless life. 1 Pet. i. 13.

The Prayer of the Apostle is *general:* "with *all* them," etc.— of whatever nation, mental quality, age, circumstance, condition, etc.

APPLICATION.

1. Imitate the catholicity of the Apostle.

2. It is high time for sectarian bigotry and hostility to cease. Christianity is assailed by virulent foes; union of Christian effort is necessary.

3. How perilous is the state of those who love not Christ!

VII.—THE TRUTH OF THE BIBLE.—MIRACLES.

"AND many other signs truly did Jesus in the presence of his disciples, which are not written in this book: But these are written that ye might believe that Jesus is the Christ, the Son of God; and that believing ye might have life through his name." — JOHN xx. 30, 31.

"PROVE all things;" says the Apostle, "hold fast that which is good." This is not like the counsel of a wild enthusiast, a sectarian bigot, or a base impostor. Such persons endeavour to persuade men to receive their dogmas with implicit confidence; to believe without inquiry. But Divinely revealed truth courts investigation. It solicits us to examine for ourselves; to compare its claims with those of opposite systems; and to receive or to reject, according to the light of evidence.

The text refers to the miracles of Christ. "Many other signs truly did Jesus," etc. That is, besides the two mentioned v. 19, 20. The other miracles which he wrought, and not related here, were such as were necessary to the disciples only, and therefore not revealed to mankind at large. Those which are revealed to mankind, Christians believe, attest the truth of Revelation. The subject to be considered is,

THE TRUTH OF GOD'S WORD IS PROVED BY MIRACLES.

Miracles are supernatural facts, occurrences which bespeak the intervention of a cause superior to, and having a supreme control over, all natural causes. That cause is the interposition of God. A miracle is a divergence from the ordinary operations of nature. There may be extraordinary floods, droughts, earthquakes, atmospherical appearances, meteors, changes in the animal economy, and unlooked-for coincidences of events; and yet all may be resolved into the laws of the natural world, without involving any special interposition of Deity.——— But a miracle is an effect produced by the special and immediate interposition of God contrary to the laws of nature, and that for the confirmation of some doctrine or message as from himself, and having his sanction, though it should be delivered to us by the ministry of men like ourselves. "These [miracles] are written that ye might believe that Jesus is the Christ, the Son of God; and that believing ye might have life through his name." Such is the design of miracles.

The miracles of the Old Testament were wrought to display the Divine power and glory, to inspire his people with confidence, and to confound their enemies. Refer to the burning-bush—the death of the first-born—the passage through the Red Sea—the Manna—the smitten Rock—the destruction of the Assyrian army—the mysterious hand-writing in the palace of Belshazzar—the preservation of the three Hebrews from the devastation of the fiery furnace—and the preservation of Daniel in the den of lions.

The miracles of the New Testament, wrought by Christ and his Apostles, were designed to prove the Divinity of Christianity. He gave sight to the blind, hearing to the deaf, locomotion to the lame, and speech to the dumb. He healed diseases, cleansed the leper, restored the withered hand, turned the water into wine, calmed the stormy ocean, and raised the dead. The same power he gave to his disciples, that their credentials might be known to be Divine. If the miracles which they performed were true miracles, Christ was the true Messiah, the Son of God. In order to ascertain their truth, consider

1. *Their number.* In a single, or even a few miracles, a plausible plea might be urged against the same; it might be said, there was some mistake, deception, exaggeration, etc. But the miracles were numerous. If there had been collusion, then the greater the possibility of detecting that collusion, the opportunities to do so being so numerous.

2. *They were publicly performed.* Neither publicity nor privacy was affected; but they were wrought as circumstances and as opportunities presented, by the acts of others rather than by any arrangement of their own. They were wrought in the presence of multitudes in all parts of the country, in populous towns and cities, in broad day, and before a whole nation for above three years.*

3. *The character of their witnesses.* Even the disciples at first were not over credulous, for they, like the Jews, had expected the Messiah under very different circumstances. They had expected wealth, grandeur, power, and great glory; but in temporal things they saw only poverty, want, suffering, and woe. If therefore they at length firmly and perseveringly adhered to him, it was on account of the miraculous evidence of his Divinity, and of which they were the witnesses.

---

* His miracles were not only of various kinds, but, as Dr. Paley remarks, "performed in great varieties of situation, form, and manner; at Jerusalem, the metropolis of the Jewish nation and religion, and in different parts of Judea and Galilee; in cities, and in villages; in synagogues, and in private houses; in the street, and in highways; with preparation, as in the case of Lazarus, and by accident, as in the case of the widow's son of Nain; when attended by multitudes, and when alone with the patient; in the midst of his disciples, and in the presence of his enemies; with the common people around him, and before scribes, and Pharisees, and Rulers of the synagogues."

The Jews had no favourable prepossessions for Christ. They, like the disciples, expected a very different manifestation. The Sadducees and the Pharisees were his most violent enemies, and were ever lying in wait to ensnare him. John ix; xi. The Jews never denied the working of these miracles. They admitted them; but instead of ascribing them to Divine agency, they attributed them to the agency of Satan. "He casteth out devils," said they, "by Beelzebub," etc. Vast multitudes of the Jews yielded to the evidence, embraced the Christian faith, and were the principal persons employed in propagating it among the Gentiles. And if the body of the Jewish nation did not believe, it has already been accounted for. Contrary to the instructions of their prophets, they expected the appearance of a mighty Conqueror, arrayed in regal pomp and splendour. But the lowly appearance of Jesus Christ had excited in their minds the most inveterate prejudices against him. Besides, the admission of Christianity stood directly opposed to the credit of the several Jewish sects, and to the worldly interests of priests and rulers, who united their efforts, in every possible way, to stir up the prejudices of the people against the religion of Jesus.

To give the question its due importance, let us summon these witnesses again to the bar; and, after a fair and impartial hearing, let us, like an upright jury, pronounce an honest verdict. Confine the case to the Apostles of Christ: — Is there any reason to believe that they were weak and credulous enthusiasts, imposed upon by false appearances? It was absolutely impossible, considering their circumstances, that they could be deceived as to the multitude and the kind of miracles which they profess to have witnessed. Is there any evidence of their being base impostors, intending, with sinister designs, to deceive others? There is the clearest proof to the contrary. They never required the belief of what they affirmed, merely on their own unaccredited testimony. ——They confirmed their report of the miracles of Christ, by the exercise of those miraculous powers with which he had endowed them for this purpose. —— So far from proposing any worldly advantage by their testimony, they knew they had nothing to expect, and they actually experienced nothing else but persecutions, imprisonment, and death. If they were neither enthusiasts, nor deceived themselves, nor impostors, intending to deceive others,—— we are bound to declare that they were true men, and this verdict is confirmed by the conduct of the primitive Christians, who had an opportunity of closely examining the Apostolic testimony; and who, from a conviction of its truth, professed the Christian faith, and maintained their profession at the hazard and with the sacrifice of their lives.

4. *The character of the miracles performed.* They were distinguished by the character of *benevolence*, emblematic of those moral miracles which he effects by his Spirit on the souls of men. He healed all manner of diseases, raised the dead; discerned, restrained, and governed the unruly wills and sinful passions of

men; the brute creation, the winds and the seas, were obedient to his command; and even devils were subject to his control. Multitudes of wretched creatures were benefited by such miracles. They were not dictated by selfishness, by the love of applause, but to display the benevolence and power of God, and to confirm his truth. That truth they have invested with the glory of Divine Omnipotency and Immutability.

How different do they appear from Pagan and Popish miracles, as weeping and bleeding pictures, of very recent relation !——— Infidels object to Scripture miracles on account of the *juggling tricks*, which have been imposed upon the world as miracles, in support of Pagan and Popish superstitions. The folly of this objection is at once apparent. It proceeds upon what Bishop Douglas very justly calls the "weak and childish argument, that because some men have been knaves and fools, therefore all must be so;— that because some men's testimony respecting miracles is false, no testimony whatever for a miraculous fact, ought ever to be taken."

——Let Pagan or Popish miracles be brought to the test, and it will appear, either that they were not announced at the time when, and the place where, they were professedly wrought; or that they were not exposed to public and minute scrutiny; or, that being closely examined, they have been detected and exposed as base deceptions. If Scripture miracles have no better evidence in their favour, let them sink into deserved contempt. But let them be fairly examined, and it will be found that they were of a different character in every respect. They were performed publicly; they were announced when and where they were wrought; and the reality of them was never contradicted by any of those who examined them.*

5. Just refer to some of *the Objections of infidels*.

Some reject the evidence arising from Scripture miracles, because they were not *eye-witnesses* of them; and because they are not *repeated* in the present day. But how unreasonable is this! Is God ever to be humouring the caprice of man?———The constant repetition of them would defeat their design, by rendering them common things. The continuance is unnecessary, because the fact of them may be clearly ascertained without seeing them ourselves. There are various kinds of evidence adapted to different cases and circumstances, and reason demands our belief of what is duly attested. The only evidence which we can justly require of the reality of Scripture miracles, is well-supported testimony; and this is com-

---

* The criteria of Mr. Leslie—the marks, that is, which he has laid down for distinguishing true miracles—remain to this day not only unanswered but unassailed. It is related, indeed, of the well-known author Middleton, that after studying these criteria for twenty years, he was not able even to conceive of a single exception to the force and universality of their application. His rules are these: 1st, that the matter of fact, that is, the miracle, be such as that men's outward senses, their eyes and ears, may be judges of it: 2. That it be done *publicly*, in the face of the world: 3. That not only public monuments be kept up, but that some outward actions should be performed in memory of it: 4, That such monuments and such actions or observances be instituted and do commence from the time that the matter of fact — the miracle — was done.

pletely sufficient. All our knowledge of ancient facts, and much even of that which relates to the present times, arises from this source; and consequences the most ridiculous would follow the rejection of it. History would, in this case, be entirely useless; persons must discredit whatever they have not themselves either seen, or heard, or experienced; and they must live confined within the circle of their senses, in their own little world, without deriving accessions of knowledge from intercourse with either men or books. ——It is the will of God that miracles should have ceased. They are not to be repeated. The record of them is sufficient—and by that record the faith of man is to be tested. Canst thou, O man, believe?——The evidence arising from miracles is so strong as to leave unbelievers without excuse.

Some infidels, like Hume, deny the *possibility* of a miracle, and declare that no evidence whatever can render it credible. This is infidelity run mad. It is Atheism itself; for it virtually denies the Being, the Power, the Providence of God. Let these be granted, and the possibility of miracles follows as a natural consequence. If what are called the laws of nature, are under the government of God for certain purposes, may he not occasionally see fit to restrain or counteract these laws, in order to serve some extraordinary and important design? and can any design be more important, more worthy of such a Divine interposition, than that of attesting a special revelation of his will? In one respect, miracles are not only possible and probable, but absolutely necessary; as the only kind of sensible evidence, by which the authority of a Divinely inspired messenger can be directly confirmed.

Lastly. The miracles of the Bible are vastly important, as *they confirm the truth of Christianity*. A miracle is the testimony of God—a Divine seal which he has placed upon the Sacred Book,— the signature of his hand bearing witness to its truth and efficacy.

One of the miracles to which the Apostles principally appealed, the resurrection of Christ, has in it a peculiar weight of evidence, arising, not only from its extraordinary nature, but also from many coincident circumstances: it had been predicted by the Jewish prophets, and foretold by Christ himself;—the unbelieving Jews, being forewarned, took all possible care to prevent it; but it happened at the appointed time, in spite of every opposition, and beyond all contradiction. On the evidence arising from this miracle, Mr. West, formerly an infidel, has expatiated with great force of argument.*

---

* But if the apostles could not be themselves deceived, then, of necessity, if the resurrection of Christ be untrue, they must have been themselves *deceivers*. Such a supposition, however, is just as contrary to all our experience of the uniformity of *moral* nature as the theory just disposed of was found to be contrary to *physical* nature. "If," says Dr. Paley, "twelve men, whose probity and good sense I had long known, should seriously and circumstantially relate to me an account of a miracle wrought before their eyes, and in which it was impossible that they should be deceived; if the governor of the country, hearing a rumour of this account, should call these men into his presence, and offer them a short proposal either to confess the imposture or submit to be tied up to a gibbet; if they should refuse with one voice to acknowledge that there existed any falsehood or imposture in the case; if this threat were communicated

To the miracles which he wrought, Christ appealed in proof of his Messiahship, when questioned on this subject by the Jews. "If thou be the Christ, (said they) tell us plainly. Jesus answered them, I told you, and ye believed not: the works that I do in my Father's name, they bear witness of me. If I do not the works of my Father, believe me not. But if I do, though ye believe not me, believe the works." John x. 24, 25, 37, 38. "When John had heard in the prison the works of Christ, he sent two of his disciples, and said unto him, Art thou he that should come, or do we look for another? Jesus answered, Go and show John again those things which ye do hear and see: the blind receive their sight, and the lame walk, the lepers are cleansed, and the deaf hear, the dead are raised up, and the poor have the gospel preached to them." Matt. xi. 2—5. The Jews felt the force of this miraculous evidence, and apprehended its consequences. Thus, after the resurrection of Lazarus, we are informed, "Then gathered the chief Priests and the Pharisees, a council, and said, What do we? If we let him alone, all men will believe on him." John xi. 47, 48. "So, likewise, a man of the Pharisees, named Nicodemus, a ruler of the Jews; the same came to Jesus by night, and said unto him, Rabbi, we know that thou art a Teacher come from God; for no man can do these miracles which thou doest, except God be with him." John iii. 1, 2. Nicodemus followed his conviction, and became decidedly a Christian.

The evidence, then, arising from miracles, is a vivid and popular demonstration, equally suited to men of the lowest capacities, and of the most exalted understandings. It is the short and lively reasoning of an Omnipotent God, and the mind of man must see, in an instant, the connection of these two ideas, *a miracle and a Divine revelation.*

Learn, 1st. The welfare of the soul is the greatest interest of man. Empires and Emperors are left to themselves; and are often allowed to conduct their various affairs in their own way; but in the affairs of the souls of men, in the affairs of eternity, God arises in his holy place; he bows the heavens and comes down; he stretches forth his hand, breathes forth his Almighty Spirit, controls and changes the powers of nature, shakes the earth, and the sea, and the dry land; all to call the attention of men to the

---

to them separately, yet with no different effect; if it was at last executed; if I myself saw them, one after another, consenting to be racked, burned, or strangled, rather than give up the truth of their account; still, if Mr. Hume's rule be my guide, I am not to believe them. Now, I undertake to say, that there exists not a sceptic in the world who would not believe them, or who would defend such incredulity." Every one who reads such a statement feels it to be conclusive and irresistible. To suppose that such men, so tried, were after all mere deceivers, were to fly in the face of our experience of the uniformity of all those laws which regulate the moral nature of man. It is superfluous to add that the apostles, as their writings prove, were more than all in point of probity, which Dr. Paley has here assumed, and that they literally suffered all he has described, rather than abandon or modify their testimony to the resurrection of Christ. To hold therefore that they were nevertheless deceivers, were undoubtedly to take for granted a series of the grossest and the most gratuitous violations of the laws which regulate our moral nature; in other words, it were to reject the miracle of the Resurrection, on grounds a million times more incredible than the Resurrection itself.

undying interests of their souls; and all to fix their eyes on him who says in mercy, "Look unto me, and be ye saved," etc.

Learn, 2d. The Reason of the perpetuity of Christianity is, its Divinity, as evinced by miracles. It could not in any age, it cannot now, and it never will be destroyed. Persecution in all its dreadful forms has attempted again and again to destroy it. But the attempts have been vain: for miracles have stamped the gospel with Divinity. Paine, Voltaire, Volney, Hume, Owen, the authors of the Vestiges of Creation, and the advocates of Nature Worship, may propose their peculiar systems to the world, as a substitute for Christianity, so hateful to them. For a while they may, by their novelty, command the attention of the superficial, and gain adherents. But will they live? No. As such systems have fared before, so it will be with those which are promulgated now. They will become stale and insipid to the mind, and cease to attract. Infidelity seldom organizes. Where are its benevolent institutions, its useful seminaries? etc. It can have no coherence, no endurance; for it has no connection with Divinity.

VIII.— RELATIONSHIP TO GOD THE PLEDGE OF EVERLASTING SALVATION.

"I am thine, save me; for I have sought thy precepts." — Ps. cxix. 94.

GOD is the only fountain of true and lasting happiness.——From every thing on earth man tries to extract happiness. Sometimes he foolishly imagines he succeeds, but the evanescent and unsatisfactory nature of his pleasures convinces him at length to the contrary.——The man who searches for substantial bliss in this world is like a ship at sea without anchorage, driven about and tossed, and in constant danger of perishing.—— But how peaceful and secure is the Christian! In all his trials he can look to God, and say, "I am thine, save me," etc.

I. THE CLAIM OF DAVID TO DIVINE RELATIONSHIP: "I am thine:" Thine in covenant, owned by thee, and devoted to thee.

1. This is a *peculiar relationship*. It cannot be claimed by all. All mankind have been created and preserved by God. They are his workmanship. He is their lawful Sovereign. They are the creatures of his power. As creatures all may say, "I am thine:" but few can claim an interest in the covenant of grace, which leads the believer to say, "My Beloved is mine, and I am his."

2. The claim is for a relationship *the most honourable and glorious*. It is a relation to God. "I am thine." I am a child of God. I belong to the King of kings, etc. — to the Almighty God, the Creator, Proprietor, and Governor of the boundless universe — to the God of infinite love, etc.——It is esteemed a great

honour to be related to a nobleman, a prince, or a monarch. But all comparisons fail here. Related to God! "I am thine."

3. *How has this relationship originated?* It implies previous impediment, as occasioned by sin. All are sinners—in a state of alienation. Isa. lix. 2; Eph. iv. 18.——In this state there is no relationship to God. There is an awful reversion of state. Sinners may say to the Prince of darkness, "I am thine." Eph. ii. 1, 2. The claim implies the following:—

(1) I am thine *by gracious purpose*. God foreseeing the fall of man, his ruin and wretchedness, made provision for his salvation, by purposing to send his Son into the world to save sinners. See Eph. 7—11; 2 Tim. i. 9. That gracious purpose includes every believer, who is warranted to say, "I am thine."

(2) I am thine *by conquest*. 2 Cor. x. 5. He subdues the opposition of the heart, and inclines it to himself. He captivates its desires and affections. "The carnal mind is enmity against God," but he destroys it. Thou hast conquered me—I am thine.

(3) I am thine *by purchase*. Christ has bought me with a price, satisfying all the claims of Divine justice; and he has rescued me from the grasp of Satan by his Almighty power. Divine justice held me in bondage, on account of the broken law, holding out no liberation till satisfaction should be given. Christ gave it. 1 Pet. i. 18, 19.

(4) I am thine *by assimilation*. I am like him, in degree. This is effected by regeneration—born again—completely changed and made like God. 2 Cor. v. 17.

(5) I am thine *by adoption*. I am not worthy to have a place in thy family; but thou hast been pleased to take me, an outcast, in. Like the father of the prodigal, thou didst run to meet me, etc. I am thy child, and thou art my Father. 1 John iii. 1; John i. 12, 13.

(6) I am thine *by dedication*. "One shall say, I am the Lord's," etc. Isa. xliv. 5. As I am "bought with a price, I will glorify God in my body," etc. Thy service is my delight. I am thine to labour — to fight — to defend in thy cause.

II. THE PRAYER OF DAVID: "Save me."

As a man, he felt himself weak, frail, dying. As a sinner, guilty and wretched, without mercy. As a Christian, opposed by spiritual foes, and weak and helpless. He might well say, "Save me."

The Lord will save his people. Isa. xii. 2, 3. "He delighteth in mercy." "I am thine," regenerated, adorned, and adopted by thee. I am thy ransomed one, thy property, thy jewel, and the object of thine everlasting love. Lord, save thine own, for I am precious in thy sight.——"Being confident," Phil. i. 6.——Men preserve that which is valuable. Hence Jehovah says, "No weapon," Isa. liv. 17. "He that toucheth you," Zech. ii. 8.

1. *Save me from sin.* That deadly poison—that destroyer of all peace — the instrument of the Old Serpent to destroy me — that which has marred the beauty and desolated the circumstances of the whole human family. Lord, save me — from the enticements, the guilt, the domination, the bondage, and the torment of sin.

2. *Save me from my foes.* Satan desires to have me. The world is full of allurements — its pleasures and amusements are made fascinating by art, and this poor treacherous heart sometimes gives symptoms of vulnerability, 'Lord, save me.' Save me from the influence of secular concerns; let not my business be my idol; may I never esteem it and my wealth as my heaven upon earth, and thereby lose the glorious heaven of eternity. Lord, save me! Save me from my deceitful and wandering heart.

The wicked often persecute the righteous. So it was with David, v. 95. Lord, save me, and let not mine enemies prevail against me.

3. *Save me from indifferentism.* This is the great sin of the church—its low estate is the effect of its lukewarmness. The children of the world—the advocates of error—the devotees of superstition—the lovers of pleasure, are not indifferent. And how miserable is their cause! Mine is an eternally glorious one, and, alas! I am indifferent! Lord, save me—from carelessness—formality — mere profession. Rev. iii. 13—18.

4. *From dishonouring my profession.* Phil. iii. 18, 19.

5. *From the errors peculiar to the times in which I live.* Infidelity and Atheism in their various shades. Their arguments, though worthless, may to the superficial mind appear plausible. And the depraved heart is more prone to error than truth. Wonder not at the existence of Atheism. The unrenewed heart is base, is daring, is demoniacal enough to hurl Jehovah from his throne, and turn heaven into hell if it had the power. Lord, save me!

Lastly. From *the depressing influence of adversity*. These personal and relative sorrows—these bereavements—these children of rebellion—these temporal losses, and the drying up of the resources of bodily sustenance. Lord, save me from my troubles. Their name is legion, and such troubles have overwhelmed thousands. Let me not be borne down by the torrent. I must soon die myself. The shafts of death are already winged. The grave is ready for me. Lord, save me, and make me a conqueror, etc.

III. THE GROUND OF DAVID'S PRAYER AND CLAIM. "I have sought thy precepts."

God's people give evidence that they belong to God. No one can be his without a sensible and visible evidence of it.

The precepts of God are loved and esteemed as an invaluable treasury of good things.

The precepts of God are regarded as the rule of conduct.

The Christian labours to understand them. He reads, compares, and searches. "I have sought thy precepts;" I have carefully inquired concerning my duty, and diligently endeavoured to do it. The word of God is not a *strange* book to the Christian. He is not coerced to read it. He regards it as a communication from heaven *specially* to him — regarding *his interests*.

This is the result of Divine operation, proving that "*I am thine!*" For, once I did not love the Scriptures.

Good men have always been attached to the Bible. Many have shed their blood, rather than even conceal their regard to it. We read in the book of martyrs, of a husbandman who gave a whole load of hay for a leaf of one of the epistles. Boyle, that great philosopher, said, speaking of the Scriptures, "I prefer a sprig of the tree of life to a whole wood of bays." Judge Hale, that ornament of his profession and country, said, "If he did not honour God's word by reading a portion of it every morning, things went not well with him all the day." Job said, "I have esteemed the words of thy mouth more than my necessary food." See also Ps. viii.

APPLICATION.

1. Examination. Do I belong to God?
2. Prayer for salvation must be united with faith.
3. Let faith be followed by works to evidence the existence of grace in the soul.

IX.—MAN VILE.

"Behold, I am vile."—Jon xl. 20.

THE text enunciates a truth which we must all know, and feel, and lament, before we can obtain Divine acceptance, and preparedness for heaven. No one ever valued Christ, and accepted his salvation, without such a knowledge and conviction.

I. THE NATURE OF THIS CONFESSION. "*I am vile.*"

Vile means inward defilement. The term is used to denote that which is base, mean, and worthless. Sometimes it means hateful, 1 Sam. iii 13; corruptible, Phil. iii. 21, and frequently, wicked, Ps. xv. 4; Isa. xxxii. 5, 6; Rom. i. 26.

1. This vileness is *natural to man.* Our first parents were created pure—they fell, and all their posterity have been involved in their fall. Rom. v. 12.

"Lord, I am vile, conceiv'd in sin,
And born unholy and unclean;
Sprung from the man whose guilty fall,
Corrupts the race, and taints us all."

"Soon as we draw our infant breath,
The seeds of sin grow up for death;
The law demands a perfect heart,
But we're defiled in every part."

2. This vileness is *internal*. It is in the soul—in its thoughts—desires—affections—purposes. How vile and wicked are these! The heart is "desperately wicked." It is a sink of iniquity; it is the habitation of the plague. Matt. xv. 19.

3. It is *outward or actual*. The conduct of man is vile. Look at what you have done—what others, the intemperate, licentious, unjust, depredators, tyrants, assassins, or murderers, have done. For the vileness of man read, Rom. i. Gal. v. 19—21.

4. Refer to the *experience of Christians*. They are often compelled to say, "Behold, I am vile." Job was an eminently pious man. But he often felt the plague of his heart. And every Christian feels it. Were it not for the blood and Spirit of Christ, believers would have no hope.

5. The *influence of this vileness*. It separates from God. Pure Deity can have no fellowship with the unclean. It is destructive of all happiness. It has converted this world into a desert—a waste-howling wilderness—an Aceldama—a field of blood. It is condemning, being a violation of the law—the law of God, and merits the penalty declared against transgression. "The soul that sinneth shall die."

II. WHAT IS REQUISITE TO PRODUCE THIS CONFESSION.

1. *Divine Influence*, to give a knowledge and conviction of it.

2. The *Instrument* used by the Spirit is *the word of God*. This shows the spirituality of the law, and convinces of transgression. Sometimes this conviction is instantaneous, as in the case of Saul of Tarsus, and the Philippian jailor, at other times it is gradual.

Happy are they who are brought to this confession! They are in the way of salvation. There is hope for them.

III. THE CONSEQUENCES OF THIS CONFESSION.

1. It produces *anxiety to obtain deliverance*. The soul groans under a burden of guilt, and cannot rest. Their vileness is disgusting and hateful to them. "What must I do to be saved?"

2. *Self-distrust*. The vileness is felt to be too great for human means to remove.

3. A *cordial approval and acceptance of salvation by the finished work of Christ*. It is hailed with rapture. The soul is placed upon that foundation. "The blood of Jesus Christ," etc. "In him we have redemption," etc.

4. Prayer for *the regenerating power of the Spirit*, to create anew, to cast out sin, to subdue the heart, and produce hatred to sin.

IMPROVEMENT.

Learn, 1. If not saved from this vileness in time, it cannot be effected in eternity.

2. Cultivate candour and tenderness in judging of the faults of others.

3. Let Christians see the riches of Divine grace. For Christ's sake, God does not regard you as vile. "Ye are complete in him."

4. You will soon enter a world where no vileness can ever exist.

X.—THE ADVANTAGES OF WAITING UPON THE LORD.

"He giveth power to the faint; and to them that have no might, he increaseth strength. Even the youths shall faint and be weary, and the young men shall utterly fail. But they that wait upon the Lord shall renew their strength: they shall mount up with wings as eagles, they shall run and not be weary, and they shall walk and not faint."—ISA. xl. 29—31.

This chapter is a very precious one. It is a cabinet of the richest treasures which Divine grace has allotted to the people of God.——It has evidently a reference to gospel times. It commences with a command to all God's ministers to administer comfort to the afflicted in Zion. The gospel is an inexhaustible source of comfort.——A reference is then made to the coming of John the Baptist, as the Forerunner of Christ, and also a reference to Christ himself as the great Saviour and Shepherd of his flock, v. 3. To the weak in Zion, and the faint-hearted, how consoling must be the description of the grandeur, the power, and the glory of God! v. 12—17. What a God the Christian has!——The prophet might well inquire the reason of the church's despondency, v. 27. This inquiry amounts to an admonition. O ye afflicted and tried, you have forgotten your Divine Refuge — God.——We often lean upon ourselves, instead of depending upon him. Self-dependance is essential in some pursuits, but it will not avail here. "Without me ye can do nothing." Without Divine efficiency none are invulnerable to the temptations that are in the world. "Even the youths," etc.

I. THE CHARACTERS DESCRIBED.

1. *The faint.* To faint, means to become weak through exertion, 2 Sam. xxi. 15; Judges viii. 4. Or, discouragement, Isa. xiii. 7; Lam. i. 22. Terror or dismay, Josh. ii. 9. A Christian may faint,

(1) From *severe and long-continued trials.*

It may be from Satanic influence — the wiles of the devil — the injection of the foulest and most malignant thoughts into the mind. He desires to have the believer—he seeks to devour.

It may arise from *adversity*. Lack of the bread that perisheth. How severe this trial! It is enough to make the heart faint. Adversity arising from lingering or painful disease — the body suspended between life and death. When this suspense is long, it is especially painful — and the heart is ready to faint. It then needs a cordial which this earth cannot supply.——Adversity arising from persecution, called tribulation. This threatened to make the Apostles faint. They had "fiery trials," but Divine strength kept them from fainting. See 2 Cor. iv. 1, 16; Eph. iii. 13.

(2) *Faint*. It is expressive of a *low state of religion in the heart*. There is the germ of religion there, but it wants Divine energy to make it productive of the fruits of righteousness. There is the bruised reed, and the smoking flax. Instead of great vitality and vigour, there is weakness, etc.

(3) *Faint*. This may be *constitutional*. Physical weakness — great nervous sensibility — mental fear and despondency. Such persons often faint at imaginary evils — what is their state, then, when trials actually come? Consoling truth! "God knows their frame," etc.

(4) *Faint*. It is expressive of *spiritual declension*. The graces of the Spirit are "ready to die." Rev. iii. 2. This has been induced by neglecting prayer—public worship—worldly attachment and devotedness.——That man's religion was once vigorous and exemplary. Look at him now. He is fast leaving his "first love."

The disuse of the means of grace resembles the disuse of food. It leads to death. God in the means of grace feeds and nourishes the soul. Neglect this, and spiritual life will faint and die. Hence the exhortation, Heb. xii. 3.

2. *No might*. Without external resources. It is an awful thing to be faint and ready to die, and to be without remedy. But so it is with the sinner. He is "ready to perish." "The whole head is sick, and the whole heart faint." Isa. i. 5.

Therefore no might to save themselves — have tried all human resources, and they have failed, as physicians of no value — completely helpless as to the performance of religious service, and the conquest of spiritual foes. "There is no health in us."

3. *The procedure of the self-confident is to be deprecated*. "Even the youths shall faint," etc. None by their own wisdom and strength shall succeed in the Christian warfare. What is a bright and vigorous intellect, or physical energy and courage, in the battles of the Lord, unassociated with Divine strength? It is he that must teach our "hands to war, and our fingers to fight." He must be our "shield and buckler." Some run well, fight well,

labour well, for a short time; but something "hinders." They become "weary and utterly fall." Alas! we expected much from them, but have been disappointed.

II. AN IMPORTANT DUTY. "They that wait upon the Lord," etc.

To "wait" signifies to serve, Num. viii. 24; Acts x. 7; 1 Cor. ix. 13. Sometimes, dependance, Ps. cxlv. 15. Also to expect, to look for, Gal. v. 5. The term in the text includes some of these senses; but it is a little more expressive. It means, APPLICATION AND EXPECTATION. *Wait upon the Lord*, humbly and believingly go to God, present thy petitions, and patiently wait for his blessing. Waiting upon the Lord,

1. Is prompted by *a sense of need*. The sinner, or the declining Christian really feels himself "faint" and without might, and that if unrelieved he must perish. Like the Prodigal, both are famished, Luke xv.

2. A recognition that it is *the prerogative of God to revive and strengthen*. "He giveth power to the faint," says the text, "and to them that have no might," etc. See Isa. xli. 10, 13, 14.

3. *They wait upon God where he is to be found*. He meets his people in his house — in the closet — in the discharge of holy service, *for strength is given in performing service*.

> Where'er we seek him, he is found,
> And every place is holy ground.

4. They wait upon him *in a manner appropriate to their own character*. With penitence. Sin has caused them to be unwatchful, weak, declining, and faint. They are humble for it. "I have sinned against heaven." With *faith*. Faith in Christ. No self-dependance.

> "Nothing in my hand I bring,
> Simply to thy cross I cling."

With *patience, and resignation*. Wait. The trial which afflicts thy soul, and makes thee faint, he may not remove at all — or not remove it yet; still he will not withhold strength from the earnest and believing applicant. Paul's thorn in the flesh was not to be removed, but God strengthened him proportionally, and kept him from fainting. 2 Cor. xii. 9, 10.

III. THE GRACIOUS RESULTS OF WAITING UPON THE LORD. "Shall renew," etc.

1. *Renewal of strength*. To renew,* means to change. Shall change the weakness and decrepitude of spiritual declension, for

---

* "They shall put forth fresh feathers, like the moulting eagle." It has been a common and popular opinion, that the eagle lives and retains his vigour to a great age; and that, beyond the common lot of other birds, he moults in his old age, and renews his feathers, and with them his youth. Whether the notion of the eagle's renewing his youth is in any degree well founded or not, I need not inquire; it is enough for a poet, whether sacred or profane, to have the authority of popular opinion to support an image introduced for illustration or ornament. — *Bp. Lowth*.

active and vigorous life, and holy enjoyment. "Renewed in the spirit of their mind." God does this by his Spirit. See Col. i. 11; Phil. iv. 13; 2 Tim. ii. 1.

The poor afflicted saint was fast fainting and sinking; now his strength is renewed by waiting upon God and "in the midst of his patience he possesses his soul."—— The tempted one was rapidly giving way; but waiting upon God has strengthened him, and given him the shield of faith, and he resists the darts of the Wicked One [amplify]. The declining Christian was almost separated from Christ, but he waited upon God, and he repaired the bruised reed, replenished the smoking flax, and supplied the lamp with new oil. He shines again, and enjoys his "first love." The fallen, God has raised up.

God strengthens for every duty, every danger, and every foe. "My grace is sufficient for thee." The way may be rough, the enemies powerful, the waters deep, but God will sustain. "When thou passest through the waters," etc. Isa. xliii. 2. O rich provision! Waiting upon the Lord will give me strength to labour ——strength to conquer——strength to suffer——and strength to die.

2. *Constant approximation towards heaven.* "They shall mount up with wings as eagles." God having renewed their strength, he will also by his Spirit lead their thoughts, affections, and desires towards heaven. Their conversation shall be in heaven— their affections fixed there. Col. iii. 1, 2. As the eagle flies a great height, so the Christian by faith and hope soars to Jehovah's throne, and says, "Whom have I in heaven," etc. "O when shall I come and appear before God." As the young eagle is assisted by its parent in its first attempts to fly, bearing it upon the wing, and teaching it to ascend, so God, on the wings of his Spirit bears up the soul to his radiant abode on high.

And there are special times in the believer's life when his thoughts are beautifully and rapturously fixed on heaven. Standing on Pisgah's top, and looking through the telescope of faith, he sees the glory of God and the Lamb. He sees the fertile plains of the heavenly Canaan, and the immense wealth and glory of the city of God. Earth then appears a shadow, wealth a bubble, etc.

While on the verge of life I stand,
And view the scene on either hand,
My spirit struggles with its clay,
And longs to wing its flight away.

Where Jesus dwells my soul would be,
I long that upper world to see;
Earth, twine no more about my heart,
For 'tis far better to depart.

3. *Great activity and perseverance.* "They shall run," etc. Strengthened with all might by the Spirit in the inner man, mounting up to heaven on the wings of contemplation and faith— in fact, seeing heaven, the prize suspended from the goal, they

may well run the race that is set before them. The crown, the kingdom, the ecstacy, the music, the company, the beatific vision, allure. Hence they gird up the loins of their minds and run —— they lay aside every weight, and run the race, etc. The voice of enchantment calls to them to stop — the gold and silver of the world, houses and land, and all earthly vanities, etc., call out, Stop! But the heavenly racer answers, No. I have seen heaven, and therefore superior joys than you can give. No, hinder me not. "I will run in the way of God's commandments." He "runs and is not weary." For God gives new strength continually — new discoveries of heaven — yes, the "inward man is renewed day by day." The strength of a Christian, as derived from God, is inexhaustible.

"They walk and not faint." They go about their spiritual business, and flag not. They serve the church without reluctance, with cheerfulness and pleasure, and never tire. Like the Saviour, they go about doing good, and they are "not weary in well-doing, for in due season, they shall reap if they faint not." They live upon their work — it is their food, and as long as they can take food they cannot faint. "It is my meat and drink to do thy will, O God."

Running and walking without weariness and fainting, must imply, *approximation to perfection*. It is a ripening for heaven. They are getting nearer it every day, and they are becoming as a bride adorned for the Bridegroom. The word *walk* in Hebrew implies progression. Hence it is said, the voice — the thunder of God walked in Eden, the trumpet walked, that is, waxed louder and louder.

In conclusion, believer, think of thy happiness. God will do all this for thee. O what an unfailing refuge!

Sinner, thou hast no refuge. —— "Thy whole head is sick, and thy heart faint." Go to Christ the Physician of thy soul, and he will save thee.

XI. — THE PERSECUTOR CONVERTED AND PRAYING.

"Behold, he prayeth." — Acts ix. 11.

THE Apostle Paul was a Jew by birth; but having been born in the city of Tarsus, he was entitled to the privileges of a Roman citizen. By trade, he was a tent-maker. He was a man of education, having studied under Gamaliel, a learned doctor of the law. As to his religion, he was a zealous, bigoted, and intolerant Pharisee, a determined opponent of Christianity, and a most violent persecutor. His opposition commenced from the martyrdom of Stephen. Acts vii. 57. See also, Acts viii. 1—3; ix. 1, 2, and in the following verses, his marvellous conversion is narrated. See also, Acts xxii. 1, etc.; xxvi.

As Saul of Tarsus was so fierce and terrible a man, the mind of Ananias had to be prepared and fortified, otherwise he would have hesitated to go and instruct him; v. 13, 14. To satisfy his fears, he was assured that he was a changed man, a chosen instrument, and a praying convert. "Behold, he prayeth." Consider,

I. The text and its connection as exhibiting a most amazing contrast.

Before, we see him aiding in the martyrdom of Stephen, and consenting unto his death. After which, with malevolent hate of Christ, "he made havoc of the church," etc. He was the prince of persecutors, and was regarded with the utmost complacency by the Jewish hierarchy, as the best instrument they could employ for the destruction of Christianity. See him in his career — mark the ferocity of his heart — like the "murderer from the beginning," he seeks to devour.

> Yes, the hate of his spirit you well might learn,
> From his pale high brow, so bent and stern,
> And the glance that at times shot angry light,
> Like a flash from the depth of a stormy night.
>
> 'Twas Saul of Tarsus, a fearful name,
> And wed in the land with sword and flame;
> And the faithful of Jesus trembled all,
> At the deeds that were wrought by the furious Saul.
>
> And Saul went on in his fiery zeal;
> The thirst of his fury no blood could quell,
> And he went to Damascus with words of doom,
> To bury the faithful in dungeon gloom.

Look at him now, and mark the contrast! What is he doing? Praying — praying to that Jesus whom he hated, and whose followers he would have murdered. He has seen his glory — heard his voice — felt his Spirit, and is now prostrate in the dust, praying. The vail is taken from his mind — the adamant from his heart — the rebel is conquered now. What a contrast! "Behold, he prayeth!" What will the Jews think? What will the high-priest say?

Have you ever been on the ocean amid the raging of a fearful storm — when the devouring wave, and the rolling billow, have assailed your frail bark? Did not your heart die within you as you were ready every moment to be engulfed? But the God who holds the winds in his fists, and the waters in the hollow of his hand, uttered his voice, "Peace, be still," and immediately there was a great calm. —— So it was with the church in the days of Saul of Tarsus. He was the chief element in the stormy persecutions which raged against the church. The storm made dreadful havoc, and threatened to engulf Christianity. But Jehovah calmed his rage as he journeyed to Damascus, made his wrath to praise him, and the remainder of that wrath restrained. —— "Then had the churches rest throughout all Judea, etc., v. 31.

II. As exhibiting the power of God, and the riches of Divine grace.

Will this man ever be converted? This man who was exceedingly mad against Christians, and persecuted them even unto death — this intolerant and bigoted Pharisee? Go to him, and ply him with the ordinary instrumentality of the church; preach to him Jesus as the Messiah, and the resurrection, with the most powerful eloquence, and the most cogent arguments, and you will find him impenetrable and invincible to conversion by human means.

No character presented so many insuperable obstacles to the attainment of such a result. His conversion is one of the greatest marvels in the history of heaven's transforming grace. It was not open profaneness; licentiousness, etc., that formed the barrier. The man who is hourly making work for repentance is far more accessible to saving convictions than he who proudly feels that he needs no repentance. The Pharisee, clothed in the panoply of his self-righteousness, is invulnerable to the shafts which the gospel aims at the hearts of ordinary sinners. And Saul was armed at all points with armour of proof.——Only the power that created the world could transform him into a Christian. For what had he done? He had not only been a blasphemer and a murderer, but he had pleaded the Divine sanction as the motive and justification of his course. He closed his eyes against all evidence of Christ's Messiahship. That must have been visible all around him. His heart must have been impregnated with the cruelty and the obduracy of a demon, when, unrelentingly, he saw Stephen die, commending his spirit to Christ, and praying for the forgiveness of his murderers. Among all enormities of human wickedness, persecution is the most hateful, and the persecutions of Saul were most inexcusable and most aggravated. Fearful is the guilt implied in the question addressed to the guilty culprit by the voice from Heaven, "Saul, Saul," etc. Why, indeed! Terrible reasons rush upon his guilty spirit — he is confounded — the "chief of sinners" falls prostrate to the earth; and in subsequent years he frequently adverted to the scene with tears of penitential sorrow, mingled with adoring gratitude and love. See 1 Cor. xv. 8.

His conversion therefore was an illustrious display of Omnipotence, and the riches of Divine grace. So he viewed it. 1 Tim. i. 12—17.

III. As giving a shock to the kingdom of Satan, and as accelerating the progress of the gospel.

By the conversion of Saul, Satan lost one of his chief instruments. He had agitated the whole church — the extent of the influence of the devastation may be ascertained from verse 31. —— Think of his eminent talents — his literary acquirements — his heroic zeal — his despite of danger — his disinterestedness and humility — his holy life — his heaven-born spirit — his vast labours and extensive success! These are the rich and triumphant trophies of Divine grace. And then those intelligent, precious, and consoling Epistles, which the Spirit dictated him to pen. What would the church have been without them? By his conversion Satan lost — the church gained.

IV. As proving the truth of Christianity. In 1 Cor. xv. 1—8, he gives his testimony to the truth of Christ's resurrection.—— He received not only the testimony of his fellow-apostles, but he was himself an eye-witness of his majesty and glory. With propriety then he said that he had received the doctrine of the gospel, not from men, but from God.

Could the Apostle have been *an impostor?* Impostors generally deceive to enrich themselves. But the Apostle abandoned the society of the rich for the society of the poor, as the first Christians were. He worked with his own hands. Is it compatible with imposture to abandon wealth for poverty?

Did the Apostle *seek power?* If he did, he adopted the most unlikely course to obtain it. Christianity was then assailed by the Jewish and Heathen governments, who incessantly sought to martyr its advocates.

Was he anxious for *honour?* To become a Christian then, and especially an Apostle, was to be defamed, and to be accounted as the filth of the world, and the offscouring of all things. He was distinguished already as a Jew, and honoured and applauded by the hierarchy. He had received the best education his country could afford, and had every prospect of rising to distinction and office. By becoming a Christian, he made his friends his most bitter foes, and how could he expect fame from them?

Did he seek *ease and pleasure?* Let his life of indefatigable labour, and constant persecution and suffering, declare. To spread the gospel, he travelled from country to country, encountering the greatest dangers, enduring the severest hardships, insulted by the populace, punished by the magistrates, scourged, beaten, left for dead; expecting, wherever he came, a renewal of the same treatment, and the same dangers; yet, when driven from one city, preaching in the next, spending his whole time in the employment, sacrificing to it his pleasures, his ease, his safety; persisting in this course to old age, unaltered by the experience of perverseness, ingratitude, prejudice, desertion; unsubdued by anxiety, want, labour, persecutions, unwearied by long confinement, undismayed by the prospect of death. See 2 Cor. xi., and 2 Tim. iv. 6—8. Is this the course of an impostor, or a man seeking fame? Recollect too his hostility to Christianity before his conversion. Infidels often say that Christians are prejudiced in favour of their religion. But here was a man, at first a bitter infidel, and foe to Christianity. All the prejudices of his education, and his worldly prospects, all his former views and feelings, were opposed to the gospel of Christ. But he became its firm advocate and friend, and it is for infidels to account for this change. There must have been some cause, some motive for it; and is there any thing more rational than the conclusion that Saul was convinced of the truth of Christianity? Nothing else *but* a religion from heaven could produce this change. Here then is the independent testimony of a man who was once a persecutor; converted, not by the preaching of the Apostles; changed in a wonderful manner; his whole life, views, and feelings revolutionized, and all his subsequent days evincing the sincerity of his feelings, and the reality of the change. He is just such a *witness* as infidels ought to be satisfied with; whose testimony cannot be impeached; who had no interested motives, and who was willing to stand forth anywhere, and avow his change of feeling and purpose. We adduce him as such a witness; and infidels *are bound* to dispose of his testimony, or to embrace the religion which *he* embraced.

V. As teaching the duty and privilege of prayer. "Behold, he prayeth."

Prayer is an evidence of Divine renovation—of spiritual life.—— An infant, as soon as born, begins to cry, an indication of life, want, and dependence. So when a sinner is really converted, he begins sincerely to pray, a sure proof of spiritual life, want, and dependence. This will be the practice of the believer till his life shall end. Grace entered the heart of Saul, and manifested its existence there by the utterance of prayer,—prayer for mercy—prayer for salvation. As soon as the churches heard he was a praying man, they instantly concluded that he was a converted man. Observe as to the excellency of true prayer.

1. It is always prompted by *a sense of need*. The publican.

2. It is *sincere*. It is the prayer of the soul, because the soul groans under bondage, and pants for deliverance.

3. It is *penitent and humble*. The prodigal.

4. It is *earnest*. "The effectual, fervent prayer," etc.

5. It is *believing*. Faith in the Mediator. "No man can come unto the Father, except by him."

IMPROVEMENT.

1. That the glorified saints before the throne of glory were once vile and sinful as we are.

2. This subject gives the greatest encouragement to those who feel their spiritual ruin. If there was grace for Saul of Tarsus, there is also salvation for them.

3. How fearful the state of those who reject salvation, and all evidence of its truthfulness.

XII.—THE EXALTATION OF THE RIGHTEOUS AT THE LAST DAY.

THEN shall the King say unto them on his right hand, Come, ye blessed of my Father, inherit the kingdom prepared for you from the foundation of the world.—MATT. xxv. 34.

THE doctrine of a future judgment is enunciated by most of the sacred writers.——It will be a solemn and interesting event.——To the wicked it presents a scene of terrors.——To the righteous it is full of interest. It will be the "day of the manifestation of the sons of God," when they shall be acknowledged, honoured, and glorified by the Judge.——The process of the Last Judgment, and its momentous results, are here graphically stated by him who is ordained of God to be the Judge of all. Acts xvii. 31

Consider the subject as follows:—

I. THE INVITATION IS GIVEN BY THE KING. "Then shall the King say." Christ is called King. And his royalty and all its exalted honours are the reward of his sufferings and death. He is now the King—Head of his church, Ps. ii. 6; John xviii. 37; Rev. xvii. 14; xix. 16. How extensive his dominion—how great his glory, according to these texts. Blessed then will they be who shall hear the favourable voice of the King of kings, &c., amid the solemnities of judgment.

II. THE GLORIOUS DISTINCTION OF THE RIGHTEOUS. "Say to them on his right hand." The whole world is supposed to have assembled at the judgment-bar. The righteous have been separated from the wicked, and placed at the right hand of the Judge.—— The right hand is the place of honour, dignity, and special favour. Eph. i. 20; Ps. cx. 1; Acts ii. 25. The left hand was the place of dishonour, denoting condemnation. Eccles. x. 2. Consider the happiness of the righteous at the right hand, as contrasted with the position of the wicked!

III. THE PLEASING AND SIGNIFICANT CHARACTER UNDER WHICH THE RIGHTEOUS ARE ADDRESSED. "Blessed of my Father." That is, made happy, or raised to felicity by my Father. Their present honours and dignities, their immediate entrance with me into my kingdom, their everlasting life, have all been effected by my Father. "Blessed of my Father," his chosen, redeemed, regenerated, adopted, and beloved children, whom he has determined to render blessed for evermore. Blessed of the Father, because

1. He *gave his Son as their ransom*. John iii. 16; Rom. viii. 32. This is the basis of their faith and hope.

2. He has blessed them with *justifying grace*. No longer cursed by the law as transgressors, but justified by the grace that is in Christ Jesus our Lord. Gal. iii. 9—13. They are not only pardoned, but *justified*, two valuable and distinct blessings. By justi-

fication, they are regarded as *innocent*, and treated as though they had never sinned. Hence, for their innocency, they are called "sheep." v. 33.

3. Blessed of the Father with the *privilege of adoption*. They have come out from the world, have been pardoned, and justified, and *renovated*, and now they resemble God, and his children. They have the Spirit of adoption. John i. 12; Rom. viii. 14—17; Gal. iv. 6.

4. Blessed with the *sanctifying influence and graces of the Holy Spirit*. This renders them obedient, and their obedience is evangelical. Hence Christ, as the Judge, will make known their good works as the effect of their faith and love, v. 35—40. These are not meritorious, but the fruits of the Spirit, proving that they have really been blessed.

5. Blessed of the Father *in contradistinction to the despite of the world*. Though despised and reproached by the world, yet the Father loves and blesses them. Deut. xxxiii. 29.

IV. THEIR FUTURE EXALTATION. "Come, ye blessed," etc.

1. He *gives them a gracious welcome*. He calls them to "come" to him, that they may behold and share his glory, and concur with him in the judgment about to be given to the wicked. —— As Matthew Henry observes, "Come," that is, welcome, ten thousand welcomes, to the blessed of my Father; come to me, come to be for ever with me, you that followed me, bearing my cross, now come along with me bearing the crown. The blessed of my Father are the beloved of my soul, that have been too long at a distance from me; come, now, come into my bosom, and rest in my love. Oh how this will gladden the saints in that day. We now come boldly to the throne of grace; but we shall then come boldly to the throne of glory, and this word holds out the golden sceptre, with an assurance that our requests shall be granted to more than the half of the kingdom. Now, the Spirit saith, Come, in the word; and the bride saith, Come, in prayer, leading to sweet communion, but the perfection of bliss will be when *the King shall say, Come*."

2. *Their everlasting destiny is to inherit the kingdom.* "Inherit the kingdom," meaning the kingdom of heaven. What a glorious inheritance! It is the dwelling-place of God. It is the abode of angels. Its glories must therefore be inconceivably great. A kingdom is reckoned the most valuable possession on earth, and it implies the greatest wealth and honour. The monarch of a kingdom wears the crown, wields the sceptre, and commands its treasures. But what is this to the Kingdom of heaven, where all the saints shall be kings?

Its glory is set forth by crowns—palms—white robes. See Matt. xiii. 43. Its riches are immense—riches of glory—its streets are paved with gold and precious stones. Its pleasures are all rational, and never satiate — always new and abundant, called "rivers of pleasure."

They shall "inherit" this kingdom. The inheritance is only for the children of the Divine family. "If sons," etc. Gal. iv. 7, but not otherwise. The sons only shall enjoy their Father's estate. There they will feel that the kingdom is their own. As they look at its vast wealth and grandeur; as they hear its delightful melodies; as their hearts pulsate with joy, they will say, "All this is mine! — to inherit — for ever!"

3. It is *prepared*. Infinite wisdom, almighty power, and inconceivable love, have prepared it. It is great like the great God. It is holy like the holy God. It is infinitely blissful like the infinitely Happy One. It is eternal like the immutable God.——It is prepared by means of Christ — by his death — and heaven is *the purchased possession*. Into it he entered as our forerunner. John xiv. 1, 2, etc.

This preparation implies its suitability and adaptation to the wants and aspirations of an immortal spirit redeemed. Nothing here can satisfy it: the novelty of every thing here departs—every thing satiates. But at the right hand of God there is "fulness of joy, and pleasures for evermore."——It is the prepared Canaan after all the trials of this world's wilderness—an exemption from all evil.

4. It is the kingdom *prepared from the foundation of the world*. God foresaw that man would fall, and his purpose to redeem was coeval with his purpose to create, that both might yield a revenue of praise to himself. Eph. i. 4. O wondrous love! before this world was made, even then did Jehovah form the plan of mercy to save sinners; and onwards till Christ exclaimed on the cross, "It is finished," and thence till now, his heart has been fixed on the happiness of believers, and it is his own blessed promise, "I will never leave thee, nor forsake thee."

Lastly. What a radiant influence then does the Royalty of Christ, and the arrangements of his grace, cast over future scenes. He is our King and our God. When we die, he will stand by our bed, having the keys of death and the invisible world suspended at his girdle. He openeth and no man shutteth. Death is entirely under his control. In those solemn moments, he will appear as the Shepherd of his flock, as the unfailing Surety of his people, and as the King of saints. Then the soul, about to leave the body, and stretching its wings for its flight, will have an Almighty arm on which it may safely recline. With one hand this gracious King shall hold the anchor of hope, and with the other signal the way to glory.

This Almighty King has power over the grave, and at the last day, he will descend from heaven, and raise the bodies of his saints from their long sleep in the dust. He will change and so fashion our vile bodies like unto his own glorious body, and reunite them to our souls, purified, immortal, and happy. O with what rapture shall we arise to gaze on the Judge descending from heaven, in "the glory of his Father, with all his holy angels." How will our souls beat with ecstacy when the same glorious and everlasting King shall place us on his right hand in glory and honour, which the monarchs of earth will covet in vain, and before which all earthly grandeur shall sink to nought. With what heavenly melody will the voice of the Redeemer sound in our ears, when he proclaims, "Come, ye blessed," etc. How will the soul distend with transport, when, accompanied by the church of the first-born, and surrounded by thrones, principalities, and powers, it shall commence its flight towards the highest heavens, to be made pillars there to go out no more for ever. What a celestial sunshine will irradiate the mind, when we shall be presented before the throne of Jehovah, and settled with angels and saints in our own immortal inheritance, and final home, and find ourselves free from sin, free from all sorrow, and our heavenly life commenced, which will be for ever vigorous and young. "Thy sun shall no more go down," etc.

XIII.—GOD A HABITATION.

A METAPHORICAL SKETCH.

"BE thou my strong Habitation, whereunto I may continually resort."— Ps. lxxi. 3. —— Or, Ps. xc. 1.—"LORD, thou hast been our Dwelling-place (or habitation) in all generations."

THE soul needs a refuge. Its circumstances are of a necessitous character. —— Regard man as a vile, condemned, and ruined sinner, as a proof that he wants a refuge. —— Regard the Christian as conflicting with sin, the flesh, the world, etc., and it will be evident that a Divine Refuge is necessary for his safety. —— God therefore bows the heavens and comes down to be the refuge of repentant and believing sinners. He is their shelter and habitation through life, and their everlasting portion in heaven. "Because thou hast made the Lord, who is my refuge, even the Most High thy *Habitation;* there shall no evil befall thee, neither shall any plague come nigh unto thy dwelling." Ps. xci. 9, 10. As a well-fortified castle or town affords safety to those within it, so is the Lord the defence of his people.

I. To every house or habitation there is a way leading to it, and a door through which to enter into it, which is freely opened only to approved friends.

The Lord Jesus Christ is the *Way* that leads to this Divine Habitation. "I am the *way*," etc. John xiv. 6. He is a Prophet to enlighten, a Priest to atone, and a King to subdue and govern. He is also called *the Door,* which lets into this Habitation. A

Door that is always open to the penitent and believer. See John x. 9.

"The happy gates of gospel grace,
Stand open night and day;
Come, sinners, here receive supplies,
And drive your wants away."

II. It is a legal right and propriety which render a habitation valuable, and interesting. A passer-by may cast a *transient* look at it, but it does not interest him because it is not his.

It is an interest in God through Christ that causes the saint highly to prize and adore him. "Thou art my God, I will exalt thee; I will praise thy name," Isa. xxv. 1; Ps. cxviii. 28; "The Lord is my portion," &c. Lam. iii. 24. O what a portion! Think of his attributes—of the riches of his grace—the gifts of his Spirit—the purposes of his love—the guardianship of his angels—the influence of his presence—the provisions of his house—the promises of his word—and the glories of his heaven; for all these are the rich inheritance of God's people. *All these are mine!* What a rich habitation! What a precious Dwelling-place!

When I can say my God is mine,
When I can feel thy glories shine,
I tread the world beneath my feet,
And all the earth calls good or great.

III. A habitation or house is a shelter or covert from heat and cold, from wind and rain, from snow and hail, and the stormy blast.

God is the soul's chief and only Sanctuary. "What time I am afraid, I will trust in thee," Ps. lvi. 3, or, as the original means, *I will retire into thee*, as my Habitation, for shelter, "for thou art a strength to the poor and needy, and a refuge from the storm." See Isa. xxv. 4. In awful convulsions of state, revolutions of kingdoms, and death-producing epidemics, which afflict the world, those who dwell in God shall be perfectly safe.

If burning beams of noon conspire
To dart a pestilential fire,
God is their life, his wings are spread,
To shield them with a healthful shade.

If vapours with malignant breath
Rise thick, and scatter midnight death,
Israel is safe, the poison'd air
Grows pure, if Israel's God be there.

Union with God prevents coldness and indifference in spiritual things. If you retire from this habitation, worldly influence, the pleasures of sin, and evil communications will soon dull your zeal, and freeze your hearts. The blights of error, apart from God, soon destroy the plants of righteousness. "Dwell in love, and dwell in God," and by the celestial fire of the Holy Spirit, you will be rendered "fervent in spirit, serving the Lord with courage, resolution, and delight."

IV. A habitation or house is a place of security against thieves, robbers, assassins. It is a man's castle for the protection of himself and family.

And God is a Sanctuary for his people when they are assailed by the fiery darts of the Wicked One, or by the malice of persecuting men, or by the corruption of their hearts. When, therefore, Christian, thou art assailed by the enemy, retire into God — throw thyself into his arms. Satan cannot follow thee there.

> Thrice happy man! thy Maker's care,
> Shall keep thee from the fowler's snare;
> Satan the fowler, who betrays
> Unguarded souls a thousand ways.
>
> Just as a hen protects her brood,
> From birds of prey that seek her blood,
> Under her feathers, so the Lord
> Makes his own arm his people's guard.

V. Our habitation is our home, for in other places we are but strangers and sojourners. It is the place of domestic comfort, and pleasant association. We love home, sweet home!

God is the Christian's home, for he dwells in God. The very business pursuits of life, which necessarily lead into all kinds of society — the customs of the world which constantly plead for adoption — and even our relationships of life have always a tendency to separate us from God. Sometimes we feel ourselves allured; — but it is always comfortable to return home to God, to dwell under the shadow of his wing, and to see his beauty, behold his glory, and partake of the riches of his grace. —— The vain amusements of this life, its scenes of gaiety, the tavern, the dance, the drama, and the tents of wickedness, afford no satisfaction to the regenerated. He could not be at home there. Spiritual vitality is in his heart — he is born of God, therefore he can only be at home in God. He is afraid of wandering from this delightful home; and if he does wander, he returns praying,

> "Create my nature pure within,
> And form my soul averse to sin;
> Let thy good Spirit ne'er depart,
> Nor hide thy presence from my heart.
>
> "I cannot live without thy light,
> Cast out and banish'd from thy sight
> Thy holy joys, my God, restore,
> And guard me that I fall no more."

This home must be a comfortable home. Ah! what are all the joys of earth compared to the "fellowship with the Father, and with his Son Jesus Christ?" "In him are hid all the treasures of wisdom and knowledge." "Whom have I in heaven but thee?"

> Let others stretch their arms like seas,
> And grasp in all the shore;
> Grant me the visits of thy face,
> And I desire no more.

VI. A habitation is the place of rest and repose after the toils and fatigues of the day.

> Night is the time for rest;
> How sweet when labours close,
> To gather round an aching breast,
> The curtain of repose,
> Stretch the tired limbs, and lay the head,
> Down on our own delightful bed.

God is a rest to the sinner at the time of his conversion. Convinced of sin — under the curse — terrified by the lightning's flash, and the thunder's roar, as they utter the curse of Sinai's broken law, he hears with rapture the invitation, "Come unto me, all ye that labour," etc. Matt. xi. 28. He is glad to repose in God, and to be saved by rich free grace. The glorious attributes of Jehovah are like so many retiring rooms, places of security, and repose. "Return to thy rest," Ps. cxvi. 7. The Psalmist uttered this language in a time of affliction and distress. And is it not a precious privilege in all our sorrows, and when puzzled with the complexity of Divine Providence, to be allowed to repose our souls on the Divine attributes? He is *omniscient*, and knows what is best for us, and we ought to bow to his will. He is *all-wise*, and commands all things to work together for our good. He is *almighty* — *faithful* — *infinitely good*, etc.

VII. A house or habitation is often a place of hospitality, to which friends are invited, where strangers are sometimes entertained, and beggars relieved.

Then look at God. He is always "waiting to be gracious." "My God shall supply all your need, out of his riches in glory, by Christ Jesus." To all distressed and anxious sinners, he utters his love, "Ho! every one that thirsteth," etc. Isa. lv. 1. —— He has given his gospel to the Gentiles, and he receives into union with himself the vilest of the vile. "Then hath God granted," etc. Acts xi. 18; Luke i. 53; James i. 5. He manifests his gracious presence in his house, and it is that presence which makes it a banqueting-house.

VIII. He that is houseless is in a very desolate and miserable state, and exposed to very great inconvenience.

He that dwells not in God through Christ, is "without God, without hope, and without Christ in the world." To him God is a "consuming fire."

APPLICATION.

1. The superiority of the Christian's privilege. He dwelleth in God, and God is his portion. All other possessions are earthly; this is Divine. Other portions are confined to the body. This blesses both body and soul. Other portions satiate; this is always satisfying. Other portions must perish; this will bless and enrich for ever.

2. It requires circumspection of life — a constant desire and

endeavour to please God, lest we should be turned out of our habitation; for can two walk or dwell together except they be agreed?

3. How great is the folly of those whose desires and aims centre in earthly things, which are but for a season, and ultimately lead to ruin!

4. Christ ever presents himself as the accessible Way, and the Open Door to fellowship with God.

IV.—DISSOLUTION FOLLOWED BY GLORY.

PART I.

"For we know that if our earthly house of this tabernacle were dissolved, we have a building of God, a house not made with hands, eternal in the heavens."—2 Cor. v. 1.

THAT which constitutes the Christian's bliss and support in this world, is the hope of a glorious immortality. This cheers his mind at all times, but especially in the time of adversity, and in the prospect of death.——Such was the experience of the Apostles, as we learn from the preceding chapter. He refers, v. 8, etc., to the severe trials which they endured for Christ's sake. But the influence of the Divine Spirit strengthened their faith and hope, v. 14—16, and by that means they were enabled to despise all their sufferings in the cause of truth, and to rejoice in prospect of heavenly glory!—v. 17, 18.—— It is as if the Apostle had said, "Brethren, see what we suffer for Christ's sake; but these are our present and everlasting profit; we are going forth weeping now, but we shall return again with joy, etc. These sufferings are great and overwhelming, and eventually they will crush us,—our bodies will soon be dissolved in martyrdom, but this trying process will last only for *a moment*, after which we are sure of a building of God, etc. Dissolved! ah! let these bodies be dissolved, and let our enemies and death do their worst, yet they cannot injure our souls, nor rob us of our house eternal in the heavens."

I. THE DISSOLUTION OF THE BODY AS REPRESENTED BY THE APOSTLE.

The various expressions by which the Apostle represents it are worthy of particular consideration.

1. *His description of the human body.*

(1) He calls it a *house*. The word house refers to the body, as the habitation, or the dwelling-place of the soul. The soul dwells in it as we dwell in a house. Thus Solomon speaks of it as a house, and when old age and death come, he describes the doors as being shut, and the windows as being darkened, Eccles. xii. 3.

It is called *a house*, because it displays the *infinite skill and wisdom of its Architect and Creator*. Just as you stand by some beautiful building, some magnificent palace or temple. You admire its symmetry, its chasteness, its beautiful sculpture, its vast extent, etc., and you say, The Architect was endowed with uncommon genius, and the builders and other workmen with elaborate skill and taste.

Contemplate the human body and all its parts — the bones, the muscles, the tendons and ligatures, the brain, the nerves, the circulation of the blood, the respiration, the organs of sight, hearing, taste, touch, smell, and speech. Consider that all the parts of the human machine are adjusted with the greatest exactness — that there is not one member superfluous, nor any thing wanting that is necessary either for ornament or use, and you will exclaim like the Psalmist, "I am fearfully and wonderfully made;" — made by God, and not come into existence by mere chance, or by the operation of some undefined chemical, magnetical, or electrical power in Nature. No. God — the Triune Deity, said, "Let us make man." "So God created man in his own image, in the image of God created he him."

Has that watch — that steam-engine — that machine which spins or weaves, sprung from chance? All have had a contriver and a creator. Apply the same argument to the creation of man's body.

(2) It is called a *house* on account of its *glorious inhabitant* — the soul. It is the residence of an immortal spirit. "There is a spirit in man, and the inspiration of the Almighty," etc. Job, xxxii. 8. This inhabitant is more valuable than the world, for "What is a man profited," etc. Matt. xvi. 26. The body then is dignified by the soul, and all the claims of the body, and all the possessions and enjoyments of earth, should be made subordinate to the infinite concerns of the soul, the tenant of the body, the glorious jewel of the earthly casket.

(3) It is called an *earthly house*, a frail tenement, whose foundation is in the dust. The word *earthly* stands opposed to "heavenly," or to the "house eternal in the heavens." The term refers to its origin, "The Lord God formed man of the dust of the ground." This is the origin of all — from the monarch on the throne, to the humble peasant in his hut. Some may boast their lineage, their proud ancestry — their noble blood — their relationship to the great — but look, ye children of vanity, down to the dust, whence you sprung, and whither you must go. "Dust thou art, and unto dust thou shalt return."

The body then is called an earthly house, on account of its origin — because it derives its sustenance from the produce of the earth — and because by the lapse of time, and the ravages of disease, it is ever tending to its mother earth. The days of childhood and youth rapidly pass away — the beauty and strength of manhood soon fade — the infirmities of age are very soon succeeded by death. "Man dieth and wasteth away, yea, man giveth up the ghost, and where is he?"

(4) The body is also compared to a *tabernacle*, which means a

booth or tent, a moveable dwelling, composed of a few slight poles put into the ground, covered with canvass, and secured by cords. The idea conveyed is this, that the body is not to be the permanent dwelling-place of the soul. The body resembles a tent, erected for a temporary purpose, and easily taken down in migrating from place to place. The body possesses no principle of permanency. It can be held together but a little time. It is like a hut or a cottage that is shaken by every gust of wind; like a tent when the pins are loose, and the cords unstranded, or rotten, and which the wind will soon sweep away.

It implies too the mutable nature of man's circumstances. Sometimes in wealth, then in poverty. Situated in this position, then it is reversed.

2. *The solemn fact:* "the earthly house of this tabernacle" must be "dissolved."

The word "dissolve" means to disunite the parts of any thing; and it is applied to the act of throwing down, or destroying a building. In the text it is applied to the body as a temporary dwelling that must be taken down,—in fact, to the dissolution of the body in the grave. It can easily be dissolved, and made to return to its primitive elements; for frail and feeble are the bodies of those "that dwell in houses of clay, whose foundation is in the dust, who are crushed before the moth."—Job iv. 9.

It will be dissolved by means of disease, which may be *quick in its operation*, dissolving the earthly house in a very short time — or *chronic*, slow in its ravaging power, but sure at length to dissolve the house of clay. The operation of disease may be gentle, or it may be violent, storming the poor clayey tenement, and dissolving it into dust

It may be dissolved by casualty, or accidents, as they are called. In a moment, in the twinkling of an eye, the body may be dissolved.

It may be dissolved by gradual decay. Life may be prolonged to the utmost extent, three score years and ten, or four score years, to the time of infirmity, sorrow, or second childhood, yet the body shall be dissolved at last.

Mark the process of the dissolution of an old man, as portrayed by Solomon, Eccles. xii. He compares the body to a HOUSE. The "keepers of the house shall tremble," the hands shall become paralytic, tremulous, and lose their grasp. "The strong men shall bow themselves,"those firm and able columns, the legs, shall sink under the weight of the body. "The grinders," the teeth, "shall cease, because they are few," and the work of mastication shall be imperfectly performed. Dim suffusion shall veil the organs of sight, for "they that look out of the windows shall be darkened." "The doors," or valves, "shall be shut in the streets," or alleys of the body, when the digestive powers are weakened, and "the sound of the 'internal' grinding is low." Sleep now loses its refreshing influence; he rises up "at the voice of the bird." His voice which once charmed an auditory with its musical cadence, now charms no more. Music once delighted him, but in a great measure it has lost its influence upon him; for all "the daughters of music shall be brought low." Timidity and distrust will predominate, and he will be alarmed at every thing; "he will be afraid of that which is high, and fears shall be in the way." As the early "almond tree," when it flourishes in full blossom, his hoary head shall be conspicuous in the congregation, the sure prognostic, not of spring, alas, but of winter; he who like "the grasshopper in the season of youth, was so sprightly in his motions, now scarcely able to crawl upon the earth, "shall be a burden" to himself; and the organ of sense being vitiated and impaired, "desire" and appetite shall fail. Thus "man" gradually, but surely, "goeth to his long home," the grave, and "the mourners go about the street," the long, hollow groans, and throat rattlings prognosticate extreme debility, and speedy extinction of life; for the spinal marrow, that "silver cord," with the infinite ramifications of the nerves, thence derived, will be relaxed and lose its tone; "and the golden bowl," the container of the brain, from which it proceeds, "shall be broken," or rendered unfit to perform its functions. The vessel, by which, as a "pitcher," the blood is carried back to the right ventricle of the heart for a fresh supply, "shall be broken at the fountain," the heart, "and the wheel," or instrument of circulation, which throws it forth again to the extremities of the body, "shall be broken at the cistern."

Thus the blood becomes stagnate; the lungs cease to respire; all motion, voluntary and involuntary, ceases; the body, the house of the immortal spirit, is no longer tenantable, and the soul takes its flight into the eternal world. The man DIES, and "the dust returns to the earth as it was." Putrefaction and solution take place; the whole mass becomes decomposed, and at length is reduced to its original dust, while the "spirit," which God at first breathed into man, even an immortal soul, "returns to God who gave it." Well might Solomon exclaim, "Vanity of vanities, all is vanity."

This dissolution will *certainly* take place; it is a *universal* law. None can evade it—nothing can prevent it. Death can never be bribed by wealth.——"It is appointed for all men once to die." Heb. ix. 27.

This truth is very *solemn* and *affecting*. However strong and robust—however beautiful and well-fed—however near and dear to us by the ties of blood and affection, the body must be dissolved, and the tabernacle taken down. The countenances which have beamed upon us with so much intelligence, and diffused life in the social circle, must all be changed and see corruption. For ever silent will be the captivating tongue, and the engaging form shall be prostrated in the dust. The man of talent, the noble philanthropist, the able minister, the munificent donor, the man of exemplary piety, and all those who have been the greatest blessing to the church and to the world, must be buried in the dust. Their lips must be sealed in silence, and their voice be heard no more.

APPLICATION.

This affecting subject should teach us,

1. *Humility.* We are sinners, and the death of the body is the consequence of sin.——Humility,—why should we be proud? The grave and its corruption are our portion. "Naked came we into the world, and naked shall we return."

2. *Gratitude.* God has provided us strong consolation in prospect of dissolution. By the gift of Christ—by his finished work on the cross—by his resurrection from the grave, he has despoiled death of his sting, and robbed the grave of its power. "All thanks to him who scourged the venom out."

3. *Watchfulness.* The time of dissolution is uncertain. Habituate the mind to think of death, to feel that this world is not our rest. Not to render life gloomy, but to endow it with Christian philosophy—which, by virtue of the redeemer's death, estimates dissolution as the process by which the soul is translated to the immortal inheritance.

XV.—THE CHRISTIAN IN THE PROSPECT OF DEATH CHEERED BY THE HOPE OF IMMORTALITY.

PART II.

For we know that if our earthly house of this tabernacle were dissolved, we have a building of God, an house not made with hands, eternal in the heavens.—2 COR. v. 1.

THE value of any pursuit is to be ascertained by its results.—— This is especially the case in spiritual things. "Say ye to the righteous, it shall be well with him; woe to the wicked, it shall be ill with him." Isa. iii. 10, 11. The great difference between holiness and sin, the saint and the sinner, is indicated by the prospect which they have of eternity. The sinner's heart is often filled with the bitterness of his own ways, and of a future glorious immortality he has no hope, but a fearful looking for of judgment. ——Hence the dissolution of the body is a dreadful subject for contemplation; but still more awful is the contemplation of his eternal state as an exile from God.——But how different is the experience of the righteous! "For we know that when," etc. Such is the Christian's hope. The body shall be dissolved in death, but immediately after that dissolution, the soul shall have a building of God, a habitation far superior to any dwelling-place ever made by human hands, a blessed mansion in the heavens, where God displays his glorious presence, and where light, purity, and felicity are found in full perfection; and' this mansion shall endure for ever.

Having considered, I. the Dissolution of the body, consider now,

II. THE BLESSED HOPE OF IMMORTALITY EXPERIENCED BY THE CHRISTIAN IN PROSPECT OF DISSOLUTION. "We have a building," etc.

This language has a two-fold aspect. It refers to heaven as the future residence of believers, and to the resurrection and glorification of the body itself.

1. *To heaven* as the residence of the Deity and all the celestial inhabitants. Into that glorious abode the soul of the believer enters to reside till the body shall be raised, glorified, and reunited to it. "It is my purpose," as if the Redeemer had said, "to build thy body afresh; in the mean time, come and live with me."

In this sense Macknight, and some others, understand the language as referring to the mansions which God has fitted up for his people in heaven, and which the Lord Jesus has gone to prepare for them. John xiv. 2, etc. What a delightful description Christ gives here of the believer's felicity! Every word is full of the sweetest melody.

It is a blessed thing that heaven has been revealed to man. That revelation harmonizes with the Christian's wishes. He longs to be at rest. It is the heaven in which he will be free from all the storms of adversity, sickness and death. It is the social home in which he will converse with all the bright intelligences of his Father's house on high. It is the region of light, where all the dark mysteries of earth shall be explained to his satisfaction and joy. It is the scene of ineffable delight, in the presence of God, where there is fulness of joy, etc. It is the promised inheritance, the abiding kingdom, the sacred temple, the heavenly Jerusalem, where he shall possess all those riches and felicities which his heavenly Father has promised him. It is the habitation of purity, where he shall sin and weep no more — the habitation of triumph where foes shall annoy him no more — the Paradise of bliss where he shall sorrow no more, and the habitation of immortal life where he shall sicken and die no more. There he shall wear the fadeless crown, wave the imperishable palm of victory, and strike the harp of lofty praise for ever. "Blessed be the God," etc. 1 Pet. i. 3.

The Apostle's description of heaven in the text is figurative, and very expressive. He compared the body to an earthly house, a frail, mutable tabernacle. But the future abode of the righteous is very different. It is "a building of God," etc.——Observe

(1) *It is "a building of God."* The apostle evidently means that it has been designed by God, and made by him, that he is

the Architect and Creator of that future and eternal dwelling. This conveys the idea of *glorious magnificence;* the infinite Jehovah has designed and built the heavenly house. What then must be its glory! It is the production of his wisdom and power. Look at this earth, its mountains and valleys, its forests and plains, its beautiful foliage and its lovely flowers, its mighty seas and noble rivers, and all the various species of living things. Look at those stellary heavens, the stars, the moon, the suns, yea, millions of suns, scattered throughout boundless space. Do not these operations of his hands proclaim his eternal power and Godhead? If he has invested these outer things with so much beauty and grandeur, then O what must be the grandeur and glory of that heaven which he has specially built for himself and his favorites! The planets may be glorious — the suns existing in boundless space may be glorious, but their light is pale and feeble, and their quality mean when compared with God's dwelling-place on high. Contrast a peasant's hovel or cot with the palace of imperial majesty; compare the indigence of a beggar with the wealthy resources of a monarch; compare the barren intellect of an idiot with the mighty devisings of extraordinary genius as put forth by some philosophers, machinists, engineers, and architects, and you will find an illustration of the statement of the Apostle. The wisest and most powerful men have been created by God. He created their genius, he invested them with power to work! O then what must be the beauty, the grandeur, and glory of the palace of God! "We have a building of God."

(2) The figure in the text conveys the idea of *social enjoyment*. It is a *house*. "A house not made with hands." A house is a home. Heaven is a large and glorious home, inhabited by Jehovah and all his holy and happy family. The Eternal dwells there arrayed in all his glorious majesty, and manifesting all his paternal love. There he communes and converses with his people. There the infinite God with the greatest familiarity of a Father opens his heart and reveals his mind to all his family. It is a large house containing a large family — consisting of angels and archangels, of cherubim and seraphim, and believers redeemed from sin and death. It is a great company which no man can number. Rev. vii. 9. It is a happy family —— a harmonious family —— a family whose hearts are full of heavenly burning love.

(3) It is "*a house not made with hands.*" Not by the hands of men, for heaven is infinite, and created man can never create that which is infinite. Not by angelic hands, for angels too are created beings, and creative agency is not within their province. God is the Creator of all things; no being in heaven or earth participates with him in the glory of creation. Heaven was not built by any creature, neither was it formed out of any pre-existent matter, but created immediately by God himself. "Not with hands." This conveys the idea of *infinite perfection* and *eternal permanence*. A mechanic may contrive and produce a machine, and deem it perfect. Another man inspects it, discovers its imperfection, and

produces a better. What appears perfect to one man, appears imperfect to another. Man cannot compete with nature. "Who can paint like nature?" How imperfect do the works of men appear to the eye of an angel — to the eye of God! "His work is perfect," and when he created heaven, the creature was perfect — perfect beauty, grandeur, purity, happiness, light, knowledge, and glory, entire and wanting nothing.

How different from the work of human hands! They are imperfect, mean, and perishable. —— But this house is

(4) *"Eternal in the heavens."* It is remarkable that nearly every promise and description of heaven is associated with some adjective or representation, indicating *eternal perpetuity.* —— It is called "eternal life," "the everlasting kingdom," "the inheritance incorruptible," etc., and "the crown of glory that fadeth not away." Such expressions abound in the New Testament. —— The house, therefore, which the Christian shall inhabit will never be subject to decay or dissolution. The revolutions of earth—the concussions of nature, and all the vast changes which affect man's condition here, will never be known there. Is heaven a state of joy? It is eternal. Is it a state of festive delight? It is eternal. Is it a state where blessed spirits commingle in holy intercourse? It is eternal. Is it a state of holy rapture and praise? It is eternal. Is it a state of glorious vision? It is eternal. Is it a state of delightful perambulation on the golden streets, under the tree of life, by the pellucid streams of the river of the water of life, with agreeable associates? It is eternal.

> Beyond this world a city stands;
> A city there not made with hands:
> Where God the Saviour reigns;
> 'Tis built for sinners bought with blood
> Redeem'd and sanctified to God,
> And cleansed from all their stains.
>
> The cities of the world must fall,
> However solid, they must all
> The common ruin share.
> But yonder city still appears,
> Unchangeable through endless years;
> For God himself is there.

Having considered the "Building of God," in which the soul shall dwell till the resurrection-day, and in which afterwards the whole glorified man shall reside for ever, consider

2. *The Resurrection of the body.* The body, the "earthly house of this tabernacle," * shall be dissolved. It shall be resolved into

---

* The word *"tabernacle"* alludes to the ancient Jewish tabernacle, which on all removals of the congregation, was dissolved and taken in pieces; and the ark of the covenant, covered with curtains, was carried by itself; and when they came to the place of rest, then the dissolved parts of the tabernacle were put together as before. Considering the simile in connection with the doctrine of the resurrection, the apostle evidently wished to convey the idea; — that as the tabernacle was taken down in order to be again put together, so the body is to be *dissolved* in order to be *re-edified;* that as the ark of the covenant subsisted by itself while the tabernacle was down, so can the soul when separated from the body; that as the ark had then its own veil for the covering. Ex. xi. 21, so the soul is to have some vehicle in which it shall subsist till it receives its body at the resurrection.— *Dr. Adam Clarke.*

its primitive elements. In innumerable particles it shall be scattered about on the face of the earth, and shall even become the source of vegetable and animal life.——But the Almighty Saviour can re-collect the scattered atoms, and reanimate the lifeless dust. Who can limit his power? Who can restrain his infinite might? He that made the body at first from the dust of the ground can surely raise it up from the dead. "I am the resurrection and the life." See John xi. 25, 26; Phil. iii. 20, 21.*

To doubt the power of Almighty God in this important affair would be more absurd than to doubt the power of a machinist to repair or reconstruct a damaged and broken instrument or machine. Though that may be broken and ruined, yet the genius of man is not destroyed. He can gather up the fragments and repair them, and probably produce a superior instrument. He constructed it at the first, and he has the same ability now as then, or very likely that ability has been greatly improved by experience.

The human machine, the body, has been broken and ruined by sin. It lies scattered in the grave; but the Almighty Saviour stands by that grave, and says, "I will raise it again at the last day. From those particles I will produce a more beautiful house for the habitation of the soul. I will endue it with the principle of immortality. All power is given unto me both in heaven and upon earth. The resurrection, though mysterious, is a small matter compared with the mighty operations of my hand. The government is upon my shoulder; I govern all worlds. Therefore weep not, doubt not. 'Thy dead men shall live; together with my dead body shall they arise. Awake and sing, ye that dwell in the dust, for the dew is the dew of herbs, and the earth shall cast out the dead.'" Isa. xxvi. 19; 1 Cor. xv., many parts of it beautifully illustrate and establish the doctrine of the resurrection.

Lastly. All true Christians *feel assured that they have a building of God*, etc. "WE KNOW." The Apostles felt persuaded that if even the body should die by martyrdom, they should enter heaven, and their bodies be raised to life again. "We know" is the language of strong and unwavering assurance. They had no doubt on the subject. And this assurance of faith may be attained by the study of God's word, by much prayer, and dependence upon the operations of the Spirit.

---

* As the finding out the particulars of the dust of our bodies discovers the vastness of the knowledge of God; so to raise them up will manifest the glory of his power as much as creation. Bodies that have mouldered away into multitudes of atoms, been resolved into the elements, passed through varieties of changes: been sometimes the matter to lodge the form of a plant, or been turned into the substance of a fish or fowl, or vapoured up into a cloud, and being part of that matter which hath compacted a thunderbolt; disposed of into places far distant, scattered by the winds, swallowed and concocted by beasts;—for these to be called out from their different places of abode to meet in one body, and be restored to their former consistency in a marriage union, "in the twinkling of an eye," 1 Cor. xv. 52, is a consideration that may justly amaze us, and our shallow understandings are too feeble to comprehend it. But is it not credible, since all the disputes against it may be silenced by reflections on infinite power, which nothing can oppose, for which nothing can be esteemed too difficult to effect, which doth not imply a contradiction in itself?"—*Charnock*.

We know from the purposes of God. It is his will to give us a building above, etc.

We know from the comprehensive and unfailing promises of God; for he is faithful who has promised.

We know from the operations of his grace upon our hearts. We have believed in Christ, washed in his precious blood, etc., etc. We are "the children of the resurrection."

We know from the resurrection of Christ, the pledge and earnest of ours. The Head has risen, the members of his mystical body shall also rise. "Christ has become the first-fruits of them that slept." Christ came to redeem our whole nature, and the body being ransomed, as well as the spirit, by no less a price than his own blood, shall be equally claimed, and renewed, and glorified.

APPLICATION.

1. How supporting to the believer is such a prospect! Is he poor? The riches of the eternal inheritance are before him. Be patient, poor brother, thou wilt be rich enough by and by. An enduring substance awaits thee in Immanuel's land.——Is he sinking under the infirmities and decays of nature? Does the earthly house give signs of falling? Is the outward man perishing? Immortal strength and vigour, immortal beauty shall be given him when his Redeemer shall come to finish his work. Does he fear death? It will soon be over. Christ will be with him in dissolution as the strength of his heart, and his portion for ever!

2. How superior is this support to every other. Some look for support to the amusements of earth, to the intoxicating cup, and to the mere creature. Some depend upon the works of the law, etc. The gospel alone can impart a hope that maketh not ashamed.

XVI.—THE DIVINE SUPPLY.

"My God shall supply all your need, according to his riches in glory by Christ Jesus."—Phil. iv. 19.

"HE that giveth to the poor, lendeth to the Lord;" and if done in faith, it shall be repaid him with the highest interest. The blessing of him that was ready to perish shall come upon the liberal soul.——Paul and his colleagues were poor—poor like their Master, who had not where to lay his head. They were often ready to perish. It was an honour, a benefit, an eternal profit, to minister to their wants. Such liberal souls were remembered by the Apostles in their prayers. Paul, in ver. 13—18, acknowledges the kindness of the Christians at Philippi; and declares his firm belief that God would enrich them for it out of the glorious treasures of his Providence and grace. "My God," etc. The Apostle draws a bill upon the Exchequer of heaven, and leaves it to God to make amends for their kindness. He shall do it, not only as your God, but as *my* God, who takes what is done to *me* as done to himself. You supplied my needs according to your poverty, and he shall supply your need according to his riches in glory.

I. THE NEED OF CHRISTIANS. "All your need." The Christians at Phillippi were in need as well as the Apostles. Under persecution, they could not well succeed in their secular affairs, ch. i. 28. It was a time of great tribulation.

The text supposes that we are very needy creatures — full of temporal and spiritual wants. Man, if left to himself, would be wretched indeed.

1. As a *sinner*, man's wants are infinite. His guilty and condemned soul requires an infinite salvation; his filthy heart Divine renovation; his rebellious will subjection and conformity to God. As an outcast from heaven, he requires a meetness and a title to it. A sinner's need is infinite.

2. As a believer there is great need. He is a sinner saved. He has received spiritual life. But he is menaced by numerous foes determined to deprive him of the grace of God, and of his heavenly crown. These foes are cunning, artful, and fascinating, and have strong and favourable allies in the heart, ever disposed to yield.

Regard the believer as a Christian *traveller;* a "pilgrim" upon earth. Journeying across the desert of this world—a desert arid, dry, and wretched, beset with wicked men—enemies to God and his people—a desert crowded with fallen spirits under the Prince of the Power of the air. Eph. ii. 2.—— How great then the Christian's need! Can he perform this journey in his own strength?—alone?—unsupported?

Regard the believer as a Christian *voyager* across the rough and boisterous ocean of life. What waves of distress—billows of trouble—storms of adversity—shoals of dangers—quicksands of error, and rocks of destruction, he has to encounter. What will be the fate of his poor bark, if he has not the breezes of Divine influence to waft, the anchor of hope to steady, the Compass Divine to direct, the voice of the Captain to cheer, and the hand of the Pilot to guide him safely to the haven of everlasting peace? Befriended by Jesus the Captain and Saviour of his soul, he shall not make shipwreck of his faith.

Regard the Christian as a *Racer* on the Course to glory. Do not a thousand voices call him back? Do not carnal scenes and amusements allure? Do not worldly cares threaten to cast him down if not girded by the girdle of truth. Is he not liable to faint and tire? Great then is the need of Divine stimulus and strength.

Regard the believer as a *Soldier.* His foes—their name is legion:

as to their character, "We wrestle not against flesh and blood" merely, "but against principalities," etc. Eph. vi. 12.——How great was Paul's need when conflicting with the thorn in the flesh —that of Peter before he denied his Lord—that of Demas before he gave up religion, having loved this present world? Omnipotence alone can uphold the Christian in battling with spiritual foes.

Consider the believer as a dying man, and as the heir of immortality. His friends die—his beloved relatives die. "Lover and friend hast thou put far from me," etc. Ps. lxxxviii. 18. This is trying, and his need is great then.——But his own death will be an event involving great necessity. Even now his body is decaying—pains and infirmities, and the advance of age tell him he must die. Death is menacing him—the grave calls for him. He will soon bid adieu to earthly scenes and the tenderest associations. How great will be his need then! Who is to bear up his head amid the swellings of Jordan? Who is to animate his fainting heart then? Will he be triumphant then?

II. THAT GOD WILL SUPPLY HIS NEED OUT OF HIS RICHES IN GLORY. A term expressive of appropriate, seasonable, ample, and everlasting blessedness.

1. *The Source of Supply.* "Out of his riches in glory." Some have rendered the original, "according to the greatness of his goodness;" and others, "out of the redundant stores of goodness which can never fail;" "the glorious treasures of his spiritual benefits;" "the abundance of his glorious grace and mercy." The expression means,

The fulness of God's grace as treasured up in, and freely dispensed through the medium of Christ, and by the power of the Holy Spirit.

Observe, (1) The riches of God's grace are gloriously manifested in our redemption by Jesus Christ. It is "fulness of grace IN HIM." As the Mediator, he was appointed to effect our reconciliation, and to bring us near to God. Eph. i. 7; ii. 13. The mediation of Christ is the rule by which we have access to God as our Father, by prayer, in order to obtain all needful blessings. John xiv. 13, 14.——All the treasures of grace, the redundant stores, and the inexhaustible riches of grace are also DEPOSITED IN HIM, that through him they may be dispensed for the supply of every want.

(2) That all the blessedness of the Christian is derived from "his riches in glory," or from the fulness of GRACE. All the blessings bestowed on a sinner must be of MERE GRACE. His awful depravity, his alienation from God, his daring impiety, necessarily cut off every other ground of hope. So far is he from meriting the Divine favour, that he justly deserves all the wrath which a violated law denounces.

(3) The phrase, "riches in glory," includes also the influences of the Holy Spirit, to enable us to approach God with acceptance,

and to enlighten, to comfort, and to cheer us. Called "the Spirit of grace," Zech. xii. 10; Eph. ii. 18; Rom. viii. 14—16; John xvi. 7.

"Riches in glory!" It is a glorious phrase. It is called "the fulness of God," "the fulness of Christ," and the "grace sufficient" in every time of need. It is the length and breadth, etc., of the love of God. It is the sun and shield which God is to his people, the grace which he gives, and the glory with which he crowns. It comprises the "things which God has prepared for those that love him." It is the "consolation in Christ," the "peace which passeth all understanding," and "joy in the Holy Ghost." It is victory over death and the grave, and "the hope which is laid up for us in heaven." It is the subject of heaven's songs, the melody of angelic harps, and the ocean of felicity to the redeemed.

"Riches in glory!" It is a mine rich and deep, full of invaluable gems, the jewels of the bride below, and of the bride in perfection above—jewels more precious than the gold of Sheba, or the topaz of Ethiopia.

"Riches in glory!" Here the diseased sinner may be healed. It is the hospital of grace, where Christ the great Physician ever waits to be gracious. Here is "eye-salve" for the blind, locomotion for the lame, the hearing ear for the deaf, the tongue of praise for the dumb, and the heart of flesh for that of stone. Sinner, touch but the hem of his garment, and thou shalt be healed.

The "riches in glory" give to the sinner the robe of righteousness to cover his naked and scathed soul—the "fine raiment of the Apocalypse by which it may be clothed and adorned." Therefore every saved sinner triumphs:—"I will greatly rejoice in the Lord, for he hath clothed me with the garments of salvation, he hath covered me with the robe of righteousness; as a bridegroom decketh himself with ornaments, and as a bride adorneth herself with jewels." Isa. lxi. 10.

The "riches in glory" provide for the Christian warrior the invincible instruments of warfare—the shield of faith, the breastplate of righteousness, the helmet of salvation, the sword of the Spirit, and victory in every battle with the foe.

The "riches in glory" secure the believer's temporal welfare, guaranteeing to him the Shield of a special Divine Providence, to deliver from danger, to preserve from disease, and to supply his bodily wants—a proof that his Heavenly Father careth for him; for "he is the Saviour of all men, but especially of them that believe." He who notices the fall of the sparrow, and clothes the lilies of the field, will he not watch over you, O ye of little faith?

2. *The Rule of the Supply.* "ACCORDING to his riches in glory." Whatever God does is done in a way worthy of himself. He will give according to his ability—and that ability is infinite.——This is not the case amongst men; the most wealthy are not the most liberal, and but few give in proportion to their wealth. A poor man may give according to his means, but how limited and ineffi-

cient must be his gifts. And even if the richest man were really to give according to his possessions, how mean would that be compared with what God can give. Nothing short of an infinite good is at his disposal. God has all things at his disposal, and "all things are yours." God then is a glorious giver. He "giveth liberally, and upbraideth not." "According to his riches in glory." Not according to one attribute only, but according to all his glorious perfections. The "riches of his grace" are the wealthy treasures of the BANK OF HEAVEN, to which all believers have free access, and from it they may be adequately supplied for time and for eternity.

The Supply will be *appropriate*, being skilfully adapted to the circumstances of his people. In spiritual things we are incompetent to judge of what is needful. We may think we need consolation, when the Lord knows we want correction. Though we may not always obtain what we desire, he will be sure to give what we need.*

3. *The Agent;* "My God." This expresses the confidence of the Apostle, arising from his knowledge of God's ability, and from the love he bears to his servants—ministers and people. God had a special regard for the first promulgators of Christianity, the Apostles. He was the Guide and the Guardian of those who directly proclaimed his gospel, and founded Christianity in the world, and he supplied "the need" of more private Christians who indirectly laboured to effect the same. Though no Christian action is meritorious, yet God will graciously reward the meanest of his servants at the last day. "Inasmuch," etc. Matt. xxv. 30. "My God shall supply." There is no question about that. In serving man you may be forgotten and neglected. But "God is not unrighteous to forget your work and labour of love." Heb. vi. 10.

III. THE MEDIUM OF THIS SUPPLY. "By Christ Jesus."

He is the way to the Father, and the only channel of communication from him. God in the supplies he grants has a special regard to Christ. Our Great High Priest is infinitely precious in the sight of God, and therefore there is nothing too good, nothing too great, to give for his sake. All the riches of his grace, and the raptures and splendours of an eternal heaven, are to be given through Christ. "This is my beloved Son in whom I am well pleased," and I will bless you for his sake. "The Lord is well pleased for his righteousness' sake, for he hath magnified the law

---

* Many of our wants are ideal, or artificial only : our real necessities are but few. We may think we need more influence, more wealth, etc., but the Lord has not promised these, nor does he allow us to covet any earthly portion. —— Jacob only asked for bread to eat, and raiment to put on, and God gave him this and much more. —— The Lord often moves in a mysterious way to provide for our necessities, or to prevent our falling into poverty and distress. Who would have thought Jacob's necessities, and those of his family, were to be provided for by the imagined death of Joseph, and by his being really banished for about twenty years from his beloved father? See Gen l. 2). —— We often imagine if we could but have our desire, it would be well for us; but if the Lord were to give after that rule, we should soon be undone. Imitate David; "Here am I, let him do unto me as seemeth good." God gives more in answer to such prayers than to those which are more specific. — *Fuller.*

and made it honorable," and he will answer every petition offered in his name, and do for us exceedingly beyond all that we can ask or think.

Christ Jesus is the channel of communication by virtue of his *atonement*. As sin destroyed the fellowship between God and man, Christ restored it.—— Then think of his *intercession*. "He ever liveth." That intercession averts wrath — secures God's favour — keeps mercies flowing — he presents our petitions, and pleads.

Were it not for the atonement, there is no more reason to suppose that blessings would be conferred on men than that they would be on fallen angels.

IMPROVEMENT.

1. How wonderful the love of God in providing such a fountain and channel of supply.

2. This Supply may be obtained by believing prayer.

3. What encouragement to do good in the church! The prayers of relieved saints — and the Divine Supply are powerful motives. See 2 Tim. i. 16—18.

XVII.— REST UNATTAINABLE HERE.

"Arise ye, and depart; for this is not your rest; because it is polluted; it shall destroy you, even with a sore destruction."— MICAH ii. 10.

SIN is destructive to every human comfort. —— It proved so to the children of Israel, who, on account of their wickedness, were expelled from their land and carried into captivity. (See Context.) —— So shall it be with all lovers of the world. This world is "*polluted ;*" we can scarcely touch it without being defiled. There is a vast deal of corruption in the world through lust, therefore Christian pilgrims must be watchful to keep their garments unspotted from the world; it is not our rest; it was never intended to be so; it was designed for our passage, but not for our portion; our inn, but not for our home. Here "we have no continuing city."

I. IT IS NATURAL TO MAN TO MAKE THIS WORLD HIS REST.

He was formed for Divine fellowship, and for a heavenly life. —— But alas! his soul has been diverted from both, and bowed down to the idolatrous love of earthly things. Sin has detached him from the Divine centre—separated him from his chief element. —— Now he seeks a rest, or satisfaction in that to which his depraved inclination leads him; as wealth, honour, pleasure, etc. This is proved

1. *By Scripture.* Solomon devoted himself to the world as his rest, but afterwards declared it to be VANITY. Then the numerous warnings, cautions, etc., not to love the world. 1 John ii. 15, etc.

2. *By Observation.* See how men scheme, plan, strive, yea, agonize to get wealth, as if they were to live for ever. Many "heap up riches, not knowing who shall gather them." Ps. xxxix. 6.

3. *By Experience.* We all feel our souls "cleave to the dust." What Christian does not sigh to be delivered from the gravitating influence of earthly things?

II. THAT THIS WORLD IS NOT THE CHRISTIAN'S REST." "This is not your rest."

1. *The Scriptures declare it.* "For here we have no continuing city." Heb. xiii. 14. The ancient patriarchs reckoned themselves as "strangers and pilgrims upon earth."

2. It is *incapable of yielding complete satisfaction to the mind.* It is not adapted to the demands of the soul. If it gains an object, and another, and another, it is not satisfied: it still aspires after something more novel, and still higher. The whole world could not satisfy its demands. This world is not its rest — it wants an eternal location in God's infinite heaven. Matt. xvi. 26.

3. On account of *its sinfulness.* There can be no rest where sin is. It is the source of all disquietude and misery: How can a defiled world be the rest of a regenerated soul? "Ye are not of the world, even as I am not of the world." "Ye are born from above;" the life of heaven is come down into your souls; then what congeniality can there be between your sanctified soul and the world? John iii. 6.

4. On account of *the Conflicts of the world.* Conflict with a deceitful heart while remaining in the world—conflict with wicked men hostile to the truth and its adherents. Numerous disappointments and losses in trade — conflicts with poverty. All these loudly proclaim, Christian, the place of thy conflict is not the place of thy rest.—— Bodily afflictions too show the vanity of the world — they show the frailty of the human structure — that it is not perfect. "We that are in this tabernacle groan, being burdened."

5. On account of the *mortality and death which pervade it.* "One generation passeth away," etc. "We must needs die." Bodily infirmities frequently indicate that we are dying — gradually approximating to the dust. Parents weep over the remains of their children — and children over their parents — husbands over their wives, and wives over their husbands. Death is no respecter of persons. The most lovely die — the most intelligent and useful fall into the icy arms of death. No one continues long here. It is not our rest.

> Friend after friend departs,
> Who hath not lost a friend?
> There is no union here of hearts,
> But what shall have an end.
> Were this frail world our final rest,
> Living or dying, none were blest.

Is this world then the Christian's rest? Is it desirable to continue where the heart is frequently riven with anguish? A voice from the sepulchre cries, the world, Christians, is not your rest! —— And where are the spirits of our beloved friends who have died in the Lord? They are gone before us, and entered the heavenly rest. They are tasting the bliss of the immortal Paradise, and to prevent us building below the skies, they seem to look down and say, Ah, that poor world is not like this—it is not your rest. Arise, depart, and come up hither to the radiant throne of God. "We who believed have entered into rest."

> Thus heaven is gathering one by one, in its capacious breast,
> All that is pure and permanent, the beautiful and blest;
> The family is scattered yet, though of one home and heart,
> Part militant, in earthly gloom — in heavenly glory, part:
> But who can speak the rapture, when the circle is complete,
> And all the children, sundered here, before their Father meet?
> One Fold, one Shepherd, one employ, one everlasting home: —
> "Lo! I come quickly." "Even so, Amen, Lord Jesus, come!"

III. THAT A SUPERIOR REST IS PREPARED IN HEAVEN.

1. This is evident from *multitudes of promises*. "There remaineth a rest," etc. Heb. iv. 9; Rev. iii. 5, 12, 21.

2. From *Christ's intercession*. It is to prepare mansions for his people. John xiv. 1, etc.

3. From the *experience* — the faith and hope *of dying* believers. "I am now ready," etc. 2 Tim. iv. 6—8.

☞ It is a rest infinitely superior. Adapted to the soul's aspirations—the scene of perfect purity—perfect intelligence—perfect happiness. There shall be no more sorrow. See Rev. vii. 15—17. "Neither shall they die any more, for they are equal to angels," etc. Luke xx. 36.

IV. PREPARATION FOR THAT REST IS REQUIRED. "Arise ye, and depart." This implies

1. *Alarm*. Alarm at having idolized the world so long. Alarm at the declaration, "It is polluted; it shall destroy you with a sore destruction."—— What is the world but the city of destruction to those who idolize it? 1 Tim. vi. 9, 10; 2 Tim. iv. 10.

2. *A Renunciation of the World*. It is now estimated as unsatisfying and worthless. The Christian comes out from the world. 2 Cor. vi. 17. The idol is surrendered. 1 Cor. vii. 29—31. "Arise, depart ye."

3. *Faith in a heavenly rest*, and the *exercise of hope to enjoy it*. This faith rests on Christ alone—and hope will always follow faith. Heb. vi. 17—20; xi. 1.

4. By *heavenly contemplation*. Look frequently at the map of it — at the pictures of it — at the descriptions of it — that is, in the Bible. Let Christians talk about it, as they are journeying on — departing to it.

5. *Constant readiness to depart* when summoned hence by death. This implies the constant use of all religious exercises as the

means of preparation. "Arise, depart ye." Arise to prayer and watchfulness. Christian pilgrim, travel onwards, and endure to the end. Many carnal scenes on the way tempt thee; but arise and depart from them. Christian racer, the crown — the rest is before thee; forget the things behind, etc. Christian warrior, continue to fight the good fight of faith, and thou shalt soon lay hold on eternal life.

XVIII.—LOOK, AND BE SAVED.

"Look unto me, and be ye saved, all the ends of the earth; for I am God, and there is none else."—ISA. xlv. 22.

IT is surprising how the minds of men are engrossed by earthly trifles, as the imagined sources of happiness. One expects it from the creature, another from commerce and wealth, another from honour and fame, another from festive enjoyment, the exhilarating cup, and the sociable companion. Then there are others who make music, the drama, the games of chance, or other worldly amusements, their principal portion — their heaven. But God proclaims the folly of such a course, "How long, ye simple ones, will ye love simplicity? Turn you at my reproof; behold I will pour out my Spirit unto you, I will make known my words unto you." "Look unto me, and be ye saved," etc.

Some are expecting salvation from idols, of their own creation — some from the works of the law — and some from the mere mercy of God. But Jehovah proclaims all these to be vanity. Instead of saving you, they will consume you. See v. 15—17. Then read the text, and following verses.

I. THE SUBJECTS TO WHOM THE DIRECTION IS GIVEN. The miserable and wretched — those who need salvation.

That man is naturally in a state to render salvation necessary is stated by the Scriptures, to which statement is required the full submission of the heart. The great principles to be embraced are these:—God has promulgated his law—he requires obedience to this law—and that the transgressor is exposed to his displeasure, and to everlasting punishment. The testimony of God's word respecting man's ruination is full and clear. Do we not read, "How abominable and filthy is man, which drinketh in iniquity like the water?" Do we not read, "The heart of the sons of men is full of evil, and madness is in their hearts while they live?" Do we not read that "The Lord looked down from heaven on the children of men, to see if there were any that did understand, and seek God: they are all gone aside; they are altogether become filthy?" Do we not read, "There is none that doeth good; no, not one?" That "the heart is deceitful," etc. Look at these affirmations of danger consequent upon that guilt. Thus:—"God is angry with the wicked every day;" "God will by no means clear the guilty;" "Cursed is every one," etc. "Whosoever shall offend in one point, he is guilty of all;" "The wrath of God is revealed from heaven, against all ungodliness, and unrighteousness of men." Refer to Rom. ch. i. ii. and iii., where the Apostle lucidly proves the existence of spiritual danger, and that there can be no salvation except by the interposition of Christ. "We have proved both," etc. See Rom. iii. 9.

This state of sinful wretchedness is borne out by observation. Look at the character and conduct of man, wherever you will, or under whatever circumstances, and you will find only one general characteristic. There are various stations, and various degrees of rank; but *all* are surrounded by guilt—*all* are exposed to danger. There may be various shades of moral excellence, or of moral delinquency; but in *all* there is hatred to God: and even those actions which seem more excellent, proceed from such motives as must be hateful to a God of perfect purity. There may be much to entitle men to commendation; there may be general propriety and uprightness of conduct;—but as to the higher duties of rendering to God the universal, the supreme homage of the heart, there is a universal failure. *All* are guilty.

To such characters then the direction, "Look unto me for salvation," is mercifully given. For their state is infinitely deplorable and dangerous.——Talk not of the dangers of insolvency—of devastating epidemics, and mortal disease. This disease is infinitely more threatening and fatal. Talk not of civil imprisonment, condemnation, and death—of situations of immense peril, as produced by conflagrations, earthquakes, and the ravages of war; there is no condemnation, no peril, to be compared with the dangerous state of the sinner, upon whom, if not saved by sovereign grace, the wrath of God will abide for ever.

II. THE DIRECTION GIVEN. "Look unto me."

This consists of two parts:—1. The object of attraction; "ME." 2. The important Duty; "LOOK UNTO ME."

1. *The Object of attraction;* "Me." The offended Sovereign—how strange!—yet the God of mercy—the God in covenant—in covenant with his beloved Son, that the Sinner should be saved. Look unto me,

(1) *As the God of compassion.* Though you have offended me, yet I commiserate your state, and will have compassion upon you. ——Hence, "God so loved," John iii. 16. Salvation in all its parts, in all its effects—and in its everlasting duration, is ascribed to rich and sovereign grace—to infinite love. Eph. ii. 4, etc.—— Look unto me,

(2) *As the God of Salvation.* I have designed it—I have secured it. By it you shall be delivered, and I will be glorified.

In the councils of the Father it was determined that Jesus should redeem sinners. Numerous types prefigured its development—the language of prophecy proclaimed its approach, and the church anxiously waited for the great salvation. In the "fulness of time," the types were realized—the predictions were fulfilled

—the Sun of Righteousness arose. He was born in the manger of Bethlehem. He of whom it was said, "His name shall be called the Mighty God;" he on whom "help was laid." And as he went on his course, all the necessary proofs of his Divine appointment were given. There was the voice from the excellent glory, "This is my beloved Son," etc.—there were the mighty miracles which he wrought.——

He is called the Saviour. "Thou shalt call," etc. Matt. i. 21. "Behold, I bring you," etc. Luke ii. 10, 11. "The Son of man is come to seek," etc. "This is a faithful," etc. 1 Tim. i. 15.—— He exhibited himself as the Saviour. At the celebration of the Passover he did it by the broken bread and outpoured wine, the emblems of his broken body and shed blood. See him in the garden, while in dreadful anticipation he cries, "O my Father, if it be possible," etc. See him as he endures the mockery of the judgment-hall, despised, and spitten upon, and scourged. Observe him in Golgotha; there the atonement is consummated— there the cross is planted—the body nailed to it—shades of darkness overspread the scene. In the extreme anguish of his soul, and amidst the terrors of the curse, he cries, "My God," etc. Struggle succeeds to struggle, and at length another cry is heard, —"It is finished!" Then he "bows the head," etc. O hear it, sinner, for then salvation was obtained! What! then? what, amidst such marks of weakness, ignominy, and anguish? Yes, for *then* the wrath of God, due to sinners, fell upon him. Yes, for *then* the fire which had descended at the first transgression, fell on Him, and consumed Him.

The Sacrifice of Christ was propitiatory. "He was wounded," etc. See 1 Cor. xi. 25; 2 Cor. v. 21, cum multis. Here then in this atonement we find refuge. It is our PROPITIATION; remove it, and we are at once exposed to all the wrath of the Divine Lawgiver. O tear us not from the Rock to which we cling; remove it not, lest you plunge us into the gulf of woe! It is our SUN; extinguish it, and you leave us in the midnight darkness of despair! It is our PORTION; deprive us of it, and you beggar us for ever. It is the BASIS on which we cast the anchor of our hope; destroy it, and we are shipwrecked for ever. This, sinner, is the object of attraction. A suffering, dying risen, and ascended Saviour, who ever liveth to make, etc. Look to him.

2. *The important Duty.* "Look." This means more than the ordinary acceptation of the term. It signifies a BELIEVING APPLICATION to Christ for salvation. This implies,

(1) A deep sense of danger, and anxiety to be saved. It is to resemble the Israelites when stung by serpents. "As Moses lifted up the Serpent," etc. They felt themselves to be dying, and were anxious to be saved. Like the Philippian jailor, etc. The sinner sees himself condemned, under wrath.——

(2) A sense of *helplessness.* He has tried to better his condition —to improve his heart, but in vain. The broken law has been

presented to his conscience, by the Spirit, and he feels he can do nothing to remove its terrible penalty. Lord, save, or I perish.

(3) A knowledge of Christ as the Saviour. A glorious perception that he is "the end of the law for righteousness to every one that believeth." Hence the mind approves the Saviour—the soul heartily welcomes his salvation.

(4) Faith, or dependence. Look at that serpent of brass, said Moses, and live. God has appointed it. Look at it; it is the symbol of Divine mercy, and you shall live. So with regard to Christ, we are saved by faith as an instrument. Look unto Christ with the eye of faith. See his adaptation—his rich and free mercy. Look unto him with the prayer of faith, saying, I rest my immortal but sinful soul upon thy great Propitiation; O God, for Christ's sake, forgive me. See Rom. x. 12, 13.

III. THE GRACIOUS RESULT; "And be saved." As with the Israelites, the sting, the bite of the serpent was healed. So shall it be with the believing penitent. The curse and sting of the Old Serpent shall be removed—the broken law shall no longer accuse him—Sinai shall flash and thunder no more. "Believe on the Lord Jesus Christ, and *thou shalt be saved!*" This is bliss—bliss to the soul—bliss for ever.

To be saved, is to be for ever free from all the debasement, the defilement, the peril of our natural condition.——To be saved, is to be freed from the guilt and power of sin, and restored to the favour of Jehovah.——To be saved is to be removed from danger for ever; to be preserved from the fear of death—from the terrors of the judgment-bar—from weeping, wailing and gnashing of teeth; and from the vengeance of everlasting fire.——To be saved, is to have everlasting life—to be conducted to the honours of immortality—to be raised to the enjoyment of celestial pleasures in the presence of God for ever and ever. This the Apostle calls "the salvation which is in Christ Jesus *with eternal glory.*" In the heavenly inheritance the believer shall be perfectly pure—perfectly intelligent—perfectly happy. He shall be exalted to the highest honours—shall see God, and enjoy blessed companionship with saints and angels. But who can describe the eternal results of salvation?

However bright and knowing the mind of man may be,
It cannot paint those glories which I am soon to see!
It would require a seraph's tongue the splendours there to tell,
Laid up for me, a sinner saved, by Christ redeemed from hell.

Look unto me, my Saviour says, look unto me and live;
Fight on, and keep the crown in view, which I will freely give
O help me, Christ, to see the goal, to run the race, and fight,
And let thy heaven cheer my soul till faith is turned to sight!

Observe, this address is VERY EXTENSIVE. All the ends of the earth," are to look unto God for salvation; meaning the extremities or most remote parts of the world, Job. xxxvii. 3; xxxviii. 13, or the people inhabiting those parts, Ps. xcviii. 3. This accords with Christ's commission, "Go ye into all the world, and," etc. Erect the cross—lift up Immanuel's standard throughout the earth—whosoever looks by faith at that cross—whosoever joins his standard, shall be saved.

We therefore can take this salvation to the shores of classic elegance, or of ignorant barbarism; we can go with it to him who shivers in the icy regions of the north, and to him who pants beneath a sultry sun in the regions of the south. We can call upon the tasked slave, and his austere lord, to "look and be saved." However guilty and vile, they may look. Dive into the depths of the dungeon—plunge into the hospitals of disease—visit the abodes of darkness and despair—take the vilest and most miserable of men—let one be brought forth on whose head, if it were possible, could be heaped all the crimes committed by mankind since the fall of Adam till now—verily such a man is commanded to look and live. "Wherefore he is able to save to the uttermost," etc.

IV. THE PROHIBITION. "For I am God, and there is none else." This implies,

1. That Christ is the only Saviour, "I am God," etc. None else appointed—the only foundation. v. 24.

2. It is therefore condemnatory of all attempts at self-salvation.

3. It implies the universal dominion of Christ. Both saints and sinners are in his hands—he rules both—he will judge both—how different the results! Read v. 23.

On HIM, then, as the Saviour, let your eye be fixed; on HIM let your heart repose. Behold HIM! Acknowledge HIM in all his offices—receive Him in all his characters.——

If you look not at the Lamb of God that taketh away the sin of the world—then your guilt will remain on your souls, and sink them to the deepest woe.

XIX.—THE CHRISTIAN DYING DAILY.

"I die daily."—1 Cor. xv. 31.

"A prudent man foreseeth the evil thereof, and hideth himself." There is one future event for which we ought to prepare. We must all die. Our time of sojourning here is short, and the time of its termination uncertain. It is true Christian Philosophy to be ready to go when the time of our departure is at hand.——but this solemn event is banished from the mind, although the mind is daily conversant with monitions of human mortality.——The man who is about to emigrate to another country, frequently thinks about it, and makes suitable preparation.—— Our bodies must soon emigrate to the grave, and our souls into eternity. Much contingency may be connected with earthly emigration. The mind's purpose may change, and many things arise to prevent it. But there is no contingency about death. It cannot be averted by human purpose, or circumstances. Nothing can reverse the decree of God. Human mortality is ever proceeding—we see it in the deaths around us,—and we ourselves are not insensible to gradual physical decay. *We die daily.*

But is it not possible daily to regard death with composure even before it comes, so that when it shall invade us, we may meet it with triumph, hailing it as the messenger to conduct us to a better state? The Apostle answers, it is. *I die daily;* and this, instead of annoying him, afforded him joy.

I. EXPLAIN AND ILLUSTRATE THE STATEMENT OF THE APOSTLE: "I DIE DAILY."

The Apostle states it with a strong asseveration: "*I protest.*" The subject was important; it deeply interested his feelings. I solemnly affirm or declare.——"By your rejoicing." Some read *our* rejoicing, but the present version appears to be correct. By their rejoicing, as the result of their conversion, and the evidence of the vitality of their hope. He hoped for their eternal salvation. He had laboured to promote it, and he firmly believed that they would be saved. Regarding that as certain, it was just as certain that he died daily on account of the belief and hope of the resurrection. By our hopes and joys as Christians; by our dearest expectations and grounds of confidence, I solemnly declare I die daily. I am every day exposed to the peril of martyrdom. I continually expect a violent death. The manifold hardships and sufferings which I endure render my life a kind of lingering execution.

1. *He died daily.* His body, as already stated, through fatigue, the hand of violence, imprisonment, nakedness, hunger, and various perils, was dying gradually every day. "For thy sake we are killed all the day long: we are accounted as sheep for the slaughter." Rom viii. 36. See also 2 Cor. i. 9; he intimates that he then supposed that the sentence of death was passed upon him. Also 2 Cor. iv. 8—12. Refer to the catalogue of perils which he endured for Christ's sake, 2 Cor. xi. 23—28. O what melting pathos in this narration!——He also says that "after the manner of men he had fought with beasts at Ephesus." Some commentators suppose that he had been subjected to combat with wild beasts in the amphitheatre of Ephesus. But if he was only speaking "after the manner of men," in a figurative sense, it denotes the fierce and bloody men who were his persecutors. Hence Whitby observes:

"If this sense, (the literal interpretation) be not liked, you may interpret 'after the manner of men,' *according to the intention of men,* it being the intention of the men of Asia to deal so with him. Note also, that cruel and bloody-minded men are often represented under this metaphor of beasts. So Ignatius, when he was carried from Syria to Rome, under a band of soldiers, who, saith he, are the worse for the kindness I show them, 'From Syria to Rome I fight with beasts.' And Heraclitus says, 'The Ephesians were turned into beasts, because they slew one another.'"

These heavy and numerous sufferings might well cause him to say, "I die daily." "So then death worketh in us, but life in you," etc. 2 Cor. iv. 12—16.

2. As he endured all these hardships to promote Christianity in the world, it indicates *his full confidence in the Divinity of the gospel* — in the reality of Christ's resurrection of the saints. The Apostle gives an epitome of the gospel and its collateral evidence in this chapter, v. 1—8.——His argument appears to be:— I have had such evidence of the truth of the gospel afforded me — I have been so fully and specially convinced that there is no collusion — that Christianity is not a cheat—that I do not regret the sufferings I have endured, nor shrink from those which, in consequence of my advocacy of Christ, must inevitably come upon me. "If after the manner of men, I have fought with beasts at Ephesus, what advantageth it me, if the dead rise not? What benefit shall I have? Why should I risk my life in this manner? Rather let us eat and drink, for to-morrow we die, if the gospel be not true." The Apostle means by this question, that if there is no future state, it is irrational to endure trials and privations so severe. We should rather make the most of this life, and make pleasure our chief good rather than look for happiness in a future state. This is the conduct of carnal men. Their affections centre in this world; they have no prospect, no desire of heaven — they give themselves up to unrestrained enjoyment in this life.

The Apostle however was fully persuaded in his own mind. His conduct in steadfastly persevering to profess and preach the gospel abundantly demonstrated that he most firmly believed a future resurrection, and the everlasting happiness of all believers. —— Therefore he was *willing to die daily*, because the gospel was true.*

---

* But the circumstance which above all others adds weight and importance to the testimony which the Sacred writers gave, was the sacrifices with which it was accompanied; the risks, the injuries, the loss of property and life, which they voluntarily incurred by giving it, and to which those were alike exposed who received it at their hands. That they had thus to lay their account to all manner of wrongs and insults, not excepting death itself, we learn not only from the accounts of Scripture, but from the notices contained even in profane historians, from the decrees of emperors, from the allusions of heathen poets, and from the whole history of that and subsequent times, of which the persecution of Christians unto death formed an essential and prominent part. We look simply at the fact, and do not stop to offer any explanation of it, though in that respect there is no particular difficulty to encounter. It is as certain as anything in history can be, that both those who gave and those who received the gospel testimony were ready, rather than renounce that testimony, to endure the loss of all things and brave the agonies of death; and not only were ready to do this, but in great numbers actually did it. This puts beyond a doubt the question of their sincerity; for no conceivable motive could have induced them, both teachers and taught, leaders and followers together, to make such sacrifices for what they knew to be a lie; as in that case, to use the emphatic expression of Paley, "They would have been villians for no end but to teach honesty, and martyrs without the least prospect of honour or advantage." But if the circumstances forbid us to consider them as deceivers, may they not possibly have been mistaken or deceived? Doubtless they might have been had the matter of their testimony been a mere opinion—had it been either

3. This dying daily *evidenced the greatness of his love to Christ and his cause.* The love which he manifested was most ardent and influential. It constrained him to despise wealth, office, honour, and ease. In labours he was most abundant. He was assiduous and indefatigable in proclaiming Christ. Before the learned, or the illiterate; in the palace or in the prison, before kings or before the populace, he was "not ashamed of the gospel of Christ." Was persecution before him? He could say, "None of these things move me," etc. Was he approaching martyrdom? He could say, "I am willing not only to be bound, but to die at Jerusalem for the name of the Lord Jesus."—— The love of Christ kindled this ardent love in his breast. He states the operation of the mighty principle, 2 Cor. v. 14. "For the love of Christ constraineth us," etc. The love which Jesus had manifested towards sinners in the great work of redemption, and in calling them to partake of this inestimable blessing, had excited in their hearts such reciprocal admiring love and adoring gratitude to him, as "constrained them," and carried them on with invincible energy in every service, by which they could glorify his name or promote his cause: nor could any fears, hopes, affections, or interests, stop their progress, when actuated by this most powerful principle.

4. Though the Apostle died daily, *yet he was inwardly supported by Divine grace, and animated by a lively hope.* "The inward man," he says, "was renewed day by day." See also 2 Cor. i. 3—9. The whole life of the Apostle was one of hope and joy— and he triumphed in death. "For me to live is Christ, and to die is gain." Phil. i. 21. Mark his consolation and heroism at the close of his life. "For I am now ready to be offered," etc. 2 Tim. iv. 6—8.

II. APPLY THIS STATEMENT TO OURSELVES.

1. It is literally true that *we are physically dying daily.* Every one — the rich and the poor, the monarch and the peasant, etc., may say, "I die daily." There may be no peculiar hardships to endure — no persecutions — no imprisonment, etc., yet the body inevitably must die daily.

> As man, perhaps the moment of his breath,
> Receives the lurking principles of death.
> The young disease that must subdue at length,
> Grows with his growth and strengthens with his strength.

Human life is daily decaying — the strength and energy of the body daily decline — the beauty of the countenance gradually

---

a doctrine or system of doctrines, which they, as many others have done, might have held in sincerity and endured martyrdom rather than recant, though their understandings might have been misinformed and their convictions ungrounded. But what the first teachers and disciples of Christianity avouched was not the truth of an opinion or the soundness of a doctrine, but the reality of facts which their own eyes had seen, and the certainty of transactions in which they had personally borne a part. Here there was no room for deception or mistake, and as their readiness to sacrifice every thing naturally dear to them in support of their testimony proves beyond a doubt the sincerity of their belief, so must it be held not less convincingly to prove the truth and solidity of the ground on which their belief was founded.

fades, and the elasticity of the limbs is constantly being relaxed. In many cases those that look out of the windows are darkened, the keepers of the house tremble, and the strong men bow themselves. Eccles. xii. All persons are not the same as they once were. They feel that they are daily going the way of all the earth—dying daily.——The lapse of time itself is proof sufficient.

The body is not merely gradually or daily declining, but it may positively die any day. Hence, "Boast not thyself of to-morrow," etc. "What is our life? It is even as a vapour that appeareth for a short time, and then vanisheth away."

Still some may, like the Apostle, say, "I die daily." Their constant afflictions, trials, domestic troubles, hardships, etc., may be wearing them down, even as the water wears the stones.

2. As we die daily, *we should be very conversant with Christ*, as the Saviour of sinners, and the Resurrection and the life. "That I may know him and the power of his resurrection." Phil. iii. 9, 10.——This is the way of conquering death and of realizing the hope of eternal life.

It should also lead a Christian daily to deposit his soul in the hands of Christ to be saved and preserved by him until the day of death.

3. As we are dying daily, and shall soon have done with the world, *it should produce a disposition to be ready at any time to resign all the interests of earth*. We are to enjoy them but for a season—we are stewards, and occupy our various stations only for a short time. We have relationships in life of the most endearing character—ties of the tenderest nature—and associations the most delightful—but they must all give way to death. Are we prepared to give them up—to part with everything below the skies? We die daily, and we should hold all terrestrial things with a loose hand. Such is the argument of the Apostle, 1 Cor. vii. 29-31. "But this I say, brethren, the time is short," etc.

4. *To cultivate a superior regard to our immortal life in heaven.* Compare this life with eternal life, and how vain and shadowy does it appear! Reckon, then, as nothing the unsatisfying and transitory joys of earth; but value and aspire after a better country, that is a heavenly one. The miser here makes gold his heaven and his god. The man of property throws his whole soul into his estate, and idolizes it. The sensualist is intoxicated with his cup of pleasure. There is no heaven to the wicked but this earth. Here they would, if they could, stay for ever.——But the believer, though sometimes he gravitates to earth by reason of imperfection, is taught and induced by the Spirit to aspire after the bliss of immortality. He "looks not at the things which are seen, but at the things which are not seen. For the things which are seen are temporal," etc. 2 Cor. iv. 17, 18.

> Sublim'd by grace, the soul aspires,
> Beyond the range of low desires,
>   To nobler views elate:
> Unmov'd her destin'd change surveys,
> And arm'd by faith, intrepid pays
>   The universal debt.

5. It includes *a pleasing realization of death as a means of attaining the utmost of our wishes.* "To die is gain." Death is the gate of Paradise — it leads to the many mansions. It conducts to the vision of God — to intercourse with the most glorious intelligences — to purity — to exalted pleasures and infinite joy.

> I yearn for realms where fancy shall be filled, and the ecstacies of freedom shall be felt,
> And the soul reign gloriously, risen to its royal destinies:
> I look to recognize again, through the beautiful mask of their perfection
> The dear familiar faces I have somewhile loved on earth:
> I long to talk with grateful tongue of storms and perils past,
> And praise the mighty Pilot that hath steered us through the rapids:
> He shall be the focus of it all, the very heart of gladness, —
> My soul is athirst for God, the God who dwelt in man!" — TUPPER.

When death comes to a believer, it is not as the dreaded monster, the King of terrors. As a friend he comes to remove him from a world of toil to a world of rest; from a life of sin to a life of glory. Death is under the power of Christ, and is the messenger sent by him to fetch his people home.

How unwise, then, to reject the gospel — which alone brings life and immortality to light! And yet infidelity seeks its chief triumph in the attempt to convince poor dying man that he has no solid ground of hope; that the universe is "without a Father and a God;" that the grave terminates the career of man for ever — it annihilates him! The Apostle therefore said, v. 33, "Be not deceived." By false teachers — by their sophistry — by their plausible arguments. Rather turn to the revealings of the New Testament; rest your souls on them as the firmest basis of hope ever propounded. Let others do as they will, hold you them fast till you die.

XX. — THE RISEN SAVIOUR.

"Come and see the place where the Lord lay." — MATT. xxviii. 6.

The resurrection of Christ is an important article of the Christian faith. 1 Cor. xv. 13—19. —— The text and its connection refer to the resurrection of Christ. The angel here addresses the visitants of the tomb. He appeals to their senses to prove the certainty of Christ's resurrection. Christ also appealed to the senses of his disciples; "Behold my hands," etc. Thus is afforded the best external evidence of the Christian religion, namely, the miracles wrought by Christ and his apostles. "If ye believe not me, yet believe the works that I do," said Christ, appealing to their senses. The invitation to see the vacated grave is a similar appeal.

I. This Declaration proclaims the actual *Resurrection of Christ.* This was predicted, Ps. xvi. 10. Christ frequently said that he

THE RISEN SAVIOUR.

would rise again. And without it his mission would have been useless.

1. The fact of Christ's resurrection is established.

(1) By the *Testimony of Scripture.* The evidence of his disciples.——They were intelligent, incredulous—men of probity—disinterested, had no worldly advantage to gain, but the very opposite. They had been very conversant with Christ, and were able to testify.—— Their testimony was harmonious and constant.

(2) *By the testimony of angels, and their appearance to different persons.* Matt. xxviii. 1; John xx. 11.

(3) *By Christ's manifestation after he rose.* To Mary Magdalene, John xx. 17; to Salome, Matt. xxviii. 9, 10. Disciples going to Emmaus, Luke xxiv. 13. To Peter, Luke xxiv. 34; and the eleven disciples, John xx. 19; 1 Cor. xv. 7. To his disciples, Acts i. 3; to Stephen, Acts vii. 55; to Paul, Acts ix. 3; to John, Rev. i. 13.

2. *His resurrection was not denied by his enemies.* Matt. xxviii. 11.

3. The Apostles constantly *declared and attested it,* and so did the primitive Christians and fathers, as Ignatius, Polycarp, etc.

4. *He rose with the same body,* John, xx. 25; Luke xxiv. 39; Acts x. 40, 41.

5. *He rose according to Scriptural types and predictions,* Jonah ii. 10; Matt. xii. 40; Ps. xxii. 15; Isa. liii. 5, 6; Dan. ix. 26; Zech. xii. 7.

II. The language of the text expresses *the great Humiliation of Jesus Christ.* "Come, see the place where the Lord lay." The Son of God lay in a tomb, in the "dust of death." What was the Saviour's mission to this world, but one scene of humiliation? He came into this vile world—he tabernacled in the flesh—he "took not on him the nature of angels," etc. Phil. ii. 5—8; Heb. ii.—he suffered and died—he was laid in the grave.

III. *It is expressive of God's infinite love.* John iii. 16. Why did he come to earth—why did he suffer and die—why was he entombed—why did he rise and ascend? The answer is, Because God loved the world, and purposed the salvation of sinners. "Come, see the place where the Lord lay." He lay in that grave, and rose from it, to fulfil all the purposes of his love.

IV. *It was the most striking evidence of Divine Faithfulness.* Faithfulness with regard to promises, types, shadows, and predictions. When Christ rose from the grave, all the arrangements of the Divine covenant which he had made known to the church by his prophets, were ratified and fulfilled. See the argument of the Apostle, Heb. viii. 6; ix. 11—15.

V. *His resurrection was an evidence of his Divine Sovereignty.* He had power over death and the grave. "He had power to lay down his life, and power to take it up again." John x. 17, 18. In like manner he can and will control the deaths of his people. "He has the keys of death," etc. Rev. i. 18.

VI. *The empty grave was an evidence of his triumph over all his enemies and ours.* Over his Jewish foes—over his murderers—over Satan, death and hell he triumphed. See Eph. iv. 8; i. 17—23.

Lastly. *It was the certain and glorious pledge of the perfecting of salvation.*

Come, see the place where the Lord lay, and you will learn that he was the "end of the law for righteousness to every one that believes.——That " he was delivered for our offences, and rose again for our justification." Christ finished all the plan of mercy on the cross. He cried with a loud voice, "It is finished," and in that empty grave, we see that his declaration was correct. "He was raised from the dead by the glory and power of God the Father." ——He has secured then for all believing penitents full pardon for every offence—complete justification—assimilation to God by his Spirit—rich enjoyment in the bosom of the church—glorious hope of heaven—successful battle with the last enemy, and an abundant entrance into the everlasting kingdom of God. "Come, see the place where the Lord lay," and behold in that empty tomb the sure pledge of thine own glorious resurrection. Phil. iii. 20, 21; Rom. viii. 11.

IMPROVEMENT.

1. Give grateful homage to Christ as the Author and Finisher of faith.
2. Frequently visit in contemplation the scenes of his conflict and conquest.
3. Rest on him alone for salvation here and hereafter.

XXI.—PRAYER.

"Men ought always to pray, and not to faint."—LUKE xviii. 1.

PRAYER to God is of the utmost importance, and absolutely necessary. Important, because God, who knows our necessities, has mercifully enjoined it upon us. The people of God in every age have loved and practised it. Patriarchs and prophets, apostles and saints, have each in effect said, "I give myself unto prayer" —"It is good for me to draw near unto God."——Christ himself loved and performed prayer. "In the days of his flesh he offered up prayer and supplications with strong crying and tears unto Him who was able to save him from death, and was heard in that he feared." Heb. v. 7.——As Christ by his incarnation entered into the circumstances of sinners, he became acquainted with the wants of humanity. He saw what a sinful soul required to make it holy and happy in this wicked and sorrowing world. He knew the willingness of his Father to supply all the wants of his needy children; and he was going soon to the cross to suffer and die, that he might open the rich and overflowing fountain of Divine mercy and love. He might well say, "Men ought," etc.

In this chapter Christ propounds the parable of the unjust judge who was overcome by the importunity of a widow to do her justice contrary to his previous purpose. He argues that if importunity will prevail with a wicked man, how much more effectual will be prayer offered to God who is infinitely good. Therefore, "Men ought," etc.

I. THE NATURE OF PRAYER.

Prayer is the humble expression of our wants, and of our desires to God. It is the soul's appeal to God in every time of necessity.

Prayer is an acknowledgement of the being and the providence of God. "He that cometh to God must believe that he is;" that is, have a full belief in his Almighty power, mercy, salvation, and faithfulness; and also a dependence upon him for the supply of all needful blessings.

Prayer is a declaration that the infinite Jehovah, the offended Sovereign, has re-established communion with man, through the meditation of Jesus Christ, in whom he is well-pleased. What condescension is this! He who receives the praises of angels, designs to listen to the breathings of a poor sinner! No wonder that Solomon said, "Will God," etc. 1 Kings viii. 27.

To pray to God implies, 1. *A knowledge of his character*, and the gracious arrangements he has made for the temporal and spiritual happiness of man, It is impossible to pray aright without such knowledge. What kind of a court would a sovereign have if his subjects could not distinguish between him and a clown? "They that *know* thy name will put their trust in thee."

2. *A deep conviction of the need of Divine aid.* This need arises from our state as fallen sinners, ever requiring an interest in the mercy of God through Christ—need arising from the conflicts of life—sickness, personal and relative, bereavements, losses, disappointments—conflicts with our own hearts, with sinners and the enemy coming in like a flood, threatening to overwhelm and destroy. Regard ourselves as the servants of God, having important offices to sustain, and arduous duties to perform—and then we are dying creatures, and must yield up our breath. Who is sufficient for these things? Every one must be wretched without God.

3. *Application to God for relief.* "If any man lack wisdom, let him ask of God." "Ask and ye shall receive," etc. "Draw near to God, and he will draw near to you." This application to God implies

(1) A faithful confession of all our offences.

(2) An honest statement of our necessities.

(3) An earnest request for God's assistance and blessing. "Lord, help me." "Save, or I perish." Disperse this darkness, and irradiate my mind with light Divine. Remove my guilt, cleanse me from my sin. Deliver me from this trouble, or sustain me under it, and sanctify it to my good and thy glory.

4. Prayer must be made to God *through the mediation of Christ.* Hence the Saviour said, "Whatsoever ye shall ask the Father *in my name* he will give it you." John xiv. 13; xv. 16; xvi. 23, 24, 26. As sinners we have forfeited all right to both temporal and spiritual blessings; sin has closed the avenue of Divine mercy, and cut off Divine communion. Christ, however, has opened the way of access to God by his death on the cross—he has broken down the wall of partition—opened the fountain of all spiritual blessings, and become the way to the Father. Hence all our petitions must be presented to God through our Lord Jesus Christ. Heb. iv. 15, 16; 1 John ii. 1.

A recognition of the Divine Mediator necessarily implies *faith.* See James i. 5, 6. "But let him ask in faith." Let him believe that in God all fulness dwells, and that he is able and willing to do more abundantly than we can either ask or think. Full of this assurance, relying upon the great Mediator, let him "ask and it shall be given him," etc. "We have boldness to enter into the holiest by the blood of Jesus," etc. Heb. x. 19—23.

5. In prayer the petititioner must be governed *by the will of God.* Man may ask many things which if granted would be injurious. So Elijah, 1 Kings xix. 4; a prayer arising from a desire to avoid persecution. See also Luke xii. 13; James iv. 3. The enlightened believer will always preface his prayer with "The will of the Lord be done." Luther could say, "Let my will be done. My will, Lord, because my will is melted into thine, there is but one will betwixt us." "If ye abide in me, and my words abide in you," said Christ, "ye shall ask what ye will, and it shall be done unto you." We ask according to the will of God, when we petition for that which tends to glorify him.——Ask in this way, and you shall obtain. 1 John v. 14, 15.

It is prayer then that must bring all our supplies from heaven. —— The experience of believers testifies, that as they decline in prayer all their graces decline also; therefore when the apostle Paul hath suited a Christian with his whole armour, he adds this to all, *pray continually;* for this arms both the man and his armour with the strength and protection of God.

> Prayer is a creature's strength, his very breath and being;
> Prayer is the golden key that can open the wicket of Mercy;
> Prayer is the magic sound that saith to God, So be it;
> Prayer is the slender nerve that moveth the muscles of Omnipotence.
> Therefore, pray, O creature, for many and great are thy wants;
> Thy mind, thy conscience, and thy being, thy rights commend thee unto prayer,
> The cure of all cares, the grand panacea for all pains,
> Doubt's destroyer, ruin's remedy, the antidote of all anxieties.—TUPPER.

II. THE PERFORMANCE OF PRAYER.

1. *It must be sincere.* In prayer especially, thou "requirest truth," O God, "in the inward parts." If we approach God, still cherishing some darling sin, we cannot expect to be heard. That sin is his rival. He demands the whole heart. Ps. lxvi. 18. When the believer sounds the trumpet of prayer, it is the breath of the soul that sounds it. The prayers of the wicked are *heartless* prayers—the heart has no place in them, and they have no place in the heart. The prayers of the righteous are heart-prayers, they are first put into the heart by God, and then they rise from the heart to God. They earnestly desire what they seek, and therefore obtain what they ask.

2. Prayer must be offered with *reverence and humility.* "God is a Spirit." He is infinitely great, holy, powerful, etc. Sinful dust and ashes must stand in awe of him.——Humility flows from penitence, and is ever associated with confession of sin. There is something delightfully affecting in the humble reverential supplications which flow from a believer's heart, and which ascend to the Most High. He employs such language as this:—Job xi. 4, 5; xlii. 2—6. The Christian finds that the prayer of the poor broken-hearted publican is never an unsuitable prayer for him, and when he comes to die he is content that the last petition ascending from his heart should be, "Lord, have mercy on me a sinner." In prayer he is led to be humble when he compares his nothingness with God's immensity; his meanness with God's glory; his folly with God's wisdom; and his deformity with God's purity.

3. *Prayer must be offered with fervency.* Not the energy and warmth of the animal spirits, but the inward, inwrought prayer, expressed in simple desires, regulated by the love of God. "The effectual fervent," etc. James v. 16. Such fervency is urged by many Scriptures. To pray, is to pour out the heart, Ps. lxii. 8. To pray, is to wrestle with God, Gen. xxxiii. 24. To pray, is to cry, Ps. ix. 12,—to sigh and groan, Ps. xii. 5,—to strive, Rom. xv. 30,—to give God no rest, Isa. lxii. 7. All these declarations teach us that prayer must be fervent. The arduous conflict in which we are engaged demands it. The immense value of the blessings for which we pray demands it.

4. *Prayer must be constant.* "Men ought always to pray, and not to faint." This duty must never be forgotten; it is so important and beneficial. We must not tire in praying for any special blessing. God loves fervency and importunity in prayer. This is illustrated by the example of the poor widow, who by her importunity, prevailed with the unjust judge. Hence Elias, James v. 17, 18.

The text teaches us that Christians should neglect no opportunity for prayer, delighting in the performance of it both publicly and privately.

Christians are liable to faint. The ardour of prayer often declines — many restrain prayer before God.

(1) The engagements of life have this tendency, absorbing the whole attention; abating, if not wholly destroying, the habit of prayer.

(2) Christians may faint from the recollection of their great unworthiness.

(3) When answer to prayer is delayed.

(4) When the favour solicited is obtained. The depravity of our hearts may cause us to forget that "Man's extremity was God's opportunity." You were humble enough in your misery, and ready to cry to God, and depend upon him, but since he delivered you, you have forgotten that in him alone is your help found.

Pray always therefore, and not faint, for

(1) We sin without ceasing, and have therefore need to pray without fainting. Till we cease to sin, we must never cease to pray.

(2) Our enemies never cease to annoy and oppose us, therefore we must pray and faint not. The hands of prayer must be lifted up like those of Moses, till the victory is won. Our enemies are ever watchful for opportunity; we must faint not in watching unto prayer.

(3) Our trials from afflictions—our bodily and spiritual wants, never cease. Every day brings fresh wants; every duty calls for fresh supplies of grace. We have scarcely emerged from one trial, but another awaits us. Is any afflicted? Let him pray and faint not.

(4) God is always waiting to be gracious. "He fainteth not, neither is he weary." "They that wait upon the Lord shall renew their strength." The Saviour ever liveth to make intercession for us. The Holy Spirit never ceaseth to make intercession for us; therefore pray and faint not.

In conclusion, how important then is prayer to a Christian—to a family—and to the community at large?

> Angels are around the good man, to snatch the incense of his prayers,
> And they fly to minister kindness to those for whom he pleadeth:
> For the altar of his heart is lighted, and burneth before God continually.
> And he breatheth, conscious of his joy, the native atmosphere of heaven:
> Yea, though poor and contemned, and ignorant of this world's wisdom,
> Ill can his fellows spare him, though they know not of his value.
> Thousands bewail a hero, and a nation mourneth for its king,
> But the whole universe should lament the loss of a man of prayer.—TUPPER.

How awful the condition of those who never acknowledge God—who live without prayer. At the day of final retribution, they will know the value of prayer. "They shall call upon me *then*, but I will not answer." Prov. i. 24–33.

XXII.—CHRIST A TESTATOR.

A METAPHORICAL SKETCH.

" For where a Testament is, there must also of necessity be the death of the Testator."
— Heb. ix. 16.

As Christ has many crowns, so he has many names. He has crowns of great glory, and he has names of unequal beauty. "Thy name is as ointment poured forth." Song i. 3. He is called the *Branch*, by Jeremiah xxiii. 5; the *Sun of Righteousness*, Mal. iv. 2; the *Bright and Morning Star*, Rev. xxii. 16; the *Surety;* "By so much was Jesus made the *Surety of a better testament.*" Heb. vii. 22. He is called the *Messenger of the Covenant*, Mal. iii. 1. Isaiah records seven of his glorious names. He calls him *the Child born, the Son given, the Wonderful, the Counsellor, the Mighty God, the Everlasting Father,* and *the Prince of Peace.* In the text he is denominated a *Testator*, a name full of glorious import. See Matt. xxvi. 26, 27, etc.

I. A Testator signifies a Disposer, a person who makes a will or testament in which he bequeaths his property to his relatives or friends.

Jesus Christ is the Testator who made his will — executed the covenant of eternal redemption. That testament derives its value from the dignity and glory of the Testator. He is "the brightness of his Father's glory," etc. "He is "the King eternal, immortal," etc. He is the high and lofty One who inhabiteth eternity — whose name is holy. He is the heir of all things.

In order to become a Testator, he entered into the very circumstances of his legatees. He became bone of their bone, and flesh of their flesh. John i. 14; Heb. ii. 14, 15. He was "made in all things like unto his brethren." Hence he felt for them, sympathized with them, and was willing to die for them. Unless he had taken our nature, he never could have become our Testator, for as God, he could not become the subject of mortality.

II. A Testator being under a natural obligation, and having affection and good-will to his friends, makes provision for them in his will.

Christ, by taking his people into covenant relation, has bound himself to provide for their spiritual and eternal necessities. He is called their Elder Brother, their Shepherd, their King; he loves them, he cares for them. As their great High-priest, he is touched with the feeling of their infirmities. It was his greatest pleasure to remember them in his will.

III. A Testator makes his will in prospect of death. He may be induced to this by age, by infirmity and decay — by the dictates of prudence, that he may not have it to do at the time of dying.

Jesus Christ knowing his hour was coming, when he should seal his testament with his blood, made his last will in favour of all his disciples. See John xiii. 1; xiv. 2, 18; xvii. 24.

IV. A Testator records the persons in his will to whom he bequeaths legacies.

Jesus Christ has recorded in his will the persons to whom he has bequeathed the blessings of his covenant, both grace and glory. His disciples, his people, his sheep, his servants, his soldiers, all that the Father hath given him, all that repent, and believe, all that are regenerated, that bear his image, that love and serve him, John x. 15, 28; iii. 36; Heb. v. 9.

V. A Testator in making his last will usually disannuls any will previously made.

Jesus Christ disannulled the law of the Old Covenant, by his establishing the New. See Heb. vii. 12, 18. "He taketh away the first, that he may establish the second." Heb. x. 9. Observe, Christ abolished the ceremonial, sacrificial law, he himself being the great sacrifice to which the Levitical sacrifices pointed. "He was the end of the law," etc.

VI. A Testator to give authority and validity to his will, has it witnessed by others.

Jesus Christ, to give validity and authority to his gracious Will, had it attested by the most credible witnesses. First, the Father; secondly, his miracles; thirdly, John the Baptist; fourthly, the Scriptures; and fifthly, his Apostles: "We are his Witnesses of all things that he did." John v. 32, 36, 37; Acts x. 39.

VII. A Testator, finally to perfect and confirm his last will, signs and seals it himself, which (according to the laws and customs, especially of Eastern nations) is done by blood. The Epistle to the Hebrews intimates that the first Testament was dedicated by blood, hence called the "Blood of the Testament."

Jesus Christ ratified his last Will and Testament with his own blood. "He shall confirm the covenant — he shall be cut off." Dan. ix. 24, 26, 27. *"For where a testament is,"* says the text, *"there must be the death of the Testator."* "This is the New Testament in my blood," 1 Cor. xi. 25; i. e. it symbolizes the shedding of my blood on the cross as a ratification of my will and pleasure concerning you my disciples.——By Christ's death there is a confirmation of the truth and authority of the Covenant, and of its efficacy and availableness to us, Heb. ix. 17.

VIII. A Testator appoints Executors in trust to fulfil the purpose and intent of his will.

Christ committed this great Trust to his Father, John x. 29, and the Holy Spirit, who are the faithful Executors of his will, dispensing according to it the treasures of Divine love to all the Redeemer's legatees. John xvii. 11; xiv. 16.

IX. A Testator makes his last will unalterable by any other person, or by himself. After death no one can legally abrogate any of its provisions. See Gal. iii. 15.

The covenant of Jesus Christ shall stand, and he will do all his pleasure. Ps. lxxxix. 34. The covenant is ratified. He will not alter it himself; much less may any man or angel presume to do it. Gal. i. 8; Rev. xxii. 18, 19.

X. A Testator takes care to have his will made known and published after his death, that the parties concerned may know what legacies are left and bequeathed to them; and their excitement and expectation will be in proportion to the wealth of the deceased.

Christ ordained and commanded his disciples to publish his mind and Will to the children of men. Mark xvi. 15. They went forth, and opened that gracious and glorious Will, and now look at its marvellous provisions.

The reading of some testaments produces disappointment; but they who consult this testament with the eye of faith, find that it contains "exceeding abundantly above all that they can either ask or think." Only think of the *wealth of Christ*, which renders his testament so important and valuable. "It has pleased the Father that in him should all fulness dwell." He hath "appointed him the Heir of all things." He is "Lord of all." "King of kings, and Lord of lords." "The Father loveth the Son, and hath given all things into his hands." How vast then must be his wealth, how unlimited his power! How capable must he have been to enrich his people for time and eternity. Read the Will of Christ—examine the blessings of the New covenant, and there can be no disappointment, but surprise, gratitude, transport.

In opening this will we read that Christ the Great Shepherd laid down his life for his flock, and that all the atoning, saving and enriching efficacy of that death is theirs. "All things are yours." "He giveth liberally and upbraideth not." Is pardon desirable to the guilty? "We have redemption through his blood, even the forgiveness of sins." Is it good for us to draw nigh to God? "We have boldness of access through him." Is faith precious? His Spirit is given to produce it, and that faith gives peace, and joy, and triumph. Are the promises valuable? "Whereby are given unto us exceeding great and precious promises." Is hope cheering, and the possession of a good hope our greatest treasure? "Blessed, etc., who hath begotten us again to a lively hope," etc. 1 Pet. i. 3. Is the gift of the Holy Spirit essential to our sanctity and comfort? This is the fruit of his death, and the gift from his throne. Do we love his house? It is his presence that fills it with glory, and there he has promised to dwell. "Where two or three," etc. Is a gospel ministry important and valuable? It is his gift. "He gave some apostles," Eph. iv. 12, 13. Do we want consolation in sorrow? It is the record of his will, "My grace is sufficient for thee." Are his dealings with us sometimes intricate and unaccountable? It is recorded in his will, "All things shall work together for the good," etc. "These light afflictions" etc. Is the path of life dangerous? Is it beset with numerous foes ready to devour? He fills that path with guardian angels — he sends them "forth to minister to the heirs of salvation." Does the dark valley of death occasion fear and dismay? The testament of Christ intimates that he will go down with them to death, and will surely bring them up again. "Death is yours, he says, fear not; fear not, for I am with you; be not dismayed, for I am thy God. Here take this staff of my atonement, lean upon it, and all your fears shall vanish."—— Then this Will announces the inheritance of the saints in light. Its mansions, its crowns, its bright shining raiment, its purity, its inconceivable felicity are prepared by him. "I appoint unto you a kingdom."

What are other wills when compared with this? They may allot to the parties thousands of silver and gold; they may apportion vast and splendid estates——but they are all vanity, because they are transitory. Death will end the enjoyment of them. But the Will of Christ is co-extensive with eternity. Its provisions are everlasting.

Lastly. Most testamentary grants are made to the dearest relatives and friends, — to worthy persons.——Sometimes a rebellious prodigal child is not provided for at all, or *cut off* with a miserable pittance.

Behold in this Testament the rich grace of the Divine Testator. "Where sin abounded, grace has much more abounded" to the guilty, to the outcast, to the lost, and undone. Those whose iniquities equalled the stars in number, and surpassed the mountains in magnitude, were chosen to drink of the rivers of Divine pleasure, and to occupy heavenly thrones. As a proof of this, behold the weeping Mary, bending over the Redeemer's feet, and bathing them with the tears of gratitude and of penitential sorrow, wiping them with the hairs of her head, and imprinting on them the kiss of love. Behold the man of sorrows, with mercy beaming on his brow, he pronounces forgiveness, for she was a sinner. Go to Calvary, and amidst its horrid scenes, behold the last glance of the malefactor's dim, languid eye, as it swims in death, trusting in the Saviour dying at his side. Listen to that faintly uttered prayer of a strong and lively faith, "Lord, remember me when thou comest into thy kingdom." Hear the soft answer of peace flowing from his lips, which death was turning pale, and from a heart convulsed with agony, "Verily, I say unto thee, to-day shalt thou be with me in Paradise." Remember to whom Jesus commanded his gracious will first to be opened — it was to his murderers—"begin first at Jerusalem"—open my Will of full and free forgiveness to the banditti that apprehended me—to those who bound me, mocked and derided me — to him who smote me on the face—to him who spat on me—to those who drove the nails —to him who platted the crown—and to him who pierced my side.

Tell them they are my legatees, and that I offer them salvation without money and without price.

Christ therefore made and issued his Will irrespective of human merit.

IMPROVEMENT.

1. Admire the grace of God as manifested in the Testator's Will. It provides salvation for the body and soul — for time and eternity — and for the vilest of the vile.

2. Ascertain whether or not you are Christ's legatees. All who are included in his Will have repented and believed — they bear his image — they do his commandments.

3. Often read this Will. You may do it in the house of God — in your dwelling — and especially at the Table of the Lord. Thus you will see the princely legacies which he has left you, more valuable than the gold and costly gems of distant India. There you will see the security and seal of the Testament — the blood and death of the Testator.

XXIII. — SOLACE IN AFFLICTION.

"Many are the afflictions of the righteous; but the Lord delivereth him out of them all." — Ps. xxxiv. 19.

No one is exempt from trouble. "Man that is born of a woman is of few days," etc. Job xiv. 1. This world has been aptly compared to a wilderness or valley of tears. What avails an honorable ancestry, or the splendours and wealth of earth —— all are heirs of sorrow, and exposed to a thousand sources of misery. "Many are," etc. —— But the Christian has a refuge in all his troubles. It is not in the giddy scenes of dissipation; it is not in sullen apathy; it is not in stoical indifference. Such refuges are unavailing, as repeated trials have proved. The refuge of the Christian is God: "The Lord delivereth," etc.

I. THE CHARACTER. "The righteous."

To be righteous is to appear just before God, and holy in heart and life.

1. *This is not their character by nature.* All persons come into this world with a depraved nature. Ps. li. 5. Depravity is visible in all human action. The thoughts, desires, affections, and conduct are full of sin. "There is none righteous; no, not one." Rom. iii. 10.—— And yet the heart of man is full of self-righteous pride. He boasts of his goodness.

2. Righteousness of state *is effected by connection with Christ.* "He is the end of the law for righteousness to every one that believes." He fulfilled the law by perfect obedience. He endured the penalty of Divine wrath, and averted it from the sinner. Rom. iii.

23—26. It is by faith instrumentally that this righteousness of state is obtained. Rom. v. 1; viii. 1; Acts xiii. 38, 39.

3. Righteousness *is produced by the indwelling of the Spirit.* This changes, quickens, and renews the soul. It is called being "born of the Spirit," "born again,"—"begotten again to a lively hope" — "passed from death unto life." The source of all moral action, is purified, and therefore

4. Righteousness *is exhibited by the conduct* — even practical righteousness. A love of justice, equity, honesty, purity, and benevolent exertion will characterize the deportment.——Mere profession is nothing. Many loudly boast of their faith in doctrines, and how they love them — but what is their conduct? Rom. vi. 1.

II. THEIR PORTION: "Many are the afflictions." All afflictions are the consequences of sin. But for sin this world would have been a Paradise. There would have been no defilement of soul— no vicious conduct — no aching hearts — no pained and decaying bodies—no wicked enemies—no lamentation, mourning, and woe. It is sin that has opened the flood-gates of misery, and deluged the world with sorrow.

Many afflictions are often the result of personal transgression— of which the intelligent mind must be conscious. In that case afflictions become correctives. Happy they who can say, "I will bear the indignation of the Lord because I have sinned against him."

Afflictions are Divinely appointed. 1 Thess. iii. 3; Job v. 6, 7. ——Observe,

1. These afflictions are *internal*, arising from

(1) The *restless operations of depravity.* What Christian does not feel that the "heart is deceitful above all things," etc. — that it is "an evil heart of unbelief, in departing from the living God." What a conflict has the Christian with that heart! Rom. vii. 18, 24.

(2) *Indifferentism.* To the most important and profitable duties — to the enjoyment of the most valuable and enriching privileges — to the most solid and lasting bliss — to the rich and splendid inheritance of heaven. —— As to worldly pursuits — nay, even to trifles, to shadows, there is often no indifference. This the Christian has to mourn over. It afflicts him.

(3) *Hardness of heart.* Experienced under the most affecting providences—at the most awful judgments—under the most tender and melting appeals, on the most solemn occasions. This is the result of unwatchfulness — neglect of prayer, self-examination, and mental discipline aided by Divine influence.

(4) *Temptations.* Often fascinate, allure, and constrain. To a pious mind, they are afflictive.

(5) *Doubts and fears.* These too often produced by indifferentism, unwatchfulness, etc. — sometimes the result of constitutional nervousness — or mental depression. But how afflictive! Often

darkness, but little light. Job xxxiii. 3—10. These afflictions are also

2. *External.*

(1) *Bodily afflictions.* Wearisome days and nights. Job vii. 3; Ps. lxxvii. 1—4, How often is this the case! The man, however previously strong, rendered helpless as an infant—the body racked with pain, scorched with fever, and wasted by pining disease. The food is bitter, the light painful, association annoying—conversation afflictive—life has lost its charms—the man is imprisoned.——There are also relative afflictions. Our beloved friends sicken——we weep with those who weep.——What anguish rends that mother's heart as she gazes upon her suffering child!——

(2) *Bereavements.* These are universal—they visit every family. To the godly they are painfully afflictive. How soon were our first parents bereaved. How intense their agony as they gazed on their beloved Abel, a silent corpse, the murdered victim of his enraged brother. Read on in the Bible, and you will find Abraham left to finish his pilgrimage without his beloved Sarah; David deprived in battle of his beloved Jonathan; Rachel weeping for her children —Jacob weeping for Rachel, who in the same hour became a mother and a corpse. David wept for his son Absalom when he died. "O Absalom, my son," etc. How affecting the announcement to Ezekiel, "Son of man, behold, I take away the desire of thine eyes with a stroke." And look at that funeral procession! The widow of Nain follows her only son to the grave. See Luke vii. 12.

> Bear forth the cold corpse, slowly, slowly bear him,
> Hide his pale features with the sable pall;
> Chide not the sad one wildly weeping near him:
> Widow'd and childless, she has lost her all!

(3) *Poverty.* It is a chilling word. It is a desolating and unwelcome visitant. With some it always lives. Some of the best of men have been in poverty. Elijah, 1 Kings xix. 4. Lazarus at the rich man's gate, though a jewel of salvation. And the blessed Redeemer could say, "Foxes have holes," etc. The Apostles were often hungry and naked. The day of poverty is the day of adversity.

(4) *The world's reproach.* Christianity and its adherents have been and are still *hated*. Look at the persecutions and sufferings endured by the Apostles, and the primitive Christians.——We live in a time of infidel opposition. Infidels think themselves wise, and laugh at the Christians. They frequently denounce Christianity, foolishly and ignorantly attributing the social evils which exist to Christianity—hence their opposition.

III. THEIR REFUGE. "The Lord delivereth him out of them all." In order to be delivered,

1. There must be *a recognition of the Divine Sovereignty, and humble submission.*
2. *Prayer*—believing prayer. "This poor man cried," etc. Ps. xxxiv. 6. "Call upon me in the day of trouble."

As to this deliverance,

1. *God can deliver.* He who appoints the affliction can remove it. Has he not wisdom, power, and love sufficient? Nothing is too hard for the Lord.

2. *God has delivered, and he will deliver.* He delivered the Old Testament saints; Abraham, Jacob, Job, the people of Israel, David, Daniel, and the three Hebrews. See Psalm xxxiv; xci.—— He delivered the Apostles frequently as recorded in various parts of the Acts. Paul alludes to one, 2 Cor. i. 8—10.——God has promised to deliver. "Call upon, etc., I will deliver thee, and thou shalt glorify me." But it must be in his own way—by his own means—and in his own time.

The last affliction—the sickness unto death will surely come—God has not promised to deliver from that—but then to manifest himself to succour and support. "When my heart and my flesh fail, God will," etc.

3. *God will not deliver till his gracious purpose in appointing afflictions is accomplished.* They are designed to correct—to enlighten—to quicken—to purify—to elevate the soul to God and heaven. When the dross is removed, the fine gold shall appear.

4. If he do not deliver, he will give an *equivalent blessing—even adequate support and consolation.* This was experienced by Paul, 2 Cor. xii. 9.

When Moses was wandering with the Israelites, in "the wilderness, in a solitary way," and found no city to dwell in, he familiarized God under the image of a home. "Lord, thou hast been our refuge and dwelling-place in all generations." When David was driven from his palace by the rebellion of Absalom, and was obliged to keep the field, he said, "Be thou my strong habitation, whereunto I may continually resort." A pious female in the most distressing bereavement was able to say,

"Thou dost but take the *lamp* away,
To bless me with *unclouded day.*"

And a good man who had endured the wreck of fortune, being asked how he bore the change in his condition so cheerfully, replied, "When I had those good things, I enjoyed God in all; and now I am deprived of them, I enjoy all in God."

Thousands can bear witness that God has made that condition comfortable which they once deemed insupportable; that "as the sufferings abound, the consolations abound also;" and that the light of his countenance, the joy of his salvation, the comforts of the Holy Spirit, are effectual substitutes for every deficiency in temporal good.

A tract distributor, in the fourteenth ward of an American almshouse, met with a poor but pious man, who had once been wealthy, but who thankfully received a tract, and said, "You see, sir, I am poor, but I have seen better days. I am sixty-five years of age. I had once a large property, but it is gone. I had children too, but they are all dead. A wife—(his tears flowed)—but six months ago she departed to her eternal rest, and on the eve of her departure, she sang,

> Jesus can make a dying bed,
> Feel soft as downy pillows are.

Ah! sir, there is no delusion here. Many would persuade me that faith in Christ is a delusion; but it is not so. Property! it is a delusion; I had it, but it has vanished. My children have vanished—my dear wife is gone—but faith in Jesus, that remains."

5. He will *finally deliver at death* for ever, and grant an abundant entrance into that world where sorrow can never enter. Rev. vii. 13.—17.

IMPROVEMENT.

1. What has been the influence of afflictions upon you?

2. Learn to regard them as visitations of Divine love — "blessings in disguise."

3. Anticipate the rest. Then "the ransomed of the Lord shall return to Zion with songs, and everlasting joy upon their heads, and all sorrow and sighing shall flee away."

XXIV.—HUNGERING AND THIRSTING AFTER RIGHTEOUSNESS.

"Blessed are they which do hunger and thirst after righteousness, for they shall be filled."—MATT. v. 6.

THESE words form a part of the renowned and instructive sermon preached by Christ. The place where he delivered it deserves notice; it was on a mountain. He preached sometimes in the temple, sometimes in the field, by the seaside, in the ship, or elsewhere; but he delivered this on a mountain. Moses received the law on a mountain, and Christ interpreted the law on a mountain, vindicating it from the corrupt glosses of the Scribes and Pharisees. It was on a mountain that the Levites pronounced the blessings and curses, Deut. xxvii. and xxviii.—blessings on Mount Gerizim — curses on Mount Ebal.

I. THE DISPOSITION MANIFESTED; "*hungering and thirsting after righteousness.*" Notice 1. The object, "righteousness." 2. The appetites, "hungering and thirsting."

1. *The object desired.* "Righteousness." This is equity in the sight of God, and equity before men. This is not peculiar to man, for he is a sinner and unrighteous. Hungering and thirsting after righteousness implies that the sinner is convinced that he has none and cannot be happy without it. The language expresses deep conviction of spiritual necessity in the mind of the awakened sinner. He has no Divine righteousness — he is miserable till he obtains it. And it is expressive too of spiritual defectiveness on the part of the unfruitful Christian. He is convinced of it, and sighs and prays for more righteousness.

(1) It is hungering and thirsting *after imputed righteousness;* that is, after pardon of sin, and acceptance with God through the finished work of Christ, who "was delivered for our offences and rose again for our justification." The sinner feels that he is unrighteous, because he is a breaker of God's law — he is under the curse — he finds all his attempts at obedience and moral excellence to be vain and fruitless. He feels as Paul did, Phil. iii. 8, 9. This perfect righteousness he finds in Christ alone.

(2) It is hungering and thirsting after *inherent righteousness;* after sanctifying and renewing grace. When a poor sinner is brought to see the corruption and defilement wherein he was born, and in which he lives, void of the image of God, which "consists in righteousness and true holiness," "dead in trespasses and sins," and in consequence "hungers and thirsts," — it is after a new nature — a renewed heart — likeness to God, "for without holiness no man shall see the Lord." O that I were holy! "Create within me a clean heart." Ps. li. 10.

(3) It is hungering and thirsting after *righteousness of life.* If a sinner, awakened by the Spirit, hungers and thirsts after imputed and inherent righteousness, righteousness or holiness of life will be sure to follow; for the existence of inherent righteousness is the purification of the heart, the fountain or spring of holy action or conduct. If the fountain be pure — so shall the streams be.

(4) It is hungering and thirsting *after the perfect righteousness of heaven.* This the Christian often does when conflicting with sin here — when harassed with temptations — when grieved by spectacles of wickedness.——Often he longs for the heavenly scenes and associations of perfect righteousness. How sweet the declaration. Rev. xxii. 27. A regenerate soul naturally longs after the purity of heaven. As spiritual things cannot support the body, so natural things cannot support or feed the soul. Col. iii. 1, 2.

2. *The appetites,* or *hungering and thirsting.* Nothing could better express ardent desire after righteousness than hunger or thirst. No appetites are so keen, none so imperiously demand supply, as these. They occur daily; and when long continued, as in the case of fever, shipwreck, or wandering in arid deserts, with a paucity of drink and food, nothing is more distressing. Thus the poet Virgil represented strong and intense desire after an obect:

"O cursed hunger after gold! What canst thou not influence the heart of man to perpetrate!"

An ardent desire for any good is represented in Scripture by hunger and thirst. Ps. xlii. 1, 2; lxiii. 1, 2. A deep sense of sin, humiliation of mind, earnest desires after forgiving love, peace, and joy, is also represented by thirsting, Is. lv. 1, 2.

1. These appetites *presuppose life*. A dead man hungers and thirsts not. The unawakened sinner discerns not his miserable state, fears no threatened danger — is dead to all spiritual necessities, and the Divine provision of the gospel.——Where these appetites exist, there is life, an awakening from the dead—spiritual apprehension of that which is super-excellent—even the salvation of the soul.

2. *Earnest, impatient, and restless desire* after righteousness. Hunger, we say, will break through stone walls. Thirst is intolerable. "All that a man hath will he give for his life," when its termination is threatened by hunger or thirst. An ancient king when suffering thirst, said, "I will give my kingdom for a cupful of water." So the poor sinner pursued by Divine justice, conscious of his guilt and everlasting ruin, says, Give me righteousness, or I perish. It is a matter of life or death with me. I cannot rest till I obtain righteousness. So the converted Jews, Acts ii. 27; xvi. 27—30.

3. Hungering and thirsting after righteousness *is an evidence of spiritual health*. The body is not healthy unless it has these appetites in full operation. So with the soul. If we feel our need of, and earnestly desire spiritual food, and go as often as we need to God's banqueting house for nourishment, it is an indubitable evidence of spiritual health. 3 John 2.

II. THE BLESSEDNESS OF THOSE WHO HUNGER AND THIRST. "*They shall be filled.*" As God never inspires desires and prayer but with a design to satisfy, those who hunger and thirst after full salvation may depend on being speedily and effectually blessed or satisfied, and well-fed, as the word implies, Ps. lxxxi. 10; cvii. 9; Luke i. 53.

1. *Christ is the source of all the blessings needed*. He is the atoning Sacrifice—the Redeemer—the Ransomer. He figuratively represents himself as the light and life of the world. How apposite are his statements;— "I am the bread of life." John vi. 35, 48, 51. He is the "Water of life," Rev. xxii. 1; John iv. 14; vii. 37, 38. He is called, "The Lord our Righteousness."

2. It implies *participation in order to "be filled."* The means of participation is *faith*, called "eating and drinking." See John vi. 51, 53—56; vii. 37; iv. 14; Isa. lv. 1. As Philip Henry observes,

"Righteousness is conveyed from Jesus Christ, through the ordinances, as water is conveyed by conduit pipes into the cistern, Zech. iv. 11. Now, if the pipes be stopped, the water flows not. Though water be in the well, if we have no bucket to draw, whence should we have it? Faith is the bucket: if faith be active in an ordinance, it proves a filling ordinance; if otherwise, we come empty, and go away empty. "According to your faith be it unto you." Matt. ix. 29. Besides, they are not only blessed because they shall be filled, but blessed because they hunger and thirst; their very hunger is a blessing.

3. *Full enjoyment.* "Shall be filled." Full pardon — complete justification — the Spirit of holiness shall be given, and all his blessed influence to renew, to purify, to comfort, and to quicken. Thou shalt be a child of God and an heir of heaven. "Of his fulness have we all received, even grace for grace." John i. 16. Ask thyself what thou needest as a sinner, as a child of adversity, as tempted, persecuted, suffering, dying, thou shalt be filled with all grace needful for thy every condition. "My God shall supply all your need," etc.

How precious and satisfying then must be this righteousness! It is more precious than gold or silver, or rubies, because it will last for ever. All earthly good satiates as the novelty dies away. A man may surfeit upon the world, but he can never be satisfied with the world. A man may be satisfied with Christ, but he can never surfeit upon Christ. In Ps. xxvi. 8, it is said, "they shall be abundantly satisfied." What can a man desire more than satisfaction? Christ abundantly satisfies — satisfies, and satisfies again.

And what a fulness will the saints have in glory! "When that which is perfect is come, then that which is in part shall be done away." Though at present we are not perfect, we shall be perfect in heaven; knowledge shall be perfect, and holiness shall be perfect. Here our imperfections cause us to hunger and thirst. But in this sense, we shall never hunger and thirst in heaven. We shall have perfect and everlasting righteousness there. "As for me, I shall behold thy face in righteousness; I shall be satisfied when I awake with thy likeness." Ps. xvii. 15.

IMPROVEMENT.

1. Learn the folly of self-righteousness. It is opposed to God's righteousness.

2. The folly of loving the world inordinately. It can never satisfy.

3. See the cause of spiritual lethargy. It is for want of appetite for gospel blessings.

XXV.—PROPHECY.

PART I.

"We have also a more sure word of prophecy; whereunto ye do dwell that ye take heed, as unto a light that shineth in a dark place, until the day dawn, and the day-star arise in your hearts: knowing this first, that no prophecy of the scripture is of any private interpretation. For the prophecy came not in old time by the will of man: but holy men of God spake as they were moved by the Holy Ghost."—2 PETER i. 19—21.

VERY expressive is Peter's address (v. 13—21,) to his fellow-Christians. It is a glorious profession of Christ in the prospect of martyrdom. His Divine Master had solemnly forewarned him of what he was to expect in the faithful discharge of his Apostolical commission. John xxi. 18, 19.—Peter knew that his labours for Christ would ultimately bring him to a violent death: therefore he could not hope for worldly advantage. His firm adherence to Christ was an irresistible proof that the testimony was dearer unto him than life itself; and therefore that he must have been confidently persuaded, both of its vast importance, and its indubitable verity. The text and its connection refer to the Evidence of the truth of the Bible arising from Miracles. See page 38. It refers also to the Evidence arising from Prophecy. "We have," etc. Consider therefore,

THE EVIDENCE OF THE TRUTH OF THE BIBLE ARISING FROM PROPHECY.

Prophecy is the prediction of such future events as are manifestly dependent on a succession of contingent circumstances, over which no created being has any control. The foreknowledge of such events belongs to God alone. He can reveal this to men, and by them to their fellow-men; but from no other source than Divine revelation can it possibly be derived. Jehovah, therefore, challenges the pretended deities of the Heathen to advance this evidence in their favour. "Produce," etc. Isa. xli. 21—23. This is a test which no imposture can endure. To predict the distant contingencies of futurity, is as far beyond the reach of human sagacity, as the working of miracles is beyond the reach of human power. "To foresee and foretell future events, Bishop Douglas says, may be called a miracle of knowledge, as properly as to raise the dead may be called a miracle of power." * And it is

---

* Prophecy, or the foretelling of future events, is possessed by no mere man; and therefore, no man, unaided by some supernatural knowledge, can foretell any future event. For example, no man could have foretold, 300 years ago, that in the island of Corsica, from a particular person there living, would rise in three centuries a man of extraordinary military prowess and political skill, who, by a succession of the most brilliant exploits and victories, should exile an old dynasty from France, raise himself to imperial dignity, affright the monarchs of Europe, and after having dazzled the world with his success, should by a more sudden descent and overthrow, die an exile in a remote island of the ocean. No man could have told, in the reign of Queen Elizabeth, that in the colony of Virginia, from an old English family, there would in less than two centuries, rise a man who should be the firm and undaunted asserter of

unreasonable to imagine that God would either by the one or the other, interpose for the sanction of imposture. Refer now

I. To some of the Prophecies recorded. These refer to Persons, Places, and Events.

1. To Persons.

It was said of HAM, "A servant of servants shall he be unto his brethren." And is not Africa, which they colonized, pre-eminently the land of slavery? Its wretched inhabitants, from the earliest periods of history, to the present time, have been bought and sold by the stranger; dragged in chains from their home and their kindred; transported in shoals to the uttermost parts of the sea; and under the whip and the lash consigned to the most grinding servitude. Four thousand years ago, Noah uttered his prediction, and we see it has been literally fulfilled.

With regard to ABRAHAM, it was predicted that his posterity should be greatly multiplied. See Gen. xii. At the time of its utterance it was apparently impossible, but the vast number of his descendants, the Jews, proves the fulfilment.

Of ISHMAEL it was predicted, "And he will be a wild man; his hand will be against every man, and every man's hand against him, and he shall dwell in the presence of all his brethren." Gen. xvi. 12. "Behold, I have blessed him, and will make him fruitful, and will multiply him exceedingly; twelve princes shall he beget," etc. Gen. xvii. 20. These prophecies have been fulfilled. Strabo frequently mentions the Arabian Phylarchs, or rulers of tribes, and Melo, quoted by Eusebius, from Alexander Polyhistor, a heathen historian, relates that twelve sons of Abraham departed into Arabia, divided the region between them, and were the first kings of the inhabitants; "whence," says he, "even to our days, the Arabians have twelve kings of the same name as the first." Ever since, the people have been governed by Phylarchs, and have lived in tribes. "I will make him a great nation;" the Saracens, his descendants, made rapid and extensive conquests, and erected one of the largest empires that ever was in the world. "And he will be a wild man," "he dwelt in the wilderness," and his sons shall inhabit it, and many of them neither sow nor plant. "And he became an archer;" such the Arabs have been, and

---

his country's rights; and by his counsel and heroic achievements, after a seven years' struggle, not only succeed in detaching thirteen colonies from the despotism of England, but in establishing a new world of republics, surpassing, in the march of intellect, in advances towards national greatness, and in all the enjoyments of rational liberty, all nations upon the earth. No mere man could have foretold such events. Now, this is precisely the species of prophecy of which we are to speak in this branch of the argument. Such prophecies do the sacred oracles present.

It has been remarked that the existence of counterfeits and hypocrites is a very stubborn and irrefragable proof that there is something genuine and authentic. No man is wont to pretend to any thing which has not somewhere a real existence: at least we have never met with such a case. All pretences prove that something real exists. Now, amongst all nations there have been false prophets. The pagans had their oracles, their auguries, and their divinations. Modern idolaters have their diviners and necromancers. Jews and Christians alone possessed, and gave the original of this idea. They alone afforded the *realities*, of which these are the pretences. — ALEXANDER CAMPBELL, *Cincinnati, America.*

continue to this day. "His hand will be against every man, and every man's hand against him." His posterity live in a state of continual war with the rest of the world, and are both robbers by land and pirates by sea. They have been enemies to mankind, and the rest of mankind have been enemies to them. They are a race of marauders, and only large caravans can safely travel across their deserts, as they rob and plunder all whom they can subdue. Such robberies they justify, by alleging the hard usage of their father Ishmael, who, being turned out of doors by Abraham, had the open plains and deserts given him by God for his patrimony, with permission to take whatever he could find there. And therefore they think they may indemnify themselves on the posterity of Isaac, and on all besides.

"And he shall dwell, (tabernacle, or dwell in tents,) in the presence of all his brethren." Gen. xvi. 12. They have dwelt in tents in the wilderness ever since. They have all along maintained their independance; and in spite of the most powerful efforts for their destruction, they still dwell in the presence of all their brethren. They have never been subdued. The Egyptians, Assyrians, and the Persians, could never conquer them. Alexander, who subdued the Persians, prepared an expedition against them, but premature death prevented. The Romans who subdued the East, were never able to reduce Arabia into a Roman province. Pompey, though he triumphed over three parts of the world, could not conquer Arabia. Thus have they maintained their independence for four thousand years. The great empires around them have in their turns fallen to ruin, while they have continued the same from the beginning. They are the only people, besides the Jews, who have subsisted as a distinct people from the beginning.

The principal predictions of the Old Testament relate to the person and advent of Christ. These are very numerous, not only referring to general events, but also comprehending the minutest circumstances.

Christ was represented to Adam as the Seed of the woman who should bruise the Serpent's head;[1] to Abraham as the source of blessing in his posterity to all the families of the earth;[2] to Jacob as the Shiloh unto whom the gathering of the people should be;[3] to Moses as the great Prophet like unto Him who should speak in the name of the Lord.[4] And then more fully and clearly the glorious scheme opens at every step. He was to belong to the tribe of Judah,[5] to the stock of David,[6] to the town of Bethlehem;[7] he was to be born of a virgin;[8] he was to appear during the existence of the kingdom of Judah;[9] before the destruction of the second temple,[10] four hundred and ninety years after the return from the Babylonish captivity;[11] his coming was to be proclaimed by a forerunner;[12] he was to be distinguished for his wisdom[13] and righteousness[14] and meekness[15] and patience;[16] he was to open the

---

1 Gen. iii. 15. 2 Gen. xxii. 18. 3 Gen. xlix. 10. 4 Deut. xviii. 15.
5 Gen. xlix. 10. 6 Isaiah xi. 1. 7 Micah v. 2. 8 Isaiah vii. 14.
9 Gen. xlix. 10. 10 Hag. ii. 7—9. 11 Dan. ix. 24, 25. 12 Mal. iii. 1.
13 Isaiah xi. 2. 14 Jer. xxiii. 6. 15 Isaiah liii. 7. 16 Isaiah l. 6.

eyes of the blind, and cause the deaf to hear, and the lame to walk, and the tongue of the dumb to sing;[17] he was to be despised and rejected of men;[18] yet called Blessed;[19] he was to be without form or comeliness,[20] yet the chiefest among ten thousand and altogether lovely;[21] he was to be a man of sorrows,[22] yet anointed with the oil of gladness above his fellows;[23] he was to be a worm and no man,[24] yet the mighty God:[25] he was to be betrayed by a familiar friend for thirty pieces of silver;[26] he was to be tried and condemned as a criminal;[27] he was to be spit upon[28] and buffeted[29] and pierced with a spear;[30] gall and vinegar were to be given him to drink in the agonies of dissolution;[31] for the sins of others he was to be slain;[32] he was to be buried in a rich man's tomb;[33] he was to rise again and become the plague of death;[34] he was to ascend on high, leading captivity captive;[35] his religion was to be established in the world on the ruins of idolatry and superstition;[36] in despite of all opposition it was to be promulgated far and wide;[37] the gentiles were to come to its light, and kings to the brightness of its rising.[38]

That particulars so numerous should be foretold and fulfilled in one individual, cannot possibly be accounted for except on the ground of Divine inspiration. The fifty-third chapter of Isaiah alone has so much force of evidence in it, that Lord Lyttleton, previously a stout infidel, on reading it, immediately renounced his prejudices, and ever after resolutely and honourably professed his faith in Christ.

Consider the following predictions as referring to Jesus Christ:—

Shem, son of Noah, stands at the head of the list of his illustrious progenitors. *"Blessed be the Lord God of Shem."* "God shall persuade Japheth, and he shall dwell in the tents of Shem, and Canaan shall be his servant." But soon the posterity of Shem became many powerful families, each of which founded a nation. Another discrimination became necessary. Abraham therefore is selected. In the seed of Abraham the blessing is now promised. But he has a son by Hagar, several by Keturah, and one by Sarah. Which of these shall be the honoured progenitor? *"In Isaac shall thy seed be called."* But Isaac has two sons, Jacob and Esau; which of these? *"The elder shall serve the younger,"* gives the honour to Jacob. He has twelve sons — which shall be the progenitor? *"The sceptre shall not depart from Judah,"* etc. Gen. xlix. 10. Then Judah became a numerous tribe, and another limitation is wanted. David, then, the son of Jesse, becomes the king of Israel, and David's son is to become David's Lord. Christ is called *"the root and offspring of David."*

But the indices pointing to the Messiah were perpetuated by the prophets. Hence his mother is described as a *virgin* by Isaiah. "Behold, *the virgin* shall," etc. Isa. vii. 14. The impious scoffs of Infidels

---

17 Isa. xxxv. 5, 6.   18 Isaiah liii. 3.   19 Ps. lxxii 17.   20 Isaiah liii. 2.
21 Can. v. 10—16.   22 Isaiah liii. 4.   23 Psalm xlv. 7.   24 Psalm xxii. 6.
25 Isaiah ix. 6.   26 Psalm xli. 9, and Zach. xi. 12.   27 Isaiah liii 8.
28 Isaiah l. 6.   29 Isaiah l. 6.   30 Psalm xxii. 16.   31 Psalm lxix. 21.
32 Isa. liii. 4—8.   33 Isaiah liii. 9.   34 Psalm xxvi. 10, and Hosea xiii. 14.
35 Psa. lxviii. 18.   36 Isa. ii. 17—19.   37 Isa. ii. 2; vii. 14.   38 Isaiah lx. 3.

at the nativity of Jesus, had they noted this oracle, would have been prevented or confounded. Let it be noted, that 700 years before this child was born, it was foretold that his mother should be a *virgin*. Also that his name should be *Immanuel*, i. e. *God with us*, a name that could never be associated with ordinary humanity.

The *place* of his nativity is also so clearly and expressly named, that all the priests and scribes in Jerusalem, could tell Herod the place, without difficulty. "And thou Bethlehem," etc. Micah v. 2.

The *time* of the birth and appearance of the Messiah was most exactly predicted. It was defined by several remarkable circumstances. The chief are

1. He was to come before the second temple decayed, or was to appear in the second temple.

2. He was to come before Judah ceased to furnish a governor.

3. He was to come while the Roman emperors were in their glory.

4. He was to come at the end of a definite number of years from the permission given to rebuild the temple.

Concerning the first prediction, observe that when the second temple was building, the old men who had seen the first, are said to have wept when they saw the second edifice progressing, because it was so inferior to that which Solomon built; but to console them it was foretold that the glory of the latter house should greatly excel that of the former. Haggai ii. 7. "I will shake all nations," etc. "The glory of the latter house shall be greater," etc. And why? The prophet Malachi delares. See Mal. iii. 1. Thus it is evident that the Lord would come while the second temple was yet standing. The first temple was destroyed by Nebuchadnezzar, on the tenth day of August, 583 years before Jesus was born; and so the second was built about 500 years before the birth of the Messiah.

The sceptre was not to depart from Judah till Shiloh came. But it was merely lingering in that tribe for some years before the birth of Christ, for the land of Judea had become a Roman province, but the remains of the ancient regal power had not been wrested from the hands of Judah. But so feebly did he grasp the sceptre, that it seemed to fall when the Harbinger appeared.

Daniel minutely describes the time in his explanation of Nebuchadnezzar's vision, Dan. ii. 36—45. By it he gives a prospective view of the history of the world from the time of the Assyrian monarchy to the end of time. In this vision, and the interpretation of it, the four great Pagan empires are accurately defined. The golden *head* of the image seen by the king was avowed by Daniel to be the Chaldean dynasty; the silver *shoulders* was the Medo-Persian dynasty; the brazen *body*, the Macedonian empire; and the iron *legs*, the Roman empire. These were the only *four* empires of the Pagan world which attained to universal dominion: they all had it for a time: they were all Pagan empires, and exactly delineated in this image. The interpretation indicates that they alone should have universal dominion. The Assyrian began 2233 years before the birth of Christ; lasted 1400 years, and ended 770 years before Christ. The Persian empire began 538 years before Christ, continued

200 years, and fell 336 years before the Christian era; the Macedonian, or Grecian, only continued 10 years; it began in 334, and ended 324 years before Christ. The Roman began 31 years before Christ, continued 500 years, ended A. D. 476.

It was predicted that in the days of the last empire, God would set up a kingdom to obtain the universal empire of the world; that it should, without human aid, break to atoms every particle of the Pagan governments; that it should resemble a stone cut out of a mountain, without hands, which, self-propelled, should roll on, increase, smite this wonderful image of Pagan government, demolish it, and fill the whole earth Such was the imagery of the vision. And was not the Messiah born in the days of the Cæsars, who first formed and governed the iron empire?

But Gabriel informs Daniel more definitely of the date of Messiah's birth: "Seventy weeks," etc. Dan. ix. 24—27. In ch. viii. 13, 14, it is asked, "How long shall be the vision," etc. The answer is, "Unto 2300 days, then shall the sanctuary be cleansed." As God said to Ezekiel, "*I have appointed one day for a year*," and as we find, in symbolic language, one day stands for a year, it is easy to arrive at the following conclusion:—

From the time of the decree to rebuild Jerusalem, until the death of the Messiah, would be threescore and nine and a half weeks, or a period of 485 or 486 years. Seven weeks make 49 years; sixty-two weeks make 434 years; and in the middle of the week, he was to establish the new institution; that is, three and a half, or four years more. From the issuing of the decree to rebuild Jerusalem, to the baptism of Jesus, was 483 years: his ministry was three years and a half, or the middle of one week; then he was cut off. And in half a week; that is, three years and a half more, Christianity was sent to all nations. This completes the seventy weeks, or 490 years of Daniel.

So clearly was Messiah's coming predicted, and so general was the knowledge of it, through the Septuagint version of the Jewish Scriptures then read through the Roman Empire, that the expectation became general that at this time some wonderful personage was to be born, who would put the world under a new government. This singular fact shows that the prophecies concerning the time of Christ's birth were so plain, in the estimation of all who read them, as to preclude all doubt as to the time of his appearance. Refer to the history and poetry of Rome:—

Suetonius, in the life of Vespasian: "An ancient and constant tradition has obtained throughout all the East, that in the *fates* it was decreed, that about that time one would come from Judea, who would obtain the dominion of the world.

From the Jewish prophets, the Pagan Sibyls gave out their oracles; so that the expectation was universal. The same year that Pompey took Jerusalem, one of the Sibyl oracles made a great noise, "that Nature was about to bring forth a king to the Romans." Suetonius says, this so terrified the Roman senate that they made a decree that none born that year should be educated. And in his life of Augustus, he says, that "those whose wives were pregnant that year, did each conceive great hopes, applying the prophecy to themselves."

Appian, Sallust, Plutarch, and Cicero, say that this prophecy of the Sibyls stirred up Cornelius Lentulus to think that he was the man who should be king of the Romans. Some applied it to Cæsar. Cicero laughed at the application, and affirmed that this prophecy should not be applied to any one born in Rome.

Even Virgil, who wrote his fourth Eclogue about the time of Herod the Great, compliments the Consul Pollio with this prophecy, supposing it might refer to his son Saloninus then born. Virgil substantially quotes and versifies the prophecies of Isaiah, applying them to this child Saloninus:

> The last age, decreed by Fate, is come;
> And a new frame of all things does begin.
> A holy progeny from heaven descends,
> Auspicious to his birth! which puts an end
> To the iron age! and from whence shall rise
> A golden state far glorious through the earth.

Then Virgil alludes to Isa. lxv. 17. "The wolf and the lamb shall feed together, and the lion shall eat straw like the ox. They shall not hurt nor destroy in all my holy mountain:"

> Nor shall the flocks fierce lions fear,
> Nor serpent shall be there, nor herb of poisonous juice.

Then the expiation of Daniel is referred to:

> By thee, what footsteps of our sins remain
> Are blotted out, and the whole world set free
> From her perpetual bondage and her fear.

Other quotations of the same nature, might be made from Virgil and other ancient poets and writers.

The Jews have been so confounded with these prophecies and events, that such of them as did not believe, have degraded Daniel from the rank of a great prophet, to one of the inferior prophets; and others have said that there were two Messiahs to come — one a suffering, and one a triumphant Messiah. But the excuses of mankind for their unbelief are frivolous and irrational. Observe also that not only the Gentiles, the proselytes to the Jews' religion, the Eastern Magi, but myriads of the Jews themselves recognized these evidences, and bowed to their authority.

The Prophecies also respect *the Jewish nation.* Many of these were delivered in the form of threatenings, and they were fulfilled. —— They were to be scattered among all people from one end of the earth to the other: "The Lord shall scatter thee," etc. Jer. xv. 4; xxiv. 9, 10; xxix. 18. The Jews, as every intelligent person knows, have been dispersed far and wide; they have been cruelly persecuted and oppressed wherever they have wandered, and been the taunt and derision of the whole world. Thus a poor wandering Jew is God's witness to the truth of prophecy. Yet, notwithstanding all they have suffered, they still preserve their national character, and cling to the customs of their fathers.

Judea is still the home of their hopes and their hearts. Empires have risen and fallen; a hundred generations have passed away; they still exist distinct — unchanged; mingling with all men, but never uniting; scattered among all men, yet never lost. By nothing less than a preternatural influence could they have been so long preserved — so long kept separate — in defiance of so many processes operating to amalgamate and extirpate them. The Jews are witnesses for God.

Even the existence of infidels and "scoffers" of religion, is a witness to the truth. By their hatred and hostility to Christianity; by their immorality, by their ridicule, by their malignant attempts to blast and to destroy all we hold sacred, they are unwittingly lending themselves to support that which they detest. In despite of themselves, they are adding to the mass of the Christian evidences, as the Apostle, 1800 years ago, predicted. "There shall come in the last days scoffers," etc. 2 Pet. iii. 3, 4.

IMPROVEMENT.

1. Prophecy should be investigated and studied by all Christians, that they may be able to put to silence the opposition of evil men.

2. Let Christians be encouraged by the Christian evidence arising from prophecy. Such evidence, if calmly considered, no infidel can withstand.

XXVI. — PROPHECY.

PART II.

"We have a more sure word of prophecy," etc. — 2 Pet. i. 19—21.

Great is the evidence of Divine truth arising from miracles and prophecies; but the latter is the more clearly demonstrative. Peter intimates this, calling it *"the more sure word of prophecy."* Miracles display the power and benevolence of God, and his vindictive justice, according to the nature of the miracle wrought; but the accomplishment of prophecy gives also a striking exhibition of the foreknowledge, the faithfulness, and the superintending Providence of God. The fulfilment of prophecy is also a more permanent appeal to the senses than miracles; and as Bishop Newton observes, "the evidence arising from prophecy is a growing evidence; and the more prophecies are fulfilled, the greater the confirmation of the truth." Consider

2. *Prophecies regarding Places.*

In examining the direct, literal, and express prophetic annunciations of the fates of the great empires and cities of antiquity, consider

Babylon. It was the wonder of the world — the glory of kingdoms — it was denominated the golden city — the beauty of the Chaldee's excellency — a queen who exulted, "I am, and none else beside me," — the battle-axe — and the hammer of the whole earth.

But the Babylonians were wicked, haughty, idolatrous, and became obnoxious to the Divine anger. While in the height of its power it was declared that the Medes and the Persians should besiege it. See Jer. l. 1 : li. 1, etc. — that its inhabitants should forbear to fight, and become cowardly as women, Jer. li. 30 — that the river which ran through it should be dried up, Jer. li. 36 — that it should be taken by stratagem during the security of a drunken revel, Jer. li. 39 — that it should be filled with soldiers as with caterpillars, Jer. li. 14 — that it should bow down in abject adulation before its conqueror.

And these remarkable predictions were literally and exactly fulfilled. See Isa. xiii, particularly v. 19—22. These predictions were delivered by Isaiah 739 years before Christ, and about 200 years before the destruction of Babylon. [*Rollin's Ancient History* may be profitably consulted.

Thus we see that Babylon, with its splendid palaces, hanging gardens, and brazen gates, etc., was to be utterly destroyed. It has been done. "Babylon the great is fallen." Recent travellers inform us that Babylon is now a "mass of ruins;" that "not a habitable spot" appears for miles around it — that "bats and all sorts of serpents infest it" — that the lion and the hyena "range it unmolested," and the wild goat "dances on its mounds as on a rock."

"Babylon shall become heaps," says the prophet; "her cities a desolation; her broad walls shall be utterly broken ; the sea shall come upon her," etc.——And the whole face of the country is covered with a vast succession of mounds of rubbish — not a vestige of those walls is to be found on which once a "chariot and four might pass and turn" — the river Euphrates, overflowing its banks, has converted the neigbouring plain into a "marshy swamp," and covered much of the ruins of the city.

"Idolatry," says one, "was fostered and protected in babylon, and from thence was diffused throughout (at least) the western world: the liberal arts, the more recondite sciences, with every power of the human mind, were rendered subservient to systematic idolatry. Its doom, therefore, must correspond with its crimes. It is enough for us that we know its punishment to be just, and that we can trace in its ruins the unequivocal, and even the verbal accomplishment of those predictions which announced its calamities " — predictions delivered so long before the event—an incontestible proof of the truth of the Bible.

Consider the fate of *Egypt*. It is unnecessary here to dwell on its great antiquity — its civil and military renown — its surpassing fertility—and of those stupendous pillars, in appearance eternal and indestructible, which have ever awakened such vast curiosity. Ezekiel thus writes;—"Egypt shall be a base kingdom." Ch. xxix and xxx. These predictions were delivered 589 years before Christ, and they have been literally and exactly fulfilled, as Rollin's History, and other writers, abundantly prove.

Not long after the era of the prophecy, Egypt was conquered by the Persians; afterwards it yielded to the Macedonians: afterwards it became a province of Rome; afterwards it came under the dominion of the Saracens; afterwards it was usurped by the Mamelukes; and now it is tributary to the Turkish Sultan, and governed by a Pacha in his name. The disgrace and oppression it has undergone are unparalleled in the history of nations. Its canals have been dried up; its fields covered with sand from the desert; its palaces have dwindled into cottages of mud; its miserable inhabitants have been under an intolerable military tyranny, and are notorious for their ignorance, laziness, idolatry, and treachery. No human sagacity could have foreseen that a country so rich and glorious, would be plunged for such a length of time into such a depth of degradation—and be compelled for 24 centuries to wear the chains of a foreign yoke, and strive in vain for liberty. Soon after Ezekiel prophesied, the far extended line of its kings was broken; *and never since has a prince of its own sat on the throne of the Pharaohs.*

Consider also *Nineveh*, a city built by Nimrod, and eternally infamous as the mistress of idolatry. It was marked by external grandeur and greatness. Its walls were 100 feet high, and sufficiently broad to admit three chariots to drive abreast on them; its towers were 1500, 200 feet high. The infants were 120,000; the entire population a million. It contained within its walls sufficient land for cultivation and pasture, which afforded food for all, and for "much cattle."

Thirst of conquest, and enthusiastic zeal to propagate idolatry, characterized both rulers and people. Pushing their conquests westward, they reached the chosen people. Their wickedness was inexcusable, because they had the opportunity of knowing the true God. But they waxed worse and worse, and ripening in sin the Divine vengeance predicted by the prophets came upon them. See Nahum ii. and iii; Zeph. ii. 12—15. The overthrow of Nineveh, before Christ 606, is attested by ancient writers. A thousand years ago, it was reckoned an old city of ruins. It was to the ancient world—a city—as if it had never been. It had sunk below the earth's surface. "I will," says Jehovah, "make thy grave, for thou art vile," and so it has long appeared a huge unshapen mound.

Modern research, however, has been able to identify it, and exhume many of its wonders. (See Layard and De Vaux's Works on Nineveh.) Its palaces—their chambers and sculptures have been brought to light; the strange shaped inscriptions have been deciphered; gods, conquerors, kings, scenes of war, national customs, etc., have been found on slabs and walls.——The records of Nineveh have been strangely preserved. The royal throne, statues, shields, seals, swords, crowns, bowls, in ivory, metal, and wood, mother of pearl, and glass, have been found in the excavations. The cuneiform writing on obelisks and marble slabs have been deciphered, and the result has been a wonderful confirmation of the inspired annals of the Old Testament. We find a veritable history parallel to that of ancient Israel, and see the actual accounts of events recorded in Kings and Chronicles. Not only do we find mention made of Jehu, Menahem, and Hazael, and many towns of Judea and Syria; but we discover Sennacherib's own account of his invasion of Palestine, and the amount of tribute which king Hezekiah was forced to pay him, 2 Kings xviii. 14. Nay, there has been found an actual picture of the taking of Lachish by Sennacherib, 2 Kings xviii. 14—17.——In short the illustrations of Scripture supplied by the marbles from Nineveh, are numerous and important. The Christian world is under great obligations to Layard and Botta for their enterprise, and to Rawlinson and Hincks, for their literary investigations and discoveries.

The prophecy respecting *Tyre*, the most celebrated commercial city of antiquity. Its wealth was immense, its merchants were princes, and its traffickers the honourable of the earth. The luxury, vice, and destruction of this mighty city, which once had the entire control of the trade with India, and into whose lap the treasures of the world were poured, form the subjects of some of the most interesting prophecies. Ezek. xxvi. 4—21; xxviii. "Behold, the Lord will cast her out; he will smite her power in the sea; he will make her like the top of a rock; it shall be a place to spread nets upon." This prophecy has been exactly accomplished.

"The stirring scenes of a seaport exhibit a picture of more constant excitement than can ever be presented by any other place. A thousand scenes of noise, and joyousness, and wealth have been exhibited upon these shores. They have passed away like the feverish dream of a disturbed sleep. Ships may be seen, but at a distance; no merchant of the earth ever enters the name of Tyre upon his books; and where thousands once assembled in pomp and pride, I could discover only a few children amusing themselves, and a party of Turks sitting in gravity, and sipping their favourite coffee. It was impossible not to think of another people, still more favoured in their priviliges, and whose commercial transactions are as extended as the world. Cities of my country! shall it be ever said of you, that ye are no more?—The patriot may sing exultingly over his cups the praises of Britannia, ruler of the waves; but the Christian will fear and tremble, and offer up prayer to God, that what we deserve in *justice*, may be withheld from us in *mercy!*"— *Hardy's Notices*.

Consider the Predictions respecting *Edom*, sometimes called *Idumea*, and *Mount Seir*. It was once a wealthy and powerful kingdom. It was of vast extent, and distinguished for the abundance of its pasturage, the number and strength of its cities, its military power, and immense grandeur and wealth. Its chief cities were Bozrah and Petra. Edom was considered the cradle of Eastern civilization.

Roman poets speak with admiration of its palm-trees, and numerous flocks. The Greeks contemplated with wonder Petra, its metropolis, and the power of its armies. The magnificent ruins of Petra, attest its original grandeur. It must have been the most wonderful city in the world—a city almost hewn and chiseled out of the Rock. It lies in the midst of a circle of almost perpendicular mountains; the faces of which are excavated into innumerable sepulchres; the interior is full of palaces, temples, grottoes, theatres, and pyramids, constructed with exquisite art. It could be no feeble race that achieved works like these; in fact, its inhabitants were celebrated for their wisdom, science and valour.

But the truth of prophecy shines bright as the sun on the wretched land of Edom. These are the words of the Lord, Isa. xxxiv. 5—17; Jer. xlix. 13—18; Mal. i. 3, 4; Joel iii. 19; Amos i. 11, 12; Obad. ver. 3—16. These predictions were delivered by different prophets at different times, when Edom was in all its glory, and there appeared no sign of its overthrow. They exhibit no mark of being shrewd guesses in the present, and leave no means of escape through a dubious sense, should they not be fulfilled in the future. The cause of the Judgments to be inflicted is clearly stated. See Ezek. xxxv. 3, 5, etc. The literal and exact accomplishment of these prophecies is fully sustained by the testimony even of the enemies of the Bible. Modern travellers declare

That Idumea is a desert. The ruins of 30 towns are traced in it absolutely forsaken. In one part it presents "an immense tract of dreary country covered with black flints," and in another "an expanse of shifting sands, with the surface broken by innumerable undulations, and without a particle of vegetation." Laborde records the awe and wonder with which he wandered up and down the deserted streets of Petra, amid silence deep as death, and surveyed its vast sepulchres, some scarcely begun—some fresh as if they had just come from the hands of the sculptor—others broken and disjointed, the abode of lizards and covered with brambles. Thus, wherever the observer looks on the desolation of Edom and the ruins of Petra, he sees not only signal proofs of past human greatness, but incontestible evidence of the truth of the Bible. Thousands of years have elapsed since the prophets of God first foretold the certain overthrow of the then powerful kingdom of Idumea; but their words spoken of old are this day literally fulfilled. And now, in view of the tenantless solitudes of the once populous Petra, and the universal barrenness of the once fertile mountains of Edom, the believer in Scripture may appeal to all who deny the faith,—"Read here in the word of prophecy what desolations are foretold—look there over the land of Edom, how all is fulfilled, and can you but confess that this book is from God?"

Christ foretold the destruction of Jerusalem and the temple, and the dispersion of the nation. Matt. xxiv; Luke xxi. Mr. Campbell, of America, thus graphically writes:

The complete desolation of the temple to the foundation, to the removing of every stone, is foretold. The compassing the city with armies, the slaughter of the inhabitants, and the captivity of those who escaped, are described. The fortunes of his disciples at this time, with all the terrors of the siege, and all the tremendous prodigies in the heavens and the earth accompanying these desolations, are named. And in the conclusion, the audience is assured that all these things should happen before forty years; "before that generation should pass away." Now this prophecy was written, published, and read through Judea, and mentioned in the apostolic epistles for years before it happened; and a general expectation of this event pervaded the whole Christian communities from Jerusalem to Rome, and, indeed, through all the Roman provinces. The allusions to these predictions are frequent in the apostolic writings. It was necessary they should, for this reason: the Jews, so long as they possessed the government of Judea, the temple and the metropolis; as long as they had any particle of influence at home or abroad, they used it with relentless cruelty against the Christians. The apostles had to succour the minds of their persecuted brethren, and exhort them to patience and perseverance, by reminding them of the speedy dispersion of them among the nations. So that all the Christians throughout the Roman empire looked for this catastrophe; and so it came to pass that such of the Christians as were in Jerusalem and Judea, about the time of the siege of Titus, fled according to the directions given by our Saviour; and thus not a believing Jew perished in the siege.

I need not detail the awful accomplishment of this prediction. Josephus has done this in awful colours. Tacitus, too, relates some of the circumstances. Every word of the prediction was exactly fulfilled, even to the ploughing up of the foundations of the temple. It is remarkable that on the tenth day of August, the very same day the temple and city were laid waste by the Babylonians, the temple was burned by Titus' army.*

II. THE CHARACTER OF THE PROPHECIES.

The fulfilment of prophecies, admitting them to have been published before the events to which they refer, is an indubitable proof of the Divine inspiration of the writers. For consider how *extraordinary* they were. Many of the events foretold were distant — some of them dependent on a great variety of causes — on the concurrent inclinations of a multitude of agents — on the will of Divine Providence. Some were connected with minute description of attendant circumstances, several of which appeared to be improbable; for instance, the piece of money in the mouth of the fish; the owner's surrender of the colt, for the use of Jesus; the treachery of Judas; the denial of Peter; the manner of the Redeemer's death; the event of his resurrection; the subsequent meeting of his disciples in Galilee, etc., etc. Such circumstances could not have been foreseen by any human sagacity.

---

* I have read somewhere, that, before the temple was burned, Titus entered the temple, got out some of the sacred utensils, among which were the golden candlestick and the table of the shewbread. These he carried as trophies home to Rome; and on the triumphal arch which was raised for him in the city of Rome, this candlestick and table were carved upon it. This triumphal arch yet stands; and even yet the Jews who now visit Rome will not pass under it. There is a side-walk and a gate through which the Jews pass. So deeply rooted is the remembrance of this indignity upon their religion and nation, that eighteen centuries have not obliterated i*

"That which distinguishes the prophecies of the Bible from all Heathen or all pretended predictions of every age, is simply that the former have not merely three specifications, or six particulars, but often very many; and many of these, too, altogether unlikely ever to come to pass. The prophecy respecting Babylon has connected with it more than twice six of these items or particulars, many of them apparently totally improbable. If you foretell the death of an individual, time will accomplish it, though you have no prophetic gift; but if you venture to add as many as three uncertain particulars, your reputation as a seer is instantly in jeopardy. Name the death 'of the man, and say that it will take place by apoplexy, on Thursday of the next week, and you are likely to fail in all the particulars; while you are an impostor should you mistake only in one. Take a thousand men, and it is not to be expected that any one of them will die just at that day, at a given hour, and with that disease. How much more difficult to sustain your pretensions to prophetic gifts, if three more specifications are added. Suppose these to be improbable particulars, and how much is the difficulty increased!"—*Rev. David Nelson, M. D.*

Consider the *vast multitude* of Scripture prophecies. Impostors, if they venture at predictions, take care that their prophecies come within the reach of strong probability, and are prudently sparing of their pretended oracular gifts. But Scripture prophecies are multitudinous; they appear almost on every page. ——Were there a fulfilment of only one or two prophecies, we might ascribe it to accident. But when we see this multitude of predictions, delivered by different persons in different ages, accomplished in chronological succession, we are compelled to acknowledge the Divine inspiration of the writers.

Their *Plainness* is also a strong evidence. How different were the prognostications of Heathen oracles; and how studiously have impostors contrived to render their prophecies capable of various meanings. Though a vail is occasionally thrown over Scripture predictions, yet the events foretold are announced in the most explicit terms; and, as time advances, the several particulars relating to them, though originally obscure, become clear and intelligible. The plain and unhesitating tone in which those prophecies are expressed, in connection with their fulfilment, is a striking proof of their Divine original.

They were *delivered by persons whose Divine inspiration was otherwise clearly attested.* Did they require men to receive them as the inspired messengers of God, merely on the ground of their own affirmation? No; they appealed to the miraculous powers with which they were endowed, and which they must have received from God.

The fact of their being real peophecies, published long before the events, is so clear, that it cannot be rejected without the most unreasonable obstinacy; and nothing is easier than to collect evidence as decisive as can possibly exist, that the New Testament was written at the commencement of the Christian era; and that the Old Testament had been in the hands of the Jews through a long succession of ages preceding. This establishes the fact that Scripture predictions were published long before the events to which they refer.

The New Testament contains many prophecies delivered by Christ before the events could possibly have occurred. One relates to the rapid spread of the gospel by the ministry of the Apostles. Considering the opposition which Christianity had to encounter, and the apparent unfitness of the Apostles for their work, it was very unlikely, humanly speaking, that their efforts would prove successful to any considerable extent. But Christ, when he commissioned them, assured them, also, that they should be endowed with supernatural powers, to qualify them for their office, and that the gospel, through their ministry, should spread with the rapidity of lightning. Acts i. 8; Mark xvi. 15—20 That these predictions were uttered before the events is clearly evident, for the Apostles acted upon them, and that they were actually accomplished is an indisputable fact, being attested not only by the Apostles themselves, but by contemporary historians.——The destruction of Jerusalem, already noticed, strongly supports our case. The literal fulfilment *after* the delivery of the predictions by Jesus, is so exactly described by Josephus, that his account of this terrible catastrophe may be justly styled a practical commentary on the Redeemer's prophecies on the subject.

Lastly. It must be conceded that the evidence derived from prophecy is abundant, though in the preceding pages only an imperfect detail of that evidence has been furnished. The field is so vast that it could not be compressed within two short discourses—yet may we defy the infidel, with all his arts, to explode the arguments adduced, on any ordinary principles of nature. Without denying all history, they cannot deny that the prophecy was in every case written before the event, even where the event is most ancient.

The two sources of external evidence, miracles and prophecy, which have now been considered, afford that rational ground of conviction which must satisfy every impartial mind, and leave infidelity completely without excuse. "Miracles," as Bishop Newton remarks, "may be said to be the main evidences of Divine revelation to the first ages who saw them wrought. Prophecies may be said to be the main evidences to the later ages who see them fulfilled." Each of them is founded on plain sensible matters of fact, as on a solid rock; and established on this basis, like the sides of an arch, they support one another, and the fabric built upon them. The miracles wrought afforded to those who saw them clear evidence of the truth of those prophecies with which they were connected; and the fulfilment of the prophecies affords unto us, who observe it, the same indubitable proof of the reality of those miracles by which these predictions were originally attested.

For further elucidation of the subject, reference may be made to

Newton's Dissertations on the Prophecies, to Keith on the same subject, and to the works of Layard, De Vaux, etc. etc.

Finally. Must not the infidelity which resists demonstration like this, be unreasonably absurd, and inexcusably criminal? If attestations so extraordinary, so unequivocal, fail to produce conviction, which is unhappily the case in numerous instances, nothing more is requisite to show the lamentable perversion, and to prove the reality of that Scripture doctrine, which teaches us the necessity of the Divine influence to enlighten the understanding, to subdue the prejudices of the heart, and to produce in us that faith which receives the gospel with child-like simplicity and humility.

Remember it is quite natural to the vastly depraved heart to be sceptical to the Divine truth. Men love darkness rather than light — infidelity is a disease of the heart, and not merely of the head. Therefore the necessity of the operation of the Spirit. Pray then for that influence as the mighty and overwhelming opponent to the scepticism of the heart.

XXVII.—THE GLORIOUS GOSPEL.

"The glorious gospel of the blessed God."—1 TIM. i. 11.

IN the context the Apostle refers to the law and the gospel, and shows that the one harmonized with the other. The gospel proclaims Christ as the end of the law for righteousness to every one that believes. Christ, by perfectly obeying its precepts, and enduring its penalty, magnified it and made it honourable. That is the source of a sinner's justification.——"The Apostle says, "The law is not made," etc. It condems not the righteous, for they are no longer under its curse. Rom. v. 1; viii. 1. This the Apostle declares is "according to the glorious gospel," etc.

I. THE GOSPEL.

The original term signifies "glad tidings," "good news." Isa. lii. 7; Luke ii. 10, 11. It announces tidings of the Divine scheme of mercy to save sinful and ruined man. The four books written by Matthew, Mark, Luke, and John, are properly called gospels, because they narrate the life, teaching, sufferings, and death of Christ, the Divine Author and Procurer of salvation, and immortal life, which is the grand theme of the gospel.

The gospel then is the intervention of Jesus Christ to save lost and perishing sinners. It is the revelation of the rich and free grace of God towards them, in giving his only-begotten Son to die for their transgressions, and in raising him again from the dead for their justification, that whosoever believeth on him, might not perish, but have everlasting life. The gospel embraces several important facts : —

1. *The Necessity of salvation.* This arises from man's ruin. How graphically is this stated throughout the Scriptures! And without a knowledge of this great fact, the gospel can never be fully understood, and its blessings never really enjoyed. It is the struggle with disease that impels us to apply to a physician, and to adopt his prescriptions. It is a sense of ruin that causes us to ask for help from our fellows.

2. *The Accomplishment of salvation by Jesus Christ.* Hence, "when the fulness of time was come," etc. Gal. iv. 4, 5. He entered into the circumstances of sinners; he obeyed the law; he made a proper atonement for sin; he met all the claims of Divine justice; he died for the ungodly: and brought in an everlasting righteousness, to cover and adorn the filthy souls of sinners.

The obedience of Christ, the sacrifice of Christ, — his whole work, was acceptable to his Father. "This is my beloved Son, in whom I am well pleased." Matt. iii. 17; xvii. 5. This is the record that God hath given to us, eternal life; and this life is in his Son. 1 John v. 11. The truth of this testimony he hath demonstrated by raising him from the dead, and giving him glory at his own right hand in the heavens, thereby declaring him to be the Son of God with power. Rom. i. 4.

3. *That it is the gracious will of Christ that this gospel should be preached to the nations for the obedience of faith.* Hence he commissioned his disciples to preach the gospel to every creature. Faith is the means by which we receive Christ. A firm belief of the truth — the love of it in our hearts — and reliance upon it by our souls. Mark xvi. 15, 16.

Previous to this commission, the knowledge of the true God was, in a great measure, confined to the Jews. Christ confined his own labours to the lost sheep of the house of Israel, and prohibited his disciples from going among the Gentiles. But now the happy time was come, when that great mystery, the calling of the Gentiles, should be unfolded; when the partition wall, which separated Israel from all the world was to be broken down, and all former distinctions for ever to cease, that in Christ Jesus there might be "neither Greek nor Jew, circumcision nor uncircumcision, barbarian, Scythian, bond, nor free; but Christ be all, and in all" sorts of people.

II. Its EXCELLENCY. "*The glorious gospel.*" All the plans and works of God are glorious, in proportion as they are marked by the impress of the Divine perfections. "Thus "the heavens declare his glory," etc. —— The gospel is glorious, because

1. It exhibits all the perfections of Deity. Creation displays his wisdom, power, majesty, and goodness; Providence also proclaims these attributes; but the gospel proclaims in addition what Nature and Providence cannot do, — the perfection of forgiving love; and in this we see the rich grace of God to a polluted, perishing world.

All these perfections appear in harmony. In some things,

there may be only one or two of God's attributes displayed, as his justice, when he executes judgment, or his patience when he bears long with sinners. But how shall God equally display his compassion and justice? Can he save the souls of sinners while punishing their sin? Can the curse of the broken law be executed, and yet the blessings of Divine love be poured down on the malefactor? Yes; go to Bethlehem — to Calvary, and learn the wondrous method by which God can be just, and yet the justifier of him that believeth in Jesus. The wrath — the curse falls upon the Saviour — the blessings are showered upon the transgressor. Hence "Christ loved the church, and gave himself for it." See also Isa. liii; Rom. iii. 24—26; v. 6, 7, 8, etc., etc. Then Christ is the substitute, the Surety for sinners. In his humiliation — in his ignominious death, a just and merciful God has had regard to the claims of his justice, while the way has been opened for the free efflux of mercy and salvation to the very persons who have sinned. "Glory to God in the highest," etc.

The perfections of God are seen more distinctly in some things than in others. His power is more visible in a sun than in a glow-worm — in a mountain than in a mole-hill — in a sea than in a brook. —— Can the Deity give a higher demonstration of his love than in the gift of Christ, and the atonement of the cross? Heavy judgments have been inflicted on men, but all such inflictions are limited by the objects on whom they fall. —— But in the sufferings of Christ for sin, there is a manifestation of justice and purity greater than has been or could be, in the sufferings of all created beings put together. When God visits created beings with his wrath, limits must necessarily be set — but in the case of Christ, we see all the vials of wrath poured out — all the fires of the Divine vengeance lighted up — all the energies exerted with which an omnipotent arm could strike. And how great must have been the love that submitted, — how great the power, which, in spite of all this, could obtain a complete victory, and take his seat at the right hand of the Majesty on high! Look, then, at that cross — you see the bush burning, but not consumed — you see God's attributes signally glorified — you see "Mercy and truth met together, righteousness and peace kissing each other."

2. It is glorious on account of its *perfect adaptation to the circumstances of the sinner*. It is adapted to *remove all his guilt*, and also to give him *complete justification*. 1 John i. 7; Eph. i. 7; Acts xiii. 38, 39. Great is the torment of guilt in the soul of the awakened sinner — terrible are his forebodings of future perdition as the desert of transgression; but when he believes — when he touches the gracious sceptre of Christ, all his sins and guilt are gone — and there comes into his soul the peace which passeth all understanding. Rom. v. 1. —— The Gospel removes all distress arising from *depraved and impure affections and rebellious passions*. So far as attempts are made by any of these to rule, all must be miserable. But when faith is exercised, the love of sin is destroyed — love to holiness is imparted; and as the tyranny of cor-

ruption is destroyed, a foundation is laid for peace and joy. —— It is *a remedy for all the natural evils of life.* For them the gospel furnishes a balm. The sweets of patience, fortitude, humility, heavenly-mindedness, are extracted from the weeds of poverty, trial, and disappointment. Present benefit is derived from present trouble, and the storms of time hurry into the joys of eternity. The evils of life we know must remain, but the gospel converts them into a furnace of purification, and makes them the means of blessedness. And, O glorious gospel of the blessed God, it is a perfect and everlasting remedy for death. It extracts the tyrant's sting; it destroys his power. 1 Cor. xv. 54, 55. It inspires the hope of immortality. —— Then think of its influence on the future. It delivers from "the wrath to come," from "the second death;" from "the blackness of darkness for ever;" from the "bottomless pit;" from "everlasting destruction from the presence of the Lord," etc. —— The body dies; but it shall be raised again. The soul departs, but it departs to heaven, the glorious and prepared habitation for God's elect, and there without sin, sorrow, or weariness, but full of joy and resplendent in glory, it shall reign for ever and ever. Seated around the tree of life amidst the everlasting hills, there is seen the Lamb slain in the midst of the throne, whom the glorified shall see as he is. The sacred fabric of our world displays God's glory — the heavens above furnish proofs of his skill; but in heaven we shall see the King in his beauty — in his essential and mediatorial glory, and gaze on him with ever-increasing rapture and admiration, and love. And while the vision is gratified, shall not the *ear* be blessed? Is there silence in heaven? Are there no tongues, no harps? Now, within the range of Christian experience, our hearts taste of heavenly joy, as in the earthly temple we raise the song of praise. But what shall we hear when the ransomed return with singing to Zion — when the redeemed multitude which no man can number, with a sound louder than that of many thunders, and in celestial music, shall utter the everlasting song—" Worthy is the Lamb that was slain," etc.

All this blessedness man requires, and the gospel profusely supplies him with it. Is not the description therefore correct? "*The GLORIOUS gospel of the blessed God.*"

3. The gospel is glorious, *because all its blessings are freely bestowed.* They are all of grace. Ruined sinners, totally depraved and wretched, ignorant, impure, and perfectly helpless — these could never have merited salvation. Let it then for ever humble the pride of our hearts when it is said, " By *grace* are ye saved." Eph. ii. 8. It is called " the gospel of the grace of God." Acts xx. 24. To gain any earthly distinction, honour, or wealth, there must be merit, worthiness of character, or patronage. —— But behold the riches of Divine grace! Sinners, God's enemies, are raised from the degradation of sin to purity, to union with the church, to heirship with Christ, to crowns and thrones of bliss in heaven. It is the *glorious* gospel.

4. *It is glorious in power.* Called "the power of God unto salvation." Its effects produce astonishment. The gospel is the rod of God's strength. Nothing has ever produced such mighty, such salutary effects. What energy attended its first promulgation. It withstood the most powerful opposition — it surmounted the greatest obstacles — it triumphed over all the policy, and all the power of idolatry and superstition: converted whole nations to a professed acknowledgment of the faith — it produced civilization, science and commerce, and spiritual blessedness wherever it came. In every age it has raised up its witnesses—inspired them openly to profess their love of its doctrines and promises, and solemnly to protest against antichristian errors. After the darkest eclipses, it has burst forth with more vigour and splendour upon the world. And as it was then, so it is now; for "the word of the Lord endures for ever." It converts the most obstinate persecutors, like Saul of Tarsus; it revolutionizes the views, the feelings, and the conduct of all its converts. It does not demand the sword of the magistrate, the aid of philosophy, the charms of eloquence; but operates by what its adversaries term "the foolishness of preaching," combined with the Spirit's influence. Hence M'Laurin, a Scotch Divine, thus eloquently speaks of its power and influence: —

"It melts cold and frozen hearts; it breaks stony hearts; it pierces adamants; it penetrates through thick darkness. How justly is it called marvellous light! 1 Pet. ii. 9. It gives eyes to the blind to look to itself; and not only to the blind, but to the dead! It is the light of life: a powerful light. Its energy is beyond the force of thunder; and it is more mild than the dew on the tender grass.

The cross of Christ is an object of such incomparable brightness, that it spreads a glory round it to all the nations of the earth, all the corners of the universe, all the generations of time, and all the ages of eternity. The greatest actions or events that ever happened on earth, filled with their splendour and influence but a moment of time, and a point of space; the splendour of this great object fills immensity and eternity. If we take a right view of its glory, we shall see it, contemplated with attention, spreading influence, and attracting looks from times past, present, and to come; from heaven, earth, and hell; angels, saints, and devils. We shall see it to be both the object of the deepest admiration of the creatures, and the perfect approbation of the infinite Creator; we shall see the best part of mankind, the church of God, for four thousand years looking forward to it before it happened; new generations yet unborn rising up to admire and honour it in continual succession, till time shall be no more; innumerable multitudes of angels and saints looking back to it with holy transport, to the remotest ages of eternity. Other glories decay by length of time; if the splendour of this object change, it will be only by increasing. The visible sun will spend his beams in process of time, and, as it were, grow dim with age; this object hath a rich stock of beams which eternity cannot exhaust. If saints and angels grow in knowledge, the splendour of this object will be still increasing. It is unbelief that intercepts its beams. Unbelief takes place only on earth — there is no such thing in heaven or in hell. It will be a great part of future blessedness to remember the object that purchased it; and of future punishment to remember the object that offered deliverance from it. It will add life to the beams of love in heaven, and make the flames of hell burn fiercer. Its beams will not only adorn the regions of light, but pierce the regions of darkness. It will be the desire of the saints in light, and the great eye-sore of the Prince of darkness and his subjects."

5. *On account of its unrestricted and boundless nature.* It offers salvation to the vilest of the vile. There are no sins too numerous to forgive, no moral turpitude too extreme to be removed, and no guilt too black to be cancelled. The most filthy sinner's extremity is the gospel's opportunity to save. Hence this gospel was sent to the Jews who crucified Christ, and to all nations, however idolatrous, infamous, and wicked. The gospel is restricted to no nation, to no sex, to no condition, to no age, to no circumstance or rank of human life. It is sent to all nations—to all people. "Go preach the gospel to every creature."

The Gentiles were condemned by the Jews, and accounted as dogs; pride led some civilized nations to regard others as barbarians; and it is true that multitudes of the human family were sunk so low in brutality as scarcely to deserve the name of men. But "preach the gospel to every creature;" make no distinctions of civilized and uncivilized; of white, brown, or black; but go into all nations; into all the world; and wherever you find a human being, however rude, base, or vile, preach my gospel, which is full of mercy for him. "The Spirit and the Bride say, Come," etc., Rev. xxii.

III. THE AUTHOR OF THIS GOSPEL: "*the blessed God.*"

In Scripture we find that all the epithets which are given to God, are given with the greatest appositeness. The gospel is not said to be the gospel of the great, the holy, or the just God, but of the happy or blessed God. The happy God desires to impart happiness to guilty man.

1. The gospel could not have emanated from any other source. It is infinite; the result of infinite contrivance and love. It saves from infinite evil — it exalts to infinite good. An angel, to say nothing about a fallen sinner, could not have produced it.

2. As it is of God, it must be true. It is like him, perfectly pure and disinterested. As one observes; "It could not be the invention of *good men or angels;* for they neither would nor could make a book, and tell lies all the time they were writing, saying, *Thus saith the Lord,* when it was their own invention. It could not be the invention of *bad men or devils,* for they could not make a book which commands all duty, forbids all sin, and threatens it with everlasting punishment."

3. As it is of God and true, it cannot fail to effect all the purposes of his mind. It shall convert men. It shall bless the world, and make the desert to blossom as the rose, etc.

4. The gospel is the greatest manifestation of Divine love. The Scriptures trace all saving benefits to Divine love: "According to his *great love*"—"according to *his mercy* he saved us"—"God so loved the world."——

Lastly. It places those to whom it is preached under great responsibility. "He that believeth," etc.

XXVIII.—CONFORMITY TO DEPARTED SAINTS RECOMMENDED.

"That ye be not slothful, but followers of them who through faith and patience inherit the promises."—HEB. vi. 12.

EVERY duty enjoined by Christianity requires diligence and earnestness. There are multitudes of foes who would ensnare us. The world is alluring, and our treacherous hearts are ever disposed for defalcation.—— Then think of the evils from which we are flying—and the unutterable bliss after which we are aspiring. Perdition is behind us—crowns of immortality are before us—they shine resplendent on the deathless brows of myriads who now inherit the promises, while ten thousand voices call to us from the heavenly inheritance, "O be not slothful," etc.—— Slothfulness is natural to us—but it is inimical to the Christian profession.

I. THE EVIL DEPRECATED; *"that ye be not slothful."*

To be slothful is to be indifferent, negligent, indolent. Slothfulness is an indisposition for, and disinclination to, the performance of duty. It is an evil which characterizes the formal, the lukewarm, and the inactive in the church. It is the very opposite of Christian zeal and activity. Hence Paul said, Phil. iii. 13, 14. See 2 Pet. i. 5, 6.

It is manifested sometimes in the *ordinary pursuits of life*—an indisposition for manual labour. And such indolence is almost sure to extend itself to religious matters.

Slothfulness in religion may be induced by various causes. There may be no real religion, the person being a mere professor. —— Extreme devotedness to the world. There is no slothfulness in secular affairs, though they are but for a season; but great indifferentism about spiritual and eternal concerns.—— From imperfect views of the nature of Christianity, and its high and responsible, yet profitable, duties.—— From the want of self-examination and prayer. For want of this, little progress is made in the Divine life. If such persons attend the means of grace, they come and go like the door on its hinges, but make no progress. Prov. xxvi. 14.

Slothfulness is an impediment to personal and relative happiness. It neglects spiritual exercises which are productive of great enjoyment—it omits important duties which would bless and save the world—it puts the light under a bushel, and the talent into a napkin—it corrodes the best and brightest talents which might act as a lever to raise the world from moral degradation and spiritual death.—— It is an injury to the church. What might the church be, and do, if none were slothful.

Slothfulness is productive of misery. It is so temporally, Prov. xix. 15; Eccl. x. 18; Ezek. xvi. 49. While an idle man is a blank in society, he is also a torment to himself; for as he knows not what it is to labour, so he knows not what it is to enjoy. And spiritually, it disqualifies for the endurance of trial, and the discharge of arduous duties. It magnifies difficulties, and esteems them as most formidable. The slothful plead exemption from whatever requires great exertion and self-denial. With them there is always some lion in the way which deters them from going forth. Prov. xxii. 13; xxvi. 13, 14.

Slothfulness, as intimately connected with unwatchfulness, and productive of spiritual debility, is the cause of spiritual delinquency. "It steals insensibly upon us, and leads on to what is positively evil. No one can begin to be inactive in the ways of God, but he will begin to be active in something else." David's fall, and Samson's destruction, were thus occasioned. Slothfulness, indifference to the means of grace, the neglect of prayer and watchfulness, are the precursors of spiritual delinquency and degradation. We start at some evils of a positive character, as intemperance, deceit, and falsehood, yet think little of slothfulness, though it is the fruitful parent of much evil in this world, and of tribulation and anguish for ever.

II. THE COURSE RECOMMENDED: "*but followers*," etc. This implies two things:—1. That religion is practical, and not merely professional. It is not mere faith in doctrines, and disputation and contention about them, because they please the fancy. It is practical—to be "followers," or imitators of "those who through faith and patience inherit the promises."——2. That success shall follow diligence—that heaven shall be the end of piety, or of faith and patience. Myriads have laboured for God, and received the reward of grace—have fought and conquered, and received the crown. That which has been done before may be done again—that which is now enjoyed in the mansions of bliss may be realized by all who are now exercising faith and patience.—— More particularly, consider,

1. *The Present Inheritance of departed Saints:* "*They inherit the promises.*" This is a conclusive proof of the *immediate* happiness of believers after death. The Apostle refers to the happiness of Abraham, Moses, Joshua, Job, and all others who lived by faith in the promises of God, and especially in the promise of salvation by Christ, and patiently waited, laboured, and suffered in the obedience of faith, and in consequence were at the time the

Apostle wrote the words, inheriting the promises of God respecting their final and everlasting salvation. "Absent from the body, they were present with the Lord."

Promises, the departed saints inherited in this world—promises suited to their every circumstance, and which the love and faithfulness of their God fulfilled—promises which cheered them on to death, and supported them in their dying moments.——— But the principal, the most glorious promises respected heaven, their rest, the scene of ecstatic enjoyment. These promises induced them "to desire a better country, that is, a heavenly one," and now they possess it. The promises of heaven here were the precious buds of grace—there they are the flowers of glory fully expanded, redolent with the fragrance of Immanuel's mediation and the delights of immortality.

Did these promises speak of "an entrance into heaven?" It has been abundantly ministered unto them. They are in full possession of it. They have entered the glorious city, and are sat down with Christ on his throne. Did the promises speak of freedom from sin? They have left all their depravity behind them, and they sin no more, Rev. xxi. 27.— Of exemption from sorrow and death? "God has wiped away all tears from their eyes," etc. Rev. xxi. 4.——Of blessed companionship? "They are come to God the Judge of all," etc. Heb. xii. 22, etc. Of mutual recognition? They sit down with Abraham, etc.—they meet and know their brethren in the Lord.——Of delightful vision? They "see God, and are like him." 1 John iii. 2.——In short, their warfare is finished — they have crossed earth's desert — the voyage of life is over — They are now "for ever with the Lord" — "they shall reign for ever and ever."

> O grandest gift of the Creator,—O largess worthy of a God,—
> Who shall grasp that thrilling thought,—life and joy for ever?
> For the sun in heaven's heaven is Love that cannot change,
> And the shining of that sun is life, to all beneath its beams:
> Who shall arrest it in the firmament,—or drag it from its sphere?
> Or bid its beauty smile no more, but be extinct for ever?
> Yea, where God hath given, none shall take away,
> Nor build up limits to his love, nor bid his bounty cease;
> Wide as space is peopled, endless as the empire of heaven,
> The river of the water of life floweth on in majesty for ever.—TUPPER.

2. *The means by which they instrumentally came to inherit the promises.* "Faith and patience."

(1) *Faith.* Their faith respected Christ, the only way to heaven — the only way to the father. By his precious death they were reconciled to God, and obtained a title to "an inheritance," etc. By his Spirit, given them as the result of faith in Christ, they were renewed, made holy, and meet for that inheritance. Their faith sustained them in difficulties — it laid hold of Omnipotent strength and they conquered all their foes. They "overcame through the blood of the Lamb," etc. Rev. xii. 11. They lived by faith, they walked by faith, they laboured by faith, and they "died in faith; not having received the promises," etc. Heb. xi.

13, etc. Faith was to them as a telescope by which they inspected and contemplated "the end of their faith, even the salvation of their souls;" by which they beheld "the king in his beauty, and the land that is afar off." Thus they were governed, supported, and animated. 1 Pet. i. 3; 2 Cor. iv. 17, 18.

(2) *Patience*. This must "have its perfect work." It is a suffering grace, and must often be called into exercise. Patience implies calmness, fortitude, resignation, and perseverance. It is enduring to the end, though the way be dark and stormy. The primitive saints endured a great fight of afflictions—they took joyfully the spoiling of their goods. See how patiently they endured, and learn to be "patient in tribulation." Heb. x. and xi. Here is the patience of the saints.

The Christian requires the "patience of hope" in all his work of faith, and labour of love." 1 Thess. i. 3. The temptation is to become "weary in well-doing."

In the endurance of affliction. Patience is heaven when compared with irritation, discontent, murmuring, etc. Rom. v. 3—5. Also in the endurance of obloquy for Christ's sake.

In waiting for the fulfilment of the promises. Rom. viii. 23—25; Heb. x. 36. In cases of glorious anticipation of future rest by the afflicted, who ardently long for it. There may be impatience—restlessness to go up and possess the land. But patience says, "All the days of my appointed time," etc.

> Says FAITH, Look yonder,—see the crown
> Laid up in heaven above!
> Says HOPE, Anon it shall be mine;
> I'll wear it soon, says LOVE.
>
> DESIRE doth say, What's there? my crown!
> Then to that place I'll flee;
> I cannot bear a longer stay,
> My rest I fain would see.
>
> But stay, says PATIENCE, wait awhile,
> The crown's for those who fight;
> The prize for those who run the race,
> By faith, and not by sight.
>
> Thus FAITH doth take a pleasing view,
> HOPE waits, LOVE sits and sings;
> DESIRE she flutters to be gone,
> But PATIENCE clips her wings.

3. *The necessity and importance of following their example.* There are three parties whom we are called upon to imitate. First, the *Deity*:—"Be followers of God, as dear children." "Christ also hath left us an example that we should follow his steps." "Let the same mind," etc. Phil. ii. 5. Second, Apostles. Hence Paul exhorts, 1 Cor. xi. 1. Third, Believers, in the text and elsewhere.

To be followers of departed saints, means that we are to follow their excellencies, and avoid their imperfections.——Observe,

(1) We must be acquainted with their history. We shall find that history in the Bible—and in Christian Memoirs and Biographies. There we shall find Christian heroism worthy of imitation.

(2) *Believing Prayer.* Prayer for a disposition and a sufficiency of grace to help us to follow them.

(3) It is *the desire and resolve of a regenerated soul to follow them.*——But sometimes the mind wanders and neglects—is fascinated by the world. Hence the necessity of exhortation. " Be followers."

Follow their *faith and patience*—their *diligence*—their *disinterestedness* and *love*—*self-denial*—*zeal* and *perseverance.* They endured to the end; they inherit the promises.

(4) It is *an honour and a great privilege to follow them.* Look at the wicked—the worldly—what is there about them worth following? Look at departed sinners, who went down to the grave overshadowed with darkness. Who desires to follow them? " Let me die the death of the righteous."

IMPROVEMENT.

1. Be ashamed of, and penitent for past slothfulness.

2. Consider the motive to diligence. Our enemies are not slothful to ruin us—worldly men are not slothful to obtain shadows—our enterprize is vast—time is short—we must give an account.

3. See the excellency of true religion in its course, and in its end.

XXIX.—THE LOVE OF GOD RECIPROCATED.

"We love him, because he first loved us."—1 JOHN iv. 19

THIS language contains two important truths:—First, the love of God, the most wonderful and interesting subject in all theology—the source of a sinner's salvation, and the cause and motive of the believer's love to God. Second, Love to God by those whom God loves, without which no one can have the Divine favour. Pretension and profession, zeal and enthusiasm, sacrifice and benevolence, are all in vain, if the love of God dwell not in the heart, 1 Cor. xvi. 22; xiii. 1, 2, etc. Consider,

I. THE LOVE OF GOD. " *He first loved us.*"

1. *Its antiquity.* The love of God was in operation before the "foundation of the world." See Eph. i. 4—6. Then he foresaw the fall—then he arranged the plan of mercy—the covenant of redeeming love, to be effected by his Son, who is called " the Lamb slain from the foundation of the world." 2 Tim. i. 9, 10; 1 Pet.

THE LOVE OF GOD RECIPROCATED.

i. 2. —— The date of his love was *antecedent to ours*, and even to our existence.

2. *This love was sovereign.* God was under no obligation to love us. He was not dependent upon us for the augmentation of his bliss and glory. As a Sovereign, an offended Sovereign, he might have consumed us in his anger——"but God who is rich in mercy," etc. Eph. ii. 4—9.

3. *The love of God is displayed in Christ.* John iii. 16; 1 John iv. 9, 10. The greatness of this love is seen in the *dignity and glory* of Christ Jesus, the great gift of God—in the *sufferings and death* which he endured—in the *debased and infamous characters* for whom he died—and in the *numerous, rich,* and *eternal blessings* which his mediation secured. Let each of these propositions be duly considered, in order to see the love of God. Each proposition might fill a volume.

4. It has ever been *a love of complacency and delight.* For Christ's sake, God has loved them, and he will love them to the end. They are made "accepted in the Beloved." Eph. i. 6. Believing and reposing on Christ, they are no more regarded as sinners—as God is well pleased with Christ, so believers, who are in Christ, are the delight of God. They are the fruits of the travail of his soul, and are to the praise and glory of his grace.

5. This love is *unchangeable and everlasting.* Man may change, but God's love is immutable. Man's works may end, but God's work is everlasting. Christ shall reign for ever and ever; and of his servants he says, "the glory which thou gavest me, I have given them."

II. THE CHARACTER OF THE CHRISTIAN'S LOVE TO GOD. "*We love him.*"

1. This *love is not natural to man.* The heart is full of enmity to God. Rom. viii. 7, 8. It is not attainable by human influence, as study, education, etc.

2. *It is caused or produced by the love of God.* "We love him, *because he first* loved us." As much as to say, Christian love is produced by God's love, because God's love appointed his Son to lay a foundation for our happiness by the shedding of his blood, and he also has given his Spirit to diffuse that grace in our hearts by which they are formed to every sentiment of gratitude and love. Hence the following observations are appropriate:—

Not that their love is *merely* gratitude for previous benefits, which, abstracted from other exercises of love, would only be a selfish affection, and not at all that holy love, which the law, as written in the hearts of all true Christians, requires: for that love is commanded previous to the consideration of redemption, and our failure in it causes us to need that love of God towards us, of which the apostle was speaking. If the Lord hath not "loved them," before they loved him, "even when they were dead in sin," they must for ever have continued enemies to him. His love suggested the plan, and provided the means of redemption; he revealed to sinners his glorious perfections and abundant mercy, in the Person and work of his Son; he sent his word to declare to sinners this great salvation, and to invite them to partake of it; he regenerated them by his Spirit, and so brought them, by repentance and faith in Christ, into a state of acceptance and reconciliation; and thus he enabled them to love his excellency, to value his favour, to be thankful for his inestimable benefits, and zealous for his glory. As, therefore, his love to them was the original source of their love to him; so, from the latter they might infer the former: if they were sure that they loved God, they might be sure that "he had first loved them," and they ought to take the comfort of the happy change which had been wrought in them, whilst they gave him the whole glory of it. — *Thomas Scott.*

3. *Christian love is influenced by the love of God.* "For the love of Christ constraineth us," etc. 2 Cor. v. 14. The believer looks at the depth of the misery from which it has extracted him, to the dignity and blessedness to which it has raised him; and his heart is touched, and filled with gratitude for God's love to him. He cannot gaze upon the cross of Christ; he cannot think upon his dying love, without a disposition to spend and be spent for him. Therefore the love of God is the *cause* and the *motive* to Christian love.

4. Love to God is *manifested in various ways.* It dwells in the heart, Rom. v. 5. Its internal operation is great and pleasant.

It *boldly professes Christ before the world;* "it maketh not ashamed." Rom. v. 5; Rom. i. 16; 2 Tim. i. 8, 11, 12.

It manifests *anxious solicitude,* and *suitable exertions to advance Christ's kingdom in the world.*

It constrains to *the consecration of our talents to God's service.* Time — money — intellectual endowments — the gift of speech — counsel — prayer and preaching.

It readily *makes sacrifices* when necessary. Witness the self-denial of Paul, Acts xx. 22—24. *Cum multis.*

It is manifested by *loving that which God loves.* As holiness — the people of God — the house of God — communion with God, etc.

5. *Love to God is necessary.* Without it we are wretched indeed. It is necessary to sanctification. Love is a powerful and transforming principle. By constant residence in the mind, the image stamps, and leaves its own resemblance; so that every man is in reality the same with the supreme object of his attachment. —— It is necessary to give pleasure in serving God, otherwise we shall act as slaves.—— It is necessary to render our services acceptable to God; "for where there is first a willing mind, it is accepted according to what a man hath, and not according to what he hath not." This will be found to be the case especially at the day of judgment. Love to God has fruits, and by these, notwith-

standing human infirmity, etc., the believer will be accepted. Matt. xxv. 40.

IMPROVEMENT.

1. Examination. "Lovest thou me?"
2. Rejoice in his love. For this purpose study it closely.
3. Woe to those who love not God.

XXX.—DIVINE FRIENDSHIP IMMUTABLE.

"I will never leave thee, nor forsake thee."—HEB. xiii. 5.

THE spiritual wealth of the Christian is great. God is his portion. All the purposes of the Divine mind, all the arrangements of his grace, and all the promises of his word, immediately concern him. "All things are yours." 1 Cor. iii. 21.——The spiritual wealth of the Christian is immutable. Human circumstances may change—earthly riches may suddenly vanish, but the riches of grace abide; unlike earthly vanities, which are transitory, the promises of God, like himself, are immutable. "The grass withereth; the flower fadeth; but the word of our God shall stand for ever." "I will never leave thee," etc.

These words were first spoken to Joshua, ch. i. 5. They were spoken also by David to Solomon, 1 Chron. xviii. 20.——And they are applicable to God's people in every age. Observe,

I. THIS PROMISE BELONGS TO THE RIGHTEOUS.

God never makes such promises to the wicked. With them he is "angry every day." It is their language, "Depart from us, for we desire not the knowledge of thy ways." "God is not in all their thoughts."——But "the Lord loveth the righteous," Ps. cxlvi. 8, and they are precious in his sight. Isa. xliii. 4; Lam. iv. 2.

"I will never leave thee," etc., means, *Thee* whom I have redeemed and purchased with the precious blood of my Son—*thee* whom I have enlightened to discover thy sinfulness, and the need of my saving power—*thee* whom I have converted, and turned from darkness to light—*thee* whom I have reconciled to myself, and slain the enmity of thy mind, by the blood of my Son, and the power of my Spirit—*thee* whom I have adopted into my family, and whom I have united to myself, and made the heir of eternal life. "I will never leave *thee*," for thou art mine—my property, having been "bought with a price," and whom I regard with infinitely more attachment than a man regards his most costly jewels. Mal. iii. 16.

Intimate then is the *union* of God with his people. It is as intimate as that of the foundation with the superstructure — as the branches of the vine with its root — as the parent with the child — as the bride with the bridegroom. These are some of the figures which show the blessed and endearing union subsisting between God and his people. There is love — almighty love — everlasting love — therefore he says, "I will never leave thee, nor forsake thee."

II. THAT THE DIVINE PRESENCE IS ACTUALLY ENJOYED. "I will never leave thee," implies that he is really with them, and that they have sensible evidence of it. This realization commenced with their conversion. Rev. iii. 20. And this Divine fellowship is constantly enjoyed. He is with his people not only essentially, but graciously, and this indicates the greatness and dignity of the privilege. He encompasses their path — he watches them by day and by night — he keeps all their bones, so that not one of them is broken — he keeps them as in the hollow of the hand — or as the apple of the eye — the very hairs of their heads are all numbered — he gives his angels charge over them, and causes all things to work together for their good.

They have constant communion with God. How beautiful the declaration of Christ! John xiv. 23.——He dwells in their hearts — that is his temple, and sweet are the whispers of his love, and cheering the witness of his Spirit. Their souls are the "abode" of God; and wherever they go, whatever they do, God is with them, and he will never leave, etc.

He is with them in the hour of solitude, and in the busy scenes of life — he is with them at his throne of grace, and in his house, to unveil his beauty, and to display his glory. "I will commune with thee from off my mercy-seat." "Where two or three," etc. Matt. xviii. 20. The Jews have a tradition: "Wheresoever two or three are sitting together, in conference about the law, there the Shekinah will be with them." This is the meaning of the passage quoted; "I am in the midst of them;" as if he had said, The Shekinah shall be there, or there I will be by my dwelling Presence, or special exhibition of myself by signs of blessing and grace. I will pour forth my Spirit to enlighten, to revive and to heal. God then is with his people in a way in which he is present with no other. The judge on the bench is present with the criminal at the bar; in his own house he is present as a father with his family. What a difference betwixt the two! God in his nature and essence is as near the wicked as he is near the righteous, but how great the difference! God is constantly with his people because he takes a special interest in them. That interest is beautifully expressed, Isa. lxii. 3, 4.

III. THE GREATNESS OF THE BLESSING ARISES FROM THE CHARACTER OF THE PROMISER. "*I* will never leave thee."

Who is the Promiser? Not a mere man; not a mighty potentate; not an angel — but God, the Almighty God, the Lord of hosts. God is infinite in wisdom, power, justice, love, and compassion, as his numerous names declare. Come, and behold a glowing constellation of titles which belong to him, and by which the hopes of his people are encouraged amid all the sufferings and conflicts of the desert. He is called Jehovah-sabbaoth, the Lord of hosts, whom he marshals in battle array against the enemies of his church;—Jehovah-repheca, the Lord thy healer;—Jehovah-tsidkenu, the Lord our righteousness;—Jehovah-shammah, the Lord is there;—Jehovah-nissi, the Lord is my banner;—and Jehovah-jireh, the Lord will provide. This is he who says, "I will never leave thee." If a poor person were to say, I will never leave you, you might answer, I value your kindness, but my difficulties are extreme, and your poverty incapacitates you to help me. A rich man might say, I will never leave thee; but his resources may be soon exhausted; and his breath is in his nostrils, and his life but a vapour.——It is very desirable to have the presence of a loving, sympathetic, rich, and powerful friend with us in our journey through life; but how few bearing this character are to be found. Do you want power to help you in time of need? You have it in God. Do you want wisdom to direct? You have it in God. Do you want sympathy? You have it in God. "In their affliction, he was afflicted." Isa. lxiii. 9. Do you want tender affection? You have it in God. "For thy Maker is thy husband," etc. "He knows our frame," etc. See Heb. iv. 15. [amplify.]

Gen. xvii. 7.—*I will establish my covenant, to be a God unto thee.*
I will establish (I thy Friend, Whose truth a world shall see,) A cov'nant time shall never rend, I'll be a God to thee.

Isa. xli. 10.—*Fear thou not, for I am with thee, be not dismayed, for I am thy God.*
Fear not, thou tender trembling saint, I'm near—thy help's divine: Be not dismayed—thou shalt not faint, The Lord of hosts is thine.

Ps. xlviii. 14.—*This God is our God, for ever and ever, and he will be our guide even unto death.*
This God is ours, through life our Friend, Our Guide, through death's dark way; This God is ours, when time shall end In an eternal day.

IV. THE PRESENCE AND LOVE OF GOD ARE IMMUTABLE. "I will *never* leave thee, *nor* forsake thee."

The words are very emphatic. In the original, there are no less than five negatives in the text, and these connected with two verbs and one pronoun twice repeated: Ου μη σε ανω, ουδ' ου μη σε εγκαταλιπω. To give a literal translation is scarcely possible:—"No, I will not leave thee; no, I will not, I will not forsake thee."

The immutability of God is declared by the Scriptures. Jehovah says, "I am the Lord; I change not." See Heb. i. 10—12; xiii. 8; James i. 17. How glorious a perfection is this in connection with the salvation of the soul. God is carrying on his work there, and he will not leave it, but nurture, guard, and defend it, and carry it on till the day of the Lord Jesus, when it will perfectly bloom with immortality. Fix thine eye, Christian, on the cross of Jesus, and "behold the blood of the covenant which the Lord thy God maketh with thee." There is given the most perfect demonstration, that "though heaven and earth shall pass away, one jot or one tittle shall not pass from the covenant of grace till all shall be fulfilled." Place the fullest reliance on the promises of God; they are yea and amen to them that believe. Delight in his mercies, for they are *sure* mercies. "Faithful is he who has promised, who also will do it." The mountain may be removed from its place; the rock, crumbling, cometh to nought; states and empires may pass away, the great globe dissolve, yet "God willing to show to the heirs of promise the immutability of his counsel, hath confirmed it by an oath," etc. Heb. vi. 17, 18.—— Observe further,

1. God will not desert his people *on account of their earthly meanness and obscurity.* Poverty will not drive him away. He has a special regard to the poor. ("He shall judge the poor of the people;" "he shall stand at the right hand of the poor;" "he will maintain the right of the poor.") How different the conduct of God from that of man! The wealthy man reduced to poverty is deserted by his former associates.——But God "hath chosen the poor of this world, rich in faith." James ii. 5. To the poor believer he says, "I will never leave thee."

2. God will not desert his people *on account of human infirmity.* When the body is weak and feeble—when the nerves are relaxed and tremble at a breeze—amid the infirmities of old age, God says, I will never leave thee.——"And even to your old age I am he." Isa. xlvi. 4. Under such circumstances, man sometimes longs to cast off dependants—they are felt to be a burden——but that is a time for Jehovah's special love and care.

3. God will not leave his people *in the time of spiritual conflict.* When they struggle with the sins which so easily beset them — when Satan comes in like a flood—when the world smiles and frowns, God is present to be their strength and shield against all their enemies. He is present to supply all their wants; to renew their vigour; to sustain their yielding constancy; to deliver them from the unequal contest, and to bless them with returning hope, peace, and safety. When their hearts wander from God, when they fall, God is there to lift them up. When weeping in the mire of sin, God says, "I will never leave thee."——

4. God will not desert his people *in the time of sickness and death.* Hear his own promise, "When thou passest through the waters,"—Isa. xliii. 2; Job v. 17—19. When they are chastened by disease, and are apparently near the gates of the grave, God says, "I will never leave thee." He is there to bear up the fainting heart, to rebuke or sanctify disease for the accomplishment of his gracious purposes.——When they have lost their parents, or their children; when they are forsaken by former friends and companions; when the world begins to seem to them a desert, and life to be a burden, God is then at hand, their Father and everlasting Friend; and will be better to them than sons or daughters.——And when they themselves come to be dissolved,— amid all the solemnities of the last struggle, God will whisper to

their souls, "I will never leave thee"—the time of dying shall be the time of triumph. Ps. xxiii. 4; 1 Cor. xv. 55.

He will not forsake their bodies *in the tomb*. He watches over their dust; he is the Guardian of their graves, and will never leave them till the morning of the resurrection, when he shall from those earthly clods raise up their bodies, and fashion them like unto the glorious body of Christ. Though their bodies may slumber in the dust for a thousand years, yet he has appointed the redeeming time, and will remember them.

And O, glorious thought, he will be with them, and they shall be with him for ever in heaven. There will be no apprehension of Divine desertion in the land of immortality. "So shall we be for ever with the Lord."

IMPROVEMENT.

1. The love of Jehovah exceeds all human love. "A friend that sticketh closer than a brother."
2. Walk worthy of the great and gracious presence of God.
3. Realize the Divine presence in every scene—and despond not of the future. "I will never."——

XXXI.—THE GOSPEL TRUMPET.

"And it shall come to pass in that day, that the great trumpet shall be blown, and they shall come which were ready to perish in the land of Assyria, and the outcasts in the land of Egypt, and shall worship the Lord in the holy mount at Jerusalem."—Isa. xxvii. 13.

THE text and the preceding verse predict the restoration of the Jews after the captivity, and under that typical event, the recovery of Israel from their present dispersions.——Thus they who had been slaves in the land of Assyria, and many of those of the ten tribes, and the outcasts who had taken refuge in Egypt, returned to rebuild the temple, and worship God in Jerusalem.——But the preaching of the gospel seems especially to be intended by the *blowing of the great trumpet*. The vail shall eventually be taken from Israel's heart—they shall be brought to acknowledge, and to believe in Christ, and worship God in spirit and truth.

I. THE PERONS FOR WHOSE BENEFIT THE GREAT TRUMPET SHALL BE BLOWN; those "ready to perish."

All men by nature are in a perishing state. They are "outcasts," and ready to perish. They are said to be "lost," "dead," in a state of "condemnation," and "ready to perish." Hence the gift of the Saviour is opposed to their condition; John iii. 14—16. They are ready to perish, because,

1. *They are transgressors*, and *under the curse.* Rom. iii. 19; Gal. iii. 10.

2. *They are impure*, and "without holiness no man shall see the Lord."

3. *They are exposed to the wrath of God.* They are called "children of wrath," Eph. ii. 2, 3. They are laying up wrath against the day of wrath.

4. *They are ready to perish every moment.* Their perishing is suspended on the death of the body, which may take place suddenly. There is but a step betwixt them and death. Death will introduce them to their offended Sovereign and Judge, who will give them the due reward of their deeds.

5. *They are helpless.* They can devise no plan — invent no remedy, to save themselves. They are insensible to their danger. Ready to perish and feel it not.

II. THE GRACIOUS REMEDY. "The great trumpet shall be blown."

The allusion here is to the Jewish trumpets. A trumpet was used in the promulgation of the law, called "the voice of the trumpet," and "the sound of the trumpet," Ex. xix. 16; Heb. xii. 19.* There was also, under the law, a memorial of blowing trumpets, to call the people to the solemn day of expiation, Lev. xxiii. 24, which was a type of the preaching of the gospel, and a declaration of the remission of sins by Christ's atoning sacrifice. But the principal solemnity connected with the blowing of trumpets was the proclamation of the jubilee, Lev. xxv. 7—9, when liberty was proclaimed throughout all the land, v. 10, and which was fulfilled in the ministry of Christ, Isa. lxi. 1, 2. To this the Psalmist alludes, Ps. lxxxix. 15. See Luke iv. 18. Thus was the gospel introduced into this world. Angels from heaven sang with rapture, as they proclaimed the birth of the Saviour. Jesus and his disciples itinerated through Palestine, proclaiming peace and joy to the people. And all ministers are ambassadors for God, etc.

1. What does the gospel trumpet announce?

(1) It announces *the mission of Christ.* It utters the "faithful saying," etc. 1 Tim. i. 15. It proclaims the death of Christ, as the needed atonement, appropriate to man's spiritual exigencies, and acceptable to God. Rom. v. 6—8

---

* It was not a real trumpet, but only the sound of one formed in the air by the ministry of angels, and rising to a degree of terror. So it waxed louder and louder to indicate the nearer approach of God; thus it was of great use in that solemnity. It had a threefold use, and a double signification: it was to intimate the approach of God, prepare the minds of men to wait on him with becoming reverence. It was to summon the people to appear before him as their Lawgiver and Judge; for on the sound of the trumpet, Moses brought forth the people to meet God, and he stood at the nether part of the mount. It was also the signal of the promulgation of the law with its penal sanction; for immediately upon the sound of the trumpet God spake unto them. And it was a type of the judgment-day, when the trumpet shall sound, etc. 1 Cor. xv. 52; 1 Thess. iv. 16.

(2) The Jubilee-trumpet announced *the remission of debts.* Those who had become poor, unable to pay their creditors, were to be free from the obligation. And has not Christ obeyed and honoured the law? Has he not endured the penalty? Yes, and therefore it is proclaimed, "Be it known," etc. Acts xiii. 38. 39; Rom. viii. 1, 33, 34. This is *liberty to the captives.*

(3) The jubilee-trumpet announced a *feast with abundant provision.* Lev. xxv. 19. The gospel trumpet proclaims a feast of fat things—the "unsearchable riches of Christ," "spiritual blessings in heavenly places," "the bread of life," and "the water of life," "wine and milk, without money and without price." It is compared to a great supper — to a royal feast. Isa. xxvi. 6—8; Matt. xxii. 1—4.

(4) The jubilee-trumpet announced *the restoration of forfeited possessions.* Mortgaged estates and possessions were to return to their original owners. See Lev. xxv. 25, etc. The gospel-trumpet proclaims the restoration of all the blessings man has forfeited by sin. Or rather it gives richer and more enduring blessings in their place:

"In Christ the tribes of Adam boast
More blessings than their father lost."

The Divine love and favour were lost; they are now restored. So with regard to the Divine image, sonship, renewal of nature, fellowship with God, and a Paradise infinitely more glorious than the first.

2. Why is it called a great trumpet?

When God sends a message from heaven, we may be sure there is something great, something extraordinary about it. When he delegates angels, as in the case of the law, and of the gospel; when he utters his voice; and specially inspires and ordains men to declare his will, we may be sure the purport of that will is great and glorious. —— Never did earthly trumpets announce tidings so significant, joyful, and glorious as the tidings of salvation proclaimed by the gospel-trumpet to fallen humanity.

The Gospel may be called great,

(1) Because it delivers from infinite evil. —— (2) Because it is the product of infinite love. (3) Because it gives the possession of infinite good—here—and for ever. (4) Because it procured salvation by an infinitely great and glorious Agent, the Son of God, who for man's redemption paid an infinite price. (5) because its influence on earth and eternity is great.

Thus the gospel-trumpet publishes *great things.* It is properly called a *great light,* a *great salvation,* and the *glorious gospel of the blessed God.*

"Never did a message of such great importance salute the ear of man. Never was any report of equal magnitude with this, — " Jesus Christ came into the world to save sinners." The news of a decisive battle, of a glorious victory, of a general peace, may be great news, and rouse a whole nation for a time; but compared with the great events reported by the gospel, they are trifles light as air, and trivial as the sports of children. The great things of the gospel affect, not a few individuals only, but all the race of Adam; they relate not only to the present concerns of a single generation, but to the everlasting interests of every succeeding age until the end of time. Much of that intelligence which inquisitive persons are anxious to receive and to communicate, is of no real consequence to them; but the truths of the gospel are inseparably connected with our dearest interests; our life, our soul, and our everlasting all, are involved in them." — *Burder.*

"O astonishing redemption, in which I see the Father in his manifold wisdom, Jesus in love that passeth knowledge, and the Spirit in grace, which defies all the power of hell to resist it, or to make it void. I might, in proof that the redemption of the soul is great and precious, appeal to the groans of the lost, doomed never to share it; to the songs of the blessed, who can find no strains too high to celebrate a Redeemer's worth, and the glory of redemption. Every era of the world hath its objects to applaud, and to cast into the shade the brilliant deeds of former generations; but the redemption of the soul shines with unfading lustre from age to age; and when the records of human glory shall have perished utterly, it will fill heaven with its wonders, and immortals with its bliss, and eternity with its praise."—*Belfrage.*

III. THE INSTRUMENTALITY OF THE GOSPEL DISPENSATION. It "shall be blown."

It is *necessary for this trumpet to be blown*. Men are perishing — the feast of spiritual blessings is "ready"— the finished work of Christ is adapted to meet the wants of dying sinners. Then let the great trumpet be blown; for "how shall they hear without a preacher?" etc. Rom. x. 14, 15.

It is the *will of God that the Gospel trumpet should be blown*. Luke xxiv. 45—48; Mark xvi. 15, 16.

But who are to be the instruments—who are to sound this trumpet?

It was *first blown by angels*, who announced the incarnation, Luke i. ii. And though their visible ministration ceased on the ascension of Christ and after the ministration of the Apostles, yet angels regard the gospel with the most profound interest. They "desire to look into these things."

The trumpet is *to be blown by men*—men of like passions as their fellows—but men of piety, of good intelligence, mighty in the Scriptures, and of ready and acceptable speech. Men disinterested, zealous, active, watching for souls, as those that must give an account.——Thus Christ commissioned his Apostles to preach the gospel—and he has never ceased since to raise up ministers, teachers, missionaries, and heralds, to blow the gospel-trumpet, Eph. iii. 6—10; iv. 11.

How is this trumpet to be blown? In *accordance with the Divine will;* not merely to please the ear, or to elicit applause—*solemnly and seriously*, in matters of life and death—*affectionately*, yearning over souls lost in sin—*faithfully*, not giving an uncertain sound, (1 Cor. xiv. 8.) "warning every man," etc.—*courageously*, fearing no foe—and *perseveringly*—depending upon God.

If the gospel be thus preached, *God will crown it with success.* He has ever done so, and will continue to do so, till the end of time. It is his own ordinance—and the trumpet shall be blown in spite of all opposition from Satan and his emissaries. Infidels labour to stop the publication—but Christ says, Blow on; for, "lo! I am with you alway," etc.

IV. ITS POWERFUL INFLUENCE; "*they shall come, and shall worship the Lord.*"

1. *They shall come to Christ.* Isaiah says, "Unto him shall men come." Christ said, "Come unto me"—Peter says, "To whom coming," etc. 1 Pet. ii. 4.

They shall come to him with conviction of their need of Christ—of his adaptedness to their wants—of the fulness and freeness of his grace.

They shall come to him believing that he is able to save, and will save them. "As Moses lifted up," etc.

2. They shall *come into his church to worship and serve God.* "Shall worship the Lord in the holy mount of Jerusalem." They shall "be added to the church," and participate in all its services. ——They shall become worshippers of God, praying to him on all occasions. They shall come to be zealous and active for the prosperity, peace, and glory of Zion.

3. They shall come to be glorified by Christ at the day of judgment. Then "the trumpet shall sound, and the dead shall be raised."

IMPROVEMENT.

Have you felt the need of Christ, as one "ready to perish?"

What a great blessing is the proclamation of the gospel.

Let those who have come be thankful. "Show forth the praises," etc.

XXXII.—GOD THE PORTION OF HIS PEOPLE.

"The Lord is my portion, saith my soul; therefore will I hope in him."—LAM. iii. 24.

"MEN of the world have their portion in this life;" but how poor and mean it is! Compare it with the portion of the righteous; they can say, "this God is our God for ever and ever; he shall be our guide even unto death." Think of his perfections—his immensity—his love—his unchangeableness—his vast dominions — his eternity: — how rich and glorious a portion has the Christian! — The sinner may be rich in worldly substance; but it is only for a moment. He may have houses and land; but it is not like "the building above," etc. His estate may be large; but it is not "the inheritance which is incorruptible," etc. He may have abundance of gold and silver; but not the Pearl of Great Price, the fairest among ten thousand.

I. GOD IS THE PORTION OF HIS PEOPLE. *"The Lord is my Portion.*

The word "portion" signifies lot or inheritance, in allusion to the allotments of Israel in the land of Canaan. Ps. xvi. 5, 6, which are called their portion. Ps. cxix. 57; cxliii. 5.—— The word refers to the blessings and enjoyments of life — domestic relationships, Eccles., ix. 9. But God is superior. Ps. iv. 6, 7; lxiii. 3. —— Observe,

1. *By sin man is deprived of God as a portion.* As God is infinitely pure, he cannot behold the sinner with complacency—there can be no communion. "God is angry with the wicked every day." Eph. iv. 8.

2. It implies the *appointment of a Mediator, and a covenant of grace through him.* "God was in Christ reconciling," 2 Cor. v. 19. —— Through Christ, God becomes the portion of his people.

3. It implies *the acceptance of this portion by faith in the Mediator.* This is always preceded by a deep sense of spiritual wretchedness without this portion. Faith is called "receiving him," and he is freely offered. John i. 12. Everything inferior is relinquished.

4. *Adoption.* The outcast, for Christ's sake, is taken in — the Prodigal returns, and is accepted. God is the father of his people, and as such he gives to his children, whom he infinitely loves, an interest in all the blessings of creation, providence, and grace; not an ordinary interest, but a special and peculiar one. They are called "heirs of God." Rom. viii. 14—17. They enjoy all good in the enjoyment of God, as every ray of perfection beams forth from him, and must be resolved into him. It is as impossible not to have *all* if we enjoy God, as it is for us to conceive of any perfection that is not involved in the idea of an infinite Being.

(1) Consider some of *the blessings of this portion.* A participation in the gracious operations of the Holy Trinity for the salvation of his church. Their Father loved them, and planned their redemption. The Son became their Ransom. The Holy Spirit dwells in them with all his quickening, renovating, teaching, and comforting influences.

An interest in all the perfections of the Deity. Wisdom to guide — grace to forgive, etc. etc.

All the promises — all his gifts and graces — all the ordinances and privileges of his house — all his guidance — his angels — his creatures — this world, as our sojourning place, and his heaven as our inheritance and home, are the great blessings of the Christian's portion.

(2) *The character of their portion.*

It is *appropriate* to their circumstances — it is suited to man's spiritual nature. Material objects may please, but they can never perfectly satisfy. It is suited to man's spiritual wants as a sinner. —— God in Christ alone can meet our case.

It is an *all-sufficient* portion. It includes everything that is great and good in God. "I am God Almighty, or the All-sufficient God." Gen. xvii. 1. There is enough in God to satisfy all the wants of an immortal soul. —— God is *infinite* in every excellency and happiness, and therefore he must be a *satisfying portion.* There is so much blessedness, and wealth, and glory in this portion, as to leave no room for monopoly, any more than for the sun or the ocean, whose fulness is not diminished by diffusion.

It is an *unmixed portion.* In this world there is a mixture of bitter with sweet, of evil with good, of deformity with beauty, and of pain with pleasure. If you pluck the rose, you encounter the thorn — if you extract the honey, it may be mixed with gall. —— But God is pure — light — bliss, and in him is no darkness at all. And he will be for ever pure, etc.

It is a *secure portion.* All earthly portions are insecure. Wealth, health, friends, and life are transitory. "We have no abiding city here. Adversity may blast our prospects, death may terminate our career, but if our faith be in God, our treasure is secure, and no mutations of earth can affect it. God our portion is immutable. Matt. vi. 20; Col. iii. 3; Mal. iii. 6; James i. 17; Heb. i. 19, 20; Rom. viii. 35.

This satisfying portion is always increasing in its possession and enjoyment. God cannot change, but our possession and enjoyment of him can be augmented.——How unlike this are all other possessions. The enjoyments of time perish in the using, they grow less by use, as every repetition of an echo is less and less till it falls into silence. While we grasp them, like snow they melt away. But believers are interested in the love of God, which, like a mighty river, enlarges its channel by constant running. There is no mortality in the spiritual life of the soul. The seed of grace, though small as a grain of mustard seed, shall spring upward. Sown and watered by the blessed Spirit, and warmed by the Sun of Righteousness, it must grow up for the harvest of glory.

It is an *everlasting portion.* Gen. xv. 1. —— My life begins on earth — death does not destroy it — it will be coeval with eternity. I therefore need a portion that is commensurate with the whole of my existence, and God himself alone is that portion. —— This is no transient good. When this sun rises upon my soul, it is the pledge of an eternal day.

Such is the common portion of all the saints, however they may vary in temporal, or intellectual endowments. It belongs to the poor widow, to Lazarus covered with sores at the rich man's gate, to the thief on the cross, as well as to the rich, the great, the honourable.

II. GOD'S PEOPLE ARE INWARDLY CONSCIOUS OF THE FACT. "*Saith my soul.*"

This is an internal witness—the voice of the soul. It is the result of Divine renovation, adoption into God's family, and conformity to God. It is the work of God speaking within—or rather the "witness of the Spirit," assuring the believer, by impressions on his soul, that he is a child of God, that Christ loved him, and gave himself for him, and that he is reconciled to God. This blessed doctrine is taught, Rom. viii. 14—16; Gal. iv. 6; 1 John iv. 13; 2 Cor. iii. 3. "We know that we are of God, because he hath given us the earnest of his Spirit in our hearts," 2 Cor. i. 22; v. 5. The Spirit excites to self-investigation, by which the believer discovers

That he has been divinely changed. In heart and life he is not what he once was. Marvellous change!

That he has been changed by Christ from the guilt and condemnation of sin—he has low views of himself, but exalted views of Christ.

That his affections and desires centre in God as the only Fountain of perfect bliss. He desires to know more of him — to commune more with him.

He feels God to be his portion, as the effect of Sovereign, rich, and unmerited grace to the chief of sinners — sees such a fulness and freeness in it as to preclude all doubt about Divine acceptance.

His conduct corresponds with the greatness of his privilege. God is his portion. Should the child of a king demean himself? —— But the "heir of God, and joint heir with Christ," orders his conversation as becometh the gospel. —— These evidences assure him that God is his portion.

"There are two senses in which Christians are able to use this language. For surely, first, you can say, *you hope* he is your God. This hope may have to war with numerous doubts and fears, but still you would not give it up for a thousand worlds. I may not at present be able to give you full relief; but then it ascends to the throne of grace, makes you familiar with the foot of the cross, concerning which you can say,—

> Should worlds conspire to drive me thence,
> Moveless and firm this heart should lie;
> Resolv'd, (for 'tis my last defence,)
> If I must perish, there to die.

This hope is like laying hold of a bough, just sufficient to keep your head above water, to preserve you from sinking, till some more effectual assistance be brought to extricate you. It is like a ray of light thrown athwart the darkness, just sufficient to show you that it is the darkness of the chamber, and not the darkness of hell in which you are placed.

And there is another sense in which this language can be used; you can say that he is your God by *preference and submission.* The ambassadors of a certain nation applied to the Romans to be admitted as their allies. They were refused: then, said they, "We will be your subjects, for we will not be your enemies." Is not this the case with you? You can say, "Lord, I am not my own; I will not be for another Lord; I am thine — save me! If thou refuse to acknowledge the relation, (and I deserve to be refused as a friend,) O make me as one of thy hired servants. Lord, what wilt thou have me to do?" Christians, you are wishing to say, "*O my God!*" Why, you *have* said it; and if the preceding language be sincere, you have effectually said the Lord is your God and portion, and therefore you may hope in him." — *Pearls of Great Price.*

III. THE INFLUENCE OF THIS PORTION: "*therefore will I hope in him.*" In most trials we can derive but little hope from any other source. All earthly refuges are of no value.

It was the refuge of Jeremiah as he wept over the captivity of God's people. They had lost their privileges, their property, their liberty, and their friends, by famine and the sword, and every earthly hope was utterly destroyed. But he consoles himself; "the Lord is my portion," etc.

"I will hope in him"

For sustaining grace. In every season of adversity and darkness, whether national, personal, or relative. "The Lord reigneth, let the earth be glad." I will trust him when I cannot see him or trace him. Isa. l. 10; li. 3.

"An able seaman," says Mr. Cecil, "once said to me, 'In fierce storms we have but one resource; we keep the ship in a certain position; we cannot act in any way but this: we fix her head to the wind, and in this way we weather the storm.'" This is a picture of the Christian; he endeavours to put himself in a certain position. He says, My hope and my help are in God; he is faithful. The man who has learnt this piece of heavenly navigation, shall weather the storms of time and eternity.

For *support and energy in serving God.* "Without me, ye can do nothing." "As thy day is, so shall thy strength be." See Isa. xli. 10; 2 Cor. xii. 9.

For *triumph over all my foes.* When Satan comes in like a flood — when the world allures — when the wicked revile — when my heart rebels. Rom. viii. 37.

In *the season of lonely solitude.* When lover and friend are gone down to the grave, and mine acquaintance to their final home. "I will not leave you comfortless, I will come unto you." John xiv. 18.

In *prospect of my own dissolution,* "I will hope in him," for he alone can save me.

For *my safe and triumphant admission to heaven.* "Thou shalt guide me by thy counsel," etc.

IMPROVEMENT.

Admire the condescension of God in becoming the portion of sinners.

"Trust in him at all times, ye people, pour out your hearts to him; God is a refuge for us."

XXXIII.—ATTACHMENT TO GOD'S HOUSE.

"One thing have I desired of the Lord, that will 1 seek after: that I may dwell in the house of the Lord all the days of my life, to behold the beauty of the Lord, and to enquire in his temple."—Ps. xxvii. 4.

ATTACHMENT to God's house—delight in the service of God characterized David throughout his life——it was an evidence of his piety.——This caused him to triumph over his enemies, ver. 1 —3. The value of God's service is known and felt when we are deprived of it.—— David was now an exile from his country, and pursued with savage fury by Saul, and that banishment caused him to value and long for God's house.——It was not military prowess that now attracted him; for he had been a great commander; it was not heroism and victory in battle that now attracted him; for he had conquered hosts of enemies;—it was not the splendours of royalty that now attracted him; for he had been anointed king of Israel. The "house of the Lord" with its glorious service, its typical reference to Christ, and the Shekinah, the symbol of the Divine manifestation, and his high enjoyment there, had supreme attractions for him.

I. THE OBJECT OF DAVID'S ANXIOUS SOLICITUDE: "THE HOUSE OF THE LORD."

By this expression he refers to the tabernacle of the Lord, where his ordinances were administered, which were types of the promised Messiah and his salvation, means of grace to believers, and acts of worship to God.——This tabernacle was succeeded by Solomon's temple, and that by another whose very foundations were ploughed up. Matt. xxiv. 2.——Well might Christ say, John iv. 21—24.

God's house is the universe. He is confined to no place; he fills heaven and earth—yet he has a *peculiar* dwelling-place on earth, and he also dwells in heaven—he dwells with the church militant, and the church triumphant.

The house of the Lord, or the church of God, is a congregation of converted and believing persons. Eph. ii. 19—22; 1 Tim. iii.

15. "Christ as a Son was faithful over his own house, whose house are we." See 1 Pet. ii. 4, 5.

It is called the house of the Lord because,

1. *God is the Proprietor of it.* It has been planned and built by his gracious purpose and power.

2. *He provides it with every thing needful for its comfort and safety—its honour and glory.* His gospel—its ministration—the influence and gifts of the Spirit.——He secures its safety, Isa. xxxiii; 29; liv. 17.

3. *Because he resides in it.* "The Lord loveth the gates of Zion," etc. "This is my rest," etc. Ps. lxviii. 15.

II. THE NATURE OF HIS SOLICITUDE.

1. *Permanent residence in the house of the Lord.* "That I may dwell," etc.

To dwell in the house of the Lord with God's people implies *Divine assimilation*—having passed from death to life like them—believed in Christ like them. Such affinity is absolutely necessary. It also implies

Union of sentiment. "Can two walk together except they be agreed?"

Social enjoyment or Christian fellowship. "Then they that feared the Lord." Matt. iii. 16.

Oneness of purpose. Entering the church of God with a desire and a resolve to be a fellow-labourer with the saints. "Go work in my vineyard." To do it willingly—from a principle of love.

He desired *a permanent residence.* "All the days of my life." Convinced that there was the greatest felicity—the highest honour and dignity.——What does the worldly man say of his wealth, his honours, and his pleasures? "Let me enjoy them all the days of my life!" And yet they are but vanity, because uncertain and fleeting. Well then may the Christian say, "That I may dwell," etc. Let me be associated with the most excellent of the earth — let me be a door-keeper in the house of my God, rather, etc. — let me be connected with Zion and all its glorious services, rather than be the servant of Satan, and the devotee of the world.—— And when death comes, let me be found a worshipper of God, among the chosen, one of the "royal priesthood," etc. — to be removed from the service of God below to the service of God in heaven.

A pillar in thy temple fixed,
To be removed no more.

2. *The design of his residence there.*

(1) *To behold the beauty of the Lord.* The services of the Jewish temple were beautiful; they were typical of gospel times. From those typical things, the pious Jews looked to "the ministration of the Spirit which exceeded in glory the ministration of condemnation." We possess the full manifestation of that glory which they "beheld through a glass darkly."——*His beauty,* or his

grandeur and glory are seen in his works; Ps. xix. 1, 2. But in his temple by the mirror of his word, there is a more glorious manifestation. —— The beauty of the Divine perfections — of his purposes of grace and mercy — the beauty of Christ's love, teaching, and example — the beauty of Christ's finished work — the beauty of the robe of righteousness, etc. This beauty is transforming. 2 Cor. iii. 18.

Though in our places of worship now, no cedars diffuse their fragrance, or sun-beams reflect from burnished gold; though we have no priests arrayed in costly vestments, nor clouds of incense wave around us — yet in the full revelation of the gospel, in the more abundant influence of the Spirit, and in the bright hope of immortality, we behold a beauty which far surpasses the beauty of the ancient temple.

In the temple, Christians have seen God as they never did before — have had joys which they never had elsewhere, etc.

(2) *To inquire in his temple.* Under the Old Testament economy, the Divine will was manifested in various ways, particularly by the Urim and Thummim. —— The Heathen inquired of their oracles, but they were vanity.

In the house of God now his word directs us—his Spirit teaches us — his ministers and his people answer our inquiries. It is the house of prayer, and we *inquire of God* in all our difficulties.

3. The *Ardour and intensity of his zeal.* "One thing," etc.

(1) He regards it as *pre-eminent.* "One thing." Above every thing else, and before every thing else. It is above all my military exploits, battles, and victories — above all earthly grandeur and enjoyment — above all my future royalty, etc. "One thing;" it is the most valuable to me — that on which my heart and purpose are fixed.

(2) *He prays for it.* "Desired of the Lord." To give a spiritual appetite for the duties of the sanctuary — and a moral fitness for church fellowship. By his providence to place my local habitation convenient to the sanctuary — to give me bodily health and intellectual vigour. To preserve me from being drawn away from God's house by the enchantments of earth.——

(3) *Exertion with prayer,* otherwise prayer would be but mockery. "That will I seek after." My wealth shall not prevent me from mingling with the poor of God's flock — I will mortify pride — I will make earthly things subordinate; they shall not have a greater claim than the service of God.——I will not love ease and worldly association better. I will not magnify the imperfections of the church into obstacles to my dwelling in the house of the Lord. I will have charity, etc. 1 Cor. xiii.

IMPROVEMENT.

1. The text affords a test of our religion. Do we prefer the service of God to every thing else? Can we say, "One thing," etc.

2. Endeavour to make the church of God attractive, so that others may desire to dwell there. By immorality, apathy, fastidiousness, lording over God's heritage, by the admixture of worldly policy with the true order of the church, persons may be repelled rather than attracted.

XXXIV.—UNEXPECTED GOOD.

PART I.

"Out of the eater came forth meat; and out of the strong came forth sweetness."—
JUDGES xiv. 14.

MAN is a short-sighted creature; his knowledge of present scenes and events is very limited and obscure. Therefore he is unable to penetrate the future, and tell what is to come.——Man is an erring creature. He often miscalculates causes and their effects. From some things he apprehends nothing but evil, when good is an inevitable consequence. From some things he calculates good, and yet they produce disappointment and grief. Man therefore needs a guide, an instructor superior to himself.—— Revelation is necessary.

We should find many deeply interesting disclosures were we carefully to study and investigate the great books of Nature, Providence, and Grace. These books are full of wonder, and they declare the eternal power and Godhead. It is true that we are not able to read them throughout, being now in a state of minority, the efficient study and perfect understanding of their contents being reserved for the immortal inheritance; nevertheless, if we investigated more, we should know more, admire more, and trust in God more, and be more happy.

The text is Samson's riddle, which, in its literal purport, implied no more than that he had got honey, for food and pleasure, from the lion, which with his strength and fury was prepared to devour him. Yet regarding it spiritually and symbollically, it is full of instruction. For illustration,

I. APPLY THIS STATEMENT TO NATURE.

1. The dead carcase of a lion was a very unlikely source in which to find honey. Under the law every dead unclean animal was considered polluting. The lion is remarkable for strength and ferocity, and for being the destroyer of man. Yet that "eater"—that "strong" beast which Samson slew, instead of destroying him, ministered to his sustenance and pleasure. So there are many things in nature which produce effects contrary to our expectations—many bitter things which produce sweetness—

many things which are awfully destructive, and without which there could be no life. A dose of poison, administered without judgment, may destroy existence; but that poison, skilfully appropriated and proportioned, may banish disease, and restore to health.

2. What is so destructive as the *elements of Nature?* Fire, air, earth, water: *fire*, as seen when destroying the cottage, the mansion, the warehouse, or the sailing ship:—*air*, when it waxes into the tempest, the hurricane, the moonsoon, or fierce tornado: — *earth*, when it quakes, and opens its mouth, and swallows up Korah, Dathan, and Abiram; or when it pours forth a river of burning lava inundating, with sure destruction, villages, towns, and cities: — *water*, when its calm surface is disturbed by the stormy wind, and lashed into foaming billows, and tremendous and irresistible waves. These elements are great "eaters," and "strong" and fearful destroyers; yet "out of the eater comes forth meat, and out of the strong comes forth sweetness."

These elements are essential to life and enjoyment; and though they may become extremely fierce and terrible, yet it is only occasionally so—occasionally to show us that none hath "an arm like God; that none can thunder with a voice like him." "God is terrible in majesty." The inclemency of winter; the operations of science and commerce, teach us the value of fire. Without air life would become extinct; without wind the oak in the forest would lose its firmness, the ship would not sail on the ocean, the sea would become stagnant, and the earth full of poisonous exhalations. —— A voice issues from the torrid zone, the arid desert, or the sultry clime, saying, "I thirst, let me drink, or I die;" and that voice proclaims the value and price of water. The earth is covered with greenness; the golden grain waves profusely in the fields, the trees blossom and are loaded with fruit; the flowers bloom and fill the air with fragrance; and thus of these destructive elements it may be said, "Out of the eater," etc.

3. The text is illustrated by a reference to *the convulsions of nature.* For instance, the deluge. What an eater, what a destroyer was that!——Yet such convulsions have produced most valuable minerals, useful and precious metals, and beautiful gems. Such effects have been produced by deluges, by subterranean fires, and by chemical process, superintended by the great Alchymist of nature.——And again, it is generally admitted, that there are cases in which complicated causes have operated through vast periods of duration, anterior to man's existence, in order to provide for the wants of the human race. Laws apparently conflicting and irregular in their action have been so controlled and directed, and made to conspire, as to provide for the wants of civilized life, long before man's existence. In those early times, vast forests growing along the shores of estuaries, dying, or destroyed by tempests, were buried deep in the mud, there to accumulate thick beds of vegetable matter, over large areas, and this, by a long series of changes, was at length converted into

coal. This could be of no use till man's existence, nor even then, till civilization taught him how to employ this substance for his comfort, and for a great variety of useful purposes. Look, for instance, at the small island of Great Britain. At this day, more than 15000 steam engines are driven by means of coal with a power equal to that of 2,000,000 of men. The influence thence emanating, reaches the remotest portions of the globe, and tends mightily to the civilization and happiness of the race. And is all this an accidental effect of nature's laws? Is it not rather a striking example of special prospective providence? What else but divine power, intent upon a specific purpose could have so directed the countless agencies employed through so many ages, as to bring about such marvellous results? Look then at those valuable minerals, useful metals, and precious stones, as being apparently the result of nature's violent operations, but really directed by God, and you will perceive that "Out of the eater hath come forth meat, and out of the strong has come forth sweetness."*

From nature's destructive power, most wonderful results have followed. Thus the diamond is formed from carbonized matter—charcoal: — and we might go back, and trace out the origin of the various ores, the marbles, the granites, and other mineral treasures so important to an advanced state of the arts, and of civilization and happiness. And we should find them originating in agencies equally remote, equally chaotic and irregular, and seemingly as much removed from all connection with man's distant subsequent appearance. But the house was being prepared for the tenant, and in the long series of preparatory agencies, we can everywhere see the finger of God's special providence, pointing to the final result. Thus "Out of the eater," etc.

Then again, how destructive is *Steam!* If restrained beyond legitimate bounds, its explosive and destructive power is tremendous; yet, as we have already shown, that destructive power has been judiciously bridled and disciplined and made to subserve the

---

* "It is already ascertained, that, by the same process of vegetable growth and decay in the hoary past, thick beds of coal have been accumulated in the rocks of the United States, over an area of more than 20,000 square miles, and probably many more remain to be discovered. Yet, upon a moderate calculation, those already known contain more than 1,100,000 cubic miles of coal; one mile of which, at the rate it is now used, would furnish the country with coal for a thousand years; so that a million of years will not exhaust our supply. What an incalculable increase of the use of steam, and a consequent increase of population and general prosperity, does such a treasure of fuel open before this country! If our numbers should become only as many to the square mile as in great Britain, or 223, there is room enough, this side of the Rocky Mountains, for 500 millions; and, including the western slope of those mountains, for 700 millions, nearly the present population of the whole globe. And yet all that has been thus seen in this country, and all that is in prospect, is *only an accidental, or incidental event in his theology who admits no special providence in nature*. We are not of that number; for we not only believe that God, through vast cycles of duration, directed and controlled the agencies of nature, so as to bury in the bosom of this continent the means of future civilization and prosperity, but that a strong obligation hence results for all its inhabitants to throw all their energies into the work of making this land a glory and a blessing to the nations." — *Edward Hitchcock's Special Divine Interpositions in Nature,* a Paper read by him in America.

useful purposes of life. —— What is so destructive as lightning? Yet that "fiery bird of heaven" has also been tamed and harnessed, and commanded to telegraph the messages and transactions of nations, and of men, from one country to another, across the earth, and under the ocean. —— then there are bitter herbs, exceedingly nauseous, yet highly medicinal; and minerals too, containing the elements of death, yet they are made to minister to health and to the prolongation of existence. What an illustration of the text! "Out of the eater," etc.

> And thus a wonder-working alchemy draineth clixir out of poisons;
> Also the same fiery volcano that scorcheth and ravageth a continent,
> Hath in the broad blue bay cast up some petty island;
> Knowledge hath clipped the lightning's wings, and mewed it up for a purpose,
> Training to some domestic task the fiery bird of heaven.
> Tamed is the spirit of the storm, to slave in all peaceful arts,
> To walk with husbandry and science; to stand in the vanguard against death.
> And the chemist balanceth his elements with more than magic skill,
> Commanding stones that they be bread, and draining sweetness out of wormwood.
> There is use in the poisoned air that swelleth the pods of the laburnum,
> Design in the venom'd thorns that sentinel the leaves of the nettle.
> Pain is useful to man, for it teacheth him to guard his life.
> And the fœtid vapours of the fern warn him to fly from danger. — TUPPER.

II. APPLY THE STATEMENT TO THE CONDUCT OF DIVINE PROVIDENCE.

1. *Personal and relative afflictions.* Distressing calamities have visited some, filling them with gloomy apprehension. Refer to the history of Joseph.

The hatred of his brethren prompted them to sell him into Egypt. To conceal their crime from their aged father, they dyed Joseph's coat in the blood of a kid, and set forwards towards the vale of Hebron. As they approach the venerable patriarch, with an anxious eye, he asks for his beloved Joseph, when they produce the blood-stained robe, and, with all the apathy of guilt, say, "behold this have we found; know whether it be thy son's coat or not." He said, "It is my son's coat. Joseph is without doubt rent in pieces; some evil beast hath devoured him; I will go down to the grave unto my son, mourning." His wounded heart was scarcely healed, when his sons, returning from buying corn in Egypt, on account of famine, informed their father that unless their brother Benjamin should be taken back by them, the governor of Egypt would sell them no more corn. Jacob might well reply, "How was it that ye dealt so ill with me, as to tell the man ye had a brother? Joseph is not, and Simeon is not, and now ye will take Benjamin away! All these things are against me! and ye will bring down my grey hairs with sorrow to the grave." Stop, venerable patriarch, stop; though thy trials are the "eaters" of thy comfort and life, yet, "Out of the eater shall come forth meat, and out of the strong" Governor of Egypt, who now menaces thy happiness, "shall come forth sweetness." "Joseph is yet alive, and is governor of Egypt." And when, a few weeks after, Jacob had embraced the long-lost exile on the plains of Goshen, he heard the same from his own lips — God hath sent me before you, to save your lives by a great deliverance." Gen. xlv. 4, 5. The following anecdotes illustrate the text: —

A good man, some years ago, wished to visit France; but on his way to the ship he broke his leg, by which he was disappointed of his voyage. The ship was lost, and all on board perished. On hearing these facts, he was thankful for his broken leg, and saw that what was a disappointment at the time was sent by the God of love to preserve his life. Little trials, as in this case, are often sent to prevent greater ones.

A man in Yorkshire once saw a book, entitled, "Vindiciæ Pietatis," by R. Alleine, at a sale; he coveted the book, and stole it. But on taking it home and reading it, it proved the means of his conversion to God. He then honestly took it back to its original owner, acknowledged his crime in stealing it, but blessed God, who had overruled it for the salvation of his soul.

2. *Worldly losses* illustrate the text. Wealth, which it has taken years to accumulate, may be swept away in a moment. National calamities, the failing of harvests, the dishonesty of men, insolvency, want of foresight, or interrupted health, may suddenly reverse the circumstances. Such visitations "eat" up the comfort of those who suffer thereby.——But they teach an important lesson — not to trust in uncertain riches, but in the living God; for "the fashion of this world passeth away." God frequently takes away the idols, lest they should destroy.—— Observe Job.

View him in his *private estate:* he heaps up silver as the dust; he washes his steps in butter, and the rock pours him out rivers of oil. View him in his *public character.* Princes revere his dignity; the aged listen to his wisdom; every tongue lauds him. View him in his *domestic circumstances:* on one hand he is defended by a troop of sons; on the other, adorned with a train of daughters; and on all sides, surrounded with "a very great household." Never was human felicity so consummate; never was *disastrous revolution* so sudden. The lightning consumes his cattle; the joyful parent is bereaved of his offspring; the man of affluence is stripped of his abundance; and he who was clothed in scarlet embraces the dunghill. The venerable patriarch is the derision of wicked men, and the late favourite of an indulgent Providence is become "a brother to dragons, a companion of owls." ——Yet "out of the eater shall come forth meat," etc. For he saw the instability of all human things—he acquired unshaken faith in the wisdom and love of God; "though he slay me, yet will I trust in him." But mark the latter part of his life; God changes the scene. See Job xlii. 10—12. Thus the "sweetness" of God's providential love more than counterbalanced all previous trials.

See the case of Habakkuk. To the prophet a time of famine, that great "eater," was a season of joyful trust in God. ch. iii. 17—19.

3. *Personal and relative afflictions* illustrate the text. Afflictions are great "eaters," and "strong" trials. Disease and pain waste the body — corrode the mind — and dry up pecuniary resources. ——How painful to the mind of a parent to tend the sick child, and mark the sad ravages of disease! The heart often bleeds by the

bed of sickness; and had afflictions no Divine counterpoise, no radiant star of hope, and no Almighty Director, they would be overwhelming. —— But "out of the eater shall come forth meat, and out of the strong shall come forth sweetness." Afflictions show the vanity of the world;—the helplessness of the creature;—they purify the soul, as gold is refined in the fire—they strengthen faith, brighten hope, lengthen patience, increase fortitude, and ripen for glory. See the glorious effects of afflictions when God superintends their operation; James i. 2, 3; 1 Pet. i. 6, 7; Rom. v. 3—5.

Sarah Howard, a poor old widow, who had been bed-ridden fourteen years, when visited by her minister, thus spoke of her afflictions:—"I can set to my seal, that the Lord has chastened me sore, but he hath not given me over unto death," Psalm cxviii. 18. "I have been chastened in my person, and am quite helpless, by long and severe illness. I have been chastened in my circumstances ever since I was left a widow: yes, I know what oppressing a widow, what bad debts and hard creditors are; I have been chastened in my family by a son, whom I was dotingly fond of, running away and going to sea. Besides all these, I have been chastened in mind, 'walking in darkness and having no light:' yet, after all, I trust I can say with David, 'Before I was afflicted I went astray, but now have I kept thy word.' And I hope I can say that I am now returned to the Shepherd and Bishop of souls." 1 Peter ii. 25.

Thus "out of the eater," etc. Darkness does not always exist, but is succeeded by the clear shining of the sun. Storms die in calms, and winter wakes spring, which passes into glorious summer and fruitful autumn. So all the trials and darkness of earth shall be succeeded, if not attended, by the light of the Divine countenance, and shall "work out a far more exceeding and eternal weight of glory."

> Were there not a need-be of wisdom, nothing would be as it is;
> For essence without necessity argueth a moral weakness.
> We look through a glass darkly, we catch glimpses of truth,
> But doubtless the sailing of a cloud hath Providence for its pilot:
> The foreknown station of a rush is as fixed as the station of a king:
> The furnace of affliction may be fierce, but if it refineth thy soul,
> The good of one meek thought shall outweigh years of torment.— TUPPER.

IMPROVEMENT.

1. Lean not to your own understandings. How ignorant is man!

2. Recognize the Divine sovereignty. The whole universe is under the government of Jehovah. "Who can stay his arm," etc.

XXXV.—UNEXPECTED GOOD.

PART II.

"Out of the eater came forth meat, and out of the strong came forth sweetness."
— JUDGES xiv. 14.

THE doctrine of Divine Providence is taught in the Bible, and is the key to the clear understanding of it. Deny his superintending power — that he directs, controls, and restrains all human events, and it will be impossible to understand a single page. If we had no other argument, the existence of prophecy would be sufficient — the foretelling of events not only the largest and most important, but even those which appear minute and insignificant. This proves God's superintendence of human affairs, in precisely accomplishing such predictions. God superintends the affairs of nations, of families, and of individuals. It is by him that kings reign, etc. He careth for his saints. See Ps. xci. and cxxxix. He can bring good out of evil, and make all things, however unpleasant and unlikely, to work together for good to them that love God, etc.

Having applied the text to Nature and to the conduct of Divine Providence in some respects,

III. APPLY THE STATEMENT TO DIVINE GRACE AND THE CHRISTIAN ECONOMY.

1. *The fall of man was followed by the declaration of the covenant of grace.* Fearful have been the effects of that fall: — "By one man sin entered," etc. Rom. v. 12. By reson of that fall, "the whole creation groaneth, and travaileth in pain together until now." Since that event what myriads of terrible calamities have come upon this earth!——Sin and death have committed the most terrible ravages!——Look, for instance, at the soul of man. How dark, impure, and pregnant with every evil work!—— Then how wretched his state. No fellowship with God — an alien, a transgressor, an outcast, and exposed to "tribulation and anguish for ever." The law proclaimed from Sinai, which the sinner has broken, thunders against him the curses of Divine wrath. Sin is a voracious "eater." It has eaten up and blasted the moral, spiritual, and everlasting happiness of man. It has separated him from God, and made him a child of Satan. It has broken the main-spring of all holy thought and action, robbed him of peace, and filled him with fear and anguish.

But "out of" sin, "the eater, shall come forth meat, and out of the strong" enemy "shall come forth sweetness." The fall of our first parents was immediately followed by the gracious promise of the Messiah. "I will put enmity." Gen. iii. 15. That glorious promise became the sweetness of man's bitter sorrows till Christ made his appearance as "the consolation of Israel." Mark the opposition of the two personages mentioned in the promise. Satan the Adversary — Christ the Friend and good Shepherd. Satan, Abaddon, the destroyer — Christ, the Life-Giver, the Ransomer, and Redeemer. Satan, the Prince of darkness — Christ, the Light of the world. Satan, the roaring lion — Christ, the atoning Lamb. Satan, the Author of death, the grave, and perdition — Christ, who hath brought "life and immortality to light by his gospel." These antitheses proclaim that, "out of the eater," etc.— that not merely shall the disorder and wretchedness produced by Satan be reversed, but that an infinitely more blessed state than the Adamic in Paradise shall be produced. Hence Paul says, "For as by one man's disobedience," etc. See Rom. v. 19—21.

On the cross the Redeemer turned the curse into a blessing. "Christ hath redeemed us from the curse," Gal. iii. 13. See there how his heart was torn with anguish; how he was "smitten of God and afflicted," when the sword of Divine justice was commanded to awake and smite the Shepherd. Mark the descending fire how it consumed him till the work was "finished."——Yes, from the drinking of that bitter cup, and from that bloody cross, and shameful death, life and salvation in rich abundance "came." "Out of the eater came forth *meat*." For he gave himself for the life of the world, and is denominated the *bread of life*, and the *water of life*. "Whoso eateth my flesh, and drinketh my blood, hath eternal life."

Look at that helpless infant, the Babe of Bethlehem; look at that despised Galilean, that root out of a dry ground; look at that condemned Nazarene at Pilate's bar; look at that bruised, crushed Jesus on the cross — is he the Sent of God — the end of the law, and the great atonement? He is. He has "made an end of sin, finished transgression, and brought in an everlasting righteousness." Then let every crown that angels wear, and every diadem that glorified saints enjoy, be cast at the feet of the exalted Jesus, while the incense of ten thousand songs in earth and heaven ascends in sweetest melodies to the Prince of Life and Peace; for "out of the eater hath come forth meat," etc.

The desolations of sin have thus been overruled for a mighty purpose. Over the grave of man's hopelessness, "mercy and truth have met together," etc. Justice has been emblazoned in awful sternness. Holiness has appeared in most unblemished purity. Sacred truth in most unbending rectitude, while mercy, gentle and unsullied, is seen bending over the godless, plucking the sinner as a brand from the burning, and setting him down among the living in Jerusalem. He has now free and joyful access to God, because he is freely pardoned, and completely justified from all condemnation. Sweet is the peace, rich the fellowship, joyful the experience, and exultant the hope, following sin's ruination. "Where sin abounded, grace has much more abounded." Suppose man had never fallen, that he had perfectly obeyed the law, and at last have been transferred to the upper Paradise, he could only have been regarded as a faithful servant of the Lord — a little lower than the angels — rendered capable of sharing their felicities, and mingling in their praises. But those who rest their souls on Christ's finished work, become the children of the kingdom, and the heirs of the covenant. They are the *redeemed* and the *chosen;* and the Eternal Word, whom angels obey, and seraphs worship is not ashamed to call them brethren. Who are these with veiled faces and covered feet, that fly throughout the measureless expanse of heaven, exclaiming in tones of deepest humility, "Holy, holy, holy, is the Lord God of hosts!" These are the angels, the cherubim that never sinned. But who are these that stand in white robes around the Lamb, hymning the praises of One who bought them with his blood? These are they who have washed their robes and made them white in the blood of the Lamb, and who dwell for ever with the Lord, exalted in his exaltation, and abundantly feeling in their super-eminent glory, how their God hath turned the curse into a blessing — how "out of the eater hath come forth meat," even the heavenly manna, and the wine of the kingdom.

> Sin is an awful shadow, but it addeth new glories to the light;
> Sin is a black foil, but it setteth off the jewelry of heaven:
> Sin is the traitor that hath dragged the majesty of mercy into action:
> Sin is the whelming argument, to justify the attribute of vengeance:
> It is a deep dark thought, and needeth to be diligently studied.
> There is then good and evil; or none could have known his Maker;
> No human intellect or essence could have gazed on his high perfections;
> No angel harps could have tuned the wonders of his wisdom;
> No ransomed souls have praised the glories of his mercy;
> No howling fiends have shown the terrors of his justice;
> But God would have dwelt alone in the fearful solitude of holiness. — TUPPER.

2. *Conversion.* The conversion of notorious sinners, who are the scourge and pests of society, "eating" up its vitals, and destroying its happiness. Look at Saul of Tarsus who made havoc of the church of God — his conversion — his call to the ministry — his invaluable letters — his illustrious example — his heroism in prospect of martyrdom. Is it not true in this case, that "out of the eater," etc.? for he "preached the faith he once laboured to destroy." Refer also to the conversion of such men as Luther, Melancthon, John Bunyan, John Newton, Whitfield and Wesley, etc. What a revenue of good has come from them! What legacies of utility have they left to the church!

3. *Spiritual Conflict.* The existence of spiritual foes is a great evil; but which our heavenly Father overrules for good. They fill the mind with dismay; they threaten to destroy spiritual life; but God clothes his child with invincible armour, and overshadows him with his presence. He gives the victory, and that victory is sweet, and more than counterbalances all the pains and fears of conflict. —— What rapturous triumph gladdened the soul of the Apostle, as he surveyed his conquered foes! "Nay, in all these things we are more than conquerors." Rom. viii. 37. It was for the "joy that was set before him that Christ endured the cross, and despised the shame." What must have been his ecstasy when he "sat down at the right hand of the Majesty on high?" —— So

the Christian, when he shall enter into rest, will regard his conflicts here as necessary to prove him, to test his love, courage, and perseverance; and when he shall experience the fulfilment of that promise, "He that overcometh shall inherit all things," then will he see that "out of the eater hath come forth meat."

Thomas Scott beautifully observes: — The remains of indwelling sin, and even the falls of *real believers*, become occasions to them of deeper humility, more simple dependence on the Saviour, more ardent love and admiring gratitude, more compassion for their fellow-sinners, more fitness for many kinds of service on earth, and greater meetness for the worship and occupations of the redeemed in glory. And if any abuse this truth, let them know that they are not concerned in it; for upright souls are always rendered more watchful, humble, diligent, compassionate, and fervent in prayer, by every false step which they make: at least no others give evidence that they are believers."

4. *Persecution.* God has permitted the most malicious devices to help forward the designs of his grace. Pontius Pilate and the Jews might crucify the Saviour, but they were carrying into effect the purposes of his grace on behalf of man. Look at the martyrdom of Stephen; it appeared as a most disastrous occurrence; apparently it threatened the destruction of the infant church. Not so; for this very circumstance was, in the specialty of God's providence, made subservient to his gracious designs, for the disciples who were "scattered abroad went everywhere preaching the word." Paul was seized by his enemies, placed in bonds, and confined in a dungeon at Rome. His presence apparently was more wanted at Corinth, or Athens, or Ephesus; but God had work for him to do in Rome; and his persecution was for the furtherance of the gospel. Hence he says, "My bonds in Christ," etc. Phil. i. 12—14.

The martyrdoms of past days were the cradlings of Protestantism. The blood of the martyrs was the seed of the church; and the light, the liberty, and the immense holy privileges enjoyed by us, we may trace to the piety and zeal, the love and fidelity of many who sealed the truth with their blood. How striking were the words of Bishop Ridley when burning: — "Be of good courage, brother Latimer, for this day we shall kindle such a fire in the good realm of England as shall never be quenched." Thus the Lord by wisely arranging apparently adverse circumstances, accomplished his great designs. "Out of the eater," etc. The text is illustrated by the following: —

The learned and pious *Bernard Gilpin* being accused of heresy to the execrable Bishop Bonner, that monster sent down messengers to apprehend him. Although Mr. Gilpin was informed of this, he scorned to fly; he was therefore apprehended, and set out for London. His favourite maxim was, *"All things are for the best!"* Upon this journey he broke his leg; *"Is all for the best now?"* said one of the attendants, jeeringly. — *"I still believe so,"* replied the good man; and so it proved; for before he was sufficiently recovered to finish his journey, Queen Mary died, and instead of coming to London *to be burned*, he returned home *in triumph* to the no small joy of his parishioners.

A pious woman, in the days of persecution, used to say she should never want, because her God would supply all her need. She was taken before an unjust judge, for attending the worship of God, who rejoiced in seeing her, and said, he had often wished to have her in his power, and would now send her to prison; "and then," asked he with contempt, "how will you be fed?" She replied, "If it be my heavenly Father's pleasure, I shall be fed from your table." This was literally the case; for the judge's wife, being present at her examination, and greatly struck with the woman's firmness, took care constantly to send her food from her table, and comfortably supplied her the whole of her confinement. In this she found her reward, for the Lord graciously made her a partaker of his forgiving mercy.

The tribulation endured by Christ, and by the church for Christ's sake, thus illustrates the text. What instruction the church derives from the spirit manifested by Christ in tribulation. Mark his patience when he said, "Foxes have holes," etc.— his meekness and forbearance under persecution, "When he was reviled," etc.— his submission and fortitude when drinking the bitter cup, "Father, if it be possible," etc. Matt. xxvi. 32—his forgiving spirit on the cross, "Father, forgive them," etc.——Had not Christ passed through such scenes, these Godlike virtues would not have been manifested.

If the Apostles had endured no persecution, their epistles would have been without the promises, consolation, and comfort peculiar to them. Being troubled themselves they were able to comfort others with the comfort by which they were comforted of God, 2 Cor. i. 4.——Had the truth encountered no opposition, the Scriptures would have been bereft of a great amount of their sweetness and preciousness.

Behold that eminent man of God, John Bunyan, suffering twelve years' imprisonment in the jail of Bedford. Had he not been confined there, we should have had no *Pilgrim's Progress*, which has been the means of so much instruction, and inexpressible delight to the church at large:—a book which has been eulogized by poets and philosophers, men of science, theologians, statesmen and legislators—a book inimitable! Persecution then may be an "eater," but overruled by God, it is the source of immense benefit. "Out of the eater, etc.

5. *Death.* It is the product of sin. "Death by sin." Rom. v. 12. Death is a plague, the king of terrors, the last enemy. Death is a great "*eater.*" The ravages of that foul cannibal have been going on for nearly 6000 years. Millions upon millions has he eaten up. At the command of that savage despot, monarchs and nobles. princes and peasants, lords and servants—all the human family have gone down to the dust.——The body may be full of strength, the countenance adorned with beauty, the eye sparkle with vivacity, and the mind be buoyant with hope, but that great

"eater" will blight all. Look down into the grave, and see what he has done.

> O great man eater!
> Whose every day is carnival, not sated yet?
> Unheard-of Epicure! without a fellow!
> The veriest gluttons do not always cram;
> Some intervals of abstinence are sought
> To edge the appetite: thou seekest none.
> Methinks the countless swarms thou hast devour'd,
> And thousands that each hour thou gobblest up,
> This, less than this, might gorge thee to the full.
> But, ah! rapacious still, thou gapest for more;
> Like one whose days defrauded of his meals,
> On whom lank hunger lays her skinny hand,
> And whets to keenest eagerness his cravings.

Death may be called the "king of terrors," not only on account of the dissolution of the body, etc., but because he has a "sting" to those who are not saved by Christ. In that case death is the messenger to usher the guilty and unchanged sinner to the bar of a despised and righteous God. This invests death with the darkest aspect.

The mediation of Christ, his resurrection, and the consequent resurrection of his people, proclaim that "out of the eater," etc. Christ has destroyed the sting of death, and dissipated the uncertainty of the future. The body is taken down to be gloriously built afresh. It is decomposed in the noisome grave to be refined and sublimated. Hence "Our conversation is in heaven." Phil. iii. 20, 21. The glorious antitheses used by the Apostle illustrate the text, 1 Cor. xv. 42—44, 49, 53—55.

If it is a blessed thing for a spirit weighed down with a sinking mortality, and groaning under sin's corruption, to flee away from its troubles, and soar amid the cloudless light of immortal day, then death has been turned into a blessing, since it merely cuts asunder the chains which bind us to earth, and usher the spirit into a land of light and joy. And when we stand on the mount of God in heaven, and retrospect our pilgrimage on earth, shall we not see that "Out of the eater," etc.

> Glorious hopes and ineffable imaginings crowd our holy theme,
> Fear hath been slaughtered on the portal, and Doubt driven back to darkness:
> For Christ hath died, and we in Him; by faith His All is ours;
> Cross and crown, and love, and life; and we shall reign in Him.—TUPPER.

If it is a blessed thing for a being pent up amid the closeness of a dungeon to exchange its pestilential air for the fragrant breath of Paradise, then death has been turned into a blessing, since it dissociates the children of the covenant from the pollution of this world, and exalts them to the regions beyond the grave, where the Lamb shall feed them, etc. —— They go from a land of darkness to the land of light — from a desert of sin and sorrow to the Canaan of purity and joy. ——

IMPROVEMENT.

1. Are you the children of God? For "all things work," etc. Rom. viii. 28.

2. As the evils which now exist, will be overruled for future everlasting good, guard against impatience and unbelief.

3. Let the sinner consider his ways. He may have good things in this life, but how will it be in a future life?

XXXVI.—BLESSEDNESS OF THE POOR IN SPIRIT.

" Blessed are the poor in spirit; for theirs is the kingdom of heaven."—MATT. v. 3.

THE beatitudes were designed to correct the mistaken notions of the Jews respecting the Messiah's kingdom.—— All seek happiness, but none but the truly enlightened know in what real happiness consists, or how it may be obtained and enjoyed. "The secret of the Lord is with them that fear him." The beatitudes may be considered as the Christian paradoxes; for they place happiness in such dispositsons of mind, and in such circumstances, as men generally deem incompatible with it.

I. DESCRIBE THE CHARACTER: *"the poor in spirit."* *

It refers not to those who are *temporally poor*. Satan has his poor as well as Christ; and O how dreadfully miserable are Satan's poor — a miserable life here, followed by a most miserable existence hereafter. Many poor persons are proud, ungodly, dishonest, profligate, and unhappy; while some of the rich are humble, holy, happy. Nor does it mean *voluntary poverty;* or to turn mendicant monks and friars, like the Roman Catholics.——By the " poor in spirit," Christ means those who are deeply sensible of their spi-

---

*1. It is not said, blessed are the poor in estate; but, "Blessed are the poor in spirit:" it is not a poverty of purse and possession, but a poverty of spirit that entitles us to the blessing. 2. It is not said, blessed are the spiritually poor, but, "Blessed are the poor in spirit:" he that is destitute of the grace and spirit of Christ, that has no sense of his spiritual wants, he is spiritually poor, but he is not poor in spirit. Further, 3. It is not said, blessed are the poor-spirited, but, "the poor in spirit." Such as act below and beneath themselves as men and as Christians, these are poor-spirited men, but these are not poor in spirit. 4. It is not said, Blessed are they that make themselves poor, by leaving their property and callings, as some do among the Roman Catholics; but blessed are they whom the gospel makes poor, by giving them a sight of their spiritual wants and necessities, and directing them to our Saviour, that they may be made rich. In sum, not those that are poor in estate, or those whom the world has made poor in possession, but those whom the gospel has made poor in spirit, that is, the truly humble, lowly spirits, have a right and title to the kingdom of heaven. Now humility is called poverty of spirit, because it is the effect and fruit of God's Spirit.—*Burkitt.*

ritual poverty and wretchedness — he refers to humiliation of the spirit.

1. They are *truly sensible of, and feel their spiritual poverty*, as caused by sin. They feel themselves reduced to a state of guilt, impurity, degradation, and alienation from God — destitute of righteousness, holiness, strength, and wisdom; deep in debt without any thing to pay; under condemnation — helpless — like the Publican — the Prodigal. Luke xv; xviii.

2. Poverty of spirit is *opposed to a spirit of self-righteousness*. This is renounced as the ground of justification. The "poor in spirit" go to God through Christ, as poor, perishing sinners, relinquishing every hope founded on their own unworthiness, and trusting simply in the mediation of Christ. Rom. iii. 24, etc.

3. Poverty of spirit is *opposed to a spirit of self-conceit* in respect of any knowledge, gifts, or attainments, which are supposed to be possessed. The proud in spirit "are vainly puffed up in their fleshly mind," thinking that they are the people, and wisdom shall die with them. But if we be poor in spirit, it will prevent our thinking too highly of ourselves; and teach us to think soberly, as we ought to think.

4. To be "poor in spirit" is *opposed to self-confidence* However others may boast of their own strength and sufficiency, such will be sensible of their weakness, will feel their danger of departing from God, and dread being left to themselves. Their present standing in religion they will ascribe to grace alone, and depend on strength Divine for perseverance to the end.

5. The "poor in spirit" are ever *sensible of their imperfect holiness*. The proud in spirit are "pure in their own eyes, and yet are not washed from their filthiness." Though their goodness is as the morning cloud, and as the early dew, yet they say, "Stand by thyself; I am holier than thou." But no such self-commendations fall from the lips of the poor in spirit. As to their graces, and their holiness, when they weigh them in the balances of the sanctuary, they consider all to be lighter than vanity. Instead of considering that they held an exalted place among the family of God, they acknowledge themselves to be "less than the least of all saints." Isa. lxvi. 2; lvii. 15; Ps. xxxiv. 18; Luke xviii. 13.

6. The "poor in spirit" are *submissive to the will of God*, under the trying dispensations of providence. The carnal man is for having his own way, and choosing his own inheritance. But Divine grace gives a better spirit—the confession of ignorance—the bowing of the will to the will of God. Micah vii. 9.

7. The "poor in spirit" *are thankful for mercies received*. The proud forget the fountain of Divine goodness from which they are every moment supplied. "Of the rock that begat them, they are unmindful, and forget God that formed them." But the poor in spirit ever feel and say, "What shall I render to the Lord for all his benefits?" Creating and preserving goodness animates their hearts to sing his praise; but, above all, the blessings of redeem-

ing grace lead their hearts in joyful accents to say, "Bless the Lord, O my soul." Ps. ciii.

II. THE BLESSEDNESS OF THE POOR IN SPIRIT: "theirs is the kingdom of heaven."

The phrases "kingdom of heaven," and "kingdom of God," sometimes signify the Christian dispensation, Mark i. 15; and sometimes the kingdom of glory, 1 Cor. xv. 50. Sometimes the privileges and blessings of the gospel, Rom. xiv. 17, and the reign of God in the soul, Luke vii. 21.

The poor in spirit have the kingdom of God in the first sense; having responded to the invitations of the gospel, they are interested in, and identified with the *blessings and privileges* of the Christian dispensation, which is God's heavenly or Divine kingdom on earth. Christ, the King, also dwells in their hearts by faith, and carries on his gracious reign there. —— And if Christ reigns in their souls, he reigns there to prepare them for eternal glory. Christ in them " the hope of glory."

For the sake of distinction, observe,

1. *The kingdom of heaven on earth is theirs*, or the dispensation of grace with all its blessings.

Its salvation is theirs. They are the saved. Poverty of spirit is followed by perfect absolution from sin — and peace and consolation. Mark their triumph. Isa. xii. 1, 2, etc.

Its Christian citizenship and sweet fellowship are theirs.

The presence of its Divine King, and communion with him are theirs.

Its gospel ministration is theirs.

Its Divine influences are theirs.

Its precious promises are theirs.

Its angelic guards and protection are theirs.

Yes, the poor in spirit — the poor worm Jacob may say of this Divine Inheritance, All are mine! 1 Cor. iii. 21.

It is theirs by virtue of Christ's mediation — and through the operations of his Spirit. They are made meet for this kingdom —have a disposition for it—none else could enjoy it. " Except a man," John iii. 5. The gates of this kingdom open only for *the poor in spirit.*

2. *The kingdom of glory is theirs.* They have "salvation in Christ Jesus with eternal glory." Enjoying on earth the former, they are hoping to enjoy the latter. " Fear not, little flock," etc. See John xvii. 24; Matt. xxv. 34.

The kingdom of glory! How rich and vast the privilege! How enchanting the prospect! An earthly crown sparkles in the eye of ambition. A throne is the pinnacle of human pride. What exertions have been made, what blood has been shed, to grasp a sceptre that rules a few miles of territory, and soon drops from the hand that wields it. But the poor in spirit have in prospect a kingdom Divine, and pre-eminently glorious. Christ is its Founder, the Governor, the Owner, the Giver;—a kingdom announced by prophets, established by miracles; prepared before the foundation of the world; a kingdom that cannot be shaken, extending into eternity, and remaining for ever; a kingdom, in comparison of which all the celebrated empires of the globe vanish into nothing; and in the possestion of which you may pity Alexander and Cæsar as grovelling worms!

Grace and glory are not so much different in states, as different degrees of the same state. Present participation, however, is imperfect. *Here*, the poor in spirit are princes; but princes in disguise; the world knoweth them not. They are like David in the wilderness, anointed but not proclaimed; and through much tribulation are entering the kingdom. Their royalties are above. There are the robes, their crowns, their harps, their palaces, and they shall reign for ever and ever.——" He raiseth up the poor out of the dust," etc. 1 Sam. ii. 7, 8.

The kingdom of glory with all its magnificence and splendour is theirs—and with its perfect knowledge—its perfect purity—its perfect happiness, etc., etc., all that which " eye hath not seen," etc., all is theirs for evermore.

> Ye palaces, sceptres, and crowns, your pride with disdain I survey;
> Your pomps are but shadows and sounds, and pass in a moment away;
> The crown that my Saviour bestows, yon permanent sun shall outshine;
> My joy everlastingly flows — my God, my Redeemer, is mine!

IMPROVEMENT.

1. If poor in spirit, be thankful, and ascribe all to grace. 2. Enjoy your privileges in the kingdom below. 3. Rejoice in hope of the everlasting kingdom. 4. Woe to the proud in spirit.

XXXVII.—CHRIST THE SUN OF RIGHTEOUSNESS.

A METAPHORICAL SKETCH.

"Unto you that fear my name shall the Sun of Righteousness arise with healing in his wings."—MAL. iv. 2.

THE beauty of this passage arises, in part, from the opposition between the different verses. In the preceding verse we are led to the torrid zone, where the day kindles into burning heat, destroying vegetation and desolating the earth. " The day of the Lord is as an oven," etc.——Then we are referred to temperate zones and milder climates, where the sun is the chief of earthly blessings—there he rises with " healing" etc.—accompanied with a healthful breeze, that clears and purifies the air. On account of its glory, and the many blessings it imparts, the Sun is an emblem of Deity. Ps. lxxxiv. 11 ; and also of Christ — text.

I. There is but *one Sun in our firmament*. Other objects in creation are numerous, as the stars, planets, mountains, seas, etc. But there is only one sun in our solar system — he has no rival, no compeer.

So in grace there is only one Sun of Righteousness. "One Mediator," 1 Tim. ii. 5. "One Lord," 1 Cor. viii. 6; Eph. iv. 5. One Saviour, Acts iv. 12. One Foundation, 1 Cor. iii. 11. One way to heaven, John xiv. 6. As there has been but one natural Sun since the creation of this world, so there has been but one Christ, and to the end of time there will be no other.

II. The Sun is the *Fountain of light and heat to this visible world*. All the light we enjoy is borrowed: the light of the moon, and of all the planets in our system, is borrowed; the Sun is the fountain of light to them all.

As all things were created by Christ and for him, John i. 3, and Col. i. 16, he is the Fountain of all light.

1. *Of natural light*, called "the Father of lights,"—the Creator of the Sun itself. When this earth was without form and void, and overspread with chaotic darkness, then he said, "Let there be light, and there was light." A word did it; a single word of the Almighty formed that most amazing, incomprehensible, and important substance, light; and collected, and concentrated it for general diffusion in the orb of day.

What a wonderful thing is light! In the *rapidity of its flight*. According to the most accurate calculations of astronomers, it travels at the rate of nearly 100 millions of miles in 8 minutes ; and yet it is most wisely ordered, that the individual particles of light should be incredibly minute and imponderous. It is said that a candle, in a second of time, diffuses several hundred millions more particles of light than there would be grains in the whole earth, if it were one heap of sand. What wisdom and mercy in the inconceivable *smallness and levity of the particles of light!* For philosophers tell us, if the finest sands were thrown against our bodies with a hundredth part of the swiftness with which light comes from the sun, each grain would be as fatal as the stroke of a dagger; and yet that tender and exquisitely sensible organ, our eye, is exposed to the light without any pain, because of the inexpressible smallness of the particles of which light is composed.

2. He is the Fountain of *intellectual light*. The structure and organization of animals and brutes is quite as wonderful as that of our bodies ; but the amazing distinction between them and us is, "There is a spirit in man," etc. Job xxxii. 8. He is the Author of the human understanding.

He has kindled such a light in the human composition, as makes man wiser than the beasts of the field, and draws a broad and everlasting distinction between him and the whole vegetable and animal world: and all the variety, all the exertions, all the productions, all the effects of intellect, are to be traced to this Sun of Righteousness. The wisdom of a Solomon, the amazing genius of a Newton, etc. [Amplify.]

3. He is the *Fountain of all spiritual and celestial light*. The light that beams forth in the Scriptures. He inspired the prophets. —— But that was only the dawn — the twilight of the day that was to come — the fulness of time, when he himself, the glorious Sun of Righteousness, should arise in the spiritual firmament, with healing in his beams, and shed light and life upon an endungeoned and benighted world. "Upon them that sit in darkness," etc. Isa. xlii. 17. "I am come as the light," etc. John viii. 12. "He hath abolished," 2 Tim. i. 10. He is the Author of spiritual light in the soul, (which will be shown hereafter.)

III. The Sun is *distinguished by greatness, magnificence and glory*. Milton calls it "the eye and the soul of this great world." It is 900,000 miles in diameter, one million times larger than the earth, and 95 millions of miles distant from it. Being the centre of the Solar system, it is the monarch of the whole, communicating its light to the celestial bodies, the firmament, moon, and stars, which derive all their light from it.

Jesus Christ is distinguished for greatness, dignity, and glory. He is "the brightness," etc., Heb. i. 3; superior to angels, Heb. i. 4—8. He was in the form of God, Phil. ii. 6. From his fulness he communicates to the angels. He is the Head of Principalities and Powers. His pre-eminent glory is stated, Col. i. 15. Before him all the shining ranks of heaven bow and worship. Rev. v. 11—14. Christ is the great Monarch of the universe.

The light of the Sun is *a pure light*; it cannot be defiled; if it shine upon a dunghill, it does not make it less glorious; so the Sun of Righteousness, if he shine upon a filthy leprous sinner, he is not defiled thereby. We cannot look at the Sun with the naked eye; but the essential glory of Christ is much more dazzling. See Acts xxvi. 13. And as we look at the natural Sun through a medium, as reflected by water, or through painted glass, so we can come near to Christ, and behold him, his glorious nature being veiled by the body incarnate.

IV. Christ resembles the Sun on account of the *benefits he diffuses*.

1. The Sun *quickens into life*. Winter freezes up the channels of life, and presents the dreary prospect of a world half dead; but in Spring, when the Sun arises with healing in his beams, he restores life and health to nature, languid and benumbed. Vegetation springs forth from the grave, and the earth is clothed with verdure and fruitfulness, "the valleys rejoice, and the little hills shout for joy."——

So Christ the Sun of Righteousness, by his word and Spirit quickens the dead sinner to life; Eph. ii. 1, 2; Col. ii. 12. "Passed from death unto life," "born again," and "have put away the unfruitful works of darkness," — now have "the fruit unto holiness," etc. Sinners are withered plants, blasted by sin; but if this glorious Sun shine upon them, they will become fertile in every good work.

2. The Sun *gives light.* It has already been shown that he is the fountain of light. So Jesus from the sinner's mind banishes the shades of night, and introduces the moral and spiritual day. He gives him a discovery of his spiritual danger—reveals his salvation—discovers to him the riches of his grace, etc. Light is opposed to darkness. Darkness is emblematic of sin, ignorance, misery, and despair. Light is the emblem of knowledge, faith, hope, happiness.

3. The Sun produces *beauty.* Contrast summer with winter; what a difference! When he shines forth in his full splendour, the grass, the trees, the flowers, all nature is full of beauty. The rich and various tints of flowers are caused by their absorbing, in different quantities, the peculiar properties of light.

All believers are beautified by Christ—being impressed with his image—sanctified by his Spirit—adorned with his robe of righteousness. They absorb light and influence from that glorious Sun, and therefore they must become like him. —— How will he beautify them at the resurrection—and in Paradise!

4. The Sun *exhilarates.* "Truly the light is sweet," etc. Eccles. xi. 7. He is the source of heat, and diffuses warmth through nature. As darkness and sadness are companions, so are light and joy. When the heavens are obscured with black clouds, the whole creation sympathizes, etc.—the clear shining of the sun is pleasant.

The Sun of Righteousness diffuses *heat*, and light, and joy into man by his Holy Spirit, which cause the soul of the believer, to burn within him, and to exult with hope. How delightful to have the shining of this Sun in affliction, adversity, and death!

5. The Sun not only quickens to vegetation, etc., but *ripens.* —— So the Saviour, by the operations of his grace—by the dispensations of his providence—by the blasts of his furnace, ripens the soul for glory.

V. The sun *gives light to all the world*—to every nation, people, etc., shining upon the just and upon the unjust.

Jesus Christ is a universal light. John viii. 12. He holds forth light and grace to all. To what nation is the gospel confined? Mark xvi. 15.

VI. The light and heat of the sun are *perfectly free.* His glorious beams are as free to the poor as to the rich.

So all the irradiating, quickening, sanctifying, comforting, and exhilarating rays of Christ, the Divine Sun, are "without money," etc., to the meanest and poorest, if they desire him.

VII. The Sun is *constant and unchangeable,* "With whom is no variableness." James i. 17. With the sun there is no real "variableness," or change, but he is one fixed, unvarying, never-failing, unchangeable source of light and heat.

To us the sun appears to rise and set — is seen in the East, South, and West — sometimes obscured by clouds — sometimes totally eclipsed; but all this is only as he appears to us. The Sun stands fixed in the heavens, while it is our earth that rises and sets. Behind the darkest clouds he shines as splendidly as on the brightest day; under a total eclipse, there is no diminution of his light; amidst the most tremendous thunderstorms his rays are as calm, as vivid, as diffusive, above the tempest, as at any other time.——It is undiminished, having shone for nearly six thousand years, and is as bright as ever.

"Jesus Christ is the same yesterday," etc. His power to save — his precious blood — his Almighty love for his church — his determination to carry on the work which he has begun in his people — his intercession — his solicitude to glorify his people — all these change not — they are immutable.——All change is in us; we obscure the Divine Sun by our clouds of sin, unbelief, ignorance.——As to Christ, every thing is clear, and perfect, and constant as the shining of the sun on a cloudy day. He is influenced by one principle, guided by one grand rule, aiming at one grand purpose — from everlasting to everlasting the same.

VIII. Persons who *feel the need of the Sun* for light, vegetation, or health, value it the most. So those who feel their need of Christ as the Divine Sun, value him the most.

IMPROVEMENT

1. Has Christ the Sun risen upon you?

2. Suffer not this world to get between your souls and the Sun, so as to cause *an eclipse.*

3. When mysterious and dark dispensations overcloud this Sun, still trust in Christ. When Jacob said, "All these things are against me," the cloud was all in him. The promise, "I will surely do thee good," was working as surely as ever! When the disciples said, "We trusted that it had been He that should have redeemed Israel," the Sun of Righteousness was only in eclipse, shining in all his glory, and hidden only behind the tomb of Joseph; the glorious morning drove away the cloud, and the Sun of Righteousness arose in all his wonted splendour.

4. As the burning sun of the torrid zone consumes all the vegetation, so will the purity and justice of Jehovah burn up "the wood, hay, and stubble," that attaches to the best human characters; and to those characters that are *all* "wood, hay, and stubble," he is a "consuming fire." His justice "shall burn as doth an oven"— it shall burn up the wicked. As a concave mirror collects and combines the force of the solar rays, so the day of judgment will concentrate upon the wicked all God's judgments.

XXXVIII.—THE BLESSEDNESS OF THOSE WHO MOURN.

"Blessed are they that mourn; for they shall be comforted."— MATT. v. 4.

MEN may bless us with their lips; but will not, or cannot help us by the hand.——Men may bless us with their lips, but curse us with the heart.——The blessing of Christ is the reverse. When he pronounces a blessing, it is with his infinite love, and it is executed by his infinite power.——Christ does not say, Blessed are the rich, the mighty, the honourable—but, Blessed are they that mourn.——

I. THE CHARACTER; "they that mourn."

1. For what do they mourn? 2. How do they mourn?

1. *For what do they mourn?*

(1) *Their sins and guilt as transgressors*—as having offended God; sin has separated them from him, and exposed them to his righteous displeasure.

(2) *They mourn the effects of sin upon the human race.* They see a whole world lying in wickedness and ruin.——Their friends and relatives affected by it.

(3) *Their imperfections as Christians.* Want of conformity to Christ—deficiency of love and zeal—imperfection of faith and hope—their feeble conflicts and conquests as soldiers of the cross.

(4) *They mourn on account of their trials.* They may be numerous—severe and oppressive—themselves brought, perhaps, to the gates of death—or following their dearest friends to the grave.

(5) *They mourn for the church.* The paucity of its members—its want of spirituality—its adoption of human policy—its pandering to the world, etc.

(6) *They mourn the prevalence of errors.* These constantly assail the church.

(7) *They mourn in prospect of death.* Fear they will never be able to endure the last conflict—they mourn on account of their unfitness to die.

2. How do they mourn? It is not the sorrow of the world which worketh death—not an habitual spirit of fretfulness. 1 Cor. vii. 10. No, it is true repentance on their own account—and heart-felt grief for the conduct and wretchedness of others.

(1) It is produced by the Spirit. Zech. xii. 10; John xvi. 8.

(2) It is self-loathing—self-abhorrence on account of their impurity—because they have sinned against God—it is not merely a dread of future wrath.

(3) It is mourning associated *with a real change of mind* as to past guilt and future godliness. A repentance to purity which never need to be repented of — a change inwrought in the whole man, producing new views, new desires, new actions. 1 Cor. vii. 11.

(4) It is mourning associated with *a feeling of helplessness and dependence upon Christ*. Sin is felt as the defilement and death of the spirit — evils which impotent man cannot remove — and having this feeling, Christ is *apprehended by faith*.

(5) And if they mourn for the church—or the world, it is heartfelt, accompanied by earnest desire, fervent prayer, and zealous exertions, to avert those evils. Rom. x. 1.

II. THEIR BLESSEDNESS; "they shall be comforted." It is the prerogative and delight of God to comfort. Isa. xxxiii. 11; 2 Cor. i. 3, 4; Isa. xl. 1; li. 3; lxvi. 13.

1. Mourning sinners shall be comforted with the pardon of all their sins. Isa. i. 18; lv. 7; Matt. ix. 6; 1 John ii. 12.

2. They shall be comforted with peace of mind. Because justified perfectly and freely. Acts xiii. 38, 39; Rom. v. 1.

3. With the privileges and blessings of adoption. Fellowship with God and his people—the possession of the Spirit. John i. 12; 1 John iii. 1.

4. They shall be comforted by sensible tokens of Christ's love. John xiv. 23 — of his grace to support them in all their trials, 2 Cor. xii. 9; and to guide them safely through death's dark vale, Ps. xxiii. 4. —— Hence they have *hope*, and that hope produces solid joy. 1 Pet. i. 8.

5. They shall be comforted at the great day of final account. Here they have wept for Zion — laboured to save sinners and to honour Christ — and "God is not unrighteous to forget," etc. Heb. vi. 10. "Inasmuch as ye have done it," etc. Matt. xxv. 40. Kings, conquerors, heroes, and statesmen will want comfort then — in vain.

IMPROVEMENT.

1. The importance of repentance. "Except ye repent," etc.

2. The importance of caring for Christ's cause.

3. Mourning here shall be followed by abundant joy hereafter. "They that sow." Ps. cxxvi. 5, 6.

XXXIX.—THE TRUTH OF THE BIBLE.

"Thy Word is truth."—John xvii. 17.

The Bible is regarded by Christians as a revelation of the Divine Will concerning the salvation of the immortal soul. It contains the plan of salvation, richly adapted to the circumstances of fallen humanity. Upon that scheme of Divine mercy the church has rested, and is still resting for eternal life.—— But the carnal mind has questioned the authenticity of God's word. Hence it becomes Christians to be fully persuaded in their own minds. The Bible courts inquiry. " Prove all things; hold fast that which is good." 1 Thess. v. 21. It encourages us to examine for ourselves: to compare its claims with those of opposite systems; and to receive or to reject, according to the light of evidence. Believing that we are not following cunningly devised fables, but the sure testimonies of the Lord, consider the following

EVIDENCES OF THE GENUINENESS AND AUTHENTICITY OF THE SCRIPTURES.

The Bible comes to us invested with just such evidences of its truth as are seen to invest other truths of a similar nature; that is, other moral truths; and the principal difference is in the *degree* of the evidence of Revealed Religion. This is incomparably greater than that which establishes any other moral truth whatever; and we are justified in expecting that it should be so: for Christianity comes to us professing to be not only *true*, but *Divine;* to be directly from God, and coming with such pretensions, it is reasonable that they should be sustained by a correspondent degree of evidence. But further,

I. *The Scriptures were written by the persons to whom they are ascribed.* Of this we have the clearest evidence. Consider,

1. The *languages* in which the Scriptures were originally written, the Hebrew and the Greek, afford considerable force of argument; for they have long ceased to be living languages. The time when they were spoken and written in their purity, was the period in which the sacred writers are said to have existed; and forbids the suspicion that the writings could be of a more recent date.

2. The *style* of the Scriptures accords with the character of the professed writers: it is evidently ancient, Eastern, and, like a book composed by a variety of authors, diversified.

3. The testimony of the first Christian fathers, and of ancient historians. They refer to these sacred books, ascribing them to the persons whose names they bear; affirming that they were received by the first Christian churches as the rule of their faith and practice; and in their own writings frequently quoting from them. Of the *Christian fathers* might be mentioned, Justin,

Irenæus, Clemens; and of the historians of that time, Tacitus, Suetonius, and Pliny, confirm the fact. Tertullian says that in his time some of the original copies of those books were extant. Even the early enemies of Christianity, Celsus,* Porphyry, Julian, acknowledge the existence and the genuineness of the Christian Scriptures; adverting to them in their writings, and quoting them for the purpose of controversy and ridicule. No person in his senses makes any doubt of Homer's or Virgil's works being theirs, by reason of the constant testimony of the Greeks concerning the one, and of the Latins concerning the other; how much more then ought we to stand by the testimony of almost all the nations in the world for the authors of these books?

4. The continual reference of the New Testament to the Jewish Scriptures. Christ and his Apostles bear witness to Moses and the prophets, as the inspired authors of the Old Testament writings. To this we have the testimony of the *Jews* through a long succession of ages: and their unanimous testimony is of the highest authority. Not only *Jewish historians*, as Philo and Josephus, but also the most ancient Heathen historians and poets, very frequently refer to the writings of Moses and of the Jewish prophets; and the early enemies of Christianity subscribe, without hesitation, to the evidence in proof of the genuineness of the Hebrew Scriptures. The writers of the New Testament refer to and suppose the truth of the facts recorded in the Old; their grand design

---

* "Celsus, one of the bitterest antagonists of Christianity, who wrote in the latter part of the second century, speaks of the Founder of the Christian religion as having lived but a very few years before his time, and mentions the principal facts of the gospel history relative to Jesus Christ — declaring that he had copied the account from the writings of the evangelists. He quotes these books, as we have already remarked, and makes extracts from them as being composed by the disciples and companions of Jesus, and under the names which they now bear. He takes notice particularly of his incarnation: his being born of a virgin: his being worshipped by the magi: his flight into Egypt; and the slaughter of the infants. He speaks of Christ's baptism by John, of the descent of the Holy Spirit in the form of a dove, and of the voice from heaven declaring him to be the Son of God; of his being accounted a prophet by his disciples; of his foretelling who should betray him, as well as of the circumstances of his death and resurrection. He allows that Christ was considered a Divine person by his disciples, who worshipped him; and notices all the circumstances attending the crucifixion of Christ, and his appearing to his disciples afterwards. He frequently alludes to the Holy Spirit, mentions God under the title of the Most High, and speaks collectively of the Father, Son, and Holy Spirit. He acknowledges the miracles wrought by Jesus Christ, by which he engaged great multitudes to adhere to him as the Messiah. That these miracles were really performed he never disputes or denies, but ascribes them to the magic art, which, he says, Christ learned in Egypt."—*Horne's Introduction, Vol. 1.*

"Lucian, the contemporary of Celsus, was a bitter enemy of the Christians. In his account of the death of the philosopher Peregrinus, he bears authentic testimony to the principal facts and principles of Christianity: that its Founder was crucified in Palestine, and worshipped by the Christians, who entertained peculiarly strong hopes of immortal life, and great contempt for this world and its enjoyments; and that they courageously endured many afflictions on account of their principles, and sometimes surrendered themselves to sufferings.

"Honesty and probity prevailed so much among them that they trusted each other without security. Their Master had earnestly recommended to all his followers mutual love, by which also they were much distinguished. In his piece entitled Alexander or Pseudomantis, he says that they were well known in the world by the name of Christians; that they were at that time numerous in Pontus, Paphlagonia, and the neighbouring countries; and finally, that they were formidable to cheats and impostors." — *Horne's Introduction, Vol. 1.*

being to show, that the Predictions of the prophets concerning the Messiah, were fulfilled in the person and sufferings of Jesus; and they take those predictions as the basis of their reasoning on that subject. So that if the Bible be an imposture, it must be carried on by a concurrence of persons, and in a manner so near to impossible, that it is absurd to mention the supposition.

II. *That the Scriptures have been transmitted to us in their original completeness and purity.*

1. *Their completeness.* There is no real evidence that any of the books generally acknowledged by either the Jewish or Christian church, have perished. As to their completeness, Josephus, in giving us an account of the sacred writings received by the Jews, records the very same catalogue of books as that which we now have in the Old Testament; exclusive of the Apocryphal writings. Some of the earliest Christian writers carefully examined the subject, and they have transmitted to us exactly the same list of canonical Old Testament writings, that the Jews have done.

2. *Their purity.* Considering that they are of the most ancient date, — that, till the invention of printing, they were circulated only in manuscript; and that since this invention, multitudes of editions have been circulated,—it is not to be supposed that every copy can be free from verbal inaccuracies.* To prevent these, nothing less than a miraculous agency would have been necessary, to preside over every manuscript transcriber, and every superintendence of the press.

Their purity has been preserved with the utmost care. For this end, the law, or the five books of Moses, were deposited in the tabernacle, by the side of the ark, Deut. xxxi. 24—26. Certain portions were read every Sabbath, as a part of public worship. Ex. xxiv. 7; Josh. viii. 34, 35, etc. The reigning king was obliged to copy the whole for his own use, Deut. xvii. 14—20. The people were to teach them to their children, Deut. vi. 6, 7. That the law has been preserved pure, appears from evidence derived from the Samaritans, whose Pentateuch, existing nearly 700 years before Christ's advent, substantially accords with its Jewish original.

So scrupulous have been the Jews on this subject, that they have formed a catalogue of not only the books, but of the chapters, the verses, the words, and even the letters of the whole of their

---

* "It may perhaps be thought, that what is advanced corresponds ill with the prodigious number of different readings that are alleged to exist in the various manuscripts both of the Old and New Testament Scriptures — of which it is said there are many thousands. But then it must be understood, that "not one hundredth part of these variations makes any perceptible alteration in the sense. They consist almost wholly of palpable errors in transcription, grammatical and verbal differences, such as the insertion or omission of an article, and the transposition of a word or two in a sentence. Even the few that do change the sense affect it only in passages relating to unimportant historical and geographical circumstances, or other collateral matters; and the still smaller number that make any alteration in things of consequence may, for the most part, be rectified by collating other manuscripts and versions. *But the very worst manuscript extant would not pervert one article of our faith, or destroy one moral precept.*"—*Horne's Introduction, Vol. 1.*

sacred writings, that no portion might be lost or corrupted. We have evidence of the radical purity of the whole, from the Greek translation, or the Septuagint, which has been circulated among the Gentiles as well as the Jews, from the period of nearly 300 years before Christ. And there is similar evidence of the same effectual care for preserving the purity of the Christian Scriptures. A great number of very ancient copies and versions of the New Testament still exist; all of them materially agreeing with our received text.

The friends and enemies of Divine revelation have acted as a check on each other, and mutually contributing to preserve the sacred writings pure and entire. The jealousy subsisting between the Jews and the Samaritans,—and between Jews and Christians, has answered the same end. And so with the differences of opinion among Christians themselves.

These books, since the first period almost of their existence, have been in the keeping. not of one party, but of several parties, who were opposed to each other in matters of faith, and exercised over each other a watchful jealousy in regard to what they mutually respected as the only rule of faith. At a very early period, while the Jews were the sole depositories of the word of God, they were parted asunder into two rival kingdoms, and after the return from Babylon, when one nation alone survived, not only did that one itself split into two hostile sects, those of the Pharisees and the Sadducees, who differed widely from each other in their views of Scripture, but the neighbouring nation of the Samaritans, in regard at least to the books of Moses, stood entirely apart from the Jews as keepers of these sacred books, and have preserved them with so much fidelity and care, that though for nearly 3000 years they have had no friendly intercourse with the Jews, and had their Scriptures written all along in a different character, yet the copies that have been preserved of these are substantially the same with the Jewish Scriptures. Then after Christianity began, the animosity that subsisted between Jews and Christians, and the spirit of controversy which they mutually cherished, caused each party to act as a vigilant guardian toward the other respecting the safe and incorrupt preservation of the Scriptures, on which they alike depended for the justification of their views. And within the bosom of the Christian church itself, since less than half a century from its first establishment, there have never been awanting sects and divisions, all forming so many separate communities, and keeping upon each other a jealous eye, lest any change should be introduced into the sacred text to suit the views of their opponents. So that what has ever been the reproach of the Church has at the same time ever proved the safeguard of Scripture; and by an extraordinary coincidence, the worst as well as the best feelings, the perversity as well as the piety of human nature have been alike serviceable in preventing the possibility of fraud or forgery in the word of God, and throwing a fence of triple security around the sacredness of its contents.—*Fairbairn*.

III. *That the sacred writers recorded a faithful narration of facts.* This is corroborated by the *highest degree of concurrent testimony*. From the most ancient, and impartial historians, we learn that the Jewish and Christian dispensations, did actually exist at the time and in the order which the Scriptures mention;—the principal incidents concerning the Founders of these two economies, are confirmed by the same indubitable witnesses, and very many of the general events of the Old and New Testaments, are related as matters of fact by contemporary historians.

The epistles of Barnabas and Clement, fellow-laborers with the Apostle Paul, repeatedly refer to the gospels as acknowledged Scripture, and quote from them their very words. The epistles of Ignatius contemporary with some of the Apostles, and the epistle of Polycarp, who had been taught by the Apostles, and conversed with many who had seen Christ, contain numerous allusions to, and quotations from the gospels and epistles: the same may be said of Justin Martyr, who was converted in the early part of the second century. Irenæus in the second century wrote five books against heresies, in which nearly all the books of the Scriptures are expressly named and referred to as authorities; and the voluminous works of Tertullian probably contain more and longer quotations from the New Testament than are to be found in all the works of Cicero.

In the third century we have a host of authors commenting upon the books of Scripture; and still more numerous in the fourth century, with catalogues of the number of Scripture books published, translations made of them, harmonies, commentaries, etc., published; and the work progressed from age to age till the world was almost filled with its fruits. —— There is nothing in the whole history of ancient learning that can once be compared to this. Why then doubt the truth of God's word?

IV. *The Scriptures possess the most convincing internal marks of authenticity.* The *fidelity* of the writers is unquestionable. When persons publish a history of their own times, self-respect urges them to be substantially correct. All attempts at imposition would be regarded with general and just contempt. In the sacred writings there is the perfect absence of every thing like artifice; there is the felt presence of every mark of truthfulness and sincerity. The writers discover no solicitude but to disclose the truth which they had heard, and report the things which they had witnessed. They tell an unvarnished tale, without the least appearance of surprise, or attempt at parade, or symptoms of deceit. They speak like men who had nothing to fear from the fullest inquiry, and nothing to gain by the most implicit credit.

The facts which Moses and the subsequent writers of the Old Testament narrate, and on which the Jewish religion was founded, were addressed to their countrymen as personal witnesses of the events recorded.—That they admitted the reality of the facts is unquestionably evident: for they espoused the religion founded upon them, and have handed down the history, to perpetuate that religion, through succeeding generations. Hence it appears that the circumstances mentioned in the Old Testament are, strictly speaking, the testimony, not merely of Moses, or of any single individual, but of the whole body of the Jews from age to age. Now can any person reasonably imagine, that the

Jewish nation would unanimously attest, and continue to attest this history of facts? and, on the ground of them, submit to a form of a religion which imposed a variety of painful restraints, if they had not been persuaded of the reality of these facts? and is there the least degree of probability that they were deceived in this matter? Being addressed as witnesses of the events recorded, they must surely know whether they had witnessed them or not; and, as the facts were of so very extraordinary a nature, it was utterly impossible that they could be imposed upon by appearances. — *Lardner*.

The Evangelists and Apostles write as eye-witnesses of what they record, and evidently defy contradiction. Their testimony is strictly harmonious, and their character highly honourable. The facts they asserted extremely irritated many, who, if able, would have proved their falsehood. They persisted in their testimony in the face of persecution, imprisonment, and death, without the most distant prospect of any worldly advantage. Vast multitudes, on the evidence of their testimony, embraced Christianity; and even they who rejected its doctrines never pretended to deny the facts upon which it was founded. If a history attended by so many external and internal evidences, is not to be received as authentic, what can be admitted as worthy of credit?

"We believe the testimony of the Apostles, because, from what we know of the human character, it is impossible that men in their circumstances, could have persevered as they did in the assertion of a falsehood; it is impossible that they could have imposed this falsehood upon such a multitude of followers; it is impossible that they could have escaped detection, surrounded as they were by a host of enemies, so eager and so determined in their resentments."—*Chalmers*.

The truth of the Bible is self-evident. The Bible records an uninterrupted series of events, during a long succession of ages, all which events were naturally and necessarily dependent on each other;—the denial of one would invalidate the rest. These events are combined with facts obviously existing now;—with facts which cannot possibly be accounted for, except we admit the truth of Bible history.

For instance, both the Jews and the primitive Christians embraced their distinct systems of religion, from a sensible conviction of certain extraordinary and notorious facts; and that, according to the rites of their religion, they began immediately to observe certain ordinances designed to commemorate these facts. A succession of the same religious bodies are now before our eyes, observing the same ordinances. How can we account for the present existence of Jews and Christians, and the peculiarities of their ceremonies, except on the acknowledged authenticity of those Scriptures by which their religious profession is directed?

The following striking and convincing arguments to prove the Divine authority of the Bible are excellent: —

I have four grand and powerful arguments, which strongly induce me to believe that the Bible cannot be the invention of good men or angels, bad men or devils, but must be from God: viz., miracles, prophecies, the goodness of the doctrine, and the moral character of the penmen. All miracles flow from Divine power; all the prophecies, from Divine understanding: the goodness of the doctrine, from Divine goodness; and the moral character of the penmen from Divine holiness.

Thus I see Christianity is built upon four grand pillars, viz., the power, understanding, goodness, and holiness of God: — Divine power is the source of all miracles; Divine understanding, of all the prophecies; Divine goodness, of the goodness of the doctrine; and Divine holiness, of the moral character of the penmen.

The Bible must be the invention either of good men or angels, bad men or devils, or of God.

1. It could not be the invention of good men or angels, for they neither would nor could make a book and tell lies all the time they were writing, saying, Thus saith the Lord, when it was their own invention.

2. It could not be the invention of bad men or devils, for they would not make a book which commands all duty, forbids all sin, and condemns their souls to perdition for all eternity.

3. Therefore, I draw this conclusion, that the Bible must be given by Divine inspiration.

Even the character and conduct of Judas Iscariot furnish us with a strong argument for the truth of the Gospel. How came it to pass that he first betrayed his Master, and then was so stung with remorse as to put an end to his life by hanging himself? How came he thus to own himself guilty of the vilest sin, when, in fact, he knew that he had done an act of justice to the world, by freeing it from an impostor? For if Jesus was not what he really professed to be, he deserved all and much more than what Judas was the means of bringing upon him. Now if there had been any base plot, any bad design, or any kind of imposture in the case, Judas, who had so long lived with Christ, and had even been entrusted with the bag (which shows he was not treated with any reserve,) who was acquainted with the most private life of Christ, must certainly have known it; and if he had known of any blemish, he ought to have told it, and would have told it; duty to God, to his own character, and to the world, obliged him to it; but his silence in this respect gives the loudest witness to Christ's innocence. — *Reminiscences of the Rev. John Ryland, of Northampton.*

Again, it is quite clear that through all ages the Scriptures have been publicly read and expounded in every congregation of believers; so that every believer, through successive generations, may be appealed to as a witness of their early existence, and their truth. The influence of the Scriptures overthrew heathenish idolatry, throughout the wide domain of the Roman world; so that every ruined temple, and every relic of deserted Paganism, is another invincible witness of the Bible's verity. Through the higher views they opened up, and the new relations which they established, and the better spirit which they diffused, they introduced another style of society, new institutions, new customs, new buildings; so that in the laws, the manners, the establishments, the very architecture of modern kingdoms, we have additional testimonies, and enduring monuments of the same. These gradual and mighty changes were all the offspring of the progressive spread of Divine truth taught *in* the Bible, and *from* the Bible, and the renovating influence which accompanied the diffusion of its sublime doctrines.

Lastly. The Bible has withstood the withering influence of time, and all the opposition of its enemies.

"Pretended friends," says Dr. Payson, "have tried to corrupt it; kings and princes have perseveringly sought to banish it from the world; the civil and military powers of earth have been leagued for its destruction; the fires of persecution have been lighted to consume it and its friends together; and sometimes death in its most horrid form has been the consequence of love to God's word. In opposing it, wit and ridicule have wasted all their shafts; misguided reason has been compelled, though reluctantly, to lend her aid; and after defeats innumerable, has been again dragged to the field. The arsenals of learning have been emptied to arm her for the contest; and in search of means to prosecute it with success, recourse has been had to the bowels of the earth, and the regions of the stars; still the Bible remains uninjured, while the armies of its assailants have melted away.

Though it has been ridiculed more bitterly, misrepresented more grossly, it is so far from sinking under these attacks, that the probability of its surviving until the consummation of all things, is now evidently much greater than ever! The rain has descended; the floods have come; the storm has arisen, and beaten upon it; but it falls not, for it is founded upon a rock. Like the burning bush, it has ever been in the flames, yet still it is unconsumed; a sufficient proof, were there no other, that God who dwelt in the bush preserves the Bible.

XL. — PARDON AND JUSTIFICATION.

"Be it known unto you therefore, men and brethren, that through this man is preached unto you the forgiveness of sins: and by him all that believe are justified from all things, from which ye could not be justified by the law of Moses."—ACTS xiii. 38, 39.

THE gospel of salvation is the most glorious subject ever announced to the world. The announcement of abundant harvests —of the termination of war and the reign of peace—of great commercial prosperity—deliverance from captivity, disease, or death, all these, as they affect nations or individuals, may be regarded with the most intense interest: yet what are they when compared with the deliverances, freedom, peace, and blessedness proclaimed by the gospel?——The Apostle Paul delivered this message to the inhabitants of the city of Antioch.

I. THE SUBJECT OF THE APOSTLE'S PREACHING. Deliverance from guilt and condemnation, called "forgiveness of sins," and being "justified."

1. *The necessity of such a deliverance.* Rendered necessary by man being a sinner — against God the Divine Lawgiver — who declares that sin shall not go unpunished.

Justification is a term used in courts of law in the sense of acquittal. If the charge preferred against a prisoner cannot be proved, or if there be positive evidence of his innocence, he is acquitted; if found guilty, the law detains and punishes him.

A charge has been preferred against man of having wilfully, knowingly, and willingly acted in opposition to the Divine law — of rebellion — of insulting and resisting Divine authority.

The charge is proved by abundant testimony. By Scripture declarations.——By observation, all around us, all on earth being sinners.——By experience, even the accusations of our own consciences. Rom. iii. 1—3.

The sentence of death is recorded. "Cursed is every one," etc. The decree has gone forth to all the world. Every sinner carries the sentence of death about him continually.——O how much is implied in that awful sentence! Rom. i. 3; ii. 9—12.

But man has not been left to perish. The infinite love of God has provided salvation. Consider therefore,

2. *The Source of forgiveness and justification.* It is said, "through this man," meaning Jesus Christ. "Being justified freely by his grace, through the redemption that is in Christ Jesus." Rom. iii. 54. The term redemption denotes a price paid for the deliverance of captives. Matt. xx. 28; 1 Pet. i. 19.

The justification of a sinner originates in the grace of God. It is not the result of human merit. It can only be obtained by perfect obedience from birth to death, which man has never rendered, and never can. Sacrifices, however costly, will not procure justification. Nor can it be obtained in a future state by purgatorial fires, etc. The grace of God is the only source.

It is "through the redemption that is in Christ Jesus." Man could not have been pardoned and justified if the honour of the Divine government had not been maintained, and the authority of the Divine law vindicated. All the claims of Divine Justice were therefore exacted from Christ, and honoured by him, who voluntarily became the sinner's substitute — his Ransomer and Redeemer.

Christ honoured the law by perfect obedience—by enduring its penalty—by rising from the dead.—See Rom. iii. 24—26; Rom. v. 1, 6—8, 16—18.

3. *The enjoyment of this spiritual freedom.*
15*

(1) *Forgiveness of sins.* The remission of sins is *through this Man;* by his sufferings and death it was purchased; in his name it is offered, and by his authority it is bestowed. Sin is taken away, Ps. xxxii. 1. It is covered. Ps. xxxii. 1; lxxxv. 2. It is not imputed, Ps. xxxii. 2. All sins are blotted out, Isa. xliii. 25; Col. ii. 14. Remembered no more, Heb. viii. 12; Isa. xliii. 25. They are entirely obliterated, Isa. i. 18.—— *All* are forgiven, Col. ii. 13.

(2) *Freedom from condemnation,* and from the *law's penalty.* Justification is the opposite of condemnation; it is a repeal of the penalty; it is the removal of punishment—the rescinding of the sentence of death; for that sentence, that death has fallen upon Christ, the sinner's righteous substitute. Rom. viii. 1. "In Christ Jesus:" not that we are so united to Christ as that what he did and suffered was actually our doing and suffering; but the sinner believing in him, God considers them as if they were one; so that his death exempts us from death, and his righteousness is imputed for our justification.—— We are treated as righteous for his sake; and he, though innocent, is treated as if he were guilty, that we might be treated as if we were innocent. 2 Cor. v. 21.

II. *The Instrumental means of justification* Faith: "by him all that believe." Faith is not the efficient cause, for it is God who justifies; not the moving cause, for it is of free grace; not the matter of it, for it is the righteousness of Jesus Christ; not the ground of it, for that would be justification by works. Gal. ii. 16.

This faith implies knowledge — of ourselves, of Christ, and of the way of salvation through him—it implies credence—confidence, reliance, Eph. i. 13.

The way in which penitent sinners receive justifying grace, is said expressly to be "through faith in the blood of Christ," Rom. iii. 25. God is "the justifier of him that believeth in Jesus," verse 26. It is also said that faith or believing is counted unto righteousness, Rom. iv. 3, 5, 9; that "with the heart man *believeth* unto righteousness," chap. x. 10; that we are "justified by faith," ch. v. 1; and that "by him all that *believe* are justified," Acts xiii. 39. All these varied expressions are of the same import, and clearly show that men actually receive and enjoy the blessings of justification, by faith, or in believing the testimony that God has given of his Son, 1 John v. 9, 11. Thus a man is justified by faith, without the deeds of the law, Gal. ii. 16.

In consequence of being justified there is the enjoyment of peace, Rom. v. 1;—comfort and joy, Isa. xl. 1, 2;—access to God with boldness and confidence. Rom. v. 1, 2;—meetness for death and heaven—hope.

III. THE PERFECTION OF THIS FREEDOM. "From all things," etc.

From all law charges—and delivered from all the guilt, pollution, and power of sin. The law of Moses could not do this.

Rom. iii. 19, 20; iv. 15; v. 20; vii. 9—11; viii. 3, 4; ix. 31, 32; Gal. iii. 10—12, 22—25; Heb. viii. 19; ix. 9, 10; x. 4, etc.

Under the law of Moses, there were several crimes for which no sacrifices were appointed, but to which the sentence of death was annexed by that law; for instance, murder and adultery. Ps. li. 16. David, therefore, was justified not by the Levitical sacrifices, but by the sacrifice of Christ. Hence Bishop Horne observes,

David in this Psalm is so evangelical, and has his thoughts so fixed upon gospel remission, that he considers the Levitical sacrifices as already abolished, for their insufficiency to take away sin: affirming them to be (as indeed they were) nothing, in the sight of God, if compared with the sacrifice of the body of sin, offered by contrition and mortification, through faith in Him, who, in the fulness of time, was to die unto sin once, that we, together with him, might for ever live unto God.

The legal sacrifices could not take away guilt from the conscience; except as the penitent offender, through them had a believing dependence on the promised Redeemer. "Ye could not be justified by the law of Moses." That dispensation was now virtually abolished; having lost all its efficacy, etc.

IMPROVEMENT.

1. Be thankful for the gospel which proclaims so great a salvation.——2. Who are justified?——3. This is a justification which gives triumph, Rom. viii. 33, 34. Its value will be found in a dying hour——at the day of judgment, when the expectation of salvation by any other means will prove but as hay and stubble.

XLI.—THE TRUTH AND INFLUENCE OF THE GOSPEL.

"For this cause thank we God without ceasing, because, when ye received the word of God, which ye heard of us, ye received it not as the word of men, but, as it is in truth, the word of God, which effectually worketh also in you that believe."— 1 Thess. i. 3.

From the epistles sent to the church at Thessalonica, we see that the gospel is the power of God to salvation to every one that believeth. The conversion of the Thessalonians was very gratifying to Paul and his colleagues; for it was an evidence that their instrumentality had been crowned with the Divine blessing. Their conversion was deemed so important by the Apostles, and so exhilarating to their minds, that they constantly gave thanks to God, ch. i. 2, and the text.——The word of God is the same in truth and power as it was then—and its dispensation in love, in fidelity, in disinterestedness, may claim the same Divine influence for success at the present time.

I. THE TRUTH OF THE GOSPEL. "Not as the word of man, but, as it is in truth, the word of God."

The Apostle was fully persuaded in his own mind respecting the truth of Christianity. In his journey to Damascus he had received ocular demonstration of it; he was an eye-witness of Christ's majesty and glory. Acts ix. 3, 4, 22; xxvi. 13; 1 Cor. xv. 8.

God has revealed his gospel in the Scriptures, and their truth is proved by abundant evidence. Consider

1. The *majesty and sublimity of the style in which they are written.* The sublimity of thought, the majesty and simplicity of expression; the beauty, the purity of the *doctrine;* — the importance, universality, and expressive brevity of the *precepts;* their admirable appropriation to the nature and wants of man; the affecting piety, force, and gravity of the *composition;* the profound and truly philosophical sense discovered in it; these are the characters which fix the attention to the Bible, and which we do not find, in the same degree, in any production of the human mind.

"I am equally affected with the candour, the ingenuousness, and the modesty of the writers, and their unexampled and constant forgetfulness of themselves, which never admits their own reflections, or the smallest eulogium in reciting the actions of their masters. The distinguishing characteristics of the true sublime appear in these writings; for when God is the object, it is sublime to say, 'He spake, and it was done;' but the sublime occurs there because the thing was of an extraordinary nature; and because the writer delivered it as he saw it. The writers are not only completely ingenuous, for they *do not even dissemble their own weakness* — nor dissemble certain circumstances and sufferings of their master, which have no tendency to enhance his glory in the world. —— It is impossible, therefore, not to feel that the purport of their writing was to bear testimony to the truth. Is it possible that these fishermen who performed miracles; who said to the man, 'Rise up, and walk!' and he walked! is it possible that they should be so destitute of vanity as to disdain the applauses of the people who witnessed the prodigies. But mark their humility and disinterestedness: 'Ye men of Israel, why marvel ye at this? or, why look ye so earnestly on us, as though by our own power or holiness we had made this man to walk?' Who then are these men, who, whilst nature is obedient to their voice, are fearful that it should be attributed to their own power? How can the mind refuse its assent to such witnesses? How can such narrations be mere inventions?"—*Charles Bonnet, F. R. S., Natural Philosopher.*

2. *The great and glorious design of their great Author.* The inspiration of the writers indicated Jehovah's design to reveal his will to the human race. "All Scripture is given by inspiration of God, and is profitable," etc. 2 Tim. iv. 15—17. Salvation is

the great and absorbing subject of the Scriptures. Other subjects of importance are revealed, but this, the salvation of the soul, is the chief. No human mind could ever have conceived and announced the plan of redemption by Christ Jesus. It emanated from the mind of the infinitely benevolent God (John iii. 16), and therefore the Scriptures must be the word of God.

3. *The harmony of the Bible in all its parts.* There is a beautiful concurrence of history, narrative, prophecy, and doctrine, among all the sacred writers throughout the Old and New Testament. One part does not contradict another. If by an honest examination of the Book, we can find a single feature clashing with another feature of it, given by any one of the writers, scattered throughout the length of duration in which they lived, and placed in the variety of circumstances by which they were surrounded, then the Bible lacks evidence of a Divine origin. But if the features of this one system are found to vary only in development, but never exhibiting a discrepancy; varying only because by some they are more fully disclosed than by others, but never contradicting one another; if we find that all the features of the Bible exhibit thus one beauteous whole, then we are warranted to declare that this uniformity of testimony was given and continued by the power of God.

Do not forget that the sacred writers lived at different times — and in different parts of the world.

"In the whole history of the world," says Dr. Chalmers, "there is nothing that bears the least resemblance to this — an authorship beginning with Moses and ending with the apostle John — that is, sustained by a series of writers for 1500 years, many of them isolated from all the rest, and the greater part of them were unknowing and unknown to each other, insomuch that there could be no converse and no possible concert between them. A conspiracy between parties or individuals so situated had been altogether superhuman. Their lots were cast in different generations; and nothing can explain the consistency or continuity of their movements, towards one and the same great object, but that they were instruments in the hand of the one God, who, from generation to generation, keeps unchangeably by the counsels of his unerring wisdom and the determinations of his unerring will. The convergency towards one and the same fulfilment of so many different lights, appearing in different ages of the world and placed at such a distance from each other, admits, we think, of but one interpretation; nor, without the power and prescience of an over-ruling God, can we account for that goodly, that regular progression of consentaneous and consecutive authorship, which is carried forward by the legislators and seers and historians of the children of Israel."

4. *The labours, sufferings, and disinterestedness, especially of the apostles of Christ.* See the *Note*, page 77.

The Apostles could expect no worldly advantage, nor reputation of character, by circulating and advocating a falsehood. They must have seen that the result of such a course would be infamy and ruin. —— In the publication and advocacy of Christianity, they had contempt, imprisonment, torture, and death before them; yet they unshrinkingly dared them all; and for this invincible reason,—they had seen Christ, had been with him as his disciples, and were "eye-witnesses of his majesty and glory." And they themselves were endued with power from on high to work miracles, as a proof that they were Divinely commissioned.—— Think too of their strict morality—of their sanctity—of their entire consecration, their souls being absorbed with the work of God—of their disinterestedness; not seeking their own, but that of others—and of their resistance even unto blood; think of these brilliant and stubborn facts with humility and prayer, and without prejudice, and the judgment will pronounce the verdict. The finger of God has written the Bible! And these men had no means of collecting together such a mass of facts harmoniously narrated; such a mass of doctrines harmoniously stated; such a mass of institutions so exalted and appropriate;—in short, they could not have written such a book but by the inspiration of God.*

5. *The testimony of God himself.* He has spoken by *Miracles*, [see page 27.] He has spoken, is now speaking, and will continue to speak by *Prophecy*, [see page 99.]

Lastly, it will appear from the preceding evidences, to every candid and unprejudiced mind, that the gospel is the message of God.—— The reason of infidel opposition to the gospel, arises from the depravity of their hearts. "Men love darkness rather than light," etc.—— It arises too from gross ignorance on their part, which is especially shown in unfamiliarity with the Scriptures. Mr. Alexander Campbell, of the United States, thus expressed himself, when discussing with Robert Owen:—

"But, after all Mr. Owen's great reading and research, there is one book which he has not often read, and which above all others he ought (*even to attack it successfully,*) often to have read. I need not tell you that this is the Bible. It is true, indeed, that he told me he read it some two or three times when an infant at school; but what of that? At this I am astonished. How dare any man attack a book of such high pretensions, from a school-boy-reading of it! But this is in unison with the sceptical school. Thomas Paine wrote against the Bible from recollections, and acknowledged that he had not much read it. David Hume acknowledged, not long before his death, that he had never seriously read the New Testament through. I have never,

---

* PLINY, the persecutor, bears witness to the patience and fortitude of the primitive Christians under *suffering.* "I have put the question to them, whether they were Christians. Upon their confessing to me that they were, I repeated the question a second and a third time, threatening also to punish them with death; such as still persisted I ordered away to be punished, for it was no doubt with me, whatever might be the nature of their opinion, that contumacy and *inflexible obstinacy* ought to be punished." Others who were accused, "denied that they were Christians, or had ever been so; who repeated after me an invocation of the gods, and with wine and frankincense made supplication to your image, which for that purpose I caused to be brought and set before them, together with the statues of the deities. Moreover, they reviled the name of Christ; *none of which things,* as is said, they who are really Christians can by any means be compelled to do. These, therefore, I thought proper to discharge."

to this hour, met with a sceptic who was well acquainted with the Holy Scriptures, or who had in his writings evinced that he had given them a close or critical examination. If it were lawful thus to retort upon Mr. Owen, I would engage to prove that his opposition to Christianity is predicated upon his ignorance of it, instead of its being predicated upon the ignorance of mankind, in his sense, or as he presumes."

II. THE RECEPTION OF THE GOSPEL: "Ye received of the word of God which ye heard of us; ye received it not as the word of men, but, as it is in truth, the word of God." This language indicates the character and conduct of the Christians at Thessalonica.

1. *The gospel had been preached to them.* This accorded with the will of Christ, who has sent his gospel to the nations for the obedience of faith. Rom. i. 5; xvi. 26; 1 Thess. i. 3.

2. *They had heard the gospel* — with attention, candour, humility, and without prejudice. It is only in this way the gospel can benefit the hearers of it. How did the Jews hear Christ? Generally with the strongest prejudice and deep-rooted hatred to the truth. So it is with modern infidels. There is nothing they hate so much as Christ and the Bible. Rom. viii. 7; 1 Cor. ii. 14.

3. The preaching of the gospel to them *was attended with Divine power*, and therefore they received it. 1 Thess. i. 5. It was not merely the power of truth itself, though this often produces a very strong effect. "By the manifestation of the truth," etc. 2 Cor. iv. 2. There is an omnipotence in truth which cannot be resisted; the consciences of men are made to echo to its authority. —— It was the power of God which brought the gospel home to their hearts. It came in demonstration of the Spirit, and not in word only. 1 Cor. ii. 1—5; iii. 6, 7.

4. *They received the gospel.* "Ye received," etc. (1) They were convinced of its truth. They did not regard it, nor treat it as "the word of men;" they believed it could not have had any human origin. They examined the evidences of its truth, and were convinced that it was indeed "the word of God." The most zealous, active, useful, and happy men are those who firmly believe in the Divinity of the Scriptures. —— They received the word of God for the purposes of salvation. They *"believed" in Christ*, obtained mercy, and peace, and joy. They were saved, and became Christ's servants. —— Hence

III. THE INFLUENCE OF THE GOSPEL. "Which effectually worketh also in you that believe."

This is the grand experimental test of the truth of Christianity. —— What was the effect of the gospel upon the Thessalonians?

It rescued them from idolatry to the service of God, ch. i. 9; v. 5.

It produced faith, hope, charity, and every Christian grace, ch. i. 3.

It gave them joy in the Holy Ghost, ch. i. 6.

It produced emulation in holiness, ch. ii. 6, 14.

It produced victory over sin and temptation, ch. iii. 5—8.

It produced brotherly love, ch. iv. 9, 10. For piety, it made them the glory of the churches, 2 Thess. i. 3, 4.

It endued them with heavenly hope, 1 Thess. ch. i. 10.

This is Christianity. It is the uniform effect of the gospel. Select a thousand conversions by its power, and the tendency will be found the same in each: — enlightening, converting, saving, sanctifying, and will ultimately glorify. It "effectually worketh in all that believe," and no other system can possibly produce such effects.

Where is the nation of antiquity that could produce one enlightened, morally enlightened principle? No such principle was known in Greece or in Rome. There was nothing there but speculation on the elements and foundation of morality. Nor will it be found that any one of these nations was ever able to embody in the divinities they had fashioned, a single moral attribute. Their gods were the vilest passions, personified and worshipped; the attributes of their divinities, were the attributes of fiends. They had gods of war, of intrigue, and of every species of iniquity; they had not a single divinity of morality; not a single god of love, in its highest and loftiest sense.——The free circulation of moral health, constituting the life's blood of a nation, was unknown in the very best days of the most exalted heathens when Christianity was unknown; but when we come within the confines of Christianity, new principles and powers are developed, exercising a commanding influence over the human mind. We can trace the plain history of these new influences of truth to the introduction of Christianity: but infidelity has never taken up this position, to trace the history of these principles and influences in connection with its own cold, lifeless, and heart-rending system.

Hence, then, we argue the Divinity of the gospel from its mighty power upon individuals, communities, and nations. ——

IMPROVEMENT.

1. As the powerful and sanctifying influence of the gospel is an evidence of its truth, — are we instances of that influence?

2. See the reason of man's hatred to the Bible. Because it is full of light and purity.

3. Let the Christian cultivate a more intimate acquaintance with the Scriptures.

XLII.—ETERNAL LIFE THROUGH CHRIST RECEIVED OR REJECTED.

"He that believeth on the Son hath everlasting life; and he that believeth not the Son shall not see life; but the wrath of God abideth on him."—John iii. 36.

THE mission of Christ to earth eminently displays the infinite love of God, and deeply involves the interests of mankind. —— This chapter contains a comprehensive epitome of the Divine scheme of man's redemption by Christ Jesus. —— It presents to the mind the most important doctrines, blessings, and privileges of Divine grace. —— The consequences of receiving Christ or rejecting him are vast indeed.

I. THE CHARACTER AND PRIVILEGE OF THE CHRISTIAN. He "hath everlasting life."

1. *The blessing.* Everlasting life.

Though man is immortal, it does not follow that he has the everlasting life here mentioned. Apostate spirits in perdition are immortal, but have the very opposite of everlasting life; they see not life, but the wrath of God abideth on them. Everlasting life has been lost, forfeited by sin—"paradise lost."

Paradise has been regained by Jesus Christ, as will be shown hereafter, and therefore he is "the author of eternal salvation unto all them that obey him." Heb. v. 9.

(1) *Believing and everlasting life, are, in some respects, simultaneous.* The commencement of the exercise and the enjoyment are at one and the same time. The text reads, "*He hath* everlasting life"—not, he shall have it. He now enjoys the beginning of it by the quickening influences of the Spirit. Eph. ii. 1, 5; John v. 21, 24. —— Spiritual life here is the commencement of everlasting life to be enjoyed hereafter.

(2) Everlasting life is freely given to all believers. Rom. vi. 23; John x. 28; xvii. 2.

(3) He has *the pledge and earnest* of everlasting life. The work of God is carried on by the sanctifying influences of the Spirit. Eph. i. 11—14. The work of God within has ever a reference, a tendency, a progress, towards everlasting life. See John iv. 14.

> Rivers to the ocean run, nor stay in all their course;
> Fire ascending, seeks the sun,—both hasten to their source:
> So a soul that's born of God, pants to view his glorious face;
> Upward tends to his abode — to rest in his embrace.

(4) That the spiritual life enjoyed by the believer on earth shall be *consummated and established in everlasting glory.* There the work of God shall be perfected—detached from all sin—associated with all that is intellectual, elevated, and sublime. It will be

everlasting life in God's Paradise—in his heaven—in his magnificent dwelling-place—with departed brethren—with blessed saints—with bright angels, etc., adoring cherubim and seraphim—with the ever-blessed Trinity. John xvii. 24; Matt. xxv. 34; Rev. vii. 13, etc.

Thus everlasting life is the Divine favour enjoyed on earth, and perpetuated in heaven—it is grace in its consummation—the full, free, and uninterrupted enjoyment of God for ever.

2. *The Author and Source of everlasting life.* "He that believeth on the Son," that is, Jesus Christ. Called the Author of it. Heb. v. 9.

(1) Christ is the *Divinely appointed Author.* John iii. 16. Delegated from heaven for that specific purpose.

(2) He was the *Revealer of everlasting life,*—in a manner clear, distinct and glorious. "Brought life and immortality to light." He did that which neither Socrates, nor Plato, nor any of the ancient sages could do.

(3) *He was able to secure it;* being *the Son of God.* He had infinite power, wisdom, love, purity, goodness.——He became flesh. John i. 14.——He shed his blood and died to purchase it. Heb. ix. 12—15.

(4) *He freely offers everlasting life to all who believe.* Indicated in the text, and other Scriptures.

3. *The means of enjoying everlasting life.* "He that believeth on the Son."

(1) He gives *credence to the Divinity of Christ's Mission.* As "the sent of God."

(2) He is *acquainted with Christ;* as to his person, offices, work, sacrifices, etc.

(3) In believing on the Son, he *distrusts all self-righteousness,* and all humanly devised plans for justification in the sight of God.

(4) *He relies alone on the meritorious and heaven-accepted sacrifice of Christ for everlasting life.* Thus the Divinity of Christ—his death, resurrection, and intercession, become the basis of his faith and hope. The result is pardon, perfect and free justification, peace, joy, and meetness for everlasting life.

He has the foretaste, the earnest of, the longing for, and the assurance of everlasting life. "I know in whom I have believed," etc.

II. THE AWFUL STATE AND PROSPECT OF THE WICKED. "He that believth not the Son," etc.

1. *His unbelief.* "He that believeth not the Son." This is the character of all the wicked—they are called, *unbelievers,* and the *unbelieving.* It arises from their totally depraved feeling—from ignorance of themselves, of God, of the nature and bitter effects of sin—from pride—from love of the world—from fleshly lusts which war against the soul. It ever manifests itself in an utter contempt of Divine things.

Unbelief presumptuously insults the Divine Majesty—blasphemes his perfections—despises his goodness—impeaches his veracity—and "makes him a liar," 1 John v. 10—it indignantly contemns and insults the Lord Jesus Christ—and impenitently rejects every blessing and privilege of the gospel, John v. 40—it is the prolific principle producing every species of impiety and wickedness. Mark vii. 21—23.

2. *The consequences of unbelief.* These are two-fold.

(1) *A painful deprivation.* "Shall not see life." Unbelief will prevent them from enjoying *the life of grace* on earth—they will remain in a state of condemnation and death. John iii. 18. They will be excluded from *the life of glory*—never taste those celestial joys—the righteous shall enter into heaven and shine like the sun in the firmament, etc.—but against the wicked "the door shall be shut."——Unbelievers could not enjoy everlasting life, having no meetness, no disposition, no relish for it.

(2) *A dreadful endurance.* "The wrath of God abideth on him." The sentence of death is not repealed—the curse is not removed—God is still "angry with the wicked every day." Sin is always productive of the Divine anger. God hates sin with a perfect hatred. Sinners are condemned by the denunciations of the law—the threatenings of the gospel—and frequently by the reproaches of a guilty conscience. Like criminals under the awful sentence of death, waiting for the day of execution, unbelievers are reserved for the day of wrath. 2 Cor. v. 10; Matt. xxv. 41.

XLIII.—THE HEAVENLY MANSIONS.

"In my Father's house are many mansions: if it were not so, I would have told you. I go to prepare a place for you."—JOHN xiv. 2.

THESE words express Christ's affectionate solicitude for the welfare of his disciples. He was about to leave the world. His death he had often predicted to them in the plainest language, yet their expectations of a temporal Messiah and Prince were so strong, that they lightly regarded such predictions.——However, it is evident that on this occasion of our Lord's address, their minds were full of painful apprehensions. The coming tragical events began to cast their shadows before. The departure of their Lord was to them a most painful event. They would be like sheep without Shepherd in the midst of wolves.——Christ perfectly understood the state of their minds; and with his own peculiar tenderness, gives them consolation:—" Let not your hearts be troubled."——

I. THE SCENE OF THE "MANY MANSIONS." "In my Father's house."

This description conveys the idea

1. *Of Locality.* Where this house is, no one can say. But it

must be where God is. Though he fills all places; though the heaven of heavens cannot contain him, yet in the boundless universe, there is one peculiar, appropriate, and magnificent place which he has allotted for himself, his attendants and saints, to dwell in for ever. It is there he holds his court—manifests his love—and reveals his glory.

That heaven is a *place* appears certain; because it is destined to receive into its capacious mansions at the last day, the glorified material bodies of all the saints; and even now that of Christ, and those of Enoch, Moses and Elias, are there. As, therefore, there cannot be body without place, it becomes obvious that there must be a place,—a place fitted for receiving and containing bodies that are material. True, those bodies will undergo some change— probably transformed into spiritual bodies, to possess no longer animal but spiritual sensations and tendencies: still it will follow that place will be as much required for the abode of the body, as if it retained all its materiality; unless we admit the wild and uncomfortable conjecture, that it will float about in some mysterious way in the regions of space for ever. Spirit being a creation, must be a substance; and to speak of a thing being created, and not requiring place, is an absurdity. That which occupies no place must be nothing.

Heaven has been too much considered as a *state* only, and not as a *place;* and thus it has lost much of the interest which it would have otherwise created in the mind. It is true that heaven derives its attractive influence from its being a *state* of happiness; for what is *place,* even the most beautiful, when the mind is unhappy? It is not in the noblest mansions, nor in the most magnificent objects, to chase sorrow from the heart. Yet still, to a gladdened mind, joy will be increased by the presence of whatever is really beautiful and grand, and a new influx of pleasure will roll in upon the soul at the sight of every fresh object of interest. And such will be the effects of contemplating heaven as a *place.* In addition to the bliss produced by the thought of infinite purity, uninterrupted intercourse with God, and unlimited knowledge, in heaven,—is there no bliss in the thought that we shall enjoy this happiness in a region more lovely than Eden, and surrounded with scenery infinitely more beautiful and enchanting than any this terrestrial orb can present to our view?

2. *The idea of Grandeur.* "My Father's house." The house of Deity. How magnificent must that house be which is the residence of the infinite Creator and Governor of all worlds—the Head of a boundless universe! On this earth there are costly mansions of beauty, and palaces of astonishing splendour; but the chief palatial residence is that assigned to royalty—that is supereminently glorious. So in the boundless universe, God's residence is the most elevated, rich, extensive, majestic, beautiful, and glorious. The Almighty Architect of the universe built it. Look at his works around you—though cursed and withered by sin, yet they still possess vast beauty, and they declare the glory of God.

God made the heavenly house — God dwells in it — that is the idea of grandeur. He has made that high and lofty place for himself and his redeemed to dwell in — the "poor worm Jacob," the broken-hearted and contrite publican, the penitent malefactor, the chief of sinners, the less than the least of all saints, and millions upon millions saved by Christ, shall dwell in his Father's house for ever — and this Divine purpose manifests *the grandeur of grace!*

The heavenly house is represented as infinitely beautiful and lovely.

When we survey the lofty and lovely scenery of nature, and gaze on her sunlit prospects, in which every object is adorned with beauty, and hear the sweetest melodies wafted on the breeze, we reason, if a world like this, wasted by the curse, be yet so fair, may there not be in the vastnesses of immensity, another world, the heaven of God, and of angels and saints, of infinitely surpassing beauty and glory, abundant in every thing to gratify the desires and wishes of the *immortal* mind?

The beauty of the ancient Eden was great; the glory of the heavenly Paradise is infinitely greater. The beauty of Canaan was most enchanting — but earth, with all its remaining loveliness, is but a miserable desert, a waste-howling wilderness, when compared with the "*Father's house.*" The foundations of the heavenly city are decorated with all manner of precious stones. Its dimensions are wonderfully great. Its wall is of jasper; its buildings are of pure and pellucid gold; its gates are pearls; its watchmen are angels. The throne of God and the Lamb is in the midst of it. Out of this throne proceeds the river of life, and on its banks stands the tree of life, yielding the various fruits of immortality. No iniquity is found here. No night overcasts the sky. No moon shines. No sun arises. The hours of darkness are unknown here. "The Lord God Almighty, and the Lamb, are the temple" of this Divine residence; the Sun which shines with the splendour of everlasting day.

Purity gives to the "Father's house" loveliness and beauty. Whatever physical, mental, and moral deformity exists in this world, it has been caused by sin. Sin has made this world a valley of tears — a place of incessant weeping — a field of blood, and the land of death. All that annoys, irritates, and distresses here, is the product of sin! O! to think of the *heavenly house* as having no sin existent there — of the church there as washed in the Redeemer's blood, sacrificed by the Spirit, "not having spot or wrinkle, or any such thing," — perfectly beautiful and glorious in the image of God, "entire, wanting nothing."

3. The language conveys *the idea of home.* "My Father's house" suggests this idea. From that house he came, and for a season sojourned in this world of sorrow. He therefore left his home, but having finished his work, was about to return. "I go unto the Father;" (John xiv. 28,) that is, I am going home. So Christ's disciples sojourn in a distant part of God's dominions; —— but they will soon reach their home. They are crossing the ocean of this life, and faith sees, and hope expects to reach, their Father's house — their home; for Jesus calls his people "brethren,"

Heb. ii. 11; and they desire to be with him in the "better country," their Father's house, Heb. xi. 16. "Behold, I ascend to my Father and your Father," etc. John xx. 17.——Hence believers especially in their dying moments, have rejoiced in heaven as their home:——

Mr. Brewer said, "O what a world am I going to! Here all is sin, and all is sorrow, but there, everlasting joy. Jesus is standing to receive my spirit. My heart, and my flesh faileth, but God is the strength of my heart, and my portion for ever."

"It will not be long, (said Mr. Toplady,) before God takes me; for no mortal man can live (bursting into tears) after the glories which God has manifested to my soul."

Dr. Rowland Taylor, when drawing near the town of Hadley, in Suffolk, where he had been a minister, and was now going to be a martyr—being asked how he did — answered, "Never better: for now I know that I am almost at home!" — And looking over the meadow between him and the place where he was to be immediately burnt, he said, "Only two stiles more to get over, and I am at my Father's house." And when the venerable Mr. Mede was asked how he did, replied, "I am going home as fast as I can, as every honest man ought to do, when his day's work is over; and I bless God I have a good home to go to."

II. THE NATURE AND EXCELLENCY OF THESE MANSIONS.

Christ alludes to the various apartments in the temple, and the vast number of persons lodged there, 1 Kings vi. 5; Jer. xxxv. 4, and by a striking simile from them he represents those numerous seats of heavenly bliss which his Father's house contained, and which were prepared for the righteous.

This representation of heaven implies,

1. *Ample accommodation.* "Many mansions." As in the ancient temple there was no lack of accommodation for the large number of officials and servants, so heaven will possess more than ample room for the "many sons," and "the great number which no man can number," whom Christ will bring to glory. The family will be innumerable, and the house will be vastly capacious. The number of apartments in Solomon's temple was limited; the number in the celestial temple will be unlimited. I am going home, says Christ, to my Father's house, and there will be ample room for you.—— O glorious thought! they "shall come from the East," etc.

2. *Variety.* "Many mansions." The sources of felicity will be numerous and diverse. God will explain mysteries—communicate light—and the wonders of redemption and grace will be constantly unfolding themselves. God will continue the operations of his wisdom and power in the boundless universe, the knowledge and inspection of which will be a source of infinite pleasure to the glorified saints. The companionship of angels — recognition and communion with relatives and brethren—the worship of God—the

lofty and melodious music—the glorious habiliments, the ethereal nature of the glorified body and soul—all these, and much more abundantly, imply most interesting variety.

3. Therefore the heavenly mansions will be *infinitely felicitous and adapted to sanctified souls*. This is evident from what has already been stated:—the locality—the grandeur—the beauty and loveliness of the Christian's home in the "Father's house." Yes, they are *mansions of purity*—of *uninterrupted and undisturbed repose*—a "rest" of *intellectual light*, etc.

4. *Mansions of Stability*. Not like a tent or tabernacle, always changing places. There are no mutations in heaven—no reversions—no change from good to evil———for they are

5. *Mansions of eternal permanency*. "Mansions," in the original Μοναι, from Μενω, which means to remain, to continue, or *abiding places*—called in another place, "everlasting habitations," 2 Cor. iv. 17, 18; v. 1. Mansions of immortality! how different from our dwelling-place here, which is full of change, sin, sorrow, and death!

III. THESE MANSIONS ARE PREPARED BY CHRIST. "I go to prepare."

Christ was going to his cross—to his grave—to his intercession in heaven, to prepare a place for his people.

1. *By his Sacrificial death*. He was going to that—going to the garden and its agony—to the Jewish tribunal with its insults, mockings, and scourging—to Calvary to suffer and to die. "I go," etc. I have fulfilled the law, glorified my Father, and now I go to Golgotha, to endure the penalty denounced against transgressors. The bitter cup is mingled for me to drink—the baptism of blood is prepared—the curse is coming upon me—the fire of Divine wrath is descending, and gathering around my soul! I go! but I shrink not; "for the joy that is before me, I will endure the cross," etc. For your salvation, I will die. I go—to rend the vail—to break down the middle wall of partition—to open a new and living way. See Eph. v. 2.

2. *By his resurrection*. He was going to the grave to rise—to triumph over mortality, that we might rise and triumph too. Rom. iv. 25; John xi. 25; 1 Thess. iv. 14, etc.

3. *By carrying our nature into heaven*. There "our Forerunner is for us entered." Heb. vi. 20. Heaven had been the abode of his Divine nature, and not as yet of his human nature. But in that nature he was going home, that by his spotless sacrifice he might appear in the presence of God for us.

Thus the believer may rejoice. "My nature is already in heaven in the presence of my Saviour. I, as a man, am now degraded by sin, wretched, sickly, and dying—my nature is subject to anguish and to mortal decay; but I see man in the person of my Redeemer on the throne of God. Mean as man may be here, he is exalted there. The great High Priest, who in human nature atoned for our sins, has carried that nature, in inseparable union with the Divine, into the celestial temple, and has taken possession of it for man in the very nature of man.

When Christ went into heaven as our High-Priest, to present his own sacrifice before the Father on our account, *he prepared a place for us*, which the Apostle expresses by his purifying or consecrating the heavenly places in which we are to dwell, which would have been polluted by the entrance of such sinful creatures into them. Heb. ix. 23, 24. So the tabernacle was consecrated, Ex. xxix. 36, 37 ; Lev. xvi. 16.

Behold, then, Christ preparing a place for us by the *administration of all his mediatorial offices in heaven*. His blood falls upon the mercy-seat — he pleads, and is heard. He commissions his Spirit, and he descends.

IV. THE CERTAINTY OF THE EXISTENCE OF THE HEAVENLY MANSIONS; "if it were not so, I would have told you."

It is not my interest to deceive you. I "take pleasure in the prosperity of my servants." "I am the faithful and true Witness." I can never deceive those whom I have loved with an everlasting love. *If it were not so:* — I know whether *it is so or not* — and I affirm that *it is so;* for I have come forth from that heaven, my Father's house, and that is "the kingdom prepared for you," etc. My mission to earth is a proof that *it is so;* for had there been no heaven lost and to regain, I should not have been sent. You have seen my miracles; they testify of me. You know my sufferings and privations — my disinterestedness, benevolence, and compassion—that I have refused earthly honours—you know my character —it is perfect, for I challenge the whole universe, "which of you convinceth me of sin? What motive then could I have had in attempting to deceive you? I speak as one having authority — "in my Father's house are many mansions" — I am "the Author of eternal life" to those that believe. "If it were not so, I would have told you."

As Mr. Jay observes, "If it had not been so, he *could* have told them. If it had not been so, he *should* have told them. If it had not been so, he *would* have told them."

IMPROVEMENT.

1. Are we prepared for these mansions? For they are prepared for a prepared people. 2. Rejoice in what Christ has done, and is now doing for you. 3. Anticipate the time when your tents shall be struck, and you shall enter the temple above. "I will come again, and receive you to myself," etc.

XLIV.—THE VOICE OF THE BELOVED.

"The voice of my Beloved! behold, he cometh."—Song ii. 8.

This Song is a Divine allegory in the form of a pastoral; and represents the reciprocal love between Christ and his Church, under figures taken from the relation and affection which subsist between the bridegroom and his espoused bride; an emblem continually employed in Scripture. To understand it aright, we must consider the Redeemer as loving and beloved of his Church. The marriage contract is already ratified, but the completion of this blessed union is reserved for the heavenly state. Let this Book be read with a spiritual mind, or it will be "a savour of death unto death."

I. THE BELOVED; "My Beloved."

The Beloved had withdrawn from the bride; but with rapture she again hears his voice, and perceives the tokens of his return, "leaping *upon*," or "over the mountains," skipping upon the hills.—— This may apply to the ancient believer's expectation of the promised Saviour coming in the flesh: they heard his voice by the prophets, and every age gave fuller intimations of his approach. Though he seemed to delay, yet he was coming with speed and alacrity; nor could any obstructions prevent his approach; but he would surmount them as the hart does the mountains and hills.*

1. Christ is *the Beloved of the Father*. Isa. xlii. 1. The expression, "the only begotten Son, which is in the bosom of the Father," John i. 18, represents the Divine affection. "This is my beloved Son," etc. Matt. iii. 17; John xii. 23, 27—30. "The Father loveth the Son, and hath given* all things into his hand," John iii. 35. He has given him the Church—its "government is upon his shoulder"—a commission and the power to redeem them —and the treasures of infinite grace with which to bless them—he has exalted him—and given him universal empire. Ps. ii. 8; Rev. vix. 6, 16.

2. Christ is *the Beloved of the Angels*, 1 Pet. i. 12; 1 Tim. iii. 10. Angels from eternity loved him — they admired and loved him in the various stages of his life—from his birth in Bethlehem to his death at Golgotha. At his birth crowds of angels descended from heaven, and hovered over the place where their incarnate God lay in a manger, Luke ii. 10—14; Heb. i. 15. At his temptation, angels ministered unto him, Matt. iv. 11. When agonizing

---

* In this sense (read verse 8th and 9th), "the wall" behind which he stood, "the windows" through which he looked, and "the lattice" through which he showed some glimpses of his glory, represent the types and ceremonies of the law, and the prophecies especially relating to that event: these in part revealed him, yet so that he was concealed from unbelievers; and but dimly seen by believers; yet his eyes were upon them, and they became in some degree acquainted with him.

in Gethsemane they were there, Luke xxii. 43. And on the cross they saw him expire! John i. 51.

> Around the bloody tree
> They press'd with strong desire
> That wondrous sight to see,—
> The Lord of life expire!
> And could their eyes have known a tear,
> It had dropt there in sad surprise.

They watched his grave — rolled away the stone from the sepulchre, and opened the prison-doors that the rising Conqueror might march forth. They formed his glorious retinue when he ascended. "The chariots of God," etc. Ps. lxviii. 17.

> Yes, when array'd in light,
> The shining Conqueror rode,
> They hail'd his rapturous flight,
> Up to the throne of God;
> And wav'd around their golden wings,
> And struck their strings of sweetest sound.

And now in heaven Jesus is the darling of angels. His name sounds from all their harps, and his love is the subject of their seraphic songs. They cry with a loud voice, "Worthy is the Lamb," etc. Rev. v. 11, 12. It is the song of the angels—it is the song of the redeemed: —

> Jesus, the Lord, their harps employs;
> Jesus, my Love, they sing:
> Jesus, the name of both our joys,
> Sounds sweet from every string.

3. Christ is *the Beloved of his people*. "Unto you therefore which believe he is precious," 1 Pet. ii. 7, or *preciousness*, all preciousness, and nothing but preciousness. The world despises him and regards him as "a rock of offence," but he is precious to God who knows him best — and precious to believers. Faith induces them to look upon persons and things as God does; conforming their sentiments to his. Christ is the Father's beloved Son, in whom he is well-pleased, and he is their beloved Saviour, in whom they are well-pleased.

Everything about Christ is excellent and glorious, and therefore they love him. For his dignity and glory — or his infinite love and condescension—for his perfect obedience to the law—for his loveliness of character—for his wise and beautiful teaching — for the work of redemption — and the gift of his grace, they love him. 1 John iv. 19.

They show their love by service in his cause — caring for it, praying for it, helping it forward—consecrating to it every talent. They are careful of his honour — guard it from reproach — and boldly avow themselves on the Lord's side.

Those that love Christ, love all that belong to him. They love the brethren. 1 John iv. 7—11.

II. THE REVELATION OF THE BELOVED. "The voice of my Beloved." He reveals himself.

1. *By his word.* There his voice is heard, whether in the private perusal of it, or in the public ministration of it. That word, which is the voice of the Beloved, speaks his character — his will — his laws — his gospel. It reveals him as the mighty Saviour. How sweet is the voice of the Beloved in the gospel! "My sheep hear my voice," John x. 27; xvii. 37. The voice of his atoning blood sounds sweetly in their ears. It "speaketh better things than the blood of Abel," or of any of the ancient sacrifices.

2. *By his Spirit dwelling in the heart.* This is the inward voice of the Beloved — a still-small voice, inspiring with light, peace, joy, faith, patience, hope, etc.

Observe this voice is *pleasant;* "Never man spake like this man."

It is *instructive,* giving information on the most important matters. It is *influential.* It raises the dead sinner to life — it calls back the wanderer, and restores the prodigal — it animates the Christian pilgrim to perseverance — and the Christian soldier to continued conflict and victory.

III. THE COMING OF CHRIST: "Behold he cometh." Then his voice is heard as the signal of his approach.

1. This was the language of *primitive and expectant saints,* "waiting for the consolation of Israel." They looked by faith over "the wall" of partition, and through "the windows" and "lattices" of types and shadows, they saw Christ in the distance, and said, "Behold he cometh."

2. He came by *his incarnation,* when he came in the form of a servant, and clothed with humility. He came to die. "I am come that you might have life," etc. "This is a faithful saying," etc. 1 Tim. i. 15.

3. He comes to *the poor penitent sinner* in his distress, and says, "Come unto me," etc. Matt. xi. "Thy sins are forgiven thee," etc.

4. He comes to *the poor, afflicted saint,* and sweet and consolatory is his voice. "My grace is sufficient for thee," 2 Cor. xii. 9. Amid the darkness and violence of earth's tempests his voice is heard; "It is I, be not afraid."

The language is expressive of all the *spiritual* visits of Christ to his people. He is ever ready to restore, revive, heal, comfort and animate.

5. It is applicable to his *coming at death* to receive the soul to glory. "Behold he cometh" to fetch his people home. Unpleasant to human nature is the messenger employed for this purpose — the "King of terrors," — "death on the pale horse," Rev. vi. 7, 8; but as he is under the power of Christ, having been conquered by him, death is a friend.

"When grim Death has lost his sting, he wears an angel's face; and he has lost his sting to a believer. I will tell you how a believer feels when he sees the pale horse and his rider. (Rev. vi. 7, 8.) He is something like a young gentleman at school. The time of vacation comes, and his father says, "I will send for you, and you shall come home." The young man has got every thing packed up, and expects his father's servant to come; he looks out at the window, and he says, "Is my father's servant coming? O yes; yonder I see my father's pale horse; I know it well enough; my father's servant is coming." And when the servant comes, on the pale horse, does he feel sick? No! He goes round to his poor school-fellows, and shakes hands, and says, "Farewell; — I shall be glad to see you at my father's house; I shall be glad to welcome you home; I shall see my father, my mother, and my companions." And there is his father's servant, on his father's pale horse.

So it is, my brethren, with an heir of God, and a joint-heir with Christ. When Death comes, upon his pale horse, he does not feel faint; his father's servant is coming; he shakes hands with all who are around him, and says, "Farewell; meet me in Heaven; I will meet you at the pearly gates: and I will welcome you. I shall see my father, my mother, my brother, my relations, and my friends — farewell." "O death, where is thy sting; O grave, where is thy victory?" Ps. xxiii. 4.—*Dawson.*

6. To his coming *in judgment* to complete the salvation of his people. "Behold he cometh." 1 Thess. i. 10; Jude 14; Rev. i. 7.

XLV. — THE IMMORTAL CONSTITUTION OF MAN IN A FUTURE STATE.

"Neither can they die any more; for they are equal unto the angels; and are the children of God, being the children of the resurrection." — LUKE xx. 36.

THE ministry of Christ consisted of revelation, teaching, and the manifestation of the Divine power and love. By the latter he proclaimed his credentials, as the "Sent of God," to be Divine; by the former he instructed the ignorant sinner, and shed a clear and brilliant light over his future existence. He who is called the "Eternal Life," and the "Way" to it, revealed heaven to man. He brought life and immortality to light by the gospel. He did that which the wisest sages, or the most renowned philosophers could not do with any degree of certainty. With them all was conjecture: with Christ all was clear and decisive.—— The doctrine of a future state was rejected by the Sadducees; they believed not in a resurrection, nor in angels or spirits. They were openly profane and licentious—the effect of regarding human life as mere animalism.

In the context Christ successfully encountered these infidel objectors. They attempted to embarrass him by proposing what appeared to them a difficulty; v. 27—33. The inference which they desired to deduce from it was the impossibility of a resurrection. The answer of Christ is sublime and overwhelming; v. 34—38.

The language employed by Christ indicates,

I. That in a future state, there will be a NEW CONSTITUTION OF SOCIETY.

Here Society is characterized by sensualism, sin, and sorrow. In heaven these will not exist at all. "The children of this world marry, and are given in marriage,"—but there they "neither marry nor are given in marriage," v. 34, 35. There will be no sexual unions, as in this world—but the absence of all sensualism. Marriage is intended only for the present world, to replenish the earth, and to repair the ravages that death continually makes amongst its inhabitants. Marriage is a Divine ordinance, and when properly contracted by the respective parties, highly honourable; but in multitudes of instances it is associated with sin, and in all cases with pain and sorrow.

The population of heaven never decreases—it is always increasing, and will do so till God shall have gathered together there all his redeemed people, who will be sinless, glorious, and immortal. "Neither can they die any more." As there will be no death there, sexual unions will be unnecessary; for they "are equal unto the angels, and are the children of God, being the children of the resurrection."

How mean and grovelling does the life of man appear here! What multitudes resemble, or exceed, "the beasts that perish." Ps. xlix. 12. "The works of the flesh are" frequently and most awfully "manifest." A perusal of Rom. i. 18—32, will exhibit to us the debased state of humanity.—— But through the blessed redemption of Christ the saints shall be constituted to mingle with ethereal spirits before the throne. Their bodies will be rendered spiritual, and all their employments and pleasures will be pure, intellectual, and angelic. Divine grace

> Will lift them from this abject to sublime;
> This flux to permanent; this dark to day;
> This foul to pure; this turbid to serene;
> This mean to mighty! And place them where
> Sin will deform no more!

II. For the Society of heaven Christians WILL BE ADAPTED PRIMARILY BY BEING DISEMBODIED, AND ULTIMATELY BY THE GLORIOUS RESURRECTION OF THEIR BODIES; v. 35.

The spirit of the believer at death quits the earthly tenement for ever. He is "absent from the body, and present with the Lord." 2 Cor. v. 1—6. Absent from a body humbled and debased by sin. Absent from a body sluggish and inert, altogether disproportioned to the activity of the mind; and often found to be an impediment to its operations;—a body which Pagan philosophers denominated the sepulchre of the soul, and the prison of the spirit. Absent from a body which is full of moral corruption and defilement; being the principal source of temptation, as the gratification of its various appetites are more sensible and urgent than that of the mental appetite. "The body is dead because of sin." Absent from a body constantly liable to pain and sickness, of frail and feeble texture, whose foundation is the dust, and which is ever tending to decay.

Therefore, being free from this corrupt and gravitating weight of earthly matter, the soul will be prepared for, and spring up, to enjoy all the felicities of the heavenly inheritance.

And even the body itself will be adapted by Divine power to inherit the kingdom of heaven. From sin, corruption, inertness, pain, sickness, and death, it will be perfectly delivered. "For our conversation is in heaven," etc. Phil. iii. 20, 21. The body will then be invested with spiritual properties; for "it is sown a natural body, but it shall be raised a spiritual body." At the resurrection, corruption shall be left behind in the grave, and through the endless ages of eternity shall never appear to deface the beauty, or interrupt the health of the blessed. "It is sown in corruption, it is raised in incorruption."——"It is sown in weakness, it is raised in power." There shall be given to it the strength and energy of an angel, to qualify it to bear and enjoy that "exceeding and eternal weight of glory." Inconceivable to our minds will be the strength of the glorified bodies of the redeemed, when they shall come forth from the tomb, fitted for being placed in the presence of the unveiled splendour of Jehovah! Wonderful contrast! a body languishing amid the weakness of approaching dissolution, scarcely able to bear the gentlest whisper of the human voice, — and this same body, in a future period of its being, fitted to endure and enjoy the matchless glories of heaven.

Thus both soul and body are prepared for God's dwelling-place, where they "neither marry, nor are given in marriage." Christians will be raised to associations more lasting—to employments more dignified, and to pleasures more satisfying than those below the skies. How mean and transitory will earthly connections appear to the glorified saint, when contrasted with the everlasting friendships of heaven! It is a pleasing thought that though no connections will exist there similar to earthly ones, yet the most refined enjoyments of a social nature will be experienced. The heavenly inhabitants will be actuated by one feeling. The Almighty Spirit, like the living creature in the wheels, moving every mind, the most entire harmony will exist. The whole will be as one family,—a family in which love will be the predominating emotion, and which will be always on the increase. They will have one name; for "of Jesus the whole family in heaven and earth is named."

III. This representation INDICATES THE TOTAL ANNIHILATION OF DEATH, and therefore A STATE OF IMMORTALITY. "Neither can they die any more." It is delightful to think of a world where death will be unknown. For only consider,

1. Death is the effect of sin.——2. It is the extinction of life: the strength departs—the blood congeals—the pulsation stops—the lungs heave no more—earthly possessions and ties are surrendered.——3. It is painful to the dying, and to surviving relatives and friends, deeply affecting.——4. Death conducts the soul to its eternal destiny—to everlasting life, or to the blackness of darkness for ever.

Ever since sin entered this world, death has committed its fearful ravages, and cast its sombre shadows over all human society. This is a dying world. "Our fathers, where are they, and the prophets, do they live for ever?" Where, under heaven, is the place in which are not deposited the ashes of the saints? In what locality find we not a sepulchre and a waving cypress? And still the "King of terrors" triumphs! Daily, hourly, every moment, he smites, and as often the church mourns. She looks around for her prophets, but they are not: for her apostles, but they are not; for her reformers, but they are not; for her missionaries, but they are not; for her pastors and teachers of former generations, but they are not: for lover, friend, and Christian brother, but they are all gone down to the shades of darkness.

But lift up your eyes to the land of immortality. "Neither can they die any more," for they are *saved by Christ*. For them he "has abolished death," and triumphed over the grave. He paid the penalty which sin had merited, which rendered death dreadful. He has entered the grave and risen from it as the first fruits of those that sleep. The exaltation of Christ is the pledge that they "can die no more." "Because I live, ye shall live also." They can die no more, because *death shall be absolutely destroyed*. "He will swallow up death in victory." "The last enemy that shall be destroyed is death." "And death and hell were cast into the lake of fire." Rev. xx. 11—15. "Neither can they die any more," for *they are immortal* as God is immortal. The bodies of the saints are gone to the grave, but their spirits "live unto God," or with him. See ver. 37, 38. Here the doctrine of immortality is clearly taught.

"Let it be observed, that Abraham was dead upwards of 300 years before these words were spoken to Moses: yet *still* God calls himself the *God of Abraham*, etc. Now Christ properly observes that God is not the God of the *dead* (that word being equal, in the sense of the Sadducees, to an *eternal annihilation*), but of the *living;* it therefore follows that if he be the *God of Abraham, Isaac, and Jacob*, these are not *dead*, but *alive;* alive *with God*, though they had ceased, for some hundreds of years, to *exist among mortals*. We may see from this, that our Lord combats and confutes *another* opinion of the Sadducees, viz., *that there is neither angel nor spirit;* by showing that the *soul* is not only immortal, but lives *with* God, even *while* the *body* is detained in the *dust* of the *earth*, which body is afterwards to be raised to life, and united with its soul by the *miraculous power of God*, of which *power* they showed themselves to be ignorant when they denied the *possibility* of a *resurrection.*" — *Dr. A. Clark.*

IV. THE HEAVENLY STATE WILL BE OF AN ANGELIC CHARACTER; "they are equal unto the angels," who neither marry nor die, but are immortal. Matt. xxii. 30. " Equal to the angels," or "as the angels."

1. *In perfect freedom from animal and sensual appetites.* Angels have never been associated with humanity. Their felicity has been infinitely greater, more refined and satisfactory than any to be derived from animal nature. When Christians shall be assimilated to angels there will not be experienced one particle of regret for the surrender of earthly associations, however tender and endearing they may have been.

2. *Equal to angels in perfect purity,* "not having spot," etc. Angels have never sinned. Goodness in them has been increasing from the dawn of their being until now. How great their sanctity! How lovely their appearance! Virtue, even in this world, is lovely and commanding; what must be its influence when seen in perfection?

3. *Equal to angels in knowledge.* The capacity will be expanded to comprehend, like them, the wondrous operations of Jehovah's hand.

4. *Equal to angels in beauty.* A man remarkably intelligent, and possessing great moral excellence, is a beautiful character. How beautiful must an angel be, perfectly free from animalism, sin, and ignorance! Sin has marred the whole creation. Whatever ugliness and deformity we see around us, all has been occasioned by sin.*

5. *Equal to angels in immortality.* In their employments, they will never tire — age will never impair their powers — their pleasures are immortal, and cannot satiate — the infinitely varied sources of their happiness can never be exhausted. Like God — like angels, the saints will be immortal, and shall "die no more."

V. For the Heavenly state, CHRISTIANS HAVE NOW THE PREPARATION AND THE HOPE. "Being the children of God, and of the resurrection." This implies,

1. Their belief in the gospel, and their reliance upon Christ for

---

* "If we were never afflicted with any disease; if we were never to indulge in any degree of sinful passion; and if we were never to depart in our affections from God, but were continually to have them in entire subjection to him, it is impossible to say what might be the effect of this on the appearance of our bodies. Had Adam remained sinless, it is a possible, if not a likely thing, that he would, down to the latest day of his residence in this world, have retained all the freshness and vigour of appearance which he possessed when he came at first out of the hands of the Creator. Sin, there is every reason to believe, has not only marred the moral beauty of the soul, but has spoiled the very appearance of our bodies. And it is perhaps in consequence of the entire absence of sin among the angels, that one of them, after the lapse of four thousand years at least, appeared to Mary still as but a young man. This idea, also, may help us to understand in what manner the saints in heaven will retain all their freshness and beauty throughout the ages of eternity." — *Leslie.*

salvation. Christ "was delivered for our offences, and rose again for our justification." As penitent sinners, feeling themselves helpless, and ready to perish, they depend upon Christ's finished work, as confirmed and rendered valid by his resurrection.

2. They are adopted into the family of God. "Being the children of God." Rom. viii. 15—17.

This is their preparation for heaven, and the basis of their hope of it. Hence at ver. 35, it is said, "But they which shall be accounted worthy to obtain that world, and the resurrection from the dead." A parallel passage occurs in Rev. iii. 4, "Thou hast a few names even in Sardis which have not defiled their garments; and they shall walk with me in white: for they are worthy." Made worthy, not by human merit, — not by self-righteousness, but by the blood of Christ. The infinite merit of his sacrifice is appropriated to them. That constitutes the robe of righteousness in which they will boldly appear in the presence of God. Hence believers rejoice in hope: "For if we believe that Jesus died and rose again, even so them also who sleep in Jesus will God bring with him." 1 Thess. iv. 14, etc.

It is evident therefore that there must be a realization of Christ's power on earth in order to realize it hereafter. In John vi. 51, it is written, "I am the living bread, etc. — whoso eateth my flesh and drinketh my blood, hath eternal life, and *I will raise him up at the last day;*" indicating the union subsisting betwixt the Redeemer and the redeemed—a union close and indissoluble. That which we eat becomes a part of ourselves; our very flesh, and blood, and bones. Those then who really by faith apprehend, or lay hold of Christ, are one with him, mystically and spiritually, and shall consequently know the "power of his resurrection," or be "raised up at the last day."

IMPROVEMENT.

1. What a glorious prospect has the Christian before him! How dreadful the prospect of the unregenerate!

2. How consoling is this subject under bereavement! We shall join our brethren who are gone before us to heaven, and we shall "die no more."

3. How thankful ought we to be for God's unspeakable gift — the suffering and dying, yet risen and triumphant Jesus!

XLVI.—INFIDELITY, OR THE REJECTION OF GOD'S WORD.

"The wise men are ashamed, they are dismayed and taken: lo, they have rejected the word of the Lord; and what wisdom is in them?"—JER. viii. 9.

A DREADFUL charge is here brought against the Jews. It is that of infidelity, or practical contempt of God's word. Yet in the pride of their hearts they valued themselves for their superior knowledge, and the possession of the law. But what ground had they for boasting, when they were guilty of the most atrocious idolatry and iniquity? They might as well have been left in ignorance with the poor Gentiles. What wisdom could there be in these Scribes who rejected the truths, precepts, and warnings of God's word? They would ultimately be ashamed and confounded with their hypocrisy and rejection of the Divine precepts. The same language may be applied to thousands now who reject Divine revelation, not for any valid reasons, but as prompted by a wicked and degenerate heart.

I. THE NATURE OF INFIDELITY.

It is "rejecting the word of the Lord." This will apply to the unbelieving world generally; to whom the gospel has been preached, and treated by them with the utmost indifference. Many of these may not deny the truth of revelation, yet they attach no importance to it. Others go so far as not to believe, and avowedly reject the testimony of Divine revelation. The infidelity of such persons is open, acknowledged, and systematic. Christianity they regard as an imposture and a falsehood; and the hatred of some to Christianity is so extreme that they would gladly dispel it from the embrace of mankind.

Infidelity has existed in every age. Our first parents became infidel when they listened to the suggestions of the Evil One in Paradise. Infidelity characterized their descendants, producing that vast amount of wickedness which was stayed by the deluge. Infidelity appeared again in the unhallowed building of Babel. Infidelity was the great destroying sin of the Jewish nation in the times of the prophets; and when Christ appeared, infidelity rancoured in the hearts of the Jews, who pronounced Christ to be an impostor, and murdered him on the cross. Infidelity excited the Greek to regard the gospel as foolishness, and to deride the resurrection from the dead. What were the Pharisees and Sadducees generally, but infidels? Infidelity instigated the church of Rome to unsheath the sword, and kindle the fire of persecution, in order to obscure the purity of religion.—— And at the present day, infidelity in various forms, determinately besieges the citadel of Divine truth, and with infernal hate exclaims, "Raze it, raze it to the ground.

The various forms of infidelity may be briefly enumerated:—The denial of the Divine Existence, or absolute Atheism; the denial of the Divine Personality, or Pantheism, (*i. e.* God in every thing, and every thing in God. Nature absorbed in Deity. God is in man, a tree, etc. —and man, or a tree, etc., is in God); the denial of the Divine Providential Government, or Naturalism; the denial of the Divine Redemption, (including the doctrine of the Trinity, Atonement, and Spirit's influences) or Pseudo-Spiritualism: to which may be added the denial of Man's Responsibility, or indifferentism, and the denial of the Power of Godliness. Such persons dismiss the doctrine of a *future* state, as a cunningly devised fable, the phantom of priestcraft and superstition, and pronounce death to be the end of all existence—absolute annihilation.

II. THE CAUSE OF INFIDELITY, or, WHY DO MEN REJECT CHRISTIANITY?

The causes of infidelity are more moral than intellectual.

This persuasion is greatly strengthened by a perusal of the productions of modern infidel writers. "Nothing can be more contemptible," says Professor Garbett, "than the argumentative resources of modern infidelity. *It does not reason, it only postulates;* it dreams and it dogmatises. Nor can it claim *invention.*" The general strain of argument brought to bear against Christianity by its modern assailants, would not be tolerated for a moment within the province of purely literary criticism. The determination to withstand every thing like reasonable evidence, contrasts very much with the feeble argumentation by which many of the truths of religion are set aside.

1. Infidelity arises from *the depravity of the heart.* As the heart is depraved, it loves neither God nor his word. The heart is impure, and therefore resists every thing like moral restraint. We might appeal to the experience of infidels, and say, What was the first step in the process by which your minds abandoned religion? Was it by a deep serious examination of the claims of Scripture, and a conviction that they were not supported? or was it not rather because you felt the claims of Christian duty to be strict, more strict than you wished, and then to be rid of their influence, denied their obligation? While the unbelief of *some* has begun in a spirit of speculation, in *more* its origin has been in an immoral life; they have indulged in and courted the speculations of scepticism to gloze over licentiousness, or to still the remonstrances of conscience.

Ah! "the heart is deceitful above all things," etc.; it hates God, and recoils, in hostility, from the doctrines and precepts of the gospel —— the corrupt heart is the grand source of infidelity. This is the polluted fountain from whence flows the most pernicious streams on human society. This is the fatal poison-tree from whose leaves has extended the wide prevailing pestilence which blasts, and withers, and destroys, and consigns all within the sphere of its influence to one uniform spiritual death and desolation. He who "saw with open eye the mystery of the soul," accounted for the rejection or feeble influence of his gospel by saying, "Men love darkness rather than light," etc.

2. *Ignorance.* (See page 178.) On this subject we quote the following striking remarks: —

"Many unbelievers desire knowledge on the great subject, but they never undergo the labour of research. We suppose that of all the scoffers who were to come in the last days, and who were to be wilfully ignorant, there is scarcely one but would be willing to receive *historic* knowledge at least, provided an angel could just grasp it in his hand, and throw it into his brain, without any exertion on his part. But the toil of research he never encounters. He may snatch at some plausible objection to truth, as he hears it repeated; but to impartial investigation he is an utter stranger. As for those who think they have investigated very laboriously, but who have not investigated at all, we will notice them in considering another part of this subject. The millions of scoffers who have come, and who now live, are ignorant of Bible facts and Bible language. The profound and the unlettered, the wealthy and the indigent, the talented and the stupid, are ignorant of Bible facts and Bible language. To some, this may sound strange, but it is not hard to prove. The matter may be easily tested. The scoffers live *now*, and you may approach and converse with them. During a ten-years' search, you are not likely to find *one* exception to the general statement. There was one who tried this for eighteen years, to see if he could meet with any one who cast away the Bible, and who was at the same time acquainted with its contents, and with the ancient literature connected with the Bible. He found some who at first declared themselves acquainted with the subject, but who really were not. After asking them, in an affectionate manner a few questions, they generally confessed that their knowledge did not extend far. But this fact can be seen more clearly while looking at examples of *wilful ignorance.*" — *Nelson.*

Infidels are ignorant of the *language of the Bible,* and that is the reason of their taking and representing mere apparent discrepancies and inaccurate translations as real or correct, and exposing them to ridicule.

Hence they refer to the conduct of the Israelites, when going out of Egypt, they *borrowed* jewels of the Egyptians. They insist that the Israelites acted dishonestly, because the "borrowing" implied they were to return them, which they never did. But the difficulty vanishes when the word rendered "borrow" is literally translated, as it should be, "ask"— "They asked of the Egyptians jewels." Hence we read in the next verse, "And the Lord gave the people favour in the sight of the Egyptians, so that they gave unto them" (lent we have it, according to the analogy of the previous word "borrowed") "such things as they required." A simple act of *borrowing* required no Divine interposition; but in the *giving* of the Egyptians, the supernatural interference was employed, that the Egyptians might be led to give them what they asked.

Infidels generally are ignorant of *philosophy.*

Not long ago, a discovery was said to have been made as to the calculation of the age of the earth, resting on Hindoo chronology, which, according to French astronomy, was to overthrow Moses, and through him Christ, but which was itself overthrown by La Place, himself an infidel, who proved that the whole proceeded in a mistake. —— Again, "How absurd," it is argued, "for Scripture to say that light was created before the sun! Every school-boy knows that light cannot exist without the sun." But no absurdity is manifest by considering that the word "light," Gen. i. 3, refers to that *substance* or *fluid* which, when operated upon in a certain manner, produces the phenomenon called light, quite irrespective of any such operation, or of the state in which it then existed. The word in the original also means, caloric, lightning, etc.

The ignorance of infidels might be further proved, but the preceding instances may suffice. Let the statement of Lord Bacon (well qualified in every respect to give an opinion) not be forgotten : — "A very little philosophy may incline a man's mind to atheism, but depth in philosophy bringeth man's mind about to religion." Multitudes, who in the outset of life, in the pride of a little learning and prating philosophy, have disbelieved in Christianity, when they have more closely investigated science and truth, have been the first to avow it, and the boldest to maintain it.

We deny not the mental distinction of some unbelievers. We disparage not the high attainments of Bolingbroke, Hume, or Gibbon, in our own land; or Voltaire, Condorcet, or Mirabeau, in France. But they have been exceeded in talent by the advocates of Christianity. Look to Barrow, Taylor, Tillotson, Butler, Paley, etc., etc., in the Episcopal church — to Howe, Baxter, Watts, Doddridge, Fuller, Hall, Wardlaw, Chalmers, etc., in Dissent. They were giants in intellect. Then, apart from the priesthood, we refer to Lord Bacon, the founder of that philosophy which has changed the character of metaphysics and morals; to John Locke, who dived into the human mind in its most secret mysteries, by the most beautiful analogies, and evolved its processes; to the Hon. Robert Boyle, a person distinguished by the greatest attainments and research; to Sir Isaac Newton; to Milton, and to hosts of individuals who in their time were the great unpaid advocates of religion, without being its priests.

Does the modern history of infidelity exhibit any instances of high and commanding talent arrayed in support of it? —— *Infidelity is not an intellectual state;* for if it were so, we should be entitled to expect among its advocates minds most transcendant — most fitted to grapple with the pretensions and expose the hollowness of religion. But in the fact that Christians have given tone to a nation's feelings and habits of thought, it is not owing to their want of intellect and reasoning power, that their belief in that religion exists; nor is it owing to the superior intellect or acuteness of the intellect of infidels, that they are infidels, — but to the moral cause previously stated. It is true that infidelity often affects an intellectual speculative air to cover its moral deformity, and that infidels often claim and too easily attain the reputation of cleverness because they doubt — but how often is this intellectuality found to be merely superficial, and the cause of infidelity found to be of an immoral character!

3. *Speculative philosophy* may be regarded as another cause of infidelity. It is the natural consequence of the mind's desire to penetrate into the mysteries of existence, and to know all things——

"This, in itself, is not to be regarded as an evil. It indicates a thinking and reflecting age, and marks the advancement of a community in mental culture. The evil is, when it spurns the investigation of palpable facts and indubitable evidence, treats as empirical the honest method of induction, and incautiously passes the bounds of all fair and legitimate inquiry. Then it becomes intolerant of the world of realities, is vainly puffed up, and, intruding into those things which are not seen, would, instead of proving a handmaid to true religion, assume the air of an imperious mistress, and decide its shape, dress, and laws. To this charge, the greater number of the systems of philosophy that have emanated from the schools must plead guilty."—*Pearson.*

4. *Political agitation.* When politicians have developed schemes designed, as they enthusiastically believed, for the amelioration of their species, they have in many instances demanded the co-operation of Christians: and because they could not conscientiously give that co-operation, Christianity and its adherents have met with their most violent opposition. It is unquestionable that misrule, unnecessary burdens, abuses both in church and state are very distasteful, but they are not to be removed by violence and inconsistency.—— Political agitation, if not regulated by true wisdom, is a withering and freezing thing—it produces indifferentism, and gradually draws away the soul from God—it has made multitudes of infidels.

5. *Sectarianism* may be regarded as another cause of infidelity:

"Sectarianism has been the bane of the church. Multiplied divisions have weakened her energies. A vast amount of zeal and power, which should have been brought to bear on the conversion of the world, has been expended in assailing and defending the several points on which the Christian community has been split into fragments. Christendom has often resembled a battle-field, in which the several detachments of the same army, instead of combining in one aggressive movement against the common foe, have raised the shout of war against each other. The enemy, meanwhile, has exulted at the sight, and not only been fortified in the belief that Christianity is a profession under which men drive low and selfish designs, but has strengthened his position in defying the armies of the living God. The storms of controversy may have been overruled for purifying the atmosphere of the church, and preserving in vigour the faith once delivered to the saints; but although good has come out of the evil, the evil has been manifested in the consumption of so much intellectual energy and effort on internal disputes, which might have been bestowed on the infinitely nobler object of converting the world to God."—*Pearson.*

6. *Disappointed pride.* Is it not to be feared that some have united with the Christian church in order to gain popularity, if not wealth? Have not some of them wished for office that they *might shine;* and others to be rulers, leaders, and sole dictators in churches? Opposition to their schemes, or the want of success, formed the great turning point where they developed their real character and designs. *Disappointed men,* they have become the most decided and virulent enemies to the gospel. We have seen such hurling, with perfect hate of heart, their spite and venom against Christianity. Because *they have not succeeded,* nothing would satisfy them but the annihilation of Divine revelation. Some, whom we know, have actually become Infidel Lecturers.———

IMPROVEMENT.

1. Let the professors of religion take care that they become not the cause of infidelity. Calamitous is the influence of Christian inconsistency.

2. Let infidels consider on what grounds they reject Christianity. Are their reasons valid?

XLVII.—THE INFLUENCE OF INFIDELITY.

"And even as they did not like to retain God in their knowledge, God gave them over to a reprobate mind, to do those things which are not convenient."—Rom. i. 28.

This language may be applied to the character, conduct, and influence of unbelievers. In the text and following verses, the Apostle gives an awful picture of the influence of infidelity. It has never been the source of goodness and happiness, and it never will be, for it is contrary to its nature. "Can we gather grapes from thorns," etc. Infidelity is like the heart, its source, only evil, and that continually.

The subject of the text is the INFLUENCE OF INFIDELITY.

I. ON INFIDELS THEMSELVES.

1. Infidels have manifested the greatest *diversity, mutation, and indecision in their opinions,* constituting *a painful experience.*

What were their views of God and of man? Hobbes taught that God exists; but he contradicted this by maintaining that whatever is not matter is nothing,—Blount that there is an infinite and eternal God, and yet at another time asserted there are two eternal independent Beings,—Bolingbroke that it is more natural to believe many Gods than one. Voltaire at first believed in a finite God, but at last doubted or denied the existence of any. Tindal expressed a similar doubt. Toland believed the world itself to be God. Hume at one time denied the existence of God, but afterwards allowed there is a God. Respecting providence, or the government of the world, Blount said the world was eternal and not created,—Chubb, that God does not interpose in the affairs of the world at all, and has nothing to do with human actions. Bolingbroke, in one part of his writings, asserts that God, having formed the machine of the world, and set all things belonging to it in motion, takes no further care of it than a mechanic does of the clock he has wound up; but in another place declares, that Providence regards his creatures not individually but collectively. Hume denied the doctrine of providence, and said it was unreasonable to believe God to be wise and good; that what we call perfections in God may be defects. On Hume's principle, therefore, injustice, folly, malice, and falsehood, may be excellencies in the Divine character.

Blount, Chubb, and Collins, declare that man is a mere machine, and that the soul is material and mortal. Hume agreed with them; but he sometimes says, that the soul is not the same this moment that it was the last; again, that it is not one thing, but many things; and again, that it is nothing at all. Bolingbroke said that thoughts are nothing but the inner matter of the body in motion; that there is no conscience in man except artificially; that man is only a superior animal, lives only in the present world, and that the soul grows in proportion to the body. Infidels reproach Christians with their different creeds and dissensions, but let them look at home. Probably the poor Heathen philosophers were not more divided in sentiment on the most important subjects than the modern Infidels of Europe.—— Such mutation and indecision must have constituted *a painful experience.*

2. Consider *the moral influence of infidelity.* What are the *merits* of that system, that boasted liberty proposed as a substitute for religion? It is the liberty of indulging in every kind of sensuality, without the fear of future consequences — the liberty of subjecting the powers of the soul to animal appetites — the liberty of laughing at the superstitions of those who are under the salutary restraint of religious scruples; the liberty of ridiculing the idea of a judgment to come ; the liberty of conjecturing that death is an eternal sleep; that God takes no notice of the moral conduct of men. And to what terrible extravagant lengths has this baseless presumption carried some infidels! Their daring assertions have sometimes shocked and repelled their most sturdy companions. Du Clos, an honest man and a liberal philosopher, disgusted with the extreme licentiousness of the doctrines broached by the infidel sect, exclaimed, "These men will do so much, that, at length, they will make me religious." Voltaire, after indulging a train of infidel reflections on the state of man, writes, "I tremble upon a review of this dreadful picture, to find, that it implies a complaint against Providence; and I wish that I had never been born."

Look at the moral character of some of the principal infidels. Infidelity has corrupted them. The rejection of all moral restraint must necessarily have a demoralizing influence.

Lord Herbert, the first author who wrote on Deism, asserts that the indulgence of lust and anger is no more to be blamed than the thirst occasioned by dropsy or drowsiness produced by a lethargy. Hobbes asserted that every man's judgment is the standard of right and wrong; that every man has a right to all things, and may lawfully take them if he can. Bolingbroke taught that the chief end of man is to gratify the appetites of the flesh; and that adultery is no violation of the law of nature; and that there is no wrong in the greatest lewdness. Hume maintained that self-denial, self-mortification, and humility, are not virtues, but are useless and mischievous; that adultery may be practised if men would obtain all the advantages of life; that if generally practised it would in time cease to be scandalous. He declared suicide to be lawful and commendable. Rousseau made his feelings the standard of morality. "All that I feel to be right," says he, "is right: all that I feel to be wrong is wrong;" and so morality is anything any men choose to make it; and it is a different thing all the world over. Ridiculing the existence of another world, Diderot said there was no difference between him and his dog except habit. Thomas Paine, a great favourite with the lowest infidels, was a profane swearer and a drunkard. It stands upon oath before a court of justice, that religion was his favourite topic when he was intoxicated. An intelligent person (Grant Thorburn) who knew him, thus describes him:— "He was an unprincipled and despicable traitor, who had sunk in his own estimation as well as of every one else. When he flew to New York from the dungeons of Paris, every good man deserted him, and even deists who had any regard for decency crossed the street to avoid him. He was the most disgusting human being that could anywhere be met with. Intemperance had bloated his countenance beyond description. A few of his disciples who stuck to him to hide him from the abhorrence of mankind, had him conveyed to New Rochelle, where they supplied him with brandy till it burnt up his liver. His deathbed was horrible, and yet this is the chosen champion of liberty and infidelity. This is the man who was to rid the world of Christianity, and conduct mankind to a millennium of purity, honour, and happiness. Lord Byron was an infidel, and given to profane swearing, intemperance, and licentiousness."

On this subject, Dr. Dwight remarks:—

"Herbert, Hobbes, Shaftesbury, Woolston, Tindal, Chubb, and Buffon, were all guilty of the vile hypocrisy of lying; professing to love Christianity, while they were labouring to destroy it. Several of them qualified themselves for civil office, by partaking of the Lord's Supper; and all of them and their brethren were guilty of the dishonesty of confounding Christianity and Popery—true Christians and nominal Christians; though, when it suited their purpose, they were forward enough to make the distinction: all showing that they themselves were chargeable with that very dishonesty and hypocrisy which they are so anxious to fasten upon Christians, and especially upon Christian ministers." President Dwight then goes on to say, "The morals of Rochester and Wharton need no comment. Woolston was a gross blasphemer. Blount solicited his sister-in-law to marry him, and, being refused, shot himself. Tindal was originally a Protestant; then turned Papist; then Protestant again; merely to suit the times; and was at the same time infamous for vice in general, and the total want of principle. He is said to have died with this prayer in his mouth, 'If there be a God, I desire that he may have mercy on me.' Hume died as a fool dieth. The day before his death he spent in a pitiful and affecting unconcern about this tremendous subject; playing at whist; reading Lucian's Dialogues; and making silly attempts at wit concerning his interview with Charon, the Heathen ferryman of Hades. With all this, I have it on good authority, that, in the absence of his friends, he was so gloomy and miserable that the person who acted as his nurse resolved his was the last infidel death-bed which she would ever attend."

3. Infidelity is *destructive of all happiness*. Happiness can never be the result of immorality. "There is no peace, saith my God, to the wicked." Rom. iii. 17. The infidel has deserted his Father's house, and gone into a foreign land of wild speculation and dark unbelief, and what can he expect but to be fed on the husks which the swine do eat, when he is reduced to beggary and want? he has gone away from the haven of peace to be tossed on the ocean of doubt and uncertainty, and what can he expect but to be driven by the tempest, and tossed by the storm? He has gone away from the living streams of consolation, and taken up his abode in the desert, and what can he expect, but the roaring of the wild beast, and the poison of the serpent? Poor wanderer! now degraded and debased, he is bereft of peace, and bliss, and hope. He may join in the festive dance, but it is the emblem of raving madness. He may repose on the couch of sensuality; he may take the intoxicating cup, and mingle with dissolute companions, but there is an aching void in his breast, wretchedness and despair.

II. THE INFLUENCE OF INFIDELITY ON THE COMMUNITY.

It is very easy to see what would be the influence of infidelity upon society. —— Infidels are ever to be regarded as the decided enemies of the country they inhabit. Their opinions are hostile to a nation's prosperity and real happiness. They may boast of their patriotism; they may occupy a few offices of trust; they may advocate their country's rights, and wish to promote its welfare, but their infidelity annuls their services, and renders them the curse of the land. . The withering effects of infidelity were awfully exemplified in the French revolution, which began in 1787. In that revolution we see the connection of Popery and Infidelity as the cause and effect. The French revolution was the natural fruit of the infidelity and atheism sown by Popery, and of the persecution and almost extermination of the evangelical Protestant church of France, many years before; but the vileness and cruelty of the Romish church was no reason for the blasphemy, the immorality, the bloodshed, and the unparalleled atrocities of the French infidels. Such crimes, and from men too who boasted of candour, charity, and liberty, is enough to persuade the world that even a corrupt form of Christianity is better than the most enlightened system of infidelity.

In the French revolution religion was trampled in the dust, the existence of God rejected with scorn, the immortality of the soul as an idle dream, and moral and religious obligation deliberately abandoned. The effect was that in Paris, and other places, the state of society appeared as if hell itself had broke loose upon a deluded people, as if demons incarnate had spread ravages and desolation, hitherto unknown in the history of mankind. No country ever furnished so frightful a picture as France, and especially Paris, when all religious obligation was renounced. On the morning of August 10, 1792, almost all the Swiss guard were massacred. Mandat, their commander, was asssassinated, and the king and royal family fled to a convent for safety. A triumvirate was formed of Danton, Robespierre, and Marat, three men of execrable memory, who presided over the period justly designated "*The Reign of Terror.*" *

A massacre in Paris lasted 4 days, by which many thousands perished. The prisons were filled by persons who were politically opposed to the triumvirate. They perished in the massacre, being driven from their dungeons, like sheep, into the streets. When outside the prison walls, they were despatched by men and women, who, with sleeves tucked up, arms dyed elbow-deep in blood, and hands holding axes, pikes, and sabres, were executioners of the sentence. Those excesses were followed by the beheading of Louis XVI, his Queen, the Princess Elizabeth, and the Dauphine. Things went from evil to worse. Force, immediate, irresistible force, was the only logic used by government. Death was the only appeal from their authority; the guillotine, the all-sufficing argument to settle all debates. Thousands were imprisoned and destroyed on mere suspicion. The number arrested was computed at 300,000, one-third of whom were women.

Gobert, the archbishop of Paris, declared in the presence of the convention, the highest court in the nation, that Christianity was a piece of priestcraft. He disowned the being of a God, laid down upon the table his pontifical garments, and received the embrace of the president of the Convention. Churches were robbed of their sacred vessels of gold and silver, which were used in their polluted feasts. The doors of the convention were thrown open. A band of musicians was introduced, and the members of the municipal body entered, singing a hymn in praise of Liberty, and escorting as the object of their future worship, in contempt of the only living and true God, a vile female, whom they termed the goddess of reason. This example was imitated in

---

* Sir Walter Scott thus describes these men. "Danton was a man of gigantic size, and possessing a voice like thunder. He was equally and excessively fond of the pleasures of vice and the practice of cruelty. Robespierre is described as a hypocrite, and as a cold, calculating, creeping miscreant. His character was composed of envy, vanity, and vindictiveness. He never forgave. As to Marat, blood was his constant demand; not in drops from the breast of an individual, not in puny streams, from the bosoms of solitary families but blood in the profusion of an ocean. The usual calculation of the heads he demanded amounted to 260,000." The following is the picture given of the three. "Danton murdered to glut his rage; Robespierre to avenge his injured vanity; and Marat from the same instinctive love of blood which forces the wolf to continue his ravage of the flocks, long after his hunger is appeased."

many places, throughout France, which at that time presented before the eye of weeping humanity, one vast frightful desert of moral desolation. The religious edifices were closed, the bells converted into cannon, and over the burying-places of the dead was written the heart-chilling inscription, "*Death is an eternal sleep.*" All distinction between right and wrong was set at nought; marriage was changed into a civil contract, which might be broken at pleasure; the nation became a nation of assassins—within the short space of ten years, it is estimated, not less than three millions of human beings perished in France alone—of these 800,000 in civil war. At first the massacres were at the rate of five per day; but under the Convention they rose to 1000 per day, and this was continued for years. In Paris, in two years there were 6000 divorces; and so little has the country recovered its moral equilibrium, that in Paris now, between a third and a half of the births are illegitimate; and over the country at large, there are not less than 1800 suicides a year.

From this horrible picture we may see the influence of infidelity upon a community. Were the world to adopt and be governed by the doctrines of France, what crimes would not mankind perpetrate; what agonies would they not suffer?

III. Its INFLUENCE ON DOMESTIC LIFE might also be noticed.

To say nothing about the selfishness, fraud, cruelty, and grasping avarice which it would engender, it would destroy the sacred bonds which cement families together. It would annihilate love, and produce a state " without natural affection." Infidelity sighs for the abolition of marriage, which it considers "unnatural, absurd, and farcical." From the system of Robert Owen, females may learn what infidelity intends for them in the paradise of Socialism.

Married to a man who is fascinated by your youthful charms, you may retain for a season your influence over him; but if disease should blanch your glowing countenance, and dim your dazzling eye; or if maternal pains, or maternal watchings, should weaken your frame, or ruffle your temper, these consequences of your conjugal devotion to that heartless man, are to become his apology for severing that tie, which should bind you till death.

Such a system as this would, as it formerly did in Rome, and latterly in France, produce open licentiousness — cruelty and wretchedness in the extreme.

IV. Its INFLUENCE ON THE PRESS.

Infidels hate Christianity with a perfect hatred. They have tried to annihilate it by persecution, by oral addresses, and by the Press. The French infidels manifested very great zeal in this respect: —

It is estimated that 20,000 men of letters were enlisted in the cause of infidelity, and in a single year expended £900,000 upon the infidel press. It was in a great measure by such means that the Revolution was awoke and carried forward. So infidel is France still, that in twelve years, ending in 1829, nearly six million copies of the works of the four most eminent French infidels had been published and sold, while under 100,000 copies of the Scriptures had in the same period been circulated, many of them gratuitously.

The Press is a powerful agency for good, and also for evil. "Out of the same mouth proceed blessing and cursing," and this fountain sends forth sweet water and bitter.——The press is ceaselessly issuing publications decidedly opposed to religion. The thirst for reading of a light and novel kind is almost universal and insatiable; and the press pours forth its shoals of novels and romances, written in the most entrancing style, full of love and intrigue, and at the same time tinctured with infidelity.——Nor are the works of some of our good writers free from infidelity. We might refer to historians, philosophers, poets, etc. How many of our polite writers have gone, or are advancing, into eternity, as John Foster says, "under the charge of having employed their genius, as the magicians their enchantments against Moses, to counteract the Saviour of the world."

"The Edinburgh Review, which is not chargeable with countenancing exaggerated statements in these matters, said, about two years ago, 'the total annual issue of immoral publications has been stated at twenty-nine millions, being more than the total issues of the Society for Promoting Christian Knowledge, the Religious Tract Society, the British and Foreign Bible Society, the Scottish Bible Society, the Trinitarian Bible Society, and some seventy religious magazines.' More recently, it has been affirmed that, during the year 1851, the purely infidel press in London issued publications to the amount of more than twelve millions; the issues of avowed atheism, during the same period, exceeded six hundred and forty thousand; and in addition to these, were issued upwards of seventeen millions and a half of a negative or corrupting character."

"Mr. Knight, the respectable publisher in Fleet Street, stated, not long ago, "During the last five years, while cheap religious periodicals have made limited progress, either in numbers or interest, the corrupt printing press has been unceasingly at work. The present circulation in London of immoral unstamped publications of a half-penny to three half-pence each, must be upwards of 400,000 weekly, which would give the enormous issue of 20,800,000 yearly! In addition to these there is the weekly importation of French prints and novels, of so indecent a character, that once they could only be obtained by stealth, but may now be purchased openly from any venders of the other periodicals." To a large proportion of this literature for the people might be applied the language which Burke applied to the French papers of his time: —'The writers of these papers, indeed, for the greater part, are either unknown, or in contempt: but they are like a battery, in which the stroke of any one ball produces no great impression, but the amount of continual repetition is decisive.'"—*Pearson.*

It is undeniable that infidelity has made great progress in Britain. Multitudes now openly profess themselves unbelievers in the verities of the Bible. The infidel press publishes, the lecturer promulgates, and the itinerant diffuses, the poison of infidelity all around. O Britain! whose soil has been red with the blood of martyrs, on whose earth has grown the trees of freedom, nourished by the hand of pure Christianity, art thou to be blighted by that pestilence that has swept other empires from the earth?

V. ITS INFLUENCE ON ETERNITY. Admitting the doctrine of the Scriptures that there is a retributive state of existence, and that God will sit on the judgment-seat, and cause every man to render an account in conformity with the principles of his law and gospel, is it not evident that the rejectors of Divine truth must encounter the infliction of his vengeance? "The wrath of God is revealed from heaven against all ungodliness and unrighteousness of men." [amplify.]

XLVIII.—NO NIGHT IN HEAVEN.

"And there shall be no night there."— REV. xxii. 5.

HEAVENLY felicity is described in the Scriptures both positively and negatively. In the Book of Revelation especially it is positively stated what in heaven the righteous *shall be*—what they *shall do*—and what they *shall enjoy*. They *shall be* pure and like God, ethereal, like angels, and perfectly happy. As to what they *shall do*, they shall see God and praise him, admire and study his works, and understand all mysteries. They shall *enjoy* emancipation from all trouble, from every foe, from all mortality, and have perfect and eternal repose.——It is also negatively stated what they *shall not be*—what they cannot and *shall not do*—and what they *shall not suffer*. Hence such expressions as these; "They shall hunger no more, neither thirst any more," Rev. vii. 16. "There shall be no more death, neither sorrow," Rev. xxi. 4. "No more pain," and "no night there." All these expressions imply the absence of such evils, and the enjoyment of positive good. So that the negative representation is as expressive as the direct and positive.

I. THE SCENE TO WHICH THE TEXT REFERS. The text evidently refers to some place from which *night* and all its evils will be excluded. "No night there."

We are not to look for such a bright and beautiful abode in this world of mutation and uncertainty, of darkness and tempest, of wickedness and woe. Not to the Elysian fields of bliss as imagined and taught by the ancient sages of Greece. Not to the Mahomedan sensual Paradise, as taught in the Koran of Mahomet. No, we must turn away from these vain imaginings, and look to the glorious Spirit-region, to the Eden of God, to the Heaven of the Bible, etc. See John xiv. 1, 2.

Yes, there is the city whose name is "Light,"
Where the radiance of God excludes the "Night;"
'Tis the "House of God," where Christ will provide
"Mansions" of rest that will ever abide!

NO NIGHT IN HEAVEN. 211

> 'Tis the land of *vision*, where mysteries all,
> God will unfold, as his light shall fall
> And clear them up, while joy shall abound,
> And the dark and complex no more be found.
>
> There is the land of eternal delight,
> Where the glory of God shall feast the sight;
> Where the eye shall be fire, and the heart be flame,
> As they gaze on the Lord, and praise his name.

The *locality* of heaven is expressed by various scriptures. It is called *Paradise* or a *garden*—a garden adorned with all that is lovely. It is represented as a *city*—a city of the most magnificent order. As a *kingdom*, in which all the inhabitants are kings and priests. As a *temple*—a temple filled with the most devout and holy worshippers.

Figurative language this may be; yet other representations of heaven, without figure, warrant us to attach the idea of place to it, or we cannot understand the declaration, "No night *there*," which evidently refers to some particular and distinguished place. In support of this idea, Enoch and Elijah were taken bodily to heaven, and the body of Christ ascended to the right hand of his Father. If Christ be in heaven, he is there in his glorified humanity, *i. e.* in his body. It is evident from Luke xxiv. 39. In this identical body he ascended to heaven. For "he led his disciples," etc. Luke xxiv. 50. That is, precisely as he was before them in his corporeal existence, he was "carried up into heaven." That his body was entirely changed, refined, and spiritualized, is evident from many recorded circumstances and declarations, but still it was in his body that he ascended to heaven. If then Christ in his mediatorial person has entered into heaven, heaven must be a place.

The resurrection of believers also conveys the idea of locality. Their bodies will certainly be changed, 1 Cor. xv. 42—44; Phil. iii. 20, 21. Admitting that the bodies of the saints will be spiritualized, still it will follow that *place* will be required for the abode of the body. [See page 184.]

According to this argument, we find that the glorified body of Christ had a distinct and tangible substance, and, therefore, appearance. So it was proved by Saul of Tarsus. He saw the radiant form of Christ. Acts ix. 3—5; 1 Cor. xv. 8. It was found so by Stephen, Acts vii. 55, 56. And by John, Rev. i. 17.——If then the bodies of believers are to be raised in the likeness of Christ, they will have tangible substance, and actual appearance and forms which can be recognized by those who have been conversant with them in the church below.——Hence heaven must be *a place*.

In what part of God's illimitable domain this habitation is built, it is superfluous to inquire; but that it now exists, and that it is not to be created at the end of the world out of the materials of which this earth is made, we have ample evidence from the word of God.

II. The Declaration, "There shall be no night there."

If we speak of heaven in the past, there never was night there. If, etc., in the present, there is no night there. If, etc., in the future, "there shall be no night there."

Literally, *night* refers to that part of the natural day when the sun is below the horizon, involving a portion of the globe in darkness.

Figuratively, *night* refers to *moral and spiritual darkness*—to a time of ignorance and unbelief. "The night is far spent;" that is, the night of ignorance and unbelief is fast passing away. "Let us cast off the works of darkness;" or put off ignorance and unbelief. "Let us put on the armour of light;" or the bright raiment of Divine knowledge and faith.

Night means a time of *adversity, affliction, and sorrow.* "The watchman said, The morning cometh, and also the night;" or the night of affliction and sorrow.

And *night* signifies *death.* "I must work the works of Him who sent me, while it is day; the night cometh when no man can work;" that is, the night of death.

1. There shall be *no natural night of darkness in heaven.*

According to the present constitution of animal nature, nightly repose is necessary.

Darkness wears an aspect of gloom and horror. It is a time of great inconvenience—of evil, danger, and death. Then the traveller is often way-laid, robbed, and maltreated. Then the murderer issues forth under the sable covering of night, bent on robbery and blood.——

But in heaven there shall be no more night. All the seasons, mutations of time, and alternations of day and night shall not occur there. No summer and winter, no seed-time and harvest, no early and latter rain, no lightning's flash or thunder's roar. No clouds shall ever darken that sky. The glorious day of heaven is one unchanging scene of inconceivable brightness and glory. "Thy sun shall never go down." Isa. lx. 19, 20.

Is it asked, what shall constitute the light of heaven? The answer is given in the words following the text; "They need no candle," etc. The glory of the ever-blessed Trinity enlightens that heaven.

> There is a land — a shining land,
> Where spirits wander pure and free,
> And saints with seraphs hand in hand,
> Together round a glory stand,
> Which burns to all eternity.
>
> That glory shrines a power supreme,
> Too bright for mortal eyes to ken,
> Besides *him* rests an holy beam
> The subject of immortal theme,
> The Son of God, the King of men.
>
> There too the Spirit's glory stays
> With radiance sanctified and bright,
> Till mixing mingling blaze with blaze,
> The mystic Godhead's triple rays —
> All blend in one excess of light.

What this glory is we may form an idea from Scripture representations of it.—— Giving of the law to Moses—the Shekinah in the tabernacle and the temple— Isaiah's vision in the temple— Ezekiel's vision of the glory of God, i. 26—28—Daniel's vision of the Ancient of Days, whose garment was white as snow, etc.—transfiguration of Christ—and from the vision of John, Rev. i.—— What metaphors are these? But do they fully represent the light and glory of heaven? No. They are the most expressive—the most graphic which human vocabularies can supply. But they are insufficient.

We may argue this subject from *analogy*. Look at the glory of the stellary heavens. The most glorious object which we can behold there is the Sun—a glorious orb—the centre of the planets, giving them light and heat. But even our Sun is but the planet of another sun, still more bright and glorious; and that other sun, no doubt, depends upon another for its light and radiance, and thus we might proceed till overwhelmed with the vastness of such glorious immensity. But this is the inference:—What must be the light and glory of heaven, God's peculiar dwelling-place, when he has invested these glorious orbs with such vast and inconceivable splendour?—— Heaven will be brighter than any of them—brighter than all of them put together.

Suppose but one million of these suns collected into one constellation of stars, one cluster of burning orbs, what a tremendous effulgence, what a deluge of light, and blaze of glory would it give! Unless placed at an immense distance, no human eye could behold it. Yet how would all this insufferable brightness disappear before the heavenly glory! When the Judge shall at last descend, attended with millions of angels, the glory of every angel will darken a sun; what then must be the light of the New Jerusalem, which the glory of God shall enlighten, and whereof the Lamb shall be the light!

2. *No night of weariness in heaven.* "No night there," conveys the idea of ceaseless activity, and unwearied enjoyment. For such a state we are not now constituted. We are soon susceptible of physical and mental weariness. Even the service of God may become irksome by the exhaustion of our powers. As glorified saints "serve God *day and night* (humanly speaking) in his temple," it is evident that we shall require a different constitution. This takes place in the first instance at death, when the soul is freed from the mortal body as a great impediment—and finally at the resurrection when the body shall be spiritualized, refined, and sublimated, and united to the soul; then the whole glorified man shall be constituted to serve God without ceasing. 1 Cor. xv. 50; Rom. viii. 23. The bodies of the saints will become ethereal, and will no longer impede, but aid the purposes of the soul.

"There remaineth a rest for the people of God." "There the weary are at rest." Rest,—not the cessation of employment, but the absence of fatigue; not the repose of indolence, or the satiety of voluptuousness, but the full, the active exercise of those reinvigorated powers, which can know no more of fatigue, exhaustion, or pain:—the untiring energies of the soul, ceaselessly occupied with enrapturing employment, as frequently some fresh extension of the field of its inquiry, some new discovery of the glory and perfections of God, are disclosed to its blissful and enraptured contemplation.

3. *No night of sin there.* Sin has spread its dismal wings, and diffused its mortal poison over every part of the habitable globe. Every individual is tainted with it. Who can say, "I have made my heart clean, I am pure from my sin?" In the world, what a black night of crime of every description. What cruelty, oppression, and injustice. On every hand "the works of the flesh are manifest." —— Sometimes believers pass through the dark night of temptation or severe conflict with remaining corruption. ever striving for the mastery, to bind the soul to earth, etc. And they feel that they will have to carry this propensity to evil as far as the grave. Yes, it will harrass, plague, and sometimes darken the atmosphere of the soul, till time shall be no more.

But there shall be no night of sin in heaven. As there is no darkness in the unclouded sky at noon-day, so there is no darkness of sin in the bright sky of spotless holiness in heaven. There are no sinful associates in heaven. There are no sinful thoughts in heaven — no sinful passions and polluted lusts in heaven — no sinful actions in heaven. No cloud of impurity, no shadow of sin, will ever appear upon the bright firmament of heaven. Rev. xxi. 27. Heaven is full of redemption, and therefore it is full of purity. Rev. vii. 14. This was the design of all the purposes of grace, Rom. iii. 29, 30. Why did Jesus die? Eph. v. 25—27. Why does the Spirit dwell in the heart? To dethrone sin, and assimilate to God. 2 Cor. iii. 18.

As one observes, "What sinful thoughts can there be when the whole soul is occupied with God? What sinful seductions can there be, when every enemy is excluded, and every temptation annihilated for ever? What sinful lusts can there be, when all that is connected with the flesh is left behind us in the grave? What sinful tempers can there be, when peace, Divine peace. everlasting peace, sheds its balmy influences over all the sensibilities of the immortal nature? No! it is impossible; "there is no night there." How can sin burst open the immovable gates, or scale the impassable walls of the New Jerusalem above? How can sin intrude into the presence of God and the Lamb? How can sin present its haggard and loathsome deformity in a world where all is the loveliness of the Redeemer's glory in the finished completing of the creations of his love? How can sin by any possibility exist in a state, where God the Father, God the Son, and God the Spirit. constitute the eternal all in all?"—(*Parsons.*) It cannot be; "there is no night there."

4. *No night of mental darkness there.* Night is the symbol of darkness, error, and delusion. Isa. lx. 2; Eph. iv. 18; Col. i. 13. The darkness of the Heathen — of sinners at large.

Christians have to mourn on account of mental darkness. How little do they know of themselves — of God — and the works of his hands!

But there is no night of ignorance in heaven. 1 Cor. xiii. 9, 10. When the soul enters heaven it is surrounded and filled with the light of Divine knowledge. In one moment there, the poorest and meanest saint will have more light than the greatest philosopher, or than the most learned theologian on earth.

There are four books which the most learned saint here cannot read and understand, but which he will be able to do in heaven. The first is, the book of God's purposes; the second is the book of creation; the third is the book of providence; the fourth is the book of redemption. Here our mental powers are so contracted and obtuse, that, the most learned can read but a few lines in these wonderful books; but in heaven they will be easily read, and perfectly understood.——All mysteries will vanish. The irradiations of the glorious Trinity will develope all that has perplexed us here. The veil that concealed Jehovah's inscrutable designs will be taken away.

5. *No night of sorrow in heaven.* As there will be no sin in heaven, there cannot possibly be any night of sorrow. Sin is the fruitful parent of all grief. In consequence of sin, "Man is born to trouble," etc. It has made this world a vast scene of weeping, and this weeping is called "*night.*" "Weeping, or sorrow, may endure for a night." There are various kinds of sorrow here, but all will be annihilated there.

The body shall be *diseased and afflicted no more.* "There is no pain among the blessed." The head shall languish no more. The heart shall throb and palpitate no more. There shall be no paralytic limbs, no palsied forms—no trembling nerves in heaven; but immortal vigour, and youth, and never-withering beauty. By thy resurrection, Christian, thou shalt possess immortal strength, and shall mount up as on the wings of an eagle, etc.

There is no night there of poverty. No perplexity how to obtain daily sustenance. You shall pass away from a world where your schemes have been frustrated, and your plans of business or philanthropy blasted, to a land of certainty and ever-increasing bliss. There you "shall hunger no more," etc. There Jesus will give you of the tree of life, the hidden manna, the wine of the kingdom, and all the felicities of his Father's house. There your hearts will never agonise on account of refractory children, their misfortunes, and ungodly conduct before you. You will never be in seasons of dark distress there. No! for there is no night there. "The ransomed of the Lord shall return," etc. Isa. xxxv. 10.

6. *No night of death in heaven.* "The night cometh," etc. Job describes the grave as "a land of darkness, as darkness itself, and of the shadow of death without any order, and where the light is as darkness."

This world is the land of the dying. All must die. That solemn and important conflict will surely come. "As for man, his days are as grass," etc. Ps. ciii. 15, 16. What suffering, what agony, what desolation is caused by death! Weeping parents, you can testify, etc.

The death of Christ involves the everlasting extinction of death —"the last enemy that shall be destroyed."—"He will swallow up death in victory." See Luke xx. 26; Rev. xx. 14; xxi. 4.

The resurrection body will possess a principle of immortality, and therefore cannot die. The elements of which it is composed are indestructible and incapable of decay. Death can never enter the territories of the blessed, or scatter among them the arrows of sickness of disease. The inhabitants of the heavenly Paradise shall no more say, "I am sick." The Redeemer lives by the power of an endless life, and he gives that power to his saints. "Because I live, ye shall live also." Blessed world of light!——"There is no night" of weariness, of sin, of sorrow, of intellectual and spiritual darkness, and of death, in heaven."

IMPROVEMENT.

1. Let Christians be cheered by this bright prospect amid the dark dispensations on earth.——2. Dark and dismal is the prospect of sinners. As it is said of heaven, "There is no night there," it may be said of the abyss of woe, There is no day there.

XLIX.—THE SINLESS CHARACTER OF CHRIST.

"Which of you convinceth me of sin."—John viii. 46.

In the preceding verses, Christ reproves the Jews.——They disregarded his teaching, hated his doctrine, and sought to kill him.——He tells them he regarded such conduct as the natural result of their alliance with Satan, whose malignant influence was visible in their disposition, language, and actions. v. 44.——The character of Satan is dark and dreadful, and his influence in this world has been overwhelming and destructive. Christ came to destroy him, and to establish the kingdom of righteousness. For this purpose he was qualified in every respect:—by his *Divinity*, or infinite wisdom, power, rectitude, and love:—by his *Humanity*, or ability to suffer and die for guilty man. These pre-eminent qualifications must necessarily have invested him with perfect purity of character, respecting which he fearlessly challenges the Jews; "Which of you convinceth me of sin?" As the efficacy of Christ's atonement, and indeed the truth of Christianity, depend upon his sinless character, consider the arguments which prove

I. THE SINLESS CHARACTER OF CHRIST.

1. *The record of Christ's assumption of human nature*, which declares that he came into this world free from that moral taint which characterizes all Adam's posterity. See Luke i. 26—35.

Mysterious this doctrine may be, yet it is the recorded plan of God to save the world, 1 Tim. iii. 16.

Hence Dr. Owen says, "The nature of Christ was perfectly holy, absolutely free from spot or taint of original defilement. And as he was consecrated from the womb, he was then and ever after God-man, the "holy thing of God." All others since the fall have had a polluted nature, but his conception being miraculous, by the immediate operation of the Holy Spirit, so in the first instant of his being he was the Holy one, unpolluted by the least taint of moral defilement."

2. *The testimony of his friends* who were the most intimately acquainted with him. They were ever with him as the witnesses of his disposition, motives, and actions. And what is their report? Can any one of them convict him of sin? No; they all describe him as innocent and faultless. John says that no one could convince him of sin. Paul declares that he knew no sin, 1 Cor. v. 21. Peter that he did no sin, neither was guile found in his mouth, 1 Pet. ii. 22. In short, all the sacred writers speak of him as without blame, as "the holy and the just," "the lamb without blemish and without spot." Their testimony was not partial, for they always proved themselves to be truthful men; they were good men, and so believed and loved the truth, that they were willing to die for it.

3. *Let this challenge be given to his enemies.* "Which of you," my foes, can "convince me of sin?" The Scribes and Pharisees were his bitterest foes. They were filled with rancour against him, and took every opportunity of displaying it, and yet they could not substantiate a single charge against him. Just before he challenged them to do it, he had severely and in the most pointed manner, reproved them. If there had been the least moral defect in his character, they would have found it out. What did Pilate testify of him? Three times did he declare before the chief priests and congregation of the people, "I find no fault in this man." And it is also recorded of Pilate's wife, "When he (Pilate) was sat down on the judgment-seat, his wife sent unto him, saying, "Have thou nothing to do with that just man; for I have suffered many things this day in a dream because of him.'" Matt. xxvii. 19. What said the centurion who stood among the crowd of soldiers, when the Saviour was crucified? "Truly this was a righteous man." Luke xxiii. 47. And then Judas, possessing the office of a disciple, had yet the heart of a traitor, and betrayed his Master into the hands of his enemies,—even that traitor testified, as he threw down the money, "I have sinned in that I have betrayed innocent blood." Then the attestation of the spirits of darkness, who knew that "the Son of God was manifested to destroy the works of the devil," even they were compelled to confess, "We know thee who thou art, Jesus the Son of God."

"It is true," says one, "that he was slandered as a wine-bibber and a gluttonous man; but it was his love to souls that subjected him to this reproach. He was also accused of 'blasphemy, in that being a man he made himself God.' John v. 18; x. 33. Nor could he be quitted of this charge, if the supposition were true, that he is only a mere man; and those who maintain this doctrine must also maintain that the Jews committed no sin in putting him to death, and that he died as a blasphemer. But if he were equal with God, by being truly the Son of God in his Divine nature, it was not blasphemy for him to affirm that he was equal with God, and the charge itself is groundless."

4. *The testimony of the Redeemer himself.* This was without ostentation, Isa. xlii. 1, 2. He said, "The Prince of this world cometh," etc. John xiv. 30. He presented himself as an example to imitate, Matt. xi. 29, 30. He declared that his actions were entirely approved by his Father, John viii. 29.——How different was he to ordinary men!——The conduct of Paul was most exemplary, and gave him great conscientiousness, but he had to mourn over the depravity of his heart, 1 Thess. ii. 10; Rom. vii. 14.

Christ's testimony to his own perfection was conscientious and sincere. It was prompted by a heart wholly impregnated and overflowing with goodness, and therefore it was a testimony naturally impelled, even as streams of water are impelled by the fulness and constant flowing from the fountain itself. It was a testimony which exhibited the beauty and excellence of the moral law, declaring what man might have been, had not sin prevented, and what man must be, through the intervention of Christ, before he can associate with pure and happy spirits in the habitation of holiness.

6. *The temptations which he successfully resisted afford proof of his unspotted purity.* He was tempted by the Wicked One, who by his frequent assaults, or by his fascinations and stratagems, casts down many who were strong.—— But Jesus Christ, the righteous one, "was tempted in all points as we are," but here is the exception, *"yet without sin.* See John xii. 31; xiv. 30.

Then mark *his resignation and patience* under numerous trials and provocations. Poverty and want did not make him repine. "Foxes have holes, and the birds of the air have nests, but the Son of man has not where to lay his head," but not one murmur escaped his lips. Ordinary men would have uttered thousands of complaints under such circumstances, yet he endured all without repining or discontent.——He wrought miracles to supply the wants of others; but none to supply his own. To do this Satan tempted him in vain, Matt. iv. 3.—— The honours and glories of this world had no attractions for him. They were offered to him by Satan, and by the Jewish populace, who wanted to make him a king; but earthly vanities could not fascinate him who truly understood the nature of all things. The minds of ordinary men would have been captivated by such proffers, and they would willingly have acquiesced, but Christ had come down from heaven—from the glory which he had with his Father—— then how could he have been attracted by this world's vanities?—— Hence the purity of his nature and actions. John vi. 15.

The ingratitude, reproach, and persecution which he endured, afford another evidence of the purity of his life. Christ suffered from ingratitude the most cruel, but "when he was reviled," etc. 1 Pet. ii. 23. When brought before Herod and Pilate, he manifested no fear, but amidst all the contempt with which they treated him, his tranquillity was undisturbed. When buffeted and spit upon in the palace of the high-priest, he meditated no revenge; when mocked and insulted by the soldiers, and derided while hanging on the cross, he prayed for them, and made intercession for the transgressors, Isa. liii. 7.

7. Refer also to *the testimony of Jehovah himself*, uttered amid the glories of the baptismal day, when the Holy Spirit was seen descending like a dove, and lighting on him, and when a voice from heaven was heard, saying, "This is my beloved Son in whom I am well pleased." This testimony was reiterated by the voice from the most excellent glory, amidst the splendours of the transfiguration. And would the eternal Father have so pre-eminently distinguished his Son, raised him up from the ignominy of the tomb, exalted him to the highest possible honours, and given him the reins of universal empire, if he had been defiled with personal guilt? The thought is impious; and the testimony of the Father unites with the testimony of friends and enemies in attesting that he was without sin.

Hence the moral superiority of Christ to every creature. We do not deny the excellencies of those other intelligences who surround the throne of God and the Lamb; but their excellence is derived and dependent. Once Jehovah "charged his angels with folly," even those unhappy spirits who fell from their first estate, and are reserved in chains of everlasting darkness until the judgment of the great day. The redeemed saints are faultless before the throne of God in heaven; but they have been purified in the blood of Christ, and by the Divine Spirit. What they have become by acquisition, Christ is essentially by nature. In the strictest sense of the term he is impeccable, without sin — otherwise he would have been placed upon a level with fallen creatures — with ourselves; and had he, in such a case, been exposed to temptation sufficiently strong, that temptation would have triumphed; and, to speak it with reverence, he might have proceeded until he had become a monster of iniquity, as he is now the perfection of purity.

II. THE IMPORTANT USES TO WHICH THE SUBJECT OF THE TEXT MAY BE APPLIED.

1. *It is a confirmation of Christ's Divine Mission.* If the life of the Redeemer was perfectly holy, the gospel must be true.—— If the gospel be not true, then Christ must have been a deceiver; but where shall such another impostor be found? Many deceivers have been in the world, but their lives have been wicked; such was Mahomet, and many others.

Christ declared that he came forth from God, and that he was sent of God. But if he had been convicted of a single sin, then the validity of these representations would have been undermined. One sin would have broken the entire evidence, and stamped as an impostor the character of Jesus Christ. But he was free from the least particle of sin. It is observed both by Paley and Dwight, that neither the Mishna, nor the Talmud, which contain the whole of the Jewish testimony on this subject — neither Celsus, Porphyry, nor Julian, who may fairly be supposed to have given the whole of the Heathen testimony, ascribe to Christ a single instance of folly or of sin; and we have the declaration of Origen, that down to his time no charge of this nature was ever alleged against him. We venture to say then that the perfect innocence of Christ is an established fact, and thus we derive substantial evidence of the truth of Christianity.

"Go," says the eloquent Bishop Sherlock, "Go to your natural religion: lay before her Mahomet and his disciples arrayed in armour and in blood, riding in triumph over the spoils of thousands and tens of thousands who fell by his victorious sword; show her the cities which he set in flames, the countries which he ravaged and destroyed, and the miserable distress of all the inhabitants of the earth. When she has viewed him in this scene, carry her into his retirements, show her the prophet's chamber, his concubines and wives: let her see his adultery, and hear him allege Revelation and his divine commission to justify his lust and oppression. When she is tired with this prospect, then show her the blessed Jesus, humble and meek, doing good to all the sons of men; patiently instructing both the ignorant and perverse: let her see him in his most retired privacy; let her follow him to the mountain, and hear his devotions and supplications to God; carry her to his table, to see his poor fare and hear his heavenly discourse; let her see him injured but not provoked; let her attend him to the tribunals, and consider the patience with which he endured the scoffs and reproaches of his enemies. Lead her to his cross, and let her view him in the agony of death, and hear his last prayer for his persecutors — 'Father, forgive them, for they know not what they do.' When natural religion has seen both, ask which is the prophet of God? But her answer we have already had. When she saw part of this scene through the eyes of the centurion who attended at the cross, by him she spake and said, 'Truly this man was the Son of God.'"

2. *The perfect innocence of Christ was indispensably necessary to his mediatorial work.* He could not have become a Mediator, if he had ever offended; neither could Moses if he had been an idolater at Horeb. But "thou hast loved righteousness and hated iniquity." Ps. xlv. 7.

If it be admitted that Jesus Christ was to become *the Lord our Righteousness*, it was essentially necessary that the righteousness which he presented, should be complete, without spot or wrinkle, or any such thing. If not his merit could not have been perfect, nor could it have been sufficiently complete to justify all those who believe in him. Was it necessary, then, that Christ should not only become our righteousness, but that he should make atonement for the sin of the world? How could that expiation be complete, if he had sins of his own, for which atonement was necessary? See Heb. vii. 26—28; 2 Cor. v. 21; 1 Pet. i. 19.

Christ was also to be the Intercessor of his people within the veil. Would an advocacy so prevalent be founded on an imperfect work? Could a peaceable man be admitted as an advocate in the high court of heaven? It is in vain to say that, like the saints, Christ dropped his imperfections in the tomb when he rose to his native heaven; for the very cause why he could not have been detained in the hands of death was, that he was without sin.

3. The sinless character of Christ rendered *him a fit model and example for his church*. God having predestinated believers to be conformed to the image of his Son, it required that he should be the model and standard of all perfection. Had we been appointed to be conformed to any of the sons of Adam, where could a sinless one be found, worthy of imitation, seeing "All have sinned," etc. Jesus could say with infinite propriety, "Learn of me." Matt. xi. 29.

Had Christ been in any respect a sinner, the worst feature of his character might have been selected for imitation; but it is the perfection of his character that constitutes him the grand, glorious original which all his followers are bound to imitate.

IMPROVEMENT.

1. Learn what constitutes a Christian. It is to be like Christ.
—— 2. How safe it is to rest for salvation on so perfect a Saviour!
—— 3. How worthy is Christ of our constant love and obedience!

L.—NO TEARS IN HEAVEN.

"God shall wipe away all tears from their eyes."— Rev. xxi. 4.

THE book of Revelation, for the most part, is a mysterious book. It contains mysteries which the most acute and intellectual mind cannot unravel.——It refers to events the most important. Mighty elements rush; mighty angels fly; the tumultuous earth sinks in trembling subjection; the seals are opened, and the vials of wrath are poured forth; till at length the chain of Divine Omnipotence binds the Old Serpent, the Accuser of the brethren, that he may deceive no more.

The Book of Revelation is the index of eternity. Not only do worldly events here rise before us, but the scenes of eternity. The dead rise; the judgment-throne is set; the books are opened; and then comes the doom of the wicked, and the glory of the righteous. Heaven opens; its rapturous songs fall on our ears; fields of light and glory, the pure abodes of the sanctified, the eternal residence of redeemed men are spread before us. Look into that Paradise! Do you see any mournful countenance, any tearful eye there? No; for "God shall wipe," etc.

I. THE TEARS TO BE WIPED AWAY.

Tears are the visible and affecting expressions of the heart's sorrows, and therefore to say that "God shall wipe away all tears from their eyes," is to say that every cause of sorrow now existing shall be eternally removed.

Tears and grief are not always inseparable. Some deeply feel, and groan in spirit, and yet have few tears. The eyes of others soon weep, and are reddened by the suffusion of tears, and yet their grief is but superficial.

Sin is the cause of all tears. There was no weeping before sin came. There cannot be any tears where sin is not. Sin has robbed us of so much honour and bliss—has so much devastated our souls and bodies—separated us from God, and deprived us of hope, revolutionized the moral and even-secular state of society, and placed us in such deplorable circumstances, that it is no wonder that this world is called, and found to be, "a valley of tears."

It is not always wrong to weep. Tears sometimes are the indication of good. When the penitent weeps for his sins; when the Christian weeps for want of more purity, and faith, and hope, it is well; they are the "mourners in Zion," and "Blessed are they that mourn," etc. When friends sicken and die, it is not wrong to weep, for "Jesus wept." Divine grace does not destroy natural sensibility; it rather increases, refines, and sanctifies it. It teaches "not to sorrow as those without hope." 1 Thess. iv. 13, 14.

1. Tears are often caused by *temporal depression*. The labouring man weeps on account of the scarcity, or inadequate remuneration of manual labour—he weeps too as he feels his failing strength for his secular pursuits. Christians desire to provide things honest in the sight of all men, and to help Zion with their substance, but their tears declare the difficulty of the performance. The insolvent tradesman, cast down from the pinnacle of comparative independence, by circumstances over which he had no control, sits upon the ruins of his estate, and weeps bitterly. Persons once well off in life are now indigent; their hearts are corroded with care and anxiety, and their eyes suffused with tears.——Now all these tears are to be wiped away. There will no poverty in heaven. "They shall hunger no more," etc. Rev. vii. 16.

2. Tears arising from *defective friendships*. Some of these are very intimate and peculiar, and must be very affecting. "Every heart knows its own bitterness," etc.——Sometimes such defection is caused by infirmity, temper, ignorance, prejudice. Some are friends just as long as the sun of prosperity shines; when that becomes obscured, their friendship, when most wanted, fails. What bitter tears David wept on account of his perfidious son, Absalom! 2 Sam. xviii. 29—33. Job too proved that it is vain to trust in man; Job vi. 14—18. Did not Christ feel such defection? His disciples "all forsook him and fled." And so with Paul when he appealed unto Cæsar; Acts xxviii. 14, 15; 2 Tim. iv. 16.—— But there will be no faithless friends in heaven. No tears will be shed on account of lover, brother, or friend proving treacherous. The whole family in heaven will be of one mind and of one soul,

and cemented together by the bond of the Saviour's love, which nothing can ever destroy.

3. *Tears caused by affliction.* How frail is the human frame! To what numerous diseases is it liable, the seeds of which are often in the constitution, and by external circumstances, ripen and bring forth fruit to death.——Affecting is the transition from health to sickness, from activity to langour and pain. How distressing the idea, this sickness may be unto death! And then when afflictions are frequent, or chronic, it is enough to cause tears,—I am a burden to myself—and to my friends. The afflicted often wet their couch with tears. Job vii. 4; xxxiii. 19—22.

The Christian*has much anxiety as he feels approaching old age and infirmities. A time of old age is often a time of weeping. ——Old age is a time in which a man is deprived of many of his relations and friends; is gazed on by a new generation; feels a thousand infirmities, anxieties, and distresses, and is reduced to dependence upon those around him. "When thou wast young," etc. John xxi. 18. From the pressure of old age, Barzillai refused the offer of a palace; "I am this day four-score years old," etc. 2 Sam. xix. 35. Such was the view of David; Ps. xc. 10; and of Solomon, Eccl. xii.——How often are the aged seen to weep!——But there shall be no affliction, no physical or mental decay in that heaven of which it is said, "Neither sorrow, nor crying, neither shall there be any more pain."——Patient sufferers from disease, you could weep though you could not murmur, but wearisome nights are no longer appointed you. Nor does the spirit, full charged with its inward griefs, pour the flood into the eyes. Martyrs, you have been racked and torn, but there is now no more pain for you; for, like your Master, you have exchanged your crown of thorns for a crown of glory.

4. Tears are caused by *bereavements*. It is a solemn and an established fact that "we must needs die, and be as water spilt on the ground, which cannot be gathered up again," yet bereavements do violence to the feelings, and deeply pierce the hearts of survivors; for the relationships of life, generally speaking, are most tender and endearing, and more especially so when sanctified and refined by Divine love.——What smiles of pleasure play upon the parents' countenances as they gaze on their beloved children! The dissolution of the conjugal bond is often productive of inexpressible sorrow. How is the heart stunned when the mandate comes from heaven, "Son of man, behold I take away the desire of thine eyes as with a stroke!" The wife of our youth is deposited in the grave, and that grave is bedewed with tears. And so it is when the husband dies, and his wife becomes a widow, and his children orphans.——Sweet sometimes is the communion between brothers and sisters, or other relatives and friends!——But death will dissolve all these connections, and mar all their delights. Instead of the smile of gladness, the countenance will be made sad, and the eyes be filled with tears.——O the agony of heart that is felt, and the bitter tears that are shed

by the couch of the dying, as they mark the progress of disease, and the approximation to death!

He must have been unhappy indeed over whose unmoistened grave no tears are shed, and whose death has caused no regrets. But the number of these is few. Death rends all hearts. Behold Jacob shaking his grey hairs, and saying, "Joseph is not, and Simeon is not, — all these things are against me." When Joseph died, the children of Israel wept sore. "My father! my father!" exclaimed Elisha, when Elijah was taken away from him. "O my son, Absalom! O Absalom, my son, my son!" said the smitten David, as he "went up to the chamber over the gate," that he might weep alone. And when his friend Lazarus died, "Jesus wept." Well; be it so. To weep, and to be wept, is the irreversible decree as to man on earth; but then so much more welcome the rest we hope for. A loud voice is heard out of heaven, "And there shall be no more death." Such a visitation would mar all the felicity of the tabernacle of God. The rigid limb, the silent pulse, the breathless lip, the pallid cheek, the fixed and darkened eye,—these, these, are not scenes for heaven. No: they shall have "joy and gladness," because "there shall be no more death."

> To lay that precious form,
>   So lovely e'en in death,
> Food for corruption's worm,
>   The mouldering earth beneath!
> Oh, worse to me than twice to part,
> Than second death-stroke to my heart!
>
> But why in anguish weep!
>   Hope beams upon my view;
> 'Tis but a winter's sleep —
>   My flowers shall spring anew,
> Each darling flower in earth that sleeps,
> O'er which fond memory hangs and weeps.
>
> All to new life shall rise,
>   In heavenly beauty bright,
> Shall charm my ravished eyes,
>   In tints of rainbow light;
> Shall bloom unfading in the skies,
> And drink the dews of paradise!
>
> Oh, this is blest relief!
>   My fainting heart it cheers:
> It cools my burning grief,
>   And sweetens all my tears,
> These eyes shall see my lov'd one then,
> Nor shed a parting tear again!

5. *Many other causes of tears may be referred to.* The Christian weeps on account of his *moral imperfections.* He is weighed in the balance and found wanting. How readily he yields to worldly influence!—he is too unwatchful, and the enemy gains the advantage. He feels himself to be a poor combatant. He has little faith, and but glimmering hope—he is like the "bruised reed, and the smoking flax." He considers how long he has known the Lord, and yet very little fruit has been produced.——The Christian weeps *over ungodly men*—and the *low estate of Zion.* —— The minister weeps for *want of success.* "Who hath believed our report?" Some are "*persecuted and reviled,*" and they weep.

Parents drop burning tears of grief for the *rebellion of their children*. So this world is a world of tears — some view it as a paradise; but observation and experience will soon produce a different conviction. ——Blessed be God,

II. THERE SHALL BE NO TEARS IN HEAVEN. "God shall wipe away all tears from their eyes."

I. *Where?* In heaven — in God's own dwelling-place. In the Canaan above, where a tear was never yet shed, and never will. In a kingdom where there is "fulness of joy" — and at "the right hand of God where there are pleasures for evermore" — in an inheritance, vast, rich, immutable, and eternal — in the "holy place," purposely designed, created, and in all things adapted, for the residence and bliss of immortal and redeemed souls. *There* God shall have "wiped away all tears from their eyes."

> No grief can change their day to night,
> Who dwell in God's immediate light.
> Sorrow and sighing God hath sent
> Far thence to endless banishment.
>
> And never more may one dark tear
> Bedim their burning eyes,
> For every one they shed while here,
> In fearful agonies,
> Glitters a bright and dazzling gem,
> In their immortal diadem.

2. *Who shall wipe them away?* "*God* shall." Their removal is Divine. His infinite love to his people insures it. His infinite power will accomplish it. The immutability of his promise and oath to save to the uttermost, is the security for it. There is Divinity in the very words, v. 4, 5. "The former things are passed away. And he that sat upon the throne said, Behold, I make all things new." Sublime and impressive is the scene thus presented. Under the throne of the Redeemer, who is arrayed in the glory of the Father, lie heaven and earth, the present seat of sorrow, pain, and death. He speaks, and they vanish; and "the former things are passed away." He speaks again, and a new heaven and earth spring into being. "The tabernacle of God is with men; and he that sitteth upon the throne saith, Behold, I make all things new." This is enough. God shall wipe all tears away.

3. *When will he do it?* "God *shall*." It is future. He wipes away many tears in this world. He wipes away the tears of the penitent, and gives pardon and peace. He many times wipes away the tears of the afflicted, and brings them forth from the furnace like gold seven times purified. He wipes away the tears of adversity, and his Providence turns their mourning into joy. ——But there is a succession of tears. "The clouds return after the rain," and the brightest sky may be blackened again. The Christian sighs for a complete removal; but this is future. "Blessed are they that sow in tears, for they *shall* reap in joy," at the last day. Hence all the promises of complete deliverance

refer to the termination of life — the resurrection of the dead — and the second advent of Christ.

4. *How will he do it?* "*Shall wipe away all tears.*"

(1) He will do it *affectionately*. God is a tender Father. Christ is "a brother born for adversity," and as our great High-priest, he is "touched with the feeling of our infirmities," etc. Then God himself, as our tender Father, with his kind hand shall wipe away all our tears; and when we hear his voice, see his face, and feel his hand wiping all our tears away, we shall never regret that we have shed them. Come, my beloved people, will the Great Shepherd say, you have wept long enough in the world's desert. I have always seen your tears, and registered them. Ps. lvi. 8. I have known your frame, and remembered that you were but dust, and I have never forgotten you, my chosen, my redeemed children. Now your warfare is accomplished, and I will save you. My beloved flock, I will turn all your sorrow into joy, and you shall weep no more. "Enter into *the joy* of your Lord."

(2) He will do it *effectually;* "*all tears*" shall be "*wiped away.*" The cause shall be removed, and the effect shall cease. Every cause of tears shall be for ever annihilated. He will destroy *sin*, the great master evil — the wide and deep ocean from which all tears have been supplied. Then all the tears of penitence, of backsliding and contrition, shall pass away. The tears of adversity and affliction, tears for the world, and for the church; the tears of bereavement, and the tears shed at the apprehension of death, — all these shall for ever cease. So *complete will be the removal*, that there shall not be found even *tears of joy!* For what do they imply? The joy which finds relief in tears implies a previous anguish, and that the change from one state to another shakes the feebleness of mortality. Or that we are so unused to strong emotion, that our measure of joy is soon filled up; that even the bliss of earth may be too copious for the contracted vessel of the heart, and therefore it so easily overflows in tears. But there shall be no such alternations in heaven; nor will the capacity for blessedness be thus limited. Joy will not be so much a stranger that we shall weep at meeting it. It will be habit, not accident. It will be, not the transient flash which dazzles, overpowers, and disappears, but the fixed and steady element in which we shall live for ever.

(3) *He will certainly do it.* The language is positive. "God *shall*," etc. The faith which believes it rests upon a Rock — the Rock of ages — the immutability of God. The hope which anticipates it springs from that stable faith, and is as "the anchor of the soul, both sure and stedfast, and entereth into that within the vail; whither the Forerunner is for us entered, even Jesus," etc. Heb. vi. 20. It is written, "God shall wipe away all tears from their eyes," and "Heaven and earth shall pass away, but not one jot or tittle of his word shall fail."

IMPROVEMENT.

1. The removal of tears implies the enjoyment of positive good. Instead of tears there will be joy — songs of triumph, and outbursts of gladness.

2. This freedom will be confined to God's people. Are you his?

3. How much we are indebted to Christ! He has entered heaven. He saves and prepares us for it.

4. How dreadful the prospect of the wicked! Their tears will never be wiped away.

INDEX.

No.	Book.	Subject.	Page.
34	Judges xiv. 14.	Unexpected Good, Part I.	143
35	xiv. 14.	" Part II.	149
9	Job. xl. 20.	Man Vile	36
33	Ps. xxvii. 4.	Attachment to God's House	140
23	xxxiv. 19.	Solace in affliction	91
4	xli. 4.	Prayer of the Diseased Soul to the Divine Physician	15
13	lxxi. 3, or xc. 1.	God a Habitation	50
8	cxix. 94.	Relationship to God the pledge of Everlasting Salvation	33
5	civ. 34.	Sweetness of Divine Meditation	19
44	Song ii. 8.	The voice of the Beloved	189
31	Isa. xxvii. 3.	The Gospel Trumpet	131
10	xl. 29—31.	The Advantages of waiting upon the Lord.	38
18	xlv. 22.	Look, and be saved	71
46	Jer. viii. 9.	Infidelity	279
32	Lam. iii. 24.	God the Portion of his People	135
17	Micah ii. 10.	Rest unattainable here	68
37	Mal. iv. 2.	Christ the Sun of Righteousness	158
36	Matt. v. 3.	Blessedness of the Poor in Spirit	155
38	v. 4.	Blessedness of those who mourn	163
24	v. 6.	Hungering and thirsting after righteousness	95
12	xxv. 34.	Exaltation of the Righteous at the last day	47
20	xxviii. 6.	The Risen Saviour	80
2	Luke vii. 34.	Christ the Friend of Sinners	11
21	xviii. 1.	Prayer	82
45	xx. 36.	The immortal constitution of man in the future state	192

No.	Book.	Subject.	Page.
42	John iii. 36.	Eternal Life	181
41	viii. 46.	Sinless Character of Christ	216
43	xiv. 2.	The Heavenly Mansions	183
39	xvii. 17.	The Truth of the Bible.	165
7	xx. 30, 31.	" Miracles	27
11	Acts ix. 11.	The Persecutor converted	42
40	xiii. 38, 39.	Pardon and Justification	172
47	Rom. i. 28.	Influence of Infidelity	203
19	1 Cor. xv. 31.	The Christian dying daily	75
14	2 Cor. v. 1.	Dissolution followed by glory	54
15	2 Cor. v. 1.	Hope of Immortality	58
6	Eph. vi. 24.	The Apostolic Benediction	24
16	Phil. iv. 19.	The Divine Supply	63
3	Col. iii. 4.	The Glorious Manifestation of Christ.	13
41	1 Thess. i. 3.	Truth and Influence of the Gospel.	175
27	1 Tim. i. 11.	The Glorious Gospel.	114
1	i. 15.	The Faithful Saying.	5
28	Heb. vi. 12.	Conformity to departed Saints	120
22	ix. 6.	Christ a Testator	87
30	xiii. 5.	Divine Friendship	127
25	2 Peter i. 19—21.	Prophecy, Part I.	99
26	2 Peter i. 19—21.	" Part II	106
29	1 John iv. 19.	The Love of God reciprocated	124
50	Rev. xxi. 4.	No Tears in Heaven	221
48	xxii. 5.	No Night in Heaven.	210

THE PREACHER'S ASSISTANT;

OR

OUTLINES OF SERMONS.

BY THE AUTHOR OF "HELPS FOR THE PULPIT."

PREACH THE WORD.

ADVERTISEMENT.

ENCOURAGED by the success of former volumes, viz., "Helps for the Pulpit," and "Pulpit Themes," the Author now presents to the Public a smaller volume of a similar nature, but of a somewhat more miscellaneous character. He also intimates that while a few of these Outlines are selected, and by different authors, whose names are appended, the greater part of them are original, and by himself.

Outlines of sermons are designed to be suggestive, and their utility in this respect may be great. Those in this volume are strictly evangelical. "Christ and him crucified," is made prominent throughout, and it is hoped that they may be rendered both instructive and profitable, and minister to the edification and prosperity of the church of Christ.

THE PREACHER'S ASSISTANT.

I.—THE SUPERIORITY OF THE CHRISTIAN'S PORTION.

"For their rock is not as our Rock, even our enemies themselves being judges."— Deut. xxxii. 31.

THE figurative language of the Bible is very expressive, and also necessary to explain subjects which are difficult to understand.——The wicked pride themselves in their possessions, etc., many of them contemptuously regard the godly poor, on account of their penurious condition. The infidel regards the Christian as deluded.—— But which of these parties is in the best position? The worldling, or the pilgrim believer — the Christian, or the infidel? The text declares, "For their rock," etc. Deut. xxxiii. 29.

I. THE CHARACTER WHICH GOD BEARS TO HIS PEOPLE. "Our Rock."

The natural scenery of Palestine supplied the Jews with figures like that in the text. Its fertile plains and rich valleys were surrounded and guarded by rocks. Rocks were the parents of the streams which watered their fields. Rocks were the basis of their fortresses, their cities, and their glorious temple itself. Hence it was natural for them to be impressed with these natural objects, and mingle the figures which they furnished with their poetry.

1. In what respect may God be called "a Rock."
The ideas conveyed by the figure are strength, stability, and permanence. By these the character of God is declared. Thus David, confiding in God's strength, triumphed over his enemies. 2 Sam. xxii. 47, 48.

(1) *Strength.* What is stronger than a rock? The rocks of the ocean have for ages sustained the violence, pressure, and immense operations of the waters of the sea — and yet they stand. God is called "the perfection of strength." "Nothing is too hard for the Lord."

(2) *Stability.* Many things are always changing. Most objects in nature, the foliage of the trees, the fruits of the earth, the sea-

sons, rivers, seas, oceans, are ever fluctuating. Look at ancient cities, temples, palaces, monuments—all have changed, but the rock of Horeb is the same to this day. And Jehovah declares his character when he says, "I am the Lord, I change not."

(3) *Permanence.* On this account the Hebrews denominated their hills and mountains, *perpetual* and *everlasting.* Christ is the "Rock of ages." The works of men, by the tide of time, are washed away, but the perpetual hills remain. So all the devices of sinners for happiness will be found vain refuges in a dying hour, and they will be swept away at the day of retribution. But "our Rock" will abide. God is the everlasting Rock. See Heb. i. 10—12.

(4) The word "rock" also conveys the idea of a *Refuge.*

It was customary, in Palestine, for the inhabitants to retire to the rocks in times of danger, and in their cliffs and caves to find refuge against any sudden incursion of the enemy. In the battle of the vale of Siddim, they who escaped slaughter fled to the mountain, and remained there in safety until rescued by Abram. When the Benjamites were nearly exterminated by the other tribes that gathered together against them, they fled for safety and secured themselves in the rock Rimmon. And David, when pursued by Saul, frequently hid himself and his followers in the strongholds and caverns of the rocks. Hence to " enter into the clefts of the rocks, and into the tops of the ragged rocks," is an image used by the prophet Isaiah to express the terrible consternation which should seize the impenitent when the Lord should visit them with his righteous judgments.

2. *When and how God is a rock to his people.*

(1) *At the time of conversion.* When the sinner is convinced of his ruin and danger—when he finds that all human devisings for salvation are but as the shifting sand, he hails with rapture the Rock Christ, as the ground of his faith and hope. Isa. xxviii. 16. He is enabled to place his guilty soul upon that Rock, and he has peace and joy in believing. Rom. v. 1.

(2) God is a rock or refuge in *a time of fear and dismay.* "Be thou my strong habitation," etc. Ps. xxxi. 2, 3. This refuge made David look with calmness and courage on all his enemies, Ps. xxvii. 1—3, 5, 6. How sweet a picture of the repose of a soul trusting in God does he draw! Ps. iii. 4—6, written when he fled from the face of a rebellious son at the head of a rebellious people.

Such is the calm fortitude of those who trust in God. Nor is this fancy. It rests upon solid grounds. "When he giveth quietness who then can make trouble?" "Hast thou not made an hedge about him?" said Satan of Job; and the first chapter of that book shows, that into the enclosure which that hedge surrounded, not even Satan could break, till Divinely permitted.——Here then is the refuge from enslaving fears for the future. Dark to us it may be; but it is all light to God; and no power, no combination of powers, can match the omnipotence which defends his people.

(3) He is their Rock *in adversity and affliction*, "Many are the afflictions of the righteous." Penury, sickness, personal and relative, etc. All these require a refuge. There is a refuge in God's wisdom that appoints them, and in his gracious superintendence of their operation. "Whom the *Father* LOVETH, (this is the rock of support,) he chasteneth," etc. Heb. xii. 6. "All things shall work together for good," etc. Rom. viii. 28. "When my heart is overwhelmed, lead me to the rock that is higher than I." Ps. lxi. 2.

Pleasing is the idea of a perfect shelter in a storm, *a rock higher than we*, and capable of giving safety while the whirlwind rages. A shelter becomes doubly calm and pleasing when surrounding tempests beat its sides harmless. The domestic hearth is more cheerful when flakes of snow gather on the windows; and when little children looking out into the darkning storm, return from the lattice with additional pleasure to a parent's embrace, while cheerful embers gild by reflected fires, their still more cheerful faces, and parental piety descants of the goodness of Jehovah. All such ideas find their substantiation in the highest sense in his experience, who in trouble takes refuge in a promising, covenant-keeping God. "He that dwelleth in the secret place of the Most High, shall lodge under the shadow of the Almighty;" like the alarmed bird, whose grasp of the bending bough becomes only the stronger for the very winds by which the tree is shaken. Hence one beautifully observes:

The passenger in an Atlantic storm remains calm while he sees the commander unruffled; and on Alpine wilds, where mountains beaten by the elements meet the clouds, how quietly slumbers the babe, unwakened at the mother's breast as she journeys, or looking up to her utterly unconscious of fear, while danger perhaps howls in every blast, and the pathway is over precipices where even a Hannibal might tremble. How can Benjamin, the beloved of the Lord, be distracted with terrors, while honoured to "dwell between his shoulders?" or how can the infant soul, borne through the world's "howling" desert, awake from time to time for any other feeling than joy, when perceiving that "underneath are the everlasting arms."

(4) He is the Rock or Fountain of *their temporal and spiritual supplies*. The idea is supported by Numb. xx. 11; Deut. xxxii. 13. Referring to the wild honey which was collected from the fissures of the rocks, and to the oil of olives supplied from the same source.

So God sends forth streams of blessings, like the rivulets which, gushing forth from the rocky hills, fertilize the valleys which lie between. "All my springs are in thee." So with all temporal blessings. He "crowns our life with loving-kindness and tender mercies."—— And spiritual blessings all come from the Rock Christ. He was smitten at Calvary, and forthwith came rich and never-ending streams of salvation. "All spiritual blessings in heavenly places," etc.

(5) God is a refuge amid all *the uncertainty and frailty of human existence*. The death of friends — of relatives —— the failing of our own strength — death near. A rock of support and refuge is

necessary then. And Christ is that Rock. "My heart and my flesh fail," etc. 1 Cor. xv. 55—57.

The great design of the gospel is to arm us against the terrors of death; when sin is pardoned, death is conquered. The Holy Spirit ever witnesses to the efficacy of Christ's mediation, and seals it upon the conscience, especially in the hour of death. Thus a precious Jesus is more desirable at last, if possible, than at first, — unlike temporal joys, which perish in the using. The great crowd of witnesses in heaven will attest that Christ never forsook them for a moment. He succoured and supported them on the couch of sickness, and unveiled to the dying eye such scenes as swallowed up mortality in life. The Spirit brought to their souls the vital gales of heaven, and whispering to them of Jesus, spread over them his immortal wings as the shadow of a great rock.

II. THE SUPERIORITY OF "OUR ROCK" TO "THEIR ROCK."

And this is so evident, that we may appeal, in proof of it, to themselves, and make them judges, though the decision may be self-condemnatory. "Even our enemies themselves, being judges."

What has been advanced respecting the character and services of this Rock, sufficiently proves its infinite superiority. Refer to the Divinity of " our Rock," to its security, its refreshing influence, to its stability, and everlasting permanence, and who will deny that "Their rock is not as our rock"?

1. Look at *idolators*. We worship the true and living God. What is the rock of idolators? Idols which "have eyes, and see not," etc.——In the time of Moses and subsequently, the outstretched arm of Jehovah convinced idolatrous enemies " that their rock was not as our rock."

2. Consider the *rock of infidels*. These reject Divine revelation, principally because of the moral restraints it imposes, and they pretend to follow the dictates of *reason*. This is their rock.

The insufficiency of such a basis is proved by three considerations:—
1. We cannot consistently reject the facts of Bible history, without rejecting history altogether. 2. If these facts be allowed, we cannot deny the argument from them to the divinity of our religion, without violating even reason itself. 3. Even if the infidel system were faultless, yet it is only of man, and is therefore altogether destitute of authority, which is essential to religion; for in this there are two parties, God and man. "Your rock is not as our Rock." Yours rests upon your own reason, and that differs in you all, and it is but human. Ours rests upon doctrine uniform in all ages, sealed by prophecies, authenticated by miracles, consecrated by the blood of martyrs, loved by the holiest and best of men, and confirmed by experience even to the present time. Examine with serious candour, and see whether your rock, etc.

3. *Socinians and Unitarians*, who deny the divinity and atonement of Christ, rejecting " our Rock " altogether. To do this they must annihilate the letter of one half of the Bible, and the spirit

of the remainder. How miserable your hope of salvation without a Divine Saviour — a Saviour who honoured the law, a matter of necessity, and which you cannot do, and who endured the curse due to the transgressor of the law! "Our Rock" is Jehovah Jesus; yours is a mere creature — mere virtue, always imperfect.

4. The *Self-righteous*, who think that moral obedience will procure Divine acceptance. This has its origin in ignorance. We feel that all our works are imperfect. We go to the atonement, etc., for righteousness and strength, etc. See Luke xviii. 10—14.

Again, some trust in the mercy of God, irrespective of the atonement. ——

And look at multitudes who are making this world their all. —— What a miserable rock is theirs! "Men of the world who have their portion in this life." But their rock is not as our Rock.

What can their rock do for them in affliction, in all their troubles, in bereavement — in a dying hour — at the judgment-day. Eternity declares "Their rock is not as our Rock."

II. — THE NEARNESS OF GOD.

"Thou art near, O Lord." — Ps. cxix. 151.

THIS declaration evinces the greatness and glory of God. His presence pervades all places, and he observes all human conduct. "He is not far from every one of us." This is a terrible subject to the wicked.——It is a pleasing one to the righteous; for they can say, "God is at our right hand, we shall not be moved." Ps. xvi. 3. My troubles, my trials may be extreme, and my enemies numerous, yet this is my consolation, "Thou art near, O Lord."

I. GOD IS ESSENTIALLY NEAR.

His presence is universal. "Do not I fill heaven and earth, saith the Lord." "Am I a God at hand, and not afar off." What an overwhelming view of the grandeur of God! Jer. xxiii. 23, 24; Ps. cxxxix. 7—12. This is the character of God. "Thou art near, O Lord." Let me therefore "take heed to my ways, lest I sin against thee with my tongue," for "thou God seest me."

II. GOD IS MANIFESTLY NEAR.

1. *In creation.* "The heavens declare," etc. Ps. xix. 1. In the sun in his glory, the moon in her softness, gleaming in the firmament, I see thee.

In the balm of the fragrant air, in the light of the cheerful day; in the redolence of these shrubs around me, whose flowery tops, as they drink in the soft and gentle shower as it falls, seem to breathe forth a fresh perfume in gratitude to him who sends it; in the melody of these birds, which fill the air with their songs, thou, O Lord, art near. I see and hear thee in the lightning's flash, and the thunder's roar. I see thee in the rolling wave, and in the rippling stream. I see thee in the cataract's foam, and in the gentle descent of the sparkling dew. I perceive thee, not with my bodily eyes, although by these I discern thy workmanship, but with the mental eye I behold thee in thy works, A PRESENT GOD.

2. *In providence.* Though sometimes thou wrappest thyself in a cloud, dark and impenetrable, yet I see thee. Thou governest the world and rulest the nations. Thou directest the flight of an angel, and arrangest the affairs of the poorest saint. ——

The book of providence is very mysterious and dark, yet there I read thy wisdom, as developed in thy world, thy church, and thy saints; yes, I discern the wisdom that guides, the wisdom that guards, the wisdom that bestows, the wisdom that withholds, the wisdom that encourages, the wisdom that corrects, that kills and makes alive. There do I read thy power, thy justice, thy faithfulness, thy holiness, thy love. Complicated and obscure is the mechanism of thy Providence, wheels within wheels, but all are working thy sovereign will, and revolving for the weal of thy church. Though thou "hidest thyself," yet I see thee there, even "the appearance of the glory of the Lord," attended by cherubims and ministering spirits. Ezek. 1.

III. GOD IS GRACIOUSLY NEAR.

Once this was man's greatest blessing and source of sweetest consolation. Nearness to God was the fairest flower which grew in Paradise; but sin withered it, the flower faded, it drooped, it died. It must be so *once more;* the flower must once again bloom, again must it revive: even upon earth must it blossom, or in heaven it will never put forth its glorious beauty and fragrance.

Contemplating man as a sinner, we see God in anger, hurling him from Paradise, and denouncing against him his wrath. God is near, but it is as an enemy, to be angry with the wicked every day. God is near, but it is as a consuming fire. Man is said to be far off, an alien, and an outcast. Eph. ii. 3, 12.

1. *God is near through Christ.* O transporting thought! "Thou art near, O Lord," in thy *Son*, thy beloved Son. So it is written; "But now in Christ Jesus ye who sometimes were far off are made nigh by the blood of Christ. For he is our peace, who hath made both one, and hath broken down the middle wall of partition between us," etc. Eph. ii. 13—22. It required nothing less than the stoop of Deity, and the sufferings and death of the humanity, to remove those hindrances which interposed between a holy God and an unholy creature. Thus Christ reconciles us to God by the shedding of his blood, which satisfied all the demands of the Law. God was honoured and satisfied, and, behold, he is *near*.

Near as a sin-forgiving God; Acts xiii. 38, 39; Rom. viii. 1.

Near as a promise-keeping God; 2 Cor. i. 20.

Near as a prayer-hearing God; John xvi. 23; Ps. cxiv. 18.

Near as a covenant-keeping God; Heb. viii. 10.
Near as a gracious tender Father; John xx. 7.

2. *God is near in every season requiring his presence.*

(1) *In the season of spiritual distress.* In the hour of penitence, to bind up the broken-heart, etc. Isa. xli. 1.——When the poor saint feels his imperfections and short-comings, God is near, and he will "not break the bruised reed," etc.

(2) *In the season of adversity and affliction*, Isa. xlviii. 10; Ps. xxxiv. 19. How near is God! See Ps. xli. 3; Isa. xliii. 2.

(3) *In the hour of temptation.* Isa. lix. 19; 1 Cor. x. 13; 2 Pet. ii. 9; Rev. iii. 10.

(3) *In the time of human desertion.* When I am left solitary by the perfidy of friends —— or by the desolation of death. Thus Paul was deserted when he was to appear before Cæsar. "At my first answer," etc. 2 Tim. iv. 16; and David was consoled *by the nearness of God.* "When my father and mother forsake me," etc. Ps. xxvii. 10.

(4) *In the valley of the shadow of death.* Amid the dissolving of the earthly tabernacle—the surrender of all earthly possessions and engagements—the rupture of the most endeared connections—when the eye gives its last look, the hand its last grasp, and the tongue its last farewell—this is the glorious privilege of the Christian, "Thou art near, O Lord." Ps. xxiii. 4.

IMPROVEMENT.

1. How unworthy are we of this great and gracious presence! 2. Let us walk worthy of it, lest God depart from us. 3. The wicked are indeed desolate, "Without God in the world."

III.—FOLLOWING GOD.

"Be ye therefore followers of God as dear children."—Eph. v. 1.

THE Apostle in this and the preceding chapter gives important advice respecting Christian conduct, and especially respecting brotherly love, and forgiveness. Stated last verse of the preceding chapter. To be thus characterized is to be like God. The text is a repetition of the important exhortation.

I. THE CHARACTERS ADDRESSED; "*dear children.*"

1. In one sense, all men are the children of God—by creation. Ps. c. 3; Mal. ii. 10.

2. They are the children of God *by adoption and grace.*

Natural or civil adoption is an act by which one is received into a man's family, as his own child, and appointed his heir. Spiritual adoption is an act of God's free grace, by which repentant sinners, believing in Christ, are received into the number, and have a right to all the privileges of the sons of God.——Such a privilege stands opposed to a state of bondage and servitude. Rom. viii. 15.——It is expressive of the relation of Christians to God.

When the Lord adopts a son, he gives him a prince-like, heaven-born nature — a "new creature," 2 Cor. v. 17; Heb. ii. 6.

3. The privilege of adoption or sonship is obtained *by a true and lively faith in Jesus Christ.* John i. 12; Gal. iii. 26. This faith supposes a previous conviction of sin, deep humiliation, and a turning from it to God.

4. Believers are called "dear children."

(1) On account of the *immense price* paid for their redemption — the precious blood of Christ, Gal. iv. 4, 5; 1 Pet. i. 18, 19.

(2) Dear because they have become in some measure *like God*, and are employed as his servants — lights of the world, etc.

(3) Dear children, on account of *the pleasure and delight which the Lord takes in them.* 1 Pet. ii. 9, 10. Called "the precious sons of Zion." Lam. iv. 2.——Esteemed as dear and precious by the highest intelligences, saints, angels, Christ, the blessed Trinity.——They will be accounted dear when others will be found to be vile; though they have been esteemed in this world as the noble, the honourable, etc.,— at the great last day when all the world shall stand at the bar of Christ the Judge.

II. THE DUTY RECOMMENDED. "Be followers of God."

The word translated "followers," signifies such as *personate others*, assuming their gait, mode of speech, accent, carriage, etc.—from this Greek word we have the word *mimic*. Though this term is often used in a ludicrous sense, yet here it is to be understood in a very solemn and proper sense. Let your whole conduct be like that of your Lord; *imitate* him in all your actions, words, spirit, and inclinations — be followers of God.

We cannot follow God essentially. We cannot imitate him in his incommunicable perfections, as the independency, self-sufficiency, omniscience, etc., of the Divine Nature.

The imitation here recommended has a reference to God's moral perfections.

1. *Be followers of God as to knowledge.* See Col. iii. 10; i. 10; 2 Pet. iii. 18.

2. *Be followers of God's holiness.* 1 Pet. i. 15, 16.

3. *His benevolence and mercy.* These are displayed in creation, providence, and grace. "The earth is full of the goodness of the Lord," Ps. xxxiii. 5. The goodness of God is unlimited, impartial, and unchangeable. How great his love—tender his compassion! Ps. cxlv. 9; ciii. 2, etc. We are commanded to imitate him. Luke vi. 36; Heb. xiii. 16; Matt. v. 7.

4. *The patience and forbearance of God.* Patience should appear in all our trials, Heb. x. 36; James i. 3, 4, in our conduct to mankind, and to the church. Rom. xii. 10; Eph. iv. 2; Col. iii. 13; 2 Tim. ii 24; Eph. vi. 9.

5. *Imitate his righteousness and truth,* or that justice and equity by which all his conduct and dispensations are governed. Let this characterize all your dealings with one another, all your promises, etc. Matt. vii. 12; Rom. xiii. 7.

Observe further. To follow God is the result of regeneration— faith in Christ— and ardent love to him.

This is not mere profession, saying, Lord, Lord; but doing the things which he has commanded.

We must follow God invariably. Openly, before the world—be anxious to do and suffer all his will; not select from his word what pleases our fancy, or accords with our prepossessions.

We must follow him perseveringly— hold fast when others forsake him. "Be faithful unto death." •

IMPROVEMENT.

1. Self-examination. 2. As we are so little like God, let us be penitent, and prayerful for the Spirit's influence to cause us to resemble God more and more. 3. Sinners have the image, the spirit, and conduct of Satan. They are ungodly, godless, Christless, and hopeless in the world. "Awake to righteousness."

IV.—BELIEVERS COMMENDED TO GOD.

"And now, brethren, I commend you to God, and to the word of his grace, which is able to build you up, and to give you an inheritance among all them which are sanctified." — ACTS xx. 32.

THE text forms part of that interesting, faithful, and pathetic address which the Apostle Paul delivered to the elders of the church at Ephesus. The address contains a declaration of his fidelity and conscientiousness as an Apostle of Christ—important advice which their circumstances render so salutary and appropriate, an affecting intimation that after this Christian and paternal interview, they would see his face no more. The time of his departure from earth by martyrdom was rapidly approaching, but this prospect did not dishearten him, v. 22—24. No wonder then that he should be solicitous for their welfare, as expressed in the text.

I. THE BLESSEDNESS WHICH THE APOSTLE DESIRED FOR HIS FRIENDS.

1. *Establishment and confirmation in the Faith.* "To build you up."

Christ is said to build up his temple by connecting his people to himself by a living faith, and to one another by mutual love, fellowship, and prayer; and he aids them by his grace to increase in all holy dispositions and practices. Matt. xvi. 18; Zech. vi. 13; Eph. ii. 22. The church is built on Christ — on his sacrificial death and resurrection. This is her true foundation, and in connection with him her whole fabric consists, Eph. ii. 20; 1 Cor. iii. 11. The saints "build up themselves in their most holy faith;" they more fully consider, more firmly believe, and more diligently practise divine truths; and receiving out of Christ's fulness, increase in faith, love, and every other grace. Jude 20.

The Apostle therefore prayed that they might feel they were resting on Christ for salvation — that they might have the assurance of faith, and the fruits of faith, and ever "know in whom they believed."

(2) *Union.* The stones of a building rest upon a foundation, and are united to it, and to one another. Christians are united to Christ by a living faith, and by love to one another. Joined to one common head, they "keep the unity of the Spirit." Eph. iv. 3. The enemies of Christianity, by persecution and violence, threatened to destroy this union. The Apostle commended them to God, that their hearts might be "knit together in love;" Col. ii. 2, 19.

(3) *Progress.* A building is carried forward till the top stone is raised, and as it progresses, its design, its symmetry, and its beauty become more apparent. So believers are to grow: Eph. iv. 15; 2 Pet. iii. 18.

2. *He desired that God might give them an inheritance.* This refers to heaven — the kingdom of glory, 1 Pet. i. 4. It is the dwelling-place of God — it was purchased by Christ — it is Paradise regained. It is pure, full of light, felicity, and glory. It is destined for the saints, being "the kingdom prepared from the foundation of the world."

(1) *It is of a social character.* "Among all them." Among all those cherubim and seraphim, angels and archangels, and the spirits of just men made perfect. "Among all them," to associate with them, converse with them, praise with them, etc.

(2) *Ample.* "Among all." Yes, it is a vast inheritance, and will ultimately have a vast population. All the members of Jehovah's house who have been saved from the fall till the consummation of all things. Rev. vii. 9.

(3) *Holy.* "Among all them which are sanctified." Those who inherit are holy. The great source of happiness there is freedom from sin. We must be justified and sanctified here, before we can be glorified there.

(4) *Perpetual.* Not transient, but eternally permanent. So described, 1 Pet. i. 4.

"The fairest inheritances of this earth must be relinquished after a few years' enjoyment. The possessor of the largest and most fertile domains has reason to say, as he surveys them, "These hills will rejoice, these vales will sing, and these trees will flourish for another, but not for me." Nay, it is not death only that drags away the great from their palaces and the fields; misfortune and oppression have often rendered the wealthy poor, and the powerful dependent on the caprice and the bounty of others. "Here we have no continuing city, but we look for one that is to come." Were the saints to be driven from the paradise of God, were they to fall from that perfection in holiness to which Divine grace hath raised them in the heavenly world, we must conclude that Jesus had ceased to be solicitous about their welfare; but this cannot be; the Lamb in the midst of the throne is the constant guardian of their interests, and the eternal security of their happiness; and perpetual obedience is the fixed choice of their hearts. Were the fear to arise in the minds of the blessed, that they would be forced to quit this inheritance, its hills of frankincense would loose their fragrance, the flowers of paradise would blossom to them in vain, and they would feel themselves incapable of relishing their best enjoyments. But the saints are not only secure from all change, but from every fear of it: Their happiness is sure in itself, and in their persuasion. They feel that they are safe for eternity. Heb. xiii. 14."

II. THE AGENCY AND INFLUENCE TO WHICH HE COMMENDED THEM. "To God, and the word of his grace."

The Apostle was ever sensible of human inefficiency. He always recognized the Divine Spirit to give success to his efforts, to promote his own salvation, and the salvation of the church at large; 2 Cor. v. 5.

1. *To God.* "I commend you to God."

(1) *To his gracious providence.* "He careth for you," and he will guide you and guard you. He does all things well;" he loves you as his saints—his Son has redeemed you, and therefore I cannot entrust you to better and safer hands.

(2) *To his special blessing.* He loved them, and he wanted them to be specially preserved. Their situation was peculiar. After his departure, grievous wolves would attempt to devastate the church, ver. 29, 30. They required a special blessing.

(3) *To the gracious influence of his Holy Spirit.* God gives this, and without it the church is nothing.

2. *To the word of his grace,* as the ground of their hope, the rule of their conduct, their direction in difficulties; support in trials; consolation in death.

IMPROVEMENT.

1. Let us enter into the circumstances of our brethren, sympathize with, and pray for them. The Apostle did thus. 2. Let us value the sympathy and prayers of our brethren, when they remember us in our trials. 3. God, for Christ's sake, will graciously regard every object which his church may "commend" to his care and attention.

V.—THE REDEEMED IN HEAVEN.

"I beheld, and lo! a great multitude which no man could number, of all nations, and kindred, and people, and tongues, stood before the throne, and before the Lamb."—REV. vii. 9.

LIFE is a journey, and Christians are travellers; but the world to which we are going is to us unknown, but as it is revealed to us in the Scriptures. Here, life and immortality are brought to light. Here, we learn what heaven is, and what its employments are. In general, we know that heaven is a place of society: when Lazarus died, he was carried to Abraham's bosom; and from the passage before us we learn that it is a very large and blessed society. Let us

I. INQUIRE OF WHOM THE SOCIETY OF HEAVEN WILL CONSIST?

1. Of *Jesus the Mediator.*—He is the Sun that enlightens that world! "I go (said he) to prepare a place for you: I will come again and receive you unto myself; that where I am, there ye may be also."—We shall "stand before the throne of God and of the *Lamb!*"

2. The *angels of God* shall form a part of this society. They even now hold an uninterrupted intercourse with the church of God on earth; are continually "ascending and descending," to "minister unto those who shall be heirs of salvation"—and at length shall lead us to "the throne of God and of the Lamb," and we shall dwell among them.

3. The society will comprehend *all good men,*—"a great multitude which no man can number, of all nations, and kindred, and people, and tongues." Those things which prevent their full society on earth, shall there no more exist. Here we are separated by distance of *time.* We have heard of Abel—of Enoch—of Abraham—of Paul, and others eminent for piety; but we have never seen them; there we shall converse with them, and—

"Walk with God high in the climes of bliss."

Here we are separated by distance of *place.* Some good men live in every quarter of the globe, too distant to hold even regular intercourse; then we shall meet in one grand society, and be no more separated. Good men are separated by *differences of sentiment;* divided into various classes, and distinguished by several peculiarities: and we necessarily feel most attached to those whose principles and dispositions are most congenial with our own. But there shall be no dissensions; God shall be our sun, and one blaze of light illuminate every heart!

II. THE BLESSEDNESS OF THE HEAVENLY SOCIETY.

1. They shall be all *holy.* One great reason of our unhappiness here is, that we have so much sin amongst ourselves, while the world around us is lying in wickedness. But there shall in no

wise enter into that state, "any thing that defileth, neither whatsoever worketh abomination, or maketh a lie; but they who are written in the Lamb's book of life."

2. Not only shall all be holy, but they shall be *eminently* so. When we meet with good men, we rejoice in their society, and feel a oneness of heart with them: but alas! we soon discover many defects, which, like spots on the sun, though they do not prevent its rays, yet in a degree veil its glory. But there, every subject shall be righteous, as his Lord; and every disciple holy, like his Master!

3. There they shall be completely *happy*, as well as holy.— Many of our sorrows in this world arise from sympathy; and religion not only allows, but teaches us "to weep with those that weep; to bear each other's burdens, and so fulfil the law of Christ." But in heaven, the "tears shall be wiped away from all faces, sorrow and sighing shall flee away," and each shall be as happy as his capacity will admit.

4. Perfect union in sentiment, affection, and worship, will form an essential part of the felicity of heaven. The want of such an agreement diminishes the aggregate of social happiness on earth, and evil passions both produce and are produced by it.——In the exercises of public worship we feel our minds elevated and dignified: here, however, our pleasures are abated by the limitation of our society: there it shall be "a great multitude which no man can number."

5. This society shall be blessed with permanence and perpetuity. Fellowship with Christian brethren on earth is sweet; but soon we are called to part, and parting divides our joy. But there shall be "no more death;" neither shall the inhabitant say any more, "I am sick!"—S. PEARCE.

VI.—DECISION FOR GOD DEMANDED.

"Who is on the Lord's side?"—Ex. xxxii. 26.

THIS chapter gives a fearful account of the idolatry of the Israelites—the wrath of God against them, v. 10. Aaron also was guilty, Deut. ix. 20, in being too pliant, etc. Their idolatry was punished— 3000 of the ringleaders were slain, after the watchword was given; "Who is on the Lord's side?"

I. AN IMPLIED CONFLICT. "The Lord's side."

He comes before us as a King—as a Commander—the "Lord of hosts is his name." The cause which he has to establish is that of *truth and righteousness*. This is opposed by Satan and his emissaries—hence the conflict—and the demand, "Who is on the Lord's side?"

This conflict is frequently expressed. "Gird thy sword," Ps. xlv. 3; Isa. lxiii. 1—3. Satan is called the Prince of darkness, and Prince of the power of the air. See Eph. ii. 2. Christ fights against Satan. Rev. xix. 11, etc. He " was manifested to destroy the works of the devil." Therefore

1. *The Cause of this struggle is Satan's conquest of the world.* In Paradise he tempted our first parents, and they fell—he stripped them of their righteousness and glory, and took them as captives. All men by nature are sinners, "children of wrath." Rom. ii. 10, etc.

2. *Christ voluntarily engaged to oppose Satan*, and to rescue sinners from his power. When Christ came the battle commenced in the wilderness, Matt. iv. 1, etc.——he opposed him everywhere; he encountered his opposition through the Jews, the Sadducees, and Pharisees. He encountered him in the garden, which is called "the hour and power of darkness;" and on the cross.——What a battle was that! "He spoiled principalities," etc.

3. *The Contest is to be carried on till the Divine purposes are accomplished.* Christ has his *army*, even all believers—these are his soldiers, who gather around his banner, and fight his battles. Their *weapons* are described, Eph. vi. 13—18. They preach the gospel, or declare the will of the Captain of salvation—they long for souls—they are anxious to be determined and valiant soldiers of the cross.

4. *This contest shall ultimately succeed.* Ps. ii.; Isa. liii. 10—12; lx. 1—5; 1 Cor. xv. 24, 25. Millennial glory shall be the issue of this contest.—— "Who then is on the Lord's side?

II. WHAT IS IMPLIED IN BEING ON THE LORD'S SIDE?

1. *Enlightenment of mind* to perceive the error of the course, and the danger of the position. To be on the side of Satan is disgraceful, dangerous, and ruinous. That cause must ultimately fail.——Enlightenment too, to discover the infinite excellency and superiority of Christ's cause, and the everlasting advantages of being *on his side.* A deep conviction of sinfulness, of guilt, of exposure to wrath for being on Satan's side.

2. *A forsaking of the opposite side, and the espousal of Christ's cause.* The heart cleaves to Christ—it is reconciled to God. 2 Cor. v. 18; Col. i. 20, 21.

3. *Submission to all the terms and conditions of Christ's service.* The terms of enlistment are repentance, faith in Christ—union with his soldiers—wearing the badge of distinction, even a renewed nature by the Spirit—putting on the Lord Jesus Christ, and taking all the weapons appointed for spiritual conflict. Eph. vi. 13.

4. *A public avowal of this to the world.* Declaring that we are on the Lord's side. Not to be ashamed of our profession.

5. *A military disposition.* A mind like Christ's, which hates sin, and is determined to oppose all the King's foes—animated by

the hope of victory, and ever panting for the glory of the Divine General.

6. *Cheerful obedience to all his commands and directions.* "Ye are my friends," etc. A full consecration of all our powers to his service.

7. Constant dependence upon Christ the Commander for all supplies of strength, deliverance, and triumph.

III. THE HONOUR AND ADVANTAGE OF BEING ON THE LORD'S SIDE.

1. *It is the most honourable side.*

It is not the side of a despot — of a tyrant; but it is the cause and service of the God of love, and spiritual freedom. It is not the side of sin, but of purity; not of darkness, but of light; not of woe, but of bliss. There is no honour in sin, in Satan, in his followers, — nothing but disgrace and torment. —— This side is honourable; for consider the worth and glory of the Divine Captain — the glorious excellency of his cause, the salvation of myriads of immortal souls.

2. *It is the strongest side.*

Though not so numerous now, yet it shall be. —— The Captain hath an omnipotent arm, valiant and undaunted courage. What was Samson, Gideon, David, Alexander, Julius Cæsar, etc., to the Lord Jesus? Think of his wisdom. "He is wonderful in counsel, and mighty in working." He is a match for Satan, being wiser and stronger than he ——It is the strongest side. Its fortifications are impregnable, impenetrable, and invincible. The outworks, walls, bulwarks, forts, and towers have been contrived by infinite wisdom, and executed by the Lord God Omnipotent.

And if it is the strongest side it must be the *safest side.* "If God be for us, who then can be against us?"

3. *It is the most happy side.*

There is no peace in the camp of the wicked — they cannot prosper who fight against God—many of them do not live out half their days— and finally with their prince they must be cast into the abode of interminable darkness. The Christian soldier has delight, peace, and confidence in his conflict—delightful exercises—and the hope of a glorious victory.

4. *It is the most useful side.* Contrast the work of Christ with that of Satan — the labours of Christians with the works of the wicked. "A sinner destroyeth much good;" but "the righteous is more excellent than his neighbour."

5. It is a side that will ultimately be crowned with victory and eternal rewards. Jesus must reign — he must conquer — he and every soldier in his army shall have repose, and honour, and glory in heaven. "On his head shall be many crowns;" and his people shall have "the crown of life." Rev. ii. 10; iii. 5, 12, 21

IMPROVEMENT.

1. Praise God that you are on his side. It is of all grace. 2. Sinners, lay down the weapons of opposition, forsake the ranks of the enemy, etc., etc. 3. Anticipate the joy and rapture of sharing with Christ the rewards of eternity.

VII.—THE CHURCH A LILY AMONG THORNS.

"As the lily among thorns, so is my love among the daughters."— Song ii. 2.

IN this book, Christ describes his church under the emblem of a beautiful female whom he has espoused. —— Christ and his church are compared to the lily, which is an apt emblem of his humiliation in assuming our nature, of his dwelling and communing with his people, once vile sinners; and it is an emblem also of his spotless purity. —— They who believe in Christ partake of his excellencies: he has humbled their pride, and given them purity and beauty, by which they are distinguished from, and exalted above sinners.

I. CHRIST'S REPRESENTATION OF HIS CHURCH. "As the lily."

"By "the lily of the valley," Song ii. 2, we are not to understand the humble flower generally so called with us, the 'lilium convallium,' but the noble flower which ornaments our gardens, and which, in Palestine, grows wild in the fields, and especially in the valleys.

Pliny reckons the lily the next plant in excellency to the rose; and the gay Anacreon compares Venus to this flower. In the East, as with us, it is the emblem of purity and moral excellence. So the Persian poet, Sadi, compares an amiable youth to "the white lily in a bed of narcissuses," because he surpassed all the young shepherds in goodness.

And Sir J. E. Smith observes: "It is natural to presume, the Divine teacher, according to his usual custom, called the attention of his hearers to some object at hand; and as the fields of the Levant are overrun with the 'Amaryllis Lutea,' whose golden lilaceous flowers in autumn afford one of the most brilliant and gorgeous objects in nature, the expression of 'Solomon in all his glory not being arrayed like one of these,' is peculiarly appropriate." Matt. xxvi. 28—30.

The church is "*as* the lily." Christ is "*the* lily," v. 1. She is "as the lily," because her beauty and glory have been derived from Christ. By union with him, and constant fellowship, the church, in degree, partakes of his excellencies. They cannot resemble him in his majesty and mediatorial excellency; but they can in his moral virtues.

1. *Christ here represents the beauty of his church.*

The lily is a beautiful flower. "Solomon in all his glory was not arrayed like one of these." Its form is excellent; it has six petals or leaves beautifully arranged; within are seven grains, internally it is of the colour of gold, and it hangs down its head. Much of the glory of the lily is internal.

The Beauty of the Church consists

In her purity. Because "justified freely by his grace," washed in his blood, and sanctified by his Spirit, the church is pure and white as a lily. Christ can see no spot in his own righteousness, and therefore he sees no spot in the believer. Ps. xlv. 13, 14.

The church has been regenerated. Once Christians were wicked — they were like the barren, prickly thorn, fit only for burning. Now Christ has put a new spirit in them. The heavenly "dew" has distilled upon their souls, and they "grow up like the lily," displaying in their disposition and conduct the "beauties of holiness." "Thou art all fair, my love, and there is no spot in thee," is the language with which Christ addresses his church. See Eph. v. 25—27. The church is beautified with the gifts of the Holy Spirit, which may answer to the leaves of the lily; and with the graces of the Spirit, which may answer to the golden grains within the lily, which are seven. 2 Pet. i. 5—8.

2. Christ here represents *the humility of the church.* "I am the lily of the valleys," says Christ. Deeply was he humbled when he took upon himself the form of a servant; Phil. ii. 5—8. And the church too is adorned with the grace of humility. Like the lily of the valley which hangs down its head, so they are "clothed with humility." See it in the Publican, Luke xviii. 13; in the Prodigal, Luke xv. 18, 19. See it in Paul; "I am less than the least," etc.

3. Christ here represents *the dignity of the church.*

The lily is a very tall flower; few flowers, as Pliny observes, are higher than the lily. So the people of God are the highest and most dignified people in the world, they dwell on high, Isa. xxxiii. 16. The beauties of holiness, their humbleness of mind, and the graces of the Spirit, confer on the church dignity and glory. —— A glorious dignity awaits the church in millennial glory; Micah iv. 1, 2. But a still brighter one in celestial glory.

II. CHRIST EXPRESSES HIS LOVE TO THE CHURCH.

Christ sees nothing so fair in all this world as the believer. All the rest of the world are like thorns, but the believer is like a beautiful lily in his eyes. He has proved his love by loving them before the foundation of the world — by taking their nature — by dying as their substitute — by calling them to repentance and grace — by his numerous promises — by his prevalent intercession — by the rich and glorious inheritance which he has provided for them. John xv. 9.

III. CHRIST REPRESENTS THE POSITION OF THE CHURCH "As the lily *among thorns.*" Observe,

The character of the unconverted world. In his sight it is like a field full of briers and thorns. So compared because

(1) *It is fruitless.* "Do men gather grapes off thorns, or figs

off thistles?" So Christ gets no fruit from the unconverted world. It is all one wide thorny waste.

(2) *Because preaching the gospel among them is like sowing among thorns.* "Break up your fallow ground and sow not among thorns." When the sower sowed, some of the seed fell among thorns, and the thorns sprang up and choked them; so is preaching to the unconverted.

(3) *Because the world is hostile to the church.* God's people are as lilies among thorns, scattered and torn, shaded and obscured by them. This they must expect, for they are planted among thorns; "In the world ye must have tribulation." See Gal. iv. 29. The ancient inhabitants of Canaan expelled by Israel were said to be "pricks in their eyes, and thorns in their sides." Num. xxxiii. 55.

(4) *Because their end will be like that of thorns;* they are dry, and fit only for the burning. "As thorns cut up shall they be burned in the fire." See Heb. vi. 8.

Observe: The lily that is now among thorns shall shortly be transplanted out of this wilderness to that paradise, where there is no pricking brier, or grieving thorn. Ezek. xxviii. 24. —— As flowers in a rich garden blend together their thousand odours to enrich the passing breeze, so, in the paradise above, you, believers, shall join the thousands of the redeemed, and blend with theirs the odours of your praise. As living flowers, you shall blend with glorified spirits, there to form a garland for the Redeemer's brow.

IV. CHRIST REPRESENTS THE GLORIOUS DISTINCTION OF THE CHURCH. "The lily among thorns." Not confounded with the thorns, but distinct.

Were we passing through a wilderness overgrown with briers and thorns, and were our eyes to fall upon some lonely flower, tall and white, and pure and graceful, growing in the midst of the thorns, it would look peculiarly beautiful. But were it in some rich garden among many other flowers, then it would not be so remarkable; but when it is encompassed with thorns on every side, then it engages the eye. "As the lily," etc.

1. They are distinct from the thorns by their *moral excellency* as produced by Christ. Refer to their purity, etc. How superior to the world! "The righteous is more excellent than his neighbour."

2. *By mutual love.* Christ loves them and they love him. But of the wicked it is said, "If any man love not," etc. 1 Cor. xvi. 22.

3. Lilies not only possess more beauty, but they are *more useful than thorns.* Formerly lilies were considered medicinal, and in that respect were often used. The righteous save souls from death — one sinner destroyeth much good.

4. A lily among thorns, exhibiting its beauty, is indicative of *life, vigour, and preservation.* Though it is surrounded and pressed on every side by thorns, yet behold, it lives and flourishes!

—— And the Christian is surrounded by wicked men, evil customs, and tempting snares, yet the Lord preserves him. He is among thorns, but he is not one of them. Great is the distinction between thorns and lilies——so with regard to saints and sinners.

Lastly, this distinction will be sublimely apparent at *the last day;* Matt. xiii. 30, 39—42; xxiv. 31; xxv. 31, etc.

IMPROVEMENT.

1. Admire and adore the grace of God, Christians, for distinguishing you from the wicked. 2. Pray to continue distinct. Be lilies among thorns — and be not turned to thorns, rendering railing for railing, etc. 3. Anticipate the celestial paradise, when you shall be free from the wicked who are thorns in your side; and from all sin. Grace in the soul is a lily among thorns — corruptions are thorns in the flesh, 2 Cor. xii. 7.

VIII.—MOCKING AT SIN.

"Fools make a mock at sin; but among the righteous there is favour." — PROV. xiv. 9.

I. WHAT THE NATURAL HEART THINKS OF SIN.

1. *Men sin easily.* As a fountain casting out its waters, Jer. vii. Such is the natural flow of their hearts.

2. *They bear the load lightly.* At ease in Zion.

3. *The heavier the load, they sin the more easily.* Like a river filled, Eph. iv. 19.

4. *It frequently excuses it;* apologizes for it—attributes it to the force of circumstances, infirmities, etc.

II. WHAT GOD THINKS OF IT.

1. He says he hates it. Jer. xliv. 4.

2. He has banished it from heaven, and prepared perdition for it.

3. He has punished it in his Son.

III. WHAT AWAKENED SOULS THINK OF IT. Rom. vii. 9; Ps. li. Those converted on the day of Pentecost. The jailor. Sin has a sting.

IV. WHAT BELIEVERS THINK OF IT. It is their plague—their enemy. Like God they hate it. Sometimes it grieves them. They long for the time when they shall be free from it. They will enter the land of rest, and leave it behind them for ever.

IX.—DIVINE SOLICITUDE FOR MAN'S HAPPINESS.

"Oh that thou hadst hearkened unto my commandments! then had thy peace been as a river, and thy righteousness as the waves of the sea." — ISA. xlviii. 18.

THE compassion of God to sinners is great. He has abundantly provided for their happiness, and he is ever solicitous for their salvation. "As I live, saith the Lord, I have no pleasure in the death of the wicked," etc. Ezek. xxxiii. 11; Hosea xi. 8. In the context the Divine compassion is expressed for backsliding Israel. By reason of their sins, God had brought them into captivity; it was their own fault, and he did not afflict them willingly. "O that thou hadst hearkened," etc.

I. GOD HAS REVEALED HIS WILL FOR THE BENEFIT OF SINNERS.

He has issued his "commandments" which are "holy, just, and good," for this purpose. At ver. 16, he intimates that he had always spoken plainly to Israel, from the beginning, by Moses and all the prophets. "I have not spoken in secret, but publicly, from the top of Mount Sinai, and in the chief places of concourse, the solemn assemblies of your tribes."

In these "last days" God has "spoken to us by his Son." Heb. i. 1, etc. The "commandments" are contained in the gospel. That gospel proclaims rich, great, appropriate, and free salvation to the guilty world. It utters its voice and says, "Repent, and believe the gospel." "Believe in the Lord Jesus Christ, and thou shalt be saved." The gospel reveals not only duty, but privilege, and promise, and Divine fellowship, and eternal life, in rich and glorious association.

II. GOD'S COMMANDMENTS ARE TO BE OBEYED. "O that thou hadst hearkened."

1. *This is perfectly just.* God has a sovereign right to command us.

2. *Obedience should be prompted by God's love.* Why does he command men to obedience? Because he loves them.

3. *It should be prompted by self-interest.* Obedience to the gospel is our life — our salvation. The "obedience of faith" instrumentally leads to deliverance from guilt and eternal perdition — and ultimately elevates the soul to the heavenly paradise. John iii. 16; v. 24.

4. Obedience should be prompt—earnest—open—sincere—and ardent.

III. DISOBEDIENCE WILL INVOLVE THE LOSS OF INCALCULABLE GOOD.

This is declared. If thou hadst "hearkened unto me, then had thy peace been as a river," etc. Such happiness have all those who love God's commandments. "Great peace have they that love thy law."

The loss of incalculable good is expressed in the text.

1. *Their peace would have been as a river.* The peace arising from God's pardoning, justifying, sanctifying, and comforting love. —— Illustrate this by the beautiful figure; "Like a river."

(1) *This peace, like a river, has a source.* It begins at the fountain of Christ's blood. That is the rich source of its glorious flow.

(2) *A river is fed from above.* Rains and showers feed the rivers. The showers of grace swell the rivers of peace. Mal. iii. 10.

(3) *A river has occasional inundations;* as the Nile, for instance. An awakening Providence often makes it overflow. Afflictions, and the consolations under them, make the peace and bliss of the believer to flow as a river. "These light afflictions," etc. 2 Cor. iv. 17, 18.

(4) *A river is fertilizing.* It conveys nourishment. Egypt owes all its fertility to the Nile. The peace of Christ makes every grace grow. Holiness and felicity always grow out of a peaceful breast. See this stated, Rom. vi. 4.

(5) *A river gets broader* as it flows on from its source to its termination. "The path of the just is as the shining light, shining more and more unto the perfect day." A river may in its course receive tributary streams, which constantly add to its strength; so a believer "grows in grace," etc. — he "adds unto his faith, virtue," etc.

2. *Their "righteousness" would have been "as the waves of the sea."* Christ is made unto believers righteousness." That righteousness, even Christ's obedience to death, etc., is as the waves of the sea.

(1) *Because it washes away and covers the greatest sins.* The waves of the sea bear down all opposition. So the righteousness of Christ is irresistible — all conquering — no guilt is too stubborn for its power. "The blood of Jesus Christ his Son cleanseth from all sin."

(2) *It covers again and again.* When the conviction of guilt distresses the conscience, we look to Christ; then the broad covering waves of Divine righteousness roll upon our souls, and obliterate all sin and torment.

(3) *It is infinite righteousness.* Who can count the waves of the sea? Who can estimate this righteousness? It exists and operates in time; its influence shall endure for ever.

3. *Of this happiness the disobedient shall be deprived.* "O that thou hadst hearkened to my commandments; then had thy peace been as a river," etc. But thou hast not hearkened — thou hast not obeyed, and therefore thy peace does not flow as a river, nor thy righteousness as the waves of the sea.

Instead of this enjoyment, there is positive wrath and misery connected with the sinner! — a fearful looking for of judgment. How vile their character — how dreadful their prospect!

Lastly, *God wishes men to be saved.* God sometimes pleads with men to be saved for his own pleasure, it would be pleasant to him; speaking after the manner of men, it would make him glad; as in the parable of the lost sheep. Sometimes he pleads for his own glory. Jer. xiii. 16; Mal. ii. 1. But here it is for the happiness of sinners themselves. Ps. lxxxi. 13. Once more, he pleads with men, because unwilling that any should perish. 2 Pet. iii. 9.

X. — THE IMPORTANT LINE.

In the year 1821, the late Rev. Daniel Tyerman, and George Bennet, Esq., were sent by the London Missionary Society to visit their Stations in different parts of the world. On the 23d June, they crossed the line, and on the following day, being the Sabbath, Mr. Tyerman preached on the event. His text was,

"His hand hath divided it to them by line." — ISA. xxxiv. 17.

And he thus considered his subject: —

1. There is a *line of being*, which we all crossed when we were born; then we were endowed with a rational and intelligent nature; and then we entered upon our state of probation.

2. There is a *line of regeneration*, dividing the moral world into two hemispheres, in one of which dwell the righteous, and in the other the wicked. This line must be crossed by all, before they can become Christians indeed, and enjoy the privileges of the gospel.

3. There is a *line of death*, which we must each cross when we have finished our probationary course, and go before the tribunal of God to render an account of the deeds done in the body; but when, where, and how, we shall cross this line, we know not.

4. There is a line which divides between heaven and hell; this none shall ever cross who have once taken up their abode in either of these regions.

In his application, the preacher remarked, that if we would not lament having crossed the line of *being*, nor fear crossing the line of *death*, we should be desirous to cross the line of *regeneration*, that when we fail on earth we may be received into everlasting habitations, on the right side of the line which divides between heaven and hell.

XI. — FREEDOM FROM CONDEMNATION.

"There is therefore now no condemnation to them which are in Christ Jesus, who walk not after the flesh, but after the Spirit." — ROM. viii. 1.

THE Apostle in this epistle dwells at large on the great doctrine of justification by faith. The text may be regarded as a summary of the whole. From it we learn the intimate connection between justification and sanctification. Its propositions are: "He that is in Christ Jesus is free from condemnation; and he that is in Christ Jesus walks not after the flesh, but after the Spirit." Being "in Christ Jesus" is that on which both depend, and it is from him that both are derived.

I. UNION WITH CHRIST. "In Christ Jesus."

1. To be in Christ Jesus is more than mere *nominal Christianity.* —— Many say, Lord, Lord; Matt. vii. 21; Luke xii. 25. Union with Christ is more than a mere profession of Christ and union with his people.

Such a union as this Judas had, apparently a branch in the vine, bearing the leaves of an outward profession, and making a fair show in the flesh. Multitudes are still the same, especially since no odium, but a degree of respectability attaches to the Christian profession. There are but few indeed who would wish to be recognized as infidels, or avowed unbelievers. The effective co-operation of various religious institutions, and the commendable zeal displayed in the diffusion of Christian knowledge, have put infidelity a little out of countenance; and the large proportion of talent, rank, and influence, which the interests of religion have associated and combined, have given it an ascendency in the public esteem which it scarcely possessed at any former period. But this nominal union will bear no genuine fruit to God after all; and though we may be instrumental in communicating good to others, we shall ourselves be cast away as fruitless branches, which are gathered and cast into the fire to be burned.

2. There is *a vital union with Christ,* by a genuine and living faith, and this is the great doctrine of the preceding chapter, iii. 25.

"In Christ Jesus" is a phrase very common in Scripture, and denotes a vital and glorious union with him. It is sometimes represented by the union of the vine and its branches, John xv. 5. As stones in a building united to the foundation stone, 1 Pet. ii. 5. By the union between the head and members of the body, Eph. v. 30. By a covenant relation to Christ, represented by marriage, Rom. vii. 4. By the bridegroom and the bride, 1 Cor. vi. 17. By the union of the food we eat with the body, John vi. 56, 57; Gal. ii. 20; 2 Cor. iv. 11. The convinced sinner has fled to Christ, and is in him, as Noah fled to the ark. Like the cities of refuge to Israel, Christ is the hope set before us, Phil. iii. 9; Heb. vi. 18.

This union is effected by *Divine power;* nothing else can ally the sinner to Christ; and it is absolutely necessary to Christian usefulness. If severed from Christ we can do nothing. Union with Christ is the only true source of practical religion.

It is a mysterious union; but of its existence believers have an inward consciousness; 1 John v. 10.

II. THE GLORIOUS PRIVILEGE CONNECTED WITH THIS RELATION. "No condemnation."

1. This implies that *there was condemnation.*

Before believing, God's people were condemned—children of wrath, and under the curse. Condemned, because the law of God was broken. The children of wrath, because God has declared that sin shall not go unpunished. And under the curse, because it is denounced—every sinner is cursed; and when the thread of existence is cut, it will fall upon his imperishable spirit with all its crushing and poignant power. Rom. ii. 9; Gal. iii. 10; Deut. xxviii. 15.

2. *This condemnation has been removed.* "No condemnation." All the curses are reversed, and all the threatenings removed; all are turned into promises and blessings.——There is now a change of state—the captive is ransomed—the sentence is gone, and the believer is accounted innocent. Rom. v. 1; Acts xiii. 38, 39.

(1) No condemnation from *conscience.* This is sprinkled from the evil of guilt by the blood of Christ, and hushed into peace, Heb. x. 22; 1 John ii. 21.

(2) No condemnation *from the law.* They are "*in Christ,*" and the law does not, and cannot condemn him. He has magnified and made it honourable; "he is the end of the law for righteousness to every one that believeth. See Gal. iii. 13.

(3) No condemnation *from God.* He is satisfied and "well-pleased" with them for Christ's sake, Rom. v. 1, 2.

3. *How is this deliverance accomplished?* It is not of works; not of faith itself as a virtue of ours, but as uniting us to Christ, 1 Cor. i. 31; Phil. iii. 9. Christ is made heir of all things; and being made one with him, we become joint-heirs of all that he possesses. Rom. viii. 17.

This delivering grace is graphically stated, Rom. iii. 23—27. All that Christ did, is imputed to believers. His death delivers them from death, and his righteousness is imputed for their justification, 2 Cor. v. 21; Rom. viii. 33.

III. JUSTIFICATION IS PRODUCTIVE OF PRACTICAL HOLINESS. "Who walk not after the flesh," etc.

The terms "flesh" and "Spirit" are here contrasted, and denote the opposite principles of sin and holiness. —— To "walk after the flesh," is to be in a carnal and corrupt state; to be governed by what is carnal; Gal. v. 19. —— To "walk after the Spirit" is expressive of an habitual course of piety; so as to prefer and seek spiritual objects and enjoyments. Gal. v. 22.

Union with Christ is attended with a real as well as a relative change, and this prevents the objection of its giving liberty to sin.—— No one is free from condemnation but by being in Christ Jesus; and no one is in Christ Jesus but such as walk not after the flesh, but after the Spirit. Justification and sanctification are therefore inseparable —— Observe,

1. *Their walk corresponds with the character of the Spirit.* He is the "Spirit of holiness;" and the Christian is holy; he follows after holiness, etc. Divine transformation is his work. 2 Cor. iii. 18.

2. The Christian is *led and influenced by the Spirit.*

The Spirit is the fountain *of light,* and Christians walk as children of light; the Spirit of *comfort*, and they walk joyfully in adversity and tribulation: a *quickening Spirit*, and their walk is active, abounding in every good work: the Spirit of *assurance*, and they repose on God, and commit their cause to him in every situation of life: the Spirit of *hope*, and they rejoice in the hope of the glory of God.

IMPROVEMENT.

1. How important to be found in Christ! What a joyful influence it throws over life:—free from condemnation—at peace with God!! 2. Examination. Am I led by the Spirit? Do I hate the "works of the flesh," and love "the fruits of the Spirit?"

XII.—AFFLICTIONS.

"Affliction cometh not forth of the dust, neither doth trouble spring out of the ground."—Job v. 6.

AFFLICTIONS, the common lot of man, particularly entailed upon good men, necessary to their character, do not come by chance. Providence, like Ezekiel's wheel, may have a terrible aspect, yet they never go but where God sends them, or without his going with them.

I. Every trouble comes according to the appointment of God.

See Ps. lxvi. 11; Lam. iii. 33; 1 Thess. iii. 3; Ezek. xvi. 21; 1 Sam. iii. 12.

II. When afflictions visit us, it is at the very time intended by God.

III. The particular object is fixed by God, to whom he intends to send affliction, or by which affliction is to come.

IV. When troubles come, it is according to a certain degree or measure.

Mal. iii. 3; Matt. xxiv. 22; Isa. xxvii. 8.

V. The continuance of trouble is not left to uncertainty or casualty.

Gen. xv. 13; Rev. ii. 10.

VI. Afflictions come for a specific purpose.

Job v. 17; Heb. xii. 6; Ps. cxix. 75.

1. They have a tendency to correct what is wrong; to mortify sin. Isa. xxvii. 9.

2. They are often sent to make manifest the energy and power of Divine grace.

3. Trials are sent by God for the peculiar manifestation of his goodness and kindness.

4. Afflictions are intended to prepare those exercised with them for a better world.

IMPROVEMENT.

1. In all our afflictions, we should view the hand of God. 2. We ought not to murmur when we are exercised with them. 3. We should feel a submissive temper under them, because, as they come from God, they must be right. 4. We should not only view God as sending affliction, but as being present to manage and control it, and to afford comfort and support under it. 5. In every affliction, we have always something to be thankful for.

JEHOIDA BREWER.

XIII.—THE SWORD OF THE SPIRIT.

"And the sword of the Spirit which is the word of God."—EPH. vi. 17.

THE Christian's life is one of warfare. He has numerous foes, stronger than he, more subtle, and they are invisible; they have also allies in his breast, even depraved appetites, ever ready to join in opposition.——A gracious God, however, has provided for the protection, conflict, and conquest of his people. He, the Divine Commander, has provided every necessary weapon, as the context declares.

"The Sword of the Spirit, which is the word of God;" the great foundation and rule of all revealed religion; the Holy Scripture,—a revelation from God, which bears the stamp of Divinity, or carries its own evidence along with it—the most ancient and excellent book in the world; and whatever the wit of infidels may rake together to shake its authenticity, it stands immovable, and will bear the strictest scrutiny of unprejudiced reason, and be found to be in every respect worthy of God, its Divine Author. The word of God is not only the ground of a Christian's faith and hope, and the rule of his conduct, but it is his Sword by which he defends himself, and attacks his enemies.

I. WHY THE WORD OF GOD MAY BE COMPARED TO A SWORD.

A sword is *a military weapon* with which soldiers are armed. In warfare it is indispensable to soldiers of every rank and quality; to the superior officer as well as to the ordinary soldier.

So the word of God is *the spiritual weapon of every Christian soldier* of whatever rank or quality, and it is indispensable. Christ, the Captain of salvation, fought with this weapon, Matt. iv. 4—8. All the soldiers in his army must therefore be armed with it.

2. A sword is a weapon by which a soldier not only defends himself, but also does *great execution against his enemies.*

So the word of God is a spiritual weapon by which the Christian not only defends himself from foes; but by it he offends, yea, cuts down and conquers all the enemies of his soul.

(1) The word is a *defensive weapon*. "By the word of thy lips, I have kept me from the paths of the destroyer," etc. Ps. xvii. 4; cxix. 92.

(2) *Offensive*. The apostles used it in defence of the gospel before Felix, etc., etc. The Bible contains truths, motives, promises, threatenings, etc., of an irresistible character.

3. A sword is *a sharp piercing weapon;* it will enter into the body, and pierce even to the heart.

So the word of God is a Sword that will pierce the hearts of sinners, and make them cry out, etc. Heb. iv. 12; Acts ii. 37.

4. A Sword is *an honourable weapon*, and of great antiquity; having been in use from the beginning.

So the word of God, the Sword of the Spirit, is *an honourable weapon*. Christ, prophets, apostles, martyrs, used it.——It is also of great antiquity; the writings of Moses are the most ancient records. Honourable too on account of the victories it has won.

5. Some swords have *two edges* and will *cut both ways*, both backwards and forwards.

So the Word of God, as used by his ministers, *hath two operations at one time*, 2 Cor. ii. 16. And when that word is received it is used by the Spirit to conquer the depraved heart of the believer, and he wields it to conquer unbelieving men. It conquers him that he may conquer others.

6. A Sword is *the instrument of victory*.

So is the word of God. See Rev. xii. 11.

7. A Sword is sometimes *carried before a magistrate* as the symbol of authority and justice. Rom. xiii. 4.

So the Sword of the Spirit is *the weapon of a minister's or Christian's authority*. In reference to doctrine, conduct, and discipline, he uses the Sword for the settlement of all disputes. "To the law and the testimony," etc.

II. WHY IS IT CALLED THE SWORD OF THE SPIRIT?

1. Because it is a *spiritual weapon*, designed to be of use in the spiritual warfare, against our spiritual foes, when the soul is attacked by Satan, etc.

2. Because *the Holy Spirit is the Author of it*. His hand alone formed and fashioned it. 2 Pet. ii. 21.

3. The Holy Spirit is *the only true interpreter of the Scriptures*, they can only be understood through the Spirit who indited them—hence the necessity of praying for illumination.

4. Because it is *the Spirit that gives the word its efficacy in the soul*. He guides the truth to the soul, there he fixes it. He makes the gospel the power of God to salvation. 1 Thess. i. 5.

IMPROVEMENT.

1. How valuable is the word of God! Without this weapon, we should be overcome and lost. Set a high value on the Scriptures.

2. We may learn the reason for Satanic opposition. The Bible being full of light is against him, and therefore he opposes it by his emissaries, Atheists, Infidels, etc. 3. See the wicked cruelty of the Roman Catholics in using all their exertions to prevent the distribution and use of the Sword of the Spirit. 4. Labour to know the proper use of this spiritual weapon. Satan is a cunning warrior, stealing insensibly into the soul.

XIV.—EJACULATORY PRAYER.

"So I prayed unto the God of heaven."—NEH. ii. 4.

REMARKS on the piety and conduct of Nehemiah—his fervent ejaculations.

I. The *nature* of ejaculatory prayer.

Prayer is presenting the *desires* to God. *Social* prayer is the united request of many—*private* prayer the supplication of an individual.

1. Ejaculatory prayer is dependent on no *place*. It may be presented everywhere.
2. It is not dependent on *time*.
3. It is not dependent on any occasion or circumstance.

II. Produce some *examples* of successful ejaculatory prayer.

Abraham's servant, Gen. xxiv. 12.——Samson, Judges xvi. 28. ——Stephen, Acts vii. 59.——Christ, Matt. xi. 25.

III. The seasons when ejaculatory prayers may be more especially necessary.

1. In sudden and unexpected calls to some important and difficult duty.
2. The sacred day of rest.
3. The hour of temptation.
4. The period of sickness.

IV. The advantages of ejaculatory prayer.

1. It would maintain in the mind an habitual sense of dependence upon God.
2. Preserve the mind in a proper tone for the exercises of devotion.
3. Prove a powerful preventive against sin.
4. Enable us boldly to contend with enemies or difficulties.
5. Quicken us to activity and zeal in the cause of God and religion.

J. A. JAMES.

XV.—LITTLE SINS VERY INJURIOUS.

"Take us the foxes, the little foxes, that spoil the vines; for our vines have tender grapes." — Song ii. 25.

I. What sins may be called *little* sins?
II. What is the harm which they do?
III. How they must be dealt with?

I. What sins may be called "little sins"?
Sins which are so comparatively.

1. Evil tempers in the church, in the family, and in the commercial world.
2. A light and frivolous spirit.
3. Remissness in religious duties.
4. Social whispering, slandering, backbiting.
5. Conformities to this world.
6. Dress — *ever veering*.
7. Conversation — earthly.
8. Light and unholy company.
9. Pride. (1) *Natural* pride, which sets us above our fellow-creatures. (2) Spiritual pride.

II. The harm which they do.

1. They injure our consciences by hardening them.
2. They make way for greater sins.
3. They relax our devotion and communion with God.
4. They hinder the presence of Christ with us.

III. How must they be dealt with?
Not tenderly, not connivingly; but they must be taken.

1. This may be a charge to ministers.
2. A charge to Christians, beware of the first approach of sin.

WILKS.

XVI.—THE SWELLING OF JORDAN.

"How wilt thou do in the swelling of Jordan?" — JER. xii. 5.

THE prophet's discomposure, on account of the conspiracy formed against him, led him into a perplexity about the prosperity of the wicked, among whom were principally the men of Anathoth, v. 1, 2.

He appealed to the heart-searching God, that he had acted uprightly, and that he was hated and persecuted for his sake, v. 3.

In the text, the Lord is thought gently to reprove the prophet's impatience. The opposition of the men of Anathoth was not so formidable, as what he must expect to encounter from the kings and rulers of Judah; and the present calamities of the nation were trivial compared with the approaching desolations.

If then he was so disconcerted by these lighter trials, how would he endure more severe afflictions? If he was so wearied running with footmen, or contending with his equals, how would he be disquieted, when required to run with horsemen, or execute his office in defiance of those in authority? If he could scarcely endure when the land remained in peace, what would he do when hostile invasions would bear down all before them, like the overflowing waters of the Jordan?*

We are apt to murmur under present trials; but more severe, solemn, and important trials are awaiting us; at any rate we are sure that death will soon break down every mortal barrier, — our health and vigour, and, like the swelling of Jordan, overwhelm us. "Then how wilt thou do in the swelling of Jordan?"

I. CONSIDER JORDAN AS TYPICAL OF DEATH.

Many persons, places, and things under the Old Testament were typical of New Testament persons, places, and events. Thus Egyptian slavery and darkness typified the dark and miserable thraldom of Satan — the despotic and cruel Pharaoh, the malice and hate of the Prince of darkness — the prophet Moses, Christ the servant of God — the wilderness, the Christian's pilgrimage through this world — Jordan, death — Canaan, heaven. —— Observe

1. *Jordan constantly flowed.* It never stagnated — it never dried. One celebrated traveller, Chateaubriand, represents it as "sluggish, reluctantly creeping to the Dead Sea; though sometimes it is very violent, turbid, and rapid; too rapid to be swam against."

So human mortality is always proceeding; its flow is incessant, ever conveying mankind to the Dead Sea, or the grave. Death is no respecter of persons — he levels all distinctions — he destroys all enjoyments — he brings all to the grave. The flow of mortality is irresistible; it cannot be swam against. No human device, no physician's skill, no human precaution, can bribe away death.

2. *Jordan overflowed all its banks*, especially at the time of harvest. Josh. iii. 15.

So the banks of every mortal will be borne down by the stream of death. Some are priding themselves in their vigour and strength — some in their riches, etc., but all these will avail nothing. —— Then again, is not death the great reaper? The time of death is the time of harvest to saints and sinners. God then gathers his saints, his precious seed, into his garner; Satan collects his tares, and deposits

---

* The overflowing of Jordan, which generally happened in harvest, drove the lions and other beasts of prey from their coverts among the bushes that lined its banks; who, spreading themselves through the country, made terrible havoc, slaying men and carrying off the cattle. See 1 Chron. xii. 15; Jer. xlix. 19; l. 44.

them in his own place. "For Jordan overfloweth all his banks at the time of harvest." O remember this! death is inevitable; Heb. ix. 27.

3. *Jordan parted the wilderness and the promised land.* The land flowing with milk and honey — the glory of all lands was on the other side Jordan, and the way to it was across that river.

So the Christian pilgrim's home — heaven, the glorious residence of God, angels, and saints, can only be attained by passing the gulf of death. Thus the poet sings: —

> "Dark river of death," that is flowing
> Between "the bright city" and "me,"
> Thou boundest the path I am going,
> O how shall I pass over thee?
>
> Let glory from Calvary streaming,
> Shine bright o'er the cold sable wave;
> Faith strong in Christ with rapt'rous hope beaming,
> To burst through the gloom of the grave.

And beautifully appropriate is the representation of Dr. Watts: —

> There everlasting spring abides,
> And never withering flowers;
> Death, like a narrow sea, divides
> This heavenly land from ours.
>
> Sweet fields beyond the swelling flood,
> Stand drest in living green;
> So to the Jews old Canaan stood,
> And Jordan roll'd between.

4. *Jordan separated the inhabitants of Canaan from those of the wilderness and other places.*

So death separates the inhabitants of the church militant from the inhabitants of the church triumphant. Some of our friends have gone over the river, and we see and enjoy them no longer. There is the father or the mother — here are the children. There is the beloved partner — gone over Jordan — here the lone and bereaved one weeps in anguish, but hopes for reunion there. Patriarchs, Apostles, martyrs, yea, legions of saints, have passed over — and Jesus himself is there.

> One family, we dwell in him,
> One church above, beneath;
> Though now divided by the stream,
> The narrow stream of death.
>
> One army of the living God,
> To his command we bow;
> Part of the host have cross'd the flood,
> And part are crossing now.
>
> Even now to their eternal home
> Some happy spirits fly;
> And we are to the margin come,
> And soon expect to die!

5. *The Jordan was a new way to the Jews.* They had never passed it before. Josh. iii. 4.

The river of death can be crossed only once; and we have yet to pass over. We have had no past experience—all will be new—solemnly new to each of us! We have seen our friends pass over; but oh! to be baptized with death ourselves — what is it — how shall we endure it — shall we go through nobly or ignobly — shall we be left to ourselves on account of our sins, or will Jesus bear up our head in the dark river? — "How wilt thou do in the swelling of Jordan?"

6. *Jordan was subject to the power of Jehovah.* At his command, "the waters rose and stood upon a heap and the people passed over." Josh. iii. 16.

So death is under the power of God. O Christian, this is thy great consolation! Pain, weariness, and wretchedness, may gather around thee in thy last conflict; thou mayst say in the evening, "Would to God it were morning," and in the morning, "Would to God it were evening;" but God shall make all thy bed in thy afflictions. To pains and agonies which threaten to overwhelm thee, like the "swelling of Jordan," he shall say, "Hitherto shall ye come, but no further; and here shall your proud waters be stayed." He will make you triumph. "O death, where is thy sting?" etc.

7. *Jordan was the last river the Israelites had to cross.* God helped them through the Red Sea ("which the Egyptians trying to pass were drowned,") and also through many rivers, and now he would help them through the last. When that was crossed, they would be in Canaan, the land of promise.

Death is the "last enemy" which believers will have to encounter. It was the last conflict which the Saviour endured. "For the joy that was before him, he endured the cross, and despised the shame, and is for ever sat down on the right hand of God." A dying saint may comfortably say, "This is the last river I have to cross, and then I shall be in Canaan. This is my last conflict—when it is over, I shall conflict no more, but enter my Father's house, and rest in his love for ever."

II. THE PREPARATION AND ARRANGEMENTS NECESSARY FOR PASSING OVER JORDAN.

1. *They were required to sanctify themselves previously.* Josh. iii. 5.

And must not we be sanctified before we can die happily? Yes, and Jesus saves his people by his precious blood — removing all their guilt, and freeing them from all condemnation: He renovates their hearts by his Spirit, and creates in them his own image, and thus they become fit to die. Titus iii. 4—7.

2. *The priests were to enter the river first.* Josh. iii. 6. How would this encourage the people!

The Lord Jesus Christ, the great High Priest, has passed triumphantly before. He left us an example. And because he has passed, we also shall go over safely; and looking down into the river, we shall discern his footsteps at the bottom.

3. *The priests stood firm in the midst of Jordan, until all the people passed over.* Josh. iii. 17. There they stood with the ark of the covenant, the evidence of the Divine favour.

Jesus stands by his people in their dying moments, and shows them the secret of his covenant. He "never leaves them nor forsakes them." He "perfects that which concerneth them; he forsakes not the works of his hands."

> Shudder not to pass the stream,
> Venture all thy care on him,
> Him, whose dying love and power
> Still'd its tossing, hush'd its war:
> Safe as the expanded wave,
> Gentle as the summer's eve;
> Not one object of his care
> Ever suffer'd shipwreck there.

4. *When they had passed over, they erected memorials of the Divine interposition,* enabling them to pass over Jordan dry-shod. Josh. iv. 5—8, 20.

So it will be with the Christian. When he enters the heavenly land, will he not erect his Ebenezer, "Hitherto hath the Lord helped me"? Will he not prostrate himself before the throne of God and the Lamb, and say along with the congregated hosts of God's elect, "Worthy is the Lamb that was slain?" etc. Rev. v. 12.

III. HOW SOME HAVE DONE IN THE SWELLING OF JORDAN.

1. *The wicked.* Look at Belshazzar—at the rich man clothed in purple, etc.— at the rich fool who resolved to pull down his barns, and build larger.

2. *The righteous.* How sweetly did some of the patriarchs and prophets pass over!—they "fell asleep"—"they departed," and were "gathered to their fathers." Look at Paul, "I am now ready to be offered," etc.

IV. PRESS THE QUESTION. "How wilt thou do," etc.

Sinner, how wilt thou do in thy dying hour. Living now in sin—seeking earthly enjoyment everywhere, and incessantly—making this world thy heaven—unforgiven, unrenewed, how wilt thou do in the swelling of Jordan?

To the *self-righteous* we propose the same question.

To the *formalist*—to the *hypocrite*.

None but the righteous can do well in the swelling of Jordan.

[Many parts of this Outline may be beautifully illustrated by a reference to the "Pilgrim's Progress;" the scene where Christian and Hopeful come to the river.]

XVII.—PRIDE.

"Only by pride cometh contention, but with the well-advised is wisdom."—PROV. xiii. 10.

WHOEVER will converse with his own heart, and carefully examine its secret workings, will find more or less of this iniquity cleaving to him, and see reason to be ashamed and humbled for it before the eyes of a heart-searching God. It is impossible, in a few words, to point out all the evils springing from this accursed root. Solomon here points out one of them, and one of the most considerable — "By pride cometh contention."

1. *Pride and ambition are the springs of those contentions that are between states and kingdoms.*

"Whence come wars and fightings?" says the apostle James; "Come they not hence, even of men's lusts that war in their members?" Haughty monarchs think they have an ability to govern the world. They are mad to think that they have any equals, or rivals. They aim at universal monarchy, and so make inroads upon their honest and peaceable neighbours, all around them. O what havoc and destruction has this cursed sin made in the world! what destruction is it still making!

2. *Pride is often the spring of contentions about religious matters, between Christians that differ in articles of faith and modes of worship.*

There are few, perhaps no churches, where the dismal effects of pride have not at times appeared in unchristian and unbrotherly contentions, which have caused and fomented divisions, and destroyed almost all their charity, that Divine and heavenly grace, the distinguishing mark of Christ's servants, as pride is of Satan's.

3. *Pride is the spring of most of the contentions that occur in families.*

Pride will invert the order of nature, and turn the family upside down. Children and servants, through pride, grow impatient of reproof, and though it is given in the most friendly and tender manner, quarrel with their reprover, and ruin the peace and order of the household.

4. *Pride is the cause of contentions between neighbours and acquaintances.*

It shows itself when men boast of their characters, abilities, and circumstances, and vainly compare themselves with others. We see it in their quick resentment of affronts; anything which touches what they call their honour. We see it in their extreme backwardness to forgive an injury, or overlook an insult. Most of the lawsuits that happen among us, have their rise here. "By pride cometh contention," and contention breeds litigation.

II. Let us consider the counter proposition. "With the well-advised is wisdom." By "the well-advised" we are to understand humble and modest men, who show their humility and modesty by consulting and taking advice. The term also implies submission to the mind and will of God, to seek direction from him. The "well-advised will not lean to his own understanding; but in all his ways acknowledge God," and submit to infinite wisdom. He pours out his heart before God, that he may lead him in the "right way," the way of truth and peace.

1. *They show that they are wise by acting a wise part.*

They manifest that they are acquainted with their own hearts: that they understand human nature; and are under the influence of religious principles, willing to do unto others as they would wish others to do to them.

2. *They are likely to increase in wisdom, for they know there is room for it, and take the proper methods to obtain it.*

The humble man is sensible that he knows but in part, and therefore he distrusts himself, and presses on to grow in knowledge. The proud man thinks all wisdom is centered in himself; and when he has got to the bottom of his line, he thinks he has got to the bottom of the ocean. He supposes himself wise enough, and despises others. Nothing shuts the heart against wisdom so much as pride. But more especially is he likely to increase in wisdom through the assistance and blessing of God, which he is always ready to bestow upon the humble. "Though the Lord be high, yet hath he respect unto the lowly." God "resisteth the proud, but giveth grace to the humble."

Let us then seek the wisdom which cometh from above, which is first pure and then peaceable. "Finally, brethren, live in peace, and the God of love and peace be with you."

Job Orton.

XVIII.—THE HAPPY PEOPLE.

"Happy is that people that is in such a case; yea, happy is that people whose God is the Lord."—Ps. cxliv. 15.

David, like a true patriot, was anxious for the welfare of his people. The close of this Psalm beautifully expresses his pious regard for them. —— It is a glorious circumstance when the honours and dignities connected with royalty do not obliterate from the mind Christian benevolence. David had been raised from a state of comparative obscurity to the throne of Israel, but in every scene of his eventful life, he regarded the blessing of the Almighty as absolutely necessary to personal and national prosperity.——How few of the wealthy and honourable of mankind are like him! Many have been raised from obscurity and poverty; but they have forgotten God, and their duties to mankind. And sometimes such men, instead of being a blessing, have been a curse to society. It is our wisdom to copy the best examples, and pray for grace to imitate them.

I. THE PSALMIST REFERS TO A HAPPY CASE OR STATE. "Happy is that people that is in such a case."

This is included in what he desired and prayed for, and which, if granted, would conduce to individual and national happiness. —— Observe,

1. The Psalmist recognizes God as *the Giver of all good.*

It is a happy case when a nation contains a goodly number of persons who regard God as the Source of all good, whose blessing alone can make prosperous and happy. They "are the salt of the earth;" and by their dependence upon Divine aid, by their prayerful applications for his blessing, and by their holy examples, perpetuate to a nation the Divine favour, and preserve it from destruction. God loves *them*, and the wicked are spared. v. 10; Gen. xviii. 23, etc.; Isa. i. 9.

2. The Psalmist prayed for *the welfare of the rising generation.* ——He was anxious that- they might fear God, and become the ornament and support of the community.

(1) He prayed to be delivered "from the hand of strange or wicked children." Such children are sure to be the source of sorrow to their parents, and the bane of society.——By their evil habits, by their pernicious principles, they threaten to debase the community.

How often may the wickedness of children be prevented by the influence of parental example, by faithful and affectionate admonition, and by earnest prayer!

(2) He prayed that their minds *might be imbued with true religion*, to render them happy, useful, valuable, and honourable. "That our youth may be as plants grown up in their youth," v. 12; Ps. cxxviii. 3; Isa. lxi. 3; that they may resemble trees or plants growing in a fruitful soil, and become vigorous and courageous, fruitful in every good work, and be the beauty and stability of society. Nothing surely on this side the grave can yield greater pleasure to the pious than to see their children walking in the fear of God, and as Matthew Henry observes, "to see them as 'plants,' not as weeds, not as thorns; to see them as plants growing, not withered and blasted; to see them healthful, quick, intelligent, and especially of a pious inclination, likely to bring fruit unto God in their day; to see them in their youth, their growing time, increasing in everything that is good, till they grow strong in spirit."*

Female virtue, on account of its influence, is represented as of supreme importance. "That our daughters may be as corner-stones, polished after the similitude of a palace." That they may be prudent, virtuous, healthful, industrious, and amiable; fitted to fill the important relations of wives and mothers. This would honour their families, and those into which they might marry. Stones, when taken from the quarry, are uneven, rough, and unsightly, but when levelled and chisselled, and subjected to the Sculptor's art, they become beautiful, and are ornamental and sustaining to the building in which they are placed.

"By daughters," says Matthew Henry, "families are united in their mutual strength, as the parts of a building are by the corner-

---

* "It is a very pleasant sight to behold a nation increasing in population; families brought up in industry, honesty, and plenty, and fitted for their several stations in public and domestic life; not cut off by war, or wasted by famine, or pestilence; and when all manner of abundance is stored in our garners, and clothes our fields and pastures. In many of these things we are a happy people; yet, alas! our numerous youth do not generally afford a pleasing prospect. Too many of the young men of all ranks in this favoured land, grow up noxious plants, being early debauched in their principles and morals, and justly to be denominated infidel, profane, licentious, and dissipated; contracting and disseminating both mental and bodily diseases; and prepared to communicate vice, and ruin, and enfeebled constitutions to the next generation."—*Scott.*

stones; and when we see them by faith united to Christ, as the chief Corner-stone, adorned with the graces of God's Spirit, polished, purified, and consecrated to God as living temples," parents and the religious community take pleasure in them. "Not when they are only polished with outward beauty and embellishments, but when possessed of that adorning which the Word of God most recommends." See Prov. xxxi. 13—31.

Happy then is that people, or nation that is in such a case—having a hopeful rising generation! No prosperity attended Israel when it was otherwise. In the times of Joshua, things were thus; "As for me and my house, we will serve the Lord;" then the nation prospered. Hence Balaam might well express himself in such language of admiration; Num. xxiv. 5—9. But when Joshua and that generation died, the next knew not the Lord, and did not prosper.

As young persons are destined to fill hereafter every department in society, and by their conduct to form its character, the prayer of the Psalmist is of the utmost importance. Let parents then live, act, and pray for the welfare of their children.

It is lamentable to see great defalcation in the discharge of this duty.——And sometimes the minds of the pious are full of painful apprehension as to the morality and happiness of the future generation. Multitudes of parents, and men in middle and advanced life, full of carnality, and haters of God and his truth, seem fully bent to warp the minds of the young from religious principles. They create for them the means of sinful pleasure; they labour to fill their minds with infidel notions; they set before them a seductive philosophy opposed to Christianity, and ·thus in many cases create a prejudice against it so strong as to be rarely conquered.——Should this state of things proceed, the effects upon society will be disastrous.—— Infidelity and Atheism, devotion to the mere idol of reason, at one period generally obtained in France, and what was the state of that unhappy country? Let the pages of history declare. That history is written in characters of blood. It is like Ezekiel's roll, full of, etc.

The prayer may be applied to the Church-as well as the State;—— It is delightful to witness young people giving themselves up to God in early life; it is the triumph of religious principle over the seductive arts of the age; it is the rescue of immortal souls from the kingdom of darkness and ruin. It is the increase and beauty, and blessedness of the Church. To see them become "olive plants" in his garden, and "corner-stones" in his building; the strength and ornament of religion, and also of society. A generation of praying, spiritual, active young people is a blessing to the Church and to the world.

3. David prayed for *temporal prosperity*. "That our garners may be full," etc. — "that our sheep may bring forth," etc. ver. 13, 14.

Jehovah is the Governor of the world. He gives the seasons; he commands and controls the elements, the showers to descend—the sun to shine. David's invocation was very important; for in the East they were liable to frequent famines and droughts which made it necessary in a season of great productiveness to fill their garners, and provide for the evil day. So Joseph during the seven years of prosperity laid up for a corresponding period of famine.

A season of great productiveness is a valuable and desirable blessing. What buoyancy it gives to the mind! It is the source of great domestic comfort. It gives an impetus to commerce. It increases the national wealth. It gives a higher tone to morals.

There have been scenes of an opposite character, when, by reason of inclement or unpropitious weather, or other causes, the crops have failed; and, strange to say, such seasons of distress are generally aggravated by the avarice of capitalists who speculate in the purchase of corn, etc., which they store up till they can obtain exorbitant prices for the same —— How different from this spirit was that manifested by the patriarch Joseph, or by David, who prayed "That our garners"! etc.

It is a sad spectacle to see a rich man increasing his wealth at the expense principally of the poor, whose miseries he has aggravated by speculative engagements.

4. David prays for *national peace, or to be secure from invasion and captivity*, v. 14.

War, in every shape, is an awful calamity. Nations in every age have been subject to the evils thereof, as prompted by a spirit of injustice and oppression on the part of the great and powerful——God's people were seldom known to engage in offensive wars, though often called to act in their own defence. When they sinned, God suffered their enemies to "break in," to invade and desolate the country. —— The Assyrians broke in upon them, and then there was a "going out" to captivity: afterwards the Chaldeans and Babylonians.

5. *He prays for contentment to pervade the minds of the people.* "That there be no complainings in the street."

It is a sign of prosperity when a spirit of oppression is crushed, and generally discountenanced; when justice and mercy pervade society, and cheerfulness and contentment are diffused throughout all classes. —— To effect this desirable object, let the wealthy become kind and friendly to the poor; and let not the poor envy the rich.

II. THE PSALMIST REFERS TO A GLORIOUS PRIVILEGE. "Happy is that people whose God is the Lord."

This constitutes the greatest happiness of all. Temporal blessings are valuable; but spiritual favours are still more so. To have an interest in God — to know that he is our portion, is the greatest privilege we can enjoy.

Without this all our other possessions and joy would be nothing. If the rising generation were ever so accomplished; though our garners were full of all manner of store; though there were no "breakings in," nor "goings out," and "no complaining in our streets;" yet we should not be really happy without the Lord as our God.

Sin has robbed us of this Divine Portion. "We are without God in the world."

Jesus Christ is the reconciling medium of access to God. By him we regain the Divine favour, 2 Cor. v. 19—21; Rom. v. 1, 2.

"Whose God is the Lord." How comprehensive is this declaration! It implies an interest in all the perfections of God—in his guardian and providential care—in all the arrangements of his grace, forgiving, justifying, sanctifying, enriching, comforting, and glorifying the soul. All that God has promised to give on earth, in every scene—and all that he has promised to give in heaven.

IMPROVEMENT.

1. We see what constitutes real personal happiness—an interest in God. 2. This too is the basis of true national greatness. The more a nation is impregnated with piety, the greater its stability and happiness. 3. Let the welfare of the rising generation be regarded as of paramount importance.

XIX.—THE BLESSEDNESS OF HONOURING GOD.

"Them that honour me, I will honour."—1 SAM. ii. 30.

THERE is an honour that comes from man. Men may be seated on thrones, and surrounded with splendour and with flattery, but this honour leads only to the grave. — There is an honour of so delicate a nature, that he who touches it must pay the forfeit of his life. "Cursed be their anger, for it was fierce; and their wrath, for it was cruel." — "Mine honour, be thou not united unto them."—But there is an honour that comes from God, and well merits our attention; "Them that honour me, I will honour." — Let us inquire,

I. How ARE WE TO HONOUR GOD?

1. *By an habitual acknowledgement of his being, providence, and moral government.*

Atheism is madness. Chance never made a watch nor a flower, and yet Atheists suppose that all things came from chance. But there is also a practical Atheism, which while it admits the being of a God, rejects his authority, and rises to assume his seat. "Is not this great Babylon which I have built?" said the Assyrian monarch; but he was soon humbled and taught another lesson; and then he says, "I thought it good to show the signs and wonders the high God hath wrought toward me. How great are his signs, and how mighty are his wonders!"

2. We are to honour God *by receiving and believing the testimony he hath given us in his word* concerning our own fallen condition, and the way of salvation through Jesus Christ.

S

3. We must honour God *by devoting to him all our talents, whether natural or acquired.*

When genius, like that of Milton — Learning like that of Leland — Science like that of Newton — Reasoning powers like those of Locke — Generosity like that of Reynolds — and Influence like that of George III.—when such talents are devoted to the honour of their Giver, then is God honoured.

4. We must honour God *by sacrificing every thing for his sake.*

Like the noble army of martyrs at the Reformation — like that worthy band of confessors, the nonconformists — we must not count our lives dear when he calls for such a sacrifice. And whenever our interests, our pleasures, or our lives are thus sacrificed, then is God honoured; and,

II. SUCH GOD WILL HONOUR — BUT HOW?

By adopting them into his family as the sons and daughters of the Almighty — by supporting them under all the trials of life, especially when called to suffer for his sake — by affording them peace, if not transport, in their death — by giving them an abundant entrance into his kingdom — by seating them with him on his throne, and making them for ever happy in his presence.—" Such honour have all his saints."

DR. RAFFLES.

XX.—THE GLORY OF THE CHURCH CONSUMMATED.

"That he might present it to himself a glorious church, not having spot or wrinkle, or any such thing; but—holy, and without blemish."—EPH. V. 27.

THE most ordinary duties of life are in the New Testament enforced by considerations the most affecting and overwhelming. Who would have thought of the affection due from a husband to a wife being enforced by that of Christ, " who loved his church, and gave himself for it!" Yet thus it is: and we are, doubtless, hereby taught, in all our civil relations and concerns, to act on Christian principles, or to carry religion into the whole of life. Many who profess Christianity never appear to think of making this use of it, but act as if the common relations of life were to be fulfilled from the common motives which influence mankind; such as a regard to decency and propriety, and the promotion of social happiness. In these words three things require particular notice; namely, the character of the church when the designs of mercy shall be fulfilled upon her — the way in which these designs are accomplished — and the end designed thereby.

I. With respect to the former she is called " a glorious church, not having spot or wrinkle, or any such thing; but holy, and without blemish." — We can be at no loss in perceiving the meaning of the term Church, in this connection. It denotes the whole assembly of the saved; "the church of the first-born, whose names are written in heaven;" the elect of God, of whom Christ was, in the eternal counsels of God, constituted the head and husband, antecedently to his giving himself for her.

The church is, in the language of anticipation, called "glorious"; not of herself, for irrespective of what is done for her, she is supposed to be altogether polluted. Her sanctification is the effect, and not the cause of Christ's love to her. What glory she has, or ever will have, is derived entirely from her Lord and Saviour. She is "comely through the comeliness which he has put upon her." The glory of the church consists in her being without spot or wrinkle, or any such thing; or, as it is literally expressed, in her being "holy, and without blemish." Purity is the beauty and glory of the church, and will be for ever. — In this description, the Apostle seems to oppose what the church will be hereafter, with what it is in the present world. She was not only originally polluted, but in her best estate upon earth is covered with spots, and her beauty marred as with *wrinkles*, the sign of declining age and vigour: but when she shall be presented to Christ, everything of this kind will be taken away. — The *spots* which at present detract from her beauty are, such as the prevalence of false doctrines, corrupt discipline, superstitious and formal worship, immoralities, conformities to the world, strifes, divisions, scandals, partialities, antipathies, jealousies, intrigues, etc. Alas, who can survey the Christian church without perceiving how her beauty is marred by the unholy influence of these things!

II. Let us notice the way in which the designs of mercy are accomplished. — "Christ loved the church, and gave himself for it, that he might sanctify and cleanse it."

What a glorious concatenation of blessings is here, the origin of which is divine love, and the end a presentation to himself in glory! Perhaps there is some allusion to the prophecy of Ezekiel, (chap. xvi. 1—10.) A humane character, passing on his way, sees a forlorn female infant, left to perish in the open field — he takes pity on it, and says unto it, "Live"; washes it, clothes it, takes it into his family; and when she arrives at years of maturity, spreads his skirt over her, and she becomes his bride. But all similitudes fail in representing the grace of our Lord Jesus Christ. The expense at which he communicated life to us, was by laying down his own. This is all represented as being the fruit or effect of love, and that to the church; consequently, of special or discriminating love.

III. The object or end of Christ's giving himself for the church was, that he might sanctify and cleanse it, with the washing of water, by the word.

The holiness of creatures is not that on account of which they are discriminated from others, but the effect of such discrimination: yet holiness occupies an important place in the scheme of redemption. We were not fit for the society of Christ as we were, and therefore must undergo a divine change, ere we could be presented to him. The word, or doctrine of the cross, when cordially believed, is a laver, which at the same time that it gives peace to the mind, imparts purity to the heart; and continues to do so, till we are meetened for the inheritance of the saints of light.

A. FULLER.

XXI. — TEMPTATION.

"And when he was at the place, he said unto them, Pray that ye enter not into temptation."—LUKE xxii. 40.

ALL mankind are liable to be tempted. Multitudes fall beneath the power of temptation, and are for ever ruined. Hence the counsel of Christ is very appropriate and weighty. It sounds like the counsels of a master to his servants, of a father to his children, of a Saviour to his disciples. It was necessary to Christ's immediate disciples, and it is no less necessary to us. Consider,

I. THIS COUNSEL IS MOST WEIGHTY AND IMPRESSIVE.

1. *Christ knew the force of temptations;* he had experienced their power for forty days in the desert. "He suffered, being tempted."

2. *Christ knew the dangers of the place.*

Judas knew it—Christ resorted thither for secret prayer, and Judas had been with him.——In this place their courage and firmness would be tested. Judas with a rabble band was approaching — the cup was about to be put into the Redeemer's hand, and he must drink it for the salvation of sinners. They apprehended no danger, but he foresaw it all. "Pray that," etc.——He knows the places where we are exposed to danger.

3. *He knew the efficacy of prayer.* He had tried it, found it successful, and recommended the same weapon to his disciples. "Pray," etc.

4. *He knew the weakness of his disciples.* He had foretold that they should all be offended because of him that night. They had heard him say to one of them, "Simon," etc. Luke xxii. 31; they had heard Peter say, "Though," etc. Matt. xxvi. 33.

The disciples did not think themselves weak. They might say, "We have had delightful intercourse in the upper chamber, where our Master offered a most delightful prayer; we are now going to the scene of his intercourse with God; we are only going from pleasure to pleasure; in that place we shall be secure from temptation; or if it comes, we shall be proof against it."——But Christ knew their weakness, and said, "Pray," etc.

II. THE COUNSEL IS APPLICABLE TO CHRISTIANS NOW. Christ knows the power of temptation still; the danger of the place: our personal weakness; the efficacy of prayer; and he says, "Pray that," etc.

1. The common evil to which Christians are exposed is *temptation*. Any thing influencing us to withdraw from God may be called temptation. No one is free, but the temptation is varied according to our particular characters, circumstances, situation, and the state of our hearts.

(1) *Temptation from the world.* 1 John ii. 16. The three great temptations of the world, Dr. Watts says, are, *honour, gold*, and *sensual joy*. Some may say, "These do not affect me; no honours adorn my brow; I have no riches, I am poor," etc. —— But you need not wear the wreath of honour to be under the power of this temptation; or to be rich to feel the tempting power of riches; we need not visit the theatre and the ball-room to feel their power to tempt; we live in a world where we witness these things, and Satan is ever ready to suggest them to our wicked hearts.

(2) *Temptations arising from our peculiar circumstances and situations in life.* Children at home have the temptations of their state and station. Apprentices who have just gone out, or the one just out of his time; the man who is just married, or who has just entered into business; the rich and the great, who move in an orbit above their fellow-creatures; and those in the lowest ranks, have all temptations peculiar to themselves. Agar's prayer is good, "Give me neither," etc. Prov. xxx. 7, 8. —— Temptations arising from office. —— Let each learn to know to what temptations he is peculiarly liable.

(3) *The devices of Satan*, 1 Pet. v. 8. His greatest device is to create in the mind doubt of his existence. —— We reason not on possibility or probability; his existence is certain — revealed — his works are manifest.

He tempted our first parents in Paradise, and brought sin into our world — tempted Cain to murder his brother; Job to curse God; David to number the people: it is he who stood by Joshua the high-priest when he stood before the Lord and resisted him; and whenever we stand before the Lord, he is not far from us. He tempted Christ, Peter, Judas, and filled the hearts of Ananias and his wife, when they lied to the Holy Ghost. How many thousands are under his power!

All the names given to Satan express his qualities to deceive and to destroy. He has many confederates — fallen spirits and wicked men. All false teachers, all ringleaders among the workers of iniquity, all who endeavour to draw men into sin, are agents for Satan. He works in a variety of ways, but he is the Old Serpent still, though he may assume the dove.

He tries to keep the ungodly secure. In order to this, he tempts them to indulge the flesh, to magnify the faults of others, and to diminish their own, and to put off the thoughts of religion. To the young he suggests that it is too soon to think about religion. that it is gloomy, and they may yet enjoy themselves in sin. To the old he suggests that it is too late, etc.

He tempts the godly to be exalted above measure. Have you never thought how fair you stand? how holy your garments — how great your talents — how much spirituality and unction there is in your prayers? etc., etc.

He tries to divide the disciples — sows the seed of discord among brethren. If God has made a hedge round his church, Satan is constantly looking for some gap at which he may step in.

His object is to cool down the warm-hearted professor. He looks with hate at young Christians full of holy love, and seems to say, "I will soon cool your zeal, and bring you into connection or company with some cool-hearted Christian who has lost his first-love; he will soon teach you by his example that there is no cause for all this zeal in religion," etc.

It is the constant aim of Satan to draw into sin — he has the advantage of *age and experience* — he has been practising these temptations six thousand years — he has *power*, but not Almighty power — he has *subtlety;* the Old Serpent selects his times and places with consummate skill — and applies his temptations to peculiar states of mind.

2. *The peculiar place of temptation.*

Young people on first leaving the parental roof are exposed to peculiar temptations. "O it would be delightful to have all our fetters broken, to go where we like," etc. Ah, take care — that very liberty may prove your ruin.

The period of making a Christian profession is a time of peculiar temptation. The Saviour's temptation was just after his baptism, and this is common with young professors. Though convinced of their sinfulness, they are but imperfectly acquainted with the deep depravity of their hearts — they are inexperienced, and Satan takes the advantage.

When forming connections for life — this is an important turning-point. At that place there is peculiar reason to pray that we enter not into temptation, etc.

Entering into business is a time of peculiar temptation — the attention may be too much engrossed — religious duties neglected, etc.

In seasons of prosperity do you say, "I have succeeded in my business, my health is good, my family comfortable, and every thing is agreeable?" Take care; these smooth paths have their peculiar temptations. —— When persons are in affliction, they frequently send to beg an interest in our prayers; but this is not often done by them in prosperity, though they are probably in circumstances of much greater danger.

Adversity has its temptations. Persons cannot submit with proper feelings to what the world calls "a reverse of fortune." There is a fine idea in Bunyan: —

Christian had to go down the hill of humiliation, and he was told that if he slipped he should meet with difficulty at the bottom, and so it was; he had a slip or two by the way, and the battle with Apollyon was the consequence, and Bunyan says, "It was the dreadfullest fight I ever saw."

The place of social company is often a place of peculiar temptation. The closet and the house of God have their temptations. We may not only lose the benefit, but bring darkness on our minds by not resisting the temptations of our Adversary.

III. THE IMPORTANT DUTY ENJOINED: "Pray." —— "Lead us not into temptation," etc.

1. *Prayer is ever a preventive to temptation.* God has prevented many temptations in answer to prayer; he has directed us into another course. In this world we shall never know the full extent of the preventing mercy of God, but it may be said of us, "The God of thy mercies shall prevent thee."

2. *Prayer*, if not a preventive, *is a preparative.* If we abound in prayer, we are prepared to meet the foe. ——

3. *It is the only weapon with which we can successfully fight.* Ps. xxviii. 6—8; cxvi. 1—5. Bunyan says that Christian found all the rest of his armour useless until he resorted to this. Pray then!

IMPROVEMENT.

1. The Christian has much cause for encouragement. He does not contend in his own strength. He has the arm of God, and he fights under an all-conquering Captain. God has promised to preserve his people. See especially 1 Cor. x. 13; Isa. lix. 19; Rom. xvi. 20.

2. Some one may say, "I know nothing of temptation!" It is very probable that you are under its power while you say this, and yet unconscious of its power; deceived by your subtle adversary. If you are not now tempted you soon may be. Watch and pray.

3. Pity the tempted. Do not triumph over them. You do not know the strength of the temptation under which he fell, nor the resistance he had previously made to it. You do not know how largely you may have to draw on the tenderness and affection of your friends.

4. We hope for a place where we can be tempted no more. Satan cannot enter those regions of purity.

XXII.— THE ATONEMENT.

"Whom God hath set forth to be a propitiation, through faith in his blood to declare his righteousness, for the remission of sins that are past, through the forbearance of God."— ROM. iii. 25.

THE doctrines of the Atonement and of the God-head of Christ lie very deep at the fountain of Christian theology. Let us consider —

I. THE NECESSITY OF IT.
II. THE ATONEMENT ITSELF IN THE BLOOD OF CHRIST.
III. THE FULNESS AND THE PERFECTION OF IT.

I. The *necessity* of the atonement. "Whom God has set forth to be a propitiation — in his blood."

The atonement is not the cause of the love of God, in the person of the Father, Son, and Holy Ghost, to sinners; for the atonement is represented in the Scriptures as the effect; and not the cause of the love of God: "God so loved the world, that he gave his Son." The necessity of it is glanced at in Rom. iii. 25, 26, "That God might declare his righteousness in the remission of sins," as well as his great love in the method of saving those he loved in their low estate.

Suffer me to introduce this simile, or metaphor. All men fell in Adam — as fallen, I suppose, they were viewed in the Divine plan. Methinks that a very extensive grave-yard makes its appearance, full of dead men's bones, like Golgotha, being walled round about with death and destruction, much stronger than the ancient walls of Babylon; having massy iron gates, bolted and locked up by the Divine threatening of the law; with this inscription on the doors — "in dying thou shalt surely die!" inscribed by an omnipotent hand. Divine love and mercy were often observed looking in through the iron gates, on the inhabitants of this dreary place, with delight and compassion, and at length exclaiming, "Let mercy be built for ever. Let love be commended by God and man. Oh! that we may be permitted to enter the graveyard, to visit the prisoners of death. We would very soon apply the balm of life; and we would plant the tree of life in the yard of death; and we would justify and sanctify an innumerable company of the poor inhabitants." But without a Mediator there was no admittance. "Mercy, break the locks and enter in!" — "No, I would not; for the locks are the locks of justice, and are under the sanction of the moral law."

Methinks I perceived, on an ever-memorable day, at the very dawning of it, Divine mercy and love resorting to the gates of the graveyard, accompanied by an august personage, in form like unto the Son of Mary; who proved to be the seed of the woman. Their very countenances appeared more cheerful, and their steps bolder. They cried out, "Divine justice, where art thou?" He sternly replied, "Here am I." The divine visitants said, "Permit us to enter thy territories, and save the inhabitants with an everlasting salvation!" "No," replied Justice; "without shedding of blood there is no remission." "Wilt thou accept a surety?" "Yes; provided he should be of sufficient worth and dignity to counterpoise the weight of sin." Then Jesus (who stood by) said, "Wilt thou accept my name instead of theirs? — behold I come." "Yes, yes;" replied Justice. "Behold, then, if thou dost acquiesce, put down my name in the roll of the book." Jesus asked, "What must be the sum I must pay for them?" Replied Justice, "Thou must make the law honourable, by living and dying in their room — die, the dead to save." "When and where dost thou fix the time of payment?" Justice replied, "At the expiration of 4000 years." "Where?" "It must be from Bethlehem Juda to the Place of Skulls. There thou must appear covered with shame, to taste their death." Jesus replied, "I accept the condition." His name was put in the bond; and the keys of the grave-yard were delivered to Mercy in the name of Jesus.

By virtue of this engagement did Mercy save the patriarchs and prophets of ancient times.

II. THE ATONEMENT ITSELF WITH ITS MEMORIALS.

"Divine Justice, seeing thou didst accept my suretyship, therefore, thou canst not be unwilling that I should set up memorials of this covenant. The price of redemption by my blood must be commemorated through the whole space of 4000 years, by bloody victims of an inferior kind. The blood of animals must perpetuate the remembrance of the blood of the Cross." "Yes," replied Justice, "I approve the plan."

Now let us view all the sacrifices slain on Jewish altars; though they made nothing perfect, yet they represented the blood of the covenant, the true atonement.

III. THE COMPLETENESS OF THE ATONEMENT IN THE BLOOD OF CHRIST.

Methinks I perceive during the long period from the sacrifice of Abel to that of Jesus, thousands of rams, lambs, bullocks, and bulls, brought to the altars for sacrifice. The fire from Heaven consumed them all to ashes. None of them ever appeared alive among their companions, as recovering from the burning altars—that was a sign of their insufficiency; therefore, the fire was stronger than they all.

Behold a new wonder comes to view. Yonder, very high, at the summit of Golgotha, a new kind of sacrifice makes its appearance; and it is drawn by Heaven, Hell, and Earth to the horns of the altar to be a burnt-offering for sin. The fire comes down from Heaven and begins to consume it, saying, I got millions of rams and bulls, but am not quenched. My flame is unquenched; I will burn to the lowest Hell if I get not satisfaction. Woe to the inhabitants of the grave-yard. It continued burning from the sixth to the ninth hour; but on the ninth, the fire touched the altar of divinity, and immediately expired; saying, "I am satisfied." Here we find a sacrifice stronger than fire. At the quenching thereof, a great shock like an earthquake penetrated through the kingdom of Satan and death; the sun darkened, the rocks rent, and many of the inhabitants of the graveyard got the doors of their prison opened, the walls broken in pieces, and a jubilee was proclaimed to them. The immaculate sacrifice himself, who was in himself both the priest, altar, and victim, after remaining three days and three nights in the ashes under the altar, revived, and came alive from the burning, and appeared alive among his companions in the midst of the throne. Death shall never have any dominion over him again.

This proves the sufficiency of his sacrifice. The way is free to mercy and love to save, to the end of time, the chosen vessels buried in the grave-yard.

CHRISTMAS EVANS.

XXIII. — THE BALM OF GILEAD AND THE PHYSICIAN THERE REPRESENTATIVE OF GOSPEL HEALING.

"Is there no balm in Gilead? Is there no physician there? Why then is not the health of the daughter of my people recovered?" — JER. viii. 22.

THE awful depravity of the human heart is frequently seen in the character and conduct of the Jews. Their hearts wandered from God, and they were frequently guilty of idolatry, ver. 19. The mind of the prophet was deeply affected on their account, ver. 21. He intimates that their case is nearly hopeless — and that though there is a balm in Gilead etc., yet they were likely to deprive themselves of the means of recovery.

I. THE LANGUAGE SUPPOSES THE EXISTENCE OF DISEASE.

The disease which affects the whole human race is sin. See Ps. xxxviii. 5; ciii. 3; Ezek. xxxiv. 4; Matt. ix. 12. This disease has various symptoms by which its nature is indicated.

1. On the part of the Jews it was *idolatry*. All mankind are idolators. Though they may not worship images, etc., yet they love the creature and various things more than the Creator.

2. *Atheism and Infidelity* are symptoms of this disease. The denial of the Divine existence—and of the verity of God's word. No wonder at this; for the human heart is as bad as Satan can make it. "The heart is deceitful," etc.

3. *Ignorance*. Even as in ordinary disease, the sight is affected; so in spiritual disease, the faculty of moral vision is impaired; Eph. iv. 18; 1 Cor. ii. 14.

Hence they see no excellency in God—in Christ—in religion. They know not themselves, and their spiritual dangers and necessities; Hosea iv. 6.

4. They have *a disrelish for all that is good*. In ordinary disease, the appetite fails. So here. The Sabbath—the house of God, etc., are disrelished. Mal. i. 13. Foolish things—earthly vanities are esteemed more than God.

5. *Apathy or lethargy of soul*. Eph. iv. 19. The severest judgments; the most bitter afflictions or bereavements, produce no effect.

6. *Sometimes delirium*. Raging fever and delirium, frequently attend bodily disease. Mark the anger, passion, the frantic madness of some sinners, as seen in their tempers, language, etc.

7. *Want of strength and energy — weakness*. —— "Without strength," Rom. v. 6, — "dead in trespasses and sins."

8. *If not cured, the disease will end in death*. "The wages of sin is death." "Sin, when it is finished, bringeth forth death."

Might mention some peculiar properties of this disease.
It is inherent in our constitution — it is infectious — it is pol-

luting—loathsome—prostrates the strength—universal—incurable by human means.

II. THE TEXT IMPLIES A REMEDY. There is "balm in Gilead," etc.

Gilead, or Mount Gilead, is a ridge or summit lying east from the Jordan. The country was noted for a tree producing a gum possessing valuable medicinal properties, called "the balm of Gilead." Strabo speaks of a field near Jericho, which was full of these balsam trees. The sap is like viscid and tenacious milk, and coagulates rapidly. It was valuable for inflammations, and, in the time of Alexander, was estimated at twice its weight in silver. Gen. xxvii. 25.

As a Physician, or Healer, he was typified by the brazen serpent, John iii. 14. By the Sun of Righteousness, Mal. iv. 2. By the tree of life, Rev. xxii. 2.

1. *Christ is the Divinely appointed Physician.* When on earth he went about healing the bodies and souls of men. He was sent by the Father for this purpose. John v. 36, 37; Isa. lxi. 1—3.

2. He possesses *infinite knowledge and skill.* He understands the disease of sin in all its symptoms and tendencies.

3. He possesses *infinite compassion.* Represented by the good Samaritan. He feels for, and weeps over the diseased.

4. He is *patient and diligent in his attention to the diseased.* "He will not break the bruised reed."

III. THE REMEDY WHICH HE EMPLOYS.

1. The Remedy, or balm, is his own "precious blood." He died to shed it. Isa. liii. 5; Rom. vi. 6—8.

2. The *Recipe for man's disease is contained in his word.* There it is graciously and sweetly written down. "The blood of Jesus Christ cleanseth from all sin."

3. The *Remedy is perfectly free.* Isa. lv. 1, 2.

4. It is given *to all believing applicants.* Feeling themselves guilty, sinners come to Christ, receive the recipe, and throwing themselves into the arms of the gracious Physician, receive and apply the remedy.

5. The Remedy is *accompanied by the influence of the Spirit.* This awakens the sinner to the danger of his disease, and urges him to speedy application to Christ.

6. The Remedy is *universally adapted.* It will meet the case of any awakened sinner, of every nation, etc.

7. It is *always available, and infallible in its efficacy.* "His word is nigh thee." "He ever liveth," etc.

IV. THE CAUSE OF THE REJECTION OF THE REMEDY. "Why," etc.

1. *Many are ignorant of their disease.* They imagine they are well and require no healing.

2. *Many apprehend no danger and are full of apathy.*

3. *Many try to heal themselves* by their self-righteousness, by formal services, etc., and neglect the great Physician.

4. Many neglect the disease, being fascinated by sin, worldly pleasure, business, etc.,—till it becomes too late. "The harvest is past," etc.

IMPROVEMENT.

1. It is dangerous to delay. 2. To be healed is to be happy. Great the difference between disease and health, pain and pleasure, death and life. 3. Let all who are healed praise Jesus the Physician.

XXIV.—LIVING EPISTLES.

"Ye are our Epistles written in our hearts, known and read of all men."—2 COR. iii. 2.

THIS was the language of the great Apostle Paul (who in his own eyes was less than the least of all saints) in an address to the Christian church, the members of which had been some of the most abandoned characters; and to whatever place the apostle went, where letters of commendation were required of the visiting ministers, he pointed to those conspicuous converts, who were living epistles, and so eminent as to be "known and read of all men." The change in them was so great, as to render it evident to every one: the drunkards were become sober; the dishonest, just; the miser, liberal; the prodigal, frugal; the libertine, chaste; and the proud, humble. To these the apostle appealed, for himself and fellow-labourers, as a letter of commendation, as a living epistle at Corinth, to the world around.

Now to pursue the apostle's allegory, we may remark, that in an epistle, there must be paper or parchment, a pen, ink, a writer, and somewhat written.

1. The *paper*, or parchment, we may consider, in these Divine epistles, as the human heart; which some people say is as clean as a white sheet of paper; but if it be so on one side, it is as black as sin can make it on the other. It may appear clean like a whited sepulchre without, but it is full of all uncleanness and defilement within.

2. The ministers of the gospel may be well compared to a *pen* used in writing these living epistles, and many of them are willing to acknowledge themselves very bad pens, scarcely fit to write with, or any way to be employed in so great a work.

It seems, they have been trying for many years to make good pens at the Universities; but after all the ingenuity and pains taken, the pens which are made there are good for nothing, till God has *nibbed* them. When they are made, it is well known, the best pens want mending. I find that the poor old one * that has been in use now for a long while, and is yet employed in scribbling, needs to be mended two or three times in a sermon.

---

* Alluding to the Preacher being much in years.

3. The influences of Divine grace I consider as the *ink* used in writing these Divine epistles on the heart; and this flows freely from the pen when it has a good supply from the fountain-head, which we constantly stand in need of; but sometimes you perceive the pen is exhausted, and almost dry.

Whenever any of you find it so, and are ready to say of the preacher, "O what a poor creature this is, I could preach as well myself;" that may be true: but instead of these complaints, lift up your hearts in prayer, and say, "Lord, give him a little more *ink*."

4. But if a pen is made well, and fit for use, it cannot move of itself; there must be an agent to put it into motion; now the *writer* of these glorious and living epistles is the Lord Jesus Christ.

Some people are very curious in fine writing; but there is something in the penmanship of these epistles, which exceeds all that was ever written in the world; for, as the Lord Jesus spake, so he writes; as never man spoke or wrote. One superior excellency in these epistles is, that they are all so plain and intelligible, as to be "known and read of all men," and the strokes will never be obliterated.

Lastly, In all epistles there must be somewhat written. Many things might be said here, but I shall include the Divine inscription of these epistles in repentance, faith, and holiness. Repentance is written with a broad-nibbed pen, in the old *black letters* of the law, at the foot of Mount Sinai. Faith is written with a crow-quill pen, in fine and genteel strokes, at the foot of Mount Calvary. Holiness is gradually and progressively written, and when this character is completely inscribed, the epistle is finished and sent to glory.

J. BERRIDGE.

XXV.—THE HEAVENLY COMPANY.

"And they shall come from the east, and from the west, and from the north, and from the south, and shall sit down in the kingdom of God."— LUKE xiii. 29.

THE Christian dispensation is full of mercy.——Its design is our salvation.——It shall have a glorious consummation; as will be manifest on the day of judgment, and throughout an eternity of repose, blissful association, inconceivable vision, and unutterable delight. "They shall come from the east," etc. —— The rejectors of the gospel now are acting a foolish part — which they will regret hereafter — and the consequences of which they will be anxious to avert. But it will be in vain. [See preceding verses.]

I. THE SCENE OF THE GATHERING. "The kingdom of God."

In the phrase, *kingdom of God*, the New Testament generally denotes either the spiritual reign of Christ over the hearts of individuals, or over his church collectively; John xvii. 36. It also sometimes denotes the state of glory beyond the grave. Matt. iii. 2; 2 Pet. i. 11.

It is *the kingdom prepared*, Matt. xxv. 34. There God has resided for ever with all his glorious attendants; but his infinite love to his people has caused him to assign and prepare this kingdom for their eternal residence. "Fear not, little flock," etc. And so it comes to pass, that a sinful guilty worm is by God's rich grace to be raised to dwell with immaculate Deity in his kingdom of glory. He has prepared it for them — and he prepares them for it.

It is a kingdom of *infinite grandeur* — of vast extent, so capacious as to contain, and afford ample room for all God's family — a kingdom of purity, order, and love — a kingdom of light, of infinite intelligence, and bliss — a kingdom of love — of durable life — a state of immortal existence. Called "an inheritance which is incorruptible, undefiled, and that fadeth not away."

II. THIS KINGDOM SHALL BE VASTLY POPULATED. "They shall come from the east," etc. The four quarters of the globe shall contribute to swell the population of heaven. It has long been populated by myriads of angels, bright and happy spirits——and has long been the blessed receptacle of departed spirits made fit for it by Divine grace.

"They shall come." They are afar off now. As far as heaven is from hell. As far as sin can make them. They are aliens — outcasts — enemies by wicked works — children of wrath. Eph. ii. 1, etc.

"They shall come." Jesus the Reconciler shall be revealed to them. The Spirit shall send a light across their path, and show them its danger. The Spirit shall direct them to the cross, and there they shall lose their guilt, and filthy stains. The spirit shall incline their hearts to the church. "They shall come" and enter it. —— They shall die, and enter heaven.

This is certain. "They *shall* come." The gospel shall be successful. Are they carried away by the world? They *shall* relinquish the world and come. Are they lovers of pleasure? God shall attract them by heavenly pleasures, and they *shall* come to enjoy them. Are they infidels, haters of Christianity? The enmity of their hearts *shall* be slain, and they *shall* come. —— All this is according to promise, to be fulfilled by Divine immutability.

God's wills and shalls are infinitely valuable and precious. If a man says "shall" or "will," it is often worthless. "I will," says man, and he never performs; "I shall," says he, and he breaks his promise. Does God act thus? He says, "They shall come." Satan says, "They shall not come." God says, "They shall." Sinners often say, "We will not come." But God says, "They shall." I will make them in love with that which they now hate, so that they shall not rest without it.

The population of heaven shall be *numerous*. "They shall come from the east," etc. It is also said in Matt. viii. 11, "Many shall come from the east and west, and shall sit down with Abraham, Isaac, and Jacob, in the kingdom of heaven."

Men of contracted views, bigots, extreme sectarians, speak and act as if the inhabitants of heaven would be few. But Christ shall "bring many sons to glory," even "a great number which no man can number,"

Heb. ii. 10; Rev. vii. 9. Satan's kingdom shall not contain more inhabitants than the kingdom of Christ. Heaven is not for the Jews alone, nor for the Gentiles alone. It will not be monopolized by one sect. It is not the heaven of Episcopalians, or the heaven of Presbyterians, or the heaven of Independents, etc., *but the heaven of Christians.*

And these Christians "shall come from the east, and from the west," etc. Palestine shall send her "Israelites indeed;" Ethiopia shall "stretch forth her hands to God," and her swarthy sons and daughters "shall sit down," etc. Multitudes from the land of China, from the vast countries of Asia, from the continent of Europe, from Australia, from the Northern parts of America, and the wilds of Russia, Siberia, and the Polar seas, from the islands of the ocean, and every country under the sun, and they "shall sit down," etc.

III. The text conveys the idea of AGREEABLE ASSOCIATION.

National distinctions will not be known. Earthly circumstances, riches and poverty, will not exist there as the barriers to association. "The rich and the poor meet together" with heavenly familiarity and harmony, because they are redeemed by the same precious blood, and equally participate in the munificence of heaven. Monarchs and peasants, princes and beggars, masters and servants, the learned and ignorant—all, all "sit down" in sweet communion there.——And that which renders their intercourse sweeter still, is,

IV. MUTUAL RECOGNITION. "They shall sit down with Abraham," etc. Matt. viii. 11. These patriarchs will be known.—— The prophets will be known.—— Apostles and martyrs will be known. Men eminent for piety, benevolence, zeal, love, usefulness, will be known. All will know one another. How sweet is this thought to those who have been bereaved! There I shall meet and know a dear mother, etc.—a father—brothers and sisters —dear children, etc.

V. REPOSE AND HIGH ENJOYMENT. "They shall sit down."

This is a peculiar phrase as applied to beatific bliss. It refers to a feast, especially to an Eastern feast, where the guests sat, or rather reclined— the position was always *recumbent*, which, in reference to heaven, is more expressive than our English "sitting."

1. They shall sit down to *rest*. They shall recline upon the pillow of heavenly peace,

> And not a wave of trouble roll
> Across their peaceful breast.

How seldom has the poor Christian sat down or rested in this world! What sorrows have encompassed him! What storms have assailed his bark! Storms of toil, affliction, cares, anxieties, persecution, mental agony, and death. O there is a blessed land where all is calm and peaceful. Believer, soon will thy Redeemer say to these dreadful tempests, "Peace, be still;" and every cloud will vanish, and every raging storm be still; and then, poor mariner, thou shalt for ever rest on the sweet and halcyon bosom of heaven.

How sweet to the working-man is the idea of rest! He often wipes the hot sweat from his brow; and if a Christian, he longs for the land where he shall toil no more. Often he comes home from his labour very weary, and he sinks into his chair, or flings himself upon his couch, perhaps too tired to sleep, and he says, "O for a blessed land, where I can sit down and for once let these weary limbs be still!"

Ah! ye afflicted ones, ye shall soon sit down, and be free from trouble. Lift up your eyes to heaven, ye sorrowing saints, and gaze upon your brethren, who now sit down, and rest

"Calm on the bosom of their God!"

"Who are these who are arrayed in white?" See Rev. vii. 13, etc.

2. They shall sit down in *triumph*. Having overcome every foe, and received the victor's immortal wreath, how sweet will it be to sit down and know and feel that every enemy is vanquished. The successful conqueror, through Christ, shall sit down on the Redeemer's throne, Rev. iii. 21. What exaltation for a vile worm!

3. *They shall sit down to converse.* What sweetness there is in this grand thought!——I shall converse with Jehovah-Jesus—angels will speak to me, and to angels I shall respond—glorified spirits will ask me how I feel in the commencement of my bliss, and my tongue to them shall utter abundantly the memory of God's great goodness.——They will converse with the utmost familiarity — in celestial language of inconceivable eloquence and beauty—without the least misunderstanding—with mutual benefit.——They will sit down to converse about the most momentous things—things connected with their pilgrimage here— connected with their Father's precious love, and heaven, and eternity.

4. They shall "sit down" *to listen*. To the revealings of God—to the explication of all mysteries—to the voice of the Triune God, speaking to them, and to all, with paternal love and familiarity, —— "Sit down" to listen to the rapturous strains of heaven's music, produced by the voices and harps of the redeemed myriads, in which they too shall unite. —— "Sit down" to listen to Jehovah's ever-occurring plans of new creations, new operations, and new sources of pleasure, to be developed in his boundless universe.

5. They shall sit down *to contemplate*. With minds unclogged — but expanded, clear, and congenial to every subject of contemplation.

IMPROVEMENT.

1. We must first sit down in the kingdom of heaven, or church of God below, previous to our sitting "down with Abraham," etc.

2. Praise God that Christ can and will prepare you to sit down.

3. Instead of sitting down in the kingdom of heaven, the wicked shall be cast into outer darkness.

XXVI.—THE SPIRIT OF ADOPTION.

"And because ye are sons, God has sent forth the Spirit of his Son into your hearts, crying, Abba, Father."—GAL. iv. 6.

GREAT are the privileges of believers. They have been redeemed by the blood of Christ, regenerated by his Spirit, and adopted into his family. The value of such a state will appear by contrast. This is given in ver. 1.——Adoption is not a mere change, or transition; it is exaltation; it is high enjoyment, and blessed hope, v. 6, 7.

I. THE DIGNIFIED CHARACTER OF BELIEVERS. "Ye are sons."

Observe, Adoption is an act by which one is received into a man's family as his own child, and becomes entitled to the peculiar privileges of that connection, as fully and completely as a child by birth, Ex. ii. 10; Esth. ii. 7. This was also done by the Greeks and Romans, who, when childless, adopted some other child, and gave it the family name, and a title to the family inheritance.——

Spiritual adoption is that act of grace by which Jehovah takes the children of Satan out of the world, and makes them his sons and daughters — members of his family.

1. *They are not the sons of God by nature.* Sin has separated them from God, and made them the children of the Wicked One. "Ye are of your Father the Devil." "Ye are his sons to whom ye yield yourselves to obey." John viii. 44; Rom. vi. 16.

2. *They become the adopted sons of God by faith in Jesus Christ.* John i. 12; Gal. iii. 26. They are convinced they are outcasts — having no interest in God — children of wrath. They feel they are guilty transgressors.

But the Spirit has led them to trust in Christ for mercy. They are forgiven all their trespasses; completely justified; and regenerated by the Spirit. Thus they, by adoption, show a change in their state and their nature.

Thus they are members of the family of God. Not slaves; but sons.

They are also *conscious of their adoption*. "We know that we have passed from death," etc. 1 John i. 3; iii. 14, 19.

3. They *participate in all the privileges of adoption.* God is their Father; "I will be a father unto you," etc. Ps. ciii. 13. His love, tenderness, and care. How feeble those of earthly parents!——

He grants supplies for all temporal and spiritual need; guidance and protection, and access to him at all times and in all places.——Employment in his service, so honourable and useful.

4. They become *heirs to their Father's inheritance in heaven.* Rom. viii. 16; 1 Pet. i. 3.

THE SPIRIT OF ADOPTION.

II. THE SPECIAL PRIVILEGE CONNECTED WITH ADOPTION. "God hath sent forth the Spirit of his Son into your hearts."

The Spirit of God and the Spirit of Christ are the same, the third Person in the Trinity. Rom. viii. 9.

1. A child of God becomes *the temple of the Holy Spirit*. 1 Cor. vi. 19.

2. The Spirit is sent into the heart *as the Comforter.* Called so by Christ. John xvii. 7.

3. This Spirit is a *Spirit of freedom and confidence.* He makes free from the law of sin and death, Rom. viii. 2,—takes away the sense of bondage and dread, and gives holy affection and confidence in God.

4. The Spirit is *the Spirit of holiness* in the heart. Called the *Holy* Spirit. By that the believer is inclined to holiness. "The fruit of the Spirit is all goodness," Eph. v. 9. "I will sprinkle," Ezek. xxxvi. 25, 26, etc.

III. THE SPECIAL OFFICE OF THE HOLY SPIRIT. "Crying Abba, Father."

1. *A special assurance created by the Spirit that God is their Father.* They look up to him as their Father; "Our Father, who art in heaven."

2. *The Spirit teaches them the need of prayer*, and how to pray. Rom. viii. 26. Called the "Spirit of grace and supplications." Zech. xii. 10.

3. It implies that *they are often in circumstances which cause them to cry*, etc. "Many are the afflictions of the righteous."

4. It implies *the certainty of Success.* Rom. viii. 27. "The effectual fervent prayer of the righteous availeth much." "If ye then be evil," etc. Matt. vii. 11.

IMPROVEMENT.

1. Happy are they who possess the Holy Spirit as the infallible witness of their Divine Sonship! 2. Let us seek the good of God's family. Being all "sons," let us love as brethren, and labour and pray for the prosperity of the family. 3. How miserable and degraded the servants of Satan! In bondage, and full of fear, and exposed to everlasting death.

XXVII.—OBJECT OF A CHRISTIAN'S LOVE.

"Saw ye him whom my soul loveth?"—SONG. iii. 3.

I. THE *object of a Christian's love may easily be identified.*
No person is named in the text who should be the object of a Christian's love but Christ: we wear his name, profess his religion, believe his Bible.

II. *Love to Christ should be personally known to ourselves.*
Do we love him more than the world, or the creature?

III. *The object of a Christian's love should be openly and publicly avowed.*
He who is ashamed of his master's livery is unworthy of him.

IV. *Love to Jesus Christ should be strong and vigorous.*
"My soul loveth him." "Thou shalt love the Lord thy God with all thy heart," etc.

V. *Love to Christ is not always enjoyed.*
There may be some cause of the Saviour's withdrawing; wandering in sinful paths, sinful company, etc.

VI. *Absence from the object will produce in his soul greater activity and zeal.* The Christian will
Review his life.——Increase his diligence.——Attend the means of grace.—— Search the Scriptures.—— Examine himself.—— Pray to be enlightened— and forgiven.

VII. *The object of a Christian's love shall be ultimately enjoyed.*
Christ will not withdraw for ever.

VIII. *The return of Christ will produce beneficial effects to the soul.*
"I held him and would not let him go."
The soul will lay hold on his merits. Will prize him now more than all besides. "Whom have I in heaven but thee?" etc.

XXVIII.—THE EFFECT OF BEHOLDING THE GLORY OF THE LORD.

[TRANSLATED FROM THE FRENCH.]

"But we all, with open face, beholding as in a glass, the glory of the Lord, are changed into the same image, from glory to glory, even as by the Spirit of the Lord."—2 COR. iii. 18.

THE day of Christ's ascension was one of the most glorious that the sun ever produced. Then he ascended to the highest heavens, after having vanquished the devil, expiated sin, triumphed over death, reconciled man with God, and received a name above every name, etc.

The day of Pentecost was no less glorious: then the Son of God sent the Comforter to his afflicted disciples, and baptized them with celestial fire——they were transformed into his image by the Spirit, and thereby rendered capable of announcing through the universe, that which they had "seen with their eyes, and heard with their ears, and handled with their hands of the word of life."

We also have contemplated the glory of the Lord, and have received his Spirit, transforming us into his image, so that we may say with Paul and the other apostles and the first Christians, "We all as with open face," etc. etc.

The words contain a magnificent description of the glory of Jesus Christ, etc.—and teach us in what true religion consists—to know the glory of the Lord, and to be transformed into his image.

Let us then inquire

I. WHAT IS THAT "GLORY OF THE LORD" OF WHICH THE APOSTLE SPEAKS?

1. *The being and perfections of God.*

2. *The manifestation of these perfections in the economy of grace.*

3. *The Divinity of Jesus Christ.*

4. *All the graces he displayed while on earth;* deep humility, infinite condescension, incomparable love, perfect obedience.

5. *All that the Father did in favour of his Son*—at his baptism—in his life, transfiguration, death, resurrection, and ascension.

6. *All that Christ did to prove his character as the Messiah.* Miracles, etc.

7. *All the celestial doctrines of his kingdom*—redemption, calling, justification, sanctification, glorification.

II. HOW WE CONTEMPLATE AS IN A GLASS (OR MIRROR) THE GLORY OF THE LORD.

1. *As He has manifested it in his glorious perfections in creation and providence.*

Nature made known a Creator, but not a Redeemer; the law discovers to us God, holy and inflexibly just; but the gospel reveals all the excellencies which constitute the glory of God, mercy and justice united—"a just God and a Saviour."

2. *As the gospel reveals Christ in his original dignity, and the infinite value of his sufferings.*

Believers under the Old Testament saw something of the glory of Christ, but it was too dazzling for them—they could not look steadfastly.

There was a vail on all things under the law: God was represented by sensible objects—a cloud—a bush, etc.; the gospel discovers Him clearly.

It was formerly a mark of slavery to cover the head with a veil — the head uncovered was a sign of liberty. Moses covered his face to indicate that the legal dispensation tended to bondage. Under the gospel the veil is removed, and we see with unveiled face as those who are called to a holy liberty.

3. *This glory is beheld in the gospel as in a mirror.*

(1) To denote the *clearness of his revelation.*

(2) The *imperfection of that revelation compared with that which we shall have in heaven.*

Among the ancients, the mirror was the emblem of meditation.

III. WHAT THIS CONTEMPLATION PRODUCES IN BELIEVERS. They are transformed, etc.

A Greek author describing the peculiarities of a temple erected to the honour of a certain idol, remarks, that those who wished to enter it must first look at themselves in a glass placed at the entrance, and that this mirror was so constructed, that at first it presented to the beholder his natural visage, but by degrees his countenance was transformed or changed into the form of the idol which was worshipped. The gospel is that mirror which they who wish to enter heaven must behold.

1. *They see themselves and their imperfections, and they see God, in whom there is nothing but perfection.*

2. *The mind is enlightened, the affections directed to proper objects, the will sanctified, and the members of the body rendered instruments of righteousness unto true holiness.*

3. *This transformation is gradual and permanent.* There is an increase of glory. "They go from strength to strength," "from faith to faith." They increase in knowledge and holiness. Like plants in the garden; like the sun which gradually advances to the meridian, or the waters of the sanctuary, first ankle-deep, and finally a river to swim in.

4. *The degree of glory through which the believer passes;* from the glory of knowledge to the glory of holiness; from the glory of the church militant to the glory of the church triumphant.

IV. HOW THIS TRANSFORMATION IS EFFECTED? By the Spirit of the Lord.

1. *He operated upon the apostles and qualified them for their great work.* Acts ii.

2. *He convinces us of the truth of the gospel.*

3. *Renders us obedient to its communications.*

4. *Renovates and sanctifies our nature.*

5. *Places before us the perfect model of Christ, and moulds us into his image.*

IMPROVEMENT.

1. Let us be thankful that we live under that dispensation in which we may behold the glory of the Lord.

2. That we are not of that communion where a veil is thrown over the gospel.

3. That we have heard and felt the power of that gospel, and are sealed by the Spirit unto the day of redemption.

4. Let the wicked remember that without the image of Christ they cannot see God hereafter.

XXIX. — CHRIST KNOCKING AT THE HEART.

"Behold, I stand at the door, and knock: if any man hear my voice, and open the door, I will come in to him, and will sup with him, and he with me." — Rev. iii. 20.

THAT it is by grace we are saved through faith, without any merits of our own, is evident from the whole tenor of the word of God. Our salvation does not imply a change in our theological sentiments, but a renovation of our hearts; yet we must not conclude that man is not to co-operate. Matthew Henry says very justly, "Man can do nothing without God, and God will do nothing without man." Man's work is to accept of Christ as he is presented to us in the Gospel; and on this acceptance his salvation now depends. Such is precisely the import of the text. We have to consider,

I. THE GOSPEL CALL.

The scene introduced is Christ knocking at the door of our hearts for an entrance. The human heart is considered as a house. It was intended for God. It is not his present residence. It is now under the power of an usurper, the dominion of Satan. This constitutes man's sin and folly. "Sin brought death into the world, and all our woe." Though Christ has been driven out of the house, he does not relinquish his claim to it. Observe, he does not force himself into the heart: hence we learn, man is a *free* agent; he cannot be saved without his consent. The door of the heart is the faculty of the will; and it is not sufficient that our judgment approves, and our conscience warns, the will must consent before we can be saved. A writer says, "The will is the *fort-royal* of the human soul, and it stands out the longest." This call is two-fold:

1. *External* — by the written word, ministry, etc.

2. *Internal* — the influence of the Spirit upon the heart. Remember that all the calls of God are intended to be *effectual*, saving calls.

II. THE GOSPEL DUTY. "If any man hear my voice, and open the door."

To knock is the Saviour's part: to open is ours. Christ will perform his work. Let us perform our duty. The will has suffered through the fall, and consequently has no disposition for spiritual things. If Christ never knocked, the will would never open. It is in consequence of the merits of Christ that light is come into the world. The will is not to be coerced: it may yield to the power of suasive reasons. The salvation of any human being does not *now* depend upon the will of God, but on man's will under the grace of God. Christ says, "Ye will not come unto me." Is a man, then, to be saved when he will? This sentiment ought to be guarded: The call is to you *now:* we have nothing to do with to-morrow: delay another hour, and that postponement may seal your everlasting doom. To open the door is to submit to the gospel method of salvation; to receive Christ as your wisdom, etc. But this requires *fixed attention.* Hence listening to the voice of Christ is necessary. The door is kept *shut* by *pride* and *highmindedness;* but when the voice of Christ is heard, the soul finds that by the deeds of the law it cannot be saved. The door is kept shut by *worldly-mindedness;* but when the voice of Christ is *heard,* these things are found to be trifles compared to eternity. It is a duty, and,

1. The *dignity* of Christ lays us under obligations to attend unto his call. Is he not the brightness of the Father's glory, and the express image of his person?

2. The claims of *equity.* He asks for what he made; and will a man rob God?

3. The claims of *gratitude*—and regard to our present and everlasting happiness.

4. *Punished for neglect.*

III. THE GOSPEL PROMISE. The blessings of the Gospel are introduced to us under various similitudes: here called a supper.

1. He that admits Christ into his heart shall feast on his *pardoning love.* His sins shall be remembered no more. This, no common part of the gospel feast.

2. Christ will bring him *peace* and *holiness.*

3. You shall have fellowship with the saints at the table of the Lord, in the house of God, in social prayer, etc.

4. If *faithful,* you shall feast with Christ in a *better world.* Christ will come again. By admitting Christ, heaven is open unto you.

CONCLUSION.

1. The natural condition of sinners—Christless. 2. Encouragement to come to Christ. 3. If not saved, all the responsibility falls on yourself, and you will go down to perdition, crying, "I have ruined myself! I have ruined myself!"

XXX.—HONEST CONVERSATION.

"Having your conversation honest among the Gentiles; that whereas they speak against you as evil-doers, they may by your good works, which they behold, glorify God in the day of visitation."—1 PET. ii. 12.

IT is necessary to have our conversation honest for the safety of the soul, and that we may glorify God. Let us consider,

I. THE INJURIOUS TREATMENT CHRISTIANS RECEIVE FROM THE WORLD. They are represented as "evil-doers." Immediately after the fall, it was said, "I will put enmity," etc. Their defamation developes itself. 1. By direct falsehood. 2. By perverting the graces of the Christian. 3. By aggravating the real action. 4. In confounding religion with its professors.

II. THE MANNER IN WHICH CHRISTIANS OUGHT TO BEHAVE UNDER THIS TREATMENT. Having the conversation, the whole deportment, honest. There is comprehended in this, 1. Purity. 2. Integrity. 3. Benevolence. This deportment can only be maintained by, 1. Regeneration. 2. Walking circumspectly. 3. By exercising yourself much in prayer.

III. THE RESULTS THAT WILL ARISE FROM THIS DEPORTMENT. 1. God will be glorified; his character manifested. 2. Gentiles will be saved.

REV. THEOPHILUS LESSEY.

XXXI.—GROWTH IN GRACE.

"Growth in grace."—2 PET. iii. 16.

BY grace is sometimes to be understood its real meaning, "favour," as in the Apostolic benediction : "The grace of our Lord." Sometimes the influence of the Spirit: "My grace is sufficient;" and sometimes the effects of the influence of the Spirit, arising from the favour of God on the heart, comprehended in one word—"experience." The first principle of grace is weak, hence compared to "a bruised reed," etc. There are babes, young men, and aged.

I. GRACE IS CAPABLE OF GROWTH. This, the proposition of the text. This, a matter of consolation.

1. To the *weak*, who are not to suppose they have no grace because they have not *all* grace,—God will not break the bruised reed.

2. To the *strong*. No degree of grace attainable which is not capable of growth; and this progression or growth extends not only to this world, but through eternity. We have an infinite

standard: Be ye perfect, as God is perfect. Man, changed from glory to glory. Ever rising higher, and sinking deeper.

II. THE EVIDENCES OF GROWTH IN GRACE. Necessary to inquire not only whether we are in the faith, but whether we grow in grace, because we are no longer in a safe state than when we are growing.

1. *Not a mere increase of knowledge.*

Though persons who increase in grace must derive it from increased knowledge of God's word, yet there may be the one without the other, — evidenced in the case of the Devil, the wisest being in the universe, possessing in himself, perhaps, the united knowledge of all saints; yet having not a single good principle; — and backsliders, who for a considerable time retain a sense of what they formerly enjoyed.

2. *Not mere attachment to ordinances.*

This is not an infallible criterion. It may be in the case of those who once hated all such means. But in these days there may be much of this without any sign of grace. Persons may come to the house of God from motives far from proper, as to a theatre, to hear,—the sermon as the performance, and the preacher as the actor.

3. *Nor mere increase of zeal.*

There will be zeal where there is grace, but there may be zeal without grace — for mere selfish opinions and purposes.

4. *Nor mere increase of painful sensations.*

This is not always a sign of increasing grace. There may be such displacency at ourselves arising from increased worldliness. But growth in grace is evidenced by

(1) Increase of *desire after spiritual attainments.* "As the hart panteth"—"followeth hard after God."

(2) Increase of *faith;*— in its twofold operations — of *affiance* in the merits and death of Christ — consciousness of need and helplessness — and of *realization* of the future: Looking at the things unseen.

(3) Increase of *moral power.* We have by nature no moral power. Without Christ we can do nothing. Power is the first effect of a gracious principle — necessary to be increased — as we grow in grace we have power over our besetting sins.

(4) Increase of *spirituality.* We have moral tastes; these are by nature sometimes earthly, sometimes sensual, sometimes devilish: when our natures are renewed, our tastes are changed; we have a relish for things we disliked before. So when we grow in grace, we have an increasing delight in God, in every thing that has God in it, however painful to our feelings, requiring however much mortification and self-denial.

(5) Increase of *delight in duty.* There is an essential connection between that which is inward and that which is outward. To separate the one from the other is like separating the root from the branch. When we love we do the most difficult duties.

III. THE MOST EFFICACIOUS METHOD OF MAINTAINING A GROWTH IN GRACE. The same as those by which grace is attained.

1. A spirit of *prayer*. Not merely an abstraction of mind whilst engaged in private or public prayer, though this is very much to be desired, we should beware lest our froward tongues outrun our languid hearts, but ever maintaining a spirit, or disposition of prayer.

2. *Watchfulness* against our danger, and for our helps. It embraces the bane and antidote, the disease and remedy.

3. *Diligence*. Not merely in reading, hearing, praying, meditating, which are very essential, but a diligent cultivation of gracious principles.

IV. THE MOTIVES FOR GROWING IN GRACE.

1. Therein we attain increase of *happiness*. This depends on our holiness. We are not to expect joy without grace.

2. Increase of *security*. Not that God is more faithful, Christ more availing, or the promises more stable; but we are in less danger of falling, though we cannot arrive in this world to any state where we shall be free from the liability of falling, yet our habits of virtue growing more confirmed, every moment renders it less likely.

3. Increase of *usefulness*. This is necessary, but we cannot be useful without growing in grace.

REV. RICHARD WATSON.

XXXII.—THE DAY OF ADVERSITY.

"In the time of adversity, consider!"—ECCLES. vii. 14.

I. THE PERIOD to which the sacred writer refers.
1. The season of public calamity.
2. The season of public embarrassment.
3. The season of public bereavements.
4. The season of paternal affliction.

II. THE SPECIAL DUTY ENFORCED. "Consider!"
1. That our afflictions are of Divine appointment.
2. That our most obvious duty is submission.
3. That our affliction is of the greatest importance.
4. That it is essential to our happiness.
5. That the only source of effectual consolation is in God.
6. That the afflictions of life have in their accomplishment led to heavenly bliss.

IMPROVEMENT.

1. Let the subject awaken us to a sense of depravity.
2. Let it impress us with a deep sense of the goodness of God.

J. BOWERS.

XXXIII.—ABUNDANT GRACE.

"Wherein he hath abounded toward us in all wisdom and prudence; Having made known unto us the mystery of his will, according to his good pleasure which he hath purposed to himself: That in the dispensation of the fulness of times, he might gather together in one, all things in Christ, both which are in heaven, and which are on earth; even in him."—EPH. i. 8—10.

THE design of this epistle is to show the union produced by the blood of Christ.

I. THE IMPORTANT TRUTH STATED. God has caused his grace to abound in all wisdom and prudence.

1. *In the formation of his plan.* Prompted by infinite love, which commiserated fallen man.
2. *In his conduct.* Sending his Son — his Spirit — providing means of grace, etc.
3. *Suspending the operations of his justice.* Accepting a mediator.
4. *In the application of his grace, and in the instruments employed.*

II. THE MEANS BY WHICH IT PLEASED GOD TO COMMUNICATE HIS ABUNDANT GRACE TO US.

Viz. By the gospel, which is called a mystery.

1. It was concealed as a secret in the mind of God, from eternity, and but faintly made known by types.
2. It is hidden now to many, who are utter strangers to Divine revelation, and from many professed Christians.
3. It has heights and depths which the most enlarged Christian mind cannot conceive.
4. The Christian feels more of it than he has utterance to express. —— The Christian joy is an unutterable joy.

III. THE DESIGN OF GOD IN THE DISPLAY OF THIS GRACE BY THE GOSPEL—WORTHY OF GOD—WORTHY THE NAME OF GRACE: viz., that he might gather into one all things, *i. e.*, all intelligent things in Christ.

1. The work of Christ is *to gather together.* We scarcely see ten men but they have ten different interests, in civil and religious things.—— Pagans, Catholics, Mahomedans: hence this is a mighty work to reconcile all these and bring them into *one.*
2. *The honour assigned to Christ.* In one head — "Christ."
(1) *The Head of conformation to the angels:* hence they are called "elect angels." 1 Tim. v. 21 ; Eph. i. 22.——" Angels, authorities, and powers, being made subject unto Him." 1 Pet. iii. 22. "Let all the *angels* of God worship him." Heb. i. 6.
(2) *Head of representation.* The Church died, rose, obeyed, and suffered in Christ, its representative, and must live with him.

(3) *Head of influence.* All the nerves and muscles come from the brain. No motion in the body without this. And without Christ there is no light, exertion, taste, sensibility, John i. 16. The Spirit acts in consequence of Christ's work.

(4) *The Head of union between Jews and Gentiles.*

IMPROVEMENT.

1. What a high value should we put on Christ! In him, the law and the gospel, the promises, God and man, heaven and earth, are united.

2. How highly should we value the gospel!

3. Let Christians unite with greater concert — striving together for the faith of the gospel.

4. Make it a matter of inquiry whether grace have united you to Christ.

DR. RYLAND.

XXXIV.—CHRIST'S INVITATION.

"Come unto me, all ye that labour and are heavy laden, and I will give you rest." — MATT. xi. 28.

I. THE CHARACTERS ADDRESSED.

They who *labour* and are *heavy laden.*

1. With a sense of sin, in its defiling, condemning, and distressing power.

2. With a sense of their own weakness. Cannot remove their misery.

3. With many doubts and fears.

4. With many sorrows.

II. THE INVITATION GIVEN.

Come to me. Rich, compassionate, kind, affable, powerful — a king, teacher, physician, friend, shepherd.

1. Possessed of a perfect knowledge of their case.

2. Willing to do them good.

3. Able to relieve.

III. THE BLESSING PROMISED. "Rest."

1. Peace of mind here, arising from forgiving and justifying grace.

2. Full enjoyment of heaven hereafter. Then there will be eternal rest from sin — from trouble — pain — death. Not merely rest; but exalted felicity — "pleasures for evermore."

XXXV. — CHRISTIAN WARFARE.

"Gad, a troop shall overcome him, but he shall overcome at last."— GEN. xlix. 19.

THE death-bed of a good man is an affecting scene. ——Sometimes it is very interesting; on account of the salutary influence of religion on the soul of the dying; the counsels administered, and the blessings pronounced on surviving relatives and friends.

Jacob was about to die.——Joseph went with his two sons to receive the patriarch's dying blessing. With uplifted hand, and with fervid pleasure, the venerable parent exclaimed, "The angel of the covenant who redeemed me from all evil, bless the lads." Gen. xlviii. 13, etc. —— He then called his own sons together; some of them he blessed; and, by the spirit of prophecy which was upon him, declared what was to happen to their posterity in the last days, v. 1, etc.

The text contains a prediction concerning the tribe of Gad. That tribe inhabited the part of Canaan adjoining the Ammonites, Moabites, and other warlike nations, who constantly annoyed the Gaddites. Yet the latter afterwards became a warlike and invincible people. 1 Chron. xii. 8; Josh. iv. 12, 13; xxii; Deut. xxxiii. 20, 21.

I. THE CHRISTIAN SOLDIER HAS ENEMIES TO ENCOUNTER.

Even as the tribe of Gad were opposed by hostile nations, so the Christian is annoyed by numerous foes.

1. *Satan* from the beginning has been the foe of man. By tempting and overcoming the first pair, what woes were introduced into this world! And now he, the Captain, sends forth his troops of snares, temptations, enchantments, blandishments, etc., to ruin the immortal soul. 1 Pet. v. 8; Eph. ii. 2.

This wicked spirit is called *the tempter*, 1 Thess. iii. 5; Matt. iv. 3 —— *the wicked One*, 1 John ii. 13 —— *Satan*, which signifies an enemy. 1 Pet. v. 8. Such he is both to God and man —— *the Serpent*, 2 Cor. xi. 3, and that *old Serpent*, incessantly labouring by his wily policy to deceive and destroy —— he is compared to a *strong man*, Matt. xii. 29; and his delegates are called *principalities and powers*, numerous! strong! though not more numerous, nor stronger than Christ —— he is called the *prince of this world*, and the *god of this world*, John xiv. 30; 2 Cor. iv. 4 —— he is called *the devil*, 1 Pet. v. 8, which means a slanderer, false accuser, and he is called the accuser of the brethren, Rev. xii. 1.

This is the great master-foe of the Christian, who has troops of emissaries possessing the same cunning, enmity, malice, etc. Satan is a host in himself! He can transform himself into an angel of light; he tries to impose upon believers the form of godliness instead of the power; zeal for party, instead of zeal for truth; warmth of natural temper, and joy of success, instead of "love to God, and joy in the Holy Ghost."

2. The Christian has to contend *with moral depravity*. "The
26

heart is deceitful above all things," etc. In its natural unsanctified state, it is opposed to all that is pure and Godlike. Rom. vii. 18; viii. 5—8.

3. The Christian has to contend *with adversity*. Depressed circumstances — bodily disease — bereavements, etc. These are enemies, disturbing the mind, trying to patience, faith, hope, resignation. And adversity cannot be considered as a blessing until we can patiently and submissively bear it.

Adversity must either be conquered, or it will conquer us. Happy are they who can be "patient in tribulation"! Thousands have been conquered here.

4. The Christian has to contend against *the world*. This is a deadly foe. It contains troops of sinful pleasures, snares, and enchantments. In contesting with these, thousands have fallen to rise no more. This world is Satan's seat and empire; it is fallen, and in arms against God. Whoever belongs to God has the world for an enemy. "The friendship of this world is enmity with God." 1 John v. 4, 5.

Sometimes the world assails the Christian by its *frowns*. It speaks against him with the tongue of slander — it traduces his character — it magnifies his imperfections, and misrepresents his motives — it persecutes him for righteousness' sake. It is often a *frowning enemy*.

Sometimes the world presents a *smiling aspect*.—— It commends talents, flatters and praises actions—your trade flourishes—your circumstances are very comfortable. —— Now take care of this smiling foe. What does it say? "I will do my best for you; forget God, and be devoted to me."

Then the world is full of *error* and *delusion*. Christianity by the carnal mind is detested — the truth is denied — apparent discrepencies of the Bible are pointed out — an attempt is constantly being made to make it appear ridiculous. Atheism, Secularism, Catholicism, Puseyism, and every kind of dogma, is proposed as a substitute for the pure principles of God's word. —— In order to conquer, the Christian hero must penetrate and explode such plausible yet truly superficial representations.

5. The Christian has to contend *with fears*. "Within are fears." 2 Cor. vii. 5. Sometimes he fears that his heart is not right with God — sometimes the formidable character of his foes makes him afraid—fears his duties, conflicts, trials—fears, on account of constitutional mental depression — fears death.

All these fears are foes—they bring a snare — they often cast down, and destroy the hope of man. Abraham, by his doubts and fears, was led to dissemble. So with Elijah, who retired to a cave, and wished to die.

II. THE CHRISTIAN IS SOMETIMES OVERCOME. "Gad, a troop shall overcome him."

1. Many are overcome in consequence of *non-resistance*. The enemy

comes, the temptation comes, and they are borne away. The voice of the charmer prevails. The stream of evil bears thousands along without the least resistance. This is especially the case with the wicked. —— And sometimes the Christian soldier resists not and is overcome for a time.

2. *Ignorance* is another cause of being overcome. Ignorance of ourselves — of our propensities — of the sins which easily beset us — forgetfulness of promised Divine aid. —— Ignorance of the character of our enemies — their policy, cunning, modes of attack — their power and determination. This ignorance often leads to

3. *Self-dependence.* Instance Peter, who by self-confidence, denied his Lord. How weak is man, to resist mighty and long experienced foes, and enchanting temptations!

> Man's wisdom is to seek
> His strength in God alone,
> And even an angel would be weak,
> Who trusted to his own.

4. *Unwatchfulness.* How many Christians have been surprised when off their guard! "Watch," said Christ, "lest ye enter into temptation."

5. *Spiritual declension.* Brought on by neglect of self-investigation, neglect of prayer, and various means of grace. A Christian so negligent soon becomes enervated, weak, and indifferent, and an easy prey to Satanic or worldly influence.

How miserable the state of one overcome! Witness Peter, who went out and wept bitterly. —— What darkness, self-reproach, grief, and agony are experienced by the fallen, when they are sensible of their condition! Witness the pangs of David. Ps. xxxviii. and li.

III. THE TRUE CHRISTIAN SHALL OVERCOME AT LAST. "But he shall overcome at last."

The defeat of a real Christian is temporary. This has been seen in many instances. From inexperience, unwatchfulness, the fierceness of temptations, he may have been vanquished. But he rises up, and returns to the fight more wary, more valiant, and more determined in the strength of Immanuel to conquer or die. "Rejoice not against me, O mine enemy," etc. Micah vii. 8, 9. —— Observe

1. He is made sensible of his fall — he feels that he has been conquered — it is a season of misery and darkness. Witness David and Peter.

2. With penitential regret, he confesses his sins to God, and seeks pardon through the blood of Christ.

3. He is willing to submit to the directions of the Captain of his salvation — equips himself afresh with the armour of righteousness; Eph. vi. 13, etc. He depends no more on his own strength and wisdom, but ever applies by prayer for guidance and strength; "Lord, what wilt thou have me to do?"

4. God has promised his efficient aid in every conflict. Isa. xli.

10; xliii. 2; xl. 29—31; Matt. xxviii. 20; 2 Cor. xii. 9; Isa. liv. 17. Thus God loves his people, and will preserve them.

5. Thousands have overcome. True, sometimes in Christian battle, they gave way — they were discomfited — but they arose again, and in the strength of their Divine Leader they conquered. All true believers "*overcome at last*" — in the hour of death — and they will finally and forever at the day of judgment. "Blessed is the man that is tempted; for when he is tried, he shall receive the crown of life." James i. 12.

XXXVI.—THE CUP OF WRATH.

"Thus saith the Lord God, thou shalt drink of thy sister's cup deep and large; thou shalt be laughed to scorn, and had in derision: *it containeth much.*"—EZEK. xxiii. 32.

THE idolatries of the sister kingdoms of Israel and Judah are represented in this chapter by the evil practices of two abandoned females; for which God brought severe judgments against them. The former proving incorrigible, and irreclaimable, God delivered them into the hands of the Assyrians, v. 9. Judah also having followed the example and plunged into all the abominations of idolatry, he would now suffer the Babylonians, who had been their confederates, to become their executioners, and to carry them away into captivity, and thus Jerusalem should share the fate of Samaria, v. 22, 23. "Thou shalt drink of thy sister's cup, deep and large — it containeth much."

I. OFFER A FEW EXPLANATORY REMARKS.

1. The "cup" is sometimes the *emblem of joy and gladness*, Ps. xxiii. 5; but here of *indignation and wrath*, in allusion probably to a very ancient method of punishing criminals, by placing in their hands a poisoned cup, and compelling them to drink it. Thus our Lord's sufferings are called a cup, which he tasted for every man. Matt. xxvi. 39; Heb. ii. 9.

2. *Afflictive dispensations are often represented by a cup*, Ps. lxxiii. 10; and though the Lord's people are made to drink deeply of it, yet the dregs only are reserved for the wicked. Ps. lxxv. 8. There is a mixture of mercy in all his judgments upon them that fear him, but to the impenitent and unbelieving it is wrath without mercy, and without end.

3. The cup is awfully *significant of future and eternal misery*, and hence is called "the cup of wrath." Rev. xvi. 19. The wrath of God and of the Lamb is put into it; the cup has been filling for many years, and wrath treasuring up against the day of wrath; and it will never be emptied. It is also called "*the cup of fury*," as containing the inexpressible fierceness of Divine indignation. Jer. xxv. 15.——With respect to the culprit, it is "*a cup of trembling*," Isa. li. 17. It will make those tremble who drink of it, more than the poisoned cup, and ought to make us all tremble to think of it. Hab. iii. 16.

4. *This cup is preparing and filling for all the disobedient and unbelieving.* The voice of Divine mercy has called them to repentance and faith. A full, rich, and free salvation has been offered them; but all has been disregarded. A voice from heaven has declared that the unbelieving shall be condemned, that they are "treasuring up wrath against the day of wrath." Rom. ii. 5; Rev. vi. 16, 17.

II. THE DESCRIPTION GIVEN OF THE CUP OF WRATH: "it containeth much.

The cup is "deep and large," containing more than we can at present imagine, but not more than we shall be made to experience, if infinite grace and mercy prevent not.

1. It contains *all the sins that we have ever committed;* and these, if not now repented of, will fill us with ceaseless remorse in the world to come. They will be found treasured up, and mingled in the cup for this very purpose. Deut. xxxii. 34. Job had imagined this to be his own case, but he was mistaken, for God had cast all his sins behind his back, ch. xiv. 17. But when the impenitent have filled up the measure of their iniquities, wrath will come upon them to the uttermost. Hos. xii. 13. If the death of Christ be not the death of sin in us, sin will be our everlasting ruin. Sins committed and forgotten will then come into remembrance, and in hell the sinner will have leisure to reflect on his folly and madness when on earth. Luke xvi. 25. Conscience keeps a faithful account of evil done; and though this account may be neglected now, it will be called over hereafter, and spread before us like Ezekiel's roll, which was written within and without: and who can stand before an accusing and condemning conscience? 1 John iii. 20.

2. As this cup contains all the sins we have ever committed, so also *all the curses of that law which we have violated.* Deut. xxviii. 15, 45. And who can tell what is comprehended in these awful denunciations, or know the power of his anger! Psa. xc. 11. The last word which the law speaks to us as sinners is misery and death, and it leaves us under the sentence till the day of execution. Gal. iii. 10. This curse it is that shall fill the sinner's cup, and shall come into his bowels like water, and like oil into his bones. Ps. cix. 18.

3. The *everlasting vengeance of God is another ingredient in this portion of misery;* and how large and deep must be that cup, which contains all the indignation and wrath that will be poured out upon the sinner to an endless eternity! As God's wrath will never be spent, so this cup can never be exhausted. The sinner's sufferings here are only temporary, but in the world to come they will be eternal, a destruction without end, 2 Thess. i. 9. A lost estate, lost liberty, or lost friends may be regained; but the loss of the soul is irreparable and intolerable. Matt. xvi. 26; Ps. xi. 6.

IMPROVEMENT.

1. If this cup "containeth much," let sinners beware how they add to its contents. Every sin committed, every mercy abused, will be a fearful aggravation. Rom. ii. 4.

2. Who will be able to drink of it? Can thy heart endure, or can thy hands be strong, in the day that I shall deal with thee,

saith the Lord. Ezek. xxii. 14; Isa. xxxiii. 14. When some drops only of this cup are tasted in the present life, they fill the soul with unutterable anguish. Ps. lxxxviii. 15, 16; Job. xx. 24—29.

3. Learn hence the evil of sin, which prepares and fills this bitter cup. Rom. vi. 23. Of every transgression it may be said, "there is death in the pot." Sin is the womb of all misery, the grave of all comfort.

4. Let this cup of wrath remind us of the cup of sorrow which Jesus drank, and drank for us. The cup did not pass from him, that it might pass from us. Let this be our plea, under a sense of all our unworthiness. Matt. xxvi. 42.

XXXVII.—SUCCESS OF PREACHING CHRIST.

"And some of them were men of Cyprus and Cyrene, which, when they were come to Antioch, spake unto the Grecians, preaching the Lord Jesus. And the hand of the Lord was with them; and a great number believed, and turned unto the Lord."— ACTS xi. 20, 21.

I. THE IMPORT OF PREACHING CHRIST.
1. The season in which these words were spoken.
2. The persons addressed — (Jews only.)
3. The impediments in the way—prejudice, ignorance, unbelief.
4. The topics announced.

(1) The harmony between Christ and the Old Testament representations of him.
(2) The certainty of his resurrection and ascension into heaven.
(3) The design of the whole in its adaptation to them as sinners.

II. WHAT WAS CONNECTED WITH THIS PREACHING.
1. The Divine authority and approbation.
2. Divine aid and support.
3. Power attending their ministry.

III. THE EFFECTS PRODUCED. "Many believed and turned to the Lord."
1. "*They believed.*"
(1) They credited the facts relative to Christ.
(2) They entered into the spirit of the whole design.

2. "*They turned unto the Lord.*"
(1) Renounced Jewish prejudices and ceremonies.
(2) They renounced justification by the Law.
(3) Became holy in their lives and manifested the fruits of the Spirit.

IMPROVEMENT.

1. God acts mysteriously in accomplishing his important designs.
2. God never wants means to fulfil his gracious intentions.
3. All instruments and means, though weak in themselves, are mighty through Divine power.

W. KENT.

XXXVIII.—CENSORIOUSNESS AND FAITHFULNESS CONTRASTED.

"I write not these things to *shame* you, but, as my beloved sons, I *warn* you."—
1 COR. iv. 14.

"HE that would be a good man must have either a friend to admonish him, or an enemy to watch over him."

The text points out the difference between censoriousness and faithfulness.

I. CENSORIOUSNESS IS A NIMROD: a mighty hunter for faults.

Jer. xx. 10. — "For I heard the defaming of many, fear on every side: 'Report,' say they, 'and we will report it.'"

Ps. lvi. 6.—"They gather themselves together, they hide themselves, they mark my steps, when they wait for my soul."

Faithfulness does not delight to dwell on a fault; but censoriousness does.

II. CENSORIOUSNESS IS A MIGHTY CREATOR; it makes faults where there are none: it puts the *worst construction* on words and actions.

Examples. The Pharisees and disciples going through the corn-fields. Matt. xii. 1, 2.
Eliab to David. 1 Sam. xvii. 28.
It calls zeal rashness. Michael to David. 2 Sam. vi. 20.
Ps. lxix. 26.—"For they persecute him, whom thou hast smitten; and they talk to the grief of those whom thou hast wounded."
Faithfulness is discreet in its decisions.

III. CENSORIOUSNESS IS AN EASY BELIEVER, WHERE HE IS NOT AN INVENTOR OF FAULTS.

Example. The two false witnesses against Christ. Matt. xxvi. 60, 61.
The people of Ephesus when Demetrius slandered Paul. Acts xix. 24—27.
The Israelites when the spies returned and brought the evil report which the Israelites believed. Num. xiii. 32, 33; xiv. 1—4.
Faithfulness is not credulous; it *believes not* every spirit; but "*tries* the spirits*."

IV. CENSORIOUSNESS IS A KIND OF OPTICIAN; it *magnifies small* things; makes a man an offender for a word: carries magnifying glasses with it.

Faithfulness endeavors to mitigate the offence. 1 Pet. iv. 8. "Charity (love) shall cover the multitude of sins."

V. CENSORIOUSNESS IS A KIND OF CRIER; it propagates the faults of men where they are not known.

Example. Ham. Gen. ix. 20—22. — "And Ham —— told his two brethren without."

Faithfulness concealeth the matter. Gen. ix. 23. — "Shem and Japheth took a garment," etc.

Prov. xi. 13.—"A tale-bearer revealeth secrets; but he that is of a faithful spirit *concealeth* the matter."

VI. CENSORIOUSNESS DELIGHTS TO DWELL ON A FAULT.

Ps. cii. 8. — "Mine enemies reproach me *all the day.*"
Faithfulness grieves and laments the failings of others.
Prov. xxiv. 17.—"Rejoice not when thine enemy falleth; and let not thine heart be glad when he stumbleth."

VII. CENSORIOUSNESS IS VERY SUPERCILIOUS IN ITS REPROOFS: it says, "stand by thyself, for I am holier than thou." Isa. lv. 5. Luke xviii. 11.—"The Pharisee stood and prayed thus with himself — God, I thank thee, that I am not as other men are," etc.

Faithfulness is tender of the reputation of others, and desires to reclaim and restore them.

Gal. vi. 1. — "Brethren, if a man be overtaken in a fault, ye that are spiritual, restore such an one in the spirit of meekness; considering thyself," etc.

James v. 20.—" He that converteth the sinner from the error of his way, shall save a soul from death, and shall hide a multitude of sins."

WILKS.

XXXIX.—CHRIST ALL IN ALL TO THE CHURCH.

"Christ is all and in all." — COL. iii. 11.

THERE is no true religion besides that which is drawn from the Bible. Many systems have been devised, but they are utterly worthless. —— There can be no true and satisfactory religion without Christ. Man's circumstances cannot be met by any human schemes of religion. —— Christ, in the dignity of his person—in his gracious atonement—in the fulness and freeness of his salvation, and as the Author of eternal life, is gloriously adapted to the circumstances of fallen humanity. He is "all and in all."

The phrase implies that the whole of Christianity is full of Christ.

The Sun is all in all to the Solar system. He diffuses light liberally to all the planets revolving around him, and his heat penetrates to the centre of the largest globes. On our earth he is the life of all vegetation; he paints the flowers, embalms the fruit, ripens the grain, and quickens all nature into life and beauty, and thus becomes *all in all* to us. And the Redeemer is the Sun of righteousness. Whatever the Sun is to the material world, that, and much more, the Son of God is to the spiritual. He is *all in all* in the system of Christianity.

1. "*Christ is all in all*" *in the scheme of salvation, as it respects God.*

Who pitied fallen humanity? Who devised the plan for the sinner's emancipation from spiritual and everlasting death? It was Christ, the second person in the Holy Trinity, and by the Sacred Three the wonderful plan of redeeming love was devised. Yes, Christ looked down from heaven, and saw man's lost estate, and said, "Lo, I come." Ps. xl. 7; Heb. x. 7. He became the Mediator between God and man.

He is the covenant-head both of men and angels, and every gracious purpose of the Divine mind toward them has an immediate respect to Christ. So in the actual communication of the blessings, both of Providence and grace, he is the only channel through which they flow. He is the spiritual ladder which Jacob saw, by which intercourse is held between God and us.

2. "*Christ is all in all*" *in the work of redemption, as it affects man.*

He paid the price of redemption, wrought out a perfect righteousness for our justification, and communicates his Holy Spirit for our sanctification. To accomplish this he passed through the fiery ordeal of suffering. From man's scorn and physical tortures—from his friends, their perfidy and desertion—from devils, their malice and infernal hate—from Divine justice, who hurled the lightning and rolled the thunder against him, the Redeemer suffered. Witness his agony in the garden, in "the hour of darkness." O what an hour was that! Divine justice approached him with the bitter cup, and said, "Drink it, or the church will be lost." With complacency and submission, he said, "It is indeed a bitter cup: Father, if it be possible, remove it from me; nevertheless, not my will, but thine be done." Divine justice again imperatively announced, "Drink it, or the law of God will be dishonoured, and every soul be lost." "I will drink it," said Christ, "that my church may be saved." And then

> At one tremendous draught of love,
> He drank destruction dry.

He was "all in all" then in the conflict. Neither men nor angels helped him to tread the wine-press of Divine fury. He alone procured salvation.——He sits both as our Prince and Advocate at the right hand of his Father; and he will ever continue to intercede for us, until all his gracious purposes are accomplished.

Happy are they who can say, Christ is *all in all* to me! I have no hope of salvation from my sinful deeds. Self-righteousness! Ah, no! rather self-defilement, self-abomination, enough to sink me to the lowest hell! Blessed Jesus, thou art my Saviour, the *all in all* in my salvation. Human merit! No; not if I poured thousands of gold and silver into the treasury of God. No; not if I were a martyr, and gave my body to be burnt at the stake. Oh, I feel no merit in my vile insolvent soul! The merit is in thee, O Christ! my *All in All.*"

> Thou hast adorned my naked soul,
> And made salvation mine;
> Upon a poor polluted worm
> He makes his graces shine.
>
> And lest the shadow of a spot
> Should on my soul be found,
> My Saviour took the robe he wrought,
> And cast it all around.

3. *Christ is "all in all" in the Sacred Scriptures.*

All Divine truths connect and harmonize in him, like the rays of light collected in the focus. The vital truths appropriate to man's undying interests, refer to Christ. The experience of the patriarchs, the sacrifices of the Levitical economy, the predictions of the prophets, the teaching of Jesus Christ himself, and the preaching of the Apostles, are full of Christ. If the Bible had not Christ, the precious Saviour, in it, it would not be worth a straw. But Christ is the Alpha and Omega of the old and new covenant.

> Here, the Redeemer's welcome voice,
> Spreads heavenly peace around;
> And life and everlasting joys
> Attend the blissful sound.

4. *Christ is "all in all" in his church.* He is its only Head, Lawgiver, Saviour, and Lord.

The church has no temporal head, but a spiritual One; no human laws, but spiritual; Christ promises no earthly honours and rewards, but spiritual and heavenly. "One is your Master, even Christ," etc. Matt. xxiii. 8. Then let no man's wisdom be substituted for that of Christ. Let not our preconceived opinions, our pride, our party, supplant Christ. Let man, and pride, and selfishness sink; but let Christ *be all in all.*

5. *Christ is "all in all" in the life of the believer.* He says, "I count all things but loss for the excellency," etc. Phil. iii. 8.

Christ is the ground of his faith, confidence, and hope. He enjoys Christ and loves him. Carnal objects he once loved, but now Christ is his all. Every grace receives its vigour from a believing view of Jesus. Amid life's adversities, and in prospect of life's dissolution, Christ alone can comfort and satisfy the Christian. "For me to live is Christ."

Yes, when a Christian comes to die, the world, riches, honour, etc., are nothing but empty things—only Christ is all in all then.

6. Christ is "all in all" in *the Christian Ministry.*

"Go and preach the gospel to every creature," was the command given to the Apostles; and the gospel is full of Christ. They did not preach the law in the abstract—they did not preach self-righteousness—or works of supererogation; they did not preach human philosophy, or mere science,——but Christ alone. "We preach Christ crucified," 1 Cor. i. 2, 3; ii. 2. "Woe unto me, if I preach not the gospel," 1 Cor. ix. 16. See also Gal. i. 8.——It is cruel to trifle in the pulpit, "when life so soon is gone." Like the Israelites stung by the serpents, sinners are dying, and they want to look up to the cross, and believe in Christ, the Physician of souls.——How cruel Moses would have been, if he had harangued the Israelites about ethics instead of lifting up the serpent of brass! So cruel is every minister of the gospel who preaches not the gospel, or who exhibits his little self, instead of Christ. He must be "all in all." O cold and sterile pulpit and sanctuary where Christ is not "set forth"!

Once, a miser, on his death-bed, called for his bags of gold, and placing the idol to his heart, he said, "It will not do; it will not do."—The poor wretch wanted Christ as his all in all, and then his gold would have been regarded as vanity.

7. *Christ is "all in all" in the enjoyment of heaven.* "The Lamb that is in the midst of the throne shall feed them, and lead them to rivers of living waters."

He is the "all in all" of the celestial anthems. The Father delights to honour him, and beams all his glory through his countenance—angels delight to honour him, and tune their golden harps to praise him. Saints delight to honour him, and cast their starry crowns beneath his feet.——He is the "all in all" in heaven—and there could be no heaven without him.

IMPROVEMENT.

1. Is Christ "all in all" to me? Without him, I am "miserable, and poor, and blind, and naked, and wretched."—2. Never substitute any thing for Christ in the concerns of your souls.——3. Let Christ be your chief good in this life. He can benefit you not only in time, but for ever. Other objects are transient.

XL.—THE COMMON SALVATION.

"Beloved, when I gave all diligence to write unto you of the common salvation, it was needful for me to write unto you."—JUDE 3.

THE most interesting subject about which we can speak or write is the salvation of man—and for this reason,—it respects our everlasting destiny. Other subjects may be important, and awaken attention, and engage our intellectual powers, but their importance and value are far inferior to the great salvation.

This salvation was denied and demoralized in the time of Jude, and the apostle knowing and feeling the value of it, thought it proper to apprize the brethren of such conduct, that they might not be seduced from the faith, v. 3, 4.

I. THE SUBJECT ON WHICH THE APOSTLE WROTE: "*salvation.*"

By this phrase is meant the *Gospel of salvation*. It is the same thing as "the faith once delivered to the saints;" "the common faith," of which Titus was a participant. "To Titus mine own son after the common faith." Tit. i. 4. In short it is that glorious system which in the New Testament is peculiarly denominated the *Gospel*——"The Gospel of the grace of God;" the grand and absorbing theme of Divine revelation—of the Christian ministry—of angelic study—of Christian delight, and of heaven's praise. Consider,

The Nature of salvation. In the New Testament, the term means the deliverance of sinners from everlasting perdition, through faith in Christ. Mark xvi. 16; John iii. 16, 17; Acts xvi. 31.

• 1. *Salvation is necessary.* Necessary on account of the dark captivity of the sinner; and his exposure to the inflictions of eternal wrath. Look at man: Can that guilty, defiled transgressor commune with God, and finally dwell with him in heaven? Impossible. The law has been broken, and God's justice demands satisfaction.——The curse of God is upon his soul, and he cannot remove it. In whatever light man is considered salvation is necessary. He cannot save himself by his own efforts, nor by the efforts of any mere creature. An angel's arm would be too weak for this mighty achievement. Legions of bright and glorious spirits would fail here. Because man is impotent—helpless—blind—dying—cursed—under the wrath of God, salvation is necessary.

2. *Salvation has been procured.* Christ is the vicarious medium of it. It was the infinite wisdom and love of God that devised and carried out the plan for man's rescue. John iii. 16.

Christ is called "the Saviour," Luke ii. 11; Matt. i. 21; Acts v. 31; Phil. iii. 20.

Christ is called a "Redeemer," Rom. iii. 24; Gal. iv. 4; Eph. i. 7. —— He is called a "Ransom," Matt. xx. 28; 1 Tim. ii. 6. —— To ransom man he paid the price demanded. 1 Cor. vi. 20; Acts xx. 28. —— He is called a "Deliverer," Luke iv. 18; 1 Thess. i. 10.——A "Mediator." 1 Tim. ii. 5. He "reconciled" man to God. Rom. v. 10; Col. i. 19, 20.

What do these expressions imply? That Christ has suffered and died to make atonement for sin. That sacrifice has been Divinely accepted — it is of sovereign efficacy — it exhibits in glorious harmony all the moral attributes of Deity. On the cross they appear emblazoned with celestial glory. His truth and mercy; his compassion and holiness; his justice and love; his wisdom and power, all meet to be magnified in the redemption of sinners. There Deity appears full-orbed in all his uncreated grandeur and glory. Creation is full of God; providence is the constant exhibition of God; but redemption is the brightness of his glory, the effulgence of the great Fountain of light and happiness.

3. *The efficacy of this salvation.* It delivers
From the *condemnation and curse of the law,* Rom. viii. 1 ; Gal. iii. 15.
It proclaims *forgiveness of sins,* and complete *justification.* Acts xiii. 38,
39. —— It delivers from *pollution.* The Holy Spirit is given to renovate
the heart. Sin no longer reigns. Ezek. xxxvi. 25—27.——It delivers
from all the tormenting fears of sin on the conscience, and gives peace.
Rom. v. 1; viii. 15. It delivers from gloomy apprehensions of future
wrath, and inspires with the hope of immortality. It delivers from the
sting of death, the terrors of the grave, and the "vengeance of everlasting
fire." Salvation is not only deliverance from evil; but it elevates the
soul to honour and glory for ever. —— Called, "the salvation which
is in Christ Jesus, *with eternal glory.*"

4. *This salvation is to be received by faith.* Acts xvi. 31. A belief that
Christ is the Saviour — a conviction that we need him — a firm reliance
on him for all we need.

II. THE PECULIARITY OF SALVATION. "Common."

Sometimes this means ordinary or usual, as a common death, Num.
xvi. 20; a common evil, Eccl. vi. 1. The word is also used in reference to that peculiar disposition of property which characterized the
infant Christian church, described, Acts ii. 44. It is called "common
salvation," because it belongs equally to all who believe, of whatever
nation, circumstance, character, or degree. For the same reason Paul
termed the belief of the gospel " the common faith," Tit. i. 4, because
an opportunity of believing it was afforded to all.

1. It is the common salvation *because it is offered to sinners in common*
—without any distinction of nation, age, circumstance, mental or moral
qualities.

It is common to *all nations.* The messages of grace under the Old
Testament were principally addressed to a single nation; but under
the gospel they are addressed to "all nations" — to "every creature."
The Gospel feast is spread, and both Jews and Gentiles are pressed to
partake of it. Rom. i. 16; Col. iii. 11; Rev. vii. 9.

It is common to *each sex, and every age.* By many systems woman is
degraded, and prohibited from her just rights, being regarded as an
inferior being. Such procedure is inculated by the atheistical religion
of China — by the Mahomedanism of Turkey, and by the cruel rites of
Hindooism. But the gospel is designed to elevate and dignify every
woman who believes in Christ. Gal. iii. 26—29. *Children* may enjoy
this salvation. "Out of the mouths of babes," etc. — the *middle-aged,*
and the *man of hoary years* may take the water of life freely.

It is common to sinners irrespective of *mental abilities.* It does not
exclude the philosopher, or the man of science. A Newton, a Locke,
a Boyle, a Milton, a Cowper, an Addison, a Sir W. Jones have drank
of its life-giving streams. It may be enjoyed by the most illiterate.

It is common to *sinners of every circumstance.* It has been enjoyed by
kings and nobles, etc. And blind Bartimeus — the lame man near the
temple—the impotent and sick near the pool of Bethesda, and Lazarus,
with his beggary and sores, may be saved. " The poor have the gospel
preached to them." " God has chosen the poor," etc.

It is common to *sinners of every degree.* To the self-righteous, the man of good moral character, decent exterior, and to the vilest of the vile. Were Mary Magdelene, Saul of Tarsus, the filthy Corinthians, or the idolatrous Ephesians, excluded? No.

> What though your numerous sins exceed
> The stars that fill the skies,
> And aiming at th' eternal throne,
> Like pointed mountains rise.
>
> What though your mighty guilt beyond
> The wide creation swell,
> And has its curs'd foundations laid
> Low as the depths of hell.
>
> See here an endless ocean flows
> Of never-failing grace!
> Behold a dying Saviour's veins
> The sacred flood increase!
>
> It rises high, and drowns the hills,
> Has neither shore nor bound:
> Now, if we search to find our sins,
> Our sins can ne'er be found.

2. *It is common to all believers.* In the enjoyment of this salvation, "the rich and the poor meet together." It does not belong to a few in the family; it is the privilege of all. Believers all meet in Christ the common head; are influenced, sanctified, and comforted by one and the same Spirit, are governed by the same laws, and meet at the same throne of grace. They have the same faith, the same hope, and the same Divine protection and love. They hope shortly to meet in one common inheritance of unspeakable grandeur and felicity. In that land the rich and the noble, if saved, will not have a more brilliant crowd, nor more ecstatic bliss than the poorest Christian who has passed through much tribulation to glory. As all the church will be "saved by grace," so there will be no inequality. *They will have all heavenly blessings common there.*

3. It is the common salvation because *it is free.* This gift of God is not to be purchased with money. Free to all who feel their need of it. Free as the air we breathe, as the rain from heaven, as the rays of the sun. It is the infinite good which God has given, and therefore a finite, sinful creature cannot merit it. Isa. lv. 1; Rev. xxii. 17.

4. The word "common" implies *value and abundance.*

Our most common blessings are the most valuable. How common it is for us to enjoy food, health, strength, our faculties, the rain, the shining of the sun, etc.! They are so common that we think little of them. Take away our food, or health — take away the sun, and we shall soon know and feel their value. And salvation so freely offered to all the world—so frequently presented to the church, and so enrapturing to the ransomed in glory; salvation, common on earth, and common in heaven, is a pearl of great and incalculable price. —— Our commonest blessings are also the most *abundant.* And so it is with this salvation. It is a "great" and abundant salvation. It is replete with every blessing. In Christ all fulness dwells.

> Wide as the reach of Satan's rage,
> Doth thy salvation flow:
> 'Tis not confined to sex or age,
> The lofty or the low.

While grace is offer'd to the prince,
The poor may take his share:
No mortal hath a just pretence
To perish in despair.

5. It is the common salvation as it is that subject in which all believers, notwithstanding their difference of opinion on other subjects, are in substance agreed. —— There may be great darkness, imperfections, and error, and many prejudices for and against distinctive names; but let the doctrine of the cross be simply stated, and it will be the joy of the renewed heart. —— Believers in Christ, of every denomination, agree as to the necessity of salvation, the vicarious medium of it, the richness and greatness of it, the freeness of it, or the holy efficacy of it. Unto all who believe, Christ is precious.

IMPROVEMENT.

1. Admire the love of God which has made such rich and ample provision for man's salvation. 2. Become so attached to it as to be ready to defend it, like the Apostle Jude. "Earnestly contend for the faith." 3. Let the penitent sinner rejoice that it is free for him.

XLI.—THE DEATH OF THE RIGHTEOUS.

"Let me die the death of the righteous, and let my last end be like his."—NUM. xxiii. 10.

Who speaks? On what occasion?

I. *He who is righteous.* He that has Christ. Given for him; living in him; and has faith, hope, and love.

II. *Their death is happy.* Freedom from sin, errors, temptation, misery. Has safe and perfect happiness, in the vision of God, Christ, angels, saints.

III. *Means.* Live the life of the righteous. Repent, and be forgiven. Make haste; do not rest in a vain wish, like Balaam; if thou doest, misery of thy life, horror of thy death. Look backward — on the present moment; but, above all, mind what will befall thee!

REV. JOHN FLETCHER.

XLII.—THE WORLD GLORIFIED.

"Brethren, pray for us, that the word of the Lord may have free course, and be glorified, even as it is with you."— 2 THESS. iii. 1.

PAUL's zeal for the gospel. The object, reason, and efficacy of the duty enjoined.

I. THE OBJECT. That "the word of the Lord may have free course." This is the case

1. When it is more extensively acknowledged.
2. When more Divine light is communicated to individuals, and their darkness is dispersed.
3. When the word exerts a more saving influence on the heart.

II. THE REASON; "That the word of the Lord may have free course, run, and be glorified." An allusion to the Olympic racers, who were opposed in their course. The word of the Lord has been *opposed* and hindered, so that it has not yet attained the goal. It has not been *glorified* as it might have been had it not been for those hinderances. The judaizing teachers and persecuting heathens hindered it in the first ages — superstition for many ages after. The causes of its being hindered in individuals and churches are

1. Indifference.
2. Secret unbelief.
3. Love of the world.
4. Indulgence of some errors, extravagant ideas of God's mercy, ignorance of religion's importance.
5. Want of light, accompanied by want of life and prosperity.

III. THE EFFICACY. The prayers of the righteous are efficacious. ——

1. Because of the interest praying persons will feel in and for the success of the word. The time to favour Zion is when "thy servants take pleasure in the stones and favour the dust thereof."
2. Because of the saving influence they diffuse around them wherever they are.
3. Because of their personal exertions.
4. Because they procure the Divine blessing and influence.

REV. R. WATSON.

XLIII.—PREPAREDNESS FOR DEATH.

"Be ye therefore ready also: for the Son of man cometh at an hour when ye think not."— LUKE xii. 40.

JESUS CHRIST was a wise Teacher. He knew what was in man, and what was necessary for man. —— The mind of man is carnal, superficial, and volatile. Things of the greatest value, and essential to his happiness, he readily forgets; yet, astonishing infatuation! mere trifles, empty and unsatisfying vanities, absorb all the powers of his soul. Are not these symptoms of a depraved appetite? —— The great Teacher, in this chapter, gives most important advice as to our behaviour in this life, and our preparation for the life to come.

I. A SOLEMN FACT. "The Son of man cometh."

Sometimes the coming of the Son of man refers to the destruction of Jerusalem, and sometimes to the day of judgment; Matt. xxiv; xxv.

1. As it regards our everlasting destiny, the day of death is to us as decisive as the day of judgment. The state of our souls is for ever fixed. The day of death is to all who die as if the last trumpet had sounded, and the Son of man appeared in all his glory to judge the quick and the dead.

2. *Christ has death under his power.* He has conquered it, and made the last enemy his servant. Heb. ii. 14, 15; Rev. i. 18. To death Christ says, Go, and he goeth to terminate the career of the wicked, or to bring his people home to himself. The Son of man therefore cometh in death.

3. *This coming is inevitable.* Inevitable, because we are mortal. Rendered so by sin. "Dust thou art," etc. Gen. iii. 19. Although man is "fearfully and wonderfully made," yet he is *frail.*

Such is the extreme delicacy of innumerable parts of the human frame, such the complicated contrivances which make up and continue what we call life, and such a total and fatal derangement does one little stoppage produce sometimes in the course of animal nature, that to those who study the structure of the body, it is astonishing that any of us should live a single day.

> Our life contains a thousand springs,
> And dies if one be gone;
> Strange that a harp of thousand strings
> Should keep in tune so long.

Death is the infallible decree of God: "It is appointed unto men once to die;" Heb. ix. 27. No human care, precaution, device, medical science and aid, can eventually ward off the attacks of the last enemy. Youth will not avail — beauty is but a superficial tincture — the strength of manhood is sure to be prostrated — for "there is no discharge in this war." "What man is he that liveth, and shall not see death?"

4. The event of death is *solemn and affecting.* It is the decay and dissolution of a being who has been loved — it is the cessation of every vital function — it is the surrender of earth with all its concerns and engagements — it is the bidding farewell to all earthly friends. Suppose the head of a family, an affectionate husband, an indulgent parent, and a kind master: by death all these bonds are broken. His wife, the desire of his eyes, and the partner of his joys, is left a widow. An incurable breach is made in the feelings of her heart. The guide of her youth, the solace of her age, is gone, and she sits pensive and solitary, and refuses to be comforted. The children exclaim, "My father, my father!" Fond expectation looks in vain for the paternal smile, and the language of love. The well-known step and the welcome voice are no more. The habitation distinguished by his name, and enlivened by his presence, now changes its owner. Those doors which readily turned on their hinges for ingress to their late master, now give him no more admission. He leaves his habitation

for the last time with the gloomy pomp of a winding sheet, a coffin, and mourning survivors! Yes, now

> The church-yard bears an added stone,
> The fire-side shows a vacant chair!
> Here sadness dwells and weeps alone,
> And death displays his banner there:
> The life has gone, the breath has fled,
> And what has been, no more shall be;
> The well-known form, the welcome tread,
> Oh! where are they, and where is he?

5. *The approach of the Son of man by death is uncertain.* "The Son of man cometh at an hour when ye think not."

(1) This coming may take place *when we least think of it* — when our minds are absorbed by other things. How often have persons who have devoted soul and body to commerce, to enterprise in various things, and to gay pursuits, been suddenly cut off! The coming of death is like the lightning that darts across the sky, without any previous warning. Previous to the deluge, the warning voice of Noah was lifted up, yet men never thought it a reality till the flood came and swept them all away. Instances of the sudden approach of death are of daily occurrence. Death may surprise us amid the pleasures of easy, gay, good nature. So it was with the sons of Job. They were eating, and drinking wine; and in one moment their dwelling was converted into a common grave. And so it was with the rich man, when he said to his soul, "Take thine ease," etc. Luke xii. 19.

(2) The event may take place *when our death appears most unlikely.* This applies not merely to the sickly or to the aged. In these cases, death seems to move in his more natural territory, for then he only levels such as were ripened for his scythe. Yet even they are often unexpectedly cut off, and the most aged are frequently vainly imagining that they are too young to die. But surely the young and the strong may flatter themselves that they shall yet see many years. Humanly speaking, appearances are in their favour. Yet how often do the strong and the vigorous fall, while the weak and the sickly stand! Ps. ciii. 15, 16; Isa. xl. 6; Job xxi. 23. Look around you, and see how the young die.

(3) This coming may take place at a time *when the circumstances of the individual render it very inconvenient to die.* Death, however, is no respecter of persons and circumstances. One person is very useful in society, and cannot well be spared, but death takes him away. Another is enlarging his commercial enterprise—his mind is full of projects—his hands are full of works, and his affairs are vast and complicated, except to himself, yet death takes him away. Behold the Father of a family—those lovely children—that fond mother: all are dependent upon that father for support and counsel; they cannot spare him, and yet he dies. How that widow mourns—and those children weep!—— So we might instance many a case.——Is it not true that "the time is short; and it remaineth that both they that have wives," etc. 1 Cor. vii. 29. Is not this uncertainty a loud call to "set our house in order, for we must die and not live?

(4) Death may come *and find us unprepared.* Our state at death is irrevocably fixed for ever. Death conducts either to eternal life, or to eternal woe. For the latter indeed death finds myriads prepared.——

For the former, how few! In such a case the sinner is hurried into the immediate presence of his God, with his heart unchanged; full of hatred to God and his ways; yes, he enters the world of spirits, with the weapons of rebellion in his hands. O what must be the feeling of that soul which is hurried from the haunts of wickedness into the presence of the God of purity!——Sinner, how awful is thy fate, standing on the brink of eternal perdition; on the very suburbs of hell! What would be thy surprise and consternation, if death should suddenly plunge thee into its awful vortex!

How dreadful to be surprised in matters that are serious! A family is reposing in the arms of sleep—they know not at what time the thief cometh—but he enters their dwelling, plunders, or even assassinates. Had they known when he would come, they would have been prepared.——An army is unwatchful, indifferent, and dreaming that the enemy is deficient in dexterity and courage to make an attack upon them, when lo! in the midst of this apathy and delusion, the enemy comes, attacks, and conquers.—— So the young man is, folding his arms in apathy, dreaming that he will live very many years — so the sinner is presuming on a long career of folly — the wealthy are idolizing their possessions — the speculator is dreaming of greater accumulations, saying, "I will pull down my barns and build larger," etc., when, behold, in a moment they think not of, the Son of Man cometh.

II. AN IMPORTANT INJUNCTION. "Be ye therefore ready also."

To be ready for death is of the utmost importance, and ought to be our great object through life.——As death leaves us, judgment will find us. "Whether the tree falls towards the north, or the south, in the place where it falls, there shall it lie," is the declaration of Scripture; and woe to the man who rests only on the forlorn hope of some after-change. A futurity unprepared for, is a gulf of darkness unilluminated by a single ray of light.

Wherein consists this readiness?

It does not consist in any specific devotional duties that can be done at last; nor altogether in unremitting devotional exercises through the course of life. It is not always praying and hearing, shutting ourselves out of the world, and declining the duties of life, that is properly a preparation for death; but true readiness consists in such things as these:—

1. *A cordial reception of the gospel as the Divine revelation of mercy to sinners.* It is examined and found to be true. It is felt to be appropriate and richly adapted to the case of helpless, hopeless sinners. Just as the Jews did on the day of Pentecost; "they gladly received the word." Like the jailor; Acts xvi.

2. *An assurance of pardoned sin, and exemption from Divine censure.* We all have sinned, and come short of the glory of God.——Our hearts are corrupted, and our lives unholy, and unless we secure Divine forgiveness for transgressions, and deliverance from Divine condemnation, there remains nothing for us but coming wrath.—— But the gospel proclaims abundant mercy to the guilty, Acts xiii. 38, 39; 1 John i. 7, 9. To die and go into eternity without sin forgiven, is to become the

victim of Divine anger. Only the pardoned and justified can be saved. John iii. 14—18, 36; Rom. viii. 33, etc.

3. *Renewal of the soul.* "Therefore if any man be in Christ, he is a new creature," and becomes like God, and meet for heaven, for Christ says, "Except a man be born again," etc. John iii. 3. No one can ever meet God with comfort, unless assimilated to his image. There must be a relish for God's service here, and a delight in God's people, or heaven can never be enjoyed; and thus we may test ourselves whether we have passed from death unto life. If a sinner could get into heaven, what enjoyment could he find there? There is enough in his disposition, unhallowed temper, and unrenewed heart to render him miserable there. To relish any thing, we must have taste and capacity for it. What gratification do the sweet strains of music yield to the deaf, or the beauties of creation to the blind? Are the society and conversation of the learned relished by the coarse and illiterate? Are the luxuries of the table relished by the sick?—Then what would the unsanctified do in God's habitation of holiness? What a weariness it would be to serve God day and night, when there is so much aversion to his service here! What a gloomy abode heaven would be to those who dislike communion with saints below, who shun them as they would a tempest, did they meet with no other company in the Jerusalem above, and were they condemned to hear thousands on Mount Zion hymning that very song which was their aversion on earth! Fellowship with God here is just a lower stage of the communion that a saint enjoys with God in heaven; and the vision of God, which is now dark, is exchanged into rapture, in beholding the same God face to face, and rejoicing in the vision.

4. *A proper disposition of soul, peculiarly befitting the approach of death.* This may embrace the following particulars:—

(1) *The graces of the Spirit in lively exercise.* Faith; "I know in whom I have believed," etc. Hope; "Rejoicing in hope of the glory of God." Joy; "We joy in God through whom we have received the atonement." Love; "The love of God is shed abroad," etc. Rom. v. 5. The *fruits of the Spirit* are described, Gal. v. 22, etc.

These holy principles must and will influence the conduct; will make us habitually and prevailingly act on what we believe, so as to be governed by it — in solitude, in our families, in our business, in our enjoyments, and in our transactions with each other, so that the gospel be not blamed.

(2) *Activity in the Church of God.* Great attachment to Zion — consecration of time, talents, and substance, and ardent prayer for its prosperity.

(3) An inward, mental, and habitual *resignation of the world* as a portion, and the choice of a heavenly one in its stead. Not retiring from the world, or despising its providential blessings; but withdrawing the heart from it, and setting the affections on things above; having the treasure and the object of supreme choice there. "Whom have I in heaven?" etc.

(4) *Expecting and waiting for the coming of Christ.* In this frame of mind was the Apostle Paul, when he longed to "depart and be with Christ." So was good old Simeon, "Lord, now lettest thou thy servant," etc. In this frame of mind was Stephen the proto-martyr, when

he said, "Behold, I see the heavens opened, and the Son of man standing on the right hand of God." True believers can say, "I am now ready to be offered," etc. They "look" daily "for that blessed hope," etc.

> O happy servant he,
> In such a posture found,
> He shall his Lord with rapture see,
> And be with honour crowned.

XLIV.—PAUL'S CONSTANCY.

"There came down from Judea a certain prophet, named Agabus: and when he was come unto us, he took Paul's girdle, and bound his own hands and feet, and said, Thus saith the Holy Ghost; so shall the Jews at Jerusalem bind the man that owneth this girdle, shall deliver him into the hands of the Gentiles. And when we heard these things, both we and they of that place, besought him not to go up to Jerusalem. Then Paul answered, What mean ye to weep, and to break my heart? For I am ready not to be bound only, but also to die at Jerusalem for the name of the Lord Jesus."—ACTS xxi. 10—14.

It is in part the design of the sacred scriptures, to furnish us with great examples, in which we may see the doctrine they teach reduced to practice, and see it in all its life and power.

In Paul we have an instance of the wonderful efficacy of Divine grace. What a change is here, from what he once was! the poor empty Pharisee and violent persecutor is now prepared to suffer martyrdom.

He was also in this an eminent follower of Christ: he met his death with constancy, and would not be turned aside from the path of duty. He went up to Jerusalem with his heart full of tenderness, but nothing could shake his resolution.

I. THE CONSTANCY OF PAUL.

1. *Its warrant* or *authority.* We might think he was rash: his friends thought so.—— In common cases we are not to run in the way of persecution, nor to go out of our way to meet the cross. But Paul was in the way of Divine appointment, and had only to take up his cross as Christ had done before him. He had a special direction to go up to Jerusalem, though he was given to expect persecution as the consequence. Acts xix. 21.—— He knew not every particular, except that he should see the churches in Asia no more: ch. xx. 25.—— We must keep the path of duty, whatever be the consequences.

2. *The trial of his constancy.* Two things were specially adapted to shake his constancy. (1) The *warning was Divine.* Agabus, however, did not pretend to command him in the name of the Lord not to go up to Jerusalem; though if he had, Paul would not have turned aside, as the old prophet did. 1 Kings xviii.——(2) *The tender affection of his friends.* He could stand threatenings and dangers, but tears and tenderness went to "break his heart."—— These also proceeded from love to him, and to the churches of Christ: but he is firm amidst it all.

3. *The strength of his constancy.* They told him of bonds: he was ready for more than bonds; he was prepared to "die." —— Liberty is sweet; life is still more so; but Christ is dearer than all. —— The motive urged by his friends was touching; the good of the churches was still more so. This consideration once caused him to be in a strait, whether to abide, or depart, and be with Jesus: but here the will of God is plain, and therefore he is ready. Nor was this a sudden flash of zeal: it continued to the end of life. 2 Tim. iv. 6.

4. *The motive which induced it.* The love of Jesus, "the name of the Lord Jesus:" this is true religion. —— It is difficult to conceive of the ideas which occupied his mind, while uttering these words: his heart is full, as the words themselves imply.——No doubt he would think of the Lord Jesus once 'going up to Jerusalem' for him: 'he loved me, and gave himself for me.' He had also himself been a persecutor of that 'name,' and had been silenced by an overwhelming question: 'Why persecutest thou me?' Christ had now honoured him as the almoner of his riches among the Gentiles: 'Unto me is this grace given.'——He had witnessed the blessed efficacy of that name, in saving thousands and thousands of sinners. —— Hence his resolution to die proclaiming it.

5. *The amiable submission of his friends.* They did not know at first what the will of the Lord was in this matter: but when this was declared, they gave him up, saying, 'The will of the Lord be done.'—— This also is true religion: it is like Christ himself. "Not my will, but thine be done."

IMPROVEMENT.

1. Let us be thankful for *the protection we enjoy*, and that we are shielded from the violence of wicked and unreasonable men. Our table is spread in the sight of all our enemies: we can go and come, without fear of persecution and of martyrdom. Ps. xvi. 5, 6.

2. Learn the importance of being *prepared for self-denial.* Having been accustomed to peace and safety, we have as it were forgotten some of the first principles of the gospel: 'deny thyself, and take up thy cross, and follow me.' Matt. xix. 29; 1 Cor. xv. 30, 31. —— Yet we are as soldiers, in a state of requisition, and ought to be prepared for action. Eph. vi. 14.

Is it not for want of entering more fully into the spirit of the gospel, that Christ is denied in far less trials than those which primitive believers had to endure; and that religion is often made to give place to the fear of man, the love of the world, and the love of ease.

3. See wherein the very *essence of Christianity* consists; it is doing what we do in religion "*for the name of the Lord Jesus.*" It is for him to be dearer to us than liberty or life itself. Acts xx. 24; Phil, iii. 8.

A. FULLER.

XLV.—THE WORK OF THE LORD.

"Therefore, my beloved brethren, be ye steadfast, unmovable, always abounding in the work of the Lord, forasmuch as ye know that your labour is not in vain in the Lord."—Cor. xv. 58.

THIS verse stands in connection with one of the most solemn portions of holy writ,—the resurrection of the body, and the eternal happiness of the righteous. We are standing before the events of the last day; we behold the great white throne; the judgment is set, and the books are open; creation vanishes; the sun is turned into darkness; the moon disappears; stars fall; the firmament is folded up; the archangel sounds; the trump of God is heard; the gates of Hades are opened; the graves yield up their dead; the righteous stand forth. To many of you I use the exhortation of the text.

I. THE NATURE OF THE WORK IS DEFINED. "The work of the Lord." This gives us two views of religion. It is

1. *Practical.* It is "labour." What has man to do? The cultivation of his personal piety. To work out your own salvation. To make your calling and election sure. The Christian is to be occupied every moment. He is never to stand still. Doctrine is valueless unless it be practical. What is repentance? I see it in the gushing tear. What is faith? Do not give me fifty axioms about it; I see it in the rising soul of the struggling penitent. What is love? The fervour of sanctified affections. What is the character of religion? Vitality. Again, the Christian is described as a labourer, a candidate for a crown, a soldier. Not every one that saith unto me, Lord, Lord.

2. *Evangelical.* "Work in the Lord." Man, of himself, is incapable of pleasing God. Regeneration is the work of the Lord. If any man be in Christ, he is a new creature. Christ is the life of all his obedience, desire, sympathy, love, exertions, conversation. He lives and labours in the Lord. Through Christ, all becomes acceptable to God.

II. THE MANNER IN WHICH IT IS TO BE PERFORMED.

1. *Stability of principle.* Instability will spoil the finest plan; will ruin a man's business. Those, in religion, who trust to temporary excitement, will do but little. Christians are temples; they are rooted and grounded. We are to increase in knowledge, and grow in grace, be much in private prayer and meditation.

2. *Unmovable.* Many have gone back to perdition. Your adversary goeth about like a roaring lion. You are not yet in heaven; are called to suffer; have numerous enemies; the frowns and smiles of the world. Many have fallen asleep on enchanted ground. Paul said, "I keep my body under;" again, "Neither count I my life dear unto me."

3. *Abounding fruitfulness.* We are not to go to a point and then stop. We must live entirely and constantly to God.

III. THE CERTAINTY OF SUCCESS IS DECLARED. "Your labour is not in vain."

1. *In reference to yourselves:* God is not unrighteous to forget your work of faith and labour of love. It is not necessary we should live in doubt. The plea of modesty is not good. You must cast yourself on the atonement. You need not wait for this knowledge until the morning of the resurrection. Now consecrate your all to the Lord. You will soon have to leave this vile body, and you shall have a glorious body.

2. *In its spiritual and individual objects.* The Christian is solicitous that his holy life should recommend religion, and by this he may bring many souls to glory. Tract distributors, missionary collectors, Sunday-school teachers, your labours shall not be in vain in the Lord.

THEOPHILUS LESSEY.

XLVI.—SEEKING GOD.

"O God, thou art my God; early will I seek thee."— Ps. lxiii. 1.

I. THE PRIVILEGE OF A GOOD MAN.
1. God is his Father.——2. Defender.——3. Counsellor.——4. Comforter.

II. THE RESOLUTION OF A GOOD MAN.
1. What is it to seek God?
2. Where is God to be sought? In his word, ordinances, by prayer, reading.
3. When is God to be sought? Early in life, early in the morning.
4. Why is God to be sought? He is lovely, and makes happy.

ALEXANDER FLETCHER.

XLVII.—CHRISTIANS THE GLORY AND JOY OF FAITHFUL MINISTERS.

"For ye are our glory and joy."— 1 THESS. ii. 20.

HERE is Paul rejoicing over his Thessalonian converts—In improving this circumstance,

I. Let us inquire into *the character of those who become the joy of faithful ministers.* Certainly, not all who hear the word are of this description. Too many are like Isaiah's hearers, over whom we have cause to lament and exclaim, "Who hath believed our report; and to whom is the arm of the Lord revealed!" Alas! to such we are made "a savour of death unto death, and must appear as swift witnesses against them another day." O that hearers of the gospel would consider this!

But the glory and joy of faithful ministers is derived,

(1) *From such as receive the truth in the love of it;* even as the Thessalonians, who "received it, not as the word of men, but (as it is in truth) the word of God, which effectually worketh in them that believe."

(2) Such characters give joy to their ministers, in proportion as they discover a temper of heart corresponding with the Gospel — when they see grace reigning in their conduct — fervent attachment to God and his cause — weanedness from the world — longing after spiritual enjoyments, and "waiting for his Son from heaven, even Jesus, who delivereth us from the wrath to come;"—"for now we live (saith the apostle,) if ye stand fast in the Lord."

(3) Those who grow in grace, as well as continue steadfast, are also the joy of faithful ministers. When benevolence towards men accompanies love to God — when Christians add to their faith, virtue, knowledge, godliness, brotherly kindness, charity — when these things are. in them, and abound, then do faithful ministers glory in the success of their labours.

II. Let us inquire WHY *it is faithful ministers rejoice in such persons?* It is

(1) *Because from their conversion they derive a proof of their own fidelity.* It is true, indeed, that usefulness in the conversion of sinners will afford no proof of personal religion in the preacher: God may honour his own truth, while he despises the instruments; yet it is an evidence that what they have delivered is substantially the truth of God. For it is the gospel only that can be effectual to this purpose: — "Ye therefore are our epistle, seen and read of all men."

(2) *In them the great object of all ministerial prayers and labours are accomplished.* The daily prayer of a faithful minister will be the success of his labours—more will he rejoice in this, than the miser in the increase of his wealth; and nothing short of this will satisfy him.

(3) *Hereby Christ is glorified.* The minister of Jesus will often remember how much his heart was set on the salvation of sinners — the sufferings he endured for their sake — and that all the reward he desired was to have them given to him "for an inheritance:" and he cannot but rejoice to see this blessed end accomplished.

(4) *The conversion of sinners secures their eternal interests.* What a source of pleasure doth it afford to view that event in connection with an eternal world! — to think what a portion of bliss that soul is to enjoy; and how unutterable that misery from which he is now rescued! "He who converteth a sinner from the error of his way, shall save a soul from death, and hide a multitude of sins."

(5) *In their conversion is seen the medium of incalculable good to others.* Of all such the Lord in effect says, as he said of Abraham, "I will bless thee, and thou shalt be a blessing." Who can tell what blessed effects may follow upon the conversion of one sinner to God! It is like "a

handful of corn in the earth upon the top of the mountains, the fruit of which shall shake like Lebanon."

(6) *Such shall be the companions of their glory and joy in the world to come.*—" We are your rejoicing, even as ye also are ours, in the day of our Lord Jesus." Faithful ministers will rejoice in delivering up their charge into the hands of their divine Lord; while believers are "presented before the presence of his glory, with exceeding joy."

S. PEARCE.

XLVIII.—SALVATION BY GRACE.

"Not by works of righteousness which we have done, but according to his mercy he saved us, by the washing of regeneration, and renewing of the Holy Ghost."—TITUS iii. 5.

THE Gospel is founded in the depravity of human nature, men being through the fall depraved, "foolish and disobedient—hateful and hating one another," until "the kindness and love of God" our Saviour, revealed the method of salvation here described; and the only one adapted to fallen and depraved creatures, as we are — namely, "Not by works of righteousness which we have done, but according to his mercy," etc. In this method of salvation, we may observe that

I. It is "*Not* by works of righteousness that we have done." This appears from such considerations as the following:

(1.) Our best duties are attended with such defects as make them sinful in the sight of God, and consequently are sufficient to condemn, instead of justifying us.

(2.) The great design of God, in the gospel method of salvation, was to magnify his own grace, in the salvation of his people; which, "if it be of grace, is no more of works, otherwise grace is no more grace."

(3.) The word of God declares expressly and emphatically, that salvation is "*Not* of works, lest any man should boast," — and so in the text — "*Not* by works of righteousness which we have done."

It may be objected, If works save not, of what use are they?—Answer: They are necessary to evidence our faith in God, and love to the Saviour, and to stop the mouths of infidels and blasphemers.

II. It is "according to his *mercy* that he hath saved us."

His salvation is abundant — complete — unchangeable — everlasting. It is founded in God's eternal purpose — in the purchase of the blood of Christ, and applied and consummated by the work of the Holy Spirit — " He hath saved us."

III. It is by the washing of regeneration, and renewing of the Holy Ghost, whose office it is

1. To convince us of sin, and of our lost estate by nature.

2. To quicken and renew our minds, by nature "dead in trespasses and sins," by a communication of divine light and life — "purifying our hearts by faith which is in Christ Jesus."

IV. Faith in this point will give peace, if not triumph, in a dying hour: the more enlarged faith is, the greater will the triumph be.

Death is an untrodden path: none of us know what it is to die; but in proportion as we believe this truth of salvation by grace alone, so will be the comfort we shall enjoy. Under this conviction we may meet the last enemy with confidence, and, appealing to our divine Lord, say, with the Psalmist, "Lord, into thy hands I commit my spirit, for thou hast redeemed me, O Lord God of truth!"

XLIX. — THE TABERNACLE TYPICAL OF THE CHURCH MILITANT, AND THE CHURCH TRIUMPHANT.

Lord, who shall abide in thy tabernacle? who shall dwell in thy holy hill?" — Ps. xv. 1, 2, etc.

THIS Psalm begins with most important questions, and proceeds to give very definite answers to them. The whole affords a test by which we may ascertain our qualifications for a residence in the church here, and in the church of glory everlasting. Self-examination in the affairs of the immortal soul is necessary, and if properly exercised, will be productive of special advantage. —— The religion of the Bible is not mere faith; but faith whose reality is proved by a life of holiness and uprightness before men. "Lord, who shall abide," etc.

I. CONSIDER THE TABERNACLE TYPICAL OF THE CHURCH MILITANT.

The tabernacle was a kind of portable temple, designed for the presence of the king of Israel, Ex. xl. 34, 35, and properly regarded as the centre of the ceremonial worship. It was a movable structure, so contrived as to be readily taken to pieces and put together, for the purpose of carrying it from place to place during the forty years of migration in the wilderness. Though called a "tent," because it was covered with canopies of cloth and skin, yet it was constructed with extraordinary magnificence, and at a vast expense, suitable to the dignity of Jehovah, and corresponding also to the value of those spiritual and eternal blessings, of which it was designed to be a type or emblem. The value of the gold and silver used in the holy service amounted to £185,568, besides the great quantity of brass, wood, pillars, and utensils; also the jewels in the high-priest's ephod and breast-plate — all these must have amounted to a great sum. It is described Ex. xxv. xxvi. xxvii.

1. *The tabernacle was built according to Divine command.*

It was his will that it should be constructed. He condescended to adjust the minutest particulars, as the loops, the taches, and the pins. And all things were done according to the pattern which God showed Moses in the mount.

The church has been designed and established by Jehovah. Every thing connected with its existence, privileges, happiness, progress, and ultimate glory, has been arranged according to infinite wisdom and love. It is not of human invention. Not even an angel interfered. — The tabernacle was executed by the Holy Spirit, who rested on Bezaleel and Aholiab to fit them for this service. The same Spirit descended on the Apostles — the wise master-builders of the gospel church, and qualified them for the work. "Walk about Zion, then; tell the beautiful towers thereof; mark ye well her impregnable bulwarks; consider her palaces;" enter her gates, and behold her privileges and immunities, and mark the infinite love of her God; read her sublime destiny, even triumph over every foe, and glory everlasting in the temple of heaven, and remember that the splendid structure is the creature of God.

2. *The tabernacle was composed of different materials, joined together, making one tabernacle.* The materials were various, as gold, silver, wood, brass, scarlet, blue, and purple cloth, fine linen, etc. These arranged by the workmen's skill produced the beauty and perfection of the structure. 1 Cor. xii. 21.

So the church of God is composed of many members in one body. See Eph. ii. 21, 22; iv. 16. The church is composed of regenerated and believing men of various nations, of different stations, different natural tempers, unequal gifts and graces, and various ministers; yet "they are all one in Christ Jesus."

3. *The tabernacle was the place of religious service, and delightful privilege.* Here was the ark, the mercy-seat, the oracles, the golden pot of manna. Here the sacrifices were offered, and incense burned. God accepted the sacrifice, and manifested his glorious presence.

The church now enjoys the Divine presence, and God communes with them from off the mercy-sent. In his power the great sacrifice is constantly exhibited. Its precious merits, its sovereign efficacy, are realized by the members of Zion. God opens the windows of heaven, and showers down all spiritual blessings upon his people in heavenly places in Christ Jesus. How sweet is the word! How delightful is praise! How precious is prayer! — The tabernacle was anointed with oil when Moses consecrated it; and the church, too, has an unction from the Holy One.

4. *The tabernacle, as previously stated, was of great cost and value.* The most valuable materials were employed in its construction; gold, silver, precious stones, and the richest embroidery.

The church of Christ, the King's daughter, is all glorious within. Believers are "redeemed with the precious blood of Christ." They are precious in the estimation of the glorious Trinity, 2 Tim. ii. 20, 21. Called "the precious sons of Zion," Tim. iv. 2; "a chosen generation," 1 Sam. ii. 9.

5. *The tabernacle was duly protected.* It was covered with fine twined linen, and with many valuable skins, which rendered it impervious to the weather. And above all, it was ever under the Divine inspection and power.

By the Omnipotence and immutable righteousness of God the church is for ever secure. Who, what, can harm that church as enveloped in the Redeemer's righteousness? The fine linen of his obedience, the purple covering of his blood, is thrown over it for its everlasting triumph. "Who shall lay any thing to the charge of God's elect?" Rom. viii.; Ps. cxxi. 5—7.

6. *The tabernacle was a migratory temple*, carried about on the shoulders of the priests and Levites from place to place, and not remaining long in any place.

It is therefore a proper type of the church militant, wandering up and down, tossed by various storms and tempests; the saints having here no continuing city; each of them feeling and saying, "I am a stranger in the earth, — a pilgrim and sojourner, as all my fathers were."——

7. *The tabernacle existed but for a season;* it was ultimately superseded by the temple at Jerusalem.

O blessed thought! these frail and dying bodies in which we tabernacle on earth must soon be dissolved, when the ransomed spirit shall ascend to the celestial temple of God. 2 Cor. v. 1. And the church on earth, so frequently encompassed with clouds, and assailed with storms; so erring and imperfect, shall soon be consummated in glory; then the Redeemer shall present her to his Father as his chosen and precious bride, "not having spot or wrinkle, or any such thing." O death, thou art commissioned to draw aside the veil of mortality that interposes between the holy and most holy place — the church militant and the church triumphant! O judgment day! on thy auspicious morning, sin shall be destroyed, death shall be annihilated, Satan for ever restrained, and the church be arrayed in splendour and beauty correspondent to the character of the New Jerusalem.

8. *The tabernacle of Moses, and even the temple on Mount Zion, typified heaven.* Expressly taught by the Apostle, Heb. ix. 24. "The holy hill" refers to Mount Zion, where the temple was built. There the ark became stationary, and was no longer carried about from place to place.

It is the happiness of glorified saints that they dwell in that holy hill; they are at home there for ever.

"Was the tabernacle of Moses divided into several parts? We know him that said, 'In my Father's house are many mansions,' John xiv. 2. Was it a place of great splendour and magnificence even to the eye? 'Glorious things are spoken of thee, O city of the living God,' Ps.

lxxxvii. 3. Was it the dwelling of JEHOVAH, where the visible tokens of his presence were seen? In the heavenly mansions he unveils the brightness of his glory to all the saints around him? Did priests always officiate there? The saints in light are both kings and priests unto God. Were the curtains broidered with cherubims? In the celestial abodes are the innumerable company of angels. Was it replenished with all necessary furniture and provision? In heaven is the true light and the living bread, fulness of joy, and pleasures for evermore. Did the voice of praise continually resound in the earthly tabernacle? The eternal regions are for ever filled with loud hosannas. Were holiness and legal purity required in all who trod the venerable courts of God's ancient dwelling-place? Nothing that is defiled can enter the heavenly Jerusalem. And, lastly, as the tabernacle was sprinkled with blood by the Jewish high-priest, when he penetrated its innermost recesses once in the year, with the names of all the tribes engraven on his heart, even so the blood of Jesus Christ has consecrated that high and holy place, that sinners of the human kind might not be for ever excluded from dwelling in the beatific presence of JEHOVAH. When the everlasting gates of heaven were by sin barred for ever against us, the blood of Christ was the key that opened them again; and the believers in his atoning blood may enter into heaven itself, with greater boldness, than the high-priest when he went into the holiest of all; than the Levites, when they officiated in the holy place; or than the people, when they approached the outward court."

II. *Inquire who shall abide in the Tabernacle, etc.* "Lord, who shall abide in thy tabernacle?" etc.

As good Matthew Henry says, "Not *who* by name, for only the Lord knows who are his; but who by description. What kind of people are they whom thou wilt own, and crown with distinguishing and eternal favours? It is a great privilege to be a citizen of Zion, an unspeakable honour and advantage. But only few are thus privileged. The majority of men follow the course of this world. None are entitled to it by birth. It is in vain to say, "We have Abraham to our Father."—Again, all are not Israel who are called Israel—some abide for a time, but fail eventually. "They went out from us; but they were not of us," etc. 1 John ii. 19, 20.

They are really members of the church, and they are characterized

1. *By sincerity.* "Who speaketh the truth in his heart." Who really loves God and fears him; who possesses a principle of grace, and true faith, corresponding to the description, John i. 47; Gen. xvii. 1; 2 Cor. i. 12.

2. *By uprightness.* "He that walketh uprightly," v. 2. Honest in his dealings, etc., ever regarding the golden law of equity. Ps. cxix. 1, 6.

3. *By neighbourly respect.* "He backbiteth not with his tongue," v. 3. He is careful not to injure him by word or deed — says nothing that might injure him in his character, person, or property; he forges no calumny, he is author of no slander, and insinuates nothing injurious, Prov. xxv. 23; 1 Cor. xiii. 5.

4. *He estimates the characters of men* by the Scripture balance, and not according to worldly rules.

(1) He thinks no better of a man's wickedness, on account of his pomp and grandeur in the world. "In whose eyes," etc., v. 4.
(2) He thinks no worse of any man's piety, on account of his poverty, etc. "He honoureth them that fear the Lord," v. 4.
(3) He is faithful to all engagements, irrespective of any sacrifice it may involve. "He sweareth," etc., v. 4.
(4) He increaseth not his wealth by injustice—not by extortion—not by bribery, v. 5.

Now all this is the result of Divine operation, the fruit of regeneration and faith. These manifestations are not meritorious;

> For when his holiest works are done,
> His soul depends on grace alone;
> This is the man thy face shall see,
> And dwell for ever, Lord, with thee.

IMPROVEMENT.

Let the church be harmonious. The symmetry of the ancient tabernacle, the nice conjunction of its parts by mortises and bars, and of the curtains by loops and taches, was not more delightful than to see brethren dwell together in unity.—Be holy. The tabernacle had the holy place—the church is God's seat.—Anticipate the time when your tents shall be struck, and you shall march forward to possess the land.

L.—THE TRUTH IN JESUS.

"As the truth is in Jesus."—EPHES. iv. 21.

THE apostle is here cautioning the Ephesian Christians against licentiousness, either of doctrine or of practice, by stating the inconsistency of either with the truth as it is in Jesus. Let this truth be the subject of our present contemplations; and we may remark,

1. *This truth comes to us attested by very high authority;* the messenger of it is the Son of God, "the brightness of his glory, and the express image of his person;" who from eternity lay in the bosom of the Father, and in the fulness of time came into our world in his name, to reveal his will for our salvation.

2. "*The truth in Jesus*" *is all truth, and nothing but truth.* He laboured under no mistake, propagated no error, practised no disguise. "All the words of his mouth are in righteousness: there is nothing forward or perverse in them."

3. "*The truth in Jesus*" *is all interesting.* Much of what is propagated by men, though it may be truth, yet it may not materially affect our most important interests; it may be often matter of curiosity, rather than of utility. But Jesus did not come from heaven to earth to propagate matters of any trifling moment; miracles were not

wrought for the confirmation of what would only gratify an idle curiosity, or merely subserve the lesser interests of mankind.

4. "*The truth in Jesus*" *is complete, though it may seem to be comprehended within narrow bounds; yet, it contains the whole will of God for our salvation.* There is nothing that can contribute to our safety, peace, or happiness — to the duty we owe to God or man, but what is fully contained in it. Here every branch of truth and duty receives due attention; nothing is overlooked, nothing disproportionate. It is sufficient to "make the man of God perfect, thoroughly furnished unto all good works."

5. "*The truth in Jesus*" *is the most eminent and glorious in its nature.* It makes discoveries which the mind of man could never reach; "what eye hath not seen, nor ear heard, neither hath it entered into the heart of man to conceive." It brings to light "the deep things of God, even the hidden wisdom which God ordained before the foundation of the world; such wisdom, that in comparison with it, all the boasted wisdom of the world is but foolishness."

6. "*The truth in Jesus shines by its native splendour.*" It needs no borrowed ornaments; it admits of no human embellishments; its own excellence is sufficient to recommend it; like the lustre of gold, or the brilliancy of a diamond. Hence its great Author, and its most successful propagators, have not come "with enticing words of wisdom," but in "simplicity and godly sincerity, words which the Holy Ghost teacheth."

7. "*The truth in Jesus*" *is level to all capacities;* as it relates to matters of as great importance to the peasant, as to the prince, or the philosopher; so it expresses itself in a way as intelligible to the one as to the other. "The wayfaring man, though a fool, shall not err therein."

8. "*The truth in Jesus*" *is most powerful in its effects.* It sets the mind at liberty from the bondage of error, and of sin. "The truth shall make you free." — It sanctifies the heart: "sanctify them through thy truth—thy word is truth." — It reforms the life: "wherefore putting away lying, speak every man truth with his neighbour; for we are members one of another."

Thus excellent, thus important is "the truth in Jesus" — revealed in him — centering in him — and in him accomplished. Let us then love and reverence — cherish and practise — "the truth" as it is "in Jesus."

LI. — GRATITUDE FOR DIVINE MERCIES.

"What shall I render unto the Lord for all his benefits towards me? I will take the cup of salvation, and call upon the name of the Lord. I will pay my vows unto the Lord now in the presence of all his people." — Ps. cxvi. 12—14.

IT is a happy effect when the numerous mercies we enjoy make a due impression on our minds. This was the case with the Author of

GRATITUDE FOR DIVINE MERCIES. 333

the text, as this Psalm abundantly indicates.—Ingratitude is a foul and hateful quality. It springs from an ignorant, unreflecting, and unfeeling mind. To every intelligent Christian the ingrate is an object of pity.—The Psalmist had experienced great deliverances, and therefore he exclaimed, "What shall I render," etc. Consider,

I. THE BENEFITS WHICH GOD BESTOWS.

The Psalmist speaks particularly of those benefits which he had received; "his benefits towards me." Many of these are frequently enumerated in the Psalms: — "O, how great is thy goodness which thou hast laid up for them that fear thee," etc. Ps. xxxi. 19—24. And so if we look back, we shall find that many benefits have been bestowed upon us — so many that they cannot be enumerated.

Christians should do with their mercies as botanists do with their flowers — class them; or as astronomers do with the stars — form them into constellations. Take a retrospect of mercies temporal and spiritual, mercies public and private, mercies personal and relative. Think of continued mercies, restored mercies, and of preventing and delivering mercies. Fix your mind on particular instances — for instances affect much more powerfully than things in a mass. Do not overlook the circumstances which enhance the benefits you have received — such as are derived from their seasonableness, their utility, etc. Look at these benefits,

1. *In creation.* "His benefits towards me." Distinguished from the beasts that perish — possessed of reason and intellect — and of a soul capable of knowing and enjoying God and all his works, for ever — some have reason to be thankful on account of the comparative perfection of their physical powers — having the use of all their limbs, etc.

2. *Preservation.* "The eyes of all wait upon thee, and thou givest them their meat in due season." Ps. cxlv. 15. Thus God every moment preserves the lives of all.—He preserves from dangers seen and unseen. What would have been our state if God had not preserved us? He preserves from snares, temptations, and the evil designs of men. God is called "the preserver of men." Job vii. 20; Ps. xxxi. 23; xxxvii. 28; cxlv. 20; Lam. iii. 22.

3. *Deliverance.* When brought low he has raised up. "Many are the afflictions of the righteous, but the Lord delivereth him out of them all." When sickness has made you fear you were about to die, has he not led you back from the gates of the grave? From what low and obscure beginnings has he raised some in the course of his wonderworking providence, and how well does it become them to compare their present state with their former one.

The Lord hath favoured many with health and gratifications suitable to their natures — with friends and relatives, and many earthly blessings.

4. *The Provisions of Divine Grace.* O what benefits are here! A Saviour for lost sinners — salvation from everlasting wrath — pardon for every sin — purity for all defilement — adoption with all its privileges — the promises with all their sweetness — the Spirit with all its power — and the hope of everlasting life. Who can estimate these benefits?

It is a benefit to know Christ — to have been enlightened and influenced to receive him — to be resting on him as the basis of faith and hope — to feel him precious. Ah! believer, once you knew him not — once you despised him! Eph. ii. 19.

II. THE INFLUENCE WHICH THESE BENEFITS SHOULD HAVE. "What shall I render," etc.

It is evident that the Psalmist recalled the Divine benefits — marked how they had crowned his existence in every stage. He reflected upon them — their richness, greatness, abundance, seasonableness, utility, and continuance. He reflected upon himself — his vast unworthiness to receive such benefits.

How much of our insensibility and ingratitude springs from inattention and the want of reflection! and of many persons it may be said, as of Israel, "Of the rock that begat thee thou art unmindful, and hast forgotten that God formed thee."

How anxious were ancient saints to keep God's benefits in constant remembrance! Let us imitate them. Thus "Samuel took a stone, and set it between Mizpeh and Shem, and called the name of it Ebenezer, saying, Hitherto hath the Lord helped us." And thus Joseph, by the very names of his children, would recall the wonders which the Lord had shown him. "Joseph called the name of the first-born Manasseh; for God, said he, hath made me forget all my toil, and all my Father's house. And the name of the second called he Ephraim; for God has caused me to be fruitful in the land of my affliction." And hence the command given to Ephraim, "Set thee up way-marks, make thee high heaps; set thine heart toward the highway, even the way which thou wentest; turn again, O virgin of Israel; turn again to these thy cities."

Observe the manner in which the Psalmist testified his gratitude:

1. *He regarded the Divine benefits as vast, innumerable, and unmerited.* "What shall I render unto the Lord?" Some render this verse thus: "All his benefits overcome me." I am so overwhelmed with his abundant goodness, that I am lost in wonder, and know not how to express my gratitude.

What shall I render? It is very little that we can render. We can render nothing as an equivalent — nothing meritorious. God is under no obligation to us. All his bounty is grace. — Yet he delights in the manifestation of a grateful heart; and who can be a Christian without it? It is his own declaration, "Whoso offereth praise glorifieth me."

2. *The Psalmist resolved to make the only return in his power, to acknowledge and declare before men the goodness of Jehovah,* ascribing all the glory where it is due. "I will take the cup of salvation," etc.

"I will call all my friends together, to rejoice with me; and taking the cup, which we call *the cup of deliverance*, (because when blessed and set apart, we are thus wont to commemorate the blessings we have received,) I will magnify the power, goodness, and faithfulness of God my Saviour before all the company; and then give it to them that they may praise his name together with me."—*Bp. Patrick.*

"It seems to have been customary among the Jews thus to take the cup of deliverance when celebrating their solemn feasts, as well as when offering sacrifices of thanksgivings for peculiar mercies; and it is thought that the Lord Jesus, complying with this custom at his last passover, thence took occasion to institute the Lord's Supper, which has ever since been to Christians "the cup of salvation," and a memorial of his immeasurable love in giving himself to death for their sins; an outward sign of their receiving him by faith as their salvation, and a grateful acknowledgment of the inestimable benefits of which they partake through his atoning sacrifice." — *Rev. Thomas Scott.*

"And call upon the name of the Lord;" that is, publish, or speak of the name of the Lord — his gracious nature, and the great things he hath done for me. See Ps. cxlv. 5; c. 4, 5.

3. *A resolution to fulfil all vows.* That is, the duties, sacrifices, and praises, which in the time of my distress I promised to render.

How many vows have we broken and forgot! In a time of extremity we made them. The extremity passed away; God interposed and delivered us — but what has become of our vows? The world has enticed us; the flesh has seduced us. Satan has ensnared us, and the vows so solemnly made have been neglected. Did we not call God to witness, that, if delivered, we would serve and glorify him?

Imitate then the conduct of the Psalmist, by paying your vows unto the Lord; — vows made when you first professed his name — vows made in affliction — in bereavement — under conviction of having sinned, etc.

The Psalmist said, "I will pay my vows unto the Lord now, in the presence of all his people." And why should any one be ashamed of publicly professing the service of the Lord? Regular and devout attention to God's service is an evidence of fidelity to our vows.

IMPROVEMENT.

1. Pray that you may ever have a grateful appreciation of God's mercies.—2. Testify your gratitude by consecrating yourselves to God's service.—3. How delightful will be the service of praise in heaven, when retrospectively we view God's mercies, and especially the riches of his grace through Christ, and in concert with all the heavenly hosts, crown the Redeemer Lord of all!

LII. — CHRIST THE FOUNDATION.

"For other foundation can no man lay, than that is laid, which is Jesus Christ."— 1 Cor. iii. 11.

It is not here alone, but in many other scriptures, both in the Old and New Testament, that our Lord Jesus Christ is held forth under the notion of a foundation. We shall

I. Show the *properties* of Christ as a foundation; what kind of a foundation he is.

1st. He is a *laid* foundation—"Behold I lay in Zion for a foundation a stone" (Isaiah xxviii. 16). "Behold I," *i. e.*, God the Father; one that knew well enough how to do it; a God of infinite wisdom and power. The Lord Jesus Christ did not take upon himself this honour of being a mediator; no, he was called to it, appointed of God for such a purpose; and this is our comfort and joy. He that could best tell what would best serve to satisfy his offended justice, pitched upon his own son for that purpose; this was the ransom he found for man (Job xxxiii. 24). "I have laid help upon one that is mighty; I have exalted one chosen out of the people" (Psalm lxxxix. 19).

2d. A *low* foundation—low laid; foundations are wont to be laid low; the lower the surer. So the Lord Jesus Christ, as a foundation, was laid very low, that he might be a meet foundation for us. He was "in the form of God, and thought it not robbery to be equal with God: but he made himself of no reputation, and took upon him the form of a servant, and was made in the likeness of man," etc. (Philip. ii. 6—9).

There were several steps of his humiliation:

1. Into the human nature. He condescended to be made a man; this was a long step downward. That the WORD should become flesh was more than if a star should turn into a cloud.

2. Into subjection under the law. "When the fulness of time was come, God sent forth his Son, made of a woman;" made *under the law* —the moral law; nay, the ceremonial law. He was to be circumcised —presented in the temple—redeemed and ransomed with two turtles— bound to go up to all the feasts.

3. Into poverty and persecution, contempt and contradiction; to be spurned and trampled on.

4. To death itself: "he became obedient unto death, even the death of the cross," a most painful, shameful, and ignominious death. This is called *a lifting up* (John xii. 32) but it was *humiliation*.

5. To the grave. When he was buried, he was, as other foundations, laid under the ground; and there was a necessity for all this; without it, there could have been no atonement, no reconciliation.

3d. Christ is a foundation of *stone* (Isaiah xxviii. 16). A stone is the fittest thing of all others to make foundations of, because it is hard and firm, and yet easily hewn. Now Jesus Christ is a stone—a foundation — a rock, 1 Cor. x. 4. Observe, again,

4th. He is a foundation *out of sight*. All foundations are so; we see the building, but we do not see the foundation: such a foundation is the Lord Jesus Christ. He is out of sight. Not below, as he once was, under the earth, but above, in glory. His *person* is out of sight, yet we love him (1 Peter i. 8.) His *presence* is invisible. He is with us every where, especially in his ordinances, but it is in an invisible way: we feel it, but we do not see it (Matthew xviii. 20, and xxviii. 20.) His *proceedings* are invisible. The proceedings of his grace within — the proceedings of his providence without (Psalm lxxvii. ult.)

5th. He is a *precious* foundation (Isaiah xxviii. 16). Though all stones in their places are useful, yet they are not all precious stones. Few buildings are built upon precious stones, but the Church of Christ is precious *in himself;* he is of great worth and value. "The chief among ten thousand, and altogether lovely." He is precious *in the account and esteem of his disciples.* To others he is a stone of stumbling, and a rock of offence; but unto them which believe he is precious (1 Peter ii. 7). Moreover,

6th. He is a *permanent* foundation (Isaiah xxvi. 4). He is the Rock of ages, from everlasting to everlasting. The saints have been building on him from the beginning, and will build on him to the end of time. He is "the same yesterday, to-day, and for ever." His righteousness is everlasting; his promises are unchangeable.

7th. He is an *elect* or *chosen* foundation (Isaiah xxviii. 16), chosen of God, and precious — " Behold my servant, whom I have chosen, mine elect, in whom my soul is well pleased" (Isaiah xlii. 1). Once more,

8th. He is an *experienced* or *tried* foundation. He was tried by *God*, who laid upon him the iniquities of us all. He was tried by *men* and *devils*, who did their best against him, but all to no purpose. He has been tried by the *saints*, who have had occasion to make use of him, and he has never failed them.

II. What is *our duty* in reference to this foundation? It is our duty,

1st. To *believe all this concerning him.* That God hath laid him purposely for a foundation; anointed and appointed him to be a Prince and a Saviour, and given him to the world, that "whosoever believeth in him, might not perish, but have everlasting life."

2d. To *behold and see our need of him.* There is no rearing a building without a foundation. We have each of us a building to rear, and what foundation have we? None in ourselves—no righteousness of our own to commend us to God—no strength or ability to anything that is good.

3d. To *renounce all other foundations.* They are but sand; and he that builds on the sand, his building will fall (Matthew vii. 24, *ad finem*).

4th. To *repair* to him. In the way of faithful and fervent prayer, tell him you are sensible of your need of him, and that you are undone without him.

5th. To *build* upon him: in the great business of *justification;* to rest our souls by faith upon his meritorious righteousness. None but Christ! None but Christ! In all our *perils* and *dangers*, personal or public, we should fly to him, trust in him, rely upon him: "Faithful is he that hath promised" (Ps. xlvi. 1, and lxii. 1, 2); and it is our duty,

6th. To *beware what we build* upon this foundation, in *opinion* and in *practice* (1 Cor. iii. 12, 13, 14, 15). If we build loose, careless walking, our hopes built, will be accordingly wood, hay, stubble, etc.

REV. MATTHEW HENRY.

LIII.—THE CHIEF CORNER STONE.

"Jesus saith unto them, Did ye never read in the Scriptures, The stone which the builders rejected, the same is become the head of the corner: this is the Lord's doing, and it is marvellous in our eyes? Therefore I say unto you, The kingdom of God shall be taken from you, and given to a nation bringing forth the fruits thereof. And whosoever shall fall on this stone, shall be broken: but on whomsoever it shall fall, it will grind him to powder. And when the chief priests and Pharisees had heard his parables, they perceived that he spake of them. But when they sought to lay hands on him, they feared the multitude, because they took him for a prophet."—MATT. xxi. 42—46.

"HE will miserably destroy these wicked men, and will let his vineyard unto other husbandmen," are words which should sound like the loudest thunders in the ears of those who make the people, or the ministers of God, the objects of their malevolence. God will destroy them, if they die impenitent. Where will he destroy them? In hell; where the worm never dies, and where the fire is never quenched; in that devouring furnace which is infinitely more tremendous than the furnace of the enraged Nebuchadnezzar. In what manner will he destroy them? He will inflict upon them the punishment of loss, depriving them of every enjoyment; and he will inflict upon them the punishment of sense, which consists of torments visited upon the miserable sufferers by God, by devils, by men, and by their own consciences. May none of us ever be left to show those indignities either to the people, or the ministers of God, which fail not to produce inevitable judgments.

In the subject of this discourse, and in the preceding part of the chapter, it was the design of our Saviour to show the priests and elders their true state, and to expose the criminality of their hypocrisy. As husbandmen, it appears, that they exceeded in guilt all who preceded them. Those who went before them killed the servants of the householder; but the priests and elders were determined to outstrip their fathers in wickedness! they determined to destroy the son and heir. They laid the cope-stone upon the fabric of their iniquity and impiety; they said, "This is the heir, come let us kill him." And what they proposed, they soon after accomplished.

I. THE STONE, ver. 48.

1. *Christ is the stone.* The passage is a beautiful quotation taken from Psalm cxiii. Is the Church an edifice? Christ is the chief stone of the building, and is thus denominated to point out his stability and duration. He is called a *precious* stone, for he is adorned with matchless excellence; a *tried* stone, because his enemies have long found that they have been foiled in every attempt against him; and his friends, that they have been disappointed in no hope they have ever founded on him; an *elect* stone, because he is the Father's choice; a *living* stone, because he has all life in himself, and animates his beloved people with life that shall never die; a *stumbling* stone and rock of offence, because proud and conceited Jews scorned the idea of a suffering, degraded, and crucified Messiah;—and the *chief corner stone*, because he connects

every part of the spiritual building of the Church, and will most securely establish her in the enjoyment of all her privileges.

2. *The stone has been rejected.* Those who were professionally engaged in building the edifice of the Church, rejected the very corner stone, without which the Church could not possibly stand. The rejection of Christ began almost as soon as he was born, it continued through every stage of his life, and it reached its most dreadful height when he was cruelly murdered upon the tree. He is still rejected when his doctrines are not received, and when his laws are cast, like broken cords, far away. Alas! we are all chargeable with having rejected him. O Lord, prevent that any of us should die with so dreadful an accusation resting on our head.

3. *The stone has been exalted.* " The same is become head-stone of the corner." This does not imply that the time ever was, when he was not head-stone. It is an expression employed to denote his humiliation, followed by his exaltation. His glory was, for a period, concealed, but it now appears — what he has always been, is fully made known. He is now highly exalted, he has received a name, which is above the name of all potentates of the earth — a name which ensures the adoring reverence, and the prostrate homage of the innumerable millions who surround the heavenly throne. May God most mercifully grant, that HE who is highly and so deservedly exalted in heaven, may be exalted in our hearts, to fill that throne in our affections which none is entitled to fill but the Saviour of men!

The glorious elevation of this "stone, is the doing of the Lord." Man's work was the rejection of Christ; but the work of God is the exaltation of Christ. Man has unjustly dishonoured him; but God has justly glorified him. Because God has exalted him, he shall be universally adored: "every knee shall bow and every tongue shall confess that he is the Lord;" and he shall be eternally praised; "blessing, and honour, and glory be to him who sitteth upon the throne, and to the LAMB for ever and ever."

The rejection, and the glory of Christ will prove an endless source of wonder. The Church on earth shall wonder at it till the revolution of centuries shall terminate; and the Church triumphant in heaven shall wonder at it, during the rolling ages of eternal duration. Happy shall we be, if our believing wonder shall begin on earth! it will be a prelude of unfading joys awaiting us, where the interruptions of sin are never felt.

II. THE KINGDOM OF GOD, ver. 43.

1. *This kingdom is the Church.* The saints of God are the subjects of this kingdom; and they are chosen out of all nations, tongues, people, and languages. This kingdom is of great antiquity, ancient as the days of Adam. The plan of this kingdom is well contrived, being devised by the unerring and unfathomable wisdom of God. This kingdom has great privileges, exceeding all the kingdoms of the earth, even when they attained the zenith of the most enviable prosperity. This kingdom shall endure for ever. The monarchies of the world are destined to dissolution; but this kingdom shall for ever remain the admired object of the Divine protection and regard.

2. Christ told the priests and elders, *this kingdom should be taken from*

them. What was then predicted, is now accomplished. The calamity has visited the nation of the Jews. They are not only without king, and priest, and ephod, but they are excluded from the Church of God, and aliens to its exalted privileges.

3. *It was predicted that it should be given to another.* The Gentiles are the nation to whom it is given. They are invested with privileges from which they were excluded for thousands of years. The following animating prophecy has now, in some measure, received its fulfilment in the descendants of Japheth, (Isaiah lx. 3.) "And the Gentiles shall come to thy light, and kings to the brightness of thy rising." The promise that this nation should bring forth the fruits thereof, has been in part fulfilled. The first-fruits were collected on the day of Pentecost, and fruit has been collecting ever since, from many of the Gentile nations.

III. THE MISERY OF CHRIST'S ENEMIES, ver. 44.

1. *The situation of those who shall fall on the stone:* they shall be broken. To fall on the stone is to stumble at the humiliation, the sufferings, and the cross of Christ. They are broken, that is, injured, who are thus offended.

2. *The situation of those on whom the stone shall fall:* "it will grind them to powder." This intimates the dreadful doom of those who sin against Christ in his exaltation. How shall persecuting magistrates, and prelates, and kings be able to stand in the judgment, when they shall be summoned to appear before his dread and glorious presence! In vain shall they supplicate rocks and mountains to fall on them, and hide them from the face of the Judge.

IV. THE MALEVOLENCE OF CHRIST'S ADVERSARIES, ver. 45, 46.

1. *They made a discovery that the word was directed to them.* It was applicable, and it was applied. It reached their conscience, but did not change their heart. It convinced them of their guilt, but it produced no compunctions of penitence. Instead of making the tears of repentance to flow, it made the fire of malevolence to flash from their eyes. May the word of God search us, and find us out: may it prove not the savour of death, but of life!

2. *The priests and elders attempted to destroy Christ.* They wished to murder him; but they were restrained. They wished to shed his blood; but his time was not yet come. What they could not then accomplish, they soon afterwards accomplished. It was not long ere they saw him suspended to an accursed tree. Holy Spirit! deliver us from enmity against God, and let divine love reign pre-eminently within us. AMEN.

A. F.

LIV.—MOSES A TYPE OF CHRIST.

"And I will raise them up a prophet from their brethren like unto me."—DEUT. xviii. 15.

Moses was the greatest legislator that ever appeared on earth. This will appear to be the case, if we consider his natural gifts, his personal accomplishments, his numerous attainments, his extensive learning, his persuasive wisdom, his unequalled meekness, his exemplary piety, or the inimitable laws which he was employed to draw up for the regulation of the civil and religious polity of the most wonderful nation that ever appeared on earth. It is to be lamented, that men, from whom better things might have been expected, have under-rated the great personages whose histories are recorded upon the sacred pages of Divine truth, and that they have much over-rated those eminent heathen sages, whose names shed lustre upon the pages of profane history. We may safely compare the greatest men and legislators of antiquity with Moses, and we shall instantly feel the irresistible superiority of the latter beyond the former. Much we have heard of LYCURGUS the lawgiver of the Spartans, and much we may admire the patriotism and wisdom of that man, who devoted all he WAS, and HAD, and DID, to render his country wise, and great, and happy. But the sequel of the discourse will testify how much the great virtues and excellence of the Spartan philosopher are exceeded by the divine graces which adorned the character of Moses, and which have deservedly given him the loftiest rank among the sons of men. Our attention will not be wholly occupied in elucidating the wonderful lineaments in the life of Moses;— a greater than Moses is here.

How was Moses typical of Christ? He was typical in his birth, his offices, and his death.

I. HIS BIRTH.

1. Moses was born of parents in mean estate. The great incarnate Saviour, who is the Legislator of the universe, was born of a mean woman, in a stable, and laid in a manger. So poor were Joseph and Mary that they could only afford to present for him, agreeably to the usages of the Jewish law, two turtle doves and two young pigeons.

2. There was great cruelty manifested at the birth of Moses. The king commanded all the male children of Israel to be put to death. There was great cruelty at the birth of Christ; for Herod the king commanded all the children of Bethlehem, from two years and under, to be slain. Then was fulfilled the prophecy, "Rachel weeping for her children, and would not be comforted, because they are not."

3. Moses was persecuted at his birth, and wonderfully preserved. How remarkably and successfully the ingenuity and care of his mother were employed for the preservation of his life! Christ was no sooner born, than he was persecuted; yea, as soon as born, an envious and impious monarch sought his life. Joseph and Mary, with great anxiety, fled with the young child to Egypt, and there remained till the monster who sought his life was dead.

II. THE OFFICES OF MOSES.

1. Moses was a deliverer. He was born to be a deliverer. Christ was born to be the deliverer of millions of the human race. For this purpose he was born, and for this end he came into the world. Moses delivered from the prince of Egypt: but Christ delivered from the prince of devils. Moses delivered by means of the blood of a passover-lamb: but Christ delivered by his own blood. Moses delivered the bodies of men by a rod: Christ delivers the souls of men by the Gospel, which is the rod of his strength.

2. Moses was a mediator. He mediated when Israel fought with Amalek, and succeeded in obtaining for them a complete victory:— Christ continues to intercede for his people while they are contending on earth with spiritual Amalekites, and he will succeed in gaining for them by his prayers a glorious triumph over all their foes. Moses mediated at the giving of the law: and Christ stands betwixt the curses of a fiery law and his beloved people. Moses, as a mediator, delivered the law: but Christ as a mediator fulfilled the law. Moses quaked at the giving of the law: Christ, when enduring the curses of the law, was so sorrowful, that his sweat was like great drops of blood falling to the ground. When the children of Israel offended God by the sin of the golden calf, Moses offered to die for them:—but Christ did more than offer to die for the sins of men—he actually laid down his precious life.

3. Moses was a lawgiver. Deut. xxxiii. 4, 5. "Moses commanded us a law, the inheritance of the God of Jacob, and he was king in Jeshurun." Of Christ we may exclaim with far greater propriety, "The Lord is our Judge, the Lord is our Lawgiver, he will save us." There is a great difference betwixt the law delivered by Moses, and by Christ. Moses delivered the law of carnal ordinances—Christ the law of spiritual institutions—Moses the law of works—but Christ the law of faith—Moses, laws which are now repealed—but Christ laws which will last for ever—Moses laws terrible for their denunciations of wrath, but Christ laws delightful for their proclamations of mercy.

4. Moses was a prophet. "There arose no prophet since in Israel like unto Moses, to whom the Lord spake face to face." Christ is a prophet of more exalted eminence. As mediator he fills the loftiest throne in heaven; and in his humanity he is taken into the closest union with the Divine Person. Moses was raised up from his brethren, so was Christ—"he took upon him the nature of the seed of Abraham." Moses was remarkable for his meekness: Christ was meek and lowly of heart. The meekness of Moses once failed him; but the meekness of Christ never forsook him. The face of Moses shone: see how Christ shone with glory on Mount Tabor! Moses covered his face with a veil: the glory of Christ for thirty-three years was concealed under the veil of his humbled humanity. Moses had a near and close view of the Divinity: but it is said of Christ, "No man hath seen God at any time, the only begotten Son, who is in the bosom of the Father, he hath declared him." Moses was remarkable for his fidelity;—he "was faithful as a servant: but Christ as a Son." Moses met with great opposition in the exercise of his office: Christ met with infinitely more. One billow of suffering after another, rolled against him without intermission, from the commencement till the close of his ministry. Moses,

by the performance of the most noted miracles, confirmed the authenticity of his call to the office he so long and so honourably sustained. It was said of these miracles, "It was never so seen in Israel;" There was a transcendent superiority in the miracles of Christ. Moses wrought miracles in the name, and by the power of another: Christ wrought miracles in his own name, and by his own power. The miracles of Moses were generally demonstrations of justice, calculated to excite terror: the miracles of Christ were, almost in every instance, manifestations of mercy, calculated to excite joy.

III. THE DEATH OF MOSES.

1. Moses died willingly, and meekly surrendered his soul on Mount Nebo. Christ died willingly. Legions of demons could never have taken away his life unless he had willingly surrendered it. His invaluable life was the free-will offering of his loving heart. Oh! how meekly he delivered up his soul to his Father on the top of Mount Calvary.

2. Moses rose from the dead. This appears from his being present in bodily form with the Redeemer on the mount of transfiguration. Christ rose from the dead as the first-fruits of them who sleep. Then was fulfilled that saying, "O death! I will be thy plagues; O grave! I will be thy destruction!"

3. Moses entered heaven. After a life of great suffering, great patience, and activity, he was admitted to the celestial paradise, though shut out from the terrestrial Canaan. Our glorious Redeemer "has ascended up on high, he has led captivity captive, he has received gifts for men." The most exalted throne of heaven is his,—principalities and powers in the heavenly places, bow before him in adoring reverence.

May I now ask — Does this blessed king of unequalled excellence reign in your hearts? If he does, you are the heirs of heaven; if he does not, you are the heirs of hell; if he does you have within you the vitals of unceasing joy; but if not, the forebodings of eternal woe. Let all of us unite in presenting before the throne of him in whom unbounded mercy presides, the following petition: — "Enter into our souls, thou King of glory, and by the influences of thy promised Spirit exercise over us the authority of thy peaceful and everlasting dominion."

A. F.

LIV.—HEAVENLY PURITY.

"They are without fault before the throne of God."—REV. xiv. 5.

WHAT an amazing contrast betwixt heaven and earth!—yonder is the region of light and beauty—here is the abode of sin, darkness, and woe. Yonder the inhabitants are pure, like God, "without fault" before his throne of inconceivable splendour—but here the heart is steeped in iniquity, and its thoughts and imaginations are only evil, and that continually.

The design of this chapter, especially the former part of it, was evidently to comfort all the children of God in times of tribulation. Those living in the time of the apostle were suffering persecution, and, in the previous chapters, he had described more fearful trials yet to come on the church. In these trials, therefore, present and prospective, the apostle directs their thoughts to the final triumph of the redeemed — that glorious state in heaven where all persecution shall cease, and where all the ransomed ones shall stand before the throne. What could be better fitted than this view to sustain the souls of the persecuted and the sorrowful? And how often since, in the history of the church — in the dark times of religious declension and of persecution, has there been cause to seek consolation in this bright view of heaven! How often in the life of each believer, when sorrows come upon him like a flood, and earthly consolation is gone, is there cause to look to that blessed world where all the redeemed shall stand before God, and all tears be wiped away, and the soul made happy for ever.

I. THE CHARACTER WHICH THE REDEEMED SUSTAINED ON EARTH, according to the description in the context.

Who are the persons "without fault before the throne of God"? First they are spoken of as the "hundred and forty-four thousand." v. I and 3.* These are evidently the same persons that were seen in the vision recorded in ch. vii. 3—8, and the representation is made for the same purpose — to sustain the church in trial, with the certainty of its future glory.

In language so figurative and symbolical as this, it could not be maintained that this proves that the same definite number would be taken from each denomination of Christians. Perhaps all that *can be* fairly inferred is, that there would be no partiality or preference for one more than another; that there would be no favoritism on account of the tribe or denomination to which any one belonged; but that the seal would be impressed on all, of any denomination, who had the true spirit of religion. No one would receive the token of the Divine favour *because* he was of the tribe of Judah or Reuben; no one *because* he belonged to any particular denomination of Christians. Large numbers from every branch of the church would be sealed; none would be sealed because he belonged to one form of external organization rather than to another; none would be excluded because he belonged to any one tribe, if he possessed the spirit and manifested the conduct of a servant of God.

The hundred and forty-four thousand is an indefinite number, and in all probability refers to the first converts to Christianity, the certain pledge and earnest of a still greater harvest. Hence they are called "*the* first-fruits unto God and to the Lamb." "After this I beheld, and, lo, a great multitude, which no man could number, of all nations, and kindreds, and people, and tongues, stood before the throne," etc. A vast host burst upon the view; *a great multitude*, instead of the comparatively few who were sealed. The number to be ultimately saved

---

* Representing those who were converted to Christianity from among the Jews.— *Dr. Adam Clark*.

by the gospel appeared so great that no one could count them; it was a number beyond all power of computation. Though great numbers will be lost, yet the triumphs of the gospel will increase, and piety will be as prevalent as sin has been, and the number of the saved will surpass all who have been lost in past periods, beyond any power of computation. God has promised to reward Christ, and the innumerable multitudes of converts will be his rich reward.

Observe then, that those who appear faultless before the throne of God,

1. *Have been redeemed*, v. 3. Enlightened by God's Spirit and Word to perceive and feel themselves as lost transgressors. Redeemed from the curse of the law — from its condemning and fear-producing power — from guilt — from sin's dominion. Redeemed from the power of Satan and the world. Redeemed by the precious blood of Christ, Gal. iii. 13; Eph. i. 7; Col. i. 14; 1 Pet. i. 18, 19; ii. 24.

2. *They boldly professed Christ;* "having the Father's name written in their foreheads," in opposition to the mark of the beast mentioned in the foregoing chapter, and in allusion to a custom among men who put their marks upon their goods, especially upon silver or golden vessels. The mark upon their foreheads denotes, (1) The precious esteem which God has for his people; and (2) Their open avowal of him as their Lord and Master, and their faithful adherence to his service. "They follow the Lamb whithersoever he goeth," v. 4. They are his disciples; they imitate his example; they obey his instructions; they make him their counsellor and guide; they love and defend his cause, and are not ashamed of it under any circumstances. Wherever the Lamb leads them they go. Be it into trouble, obloquy, and persecution; be it in Christian or Heathen lands; be it in pleasant paths, or in roads rough and difficult, they submit wholly to his guidance, and continue steadfast in his cause.

3. *They were distinguished by purity.* See v. 4. "Being born again, they had their fruit unto holiness, and the end everlasting life." The word "virgin" is applicable to male as well as female; and, morally, it implies freedom from licenciousness. Those now in heaven were distinguished by chastity. They were chaste as it regards the doctrines and precepts of Christ; not departing from them, and espousing those of human invention.

4. *They were sincere.* "And in their mouth was found no guile." They were Israelites indeed. Not mere professors, but possessors of the grace of God.

Such were the characteristics of the redeemed when in this world. And let it not be forgotten that redeeming love must be enjoyed here before we can unite in singing "the new song of redeeming love in heaven;" we must, in degree, have the spirit of heaven here, or we cannot enjoy heaven hereafter.

II. THE CHARACTER OF THE REDEEMED IN HEAVEN. "They are without fault before the throne"; that is, spotless, without blemish. 1 Pet. i. 19. Observe

1. This is not their state *by nature;* being in that state *filthy and unclean.* Rom. iii. 10, etc.; Tit. i. 15.

2. *They are not so by human effort.* In heaven they never cry, "salvation by man;" but "salvation to God and the Lamb."— Afflictions, persecutions, and martyrdom, endured in the cause of Christ, cannot purchase a position before God's throne. No physical laceration, no human ceremonial laver, no penance, no pilgrimage, etc., can render them "*without fault*" before God's throne. "These are they which came out of great tribulation," but tribulation has not been the lever to raise them to celestial glory: no, for "they washed their robes and made them white in the blood of the Lamb." Rev. vii. 14.

3. *They are without fault through the expiatory sacrifice of Christ.* This is the robe of righteousness which covers them — this is the fine linen of the saints, clean and white, Rev. xix. 7, 8. They were made white in the blood of the Lamb. The shedding of that blood appeased the Divine anger, satisfied the demands of Divine justice, and honoured the broken law, Rom. v. 6, 7, 8. —— Christ thus became "the new and living way" to heaven.

The frequent reference to the blood of the Lamb proves the reality of the atonement, by which the soul is saved. If Christ shed his blood merely as some men have done, if he died only as a martyr, what propriety would there have been in referring to *his* blood more than to the blood of any other martyr? And what influence could the blood of *any* martyr have in preparing the soul for heaven?

Thus the operations of Divine grace alone can make vile sinners *without fault* before the throne. It is the Redeemer's brood that makes them white—his Spirit that new-creates them, and gives them a relish, a nature, and organization for heaven. That they are without fault before the throne is evident from many considerations. The infinite purity of God, and of all the heavenly inhabitants, is frequently stated. The design of Christ's death was to redeem from all iniquity, and to present the church without spot and blemish before his Father, Eph. v. 27. He possesses Almighty power to keep his disciples from falling, and to present them faultless before the presence of his glory with exceeding joy. Jude 24. Holiness is the attribute possessed by all in heaven; and "without holiness no man shall see the Lord." Rev. xxi. 27.

4. Consider the happiness of such a state. They are "without fault." Then

(1) *They are for ever free from the physical effects of sin.* Sin has scathed and desolated this earth—it might have remained a paradise; but now "the whole creation groaneth and travaileth in pain together until now," Rom. viii. 22. How felicitous must be the New Jerusalem, where sin never can contaminate and destroy!

Sin has ruined the body—filled it with disease, and exposed it to death. But in heaven the body shall be *without fault.* for ever youthful and vigorous, and shall sicken and die no more. What a glorious thought!

(2) *They are for ever free from the moral effects of sin.* Temptations, falls, injurious treatment, the effects of evil passions, will not exist there.

(3) *No social evils can exist* where they are "without fault." What is this world but a disorganized family, where they often bite and de-

your one another? —— But before the throne every soul will be full of love and benevolence. They will *really* love as brethren. Hence there will be perfect harmony, and the most delightful companionship.

(4) *Perfect repose.* "They will rest from their labours." Rest from the burden of sin, from the sorrows of life, from conflict with foes, from gloomy apprehensions, from fear and despondency. Sin has been the cause of all these.

III. THE SCENE OF THIS PERFECT PURITY: "Before the throne of God."

The throne of God! No mind can conceive its glorious splendour; no human tongue can describe it. The thrones or seats where earthly monarchs sit are characterized by wealth and grandeur, being composed of silver, gold, and precious stones, etc., consequently their value is immense. These give but a faint idea of the throne of God and the Lamb.

To sit or stand before the throne, is to behold the Divine Majesty ——Isaiah saw the glory of the Lord, Isa. vi. He saw the likeness of a glorious person embosomed in Divine Majesty, surrounded and encompassed by transcendent light, and majesty, and beauty. The same Being had appeared nearly in the same form, in earlier times. Our first parents in the garden, Enoch, and Abraham, were permitted to behold the Divine glory; and of Moses it was said, "I will speak to him in no dark speeches, and the similitude of the Lord shall he behold;" and they who went up into the mountain "saw the God of Israel, and there was under his feet as it were a paved work of sapphire stone, and as it were the body of heaven in its clearness." Ezekiel beheld him in the same mode of manifestation; there were the great cherubic figures, the vast revolving wheels, and these sustaining a crystal expansion, a vast slab, as we should call it; and upon this a throne, and upon the throne the likeness of the appearance of a man in glory; and round about the throne there was a rainbow, in sight like unto an emerald. Read the overwhelming description, Ezek. i. 26, etc., and remember that splendid and glorious as it was, still it was only "the appearance of the likeness," a faint representation of the real thing. Daniel saw him also clothed in gold of Uphaz. The apostle John says, "His countenance was as the sun shineth in his strength," etc., Rev. i. 10—20.

To be before the Divine throne implies,

Assimilation to God. "Without fault;" as previously stated.

The Vision of God in all his majesty and glory. "They shall see his face;" "They shall see him as he is." 1 John iii. 2.

Intercourse with Deity. Communion with the King of kings — with the Lord of angels, the infinite Governor of the universe. To be before the throne implies familiarity.

To be a witness of all his operations throughout his boundless universe.

To praise and adore. This is the employ of the hundred and forty-four thousand, v. 2. The sound of praise was heard by John as the sound of the ocean, or of a mighty cataract; so loud that it could be heard from heaven to earth, for it was *as the voice of a great thunder.*

The singing of the "new song," the song of redeeming love in its glorious completion, was accompanied by *harpers, harping with their harps.* This image gives new beauty to the description. Though the sound was loud and swelling, yet it was like the sweetness of symphonious harps. The music of heaven, though elevated and joyous, is sweet and harmonious; and perhaps one of the best representations of heaven on earth is the effect produced on the soul by strains of sweet and solemn music.

What a vast company will heaven contain when time shall be no more, and the present dispensation shall be closed! Then shall the Redeemer gaze with ineffable delight upon the immense multitudes whom he has saved by his blood. They will be the trophies of his grace, and they shall praise him; yea, they shall all be harpers, harping with their harps in praise to the Lamb. O what will it be to hear the angels and archangels, the cherubim and seraphim, and the glorified saints, sing! This earth could not bear the loud sound, as the voice of many waters, as the loudest thunder, the voice of praise to the Saviour.

Once on a great musical occasion in Westminster Abbey, in the reign of George the Third, there was one stroke, a swell so deep and so amazing, that the building shook, and they were afraid of its repetition. But infinitely more sublime, harmonious, and enrapturing anthems are sung in heaven! When they laid that stone, that poor paltry stone, at the building of the second temple, there was shouting which filled all heaven again. But when Christ's great work is done, when all the myriads of the saints shall be gathered home, and all the unsinning creatures in the universe shall be gathered together to be the witnesses, they will raise such a chorus, they will hold such an anthem, as shall make the arches and the canopies of the universe to quiver again, as in sympathetic joy.

IMPROVEMENT.

1. The vanity of this world. How this view of heaven reproves us for setting our affections on earth! 2. Pray for more purity here as a preparation for a faultless state in heaven. 3. Anticipate a state of endless perfection.

LV.—IMPORTANT ADMONITION.

"O Jerusalem! wash thine heart from wickedness, that thou mayst be saved: how long shall thy vain thoughts lodge within thee?"—JER. iv. 14.

THERE are certain fundamental truths in religion, which cannot be too well understood, or too deeply felt. The depravity of human nature is one of these; and Dr. Owen well observes, that a defective sense of this, and of the evil of sin, lies at the root of all error. A proper conviction of sin destroys all idea of human merit, and leads us to prize the atonement of our Saviour. A sense of sin, and the necessity of reformation, are also essential to national repentance and reform, and are therefore urged upon the Jewish nation, to whom the text was principally addressed; in which we may observe—the pollution of man by sin—the cleansing here required, and its necessity to our salvation.

I. THE POLLUTION OF MAN'S HEART BY SIN. "Wash thine heart from wickedness."

The same prophet hath said in another place, "The heart is deceitful above all things, and desperately wicked." And our Lord expounds this, when he informs us, that "out of the heart proceed evil thoughts"—namely, "murders, adulteries, fornications, thefts, false witness, blasphemies." This is the corrupt fountain from which flow these evil streams, these vain and wicked thoughts and actions. Good men in all ages have felt and lamented this, and traced up their sin, like David, to this cause. "Behold! I was conceived in sin, and shapen in iniquity."

II. THE HEART MUST BE WASHED FROM WICKEDNESS. "Wash thine heart," etc.

Not indeed that we are able of ourselves to effect this change: as the prophet says, "Can the Ethiopian change his skin, or the leopard his spots?" Nor will a mere external reformation suffice, a feigned penitence, or an outward reform.

> "No outward form can make us clean:
> The leprosy lies deep within."

But the washing here spoken of includes the following particulars.

1. *Evangelical repentance*, "godly sorrow, which worketh repentance unto life."
2. *Faith in the Redeemer*, whose blood alone "cleanseth from all sin."
3. *Prayer for the sanctifying grace of God's Holy Spirit.* Thus David prayed: "Create in me a clean heart, and renew a right spirit within me."
4. *An experimental acquaintance with the word of God.* So prayed our Divine Redeemer: "Sanctify them through thy truth: thy word is truth."
5. *The hearty forsaking of sin*—and of all sins without reserve. Some kiss the Saviour, and betray him: some, (like Joab,) conceal beneath the cloak of their religion some favourite lust, which is like a dagger to the Saviour's heart. But "let the wicked forsake his way, and the unrighteous man his thoughts"—his vain and wicked thoughts, if he expect the Lord to have mercy on him.

III. THE NECESSITY OF PURIFICATION. "That thou mayst be saved."

"If I wash thee not," said our Redeemer to Peter, "thou hast no part in me." There must be a meetness for heaven before we can enter it—for "nothing that defileth, or maketh a lie, can ever enter there." "The pure in heart" alone can "see God;" and "without holiness no man can see the Lord." Let our prayer, therefore, with the Psalmist, be—"Wash me thoroughly from my iniquity, and cleanse me from my sin."

IMPROVEMENT.

1. Be thankful for the Fountain that is opened to cleanse from all sin and uncleanness.
2. Promptly avail yourselves of the opportunity of being morally cleansed. "Time is short." The season of grace will soon pass away.
3. If not cleansed in time the responsibility will rest upon yourselves —— and awful will be the reflections of those who will have to say, "The harvest is past," etc.

LVI. — REDEMPTION.

"In whom we have redemption through his blood, the forgiveness of sins according to the riches of his grace."— Eph. i. 7.

REDEMPTION is the most glorious work of God. Creation is glorious, but Redemption exceeds it in glory. —— The mind of the Apostle delighted to dwell on this theme. He prized it above every other subject. —— By Christ he had been redeemed from the error of his ways, from the curse and bondage of the law, had been washed in his blood, and endowed with his Spirit, and made an Apostle of the Cross. Well then might he delight in the subject, and count all things else but loss.

Redemption denotes recovery from sin and death by the obedience and sacrifice of Christ, who, on this account, is called the *Redeemer*, Isa. lix. 20; Job xix. 25.

I. THE NECESSITY OF REDEMPTION.

The Scripture doctrine of Redemption implies the entrance of sin into the world; that men in their natural state are universally the subjects of it, and that for the perpetration of it, they are exposed to everlasting death. Man is represented as a miserable captive, needing the interposition of a Redeemer.

The sinner is a captive,

1. *To sin.* John viii. 34. Sin rules and reigns in him. He is a captive to his lusts. 2 Pet. ii. 19.
2. *To Satan,* 2 Tim. ii. 26; he rules in every sinner's heart, Eph. ii. 2.
3. *To the Law.* As a captive, the Apostle says, he is *shut up in prison*, as the phrase "concluded all under sin," Gal. iii. 22, implies. Not having performed the requirements of the Divine law, Divine justice has seized, and now retains him as a prisoner doomed to execution; even now the wrath of God abideth on him.

What a wretched state is this! For only consider,

A state of captivity is *a state of darkness.*—The darkness of a dungeon is a fit emblem of a sinner's mind. In ancient times it was customary to put out the eyes of the prisoners of war, and otherwise maim them. Samson suffered this privation from the Philistines, so did Zedekiah, the last king of Judah, at the hand of the king of Babylon, 2 Kings xxv. 7.———Satan blinds the sinner's mind, Eph. iv. 18; 1 Cor. ii. 14.

A captive is *bound in fetters*, so are sinners who are "in the gall of bitterness and in *the bonds of iniquity.*" See Isa. lxi. 1.—the bond of fleshly lusts, of a hard heart, of unbelief, hatred to the truth, of worldly allurements, etc.

A *captive is an exile*—often in a distant, foreign country. ——The sinner, through Satanic and worldly influence, has been carried away from his Father's house, far away from his love, his image, his fellowship, Eph. ii. 11, 12.

A captive is in *a state of wretchedness and misery.* He is in want; he is often supported by the coarsest fare, etc., Isa. lv. 1, 2. Sinners feed on the wind, on husks, on ashes, etc., Isa. xliv. 20; Hosea xii. 1; Prov. xx. 17.———A captive is frequently stripped naked———the sinner is naked, stripped of the robe of righteousness, Isa. lxiv. 6.— A captive may be in a state of disease, induced by imprisonment, —— Isa. i. 5, 6——of extreme poverty, helplessness, Rev. iii. 17,—and under sentence of death, Rom. vii. 23; 2 Thess. i. 9. In that cell the captive lingeringly waits for the execution of the sentence passed against him. So the sinner has a fearful looking for of judgment, etc.

II. THE AGENT OF REDEMPTION. In whom, etc.

Jesus is the Redeemer. This is his name and memorial to all generations. "For even the Son of Man came not to be ministered unto, but to give his life as a ransom for many," Matt. xx. 28; 1 Tim. ii. 6. Christ, then, was the appointed *Ransomer,* Job xxxiii. 24. As the Redeemer or Ransomer,

1. Jesus Christ was possessed of *the highest dignity and glory.* John i. 1—5. "In him dwelt all the fulness of the Godhead," Heb. i. 2, 3, 6. ———An angel, or legions of angels could not have redeemed man. Hence, "when the fulness of time was come, God sent forth his Son," etc. Gal. iv. 4, 5.

2. *He became incarnate*, and entered into the circumstances of guilty men to redeem them. John i. 14. He could not have become a sacrifice without this, Heb. x. 4—8, nor have entered into the feelings and trials of his people.

3. Christ was *perfectly holy.* The sacrifices under the law were to be without spot or blemish, or they could not have been accepted, Lev. xxii. 19—26. Christ "knew no sin." "He offered himself through the Eternal Spirit without spot unto God." Had he been stained with sin, his sufferings would not have sufficed for himself. In that case what would have become of fallen humanity?

III. THE MEANS OF REDEMPTION: "through his blood."

The Apostle Peter uses a similar expression; "by the *precious blood* of Christ." 1 Pet. i. 19."

Christ stood *charged with sins*, as one who had undertaken to put them away by the sacrifice of himself. He took the sinner's place, Isa.

liii. 6. This undertaking was a voluntary one, "he had power to lay down his life," etc. It is as if he had said, "Let me die for the rebel—let me endure his curse—let me prevent my Father's vengeance from falling upon the guilty sinner—rather let the wrath of God come down and consume me."

O what a burden the Redeemer sustained! It was the heaviest burden that ever was borne! What pain and anguish he endured! O how intense was his agony! See it in Gethsemane, and on the cross, where the immaculate Lamb trod the wine-press of God's wrath alone! See Isa. liii.; Dan. ix. 24; Rom. iii. 23—26.

Christ effectually redeemed sinners,

1. *By honourably paying the price demanded by Divine Justice.* By his power he might have rescued man; but it would not have been honourable. All the claims of God's insulted honour and government were met by Christ. He conformed to the law in every precept—and he paid the penalty due to the transgressor.

And Christ redeemed the sinner,

2. *By power.* He not merely paid the ransom price, but he destroyed the power of man's enslavers. See the argument of Christ, Luke xl. 21, 22. Satan is the strong man armed, and Jesus Christ the man who is stronger than he;—he can destroy sin, Satan, death, 1 John iii. 8. He delivers the penitent from the bondage of Satan, and gives him the liberty of the sons of God.

The redemption of Christ was effectual, for it received the approval of God the Father; "This is my beloved Son in whom I am well pleased." It is proved by his resurrection; for "God raised him from the dead," and by the determination of Jehovah to crown his mediation with triumphant and everlasting honours.

IV. THE BLESSED FRUITS OF REDEEMING LOVE: "Even the forgiveness of sins."

This is a great blessing—the greatest we can have in this world—and the fruitful source of all true blessedness in time and in eternity.

"If sin be pardon'd, I'm secure,
Death has no sting beside;
The law gives sin its damning power
But Christ my Ransom died."

All sins are forgiven—the most flagrant and long continued. How frequently stated in the Scriptures! Isa. i. 18; Ps. ciii. 3; xxxiii. 1; lxxxv. 2; Isa. liii. 25; lv. 7; Heb. x. 17; Matt. i. 21; John i. 29; Acts xiii. 38; 1 John i. 7; Rev. i. 5.

The forgiveness of sin is followed by justification, Acts xiii. 39—peace, Rom. v. 1—adoption, John i. 12—hope, Rom. v. 5.

V. THE SOURCE OF REDEMPTION. "According to the riches of his grace."

This teaches us,

1. *That salvation is not by works;* Eph. ii. 8, 9. Human merit can never purchase the Divine favour.

2. *The source of salvation is Divine Grace,* the free unmerited love of God, 2. Tim. i. 9; Gal. ii. 21.

3. The Gifts of God are munificent. *"According to the riches,"* etc. God gives not with a niggardly hand. How few give according to their means!———God gives according to his—according to the riches of his grace. A poor man may give according to his means, and so may a monarch; but what a difference in the value! What must be the liberality of the God of the universe! He is not merely possessed of infinite ability, but of perfect willingness and delight, peculiar to Deity, to bless his people. "He that spared not his own Son, but freely delivered him up for us all, how shall he not also with him freely give us all things?"

IMPROVEMENT.

1. Study this interesting subject as that in which your eternal interests are involved. 2. Pray to realize an interest in it by faith alone. 3. How fearful to despise Redemption, God's greatest work!

LVII.—ZEAL FOR THE GOSPEL.

"It is good to be zealously affected always in a good thing."—GAL. iv. 18.

FROM this universal maxim observe,

I. THAT THE DOCTRINES WHICH COMPOSE THE GOSPEL OF CHRIST ARE SUPREMELY EXCELLENT.

1. As to their origin, not as the doctrines of any man or any set of men, of any denomination, but as the doctrines of Christ.

2. They are excellent in their own nature. As rays of light issuing from the sun of righteousness. Compared to sincere milk and pure gold.

3. They are peculiarly adapted to the nature, condition, and local circumstances of fallen, debilitated, and helpless man.

4. From the great designs they promote. More efficacious than philosophy, etc., etc.

II. THESE DOCTRINES DEMAND THE EXERTION OF THE WARMEST ZEAL.

1. Inquire what is essential to the nature of zeal.

(1) That it be founded in a knowledge of ourselves, God, Christ, etc., etc.

(2) An ardent affection for the doctrines of the cross of Christ.

(3) Sincere and earnest exertion.

Unremitted mental exertion in studying them.
Exertion of life to exemplify their moral beauties.
Exertion of authority and moral influence to bring others under the truth.
Exertion of property to circulate it in various parts.
Exertion of prayer to God for his blessing.

(4) A mingled grief and indignation on account of whatever opposes itself to the doctrines of Christ. "The men who sigh and cry."— Ezek. ix. 4.

(5) A readiness to make every sacrifice for the glory of Christ.

2. The peculiar characteristic of its operations.

(1) It must be characterized by right motives.

(2) Uniformity in its operations. It must partake of the nature of Christ as to its objects, if not as to its degree.

(3) Prudent and wise in difficulties.
Not precipitate or rash.
Cautious but determined.

(4) Meek in provocation.
Like charity, true zeal will not call for fire from heaven.
Every wound inflicted for the cause of Christ, is in itself a wound to that cause.

(5) Its subjects are cheerfully willing to suffer, and are resigned to the Divine will in suffering.

(6) It is unostentatious in its usefulness.

III. THE IMPORTANCE OF THE EXERCISE OF SUCH ZEAL IN THE CAUSE OF CHRIST.

1. We cannot be Christ's disciples without.
2. It is an evidence of compassion for the souls of men.
3. It is adapted to stimulate others.

PARSONS.

LVIII.—PRAYER TO BE PREPARED FOR DEATH.

"Lord, make me to know mine end, and the measure of my days, what it is, that I may know how frail I am."—Ps. xxxix. 4.

It is probable that David wrote this Psalm during Absalom's rebellion. It is evident that the writer's mind was greatly discomposed by heavy trials. He, however, resolved to walk circumspectly, and to watch over his words, and stop his mouth, as the mouths of animals are confined by a muzzle—so the word signifies. Aware of the baseness of his enemies, he determined on a total silence before them; he would neither speak anything in his own vindication, nor complain of them; nor utter any pious discourse, which would be like throwing pearls before swine. Still the treatment which he received, his indignation at the crimes which he witnessed, his zeal for the honour of God, excited in his mind a violent and painful commotion, v. 3.—It appears probable, too, that mental excitement produced bodily indisposition, v. 10, 11, 13.——These troubles led him to prayer, v. 4.——He prayed that he might know his end, the measure and limit of his days, and how near he was to the closing scene; that being suitably affected with the shortness of life, and his own frailty, he might be the more engaged to prepare for death and eternity, and less concerned about his temporal interests.

I. THE END OF HUMAN EXISTENCE: "Lord make me to know mine end."

1. *It is not the end of man by annihilation.* Death is not the extinction of our being; and to die is not to terminate our existence. The future existence of the soul, or its immortality, is taught by reason and by Scripture.

By reason.—When we consider the exalted station of man—the surprising powers and vast capacities of his soul—his undying thirst for happiness—his inherent desire to live for ever—the fears of infidels—and the hopes of Christians,—these are presumptive evidences of man's immortality. It is proved

By Scripture.—Throughout, the Bible speaks of a future state. God took Enoch to himself—translated Elijah, and cheered his people by promises and representations of heaven. And how full of immortality was the teaching of Christ, and the writings of the Apostles! These are too numerous to be quoted. They prove that the soul is immortal, and survives all the scenes of mortality, Ec. xii. 7. When it takes its flight from earth to explore regions unknown to it, it will exist in the participation of a blissful immortality, or the endurance of eternal perdition, Rom. ii. 6—11. Its salvation then is more important than the possession of the whole world. Look not then "at the things which are seen," etc., 2 Cor. iv. 18.

2. *It is a certain End.* Death is the punishment of sin. "The wages of sin is death." See Gen. iii. 9; 2 Sam. xiv. 14; Heb. ix. 27. ——Observation convinces us that our end must come. Look back on the unnumbered millions of mankind that have existed in the world, the long line of Adam's descendants, the mighty monarchs of the earth, the young, the old, the serious, or the gay, where are they now? once they engaged in social scenes of mirthful festivity, they chanted to the sound of the viol and the harp; the tabret and the pipe were in their feasts; they had the same fond attachments and endearing sympathies, that we now have; but, alas! they are quenched in death, and the same power that laid them low is sure to terminate our career. "There is no man that hath power over the spirit to retain the spirit," etc. Eccles. viii. 8.

3. It is *the end of the connection subsisting between the body and the soul* in this world. Dissolution will separate them. They are now linked together more closely than any wedded pair. How tender yet mysterious the union! Death dissolves that union; the silver cord is loosed, and the golden bowl is broken; the soul escapes, and heaven or the abyss of woe, receives it. The body, like a house without an

inhabitant, falls into ruins, and the particles of matter which composed it, hasten to their kindred elements.

4. *It is a painful, solemn, and deeply affecting end.* It is so even to the righteous ——— but in some respects more especially so to the wicked.

Painful. Generally so. Life is wrung out by pain and prostration. Troops of malignant diseases attend the King of terrors — the stone racks — fevers burn — consumptions waste — plagues depopulate, and disorders of every class attack the human frame, Isa. xxxviii. 13; Matt. viii. 6; Acts ii. 24.

Solemn. It is a serious thing to die. We shall then have done with the world for ever. Death will end all human employments—will take us from all secular pursuits, and for ever separate us from the idols of our own creation. Man of pleasure, you will no more doat on the objects that now charm and attract you. Man of business, you will leave your shop, your warehouse, your manufactory, for ever. Miser, your gold will charm no more,—you will press it to your heart no more for ever. — Statesmen, legislators, orators, there is an end for you! Young and old, rich and poor, learned and illiterate, monarch and peasant, yea, and all living, there is an end for you! Death is the end of all! "What man is he that liveth, and shall not see death?"

Affecting. Sometimes the circumstances are peculiarly affecting—— when the end is characterized by unbelief, destitution of hope —— sometimes the dying experience of believers is beautifully affecting. Consider again how many ties of endearment — bonds of strong relative affection, death rends asunder. Being no respecter of persons, he tears the beautiful child from the parent's embrace, the loving wife from the husband's arms, and relentlessly separates brothers and sisters, etc., etc.

5. *It is the end of all the trials incident to our sojourn in this world.* The end of the race — the end of life's weary journey — the end of every storm and danger incident to the voyage of life — the end of the conflict—the end of every battle with all our foes. Isa. xxxv. 10.

6. *The end of human probation, and all the means of grace.* "The harvest will be past, and the summer ended," and many will have despised the advantages, and will not be "saved."

II. THE BREVITY OF HUMAN LIFE! "And the measure of my days, what it is."

And is not the measure of human existence *very short?* Some die in infancy—some in the youthful period—some in manhood, and some in middle age. How short the measure!

Life at the longest is but short. Suppose it be extended to the utmost period allotted to the existence of man, or more than "threescore years and ten," yet how soon will life pass away! and looking back, how short does the longest life appear!

How short is life when compared with eternity!

What is to be the measure and extent of our days, we cannot tell. All this is known to God alone. "My days are determined," etc., said Job, ch. xiv. 5. The Psalmist adds, v. 5, "Behold thou hast made my days as an hand-breadth; and mine age is as nothing before thee."

"Hand-breadth,"—the breadth of four fingers, a certain dimension, a small one, and that measure we have always about us, always before our eyes; and as good Matthew Henry observes,

"We need no rod, no pole, no measuring line wherewith to take the dimension of our days, nor any skill in arithmetic by which to compute the number of them; no, we have the standard of them at our finger's end, and there is no multiplication of it; it is but one hand-breadth in all. Our time is short, and God has made it so; for 'the number of our months is with him.' Life is short, and he knows it to be so; 'it is as nothing before thee.' All time is nothing to God's eternity, much less our share of time."

O how important is this prayer, "Lord, make me to know mine end, and the measure of my days what it is"! For we are very apt to forget it—we often act as if we were to live forever. When we look upon death as a thing at a distance, we are tempted to adjourn the necessary preparations for it; but if we consider how short life is, we shall see ourselves concerned to be always "*ready*."

III. THE FRAILTY OF HUMAN EXISTENCE. "That I may know how frail I am."

Man's life is not only short; but very frail.——The withering of the grass—the fading of the flower—the fleeing of the shadow—and the dispersion of the vapour, are used to illustrate it.—"The voice said, Cry," etc., Isa. xl. 6—8.

At the creation of man, God pronounced him to be "very good." His soul was untainted by sin, and his body, as its vehicle, was pure and beautiful, strong and undecaying. "In the day thou eatest thereof thou shalt surely die." Man transgressed the Divine law, and then the penalty was inflicted. "Sin brought death into the world, and all our woe."

"How frail I am!" "My foundation is in the dust." "Dust thou art, and unto dust thou shalt return." The principles of disease, of decay and death, are born with man, inwoven in his constitution.

"As man perhaps the moment of his birth,
Receives the lurking principles of death,—
The young disease, which must subdue at length,
Grows with his growth, and strengthens with his strength."

Human life may terminate when we little expect it; when, according to human probability, we calculate upon its prolongation.——See the frailty of man arising from feebleness of constitution—from hereditary predisposition to disease—from infectious diseases—from casualties—from ungenial climates—from weather inclement—from excessive fatigue—from mental depression—from causes the most trivial, and whose minuteness astonishes us.

Human frailty is strikingly set forth in Scripture. Some of these have already been alluded to; consider also the following:—Job vii. 6, 7; xiv. 1, etc.; Gen. xlviii. 9; 1 Chron. xxix. 15; Job iv. 19, 20; xxi. 23; xxiv. 24.

II. THE IMPORTANCE OF THE PRAYER.

1. It implies that *we are very apt to forget our "end, the measure of our days,"* etc. The engagements of life, etc. etc., drive the subject from our minds.

2. *That nothing less than Divine power can cause us to know our end.* The subject is very distasteful to us, and we are disinclined to know it.
——— The Psalmist recognizes the necessity of divine influence.

3. *That to know our end would have a very happy influence upon us.*

(1) It would lead to *a proper estimate of this world, and all its possessions.*

(2) It would *endear heaven to us.* "For here we have no continuing city, but we seek one to come,"—"a city which hath foundations," substantial and enduring—"An inheritance which is incorruptible, undefiled, and that fadeth not away."

(3) *It would promote faith in Christ,* the Divine preparer for, and consoler in the hour of death. Heb. ii. 14, 15.

(4) *It would lead to holy activity in God's service.* Our time and talents would be consecrated to him. "Whatsoever our hand should find to do, we should do it with all our might," etc., for "time is short."

(5) *It would reconcile us to death.* Faith in Jesus, intercourse with him, and the faithful discharge of our duties, would have this beautiful tendency. "Be thou faithful unto death," etc.

LIX.—THE BLESSEDNESS OF HEAVEN.

"And I saw a new heaven and a new earth: for the first heaven and the first earth were passed away; and there was no more sea. And 1 John saw the holy city, new Jerusalem, coming down from God out of heaven, prepared as a bride adorned for her husband. And I heard a great voice out of heaven saying, Behold the tabernacle of God is with men, and he will dwell with them, and they shall be his people, and God himself shall be with them, *and be* their God. And God shall wipe away all tears from their eyes; and there shall be no more death, neither sorrow nor crying, neither shall there be any more pain; for the former things are passed away."— REV. xxi. 1—4.

THE hope of victory animates the general in the midst of the contest; and the prospect of home comforts the pilgrim amidst the dangers of the journey. The believer on earth is contending with enemies numerous, powerful, and malicious; but he is animated with the hope of a most triumphant victory. He is a pilgrim surrounded by many dangers, exposed to many storms; but he is comforted with the prospect of a most delightful home—and that home is heaven. Sometimes tears of sorrow trickle down his cheeks; but he knows that though he sows in tears, he shall doubtless come again with rejoicing, bringing his sheaves with him. Even in the dark night of human calamity, he knows from experience what it is to rejoice in hope of the glory of God. An interesting account of that glory is given in the verses which constitute the subject of the following discourse. Happy shall we be while we are engaged in the contemplation of a subject so animating and sublime, if we are enabled to rejoice in hope of the glory of God!

I. THE VISION WHICH JOHN SAW. Verses 1, 2.

1. *He saw the first heaven and the first earth* disappear, and also the departure of the sea. The disappearance of the first heaven may denote the great change which will take place in the visible heavens, which are represented by the very striking metaphorical expression of the "rolling together of a shrivelled scroll." The departure of the earth and the sea intimates, not the annihilation of this globe, but the destruction of everything connected with it, which has been the result of sin. This change will be greater than if a waste, howling wilderness were converted into a paradise of luxuriance and beauty; than if a dungeon were changed into a palace of magnificence and splendour. The present glory of the earth shall be destroyed, with all its treasures, sceptres, thrones, diadems, kingdoms, and empires. The pleasures after which the foolish and the gay pursue with the most deluded earnestness, shall pass away; the objects on which the ambitious have placed their hearts shall pass away; hoards of shining wealth, which the avaricious worship with such devoted admiration, shall pass away. How much these solemn realities illustrate the vanity of things terrestrial being sought as a portion! and how much the transitory nature of all the objects of time illustrate the unchanging glory of Him, respecting whom it is said, "They shall perish, but thou remainest; they shall wax old as doth a garment, and as a vesture thou shalt change them, and they shall be changed; but thou art the same, and thy years shall not fail!"

2. *He saw new heavens, and a new earth.* Though this expression does not exclude the pleasing idea of the animating change which the earth and the visible heavens shall undergo by fire at the resurrection; yet it may be understood as chiefly to denote the glories of the heavenly state. The residence of the Church of Christ compared with what it is now, will be completely *new;* it will be a new order of things, exceeding the present, more than the blooming, verdant paradise surpasses the barren waste. The Church itself will be wonderfully changed, and arrayed in robes of inimitable beauty, and the residence of the Church will correspond completely with the glory of the inhabitants.

3. *John saw the new Jerusalem.* Verse 2. Jerusalem was once the most glorious city upon the face of the earth, and the visible residence of the King and Head of the Church, during the succession of many generations. That city is sometimes employed in figurative language, as typical of heaven; at other times as typical of the Church. From the description of Jerusalem in the vision, it appears to signify the Church triumphant. As God dwelt in ancient Jerusalem, so he dwells in the midst of his Church in heaven. Glorious was the Shekinah, which was the visible manifestation of God's presence; but infinitely more glorious the displays of the Divine Majesty, which are the delight of the Church triumphant in heaven. Saints on earth who are renewed by the Spirit of God, and the general assembly of the saints in heaven, are called the New Jerusalem, because of the completion of that holiness which will form their bright and unfading ornament.

4. *John saw the new Jerusalem descending from heaven.* Every believer is of heavenly origin and descent — he is of the blood-royal of heaven — he can boast of a more ancient, and honourable, and glorious heraldry than any of the princes of the earth. "He is born again, not of blood, nor of the will of man, but of God." It is probable that there was, before the eyes of John, the actual appearance of a city coming down from on high, and delineated in all its splendour upon the firmament of the sky. There was something infinitely imposing in the general outline of the city — it resembled a bride adorned for her husband. Christ, the author of perfection and beauty, imparts beauty and perfection to his Church. Are they comely? It is by his comeliness put upon them. Are they arrayed with a robe of righteousness? It is a robe of righteousness of his making. Are they adorned with the garments of salvation? They are garments which he prepares, and which he gives. Who can conceive the beauty and perfection of saints in heaven? It is such as to be admired by God himself. Oh! what must that created glory imparted to the triumphant Church be, which God himself shall look upon — and look upon with delight! Well may the redeemed on earth lift up their voices, and sing: "It doth not yet appear what we shall be, but we know that, when he shall appear, we shall be like him, for we shall see him as he is."

II. THE GLORIOUS THINGS WHICH JOHN HEARD.

He was alone in Patmos Isle, but his eye was gratified with the most magnificent displays of celestial glory, and his ear was delighted with the most captivating sounds of heavenly music. He heard the songs of saints, and the songs of angels; but above all, he heard the voice of God. O Lord! make us to hear the voice of thy spirit, that we may live for ever.

What were the utterances of the voice which the apostle heard?

1. The voice said: "*Behold the tabernacle of God is with men.*" The ancient tabernacle was God's visible residence among the Jewish Church, before the temple was erected. God is no less present with his Church now, than he was then. Miraculous evidences of his presence are withdrawn, but his presence remains the same, and his gracious and constant communications never cease. Can we contemplate, without astonishment, the merciful condescension of God in taking up his residence with the sons of men, never to be withdrawn? "He will dwell among them."

2. *The voice said:* "*They shall be his people.*" From eternity they were his, by sovereign gracious choice; in time they became his by creation and by preservation; but in a sense more important than them all, they became his by redemption. They shall be his to know him — to behold his attributes glorified by the righteousness of Christ; they shall be his to love him, to surrender to him all the affections of their nature; they shall be his to praise him, and to ascribe to him that glory and honour which it is God's right to receive, and man's highest felicity to give; and they shall be his to enjoy him as the fountain of all their joy, as the strength of their heart, and their portion, for ever.

3. *The voice said:* "*God himself shall be with them, and be their God.*" God was with them on earth; he never left them, no, not for an hour, and he shall be for ever with them in heaven. On earth, they knew

God's presence through a medium, but in heaven they shall have his presence without a medium, seeing him face to face. What God has been to them in time, he will be to them for ever — "he will be their God." He will be theirs, to admit them to the most delightful fellowship with himself — he will be theirs, to admit them to the most glorious discoveries of his nature, essence, perfections, purposes, and works, — and he will be theirs, to fill their expanded minds, and the wide capacity of their desires, with the richest communications of his boundless goodness.

When these splendid blessings are given to the people of God, every description of misery shall have disappeared, never to becloud the comforts of the Church, or to interrupt her refined enjoyment. The tears of sorrow shall no more bathe the cheeks of the followers of the Lamb; they shall no more become the victims of death's tyrannical dominion; the cup of mingled sorrow shall no more be presented to their lips; as the cause of sorrow shall be removed, there shall be no more weeping and crying, the expression of sorrow; there shall be no more pain, either of body, produced by maladies lingering and acute, or of mind, produced by afflictions perplexing and severe. When these mighty deliverances are effected, then "the former things shall have passed away." Sin shall have passed away, and unspotted holiness shall enjoy the exercise of undisturbed authority; enemies shall have passed away, to be exchanged for friends whose love shall never decay; powerful temptations shall have passed away, to be substituted by the most secure enjoyments; and stormy tempests shall have passed away, to be followed by the tranquillity of eternal peace. Let all hear the encouraging voice of God: "Be thou faithful unto death, and thou shalt receive a crown of life." O hear the following encouraging accents! — and when you hear them, may the Spirit effectually apply them: "He that overcometh shall inherit all things, and I will be his God, and he shall be my son." Amen.

LX.—THE CHRISTIAN A SOJOURNER.

"Pass the time of our sojourning here in fear."—1 Peter i. 17.

WE are so wedded to this world, that we have constant need of exhortation. The Apostle Peter, in the previous verses, endeavours to cheer Christians with the hope of immortality, v. 13, and then exhorts them to maintain a holy deportment; and as they called on the Father, or called God their Father, who was an impartial judge of all human conduct, it became them to pass the time of their sojourning here in fear.

I. THE CHRISTIAN IS A SOJOURNER.

A sojourner is one who dwells in a strange country, and has no possession in it of his own. Thus, "Abram went down to Egypt to sojourn there." He felt himself a stranger and a pilgrim, and by his unsettled state, he was kept in mind of the city which hath foundations—that is permanent and stable, whose building is the living God. See Heb. xi. 8, 9.

So a Christian is absent from his native country. He is born from above. His home is heaven. The body is but the house of the soul's pilgrimage, in which she is confined during her exile from home.

II. *A sojourner is at a distance from his relatives.*

Some of these may be with him, but how many have departed to the land of the blest!

> There his best friends and kindred dwell,
> There God his Saviour reigns.

III. *A sojourner is sometimes exposed to rough treatment from the natives.*

They cast out his name as evil. They deride and persecute him. His principles, pursuits, exertions, and hopes are hated by the wicked.

IV. *A sojourner is but little known.*

His friendship, his companionship, are not courted. He has pleasures, and bright anticipations of future bliss, to which sinners are strangers.

V. *A sojourner has no inheritance in the country through which he is travelling.*

"This world is not our rest; it is polluted." He seeks a "better country," that is, a heavenly one. Why fix his affections on earthly things, which are transient and unsatisfying?

VI. *Their pilgrimage here is but short and fleeting.*

They are in this world for a certain season, and for some certain end; they have their work to do, and their measure of suffering to endure. Christ has called them to work in his vineyard, and he will soon call them to their reward.

VII. *The Christian must pass the time of his sojourning here in fear.*

Not in slavish fear, for there is no necessity for that. Rom. viii. 15. But in reverential fear — in fear of sin — in fear of offending God — in fear of temptation — in fear of loving the creature more than God. But more particularly,

1. Let us live as though we are really not at home, manifesting by our conduct, deadness to the world, and earnest pursuit of spiritual and celestial happiness, that we belong to a better country, that is, a heavenly one.

2. Let us not strike deeply our roots here, nor encumber ourselves with the clay of this world, considering what a journey we have to take, what a race we have to run.

3. Are you sojourners? Remember that the eyes of the natives are

upon you; they will make no allowance; show you no mercy; scrutinize your actions.

4. Recommend the gospel while you sojourn to those around you, by a corresponding temper. Make up your mind to suffer. A traveller does not expect to find at an inn, all the comforts of home.

5. In a short time you will be at home in your Father's house. What is dying? It is going home, entering the port, taking the spoil, and enjoying the fruits of a glorious victory. Soon you will have done with all the unkindness, suspicions, and censures of those who surround you.

LXI.—PRESUMPTION IN THE CHRISTIAN WARFARE FORBIDDEN.

"Let not him that girdeth on his harness boast himself as he that putteth it off."—
1 KINGS xx. 11.

PRIDE dwells in the heart of man. Pride frequently induces presumption, the fruitful source of misery and ruin. Hence we need to be cautioned against it, that we may be clothed with humility; for "before honour is humility."

For once Ahab the king of Israel speaks sensibly, in the answer which he sent to Ben-hadad, the king of Syria. Ben-hadad, priding himself in his military valour, in the vast number of his hosts, v. 1, expected no less than the defeat of the Israelites, and the capture of Samaria, v. 10.—It is not numerous and potent armies that always succeed,—as history proves. God is the Governor among the nations, and often "brings the princes of the earth to nought." "The race," says Solomon, "is not to the swift, nor the battle to the strong." Beautifully appropriate, therefore, was the answer of Ahab, "Let not him that girdeth," etc.

The text may very properly be applied to the Christian warfare, and act as a check to presumption and self-dependence.

I. THE CHRISTIAN IS ENGAGED IN A WARFARE.

The exhortation in the Scripture to "war a good warfare," "quit you like men, be strong;" and, "wherefore take unto you the whole armour of God, that ye may be able to stand in the evil day, and having done all to stand," and many others, imply that the Christian is a soldier called to do battle against powerful adversaries. These adversaries are,

1. *Satan and the powers of darkness.* Believers have been translated by Divine power from the kingdom of Satan into the kingdom of God's dear Son. This conquest is ever galling to the prince of the power of the air, who is restless to retake the captive he has lost. Therefore he constantly invades the Christian with all his subtlety and fascinations. Hence we read of the "wiles of the devil," Eph. vi. 11; of "the fiery darts of the wicked one," Eph. vi. 11; and of the "snares of the devil;"

1 Tim. v. 7. "We wrestle not against flesh and blood," merely, "but against principalities," etc. Eph. vi. 12.

2. *The world.* This is Satan's seat and empire; he is called "the God of this world;" "the friendship of the world is enmity against God." Is there any thing in this world friendly to the Christian's growth in grace? Is it not full of snares? The world must be overcome. Its maxims, pleasures, riches, etc., must be made subordinate to the higher pursuits of Christian profession. What multitudes have been seduced and conquered by the world!

3. *The human heart,* which naturally is "deceitful above all things and desperately wicked." What Christian does not exclaim, "In me, that is, in my flesh dwelleth no good thing." Thus the Apostle felt the struggle, Rom. vii. 14, etc.

4. *There are many contests incident to human life, and also to the Christian profession.* There is adversity—poverty with its chilling influence—sickness with all its pains and languor—bereavement with all its mourning and bitter pangs—temptations, with all their power and darkness, and persecution with all its enmity and cruelty.——What is the design of all these foes, but to cast down and destroy the Christian?

II. ARMOUR IS PROVIDED FOR THE CHRISTIAN WARFARE.

The Christian soldier must have arms, or he cannot resist his foes; he is not sufficient to select weapons for himself. This is never left to the soldier's choice. Divine and not carnal weapons must be used. "The weapons of our warfare are not carnal," etc. God has provided every weapon of combat, and all the armour of defence, and given directions for their use.

This Armour is distinctly specified, Eph. vi. 14, etc.

This armour must be girded on. The "*whole*" of it must be put on, Eph. vi. 13. Every part of the man is vulnerable, and must therefore be defended. Which of the weapons can be dispensed with? Not the sword, not the shield, not the breast-plate, not the helmet, etc. Neglect to take one of these, and you insult the Captain of salvation, and peril your souls.

This armour must be employed against every opposing power—must be kept in use, and never be relinquished till the earthly tabernacle itself is dissolved.

III. SUCCESS, OR TRIUMPH IS GUARANTEED.

That is, if a person properly becomes a soldier of the cross, possesses the martial spirit, and submits to the directions of the Divine General, opposes and resists his adversaries in the name of God and his strength, he shall obtain the victory. That such shall obtain the victory is certain,

1. *From God's love to them.* Those who trust in him and fight for him he will preserve. "No weapon," etc., Isa. liv. 17.

2. *From the Divine aid afforded.* He will instruct them—strengthen them—cheer them by his promises, etc.—by the prospect of victory and reward. Eph. vi. 10; Rev. ii. 7, 11, 17.

3. The armour provided is *all-sufficient.* With this we may go forth,

like our illustrious Captain, from conquering and to conquer. This armour was never known to fail.

4. *Multitudes have overcome.* Look at the general assembly of the church of the first-born—to the spirits of just men made perfect, for a proof. "A great number which no man can number." Rev. vii.

IV. THAT THIS WARFARE MUST BE UNDERTAKEN IN A PROPER WAY.

" Let not him that girdeth on the harness boast," etc.

" He that putteth it off;" this is expressive of victory; it is spoken of one who had reason *to boast.* Great is the pleasure of the successful warrior as he lays aside his armour after victory. Imagine the spectacle.

" He that putteth it on " is a mere recruit. To him conflict is prospective, and not retrospective. It is therefore absurd to boast. For, observe —

1. He that putteth on the armour *is inexperienced.* Boasting or confidence, if admissible at all, is only for the experienced warrior who understands military tactics, the cunning, malice, and strategems of the enemy. —— How inexperienced is the young Christian! Let him not boast, but rather pray for an increase of wisdom — a better knowledge of himself and the character of his enemies. Let him study the lives of Christian warriors as narrated in the Bible, and the biographies of good men.

2. *He that putteth on the armour has not obtained the victory;* he that putteth it off has; therefore the former has nothing to boast of. The cause for boasting has yet to come. How absurd to boast of that which to us appears uncertain.

3. *He that engages in Christian warfare has nothing, and can do nothing in which he may boast.* All his armour is Divine—his wisdom, strength, and success, come from God. It is "he that reacheth the hands to war, and the fingers to fight." Ex. xv. 2; Ps. xviii. 32; 2 Cor. iii. 5. Therefore,

Put on the armour with humility. It is an honour of which we are unworthy to be made Christian soldiers.

Put on the armour with self-distrust, but with trust in God. The most confident are the most exposed; and the most humble the most safe. "When I am weak then am I strong." Why? Because the deep consciousness of my own weakness will induce me to shun scenes of temptation; keep me from aspiring after high and responsible stations, and to pray without ceasing, " Hold thou me up, and I shall be safe."

Put on this armour with courage, and in expectation of overcoming, and receiving the warrior's crown.

Think again how many boasters have come short. Witness Benhadad, Goliath of Gath, Nebuchadnezzar, the Pharisee in the temple, Peter, etc. " Let him that thinketh he standeth take heed lest he fall."

LXII. — THE DAY OF SALVATION.

"Behold now is the accepted time; behold, now is the day of salvation." — 2 COR. vi. 2.

NOTHING is so important as the salvation of the immortal soul— Nothing in this world is so worthy of our thought and attention. Other things are temporary; salvation is everlasting. Hence all the Scriptures are in earnest about it. God is in earnest, Christ is in earnest, and the Holy Spirit is in earnest for the salvation of guilty man.

The second verse of this chapter ought to have followed the last verse of the preceding chapter. In its present position it greatly disturbs the connection between the first and third verses.——The text embodies the following sentiments:

I. *All mankind as ruined transgressors need salvation.*

Man has broken the righteous law of heaven — he is a rebel — under the dominion of sin — defiled — under sentence of condemnation.

II. *Salvation has been provided.*

The terms, "the accepted time," "the day of salvation," imply this. See Isa. xlix. 8. The advent of the Messiah was the time of God's pleasure or benevolence, of which all the faithful were in expectation; and the day of salvation was the time in which his salvation should be manifested and applied.

1. *Christ became the Author of salvation.* In covenant arrangement he was accepted as the Mediator. He was eminently qualified for the undertaking. Possessed of a Divine nature —— Became man.

2. *He made reconciliation for iniquity.* He shed his blood for the remission of sins; 2 Cor. v. 20, 21. As a proof of the acceptance of his sacrifice, God raised him from the dead.

3. *All sinners who believe in him are fully accepted* — "made accepted in the beloved." Christ is their substitute — their Ransomer, and Surety.

4. *This Salvation is freely offered* to the vilest of the vile—without any preparation on the part of the sinner. Rev. xxii. 17; John vi. 37; vii. 37; 1 Tim. i. 15.

III. *Now is the day of salvation.*

It has been so since the birth of Christ, and will be till time shall be no more. The first promise was the first glimmering of light — the patriarchal age was the beginning of the dawn — the time of the prophets was the approach of the morning. But Messiah's birth ushered in the full and glorious day of salvation.

It is the day of salvation — for we have the ministry of salvation in abundance. We have the means of salvation. We have the privileges and enjoyments of salvation.

IV. *Now is the accepted time.*

While we have life—this is frail and uncertain—and will soon end. There can be no acceptance after death, if not reconciled now.

While we are placed in favourable circumstances. Our position in life may be changed, and we may be placed under unfavourable influences, etc.

While we are young and healthy—while our intellectual powers are in vigour—while we have powerful and favourable convictions—now is the accepted time.

V. THE NEGLECT OF THIS SALVATION *will be followed by punishment.*

To neglect is to abuse the love of God—to insult Christ as the unspeakable gift of God—it will produce bitter regret, guilty remorse, and a consignment to perdition.

LXIII.—MESSIAH'S WORK FINISHED.

"It is finished."—JOHN xix. 30.

I. THE HUMILIATION AND SUFFERINGS OF CHRIST WERE FINISHED.

1. *His humiliation was profound.* He became man—poor—had not where to lay his head.

2. *His sufferings were intense,* arrayed in mock royalty—was crucified—endured Divine vengeance.

3. But the sufferings and humiliation of Christ *were now terminated.*

II. THE PROPHECIES OF THE OLD TESTAMENT WERE NOW FULLY ACCOMPLISHED.

1. The prophecies had predicted all the remarkable events in the Saviour's life. Birth—rejection by the Jews—meek in sufferings—numbered with transgressors—bone not to be broken.

2. These prophecies received their full accomplishment.

III. THE MOSAICAL DISPENSATION WAS NOW FOR EVER ABOLISHED.

1. It was only a *typical* dispensation.

2. It was abolished; oblation and sacrifice ceased—veil of temple rent; indication of Divine authority for its abolition.

3. The Jews no longer the exclusive objects of Divine favour, gospel to be preached to Gentiles also.

IV. THE REDEMPTION OF THE GUILTY WAS NOW COMPLETED.

1. Man required redemption.

2. Justice and veracity of God required satisfaction for sin.

3. Satisfaction was rendered by the Saviour in the nature that had sinned, and to the extent that the law required.

V. THE EMPIRE OF SATAN WAS FOR EVER DESTROYED.

1. The world was in bondage to Satan — led captive by him at his will.

2. This enemy was conquered by Christ — at his temptation in the wilderness — when he expelled him from those whom he had possessed — at his cross.

CONCLUSION.

Be grateful for the dispensation under which you live.

LXIV.—THE SOUL NEGLECTED.

"And as thy servant was busy here and there, he was gone."—1 KINGS xx. 40.

THE prophet, under the parable of a prisoner, as appears from the context, v. 35, making Ahab to judge himself, denounceth God's judgment against him for sparing the life of that infamous king, Ben-hadad. "Thy life shall go for his life," v. 42. This was fulfilled at the battle of Ramoth-gilead, where he was slain by the Syrians, ch. xxii. 34, 35.

In applying the subject to ourselves, it is evident from God's word, that we have all a trust committed to us. All Christians, as well as ministers of the Gospel, are called upon to labour for God, and to save souls from death. Hence he has endowed us with ability, and placed us in suitable spheres, and promised his blessing to crown our efforts with success.

I. THAT MAN POSSESSES THE ABILITY TO DO GOOD.

Man is not created to live for himself alone. He is a social being, and designed by his great Creator to minister to the welfare of the human family. Man cannot renounce his responsibility, and say like Cain, "Am I my brother's keeper?"——— Jesus Christ taught by his precepts, and by his holy, devoted, and benevolent life, what should be the characteristics of man. "He went about doing good."

1. *God has given to some intellectual ability.* They have learning—are possessed of useful knowledge. They should be lights in the world, irradiating the surrounding moral and spiritual darkness. Phil. ii. 15.

Some have a good understanding of Bible truth — of the doctrines of Christianity—and have an experimental acquaintance with Christ's mediatorial love. Let such enter into the Sunday School and become "teachers of babes," or ascend the walls of Zion, and "cry aloud and spare not;" let them blow the gospel trumpet, that they who are ready to perish may come to Christ.

2. *To some God has given wealth;* and of that which he has so freely

given they should be willing to communicate. "The gold and the silver are his, and the cattle upon a thousand hills." Who has given them mental ability, enterprise, health of body, and favourable circumstances for the accumulation of wealth? God has done it—made them stewards of his bounty, and "it is required of stewards that a man be found faithful."

3. *Some have influence.* And this exercised in a Christian spirit may produce happy results. The influence of a parent, of a master, of a friend, is often felt.—Such influence is not to be of a coercive character, —but gentle, loving, and persuasive.

II. THAT THE SALVATION OF SINNERS SHOULD BE THE SPECIAL OBJECT OF ZEAL AND LABOUR.—Rom. x. 1.

It is good to promote the temporal welfare of man—to ameliorate distress—to bless the sons of poverty—to visit the afflicted—to contribute to institutions designed for the relief of the wretched, etc.; but the salvation of the sinner outvies all these.

1. *The soul is ruined by sin*—it is exposed to everlasting perdition.

2. *The soul is of immense worth*—formed for God and eternity—capable of enjoying infinite bliss in heaven, or of enduring infinite evil in a state of retribution. Then think of its vast and capacious powers —of the value which God and all heaven fix upon it. Mark viii. 36.

3. *The soul may be saved.* Jesus has died to save it. That salvation is adapted—it is rich and free; 1 Tim. i. 15; John vi. 37; Rev. xxii. 17.

4. The salvation of sinners may be effected;—by preaching—by personal entreaty—by believing prayer—by the circulation of knowledge. Thus acted the Apostles, and all who have been eminent for winning souls to God.—Parents should be anxious for the salvation of their children. Solemn and responsible is their trust!——Ministers are responsible for the salvation of their hearers—they must " warn every man," etc.—must "watch for souls as those that must give an account."

III. THAT THE PRESSURE OF TEMPORAL ENGAGEMENTS OFTEN PREVENT SUCH AN ACCOMPLISHMENT. "Thy servant was busy here and there, and he was gone."

The minds of some persons are *absorbed by trade.* This occupies their constant attention. They never make it subordinate to holier and loftier pursuits. "Busy here and there," many neglect their own souls, and those of others. And yet they must soon die, and what will this total absorption do for them then?

The minds of some are *absorbed by domestic concerns.* They are "busy here and there" to promote bodily happiness, and domestic comfort, which they seem to regard as supremely important. Always solicitious what they shall eat, with what they shall be clothed, etc. Death comes and takes them away amid all their anxious solicitude— their souls unsaved, etc., and immense good left undone; Luke x. 40—42.

Some are carried away by worldly pleasure—vain amusements, etc.

It is not to be denied that many professors of religion are thus characterized; are "busy here and there," while religion and its various services and duties are neglected.

Thus through an inordinate attachment to the busy concerns of life, solemn trusts are neglected. Faculties are not improved — property not rightly applied — influence not turned into a right channel — the soul subjected to the body, etc.

And what is the consequence? "And as thy servant was busy here and there, he was gone." Apply this to the souls committed to your care, and whose salvation you have neglected.

It may be the case of a youth whose mind was tender and susceptible of impression. But while you were busy here and there, he "was gone" up into manhood; the propitious period of youth passed away, and through the influence of temptation, and different associations, the mind is no longer susceptible of impression.

It may be the case of a friend, neighbour, or relative. You might have blessed them, but you were "busy here and there," and God, who appoints the bounds of human habitation, removed them from the reach of your solicitude. You looked, but they *were gone*, and not saved by your instrumentality.

Then how many die before you are aware, and whom you intended to bless. This will apply to some in the congregation, upon whom the attention of the minister was fixed — some in the Sabbath School whom the teacher intended to warn and advise — some brother in the church who required quickening or strengthening; — but while you were "busy here and there" with the trifles of earth, death has cut them down — they are "gone" to the chambers of the grave, and their faces will be seen no more.

Do you wish to bless any one? O do it quickly! He will soon be gone. Your children, your relatives, your friends, etc., will soon be in the grave.

IV. THAT SUCH NEGLECT INVOLVES MOST PAINFUL CONSEQUENCES.

1. *Bitter regret.* That the world and its trifles have been allowed to prevent the accomplishment of a mighty purpose.

2. *Immense loss.* Probably the loss of a soul or souls. Oh! if we had warned them — instructed and guided them, they might have been saved. O fearful loss! "What is a man profited if he gain the whole world and lose his own soul?"

3. *Irreparable loss.* "The harvest is past," etc. You can warn him no more — offer Christ to him no more!

4. *Criminality before the judge.* What a poor excuse to make! "Thy servant was busy here and there." How mean will all worldly possessions then appear! All our excuses will be inadmissible at the great day. We must then give a true account, and shall be punished for abusing our trust. Matt. xxv. 30.

LXV.—REDEMPTION BY THE PRECIOUS BLOOD OF CHRIST.

"Forasmuch as ye know that ye were not redeemed with corruptible things, as silver and gold, from your vain conversation received by tradition from your fathers; but with the precious blood of Christ, as of a lamb without blemish and without spot; who verily was foreordained before the foundation of the world, but was manifest in these last times for you, who by him do believe in God, that raised him up from the dead, and gave him glory, that your faith and hope might be in God." — 1 Pet. i. 18—21.

THE Apostle Peter, in the preceding verses, advises Christians as to their behaviour in the world; and was anxious, as it appears, that they should no longer cling to ancient Jewish ceremonies and usages, which by the coming of Christ had been entirely abrogated. They had been redeemed by the precious blood of Christ, from their vain conversation, etc., and introduced into the glorious liberty of the children of God.

I. *Redemption is necessary.* The introduction of sin into this world renders it needful; for consider what sin has done.

It has alienated the soul from God. Man is now a "hater of God, an enemy by wicked works." Eph. iv. 18; Col. i. 21.

Alienation leads to transgression. The righteous laws of heaven are treated with contempt. "There is no fear of God before their eyes." Rom. iii. 9, etc.

Sin has defiled the soul. It has defaced the image of God. It has corrupted the desires, affections, thoughts, purposes, etc. The apostle dwells at large on the corrupt state of the soul. Rom. i.

Sin has blinded the soul. See 2 Cor. iv. 3, 4.

Sin has enervated the soul. It is "without strength," Rom. v. 6. And as to spiritual exercises, the soul is dead, Eph. ii. 1.

Sin, therefore, is the death of the soul. Not only enervated its powers, but placed it under arrest to the Divine law. The sentence has gone forth. "The soul that sinneth shall die." The transgressor is "cursed."

II. *Christ was foreordained before the foundation of the world as the Redeemer.*

The God of Love, foreseeing the lapsed and ruined condition of man, devised the plan of redemption — and entered into covenant with his only begotten Son to become the Redeemer. See Gen. iii. 15; Micah v. 2; Rom. iii. 25; xvi. 25, 26; Eph. i. 4; iii. 9—11; Rev. xiii. 8.

What a delightful thought is this! — the Almighty was interested in my elevation from the fall, ages before that fall took place! How great, nay incomprehensible, was that love that rested upon objects so vile and odious!

Jesus Christ, then, is the appointed Redeemer. This is his name and office to all generations. It is a rich and glorious name, fragrant as "ointment poured forth." Millions on earth and in heaven ascribe to him this character, and will do it for ever, for they have been redeemed by his precious blood. To each of them he said, as he hushed their fears and inspired their hopes, "Fear not, I have redeemed thee; I have called thee by my name; thou art mine."

III. *Christ came into the world to effect the work of redemption.* "Was manifest in these last times for you."

Manifest in the likeness of men — took upon himself the form of a servant — became "a partaker of flesh and blood." How great the condescension of the Son of God! Think of his pre-existent glory in contrast with his humiliation on earth, those sad scenes of hunger and thirst, of contempt and persecution, of mental darkness and anguish, of bodily inflictions and the shedding of his blood.——Yet all this was necessary. The objects of his redemption were human; "it behoved him to be made like unto his brethren."

IV. *Jesus Christ was perfectly holy.* "A lamb without blemish and without spot." This was absolutely necessary. Heb. iv. 15; vii. 26—28.

This perfect purity was proved by his perfect conformity to the Divine law. "I came not to destroy the law, but to fulfil the law." The testimony of Jehovah is sufficient. "This is my beloved Son, in whom I am well pleased."

V. *Jesus Christ redeemed by his precious blood.* "Not redeemed with corruptible," etc.

Created things could not purchase the souls of men; else the sacrifice of Christ had not been offered; could anything less have done, Jehovah would not have given up his only begotten Son. Even *silver and gold*, the most valuable medium of commerce among men, bear no proportion in their value to one lost soul, for there should be a congruity or agreement between the worth of the thing *purchased*, and the *valuable consideration* which is given *for it;* and the laws and customs of nations require this. On this ground, perishable things cannot be placed against the soul which is immortal. Nothing, therefore, but such *a ransom price* as God provided could be a sufficient ransom.

Levitical sacrifices were insufficient to procure redemption. Graphically stated by the apostle, Heb. x. 1—14.

The precious blood of Christ alone paid the penalty, satisfied Divine justice, and rolled away the curse. This is most graciously stated, Isa. liii., Rom. iii., and Heb. ix. 10. The cattle upon a thousand hills might have bled; the gold of a thousand treasuries might have been piled up in vain. Blood divine was its only price; and for the soul's redemption that blood was shed. On Calvary this ransom was paid; and in the salvation of the penitent malefactor, a pledge of its acceptance was given. "God gave Egypt for his people's ransom of old, Ethiopia and Seba for them, because they were precious in his sight and honourable." But in the redemption of man from sin, "no mention shall be made of the gold of Sheba, the topaz of Ethiopia, or the fine linen of Egypt;" "the precious blood of Christ" was the only sufficient ransom.

It is called the PRECIOUS *blood of Christ*, because of his Divine nature —because it *has* redeemed, or done that which nothing else on earth or in heaven could have done —— because it is productive of the most valuable blessings. From every pang to which they were liable through eternity, the redeemed are saved. To every enjoyment to which they can rise through eternity, they are elevated. The robes of glory are washed in the Redeemer's blood. The crowns of glory are placed on the heads of the redeemed by the Redeemer's hand. From his everlasting merits flow their everlasting joys.

VI. *Christ's redemption was accepted by the Father.* He raised him from the dead, and exalted him to his right hand. "That raised him up from the dead, and gave him glory;" v. 21.

If Christ had not risen, his sacrifice would have been fruitless — our faith and our hope would be in vain; 1 Cor. xv. 12, 13, 14, etc. — But as Christ rose from the dead, our hope of eternal life rests on an imperishable basis. "That your faith and hope might be in God." Ver. 21.

VI. *Redemption by the precious blood of Christ is enjoyed by faith.* "Who by him do believe in God."

That is, by the preaching of his gospel, attended by the influence of his Spirit, sinners see and feel themselves to be lost, and by faith are brought nigh to God by the blood of Christ.

And what is the effect of this? The Christians to whom Peter wrote had been redeemed from *their vain conversation*, or former empty, foolish, and unprofitable conduct; and from unmeaning ceremonies and useless ordinances, which they received by tradition from their fathers, rabbins, or doctors.

All believers are redeemed out of the hand of offended justice—from the guilt, pollution, and dominion of sin. All this they enjoy now, yet it is but the earnest of future bliss.

IMPROVEMENT.

1. How precious must the soul be when its redemption required such a price! 2. How important to have a sensible evidence that we are redeemed! 3. If not redeemed by the blood of Christ, we must perish. "There remaineth no more sacrifice for sin."

LXVI.— THE RIGHTEOUSNESS OF THE SCRIBES AND PHARISEES.

"For I say unto you, that except your righteousness exceed the righteousness of the Scribes and Pharisees, ye shall in no case enter into the kingdom of heaven." — Matt. v. 20.

"I AM the Searcher of hearts," is the prerogative of Jesus Christ. This was proved by his teaching. While his auditors were unaware of his scrutiny, he "perceived the thoughts of their hearts;" he "knew what was in man." What appeared beautiful and complete in human conduct to superficial observers, appeared odious and defective to him. What was condemned by the formal and presumptuous received his commendation. See Luke xviii.

In the context Christ maintains the authority and permanency of the moral law. He came "not to destroy it, but to fulfil it."——— He strictly conformed to it, and therefore was fitted for his Mediatorial office. "Such an high priest became us," etc. This is the consolation of the church. See Rom. iii. 20—26.

I. THE RIGHTEOUSNESS OF THE SCRIBES AND PHARISEES.

In the time of Christ, the Pharisees were a large and powerful sect. Among them were the Scribes or Doctors of the law, or lawyers. They copied the law for the people, and expounded it. The word Pharisee means separatist; and it originated from their separating from the rest of the Jews 144 years before the birth of Christ, on account of the national corruption; their aim was to restore the pure worship of God; but in the time of Christ they had greatly degenerated into mere formalism and hypocrisy, on account of which Christ frequently exposed and censured them.

They professed to conform their lives to the law of God in its external requirements; and probably there was in them much that was commendable; of which many now are deficient, and yet expect the kingdom of heaven.

1. *They were frequent in prayer.* None prayed more frequently—they had eighty set forms of prayer, and never went into a house or came from it without prayer. They prayed at the corners of streets, they went up to the temple to pray, and prayed at home.

2. *They practised self-denial.* They fasted twice in the week, on Mondays and Thursdays, with great constancy, and frequently on other days. They subjected themselves to great austerities, and denied themselves many indulgences.

3. *They were liberal.* Gave tithes of all they possessed, and alms to the poor in great profusion, accounting the same to be meritorious.

4. *Very zealous.* Would compass sea and land to make one proselyte. The Apostle Paul was thus zealous. See Acts xx. 3, 4; xxvi. 5; Phil. iii. 5, 6.

II. THEIR RIGHTEOUSNESS WAS DEFECTIVE.

1. *In its nature;* it was altogether carnal, not spiritual. It was the righteousness of the mere creature, which is declared to be as filthy rags, and which the Scriptures condemn; Rom. iii. 20; Rom. ix. 30—33: x. 2—4.

2. *In its extent.* It reached only the external part. What were their prayers, but the service of the lips?

3. *In its objects.* They sought the praise of men more than the approbation of God.

4. *In its effects;* pride; "I am not as other men"—hardness of heart—blindness of mind—hatred of others—persecution.

III. THE RIGHTEOUSNESS OF A BELIEVER EXCEEDS THE RIGHTEOUSNESS OF THE SCRIBES AND PHARISEES. "Except," etc.

1. *It is Divine.* A believer's righteousness of state, heart, and life, is the creation of God. "We are God's workmanship," etc. — That of the Scribes and Pharisees was human, and self-created, and abhorred by God.

2. *It is internal.* "The kingdom of God is within you." Rom. ii. 28, 29. That of the Scribes and Pharisees was outward pomp and show. Matt. xxiii. 25—28. —— And if it is internal, it must be *spiritual*, seeking the approval of God alone. Theirs was carnal; they "loved the praise of men." They "appeared to men to fast."

3. The righteousness of a believer is a *surer ground of trust, and expectancy of eternal life.* "They trusted in themselves," etc. Defective as was their practice, lax as were their doctrines, they expected to enter heaven. But "except your righteousness," etc. Man is not accepted on the ground of his own righteousness, for "there is none righteous, no, not one." He is justified by faith in Christ. Rom. v. 1; Acts xiii. 38, 39. His sins are forgiven, he is delivered from the law's condemnation and curse, through the grace of God, and this is the ground of his hope of eternal life. "By grace are ye saved," etc. Eph. ii. 8.

4. The righteousness of a believer is *superior in its fruits.* It makes the heart humble, benevolent, kind, ardent to do good. Not despising others, but anxious to benefit them. The righteousness of the Scribes, etc., left their hearts unsubdued, and they were characterized by pride and vain glory. They possessed an illiberal and uncharitable spirit. —— The Christian walks in love; 1 Cor. xiii.

IMPROVEMENT.

1. The folly of trusting to self-righteousness. It excludes from the kingdom of grace and the kingdom of glory. 2. How great the happiness of those whose righteousness exceeds! etc.

LXVII.—LIGHT IN DARKNESS.

"Unto the upright there ariseth light in darkness."—Ps. cxii. 10.

GODLINESS profitable for all things. Its advantages are principally future; but it has also the promise of the life that now is. Religion meets the present state of man; in his dangers, difficulties, sorrows, etc. etc.

I. GIVE AN OUTLINE OF THE CHARACTER "UPRIGHT."

1. An upright man is so as it regards *himself;* looks to his motives, as well as to his *actions*, and particularly in time of trial.

2. He is so as it regards *others.* He is not the fine marble chimney-

piece that hides a smoky chimney, nor the painted tomb that covers corruption and worms.

3. He is so as it regards *God;* as to the *path* he treads, and the *creed* he embraces.

II. REMARKS ON THE CHARACTER.

1. This uprightness is not to be considered as a particular grace or duty, but a general quality, that is to attend every grace, and the performance of every duty.

2. Such a character may be found with very considerable imperfection.

3. Such a character is by no means common in the world and the church.

III. EXEMPLIFY THE MEANING OF THE BLESSEDNESS AND PRIVILEGE ATTACHED TO IT.

1. Light in the darkness of Ignorance.
2. Light in the darkness of Perplexity.
3. Light in the darkness of Doubt.
4. Light in the darkness of Affliction.
5. Light in the darkness of Death.

LXVIII.—THE ARK A TYPE OF CHRIST.

"And the ark of the Lord continued in the house of Obed-edom three months; and the Lord blessed Obed-edom, and all his household." — 2 SAM. vi. 11.

THE history of the Jews is a striking detail of the Providence of God towards them ——— The tabernacle with its furniture and services had a typical character. The ark of the covenant, typical of Christ the substance of all the shadows connected with the ceremonial of the Levitical economy. See Ex. xxv. 10—22; Heb. ix. 4, 5.

I. The Ark represented the purity and incorruptibility of Jesus Christ. It was made made of the best cedar or shittim wood, to denote its duration and value.

Jesus Christ is the same yesterday, to-day, and for ever; and he is precious to all his people.

II. The Ark represented the divinity of Christ. It was overlaid with pure gold both within and without.

Jesus Christ was the "brightness of his Father's glory, and the express image of his person." Fine gold is but a faint representation of Christ's Divine excellencies. "In him dwelt all the fulness of the Godhead bodily."

III. It represented the legal dignity and glory of Christ. On the ark, and about it, were set golden crowns.

This indicated the future kingly glory of Messiah. On his head, as the King of kings, and Lord of lords, shall be placed many crowns. Rev. xix. 11.

IV. In the Ark were deposited the two tables of the moral law.

The law was written upon the heart of Christ, illustrated in his life, and glorified in his death. Rom. viii. 2—4. Thus "he magnified the law, and made it honourable."

V. The Ark had the mercy-seat, and the cherubims of glory overshadowing it.

In Christ, and in him only, there is mercy for guilty man. John i. 51. "Here," said God to Moses, "here will I meet with thee, and commune with thee from between the cherubims, before the mercy-seat, upon the ark of the testimony." Ex. xxv. 22. So Christ is the meeting-place of God with man, in whom he designs to reveal his gracious will and pleasure to the fallen creature.

VI. The ark contained the golden pot of manna, preserved as a memorial of the miraculous interposition of Jehovah on behalf of the Israelites.

So Christ came down from heaven to suffer and die for man's salvation. His death is the life of all believers'. This is beautifully stated. John vi. 31—35, 48—58.

VII. The ark contained Aaron's rod that budded.

Typifying Christ's resurrection, exaltation, and unchanging priesthood. Though he was crucified through weakness, yet he was raised in power. He was esteemed as a root out of a dry ground, yet he arose as the immortal Saviour, and the mighty God. "I am he that liveth, and was dead; and behold, I am alive, for evermore, Amen; and have the keys of hell and of death." Rev. i. 18. Though cut down by the hand of divine justice, yet he lives, and blooms, and bears the rich fruits of grace for the healing and life of the nations.

VIII. The Ark was the companion and the blessing of Israel in all their journeys through the wilderness. It was the sure indication that God went with them.

Christ is with his people always — in all their afflictions and sorrows — in all their temptations, bereavements, and death. He will be with them to the end of their journey. "Lo, I am with you always," etc.

IX. When the Ark was carried into the Jordan, the waters divided for the children of Israel to pass through to the promised land.

It is by Christ that believers safely pass through the Jordan of death. His everlasting covenant, ordered in all things and sure, is the ground of their faith and hope. Resting on him they will have peace, and triumph, and joy, and an abundant entrance administered unto them into the everlasting kingdom. 1 Cor. xv. 55—57.

X. The presence of the ark conquered every opposing power, and was ever signalized by complete triumph.

It overturned the walls of Jericho when carried round them seven days. So shall the walls of Babylon fall, and every high thing that exalts itself against God be cast down by the preaching of the gospel, which is the power of God to salvation. He shall reign from sea to sea, etc.

The ark overthrew Dagon of the Philistines in his own temple, and broke him to pieces. So by Christ, shall all the idols of the heathen utterly perish. He will destroy the Man of sin, even him who sits in the temple of God, and shows himself that he is God — he shall be destroyed by the spirit of his mouth, and brightness of his coming. Christ alone shall receive the worship and homage of all the nations, and be crowned Lord of all. Rev. xi. 15.

IMPROVEMENT.

1. No one can be happy without an interest in Christ. For the ark of the covenant sanctified the places to which it came; and blessed the house of Obed-edom, where it continued for a short time. So it is the presence of Christ that makes holy and happy. 2. Constantly approach this ark, and receive the richest blessings deposited there. 3. Despise not Christ. He that does so will perish. See the case of Uzzah.

LXIX.—HEAVEN A BETTER COUNTRY.

"But now they desire a better country, that is, a heavenly." — HEB. xi. 16.

THE land of Canaan was a glorious land — the land of promise and high expectation. The possession of it animated the Israelites in all their journeys.———But the Patriarchs valued heaven more——— that they sought by faith, accounting themselves strangers and pilgrims on earth. V. 13.———It is a pleasing feature in a believer, when his mind is becoming gradually detached from this world, and aspiring after a better country, that is, a heavenly. By this he proves his regeneration by the Spirit, being born from above.

I. HEAVEN IS A BETTER COUNTRY.

Heaven has various appellations in Scripture. It is called mansions, my Father's house, a city, a kingdom, a temple, an inheritance, the purchased possession; and here a country, doubtless in allusion to the land or country of Canaan, which was typical of heavenly and eternal rest.

This country has been revealed. "Life and immortality have been brought to light by the gospel."

It is impossible to give an adequate description of its unparalleled excellency and glory.

In what respects is it a better country?

1. *Because of its vastness and magnificence.* How poor and limited was Canaan — how contracted is this world, or any of the planets, compared with Jehovah's boundless residence! What is worldly grandeur compared to the grandeur of heaven! How poor its crowns, sceptres, thrones, etc. — Rev. xxi. If one soul outweighs this world in value, how valuable must be a heaven of redeemed souls!

2. *Because it has never been revolutionized by sin.* True, some of the angels kept not their first state —— but the atmosphere of heaven, its employments, etc., etc., have never been scathed by sin. It retains its pristine beauty and glory. *Its government is perfect.* The best governments in this world are imperfect, etc.

3. *It is a more holy country.* Satan reigns not there. No depraved hearts there. No polluted associates there. No prevailing lusts there. "They have washed their robes," etc. "They are without fault before the throne." Rev. xxi. 27.

4. *It is a happier country.* Because no sin. All the misery of this world is to be traced to sin. —— No bodily disease — no temptations — no persecution — no adversity — no bereavements — no death.

5. *The associations are more refined, exalted, and agreeable.* With angels, and the spirits of just men made perfect. All pure, all happy — saints will know each other. Shall reign with Christ.

Contrast the inhabitants of heaven with those of earth. Here they are earthly, sensual, and devilish. This is a world of commotion and moral evil.——But in this better country dwells every excellency that can ennoble the Christian.

6. *Its employments are better.* They stand in the immediate presence of the Triune Jehovah — they are favoured with peculiar discoveries of the nature and perfections of God — and with the great mysteries of providence and grace.

7. *It will abide for ever.* Every thing in this world is evanescent — fading — yea, the world itself shall pass away. 1 John ii. 17. But that inheritance is incorruptible — that crown fades not. It is the everlasting kingdom of our Lord Jesus Christ. 1 Pet. i. 4.

II. BELIEVERS DESIRE THIS BETTER COUNTRY.

1. *Once they did not.* They were content with this world. And so it is with all the unregenerate.

2. *They desire this country because they are regenerated by the Spirit.* It is natural for them to desire it. By faith in the blood of Christ they have a title to it. Their names are written in heaven.

3. *They are dissatisfied with this world, and charmed and attracted by the better country.*

4. They express their desire for it *by constantly engaging in those spiritual exercises which are akin to those of heaven.* They love prayer and praise, and all the means of grace, as the preparatives for their heavenly rest.

Thus they imbibe a disposition kindred to that of the heavenly inhabitants.

5. *They desire it as the result of constant dependence upon Christ.*—They hope for it, and daily expect to enjoy it.

6. *They desire it above every other thing.* "Whom have I in heaven but thee?" etc.

IMPROVEMENT.

1. Have we seen the vanity of this world, etc. 2. The desire of the saint will soon be realized. "Your salvation is nearer than when you believed." 3. Let sinners forsake the world because unsatisfying and ruinous.

LXX.—THE AXE LAID TO THE ROOT.

"And now also the axe is laid unto the root of the trees; therefore every tree which bringeth not forth good fruit, is hewn down and cast into the fire."—MATT. iii. 10.

THE Metaphor is taken from the Keeper of a vineyard, who, when he has an unfruitful tree, takes the axe, and cuts it down, Luke xiii. 9.
—— John the Baptist reminds the Jews of their disobedient and unprofitable conduct. They had been favoured with rich and distinguished privileges, with the Levitical worship, the ministry of the prophets, and had seen again and again the terrible effects of disobedience, yet they had made little improvement. And he tells them that the time had come when such unfruitful professors should be removed as cumberers of the ground. "And now the axe," etc.

I. *Point out some instances in which the axe of Divine vengeance has been lifted up against sinners, and which may now be said to be at the root of the trees.*

1. The first instance is *the deluge of the antediluvian world.* Gen. vi. Noah was sent to warn them, but they regarded him not, and they were hewn down as unfruitful trees.

2. *Sodom and Gomorrah*, Gen. xix. 14. Lot faithfully admonished them from the Lord. They were refractory, and Divine justice cut them down.

3. The fate of *Korah, Dathan, and Abiram.* See Num. xvi. 31.

4. *The destruction of Jerusalem.* Even when John the Baptist uttered the warning voice, the axe was at the root of the trees. Such an awful stroke was this, that it cannot be equalled in history. The Scripture was fulfilled, Luke xxi. 6; Matt. xxiv. 21; Luke xxi. 24.

5. *The axe of Divine vengeance is now at the root of every sinner, ready to strike the fatal blow.* For life is short and uncertain—and death may be very near. As it respects the aged and infirm, death has already begun to strike—the tree shakes, and gives symptoms of its approaching fall—another stroke, and they are gone. "There is but a step between me and death."

II. *The objects against whom this axe may be said to be lifted up.* "Every tree that bringeth not," etc. Many bring forth the fruits of sin; but how few those of holiness!

1. *All open and profane sinners.* These bring forth bad fruit—wild grapes. Isa. iii. 10; v. 4.

2. *All prayerless Christians.* Many who would be thought Christians, yet live without prayer. There can be no good fruit there.

3. *Such as rest satisfied with the outward form of religion,* but deny the power thereof, Matt. xxiii. 33.

4. *Such as rest in their former attainments,* and think because they once had good desires and resolutions, and felt their minds occasionally affected with Divine things, they must belong to the people of God, and shall surely arrive in heaven at the last. This is a common deception which Satan injects into the mind. Jude 12.

III. *The awful consequences of being found unfruitful.*

Death is the executioner. He conducts from earth to the bar of God; and as the tree falleth so it lies, etc. "He that is holy will be holy still; he that is filthy," etc. As death leaves us so judgment finds us. What an influence has conduct here upon our future destiny! "The wicked shall be cut off from the earth," Prov. ii. 22. "The wicked is driven away in his wickedness."

The final doom is awful. "And cast into the fire, being worthless," Rev. xxi. 8; Ps. ix. 17. This is a doom of which we can form but an imperfect conception; and therefore it is indescribable.

It is one of severe mental agony—of torturing recollection—of unavailing regret—and it is entirely without hope.

What meanest thou, O sleeper? Arise, and call upon thy God, lest thou perish. Turn to the Lord with a contrite heart—look to Christ for his saving grace, and to the Spirit to strengthen thee with all might by his Spirit in the inner man.

LXXI.—GOD'S PRESENCE CONDUCTING TO HEAVENLY REST.

"My presence shall go with thee, and I will give thee rest."—Ex. xxxiii. 14.

It appears from this chapter that the situation of Moses was a very painful one. On his return from the mount where he had intimate fellowship with God, he found the children of Israel worshipping the golden calf which they had made. Jehovah threatened to leave them in the wilderness, and to destroy them. The people were so alarmed that they instantly stripped themselves of their ornaments, and wept. While in this dreadful dilemma, God called Moses to enter the tabernacle.——There Moses interceded for them, and the text is the gracious answer of God to his prayer.

I. OBSERVE THE ANALOGY IN THE CONDITION OF THE ANCIENT ISRAELITES, AND GOD'S PEOPLE NOW.

There is a striking analogy in the condition and circumstances of ancient Israel, and God's Israel now. For instance, the ancient Israelites were in the land of Egypt, and in the house of bondage. It was a land of toil, wretchedness, and misery. God mercifully interposed and delivered them from the yoke of the oppressor. Is not this representative of God's people now? They have been in bondage to Satan, to sin, and the law. But God by his marvellous grace has made them free. Col. i. 12, 13.

The children of Israel journeyed through the wilderness, and were subject to hunger, thirst, and various dangers. And what is this world but a desert through which all true believers are travelling? It is a dreary desert, beset with troubles and dangers on every hand.

The Israelites were journeying to Canaan, the promised land. The land promised to Abraham, Isaac, and Jacob—that goodly land which Moses desired to see—"a good land, a land of brooks of water, of fountains and depths that spring out of valleys and hills; a land of wheat and barley, and wines, and fig-trees, and pomegranates," etc. Deut. viii. 7—10.——Believers are journeying to that heaven of which Canaan was but a faint type. It is a "better country, that is, a heavenly" one. It has been purchased and prepared by Christ, and he prepares all his people for it. It is the land where Jehovah dwells and reigns, and all his angels and saints appear with him there in glory.

But numerous enemies, conflicts, adversities, afflictions, and death itself, await the Christian before he can enter the heavenly Canaan. "It is through much tribulation that he must enter the kingdom of God." Hence he needs the Divine presence to conduct him on his journey.

II. THE PROMISED PRESENCE. "My presence shall go with thee." The presence of God is frequently declared in the Scriptures.

1. *We read of his essential presence.* His universal presence, Ps. cxxxix. 7. His presence pervades all space. His perfections and glory are displayed everywhere. "Do not I fill heaven and earth, saith the Lord?"

2. *God manifested his presence symbolically.* To Moses he appeared in the bush. To the Israelites he appeared in a pillar of cloud by day, and in a pillar of fire by night. In the temple the bright cloud of the presence of the Lord filled the house. In a symbolical way he manifested his presence on the day of Pentecost, Acts ii.

3. The Scriptures also record *God's judicial presence.* Hence he has come down from heaven in terrible majesty to punish the nations of the

earth. How awful his appearance at the deluge—at the destruction of Sodom and Gomorrah! etc. It is thus that God comes near to the wicked in judgment, Mal. iii. 5.

4. *Also God's Providential presence.* By this he is present with all his creatures; providing for their wants and necessities, and causing his sun to shine upon the evil as well as upon the good, etc. But there is a special providence which watches over, defends, and guides his saints, Matt. vi. 27. This leads us to observe,

5. That God's presence is of *a gracious character.* As sinners, he is far from us, and we are far from him. " But we are made nigh by the blood of Christ." Now his presence is felt and enjoyed in his house, in his ordinances, in the closet, etc.

God therefore by his gracious promises says to his people,—

My *comforting presence* shall go with thee. Is the sinner penitent? He will appear to heal his broken heart and forgive all his sins. He will comfort the returning prodigal, and throw around him the arms of compassion. Is the Christian afflicted—a mourner? He will appear as the God of comfort and consolation, 2 Cor. i. 3, 4.

My *protecting presence* shall go with thee. The way to heaven is full of enemies and dangers. But God is a sun to shine upon their path, and a shield to defend them, Gen. xvii. 1.

My *supporting presence* shall go with thee. In how many conflicts, distresses, straits, do believers need support! How sweet then is the promise, "My presence"! etc. Isa. xli. 10.

My *guiding presence* shall go with thee. It is not in man to direct his steps. Thus he guided Israel through the intricate paths of the wilderness; and he will guide his people safely across the desert of this world. See Ps. xxv. 9; cxliii. 10; lxxiii. 23, 24.

My *communing presence* shall go with thee. John xiv. 16, 17. I will hear thy prayers; I will commune with thee from off the mercy-seat. Thou shalt see my power and glory in the sanctuary. "In all places where I record my name, I will come unto you and bless you."

My presence *shall ever go with you.* "I will never leave you, nor forsake you." To a time of old age, to your grey hairs, to your struggle with death, my presence shall go with you—and after your last conflict and victory, I will give you rest.

III. THE PROMISED REST. "I will give thee rest."

As it respected Israel, it implied a quiet resting-place in the land of Canaan. There they had done with all the toils of the wilderness, and enjoyed the fertility and beauty of that " goodly land."

Canaan was a type of heaven, because,

1. It was *the promised land.* During a period of 400 years the posterity of Abraham had their hopes directed towards it as the country which God had promised to bestow upon his chosen people as a possession, where they should serve him, and enjoy his favour, Gen. xii. 7; xiii. 15.

Thus believers are promised a possession in that better country, that is, a heavenly one, John xiv. 2, 3; Col. i. 5.

2. It was the land in which the Israelites should *enjoy rest and peace* after all their toils, warfare, and journeyings should be ended. Deut. xii. 9; Ps. xcv. 11.

And in heaven, the glorified saints shall rest from sin, and all its consequences—from afflictions—from temptation—from persecution—and from death.

And being admitted into the immediate presence of God to worship, they shall pass a perpetual sabbath in those elevations of pure devotion which the sublimest moments of our happiest days here can teach us but imperfectly to conceive. For being free from sin, from sorrow, and the curse, they shall have access to the throne of God, and "serve him day and night in his temple, and he that sitteth on the throne shall dwell among them," etc. Rev. vii. 15—17.

The land of Canaan was a type of heaven because it was *an inheritance freely bestowed upon them*, a gift which flowed wholly from the good pleasure of God; and in this respect it was a figure of "the inheritance of the saints in light," Col. i. 12; Acts xxvi. 18. "Eternal life is *the free gift of God*, through Jesus Christ our Lord," Rom. vi. 23. And in every part of the salvation of sinners, the grace of God reigns to the exclusion of all worthiness in the creature, Eph. ii. 8, 9.

IMPROVEMENT.

1. We must be Israelites indeed, etc., before we can lay claim to this promise.——2. How miserable the state of those persons who pass through life without the presence of God!——3. How cheering the prospect of Christians! They are journeying to the rest.

LXXII.—CHARACTER AND PORTION OF GOD'S PEOPLE.

"O how great is thy goodness, which thou hast laid up for them that fear thee, which thou hast wrought for them that trust in thee before the sons of men." — Ps. xxxi. 16.

THE goodness of Deity is a delightful theme, and forms the principal glory of the Divine character. Great as he is in majesty, power, and dominion, he prefers to be known as the God of love and of all grace; for mercy is his chief delight.——The ordinary goodness of God extends to all; for "his tender mercies are over all his works:" but there is a special goodness which is enjoyed only by his people, and of this the text speaks.

I. THE CHARACTER OF GOD'S PEOPLE: "them that fear thee;" "them that trust in thee before the sons of men."

The union of these two principles is what constitutes the Christian character.

1. *They fear God.* The fear of God is frequently put for the whole of religion, Mal. iii. 16. "Then they that feared the Lord," etc. There is a fear which is of a slavish kind, and which torments the soul, Rom. viii. 5.——But this is not the fear intended in the text. Sinners fear the effects of their deeds in a future state; they have an evil, a defiled conscience, and a fearful looking for of judgment. From all this believers have been delivered, Rom. viii. 1.

It is a filial fear—a child-like fear, accompanied by faith, hope, and love, Ps. xxxiv. 9. It is the effect of Divine operation. "I will put my fear into their hearts."——This fear is a powerful preservative from sin. "Fear the Lord and depart from evil," Prov. iii. 7.——it stimulates to holy obedience, Ps. cxii. 1—3.

2. *They trust in God.* "Them that trust in thee." They feel their own unworthiness—their own weakness and insufficiency. They trust in God through Christ, who is the way to the Father. They trust him for all the purposes of salvation—in every time of need—in prospect of death and eternity.

This distinguishes real believers from Pharisees, whose religion is all fear, and whose services result from the mere dread of future misery. They would neither serve God, nor do any thing to please him, but for this, or the hope of being well rewarded. In the same way real Christians are distinguished self-confident antinomians, whose religion is nothing but unfounded assurance, and an arrogant assumption of the promises, unaccompanied by the fear of God.

3. *Their conduct is manifest and exemplary.* They "fear God, and trust in him before the sons of men." They are not ashamed of their religion. They show to the world what they are. They are "the lights of the world." They are not intimidated by persecution, being fully persuaded in their own minds that religion is the one thing needful. This honours God, and God will honour them. Their conduct reproves the world, and they are God's witnesses against it. Mark viii. 38; Luke ix. 26.

II. WHAT GOD HAS LAID UP AND WROUGHT OUT FOR HIS PEOPLE. "O how great," etc.

God is good to all his creatures in the supply of all their temporal wants and necessities. "The Lord is good to all, and his tender mercies are over all his works." But this goodness is peculiar and special to the people of God only. For them alone it is laid up, and wrought out.

1. There is much *temporal good* laid up for them. God feeds the fowls of the air, etc., and will he not take care of his people? Matt. vi. "Casting all your care upon him; for he careth for you."

2. There is an infinite amount of *spiritual good* laid up and wrought out for them.

(1) See this in the work of *Redemption.* Rom. v. 6—8; Eph. i. 7; John iii. 16. No goodness ever equalled this.

(2) See it in the *blessings of Redemption.* Pardon for every offence—justification from all condemnation—enlightenment by the Holy Spirit—his teaching, sanctifying, and comforting influence.

(3) See it in *the sufficiency of Divine grace for every time* of need. Isa. xxvi. 4; xli. 10: 2 Cor. xii. 9. —— In all his conflicts and distresses, how much the Christian needs!

3. But this goodness *refers especially to a future state.* "O how great is thy goodness which thou hast *laid up in heaven!*" It is the inheritance, 1 Pet. i. 4.—It is the building of God, 2 Cor. v. 1.—Mansions of rest, John xiv. 1, 2.—Crowns of glory are laid up, 1 Pet. v. 4.—A fulness of joy is prepared, Ps. xvi. 14.

III. THE MAGNITUDE OF THIS GOODNESS: "O how great," etc.

1. *Great in the contrivance and arrangement of it,* Rom. ii. 33. It was "laid up" in the councils of heaven.

2. Great, if we consider *the guilt and wretchedness of its recipients.* They are lost, ruined, and undone. How great is that goodness which could provide for the pardon of all their sins—the moral renovation of their nature, and for perfecting the work of grace with a crown of glory!

3. *The abundant provision* which God has made for his people, affords a still greater display of his mercy. It is what eye hath not seen, nor ear heard, etc.; exceeding abundantly above all that we can ask or think; Col. i. 19.

4. *The security of it.* It is deposited in safe hands. God himself has laid it up, and he himself will give the inheritance.

5. *Its free dispensation,* without money and without price; yet in a manner corresponding with infinite wisdom.

IMPROVEMENT.

1. Pray for a rich and joyful participation in this goodness now. The greater part of the portion is still to come, yet in every time of need a present supply is given, sufficient to carry us to our journey's end, and to give us a foretaste, and an earnest of the future inheritance.— 2. Be grateful for this goodness, which was wrought out by the gracious purposes of God, and the sacrificial death of Christ. This goodness was wrought out by the agony in the garden, by the bloody sweat, and by the terrible inflictions of Divine wrath when nailed to the ignominious tree.

LXXIII.—CHRIST THE GOOD SHEPHERD.

"I am the good Shepherd, and know my sheep, and am known of mine."— JOHN x. 14.

THIS is not the language of self-adulation; but of sincerity and truth on the part of Christ, and of gracious intimation to his people. Jesus Christ was never known to boast; for he was "meek and lowly in heart." He merely proclaims his own character in the text.

I. THE CHARACTER OF CHRIST. "I am the good Shepherd."

1. HE IS GOODNESS ITSELF. "God is love." "He delighteth in mercy." And this goodness is the source of all the good he manifests towards his flock.
2. HE HAS PURCHASED HIS FLOCK by the shedding of his blood. They are a redeemed people. Acts xx. 28.
3. HE FEEDS THEM. In the green pastures of his word, church, ordinances, etc. Ps. xxiii. 1. 2.
4. HE GUIDES THEM. They are ignorant—short-sighted, etc. He guides them by his Providence, word, and Spirit.
5. HE DEFENDS THEM. Ps. lix. 9, 16; xciv. 22

II. HIS KNOWLEDGE OF HIS PEOPLE.

1. HE DISTINGUISHES THEM FROM OTHERS. "And know my sheep."
(1) HE HAS CHOSEN THEM. —— (2) He has drawn them to his fold. (3) He has formed in them his image.
2. HE KNOWS THEM INDIVIDUALLY— In their various situations, and circumstances of life.

III. THEIR KNOWLEDGE OF HIM. "And am known of mine."

1. They know and value His person.——2. They know his will.——3. They know his voice. —— 4. They know his present power to save them. —— 5. They know his intentions as to the future.

IMPROVEMENT.

1. How condescending is Christ's love! — 2. How necessary is self-examination!—3. How blessed is the true believer's condition!

LXXIV.—CONSTANCY IN PRAYER.

"Praying always with all prayer and supplication in the Spirit, and watching thereunto with all perseverance and supplication for all saints." — EPH. vi. 18.

PRAYER is the Christian's "vital breath." It is a part of spiritual life. —— Prayer is indispensable. Without it we shall be miserable, weak, and helpless, and ever liable to be cast down by Satan. —— In the context the Apostle refers to the formidable enemies of believers, and urges them to avail themselves of the Divine armour provided, which he specifies, ver. 11, etc. The weapon of All-prayer is the subject of the text. Without this all the others would be of no avail; in fact, without it they could not be used at all.

The Apostle contemplates a Christian soldier fully armed, ready for battle, and exhorts them in that condition to look up to God for success in warfare. As it was the custom of the Grecian armies, before battle, to *offer prayers* to the gods for their success, the apostle shows that these spiritual warriors must depend on the Captain of their salvation, and pray with all prayer for triumph over all their foes. He alone can save, and he alone can destroy all Satan's machinations.

I. THE APOSTLE URGES THE PERFORMANCE OF PRAYER.

Prayer does not consist in any form of words—nor in any extempore addresses. These may be very correct, expressive, and eloquent; yet they will be of no avail without the heart. Prayer is prompted by a deep conviction of need — a deep conviction that God alone can supply that need, and an application by faith in the Redeemer for the blessings required. In short, prayer is the desire of the soul going out after God,* whether in a form, or without one. "As the hart panteth," etc. Ps. xlvii. 1. Hannah of old prayed in her heart, 1 Sam. i. 13, etc.

Prayer might also be represented as consisting of *Adoration*, or reverencing of God — *Thanksgiving*, for the mercies bestowed — *Confession* of sins committed — and *Petition*, or pleading for needful grace in the name of Jesus Christ.

2. PRAYER MUST BE CONSTANT. "Praying always."

Wherever we are, whatever we are doing, in all conditions of life, we must pray. Happy is the Christian who has his heart ready for prayer! "In every thing, by prayer and supplication, with thanksgiving, let your requests be made known unto God," Phil. iv. 6. "Pray without ceasing." 1 Thess. v. 17.

A number of ministers were assembled for the discussion of difficult questions, and it was asked, how the command to "pray without ceasing" could be complied with? Various suppositions were started, and one of the number was appointed to write an essay upon it, to be read at the next monthly meeting; which being overheard by a plain, sensible servant-girl, she exclaimed, "What! a whole month wanted to tell the meaning of that text! it is one of the easiest texts in the Bible." "Well, well," said an old minister, "Mary, what can you say about it? how do you understand it; can you pray all the time?" "O yes, sir." "What, when you have so many things to do?" "Why, sir, the more I have to do, the more I can pray." "Indeed? well, Mary, do let us

---

* An old divine has the following beautiful passage on the approach of prayer to the mercy-seat, and her success there. — "Hope calls to prayer, and says — 'Lo, here is a messenger speedy, ready, trusty, knowing the way. *Ready;* you can no sooner call her than she comes. *Speedy;* she flies faster than eagles, as fast as angels. *Trusty;* what embassage soever you put in her tongue, she delivers with faithful secresy. She *knows the way* to the throne of mercy; and never faints till she comes to the chamber of the royal presence. Prayer hath her message. Away she flies, borne on the sure and swift wings of faith and zeal, wisdom having given her a charge, and hope a blessing. Finding the gate shut, she knocks and cries; 'Open, ye gates of righteousness, and be ye open, ye everlasting doors of glory, that I may enter, and deliver to the King of Jerusalem my petition.' Jesus Christ hears the knock, opens the gate of mercy, attends her suit, promiseth her infallible comfort and redress. Back returns prayer, laden with consolation. She hath a promise, and she delivereth it into the hands of faith — that were our enemies more in number than the locusts of Egypt, and more strong than the giants, the sons of Anak, yet power and mercy shall fight for us, and we shall be delivered. Pass we then through fire and water—through all dangers and difficulties, yet we have a messenger holy, happy, acceptable to God; that never comes back without comfort — that messenger is, *Prayer*."

know how it is, for most people think otherwise." "Well, sir," said the girl, "when I first open my eyes in the morning, I pray that the Lord would open the eyes of my understanding; and while I am dressing, I pray that I may be clothed with the robe of righteousness; and when I have washed me, I ask for the washing of regeneration; and as I begin to work, I pray that I may have strength equal to my day; and when I begin to kindle up the fire, I pray that God's work may revive in my soul; and as I sweep out the house, I pray that my heart may be cleansed of all impurities; and while preparing and partaking of my breakfast, I desire to be fed with the hidden manna, and the sincere milk of the Word; and as I am busy with the little children, I look up to God as my Father, and pray for the spirit of adoption that I may be his child; and so on all day: every thing I do furnishes me with a thought for prayer." "Enough, enough," cried the old divine, "these things are revealed to babes, and often hid from the wise and prudent. Go on, Mary: 'pray without ceasing;' and as for us, my brethren, let us bless the Lord for this exposition, and remember that he has said, 'the *meek* will he guide in judgment.'" After this, the essay was considered unnecessary.

There are some special seasons for prayer, which call for more than ordinary exercise — which require fervency and perseverance:—

(1) *When the Christian has great duties to perform.* Then he must pray for help. It is a time of need. The Apostle Paul regarded the duties of his office to be great, and therefore he prayed, and requested the prayers of others; "Brethren, pray for us." "Praying always—and for me, that utterance may be given unto me," etc. Eph. vi. 18, 19. We need omnipotence to help us to do the Lord's work.

(2) *When the Christian has to endure afflictions.** The Psalmist was afflicted, and it brought him to the throne of grace: Ps. xxv. 16; cxix. 107; James v. 13.

(3) *When sin abounds, and the flood-gates of wickedness are let loose.* So Hezekiah prayed; Isa. xxxvii. 15.

(4) *In the time of persecution and distress.* When Haman plotted the destruction of the Jews, they prayed. When Esau came out to meet Jacob, Jacob prayed for protection and deliverance; Gen. xxxii. 9, etc. When Peter was in prison, the church prayed; Acts xii. 5.

(5) *In the hour of temptation.* When Christ was assaulted, and his

---

* Believers are afflicted as other men. They endure pains and weakness of body—domestic trials—family bereavements—worldly losses—and distress of mind. In addition to all these, which are the common sorrows of our race, they have trials peculiar to themselves. Many are the afflictions of the righteous. These afflictions do not proceed from chance, nor do they proceed from the will of a capricious and despotic tyrant. They are the chastisements of a father's hand — the proofs of paternal love. What then should be our conduct under them? We should pray. *Pray in submission to the Divine will, that your afflictions be removed.* Take as your examples David, Jonah, Hezekiah, Manasseh, Paul, and even Christ himself. *Pray for grace to endure affliction while it continues, so as to glorify God.* Certain graces thrive best in affliction. Gold shines brightest when burnished. Stars are most lustrous in the darkness of night. Spices emit their sweetest odours when bruised. So patience — meekness — acquiescence in the will of God, are most conspicuous in the time of affliction. *Pray that your afflictions may be sanctified.* Sanctified afflictions are among the best blessings of the new covenant. What a mercy that we can pray, even in the darkest hour! Avail yourself, my friend, of this relief. The returns of prayer will be more precious than the richest cargoes — more refreshing than the most genial showers — types and foretastes of heaven.

hour was come, etc., he prayed earnestly. Matt. xxvi. 44. When Paul was buffeted with the thorn in the flesh, he prayed; 2 Cor. xii. 8, etc.

3. The exhortation comprehends *various kinds of prayer.* "With all prayer."

It may embrace prayer performed in public, in the family, in the closet, in business, on the way, *in the heart* without a voice, and with *the voice* from the heart. All these are necessary to the genuine Christian; and he whose heart is right with God will embrace every opportunity for prayer. Mr. Wesley says, "Some there are who use only *mental* prayer or ejaculations, and think they are in a state of grace, and use a way of worship far superior to any other; but such only fancy themselves to be *above* what is really above *them;* it requiring far more grace to be enabled to pour out a fervent and continued prayer than to offer up mental aspirations.

"Praying with all prayer *and supplication.*" There is a difference in the Greek between the word *prayer* and the word *supplication.* Some think the former means prayer for the *attainment of good;* the latter prayer for *averting evil.* Supplication, however, seems to mean prayer continued in strong and incessant pleading, till the evil is averted, or the good communicated—wrestling like Jacob—pleading earnestly with the Lord. "The kingdom of heaven suffereth violence, and the violent take it by force."

4. *Prayer must be dictated by the Spirit.* "Praying —— in the Spirit." The Spirit was promised by Christ; John xiv. 16; xvi. 7, 14, etc. Matt. vii. 11.

We need the assistance of the Spirit. Our *infirmities* render it necessary. Rom. viii. 26. Our infirmities will be assisted. Let us not pray in the strength of our genius, or our natural eloquence—but seek the aid of the Spirit.

5. Prayer must be *combined with watchfulness.* "And watching thereunto."

Watching that you may be assisted to pray—watching against improper motives to pray—watching the movements of your enemies, lest they should surprise you—watching, striving with your prayers to accomplish at least some of the good you seek—watching over your conduct, words, and actions, that they be suitable to praying persons—watching, waiting, wrestling for answers to your prayers. Hence the Redeemer said, "What I say unto one, I say unto all, Watch."

6. The Apostle recommends *perseverance in prayer.* "With all perseverance."

Being always intent on your object, and never losing sight of your danger and interest. The word implies *stretching out the neck,* and looking about, in order to discern an enemy at a distance. Never give over praying, though God may not answer you immediately. "The vision is for an appointed time," etc. Hab. ii. 3; Luke xviii. 1. Spiritual, heavenly blessings are worthy of perseverance.

7. *Prayer is not to be selfish.*

Pray for ourselves in the first instance; but forget not the saints — forget not ministers — pray for all the church. See text and following verse.

IMPROVEMENT.

Pray according to the will of God. 1 John v. 14.
Let not sin be indulged, or unrepented of. Ps. lxvi. 18.
Pray in faith. Unbelief hinders success in prayer; James i. 16.
Pray in the name of Christ. Depend upon his mediation, and intercession.

MATERIALS OF THOUGHT FOR THE PRECEDING OUTLINE.

CHRIST PRAYED.

The Lord Jesus was a man of prayer. He came to do his Father's will, and his prayers had reference to his life-work. He knew the Divine mind; hence his prayers were always in harmony with it, and were put up in faith. He prayed in public and in private; but more in the latter way than in the former. In public his prayers are short ; but in private he "continued all night in prayer to God." He prayed for himself — for his friends — and for his persecutors and foes. He prayed always, and maintained a constant habit of communion with his Father. In this, as in the other parts of his life, he has set us an example. Many are the temptations to neglect prayer; especially PRIVATE prayer. Many excuses are ready to abridge it, if not to slip it entirely. We may plead cares, calls, fatigue. Let us think of Jesus. He never allowed the pressure of engagements (and his was a busy life) to cheat him out of his season for prayer. If he found this exercise so important, how essential must it be to us! the nearer we come to him in his solitary devotions, the more shall we be like him in his public life. Prayer will give us power with God and with men. We shall experience the fulfilment of that promise, "My Father which seeth in secret shall reward thee openly."

SUCCESS IN PRAYER.

Shortly after the settlement of the Pilgrim Fathers in New England, they were visited by a long and terrific drought. Providence seemed to frown upon them, and threaten their destruction. In their distress they appointed a day of fasting and prayer; and thus one of themselves records the result of their united supplications:—"O! the mercy of our God, who was as ready to hear as we to ask! for though in the morning, when we assembled together, the heavens were as clear, and the drought was as likely to continue, as ever it was, yet (our exercise continuing some eight or nine hours) before our departure the weather was overcast, the clouds gathered together on all sides, and on the next morning distilled such soft, sweet, and moderate showers of rain, continuing some fourteen days, and mixed with such seasonable weather, as it was hard to say whether our withered corn or drooping affections were most quickened and revived,—such was the bounty and goodness of our God." Thus God, in every age, proves himself to be the hearer and the answerer of prayer. Let us, then, at all times, and under all circumstances, by prayer and supplication, make known our requests unto him!

IMPORTANCE OF PRAYER.

"There was once a husbandman," says Flavel, "that always sowed good seed, but never had good corn. At last a neighbour came to him, and said, 'I will tell you what probably may be the cause of it. It may be,' said he, 'you do not STEEP your seed?' 'No, truly,' replied the other, 'nor did I ever hear that seed must be steeped.' 'Yes, surely,' said his neighbour, 'and I will tell you how: it must be STEEPED IN PRAYER.' When the party heard this, he thanked him for his counsel, reformed his fault, and had as good corn as other persons." Those who sow the good seed of the gospel may obtain instruction here. John Owen somewhere remarks, that, " to preach the word, and not to follow it with prayer constantly and frequently, is to believe its use, but to neglect its end, and to cast away all the seed of the gospel at random." And Leighton observes beautifully on the same point, that, " In the 10th of St. Luke, the disciples are sent forth and appointed to preach; and in the 11th we have them desiring to be taught to pray; LORD, TEACH US TO PRAY. And without this there can be little answer or success in the other: little springing up of this seed, though ministers sow it plentifully in preaching, unless they secretly water it with their prayers and tears."

LXXV. — SELF-EXAMINATION.

BY THE REV. MATTHEW HENRY.

"Examine yourselves, whether ye be in the faith."—2 COR. xiii. 5.

BLESSED Paul was famous not only for love to Christ, but also to the precious souls of men—a principle which should act in all of us. The effects of this were:

1. An earnest desire of the salvation of precious souls, Rom. x. 1. This was his heart's desire; for this he (as it were) travailed in birth; he spent his strength, and was ready to spend his blood.

2. This desire was accompanied with a holy fear of the miscarrying of souls. I am *jealous over* you — afraid of you, Gal. iv. 10.

You cannot think what a terror it is to a faithful minister to think of the perdition of any of the souls that he preaches to: it is sad to think that we labour in vain ; yet if it were only the loss of labour, it were not so much ; but it is the loss of the precious souls that I fear— lest I should meet any of you in an unconverted state in the great day. It is in pursuance of this, that this great apostle gives the exhortation here, "*examine yourselves.*" It must be *your own* work. Ministers cannot do it for you — only help you in it.

1. It supposes a doubt, whether you be in the faith or not.
2. The method for deciding this doubt. *Examine:* we must not expect revelation; try yourselves, what principle are you actuated by? You cannot judge by the outside; you must search and examine, prove your ownselves.

Doct. All that profess themselves to be Christians, ought strictly to examine whether they be Christians indeed.

We are all professing Christians by our joining ourselves to religious assemblies; but if we be not Christians indeed, our profession will signify nothing; we must be converted, born again, and be really what we seem to be. It is the soul's deliberate renouncing the world and the flesh, and resigning itself to God as its ruler and portion. You must be delivered into gospel duties as into a mould. He only is the true Christian that is one inwardly. You must try your state, and, if you are real Christians, your title is clear to all the benefits purchased by Christ.

Show 1, what it is thus to examine ourselves: it is a work that requires time, pain, skill, and care.

1. We must concern ourselves about our spiritual state: this is the first step. It is too true, but very sad, that it is very possible for men to make a profession, attend on ordinances, and yet have no true concern about their souls. Oh, the amazing stupidity of the most of men!

2. We must consider with ourselves concerning it. "Commune with your own hearts," Ps. iv. 4. Talk this matter seriously with yourselves, — to what end have we our thinking faculties? Men never begin to be religious till they begin to think. If you have some great worldly affair in hand, how do thoughts fill your minds about it!

3. We must suspect the goodness of our spiritual state—indeed some are too suspicious; I am not persuading to that; but a holy, religious fear, which is a means of our preservation—as the disciples,—"Lord, is it I?" Many have a hope for heaven which they sucked in with their milk, and, such as it is, serves to keep them from melancholy; but though many are going heavily, yet it is toward heaven, and will end well.

4. Make a strict inquiry, and bring the matter to an issue. Many have some secret misgivings which yet comes to nothing. Examine closely, call a court, command silence; it is not a thing to be done in a hurry. "If ye will inquire, inquire ye," Isa. xxi. 12.

5. Make an impartial trial, as thus: — You call God Father; but upon what ground? Have you the nature and disposition of a child? Upon what ground do you hope for heaven? The word of God is the touchstone. Let that book be opened; let nothing false be given in for evidence; let conscience speak the truth, the whole truth, and nothing but the truth. Are you prepared for glory by a work of grace? Try this impartially, without favour or affection.

6. You must pass an impartial judgment; judge by the acts. The tree is known by its fruits. If it appear upon evidence that thy hopes are false, that the love of the world prevails above the love of God, pronounce thyself unclean. Give not sleep to thine eyes till the matter be mended. Give all diligence about it, 2 Pet. i. 10, and if you can make it sure to yourselves that you are effectually called, you are made for ever; if the Spirit of God has been at work with you, to justify and sanctify you, you shall be eternally saved.

Obj. What needs so much ado, such close examination?

Ans. Such is the folly of the most of men—to be earnest about trifles, and unconcerned about things of the greatest moment.

Some motives to this duty:

1. The matter to be examined is of great concernment: are you in the faith? It is not, am I a scholar? am I in the way to preferment? No; but am I a good Christian? have I a principle of grace in my heart? Man, woman, it is not thy livelihood, but thy life—the life of thy precious soul—that lies at stake. Is it an indifferent thing whether thou be a saint or a brute, a child of wrath or a child of love? If you have any regard to your precious souls, be convinced these are not trifles.

2. The rule we are to go by is very strict. In a great road it is obvious we do not inquire; but if it be narrow and have many turnings, we are often inquiring; the gate is straight, the way narrow, many called, but few chosen; and we must be of those few, or we are undone. When Christ was asked a curious question, "Are there few that be saved?" he answered with a serious exhortation, "Strive to enter into the straight gate."

3. It is an easy matter to be deceived: to be in the faith is an inward thing. You can see in a glass the complexion of your natural face; but no glass can discover the heart. "The heart is deceitful above all things; who can know it?"

4. Multitudes have been deceived in this matter. The Church of Laodicea, Rev. iii. 17, thought herself rich, and in need of nothing, when really wretched, miserable, poor, blind, and naked.

A careful tradesman that sees others break, (who seemed thriving,) is alarmed to look to himself. "There is a way that seemeth right to a man, but the end is death." The Pharisee, Luke xviii., went down not "justified." Many have a hope for heaven ready to swear by, (as I hope to be saved,) and, perhaps, the next breath challenges God to curse them.

5. It is a matter which must be examined shortly; therefore we are concerned to examine it now. Shortly this will be the decisive question, Were you in the faith? not whether you went to this church or that; whether Greek or Jew, high or low, rich or poor, bond or free, learned or unlearned? but whether you were in the faith, and were really what you seemed to be? You cannot avoid God's inquiry, therefore must examine yourselves.

6. A mistake in this matter will be of fatal consequence. Those that cried, "Lord, Lord," were bid to depart. The higher men are lifted up in their hopes, the more sad will their fall be, Hos. xii. 8.

What a surprise was it to her that came in disguise! 1 Kings xiv. 6,

"Come in, thou wife of Jeroboam." Allude so here: Come in, thou hypocrite; why feignest thou thyself to be a true Christian? The house built on the sand fell in the storm.

7. The true discovery of our state will be greatly to our advantage; therefore we are concerned to inquire,—1. If our case be bad, there is hope that it may be mended; if you are not in the faith, get into it without delay; while there is life there is hope. A wound that is only skinned over is dangerous and threatens the patient's life, but when opened, more hopes of a cure. 2. If good, if you are in the faith, take the comfort of it; rejoice, and be exceeding glad.

Inf. 1. We have all cause to lament our neglect of this great duty of self-examination, as if it were an indifferent thing. Hence it is that many good Christians labour under such doubts; they are wanting in this great duty.

2. Examine your settled judgment. What are your thoughts of God and Christ and another world? Do you discern the glory of an invisible God above that of a dark, blinded world? If you are in the faith, invisible things will be great and real to you.

3. Examine your deliberate choice. You are of age to choose for yourselves—which has your choicest love, your best affections, God or the world? Is your religion subservient to the world, or the world to your religion? All that are in the faith have chosen God's testimonies as their heritage for ever.

4. Examine your commanding principles. What do you govern yourselves by? The world says,—Please men to serve a turn,—Every one for his gain,—Let every man look to himself, etc. ; but then there are other and better principles to steer by, — that the favour of God is better than life,—that the salvation of the soul is to be first and chiefly sought after.

5. Examine your indwelling cares. I know not what should most fill you; you know what doth. Is it care for the world and body, or for the soul and eternity? Rom. vii. 5. If in the faith, your chief care is to please God and get to heaven. I would hope that some are more careful for their souls than they seem to be. You should keep under your body; bring it into subjection.

6. Examine your outgoing affections. What is it you most delight in, most earnestly desire? Is Christ your chief good, fairest of ten thousand? Only you must not judge by the flaming of affection outwardly, for that is an uncertain rule.

Lastly; examine your constant and allowed practice. Try your state by your walk. If you live in the neglect of any known duty, it is a sign you are not in the faith. "Be not deceived; his servants you are to whom you obey." Conscience is the candle of the Lord; then light it up and make a strict search, and if you find you are in the faith, take you the comfort and give God the glory. Those that are in the faith now, if God be true, shall be in heaven shortly.

LXXVI.—IMPROPRIETIES REPROVED.

'My brethren, these things ought not so to be."—JAMES iii. 10.

THE epistle of James is not addressed to any particular church, or individuals, but to believers generally among the Jewish nation, or to the twelve tribes which are scattered abroad. The design of the Apostle was to correct the errors into which many of the early Christians had fallen. His admonition is gentle and kind, and such as became the dignity of an aged apostle. With all their imperfections, he still calls them "brethren;" and instead of dealing in invective or reproach, he merely states the impropriety of their conduct, saying, "These things ought not so to be" — a lovely example of that meekness of wisdom which the Apostle endeavoured to inculcate.

I. THE REPREHENSIBLE CONDUCT REFERRED TO.

No Christian church on earth is perfect. None were so in the Apostolic age—though some were superior to others. To how many churches at the present day may this text be applied, " My brethren, these things ought not so to be."

1. He refers to *unbelief and instability*, ch. i. 5—7. Unbelief will produce instability — a state of wretchedness and unfruitfulness.

2. *Extenuation of sin, and charging it upon God*, v. 13 — 15.

Sin should never be regarded lightly, for it is an "evil thing and bitter." Sin must not be charged upon God, for he hates it, and cannot promote it. When a sinner feels the pressure of guilt, he may be induced to say, Why hast thou made me to err? There is a disposition to charge God with that which is produced by man's lusts.

3. *Mere attendance upon the means of grace*, and impractically hearing the word; ch. i. 22.

An evil of fearful magnitude, and very common. Hearing is good when it becomes the means of knowing and doing the will of God; otherwise it will only tend to our greater condemnation; Matt. vii. 24—27; Luke xii. 47.

4. *Partiality for the rich, and despite of the poor;* ch. ii. 1.

Christianity was never intended to destroy those natural and civil distinctions which necessarily exist among men, nor to lessen the respect which is due to superiors; but in the church of God it requires at the same time that fraternal affection and lovely equality which should exist in a family of equals. When preference is shown, not to office or character, talent or virtue, but merely to wealth, it is a violation of the law of love, Matt. xxiii. 8; Ps. xv. 4.

5. *An uncharitable and unmerciful disposition;* ch. ii. 12, 13.

This respects *charity to the poor.* A righteous man will draw forth

IMPROPRIETIES REPROVED. 397

his soul, and deal out his bread to the hungry; and if rich in this world, they will be rich in good works. Severely and justly the Apostle condemns wealthy professors who had nothing for their poor and needy brethren, but a few smooth words; ch. ii. 14—16. —— An *unforgiving spirit* is also reprehended, v. 13. Christ said, "If ye forgive not men their trespasses, neither will your heavenly Father forgive you."

6. *Detraction and slander.* Evils which ought never to have existed among Christians, ch. iii. v. 5—10.

The Apostle states the difficulty of governing the tongue, that it is easier, etc. He also allows that a person who can command his tongue, has made no ordinary attainment, and may be esteemed "a perfect man." —— The Scriptures condemn wrath, malice, bitterness, and evil speaking; and among Christians especially these things ought not to be. —— See Matt. vii. 1; 1 Pet. ii. 1.

II. THE EVIL OF SUCH CONDUCT.

1. *It is utterly inconsistent with a profession of the gospel.* However it might have comported with a state of unregeneracy to live in envy, hateful, and hating one another, it is contrary to that spiritual regeneration passed upon every believer, Eph ii. 2, 3, 10; Col. iii. 1, 5. —— To profess to be alive to God, and yet to be dead in sin, etc. —— to be a follower of the meek and lowly Jesus, and yet to be litigious, implacable, unmerciful, certainly these things ought not so to be.

2. This conduct is evidently *inconsistent with growing in grace, or spiritual advancement.* The great object of the Christian profession is to be "pressing towards the mark," etc.; but the cherishing of carnal, worldly, and malevolent dispositions is utterly incompatible with such a progress, and will render our religion more than doubtful. "But he that lacketh these things is blind and cannot see afar off, and hath forgotten that he was purged from all sin;" 2 Pet. i. 9.

3. The evils reproved *are clearly opposed to the rule of duty, and the love we owe to Christ and his cause.* When professors are living too much like men of the world, wanting in circumspection, zeal, and spiritual-mindedness; when they have left their first-love — are immersed in the cares of the world, and think of little besides their secular interest ; when religion lies bleeding and dying amongst them —surely "these things ought not so to be." —— It shows the want of religion.

4. Evil tempers and dispositions among Christians tend greatly to dishonour God, to bring reproach upon his cause, and to injure the souls of men; Rom. ii. 24. —— Unbelievers are hereby furnished with an excuse, and become hardened in their impiety.

5. *Such a spirit is the very opposite to the spirit of heaven.* Heaven is love. The atmosphere of heaven is peace and love.

"There all the millions of his saints
Shall in one song unite,
And each the bliss of all shall view
With infinite delight."

IMPROVEMENT.

The imperfect state of the church should endear to us the prospect of a purer and brighter state, when Christ shall take out of his kingdom all things that now offend; when the Canaanite shall no more be in the land, and nothing that defileth, etc.,—but when the righteous shall shine forth as the sun, etc.

LXXVII.—THE DIGNITY OF ADOPTION.

"For as many as are led by the Spirit of God, they are the sons of God." — Rom. viii. 14.

No earthly position or office can be compared with the dignity of being a child of God. The honour and pleasure connected with them may please for a time only——but the privileges and honours connected with Divine sonship are great and everlasting.——This great privilege is not of self-creation. It is of Divine origin. It is induced by the leading of the Spirit. "For as many as are led by the Spirit," etc

I. THE DIGNITY OF BELIEVERS: "*They are the sons of God.*"

They obtain this honourable title through the grace of God — through faith in the sacrifice of Christ, and not as the result of any good in themselves; John i. 12; Gal. iii. 26.

1. The dignity consists *in being related to the most glorious Being in the universe;* "*The sons of God.*" He is the King of kings, and Lord of lords, God over all, blessed for evermore. The infinite Jehovah declares to repentant and believing sinners, "I will be a Father to you, and ye shall be my sons and daughters; 2 Cor. vi. 18; Rev. i. 6. —— What are earthly princes, or their sons, compared with this dignified relation?

2. The dignity consists in *separation from the world and living above it*—in a more exalted situation——more suitable to the nature of man, as rational and immortal—— like Jabez of old, who was more honourable than his brethren, 1 Chron. iv. 9; Eph. i. 3.

3. In nearness of access to God—and constant communion with him. It is a great honour to be admitted into the presence of the great God. Rom. v. 2; Eph. ii. 18.

Speaking to God *will result* in great mental peace—in high elevation of character — and in the gracious manifestations of God's mercy and aid. Never may we slight the privilege which is thus before us. If we were invited to speak with an earthly monarch, we should embrace the favour at once; especially if we were assured that any request we presented would be granted. How much more gladly should we hasten to avail ourselves of the privilege of laying our petition before the King of kings! Let us ask, that we may receive, and that our joy may be full!

"Lord! there is a throne of grace;
May we ever seek thy face!
Thou wilt hear the humblest prayer
Of the soul that seeks thee there."

THE DIGNITY OF ADOPTION.

4. This dignity is visible in their *Christian deportment in the world.* Persons of high rank may be easily discovered by their behaviour. — The real dignity of believers consists in holiness, and some degree of likeness to God. Ps. xlv. 19; Isa. lxi. 10. — Believers are easily distinguished from the men of the world.

5. It appears in *their legal right and title to all the blessings of the New Covenant, and to the heavenly inheritance,* v. 17 ; "If children, then heirs of God," etc.—"To an inheritance," etc. 1 Pet. i. 4. All the honours and riches of this world are contemptible, when compared with the glories of the Divine kingdom.

II. THE PERSONS UPON WHOM THIS DIGNITY IS CONFERRED. "As many as are led by the Spirit of God."

1. *They are enticed or sweetly drawn by the Spirit of God.* They are drawn from sin; or led by the goodness of God. Rom. ii. 4.

2. *They are led by the Spirit,* as a scholar is led by his tutor — a tutor uses various methods to convey instruction. "And they shall all be taught of God." John vi. 45.

3. They are *led by the Spirit, as a traveller is led by his guide.* The guide shows him his way, and the dangers and enemies he may expect. This world is a wilderness; but the Spirit is a sure guide. The *counsel* of God is imparted through the Spirit. Ps. lxxiii. 24.

4. *Led as a soldier is led by his captain.* The captain trains the soldier for duty, and leads him on to battle. So the Spirit trains the believer — teaches him the character of his spiritual foes — stimulates him to offence and defence — strengthens him, and animates him with the hope of complete ultimate triumph.

5. As the word signifies to rule and govern, so the sons of God *are under the government of the Spirit of God.* The Spirit dwells in them — they obey its dictates. "If we live in the Spirit, let us also walk," etc.

More particularly, observe how the Spirit of God leads them.

1. By opening and enlightening their understanding—showing them their danger, and the remedy God has provided. John xvi. 8; 2 Cor. iv. 6.

2. *By subduing and renewing their will*— removing its carnality — influencing it to close in with the overtures of mercy — bending the mind to the plan of mercy.

3. *By sanctifying the affections*— leading them to the right object of love — to love God and the things above — "sanctified by the Spirit of God." 1 Cor. vi. 11.

IMPROVEMENT.

1. Are you under the influence of the Spirit? 2. If adopted children of God, walk as such. 3. If sons of God, your prospect of future glory is enrapturing — let this cheer you.

LXXVIII.—ANOTHER OUTLINE FROM THE SAME TEXT.

I. THE CHARACTER OF THE SPIRIT.

1. A Divine person.
2. The Spirit of Grace.
3. The Spirit of Love.
4. The Spirit of Wisdom.
5. The Spirit of Holiness.

II. WHAT IT IS TO BE LED BY THE SPIRIT.

1. To experience His influence in regeneration.
2. To be instructed in the truth.
3. To be led to Christ for salvation.
4. To be led into the path of communion with God.
5. To be led into evangelical obedience.
6. To be led into glory.

III. THE PRIVILEGE CONNECTED WITH BEING THUS LED.

1. Adoption into the family of God.
2. An interest in all the blessings of grace and glory.

LXXIX.—CHRISTIAN STEADFASTNESS.

"For now we live, if ye stand fast in the Lord."—1 THESS. iii. 8.

I. THE IMPORT OF THE EXPRESSION, "*standing fast in the Lord.*"

1. A Christian is said to be in Christ — to *put on* the Lord Jesus — to be *grafted into Him* — to be *built upon* Him. By this is denoted the *nature, source,* and *support* of a believer's holiness.
2. Standing fast in the Lord denotes adherence to the doctrines of the gospel.
3. Consistency of conduct.
4. Growth in grace.

II. HOW THE STABILITY OF THE CHRISTIAN MAY BE PROVED.

1. By the assurance of understanding in the doctrines of the gospel.
2. By the adherence of the *heart* to these doctrines.
3. By standing fast *in Christ*, according to 1 John ii. 6.

III. The Dangers which threaten Religious Steadfastness.

1. False teachers.
2. The hostility and terrors of the world.
3. Worldly stratagems and fascinations.
4. The difficulties of a religious course.
5. Spiritual pride.

IMPROVEMENT.

1. It is by the help of the Holy Spirit alone that we stand fast in the Lord.
2. Pray for Divine aid
3. The effects of a steadfast abiding in Christ will be increasing sanctification, and an assured hope of heaven.

LXXX.—THE DEMONIAC OF GADARA.

BY CHRISTMAS EVANS. A SPECIMEN OF WELCH PREACHING.

"And when he went forth to land, there met him out of the city a certain man which had devils a long time, and wore no clothes, neither abode in any house, but in the tombs." — LUKE viii. 27.

It is said, that it was his desire to arouse the attention of the people, which had not been excited during the whole meeting, though many excellent sermons had been delivered. If I remember right, this meeting was held in the open air, and I think it was stated that there was a fair in the adjacent neighbourhood, which had a tendency to divide the attention of the people from hearing the word of life. I think in a few moments after Mr. E. began, the whole congregation gave profound attention to the following sermon from the above text.

I imagine, said Mr. E., that this demoniac was not only an object of pity, but he was really a terror to the country; so terrific was his appearance, so dreadful and hideous his screams, so formidable, frightful, and horrid his wild career, that all the women in that region were so much alarmed that none of them durst go to market.

And, what made him still more terrible, was the place of his abode; it was not in the city, where some attention might be paid to order and decorum — though he would sometimes ramble into the city, as in this case. It was not in a town, or village, or any house whatever, where assistance might be obtained in case of necessity; but it was among the tombs, and the wilderness, not far, however, from the turnpike road. No one could tell but that he might jump at them like a panther and scare them to death. The gloominess of the place made it more awful and solemn. It was among the tombs, where, in the opinion of some, all witches, corps, candles, and hobgoblins abide.

By this time, the devil became offended with the Gadarenes, and in a pout he took the demoniac away, and drove him into the wilderness. He thought the Gadarenes had no business to interfere and meddle with his property — for he had possession of the man; and he knew that "a bird in the hand is worth two in the bush." It is probable that he wanted to send him home; for there was no knowing what might happen now-a-days. But there was too much matter about him to send him away as he was; therefore, he thought it the best plan to persuade him to commit suicide, by cutting his own throat. But here Satan was at a nonplus — his rope was too short; he could not turn executioner himself, as that would not have answered the design he had in view, when he wants his people to commit suicide; for the act would have been his own sin, and not the man's. The poor demoniac, therefore, must go about to hunt a sharp stone, or any thing he could get. He might have been in search of such an article when he returned from the wilderness into the city whence he came, when he met the Son of God.

Jesus commanded the unclean spirit to come out of the man. And when he saw Jesus, he cried out, and fell down before him, and with a loud voice said, "What have I to do with thee, Jesus, thou son of God most high? I beseech thee, torment me not."

Here is the devil's confession of faith. The devils believe and tremble, while men make a mock of sin, and sport on the verge of dark damnation. To many of the human race, Christ appears as a root out of a dry ground. They see in him neither form nor comeliness, and there is no beauty in him that they should desire him. Some said that he was the carpenter's son, and would not believe in him; others said, that he had a devil, and that it was through Beelzebub, the chief of the devils, that he cast out devils. Some cried out, Crucify him, crucify him; and others said, let his blood be upon us and our children. As the Jews would not have him to rule over them, so, many who call themselves Christians say that he is a mere man; as such, he has no right to rule over their consciences, and demand their obedience, adoration, and praise. But Diabolus knows better — Jesus is the Son of God most high. Many of the children of the devil, whose works they do, differ very widely from their father in sentiments respecting the person of Christ.

Jesus commanded the legion of unclean spirits to come out of the man. They knew that out they must go; but they were like some Irishmen — very unwilling to return to their own country again. And he suffered them to go into the herd of swine.

Methinks that one of the men who fed the hogs, kept a better look-out than the rest of them, and said,

"What ails all the hogs? look sharp, there, boys — keep them in — make good use of your whips. Why don't you run? Why, true as I am alive, one of them has gone headlong over the cliff! There! there, Morgan, yonder goes another! — Drive them back, Tom."

Never was there such running, and whipping, and hallooing — but down go the hogs, before they were aware of it. — One of them said,

"They are all gone."

"No, sure, not all of them gone into the sea?"
"Yes, every one of them; and if ever the devil entered anything in this world he has entered into those hogs."
"What!" says Jack, "and is the noble black hog gone?"
"Yes! yes! I saw him scampering down that hill as if the very devil himself was in him; and I saw his tail take the last dip in the troubled element below."
"What," says Tom to Morgan, "shall we say to our Masters?"
"What can we say? We must tell the truth, that is all about it. We did our best—all that was in our power. What could any man do more?"
So they went their way to the city, to tell their masters what had happened.
"Jack, where are you going?" exclaimed one of the masters.
"Sir, did you know the demoniac that was among the tombs!"
"Where did you leave the hogs?"
"That madman, Sir—"
"Madman! Why do you come home without the hogs?"
"That wild and furious man, Sir, that mistress was afraid of so much."
"Why, Jack, I ask you a plain question—why don't you answer me? Where are the hogs?"
"That man who was possessed with the devils, Sir—"
"Why, sure enough, you are crazy! You look wild! Tell your story if you can, let it be what it may."
"Jesus Christ, Sir, has cast the unclean spirits out of the demoniac; they are gone into the swine; and they are drowned in the sea; for I saw the tail of the last when it went out of sight! Now, master, it is even so, you may depend."

The Gadarenes went out to see what was done; and finding that it was even so, they were afraid, and besought Jesus to depart from them.

How awful must be the state and condition of those men, who love the things of this world more than Jesus Christ!

"The man out of whom the unclean spirits were cast, besought Jesus that he might be with him. But he told him to return to his own house and show how great things God had done for him. And he went his way, and published throughout the whole city of Decapolis, how great things Jesus had done unto him."

The act of Jesus casting so many devils out of him, was sufficient to persuade him that Jesus was God as well as man.

I imagine I see him going through the city, crying, "O yes! O yes! O yes!—Please to take notice of me, the demoniac among the tombs. I am the man who was a terror to the citizens of this place; that wild man, who could wear no clothes, and that no man could bind. Here am I now in my right mind. Jesus Christ, the friend of sinners, had compassion upon me, when I was in my low estate. When there was no eye to pity, and no hand to save, He cast out the devils, and redeemed my soul from destruction."

Most wonderful must have been the surprise of the people to hear such proclamation. The ladies running to the windows—the shoemakers throwing their lasts one way, and their awls another—running out to meet him, and to converse with him, that they might be positive there was no imposition; and found to be a fact that could not be contradicted. O the wonder of all wonders! Never was there such a thing! must, I think, be the general conversation.

And while they were talking, and everybody having something to say, homeward goes the man. As soon as he came in sight of the house, I imagine I see one of the children running in, and crying, "O mother! father is coming, and he will kill us all!"

"Children, come all into the house," said the mother. "Let us fasten the doors. I think there is no sorrow like my sorrow!" said the broken-hearted woman.

"Are all the windows fastened, children?"

"Yes, mother."

"Mary, my dear, come from the window; don't be standing there."

"Why, mother, I can hardly believe that it is father! that man is well dressed."

"O yes, my dear children, it is your own father. I knew him by his walk the moment I saw him."

Another child, stepping to the window, said, "Why, mother, I never saw father coming home as he comes to-day. He walks on the footpath, and turns round the corner of the fences. He used to come towards the house as straight as a line, over fences, ditches, and hedges; and I never saw him walking as slowly as he does now."

In a few moments, however, he arrives at the door of the house, to the great terror and consternation of all the inmates. He gently tries the door, and finds no admittance. He pauses a moment, steps towards the window, and says, in a low, firm, and melodious voice, "My dear wife, if you will let me in, there is no danger. I will not hurt you; I bring you glad tidings of great joy."

The door was reluctantly opened, as it were between joy and fear. Having deliberately seated himself, he said:

"I am come to show you what great things God has done for me. He loved me with an everlasting love. He redeemed me from the curse of the law, and the threatenings of vindictive justice. He saved me from the power and the dominion of sin. He cast the devils out of my heart, and made that heart which was a den of thieves, the temple of the Holy Spirit. I cannot tell you how much I love the Saviour. Jesus Christ is the foundation of my hope, the object of my faith, and the centre of my affection. I can venture my ignorant soul upon him. He is my best friend — he is altogether lovely — the chief among ten thousands. He is my wisdom, righteousness, sanctification, and redemption. There is enough in him to make a poor sinner rich, and a miserable sinner happy. His flesh and blood are my food — his righteousness my wedding-garment — and his blood is efficacious to cleanse from all sins. Through him I can obtain eternal life; for he is the brightness of the Father's glory, and the express image of his person—in whom dwelleth all the fulness of the God-head bodily. He deserves my highest esteem, and my warmest gratitude. Unto him who loved me with an eternal love, and washed me in his own blood — unto him be the glory, dominion, and power, forever and ever. For he has rescued my soul from hell; he has plucked me as a brand out of the burning. He took me out of the miry clay, and out of a horrible pit. He set my feet upon a rock, and established my goings, and put in my mouth a new song of praise and 'glory to him! Glory to

Him forever! Glory to God in the highest! Glory to God forever and ever! Let the whole earth praise him! Yea, let all the world praise him!—Hallelujah! The Lord God omnipotent reigneth!"

It is beyond the power of the strongest imagination to conceive the joy and gladness of this family. The joy of sea-faring men delivered from being shipwrecked—the joy of a man delivered from a burning house—the joy of not being found guilty at a criminal bar—the joy of receiving pardon by a condemned malefactor—the joy of freedom to a prisoner of war—is nothing in comparison to the joy of him who is delivered from going down to the pit of eternal destruction. For it is "joy unspeakable and full of glory!"

LXXXI.—CONFIDENCE IN CHRIST.

"For I know whom I have believed, and am persuaded that He is able to keep that which I have committed unto him against that day."—2 TIM. i. 12.

I. THE DECLARATION OF THE APOSTLE.

1. He had known the necessity of salvation as a lost and ruined sinner.
2. He had known the power of Christ to save.
3. He had committed his soul and body to his care
(1.) For salvation.
(2.) For government.
(3.) For preservation.

II. HIS SECURITY.

1. Because, He was the author of his soul.
2. He died to redeem it.
3. All things are under his power.

III. HIS ASSURANCE.

1. It was the language of experience.
2. It was the language of an authorized confidence
(1.) In the principles of the gospel.
(2.) In God himself.

APPLICATION.

1. Are you a believer in Christ?
2. Have you committed your soul to Him?
3. Have you this confidence?
4. How great are the privileges of believers!

LXXXII. — RECONCILIATION.

"And you, that were sometime alienated and enemies in your mind by wicked works, yet now hath he reconciled, in the body of his flesh through death, to present you holy, and unblamable, and unreprovable in his sight." — COL. i. 21, 22.

WHAT a congratulation is this to the church at Colosse! They had become the subjects of a marvellous transformation anterior to their exaltation to eternal life. —— O what a change! Once alienated — children of wrath, even as others. Now made richer and more honourable than the kings of the earth.

I. THE STATE OF MAN BY NATURE. "Alienated and enemies in," etc.

Alienated; estranged from God in your affections, which are fixed on improper objects—the creature, the world. No love to God—no relish for his service — nor for his people. Carnal objects more attractive.

"*And enemies in your minds;*" — a fixed enmity in the heart against God—"the carnal mind is enmity against God." A manifest dislike to God and all his appointments—is in a state of active rebellion—trampling on the law and government of Jehovah.

This enmity discovers itself by "*wicked works.*" Sometimes called the "works of the flesh." Sins of omission and commission — open acts of wickedness. All are more or less guilty; Rom. iii. 10.

What a dreadful condition the sinner must be in—under the curse of the law!

II. THE GREAT CHANGE EFFECTED BY THE GRACE OF GOD. "Yet how hath he reconciled," etc.

Reconciliation is the reuniting of persons at variance, which is the case between God and sinners. But God has graciously proposed terms of reconciliation in the gospel. Mercy is graciously offered to rebels.

Sinners are invited and entreated to accept salvation—to be reconciled to God. "We are ambassadors for Christ, as though," etc. 2 Cor. v. 20. — This implies,

1. That the sinner be *truly sensible of his rebellion, and forsake his sins.* Isa. iv. 7.

2. That he be *truly humbled before God on account of it* — there must be penetential sorrow, like that manifested by David; Psal. xxxviii. 5, 6.

3. *A hearty acquiescence with the terms of mercy, and a closing in with the Lord Jesus as our great Reconciler*—receiving and embracing him as our only Saviour.

4. *The happy effect of this is peace and reconciliation to God.* Rom. v. 1. It leads to Divine worship; to communion; to exhilarating hope.

III. THE MEANS BY WHICH THIS IS EFFECTED. "In the body of his flesh through death."

Reconciliation to God is by Jesus Christ. He is the only person qualified for this work. He is the "one Mediator." "There is no other name given under heaven by which we can be saved." It is effected

1. *By his incarnation.* "In the body of his flesh through death." It was necessary that he should become man, that he might suffer in our nature and stead. "The word was made flesh," etc. John i. 14. "He took not on him the nature of angels," etc.

2. *By his Sacrifice.* "Through death." It was necessary that he should suffer and die — to pay our debt — to make satisfaction for the broken law — to appease Divine justice. See Isa. liii. 5; Dan. ix. 24; 2 Cor. v. 21; 1 Peter ii. 24.

IV. THE DESIGN OF THIS GRACIOUS ARRANGEMENT; "To present you holy, and unblamable, and unreprovable in his sight."

1. *To present you holy;* that you may be a renewed, sanctified people — devoted to God — loving holiness, and holy pursuits.

2. *And unblamable.* In the sight of the world — that the world, instead of having cause for censure, may have cause to admire. "Let your light so shine," etc. No one can injure you while you are in Christ. Rom. viii. 31, 33—35.

3. *And unreprovable in his sight.* That your consciences may not condemn you. The work of Christ has been so complete in you, that the Judge will look on and approve, when, as naked spirits, you stand before him.

"In his sight." Blessed operation! by which you will be able to stand peaceably before your Judge. Your sins forgiven; clothed with a Divine righteousness, etc., you will have joy and triumph when his scrutinizing eye shall investigate you, and you shall be found unreprovable even by him. He will then exclaim, "Thou art all fair, my love; there is no spot in thee."

IMPROVEMENT.

Be thankful for Christ. Are you reconciled? Now is the accepted time. Dreadful thought! to be alienated for ever.

LXXXIII.—PREPARATION FOR DEATH.

"Thus saith the Lord, Set thine house in order: for thou shalt die, and not live."— Isa. xxvii. 1.

HE is a wise man who regards this advice in the time of health: for we cannot tell what a day may bring forth. It is well to be always ready to die. — But when we are afflicted, the exhortation is peculiarly applicable; for that sickness may be unto death. "Set thine house in order; for thou shalt die." Such was the declaration of the prophet Isaiah to Hezekiah the king of Judah, who was sick unto death.

The text may have a two-fold application:—

1. Respecting *temporal things*. For the good of survivors it is important especially for the head of a family so to arrange his temporal affairs as to prevent confusion and unpleasantness. From the neglect of this, what scenes of disorder, bitterness, and wrath, have ensued!

2. Respecting our *spiritual concerns, and a due preparation for death.* In this sense, let the subject be considered.

I. WHAT MAY BE IMPLIED IN A DUE PREPARATION FOR DEATH? "SET THINE HOUSE IN ORDER."

1. *All carnal, open, and profane sinners are unprepared for death.* "Without holiness no man shall see the Lord." This settles the matter. The wicked are unprepared to die.

2. *The proud, self-righteous, and formalist, are unprepared for death.* They are resting on an unstable foundation, Matt. vii. 26. "Except your righteousness exceed;" Matt. v. 20.

3. *All who depart from the truth of the gospel,* and embrace errors of a fundamental nature—ridiculing the doctrine of regeneration—denying the Divinity of Christ, and the eternity of future punishment, are not fit to die; indeed it is possible for God to give them up to strong delusion. 2 Thess. ii. 13.

But more directly, To set the house in order implies, that the soul be made acceptable to God according to the method prescribed by the gospel.

The means of preparation have been provided. Christ has died, given his Spirit, communicates his grace, etc.

1. *The conscience must be delivered from guilt, sin pardoned, and peace and hope enjoyed;* Gal. iii. 13; Eph. i. vii; Rom. iv. 3.

2. *The soul must be regenerated, and renewed by the Holy Spirit.* John iii. 3; 2 Cor. v. 17.

3. *Frequent self-examination is necessary.* Matt. xxxv. 7. "Examine yourselves," etc.

4. *Constant watchfulness;* Matt. xxiv. 42. Maintaining the graces of the Spirit in lively exercise—living by faith in Jesus Christ—watching for the approach of death, and being ready to meet him. "I know whom I have believed."

II. THE ARGUMENT EMPLOYED TO ENFORCE THE NECESSITY OF SUCH A PREPARATION. "For thou shalt die, and not live."

1. *Death is the common lot of all men,* rich and poor, etc. Heb. ix. 22.

2. *Death is the sentence of Jehovah on account* of sin. It is the effect of sin; Rom. v. 12. "As by one man sin entered into the world," etc.

3. *The words are very emphatical.* "Thou shalt most assuredly die." Death is inevitable. There is nothing of which we have more incontestible evidence. "Our fathers, where are they? And the prophets, do they live for ever?" How frequently we hear of people dying! A proof that we also must die.

4. *It is as if God had said, Thou shalt shortly die.* How short and

uncertain is the life of man! It is as *grass*, Isa. xi. 6; it is like a *vapour*, James iv. 14; it is a *shadow*, Job xiv. 2; it is a *dream*, Job xx. 8; yea, even *nothing* before God; Ps. xxxix. 5.

5. *The argument gains additional force* by considering the consequences of death.

The state unalterably fixed either in bliss or woe.

That there will be a future judgment.

That man is an accountable creature. See 2 Cor. v. 10; Eccles. xii. 14; Matt. xxv. 31.

APPLICATION.

You are all dying creatures. Are you prepared to die? Upon what foundation are you resting?

Let the followers of Christ gird up the loins of their minds; be sober and hope to the end. Blessed will you be, if your house be set in order. Death will introduce you to the glories of your Father's house.

LXXXIV.—THE CHRISTIAN'S GLORIOUS PRIZE.

"I press towards the mark, for the prize of the high calling of God in Christ Jesus."
—PHIL. iii. 14.

THIS text has an evident and beautiful allusion to the Olympic games among the Greeks, in which rival candidates fought, wrestled, or ran, to obtain a prize, in itself indeed of little value, but anxiously sought as an honourable distinction bestowed on the successful candidate. To those exercises St. Paul frequently alludes; and in the present case,

I. We are called to consider eternal life and glory under the figure of a prize.

(1) It is an honourable and valuable object—a crown;—and not like the perishable garlands bestowed in those races, but a crown that fadeth not away. It is a throne, but not an earthly, transitory throne; a throne in heaven — the throne of God and the Lamb: "To him that overcometh will I grant to sit with me in my throne, even as I also overcame, and am set down with my Father in his throne."

(2) This prize is *held up* to excite and animate us. The world subsists by hope. The mind of man naturally turns to futurity. Hope animates the soul, and gives life to action; like the Highland stream that dashes from the rock, and purifies itself as it pursues its course. Not only did Moses have "respect to the recompense of reward," but even Christ Jesus himself was animated by hope, when "for the joy that was set before him he endured the cross, and despised the shame" attending it.

(3) This prize shall be *publicly and honourably bestowed*, and shall bear a proportion to our activity and exertions. "One star differs from

another star in glory;" and so shall it be in "the resurrection of the just." "Every man shall be rewarded according to his works." And this reward shall be greatly enhanced by the hand which doth bestow it: "Henceforth there is laid up for me a crown of righteousness, which the Lord, the righteous Judge, shall give unto me in that day, and not unto me only, but unto all them that love his appearing."

(4) It is the prize of *God's* high calling: we are not called by an earthly prince, nor to earthly honours, but to "glory, honour, and immortality."—It is "in Christ Jesus:" the Apostle drew all his motives from the cross: "there strongest motives spring:" not from pagan philosophy, nor from moral suasion, but from the Gospel.

II. We are with eager eye and outstretched hands to press towards the mark—the perfection of holiness. And as the ancients contended in the presence of fathers and brothers, wives and sisters, magistrates and their country; so we are encompassed with "a great cloud of witnesses"— patriarchs and prophets — apostles and evangelists — saints and martyrs.

This *pressing* toward the mark implies,—

(1) An eye towards the prize: "We look not at the things which are seen, but at the things which are unseen; for the things which are seen are temporal, but the things which are unseen are eternal."— (2) A confidence in the Judge: "I know in whom I have believed, and that he is able to keep that which I have committed to him."—(3) Perseverance in the path pointed out by the law of God, and the example of Jesus Christ.—(4) Reliance on Divine strength.

"Man, like the generous vine, supported lives;
The strength he gains, is from th' embrace he gives."

It is our duty to exert ourselves as if everything depended on our exertions, and at the same time to trust in Divine support, as knowing we can do nothing of ourselves.

DR. WAUGH.*

LXXXV.—APATHY OF THE CHURCH.

"Woe to them that are at ease in Zion." — AMOS vi. 1.

DESIRABLE as ease may be, both to the body and to the mind, there is an ease more to be dreaded than distress or pain. It is like the calm of the Dead Sea, or like that fatal stillness which often precedes a tempest or an earthquake. "Woe to them that are at ease in Zion!" —Who are they?

Some are at ease through selfish *insensibility*. They will not spoil their enjoyments, or wound their feelings with sights of human misery —they will not "visit the fatherless and the widow in their affliction;"

---

* See the Outline in "Helps for the Pulpit," Second Series, page 253.

and if they meet the wounded traveller in the way, they "pass on the other side." They "lie on beds of ivory," and stretch themselves on their couches — they eat the lambs out of the flock, and the calves out of the stall — they chant to the sound of the viols, and drink wine in bowls, but they are not grieved for the affliction of Joseph — "Therefore (saith the Prophet) shall they go captive, with the first that go captive."

Two objects should particularly interest the Christian, the welfare of his country and the church. So Jesus wept over both — "O Jerusalem! Jerusalem!"—But "woe to them that are at ease in Zion."

Others are at ease through infidel *presumption*. They cry, "Thus! doth God see, and is there understanding (of this) with the Most High? —Where is the promise of his coming?—for all things continue as they were from the beginning." They presume, either that the threatenings of God's word are not true, or at least that they are not nigh; till, lo! "sudden desolation cometh upon them, and their destruction cometh as a whirlwind." Then "woe to them that are at ease in Zion."

Some are at ease through *self-confidence;* trusting in themselves that they are righteous, they despise others, and say, with the church at Laodicea, "I am rich, and increased with goods, and have need of nothing:" whereas in the sight of God they are wretched, and miserable, and poor, and blind, and naked. Alas, for these men! they build for eternity, and yet build upon the sand; and when the storms of life — or, at farthest, when the hurricanes of death come, they are swept away into the pit of everlasting destruction. — "Woe to them that are at ease in Zion!"

Lastly, others are at ease through practical *indifference*. They come to God's house when his people come; they sit as his people sit; the sound of the Gospel is as a very lovely song, or as "the sound of one that playeth skilfully on an instrument;" they profess to believe in a hell and a heaven—a world of everlasting joys and endless pains — and yet act as if it were impossible there should be either. They are like a man sleeping on a mast in a storm, or amidst a house in flames. "Woe to them that are at ease in Zion!"

But peace be to those who are distressed in Zion. The dead feel not, but pain is an indication of returning life. "Blessed are they that mourn in Zion;" they shall be comforted with many consolations here, and hereafter crowned with everlasting joys.

> Life and immortal joys are giv'n
> To souls that mourn the sins they've done;
> Children of wrath made heirs of heav'n,
> By faith in God's eternal Son.

LXXXVI.—JESUS WEPT.

"Jesus wept."—JOHN xi. 35.

1. WHO WAS IT THAT WEPT?

That the children of men should frequently be in tears is nothing strange: this world is a place of sin, and therefore it is no wonder that it is also a place of weeping. Sin and sorrow must be companions. But what shall we say when we read that Jesus wept? Was it not strange that he, who was "holy, harmless, undefiled, and separate from sinners," should be in tears? "Jesus wept!"—Let us contemplate this weeping Saviour.

2. "JESUS WEPT." And was it not the tear of *sympathy* he shed?

When he saw Mary weeping, and the Jews who came with her, also weeping, "he groaned in the spirit and was troubled." On some other occasions he had forbidden weeping for the dead. He had said, "Why make ye this ado, and weep?" We do not find that Jesus wept, when he first said, "Our friend Lazarus sleepeth"—nor when Martha met him—nor when Mary came unto him; but afterwards when he saw the tears of Mary, and her sympathizing friends, who came to comfort them concerning their brother, then he mingled his groans and tears with theirs. Thus did he "weep with those that wept;" and recommended the precept by his own example.

"JESUS WEPT." And was it not the tear of *friendship?* "Our friend Lazarus sleepeth."

By his own example then hath he sanctified the soft endearments of friendship; and in the beloved Apostle, and his friend Lazarus, he hath fastened, as it were, its tender ties with his own hand.—"Jesus loved Martha, and her sister, and Lazarus." Was it therefore strange if Jesus wept for Lazarus? If he were capable of tears, was not this an occasion to draw them forth? He wept, as a man might weep for his departed friend: and therefore the Jews observed, "Behold, how he loved him!"

"JESUS WEPT:" And let us recollect the scene that was then before him.

A grave, the awful consequences of sin, was in his view. The grave had opened its mouth and seemed to say, Behold the cursed effects of transgression! "In the day thou eatest thereof, thou shalt die." The people of God have all seen the evil of sin in some degree, and have been affected with it; but they do not, they cannot, in this world, have a sufficiently comprehensive view of all its deformity, and horrid consequences. But Jesus could view it exactly as it is. His all-comprehending mind knew its height and depth; and, as a man, when he saw its effects in the death of Lazarus, when he saw the place where he himself was shortly to be laid," he wept. So when he foresaw the destruction that awaited impenitent Jerusalem; he "beheld the city, and wept over it." We know that in the view of approaching suffering, he was "exceedingly sorrowful;" and we know, because an Apostle hath informed us, that "in the days of his flesh, he offered up prayers and supplications, with strong crying and tears," in the discharge of his mediatorial work.

"JESUS WEPT:" But it was in the way to glory.

There was a joy set before him; and therefore he endured the cross, despising the shame; and he is now sat down at the right hand of the throne of God. Thus should we be "looking unto Jesus" as our glorious example! In this world we must expect occasions of sorrow. But it is well for us that our tribulations are in the way to an heavenly kingdom. "They that sow in tears shall reap in joy." This is the order of these things: "Before honour is humility." Afflictions are the royal road to heaven.

"JESUS WEPT," when he was on earth; and he has still the same affection for his people.

When he went to heaven, he did not leave behind him his heart of tenderness. He is now at the Father's right hand, as our friend and advocate. There he pleads our cause: "For we have not an High Priest which cannot be touched with the feeling of our infirmities." What encouragement is this to approach the heavenly throne! "Let us, therefore, come boldly to a throne of grace, that we may obtain mercy, and find grace to help in time of need."

J. JEFFERSON.

LXXXVII.—CONTEMPT OF DIVINE GOODNESS.

"Despisest thou the riches of his goodness, and forbearance, and long suffering: not knowing that the goodness of God leadeth thee to repentance." — ROMANS ii. 4.

IN this passage we may notice the goodness of God, and its design— the contempt of that design, and the punishment of that contempt.

1. To estimate rightly the *goodness* of God, we should think of the number of offences committed against him; the offences of a single individual this day—of an individual in his whole life—the offences of a city, a nation, the globe—a world of rebels. How many oaths have been sworn to-day—in this city—in the nation—in the world? And yet the world has not been burned with fire, nor overwhelmed with water. How would you be enraged, if you knew all that was said and done against you in secret? This you cannot know; but it is otherwise with God: he knows all that is said and done against him, and bears with all. When Moses provoked an Egyptian, he preserved himself by flight; this could not be your case, for whither would you fly from his presence?

2. The design of God's goodness is to lead us to repentance. The

necessity, the expediency, and the means of repentance are inferred from this passage.—How may the goodness of God lead us to repentance? Three ways.

(1) By affording opportunity: while the execution of a criminal is delayed a pardon may arrive.

(2) By affording us encouragement; punishment is delayed, and who can tell?

(3) By furnishing us with the most affecting motives. We are not driven, but attracted. Cain and Judas were driven to repentance, and we see what their repentance came to. Peter was led to repentance; Jesus looked on him, and that look said, "Peter, with all thy faults, I love thee still." David was led to repentance; "I have sinned," said he. "The Lord has put away thy sin," says the prophet; and did David put it away too? No: so soon as God had put it away, David set it before him, and kept remembrance of it as a memento to the end of his days: "My sin is ever before me." An old divine, when dying, said, "I weep, not because I cannot be pardoned, but because I am pardoned." The religion of the gospel is the fond mother tenderly alluring the disobedient boy to return, and hide his blushes in her bosom; and not the stern angry father. We must now consider,

3. The *contempt* of God's design. How does the sinner show this?— By his inconsideration—by his disobedience—by his perversion of the design. "If I thought, (says the sinner,) that he would cut me off so soon as I commit sin, I would sin no more: but as he bears with me, I will still go on."

4. Let us mark the *punishment* of that contempt. He goes on; but observe the issue—"treasuring up wrath against the day of wrath." We have heard of the riches of God's goodness in the former part of the text, now we hear of the treasures of his wrath: both expressions denoting abundance and variety. This is an awful subject: let us dismiss it with three remarks.

(1) All this misery is of the sinner's own procuring. Hell is the sinner's "own place;" he made it, he furnished it; he breeds within him the worm which never dies, and the fire which cannot be quenched.

(2) The sinner is making continual accession to his misery: "treasuring up wrath unto the day of wrath."

(3) The whole amount of his wickedness will not be known till a future day, called "the day of wrath," and this, says the apostle, will be the day of retribution—"the revelation of the righteous judgment of God."

> Lord, we have long abus'd thy love,
> Too long indulg'd our sin;
> Our aching hearts e'en bleed to see
> What rebels we have been!
>
> No more, ye lusts, shall ye command,
> No more will we obey;
> Stretch out, O God, thy conquering hand,
> And drive thy foes away.

W. JAY.

LXXXVIII.—COMFORT IN TROUBLE.

"Let not your heart be troubled: ye believe in God, believe also in me." — JOHN xiv. 1.

CHRIST is the Fountain of Divine consolation. He is styled "the Consolation of Israel," and "the God of comfort." How cheering such a character to the mind of the believer amid the troubled scenes of life! The great High Priest loves him, and compassionately looks from his high abode upon his suffering servant. The glories of his heaven, the grandeur of his nature, the acclamations of celestial spirits, and the love he has for them, do not prevent him from sympathizing with his afflicted people, and saying from his throne, "Let not your heart be troubled," etc.

When these words were uttered, the disciples of Christ were in distress. Jesus their Master was about to leave them. He was going to his cross to die. The purport of his death they did not clearly apprehend; yet his departure was distressing to them. Jesus knew their perturbed state of mind, and he gave them instruction and appropriate consolation. As sorrow filled their hearts, and tears suffused their eyes, he said, "Let not your hearts be troubled," etc.

I. THE HEART IS SOMETIMES TROUBLED : " Let not," etc.

The word troubled denotes an agitated and painful state of mind, created by something unpleasant and disagreeable. The heart heaves, and sometimes agonizes under the pressure of fear, grief, anxiety, despondency, or apprehension of future evils. Thus the disciples were troubled by the loss which they were about to sustain. They gazed upon the lovely and majestic person of the Redeemer, and were distressed to think they would soon see him no more. They thought of his delightful companionship, his constant kindness and peculiar tender sympathy, and his wonderful teaching, and O what a sad blank would his departure create ! His loss they felt to be irreparable. And not only so; they were troubled also by his intimations of approaching tragical sufferings. Disappointed at his not erecting a throne of regal power and grandeur, and causing them to sit in dignity on his right and on his left hand in his earthly kingdom, the very idea of his departure to the ignominious cross was appalling to their minds. Their hearts were troubled. The prince of this world was collecting his forces against him; the Jewish rulers were full of bigotry, and their determination to destroy him was complete. He was about to close his career by unparalleled sufferings, and by a shameful and accursed death. This he had intimated to them. But he told them that they also should be baptized with sufferings. "These things have I spoken to you, that ye should not be offended. They shall put you out of the synagogues; yea, the time cometh, that whosoever killeth you will think that he doeth God service." It is not surprising then that they should be distressed by the dark prospect which they had before them.
—— Observe,

I. That the people of God, even the most holy and devoted of them, are subject to various troubles and perplexities.

The trouble which agitated the disciples is not applicable to believers. The departure of Christ to heaven as their Intercessor and Forerunner is a source of joy. But they have trials.

Adversity. Scarcity of manual labour—inadequacy of remuneration for manual labour—plans unsuccessful—losses through the mismanagement of others,— or adversity produced by lengthened affliction—incapacity for labour.

Afflictions, personal or relative. These are painful and cause serious apprehension. They may be the precursors of death.

Bereavements. Here, "the heart knows its own bitterness." To part with beloved relatives and friends is very trying. "Lover and friend hast thou put far from me, and mine acquaintance into darkness."

Family troubles. Millions of hearts have been troubled by the ungrateful conduct of their children. Their best counsels neglected — bent on a course of impiety. Instance Eli, and David.

"How sharper than a serpent's tooth it is
To have a thankless child!"

Troubles in the church. Disunion — lukewarmness — unproductiveness—want of religion—To a real Christian these things cause sorrow. Phil. iii. 18.

Heart trouble. "Let not your heart be troubled." What trouble arises from the evil heart of unbelief, ever prone to depart from the living God! Rom. vii. 24.

What crowds of evil thoughts,
What vile affections there!
Distrust, presumption, artful guile,
Pride, envy, slavish fear.

Apprehension of death. The believer is sometimes troubled by thinking of his death. He has yet to die. To meet the tyrant. To part with all — to pass into the invisible state. Heb. ii. 14, 15.

The foregoing may be illustrated by the following: —

Believers are afflicted as other men. They endure pains and weakness of body—domestic trials—family bereavements—worldly losses—and distress of mind. In addition to all these, which are the common sorrows of our race, they have trials peculiar to themselves. "Many are the afflictions of the righteous." These afflictions do not spring from chance, nor do they proceed from the will of a capricious and despotic tyrant. They are the chastisements of a father's hand — the proofs of paternal love. What then should be our disposition and conduct under them? We should pray. *Pray, in submission to the divine will, that your afflictions be removed.* Take as your examples David, Jonah, Hezekiah, Manasseh, Paul, and even Christ himself. *Pray for grace to endure affliction while it continues, so as to glorify God.* Certain graces thrive best in affliction. Gold shines brightest when burnished. Stars are most lustrous in the darkness of night. Spices emit their sweetest odours when bruised. So patience—meekness—acquiescence in the will of God are most conspicuous in the time of affliction. *Pray that your afflictions may be sanctified.* Sanctified afflictions are among the best blessings of the new covenant. What a mercy that we can pray, even in the darkest hour! The returns of prayer will be more precious than the richest cargoes—more refreshing than the most genial showers—types and foretastes of heaven.

The Rev. George Whitfield said, when preaching from the text, "Wherefore glorify ye the Lord in the fires," Isa. xxiv. 15. "When I was some years ago at Shields, I went into a glass-house, and, standing very attentive, saw several masses of burning glass of various forms. The workmen took one piece of glass, and put it into one furnace, then he put it into a second, and then into a third. I asked him, 'Why do you put that into so many fires?' He answered me, 'Oh, sir, the first was not hot enough, nor the second, and therefore we put it into the third, and that will make it transparent.' Oh, thought I, does this man put this glass into one furnace after another that it may be rendered perfect? Put me, my God, into one furnace after another, that my soul may be transparent too!"

> 'Tis my happiness below,
> Not to live without the cross,
> But the Saviour's power to know,
> Sanctifying every loss.
>
> Trials must and will befall,
> But, with humble faith to see
> Love inscribed upon them all,—
> This is happiness to me.

II. *That the Lord Jesus is ever ready to comfort his people in their distress.* "Let not your heart be troubled." I wish your happiness, and will endeavour to promote it. My heart deeply feels and sympathizes with yours. I know what you have to suffer; and I will never leave you, nor forsake you.

He had this peculiar end in view in assuming our nature. He came to bind up the broken-hearted, Luke iv. 18; Heb. ii. 17. "Wherefore, in all things," etc.

For this purpose he procured the Spirit, and sent him into the world, John xiv. 16.

For this purpose he raises up ministers, and sends them forth to console his people; "Comfort ye, comfort ye, my people, saith the Lord; yea, speak comfortably unto Jerusalem," Isa. xl. 1, 2.

III. THE ADVICE WHICH HE GIVES THEM: "*Ye believe in God; believe also in me.*"

It accords with the original to read both the verbs in the imperative mood;—Place your confidence in God, and in me as the Mediator between God and man; expect the utmost support from God, but expect it to flow from me. My father has appointed me as the channel through which my church is to receive all spiritual and celestial happiness.

"Ye believe in God." You believe him as the Creator of all worlds —you believe in the spirituality of his nature—in his benevolence in supplying all the wants of his creatures—in his power shielding his servants from the malicious designs of their foes, and in his wisdom, ordering all things for the best. If you believe in him, believe in me; for I came forth from my Father—I was delegated by him to save the world. My great object in going away is to secure the salvation of my people. I go to die that they may live. I go to rise from the grave that death and the grave may not destroy them. I go to ascend to my Father's house, there to reign, there to intercede. I go to open the windows of heaven to pour down, in rich profusion, the richest blessings upon my church. Therefore, "believe in me."

The exhortation of Christ therefore means,

1. *Believe in the Divinity and authority of my mission.* You have seen my miracles — you have witnessed my power — you have heard my Father's voice from the most excellent glory proclaiming me his beloved Son, in whom he is well pleased. Do you not perceive then that my credentials are divine? Believe this, and it will embolden you in the office which you have to discharge. Ever remember that you have an Almighty Saviour to serve, and to protect you. I commit my cause into your hands. Believe, trust in me, and it shall succeed. So Jesus speaks to all his people. The Divinity of Christ makes our religion sweet and precious. "Believe in me," says Christ, "and you shall be happy." "Unto you who believe, he is precious," says the Apostle Peter.

2. *Believe in my mediating love and death.* "I lay down my life for my sheep." Your souls, my disciples, are lost, guilty, and defiled by sin. You cannot save yourselves. Believe in me as your Saviour. I am the end of the law for righteousness to every one that believeth. I will save you to the uttermost. Faith in the precious blood of Christ. O what a magic power has that! It turns the curse into a blessing. It gives peace, and joy, and hope. It rescues from perdition, and elevates to glory. Blessed are they who believe in Christ!

3. *Believe in my kind and constant care.* "I will not leave you comfortless; I will come unto you." I am the chief Shepherd and Bishop of your souls — how then can I leave you? Amid all the glories of my kingdom, my care and love will be for you. Though cherubim and seraphim, and myriads of angels and saints will adore me when I put on my coronation robes, yet I will not forget you. Believe in me; for "I am with you alway, even to the end of the world." Commit all your cares into my hands. I care for you. I shall see you, and feel, and care for you when you are poor and destitute. When they hail you to prison and to the tribunal, I shall see you. Believe in me then. I will teach you what to say. I will be your invisible counsellor, and plead your cause. But eventually for that cause you must die. As the master is persecuted to the death, so you must be. You must be martyrs for my sake. O believe in me then! I will comfort and cheer you amid the pangs of martyrdom. I will open heaven, and let you see my glory, and that I live observant of you. I will give you my Spirit, and you shall sweetly fall asleep in me — in Jesus!

O Christian, great is the love, and constant the care of thy Saviour. Thou believest in God, believe also in him. He careth for thee when thou art in straits and difficulties — when thy circumstances are indigent, Jesus loves thee. In the days of his flesh, he loved the poor, and on his throne he still anxiously remembers them. Art thou afraid of perishing by the hand of thine enemies? Believe in Christ, and they will be vanquished. Thou art weak but Christ is strong; thy foes are mighty, but he is Almighty; thy sufficiency is of him. The supplies of his Spirit are exhaustless. When the enemy comes in like a flood, his Spirit will lift up a standard against him."——When on thy sick-bed, languishing in pain, burning with fever, tossing to and fro, Jesus cares for thee. Believe in him then. He will make all thy bed in thy affliction, and make it a bed of roses. "My grace shall be sufficient for thee."——When thy friends die and are covered by the sod, he will give thee "oil of joy for mourning, and the garments of praise for the spirit of heaviness." At the grave of Lazarus "Jesus wept," and on his radiant throne he still sympathizes with all his bereaved people. "Leave thy fatherless children, and let thy widows trust in me." —— Christian, thou must die, but let not thine heart be troubled; believe in me; I am the conqueror of death, and will make thee more than a conqueror. Fear not to go down to the grave; I will go down with thee, and will surely bring thee up again. Believe in me when thou art dying, and think I died for thee. I am thy righteousness and strength.

Lavater has the following allegory illustrative of the Christian's triumph over Death. "It happened one day that Death met a good man; 'Welcome, thou messenger of immortality!' said the good man. 'What!' said Death, 'dost thou not fear me?' 'No,' said the Christian; 'he that is not afraid of himself, needs not be afraid of thee!' 'Dost thou not fear the diseases that go before me, and the cold sweats that drop from my finger ends?' 'No,' said the good man, 'diseases and cold sweats announce nothing but *thee!*' In an instant Death breathed upon him, and Death and he disappeared together; a grave had opened beneath their feet, and in it lay *something*. I wept, but suddenly heavenly voices drew my eyes on high. I saw the Christian in the clouds. He was still smiling, as when Death met him, angels had welcomed his approach, and he shone as one of them. I looked into the grave, and saw what it was that lay there; nothing was there but *the garment the Christian had laid aside.*"

IMPROVEMENT.

Be very thankful for Christ. What a sympathizing friend is he! He may well be styled, "THE CONSOLATION OF ISRAEL;" "The Comforter of those who are cast down."

In all your troubles, go to him for support. Trust in his mighty love and power. Ever believe in him. The life which you live in the flesh, let it be by the faith of the Son of God.

How comfortless must sinners be in their troubles! They go not to God for support; but to artificial means—physicians of no value.

LXXXIX.—THE GREAT QUESTION.

"Dost thou believe on the Son of God?"—JOHN ix. 35.

THE chapter relates the extraordinary cure of the man born blind. By this miracle Jesus declared himself to be the Son of God with power. —Observe the malice and envy of the Jewish authorities—the fear and duplicity of the parents—the honesty of the man healed—his expulsion from the synagogue. Jesus sympathized with the man, and went in search of him after his expulsion. When he had found him, he proposed the question, "Dost thou believe," etc. Great was the miracle for the body — but a greater miracle was effected for the soul.

I. THE OBJECT OF FAITH. "The Son of God."

A glorious and complex personage — possessed of two distinct natures, human and divine — a glorious person, God and man. The appellation, *Son of God*, is applied both to angels and to men. Angels are so called. Job xxxviii. 7. It is applied to believers. John i. 12; Rom. viii. 14; 1 John iii. 2. Angels are the sons of God by creation; believers are the sons of God by regeneration and adoption; but Christ is the Son of God in a special sense, only applicable to himself. He possesses the nature of God — equality with God; has the names of God, and the perfections of God.

1. His Divinity and Godhead appear from the following considerations: —

(1.) *From the express declarations of Scripture.* While he is the child born, and the Son given, he is the mighty God, the everlasting Father, and the Prince of peace. See Isa. ix. 6; John i. 1, 18; Rom. ix. 5.

(2.) *From the perfections ascribed to him, which are peculiar to Deity.* Eternity; "Before Abraham was I am."— Unchangeableness; "Jesus Christ, the same yesterday," etc. Heb. xiii. 8. — Almighty power; "Christ the power of God." 1.Cor. i. 24. — Infinite wisdom; "Light of the world;" "the only wise God."—— *Infinite love;* "Ye know the grace," etc. 2 Cor. viii. 9. Creation is ascribed to him. And so is redemption. All these attributes are therein displayed.

(3.) *From the works which he did.* These could not have been done by a person inferior to God. Such as searching the heart, and perceiving what was in it — healing the sick and raising the dead — the forgiving of sins.

2. *But he was perfect man as well as God.* He assumed our nature in all respects — flesh of our flesh, and bone of our bone. He was subject to pain and weariness of body — he needed meat and drink for his sustenance — he slept for the refreshment of nature.

This human body was animated by the Divine nature, which made Christ a Godlike man. His mind was endowed with faculties of the most exalted rank — far superior to angelic minds. "Being made so much better than the angels," Heb. i. 4. Yet as man, he sorrowed, feared, hated, loved, etc.

In our nature, he undertook our cause — suffered and endured the punishment due to our sins. Isa. liii. In our nature he is exalted at God's right hand. This is the glorious object of our faith.

II. THE NATURE OF FAITH. *"Dost thou believe?"*

It is not merely giving credit to the Scriptures. It is not merely confessing the doctrines of any particular creed — it is not a mere professing of faith.

Faith is confidence, trust, or reliance upon the sacrificial death of Christ for salvation and everlasting life. It is the act of the heart by which we heartily welcome him into our souls. The Scriptures figuratively represent this grace, as *beholding him*, or *looking to him; it is coming* to Christ, *laying hold* of him, *receiving* him, *resting* on him, etc. Figuratively, he is called "the bread of life, and the water of life," and faith is participation, called "eating and drinking."

1. *Faith is always preceded by a deep conviction of sinfulness.* The sinner must feel that he is a transgressor of God's holy law, and in consequence is in a state of condemnation. If so, he will say, like the Jailor, "Sirs, what must I do to be saved?"

2. *This faith implies a knowledge of Christ as the Saviour.* Rom. x. 14. No gospel faith without gospel knowledge. Knowledge of Christ as the great Prophet and Teacher. As the Priest, the Mediator, the Atonement.

3. *Faith implies the assent of the mind to Christ in all his saving power, and dependence upon him.* It is venturing the soul upon him. It is an appropriating faith. "He loved me, and gave himself for me." "My Lord and my God." Isa. xii. 1, etc.

III. THE EFFECTS OF FAITH.

By these we may be assisted in the duty of self-examination. "Dost thou believe on the Son of God?" If so, the effects of faith will be mental comfort and satisfaction, and holy fruits, showing to the world that we are the subjects of a very important change.

1. The inward effects of believing on the Son of God will be

(1.) *Justification.* A full and free acquittance from all law charges. Acts xiii. 39; Rom. v. 1; viii. 1.

(2.) *Peace and tranquillity* of soul. Rom. v. 1. Christ is the Prince of peace, the Author of peace; and his gift to all believers is the enjoyment of peace. Anxiety, restlessness, dread, and torment, are vanished, and the mind is comfortable, joyous, serene, and calm.

(3.) *Adoption into the family and household of God.* Gal. iii. 26; 1 John iii. 1, 2; John i. 12.

(4.) *All such have the Spirit of God*, as their witness, comforter, helper, and sanctifier.

(5.) *Hope of heaven.* Faith leads to this. Heb. xi. 1.

2. *The Outward Effects of true Faith.*

(1.) A new creation and reformation of life. 2 Cor. v. 17.

(2.) *A conscientious regard to the authority of Christ.* His laws will be regarded — a desire to please him — a desire to promote his glory in the world — great love to his cause. Faith works by love — love to God, to saints, to our fellow-men.

(3.) *Victory over the world.* 1 John v. 4.

IMPROVEMENT.

1. The text applies personally, "Dost THOU believe on the Son of God?" It does not relate to others, but to ourselves. It does not refer to mere information or opinion, but to faith. It refers not either to past or future, but to the present: "Dost thou believe?"

2. If you believe, be thankful for the means by which you have been brought into that happy state. Faith is not natural to you; by nature you are unbelievers, far from God, and strangers to his Son. An important change has taken place. The eyes of your understanding have been enlightened, and you behold the glory of Christ. You are interested in him. He is your Saviour, and he will take pleasure both in time and eternity to make you happy.

3. Let the Christian cultivate the evidences of his faith. Let the world see and feel that you are believers. This will afford sweet satisfaction to yourselves.

4. He that believeth not must perish. Mark xvi. 16; John iii. 18.

XC. — THE COMING OF SATAN.

"The prince of this world cometh, and hath nothing in me." — JOHN xiv. 30.

By the prince of this world we are to understand Satan; called Apollyon, the old serpent, the roaring lion, the god of this world, the prince of the power of the air.

I. THE MANNER OF HIS COMING.

1. His influence is sometimes sudden, alarming, formidable, as a lion springing on his prey. Witness his attack on Judas, Peter, etc.
2. A slow or gradual approach like the serpent.
3. He comes under the mask of friendship.
4. He comes by the slavish fear of man.
5. He comes by plausible and fundamental error.

II. THE DESIGN OF SATAN'S COMING.

1. It is directed against God.
2. To bring the children of men into the same condemnation with himself.

"Lest being lifted up with pride, he fall into the condemnation of the devil." — 1 Tim. iii. 6.

3. To prevent the influence of divine truth on the heart.

"The god of this world hath blinded the minds of them that believe not, lest," etc. — 2 Cor. iv. 4.

He blinds the understanding, raises prejudices, etc., against the truth.

4. To hinder saints in the works and ways of God.

"But Satan *hindered* us." — 1 Thess. ii. 18.

5. To overthrow our goings and to ruin the soul.

"But I fear, lest by any means, as the serpent beguiled Eve," etc. etc. — 2 Cor. xi. 3.

III. THE CONSEQUENCE OF HIS COMING. "He hath nothing in me."

1. No native depravity in Christ. In us there is every thing friendly to the designs of Satan.

2. The impossibility of Satan's prevailing against Him.

He never did sin. He could not sin, because perfect purity was his nature. "He did no sin, neither was guile found in his mouth."

IMPROVEMENT.

1. Though Satan be powerful, he is not omnipotent.
2. Commit your soul to the care of Christ.

J. BODEN.

XCI. — HOPE A SUPPORT IN TROUBLE.

"Why art thou cast down, O my soul? and why art thou disquieted within me? hope in God; for I shall yet praise Him, who is the health of my countenance, and my God." — Ps. xliii. 5.

A CHRISTIAN has been justly compared to an exotic, a plant which flourishes in its own climate; but which, when brought into one unfriendly to its nature, is alive indeed, but sickly. There is something paradoxical, an apparent contradiction in the Christian's character; he is sorrowful, yet always rejoicing.

From these words, observe,

I. That the best of men, and men of the deepest experience, may, at times, suffer great depression.

1. From the corruptions of the heart.
2. From his near connections.
3. From bodily disease.
4. Privation from ordinances.

II. It is the duty of good men to resist such despondency.

1. Because if this despondency be not arrested in its progress, they are in danger of dishonouring God.
2. It has a tendency to weaken exertion.
3. It is a snare to his neighbour, an injury to his family, and a scandal to religion.

III. The infallible resource of the godly in all cases of trial, is — Hope in God.

1. This is according to His word.
2. A Christian has experienced this confidence.
3. The Omnipotence of God warrants this confidence.

IMPROVEMENT.

1. You must often hope in an inexplicable providence, and depend on God in the order of His dispensation.
2. Exercise hope in the path of duty.
3. Exercise your confidence with respect to your best interests.

XCII.—THE BEAUTY OF THE LORD IN HIS HOUSE.

(AT THE OPENING OF A PLACE OF WORSHIP.)

"Let thy work appear unto thy servants, and thy glory unto their children. And let the beauty of the Lord our God be upon us: and establish thou the work of our hands upon us; yea, the work of our hands establish thou it."—Ps. xc. 16, 17.

I. THIS IS A PRAYER FOR THE WORK OF GOD.

A work infinitely interesting to angels and believers.

A work early begun—carried on—gradual—opposed—imperceptible — by human instruments — in answer to prayer.

II. The Church prays that the glory of the Lord may be visibly displayed in this work. God brings all the glory of His essence and perfections into this work.—All the wisdom of His mind; the love of His heart; the power of His arm; fidelity of His care; the plenitude of His grace.

III. Estimating the interests of the Church, we pray that the beauty of the Lord our God may be upon us.

Beauty which consecrates all the beauty of our places of worship. Nothing is of importance unless the beauty of the Lord be there.

1. The beauty of the administration of the ordinances of God.

Isa. iii. 7. — "How beautiful upon the mountains are the feet of him," etc.

All the ordinances are the beauty of the Lord *upon* us, and *amongst* us.

We must lay no stress on *doctrinal* preaching but in connection with the heart and life.

2. The spirit in which the Head of the church is worshipped, the gospel is heard, and the ordinances are observed.

3. The presence of the Lord our God.

His presence will be the glory of the place. He has promised His presence to His church under all circumstances. They shall feel His presence and be made happy as they proceed on their Christian course.

A church of Christ bears the most striking resemblance to heaven.

The beauty of the Lord is His resemblance. Every believer is a living epistle of Christ.

IV. The prayer of the text is for a blessing upon every plan tending to promote the glory of God.

4. The beauty of the Lord includes all immunities, blessings, consolations, and joys of His love. Isa. lxi. 3.

We must have clear views of His work and of our work; act in the true spirit of our character and of the magnitude of our work, and the awful responsibilities of its glorious result: not grow cool or indifferent, but continue to do all His will with increasing animation, warmth, and ardour. Not forsaking it, not looking back, not doing it deceitfully.

We pray that God would counsel and lead us; make our way plain, and that in whatever way the church may be assailed we may still go on; prepared for all difficulties and ready to make every sacrifice. That the work may be permanent and progressive. "Let it not die with us, raise up labourers, adequate to the extent of the harvest."

V. That you may enjoy clear, satisfactory, exhilirating evidence of the *prosperity* of the work. "Let thy work *appear.*"

Ministers cannot rest in preaching faithfully; they must see the work of God is in progress, by their own instrumentality or not. If they see it going on they rejoice, whoever is the instrument. "Let thy work appear to *all* thy servants!"

God will let his work appear for our encouragement, that we may feel more of the power and enjoy more of the renovating, comforting, and sanctifying influence of His Spirit.

Every appearance of the work of God is the crown of exertion, and the harbinger of greater things about to be accomplished.

VI. The Church prays that this blessedness may be extended to succeeding generations. "Thy Glory unto their children."

The spirit of prayer connects itself with futurity. The believer looks forward in the spirit of devotion, desire, hope, confidence, and joy, when the earth shall be filled with the glory of the Lord. This is the true spirit of benevolence. Ps. lxxii.

VII. This prayer in its bearings on parental affection, fixing on the highest object of eternal realities, desires the Salvation of Children.

One generation of pastors, church members, friends, and contributors pass away after another. The world is constantly changing. Let children be admonished to pray that the beauty of the Lord may be upon them. And let all unite in the prayer of the text.

PARSONS.

XCIII.—THE FADING LEAF.

We all do fade as a leaf."—ISAIAH lxiv. 6.

THESE words will admit of several applications. They could be applied to religious declension, and to national declination. But let us consider them as applying to physical corruption, or the mortality of man.

1. *The decay of the leaf is natural.*

It is what constantly occurs. After the summer is gone, and the fruit is fully ripe, the leaves begin to change their colour, to lose their interesting hue, and at last to fall in quick and rapid succession to the ground. It is true there are some trees and shrubs, which retain their verdure through the year; yet even these have faded leaves, and are constantly putting on a new attire. Thus, the decay of the leaf is natural.—So it is with the physical existence of man. We no sooner begin to live, than we begin to die. Mortality is inseparable from our present existence. Hence the language of inspiration.—"Man that is born of a woman is of few days and full of trouble." "We must needs die and be as water spilt upon the ground that cannot be gathered up again." "By one man hath sin entered into the world, and death by sin." And in turning over the pages of history, what confirmations of the truth are there, that all men are mortal! Where are the builders of Babel? Where Abraham and his numerous seed? Where the patriarchs and prophets of succeeding ages? They are gone, and the place which once knew them now knows them no more. Where are the vast armies of the Assyrians, Persians, Grecians, Romans: the myriads of the four great monarchies? They are not, and are as though they never were. And as with warriors, so with the most peaceful; as of enemies, so of friends. Death is no respecter of persons.

"Should his strong hand arrest,
No composition sets the prisoner free."

Whatever the tears of friends, or the prayers of the good, death, alike regardless of our tears and prayers, obeys his mandate, and summons us away. The death of man is natural.

2. *The decay of the leaf is gradual.*

It does not fade away and come to corruption in a day. A gradual process of decay is going on long before we perceive it, and after it is discovered, weeks may elapse before it is entirely withered and falls as a thing of nought to the ground.—So it is with man. The corruption of his nature is gradual. Having attained to its full strength, and put forth and expended its greatest vigor, the infirmities of nature begin to appear. The energies of youth are gone; the strength of mature age is commanded no more. Aged persons cannot see so well; cannot walk so far; cannot labour so hard. The difference between their physical constitution *as it was* and *as it is*, is as the difference between a tree full of leaves and fruit, and a tree whose leaves are falling, whose branches are decaying, and whose stem is becoming daily more corrupt. May the aged professor find that as his outer man decays, his inner man grows stronger and stronger; that as his body bends more and more towards the earth, his spirit soars with greater vigour towards heaven, and that in him is seen an illustration of those beautiful lines,—

> "The plants of grace shall ever live,
> Nature decays, but grace must thrive;
> Time, that doth all things else impair,
> Still makes them flourish fresh and fair."

3. *The decay of the leaf is often hastened by external circumstances.*

It may be effected by insects, by blight, by excessive moisture, or excessive cold. Each of these things may hasten the decay of the leaf, which otherwise would die, though at a later period, from an inherent principle of corruption.—Thus it is with man. Though he will surely die, because his nature is mortal, yet many die sooner than they might have died, from their situations, occupations, habits, and pursuits. Hot climates are prejudicial to longevity. The average existence of many artisans, is only from thirty to forty years. But in most cases life is shortened by reckless habits. "The wicked do not live out half their days." Thus with the drunkard, who often finds an early grave. How lamentable to think that many make life, at its longest period short, still shorter than it is intended to be! "Oh, that they were wise, that they understood this, that they would consider their latter end!"

Thus, as the decay of the leaf is natural, gradual, and often hastened by external circumstances, so it is with the mortality of man. But if this be admitted, what are the effects which this representation should have upon us?

(1) *Should it not produce humility?*

Many are proud, and proud of their persons. Hence their gay and costly attire. They dress to adorn their persons, or to cover their circumstances, to make themselves appear what they really are not. How great their folly! and often great is their fall. "*Pride goeth before destruction, and a haughty spirit before a fall.*" But would not a habit of reflection on our mortality tend to diminish our pride? What is there in a corruptible body, about which to take so much pains, or make to appear so gay? Does it not possess the elements of destruction? Is there not a process of decay constantly going on within? Is it not a little while, and a shroud shall enwrap it, and a grave shall receive it? Shall we not return to the earth from whence we came, and find that the worm is our companion, and our body its aliment and its home? Would you find a remedy for personal pride,— Think of the coffin which is to contain you, the grave which is to receive you, and the worm which is to feed upon you. And never forget that

> "Pride, self-adorning pride, was primal cause
> Of all sin past, all pain, all woe to come."

(2) *Should it not produce sorrow?*

Jesus wept at the grave of Lazarus, not so much because he sympathized with the bereaved condition of Mary and Martha, as in contemplating what sin had done. "The wages of sin is death." But for sin, death would no more have been known on earth, than it is known in heaven. No funeral knell would have been sounded; no funeral procession would have been seen; no funeral obsequies would have been performed; no funeral sermon would have been heard. But for sin, the evils which are now committed in the world (oh, how vast and iniquitous!) would have been unknown, and the consequences of those evils would have been unfelt. No parent would exclaim with David, "O Absalom, my son, my son." No minister would employ the language of a Psalmist, "Horror hath taken hold upon me, because of the wicked they forsake thy law." But for sin, this world would be a paradise, where man would luxuriate in communion with his Creator. But, alas, the world is corrupt, it is in the arms of the wicked one, and is covered with the gloom of the sepulchre, with the darkness of the shadow of death! Mourn, Christian, mourn, and give vent to the feeling of sorrow, as you contemplate the universal ravages of sin.

(3) *Should it not produce self-examination?*

We are fast hastening to another world. Does it not behove us to inquire, "What is the character we sustain?" Are we new creatures in Jesus Christ? Have we been born again of the Spirit? Are we conscious of a change produced in our feelings, answering to the demands of God's word? Know we anything of the feeling of repentance?—that feeling which contains a horror of sin, sorrow for its commission, and a resolution to avoid and abandon it? Know we anything of the principle of faith?— that principle which works by love, which overcomes the world, which rests alone on Christ for pardon and salvation, saying,

> "Other refuge have none,
> Hangs my helpless soul on Thee!"

Know we anything of the exercise of prayer? — that exercise in which the mercy-seat is approached, in which the soul pours forth its desires to the Great Intercessor, that sin may be pardoned, and the Holy Spirit received as our teacher, comforter, and guide, whilst passing through this vale of tears? Are we living so as always to be ready for death?

If it is so, our love to the world is moderated, and subordinated to the love of God. If it is so, our diligence in the things of time is accompanied with an equal diligence about the things of eternity. If it is so, we shall seek and, in some measure, obtain a character and existence approaching to what is found in heaven.

"Oh, happy servant he,
In such a posture found;
He shall his Lord with rapture see,
And be with honour crowned."

XCIV.—ESTRANGEMENT FROM GOD.

BY THE REV. JOHN FOSTER.

"They did not like to retain God in their knowledge."—ROM. I. 8.

THIS plainly tells us, that it may be a very bad reason to show for doing a thing or not, for men to say that they do, or do not *"like"* it. Men should *suspiciously* bring their "liking" and "not liking" under judgment.

The apostle is describing the state of the heathen world, sunk into a frightful depravity, to show it was high time for a *new dispensation*. Their *estrangement from God* was both a *cause* and a *consequence* of that depravity. He shows that, though they were without a special revelation, yet "they were without *excuse;*" for they did, or might, know something of God. But, besides there *had been* a revelation, the loss of which was owing to the depravity of the successive generations (Noah). But not liking to retain the true God in their knowledge, they had changed religion into idolatry (they could not become *Atheists;*) and that wickedness had hastened their desperate descent into all other.

Such was the heathen world; but this is not a thing *peculiar to them.* No; it is the fallen nature of man, in all ages and regions. It is so, all but as far as divine grace repairs. Let any one soberly *look at the fact* and judge. Is it not the fact, that men in general, with regard to the state of their minds, do not like to take special care that God be *retained there?* In passing through the vast succession and variety of thoughts about things they know, do they often *check* themselves, as it were, to say, "But there is *God* for me to think of?" On looking into them, and being conscious that He is too little there, is it a matter of sincere grief and self-reproach? Is it a *welcome* thought when suggested? Are those things that suggest it particularly acceptable? Is there an earnest wish and *endeavour to keep* it much in the mind? and to recall it, that it be not too long absent? and an attention to those things that, as means, tend and contribute to do so? to look unto His word? to look on the creation as *His?* to look at events as His doing? No, no; the mournful truth is, that there is an indisposition, a reluctance to retain or to admit the thought of God. It may be added, as to one large portion of men (even in this so-called Christian land), that they are very little and seldom troubled with *any* thought of God at all.

(Even His *name*, very often profanely uttered by them, hardly raises the thought.)

But, now, is not all this very *strange*, as well as very wrong, if we consider that God is infinitely the greatest and most glorious Being in existence?—that all things in the universe have had their existence from Him, and are *kept* in existence by Him?—that, therefore, all things, ourselves as much as everything else, strictly *belong* to Him?—that we, as *individuals* (one and one), are sustained by Him, especially and singly "in Him we live, and move, and have our being?"—that every good, of every kind, is His gift *directly?*—that, being ever *present* everywhere, He observes and knows everything about us?—that we are accountable to Him, and shall be *brought* to account to Him as our Judge?—that we can be happy *no way*, now and through all eternity, but in His favour? And yet—*not to like to think of him!* Oh, it is amazingly strange!

How comes it, a thing so monstrous, so plainly contrary to all reason?

One thing may be, that we live so much in and by our *senses*—our mere bodily state—that we do not easily realize what is invisible, spiritual. There is a degree of excuse in this. Faith is not so easy a thing as sight.

But, far worse than this, we do not like the thought of a Sovereign, absolute *Lawgiver*, that says in an *awful voice*, I REQUIRE YOU TO SUBJECT YOURSELVES TO MY WILL (for we should like the privilege of doing and being *what we "like"*). To our corrupt nature there are *attractions in sin;* we do not like that there *should* be an authority that, as it were, writes on each sinful thing that pleases, "Do this, and I will *punish* you for it." Men do not like the idea of a Power that they cannot escape from, here or hereafter.

And then, to be reminded of great and continual obligations of *gratitude* to a Being not loved increases the dislike. Many would be glad if the good could be had otherwise than by *God giving it.*

And the judgment at last—to meet Him there—is an unwelcome thought.

In all this, God is regarded more as an enemy than a friend. We do not *love* to think of that which we fear—*if we can help it.* And it is very marvellous how much, in this instance, it *can* be helped, avoided; astonishing to reflect how long the thinking spirit can be in exercise, *with how little thought of God.* (As man may look at a thousand things, and never think of the *sun* that gives the light on them all.)

But, now, what is the *tendency*, the natural *consequence*, of this estrangement of the mind from thoughts of God? The apostle describes such as resulted among the heathen people. And every where, and always, the *tendency* must be to *give men up to sin.* Other considerations and circumstances may contribute to restrain and limit; but the thought of *God* being rejected will take off the most solemn restraint of all. Then the evil propensities of the heart will have all their power, and temptation coming in will not meet the chief *resisting* power (like a city assailed, with no great captain to *command in its defence*).

The just ideas of God being excluded, there are certain to be a great many vain, and useless, and evil things at work in the mind. This wanting, there will be but a very faint, uncertain discernment between good and evil, and a slight sense of the importance of the difference (the right knowledge of God is the only light); a delusive self-judgment, and a dangerous security. Without right knowledge of Him, there will be none of *ourselves*. This estrangement from the thoughts of God will "*increase unto more ungodliness*," — it will *confirm* itself by degrees into a hopeless insensibility; so that the thought of Him will less and less come into the mind, and with still less impression (as in the case of thoughtless old age).

But, now, all this is miserable, and dreadful to think of. The danger, the possibility, of being in such a case, ought to alarm and arouse us. If we feel the dislike in the text, — if we feel it *in any degree*, — it is not a thought to be let alone. It is a mortal enemy, as if an evil spirit possessed the soul. So far we reject our best and Almighty Friend, and all that His favour would confer on us in time and eternity. What is it but to dislike the consideration of what He can give to us and do for us? For "not liking" to have *Him* in our thoughts, there is no reproach too indignant, too bitter for us to pronounce on ourselves; and in this we should "judge that we be not judged."

We should resolutely set ourselves to strive against this hateful and fatal disposition of the soul; and earnestly implore Him not to let us forget Him,—be estranged from Him; lament to Him, penitently, that there should be such a thing in us; entreat Him, in the name of our Lord, to take strong and absolute possession of us,—to make the knowledge of Him clear and bright upon our spirits, shining more and more unto the perfect, the everlasting day.

XCV.—THE CHRISTIAN'S PROSPECTS.

"For they are without fault before the throne of God."—REV. xiv. 5.*

THAT may be affirmed of man which is not true of all the objects that surround him — never was an individual lost.

The trees that bloomed in Paradise are uprooted and gone. No fragment remains of the ark which floated over the deluged world, — nor of the temple reared by Solomon — nor of the cross on which the Saviour expiated sin. They are all confounded with the lumber of creation. They are lost.

But survey the generations of men. Contemplate their millions — sixty-six, it has been computed, die in a minute. Where have they fallen? Some into the hands of robbers,—some into the abysses of the ocean, — diseases, volcanoes, executions, are even now thinning our race. But let these adversaries of human life enter into a grand conspiracy to annihilate or conceal a single victim — the Deity shall cast down a direct ray upon him.

How vain the love of fame, that passion which so agitates the heart,

---

* See Page 343.

and as so often controlled all other emotions in death itself! Mean, unnecessary efforts, we may say to the ambitious,—Your mausoleums, your pyramids, your splendid villany, may be dispensed with; we shall find you without your wishing for it. You belong to an Eternal train. Of that train how wide the extent! You may cross hills, and plains, and deserts, and rivers,—every where you may read some solemn intimations of man, some of his works, of his follies, of his crimes.

Oceans are navigated, and serve as the measure of distance between nation and nation, between man and man. But the vast family have travelled further. Go to the confines of the visible creation, the extensive boundaries of time, you are still behind them; they passed the gates of death, they are fled in various directions, some on high "before the throne of God." Once they were here. Let us congratulate each other. Our friends are gone up; they see the central God. And we shall see him. Our hopes may fix themselves where our friends are. He will make our actions a progress to their abode. Successive moments shall form the several steps in our journey.

WHENCE came they? From meanness; from sorrow; from degradation and want; from a subjection to all the inequalities of the elements; from the dread of death, which hath given to them such felicities. The mortal tabernacle fell asunder, and let the captive spirit free. Now they discern a throne of which their conceptions were as grovelling as ours.

WHO are they? One was Lazarus, lying cold and disordered at a rich man's gate. Another was pointed at by the finger of scorn. A third heard on such a day as this the cold wind singing shrilly through his iron grates. A fourth perished in the martyr's flames. *Now* they are rich. *Now* they are ennobled. *Now* they live, they greatly live, alike enkindled, unconfined. They see the sapphire blaze. " They are before the Throne of God."

BY what track did they ascend? How did they measure the aërial space? What are the way-marks? What human eye has glanced the celestial map? One hour before this dissolution they knew as little as ourselves whether they should graze the sun, or pass gloriously through a constellation. Once darted through their smitten clay, their spirits could not touch again on earth, or stop short of heaven.

WHO gave them their confidence and a claim?

JESUS, THE FAVOURER.

He is there for the purpose—the righteous Advocate. His meritorious actions, his extreme sufferings, his perpetual pleadings, could not secure a less privilege.

What characters do they exemplify? "They are without fault." Yet they are described as a large company. Here there are many faults in *one man*, in one believer. You fold me round in the arms of charity, but you cannot hide my spotted nature. No candour is wanted on *their behalf.* They are pure. They are in the glare of glory.

Oh! to join with such, to become one of them: to use their language — " I hail thee, Brother; our feelings are in unison, in full glow." — " I rejoice in thy newly-attained felicity." — " I congratulate thy late arrival."

THE CHRISTIAN'S PROSPECTS.

What is it to possess innocence pure as air, mirrowy as water, serene as the summer's evening sky: each thought brilliant as a star: the whole character in alliance with God?

In some lands we are told that there are no vegetable poisons. In heaven no faults can grow. The soil is luxurious; without a weed. Faults deform us daily. Each day we have to accuse ourselves — we have been impatient, or idle, or unjust, or impious. Faults divide human affairs with so many opposing interests, occasion all our petty, all our ruinous disasters. In heaven the light which reveals happiness imparts it. There, under the influence of *this* light, stands the faultless immortals, waiting till their late friends reach them. They anticipate the entire tone of praise. They call us to the same place. That place is magnetic, compelling towards it all the faithful, attracting from all distances and communities.

What moral course did they pursue? They bowed in prayer. They repented. They put off the old affections which war against the soul. They were disciplined by chastisement. They washed their robes and made them white in the blood of the Lamb. Sin, so amented with their frame, *that blood* dissolved — dissolved it wholly.

With what cheering accents then may the Christian expire, and say, "My friends, be not despondent on your own account, nor on mine. I am going to be made happy, and ere long you shall see and share my happiness. I shall be 'before the throne of God.' THERE rejoin me."

What is their employment? Let their general character, their society, their enjoyments tell. They take a wide survey of a wide scene. The laws of nature, the divine counsels, redeeming love, they adore, they serve, they do *all* things God appoints. You wish to be with them, but you distrust your purposes.

Behold, as they did Him, the Conqueror of faults. Are you combating them? You are on His side, opposing His enemies, and verging to the same point with His friends. Success attends such a combat; and promises, the same promises, of heaven, ensure continued success.

Let us then become competitors! Not one shall fail. We shall survive every element. We shall soar above the shock of death. We shall be borne up to pass by the pearly gates. We shall appear and dwell for ever "WITHOUT FAULT BEFORE THE THRONE OF GOD."

REMARKS ON PREACHING.

1. PREACHING should be *conversational* and colloquial. A minister must preach just as he would talk, if he wishes fully to be understood. Nothing is more calculated to make a sinner feel that religion is some mysterious thing that he cannot understand, than this mouthing, formal, lofty style of speaking. The minister ought to do as the lawyer does when he wants to make a jury understand him perfectly. He uses a style perfectly colloquial. The gospel will never produce any great effects until ministers *talk* to their hearers in the pulpit, as they talk in private conversation.

2. It must be in the *language of common life*. Not only should it be colloquial in its style, but the *words* should be such as are in common use, otherwise they will not be understood. In the New Testament Jesus Christ invariably uses words of the most common kind, that any child can understand. The language of the gospel is the plainest, simplest, and most easily understood of any language in the world.

Some ministers use language that is purely *technical*, and try to avoid the mischief by explaining the meaning fully at the outset; but this will not answer. If he uses a word that people do not understand, his explanation may be very full, but the difficulty is that people will forget his explanations, and then his words are Greek to them. Or if he uses a word in common use, but employs it in an *un*common sense, giving his special explanations, it is no better; for the people will soon forget his special explanations, and then the impression actually conveyed to their minds will be according to their *common* understanding of the word. It is amazing how many men of thinking minds there are in congregations, who do not understand the most common technical expressions employed by ministers, such as regeneration, sanctification, etc.

Use words that can be perfectly understood. Do not, for fear of appearing unlearned, use language half Latin and half Greek, which the people do not understand. The apostle says, the man is a barbarian who uses language that the people do not understand. In the apostle's days there were some preachers who were proud of displaying their command of language, and variety of tongues they could speak, which the common people could not understand. The apostle rebukes this spirit: "I had rather speak five words with my understanding, that by my voice, I might teach others also, than ten thousand words in an unknown tongue."

I have sometimes heard ministers preach, even when there was a revival, when I have wondered what that part of the congregation would do, who had no dictionary. So many phrases were brought in, manifestly to adorn the discourse, rather than to instruct the people, that I have felt as if I wanted to tell the man, "Sit down, and do not confound the people's minds with your *barbarian* preaching, that they cannot understand."

3. Preaching should be *parabolical*. Christ thus constantly illustrated his instructions. He could either advance a principle and then illustrate it by a parable, that is, a short story of some event, real or imaginary, or else he would bring out the principle *in* the parable. There are millions of facts that can be used to advantage, and yet very few ministers dare to use them, for fear somebody will reproach him. "O," says somebody, "he tells stories." Tells stories? Why, that is the way Jesus Christ preached. And it is the only way to preach. Facts, real or supposed, should be used to show the truth. Truths not illustrated, are just as well calculated to convert sinners as a mathematical demonstration. Is it always to be so? Shall it always be a matter of reproach, that ministers follow the example of Jesus Christ, in *illustrating* truths by facts?

4. The illustrations should be drawn *from common life*, and the common business of society. I once heard a minister illustrate his ideas by the manner in which merchants transact business. A minister who was present objected to this illustration; he said, it was too familiar, it was letting down the dignity of the pulpit. He said all illustrations in preaching should be drawn from ancient history, or from an elevated source, that would keep up the dignity of the pulpit. Dignity indeed! Why, the object of an illustration is, to make people see the truth, not to bolster up pulpit dignity. A minister whose heart is in the work, does not use an illustration to make people stare, but to make them see the truth. If he brought forward his illustrations from ancient history, it could not make the people *see*, it would not illustrate anything. The novelty of the thing might awaken their attention, but then they would lose the truth itself. For if the illustration itself be a novelty, the attention will be directed to this fact as a matter of history, and the *truth itself*, which it was designed to illustrate, will be lost sight of. The illustration should, if possible, be a matter of common occurrence, and the *more* common the occurrence the more sure it will be not to fix attention upon *itself*, but serve as a medium *through* which the truth is conveyed.

The Saviour always illustrated his instructions by things that were taking place among the people to whom he preached, and with which their minds were familiar. He descended often very far below what is now supposed to be essential to support the dignity of the pulpit. He talked about the hens and chickens, and children in the market-places, and sheep and lambs, and shepherds and farmers, and husbandmen and merchants. And when he talked about kings, as in the marriage of the king's son, and the nobleman that went into a far country to receive a kingdom, he had reference to historical facts that were well known among the people at the time. The illustration should always be drawn from things so common, that the illustration itself will not attract attention away from the subject, but that people may see, through it, the truth illustrated.

5. Preaching should be *repetitious*. If a minister wishes to preach with effect, he must not be afraid of repeating whatever he may see is not perfectly understood by his hearers. Here is the evil of using notes. The preacher preaches right along just as he has it written down, and cannot observe whether he is understood or not. If he interrupt his reading, and attempt to catch the countenances of the audience, and to explain where he sees they do not understand, he gets lost and confused, and gives it up. If a minister has his eyes on the people he is preaching to, he can commonly tell by their looks whether they understand him. And if he sees they do not understand any particular point, let him stop and illustrate it. If they do not understand one illustration, let him give another, and make it all clear to their minds before he goes on.

I was conversing with one of the first advocates in America. He said the difficulty which preachers find in making themselves understood is, that they do not repeat enough. Says he, "In addressing a jury, I always expect that whatever I wish to impress upon their minds, I shall have to repeat at least twice; and often I repeat it three or four times, and even more. Otherwise, I do not carry their minds along with me, so that they can feel the force of what comes afterwards." If a jury cannot apprehend an argument, unless there is so much repetition, how is it to be expected that men will understand the preaching of the gospel without it?

In like manner, the minister ought to turn an important thought over and over before his audience, till even the children understand it perfectly. Do not say that so much repetition will create disgust in cultivated minds. It will not disgust. This is not what disgusts thinking men. They are not weary of the efforts a minister makes to be understood. The fact is, the more simple a preacher's illustrations are, and the more plain he makes everything, the more men of mind are interested. I know that men of the first minds often get ideas they never had before, from illustrations which were designed to bring the gospel down to the comprehension of a child. Such men are commonly so occupied with the affairs of this world, that they do not *think* much on the subject of religion, and they therefore need the plainest preaching, and they will like it.

6. A minister should always deeply feel his subject, and then he will suit the action to the word, and the word to the action, so as to make the full impression which the truth is calculated to make. He should be in solemn earnest in what he says. I lately heard a most judicious criticism on this subject. "How important it is that a minister should feel what he says! Then his actions will, of course, correspond to his words. If he undertakes to *make* gestures, his arms may go like a windmill, and yet make no impression." It requires the utmost stretch of art on the stage for the actors to make their hearers feel. The design of elocution is

to teach this skill. But if a man *feels* his subject fully, he will *naturally* do it. He will naturally do the very thing that elocution laboriously teaches. See any common man in the streets, who is earnest in talking; see with what force he gestures. See a woman or a child in earnest—how natural! To gesture with their hands is as natural as it is to move their tongue and lips; it is the perfection of eloquence.

No wonder that a great deal of preaching produces so little effect. Gestures are of more importance than is generally supposed. Mere words will never express the full meaning of the gospel. The *manner* of saying it is almost everything. Suppose one of you that is a mother, goes home to-night, and as soon as you get to the door, the nurse comes rushing up to you, with her soul in her countenance, and tells you that your child is burnt to death. You would believe it, and feel it, too, at once. But suppose she comes and tells it in a cold and careless manner. Would that arouse you? No. It is the earnestness of her manner, and the distress of her looks, that tell the story.

I once heard a remark made respecting a young minister's preaching, which was instructive. He was uneducated, in the common sense of the term, but well educated to win souls. It was said of him, "The manner in which he comes in, and sits in the pulpit, and rises to speak, is a sermon of itself. It shows that he has something to say that is important and solemn." That man's manner of saying some things I have known to move the feelings of a whole congregation, when the same things said in a prosing way would have produced no effect at all.

7. A minister should aim to *convert his congregation*. But, you will ask, Does not all preaching aim at this? No. A minister always has some aim in preaching, but most sermons were never aimed at converting sinners. And if sinners were converted under them, the preacher himself would be amazed. I once heard a fact on this point. There were two young ministers who had entered the ministry at the same time. One of them had great success in converting sinners, the other, none. The latter inquired of the other, one day, what was the reason of this difference. "Why," replied the other, "the reason is, that I *aim* at a different end from you in preaching. My object is to convert sinners, but you aim at no such thing. And then you go and lay it to sovereignty in God that you do not produce the same effect, when you never aim at it. Here, take one of my sermons, and preach it to your people, and see what the effect will be." The man did so, and preached the sermon, and it did produce effect. He was frightened when sinners began to weep; and when one came to him after meeting, to ask what he should do, the minister apologized to him, and said, "I did not aim to wound you; I am sorry if I have hurt your feelings." O horrible!

8. A minister must *anticipate the objections* of sinners, and answer them. What does the lawyer do, when pleading before a jury? O how differently is the cause of Jesus Christ pleaded from human causes! It was remarked by a lawyer, that the cause

of Jesus Christ had the fewest able advocates of any cause in the world. And I partly believe it. Does the lawyer go along in his argument in a regular train, and not explain anything obscure, or anticipate the arguments of his antagonist? If he did so, he would lose his case, to a certainty. But no. The lawyer who is pleading for money, anticipates every objection which may be made by his antagonist, and carefully removes or explains them, so as to leave the ground all clear as he goes along, that the jury may be settled on every point. But ministers often leave one difficulty, and another, untouched. Sinners who hear them feel the difficulty, and it is never got over in their minds, and they never know how to remove it, and perhaps the minister never takes the trouble to know that such difficulties exist, and yet he wonders why his congregation is not converted, why there is no revival. How can he wonder at it, when he has never hunted up the difficulties and objections that sinners feel, and removed them!

9. If a minister mean to preach the gospel with effect, he must be sure *not to be monotonous*. If he preaches in a monotonous way, he will preach the people to sleep. Any monotonous sound, great or small, if continued, disposes people to sleep. The falls of Niagara, the roaring of the ocean, or any sound ever so great or small, hath this effect naturally on the nervous system. You never hear this monotonous manner from people in conversation. And a minister cannot be monotonous in preaching, if he feels what he says.

10. A minister should address the feelings enough to secure attention, and then, *deal with conscience*, and probe to the quick. Appeals to the feelings alone, will never convert sinners. If the preacher deals too much in these, he may get up an excitement, and have wave after wave of feeling flow over the congregation, and people may be carried away in the flood, with false hopes. The only way to secure *sound* conversions is to deal faithfully with the conscience. If attention flags at any time, appeal to the feelings again, and rouse it up; but do your *work* with conscience.

11. If he can, it is desirable that a minister should learn the effect of one sermon, before he preaches another. Let him learn if it is understood, if it has produced any impression, if any difficulties are felt in regard to the subject, which need clearing up, if any objections are raised, and the like. When he knows it all, then he knows what to preach next. What would be thought of the physician who should give medicine to his patient, and then give it again and again, without trying to learn the effect of the first, or whether it had produced any effect or not? A minister never will be able to deal with sinners as he ought till he can find out whether his instruction has been received and understood, and whether the difficulties in sinners' minds are cleared away, and their path open to the Saviour, so that they need not stumble, and stumble, till their souls are lost.

BY REV. C. G. FINNEY, NEW YORK.

INDEX.

No.	Book.	Subject.	Page.
35	Gen. xlix. 19.	Christian Warfare	301
6	Ex. xxxii. 26.	Decision for God	247
71	Ex. xxxiii. 14.	God's Presence	381
41	Num. xxiii. 10.	Death of the Righteous	315
54	Deut. xviii. 18.	Moses typical of Christ	341
1	Deut. xxxii. 31.	The Superiority of the Christian's Portion	235
19	1 Sam. ii. 30.	Blessedness of honouring God	273
68	2 Sam. vi. 11.	The Ark a type of Christ	376
61	1 Kings xx. 11.	Presumption Forbidden	363
64	1 Kings xx. 40.	The Soul Neglected	368
14	Neh. ii. 4.	Ejaculatory Prayer	262
12	Job v. 6.	Afflictions	259
49	Ps. xv. 1, 2.	The Tabernacle Typical	327
72	Ps. xxxi. 19.	Character and Portion of God's People	384
58	Ps. xxxix. 4.	Prayer to be Prepared for Death	354
91	Ps. xliii. 5.	Hope a Support in Trouble	423
46	Ps. lxiii. 1.	Seeking God	324
92	Ps. xc. 16, 17.	The Beauty of the Lord in his House	424
67	Ps. cxii. 10.	Light in Darkness	375
51	Ps. cxvi. 12—14.	Gratitude for Mercies	332
2	Ps. cxix. 151.	The Nearness of God	239
18	Ps. cxliv. 15.	The Happy People	269
17	Prov. xiii. 10.	Pride	267
8	Prov. xiv. 9.	Mocking at Sin	253
32	Eccl. vii. 14.	The Day of Adversity	298
7	Song ii. 2.	The Church a Lily among Thorns	250
15	Song ii. 25.	Little Sins very injurious	263
27	Song iii. 3.	Object of a Christian's Love	291
83	Isa. xxvii. 1.	Preparation for Death	407
10	Isa. xxxiv. 17.	The Important Line	256
9	Isa. xlviii. 18.	Divine Solicitude for Man's Happiness	254
93	Isa. lxiv. 6.	The Fading Leaf	426

INDEX.

No.	Book.	Subject.	Page
55	Jer. iv. 14.	Important Admonition	348
23	Jer. viii. 22.	The Balm of Gilead	282
16	Jer. xii. 5.	The Swelling of Jordan	263
36	Ezek. xxiii. 32.	The Cup of Wrath	304
85	Amos vi. 1.	Apathy of the Church	401
70	Matt. iii. 10.	The Axe laid to the Root	380
66	Matt. v. 20.	The Righteousness of the Scribes and Pharisees	373
84	Matt. xi. 28.	Christ's Invitation	300
53	Matt. xxi. 42—46.	The Chief Corner-Stone	338
80	Luke viii. 27.	The Demoniac of Gadara	401
43	Luke xii. 40.	Preparedness for Death	316
25	Luke xiii. 29.	The Heavenly Company	285
21	Luke xxii. 40.	Temptation	276
89	John ix. 35.	The Great Question	420
73	John x. 14.	Christ the Good Shepherd	386
86	John xi. 35.	Jesus Wept	412
88	John xiv. 1.	Comfort in Trouble	415
90	John xiv. 30.	The Coming of Satan	422
63	John xix. 30.	It is Finished	367
37	Acts xi. 20, 21.	Successful Preaching	306
4	Acts xx. 32.	Believers commended to God.	243
44	Acts xxi. 10—14.	Paul's Constancy	321
94	Rom. i. 8.	Estrangement from God	429
87	Rom. ii. 4.	Contempt of Divine Goodness	413
22	Rom. iii. 25.	The Atonement	279
11	Rom. viii. 1.	Freedom from Condemnation.	256
77	Rom. viii. 14.	The Dignity of Adoption	398
78	" "	" "	400
52	1 Cor. iii. 11.	Christ the Foundation	335
38	1 Cor. iv. 14.	Censoriousness, etc	307
45	1 Cor. xv. 58.	The Work of the Lord	323
24	2 Cor. iii. 2.	Living Epistles	284
28	2 Cor. iii. 18.	Beholding the Glory of the Lord	291
62	2 Cor. vi. 2.	The Day of Salvation.	366
75	2 Cor. xiii. 5.	Self-examination	392
26	Gal. iv. 6.	The Spirit of Adoption	289
57	Gal. iv. 18.	Zeal for the Gospel	353
56	Eph. i. 7.	Redemption	350
50	Eph. iv. 21.	The Truth in Jesus	331
3	Eph. v. 1.	Following God	241
33	Eph. i. 8—10.	Abundant Grace	299

No.	Book.	Subject.	Page.
20	Eph. v. 27.	The Glory of the Church Consummated..	274
13	Eph. vi. 17.	The Sword of the Spirit	260
74	Eph. vi. 18.	Constancy in Prayer	387
84	Phil. iii. 14.	The Christian's Glorious Prize	409
82	Col. i. 21, 22.	Reconciliation	406
89	Col. iii. 11.	Christ All in All	308
47	1 Thess. ii. 20.	Christians the Joy of Ministers	324
79	1 Thess. iii. 8.	Christian Steadfastness	400
42	2 Thess. iii. 1.	The Word Glorified	315
81	2 Tim. i. 12.	Confidence in Christ	405
48	Tit. iii. 5.	Salvation by Grace	326
69	Heb. xi. 16.	Heaven a Better Country	378
76	James iii. 10.	Improprieties Reproved	396
60	1 Pet. i. 17.	The Christian a Sojourner	361
65	1 Pet. i. 18—21.	Redemption, etc	371
80	1 Pet. ii. 12.	Honest Conversation	296
31	2 Pet. iii. 16.	Growth in Grace	296
40	Jude 3.	Common Salvation	311
29	Rev. iii. 20.	Christ Knocking at the Heart	294
5	Rev. vii. 9.	The Redeemed in Heaven	246
54*	Rev. xiv. 5.	Heavenly Purity	343
95	Rev. xiv. 5.	The Christian's Prospects	431
59	Rev xxi. 1—4.	Blessedness of Heaven	358

THE END.

www.ingramcontent.com/pod-product-compliance
Lightning Source LLC
Chambersburg PA
CBHW032138010526
44111CB00035B/608